CLAIMING TRIBAL IDENTITY

Claiming Tribal Identity

The Five Tribes and the Politics of
Federal Acknowledgment

Mark Edwin Miller

University of Oklahoma Press : Norman

Also by Mark Edwin Miller

Forgotten Tribes: Unrecognized Indians and the Federal Acknowledgment Process
(Lincoln, Nebr., 2004)

This book is published with the assistance of Southern Utah University, Cedar City.

Library of Congress Cataloging-in-Publication Data

Miller, Mark Edwin, 1966–
    Claiming tribal identity : the Five tribes and the politics of federal acknowledgment / Mark Edwin Miller.
        pages cm.
    Includes bibliographical references and index.
    ISBN 978-0-8061-4378-1 (pbk. : alk. paper)
    1. Five Civilized Tribes—Tribal citizenship. 2. Five Civilized Tribes—Legal status, laws, etc. 3. Five Civilized Tribes—Politics and government. 4. Federally recognized Indian tribes—History. 5. Indians of North America—Tribal citizenship. 6. Indians of North America—Legal status, laws, etc. 7. Indians of North America—Government Relations. I. Title.
    E78.O45.M56 2013
    323.1197—dc23   2013001308

Contents

Illustrations

Foreword

A sense of identity is a powerful emotional driver. In Indian country, it seems that tribal identity is the last attribute and asset that tribes retain when all else is taken away. Regardless of their nationality, color, or race, Indians called all non-Indians "white men." It seems that throughout history, white men have always wanted and took what Indians had. First, it was Indian land, then their political territory, then their independence, then their assets such as timber, minerals, and water, then their tribal governments, then their art, history, and culture, then their children, and currently, it is their identity.

We have heard people claiming Indian ancestry based on their having high cheekbones, having an affinity for nature, having long black braided hair, and even having "Indian" fingernails. Of course, many people claim to have a great Cherokee grandmother who was an "Indian princess," *even though no such thing existed.* Unfortunately, there are fakes and imitators who try to take advantage of programs offering Indian preference, and "T-shirt Indians" hungry for a tribal identity (wearing culturally incongruent T-shirts showing an "Indian princess" with classic European features paired with a wolf). These are some of the people who offend the cultural body of the Five Civilized Tribes and often try to take things that do not belong to them.

Many of their family stories are dubious. For example, some say that their ancestors were ashamed of being Indian and that is why they did not enroll in their tribe. History shows, however, that when the Dawes Commission enrollment ended in 1906, tens of thousands of white men clamored to be enrolled with the Five Civilized Tribes so they could get an allotment of land. Others say their ancestors did not enroll because they "dropped off" the Trail of Tears, which was the forced 850-mile removal of 16,000 Cherokees in 1839 from northern Georgia to Indian Territory, a march on which 4,000 Cherokees died. The only reason Cherokees dropped off the Trail of Tears was that they died.

On the other hand, many people who are not enrolled have legitimate family stories of Cherokee ancestry. Doc Watson, for example, was a blind folk and country musician with phenomenal talent; he recently passed away. I always wanted to meet this gentleman and thought his voice should be used in a movie as that of God. I met him several years ago, after one of his shows. A charming man, he told me that he was one-eighth Cherokee. I was ready for the standard story of "my great-grandmother was full-blood Cherokee." But instead, he told the story about his great-grandfather in eastern Tennessee who was a "rounder" and often got into fights. Doc Watson's story is believable and authentic. His is not an isolated case. In the 2000 U.S. Census, 750,000 Americans claimed to be Cherokee; however, there were only 250,000 enrolled as Cherokee citizens. In other words, half a million Americans who claimed they were Cherokee did not or could not enroll in the Cherokee Nation.

American Indian identity, and the seizing of that identity by non-Indians, is a bit complicated, but worthy of investigation, because it provides insight into the national character of America and Americans' own search for identity. That search becomes contentious when appropriation of Indian identity infringes on tribal governments' very keen sense and protection of sovereignty. An individual may say he or she is part Indian or claim Indian heritage or affiliation, but it is another issue for that individual to say "I am a tribal citizen or member," or even worse, to attempt to establish his or her own tribe. A tribe or Indian nation is a family of families and a community of communities. However, an Indian nation is also a government with all the incidents of sovereignty that any government in the world possesses; except for those taken away through treaties or by federal law. The greater conflict occurs not when individuals claim Indian ancestry or heritage, but when groups claim to be Indian nations.

For decades before the United States was founded, the Five Civilized Tribes existed in the world community of governments, and since those early times, they have fought to maintain their sovereignty and national identities. In 2010, the staff at the Cherokee Nation identified some two hundred groups that claimed to be Cherokee organizations and tribes. By using the subterfuge of state recognition to legitimize often silly claims of nationhood and playing "Indian," some of these groups demean the national identity of the Five Civilized Tribes. An Indian nation is not a grandmother society, a culture club, or a fake tribe; quite simply, it is a nation.

In this book, *Claiming Tribal Identity: The Five Tribes and the Politics of Federal Acknowledgment,* Mark Miller provides an exhaustive and poignant study of how identity and sovereignty intersect, and relate to and influence each other. He thoroughly reviews the Five Civilized Tribes' history, the stories of those groups that try to maintain or create a tribal identity, and the charade of apparent fakes. He examines the external and internal influences that challenge the Five Civilized Tribes' national existence.

Miller offers valuable insight into the complexity of this conflict. There were families and communities that during the removal period, because of treaty provisions or to avoid removal, expatriated from their tribal governments; their descendants now seek recognition as a nation. There are imposters seeking public and federal recognition as Indian nations and snake oil artists exploiting the public's ignorance of Indians for their own personal gain. There are also people of good will trying to complete their identity with family stories of being "part Indian." There are self-identifying descendants of Indians who left Indian Territory during the American Civil War, settled in surrounding states, and did not return during the Dawes enrollment period. There are federally recognized Indian nations and their citizens who have survived horrific episodes of genocide, germ warfare, removal, abandonment, federal seizure of tribal assets, forced governmental disintegration, termination, and relocation. Unfortunately, today all of these histories and stories have become intertwined and are blindly called "being Indian."

Miller does not shy away from handling any of these sensitive identity issues. He judiciously, but directly cuts through cloudy and spotty family stories, differentiating those legitimately seeking an ancestral identity from charlatans parading and "chiefing" for the public.

Against this backdrop, Miller examines the Federal Acknowledgement Process, by which the United States establishes a government-to-government relationship with Indian nations. He addresses the questions of why the federal government should determine the political legitimacy of an Indian tribe or nation, and whether the criteria are fair. A review reveals that the tribal acknowledgment criteria are common-sense evidence of a legitimate government. Further, if not the federal government, then who should determine whether the United States should establish a government-to-government relationship with a tribe? The federal executive branch administers the Indian nation acknowledgement process, just as it establishes foreign policy and determines which countries the United States diplomatically recognizes.

Miller's book is an important work not only for the Five Civilized Tribes and those groups seeking an Indian identity but also as a study for all Americans lost in filling a void in their ethnic, cultural, genealogical, and personal history and identity. *Claiming Tribal Identity* is well researched, exhaustive, insightful, nonjudgmental, and scholarly, and it contributes to the body of knowledge of the Five Civilized Tribes and the larger issues of personal and tribal identity.

Chadwick Corntassel Smith
Principal Chief of the Cherokee Nation,
1999–2011

Acknowledgments

This book had its genesis at the Western History Association Annual Meeting in Oklahoma City in the fall of 2007. I gave a paper there on the conflict between the Five Tribes and unrecognized tribes, and was surprised at the interest in my talk. What I thought was a minor paper I had extracted from my first book, *Forgotten Tribes*, turned into a project that kept me fascinated for over four years.

I would like to thank the individuals, including tribal leaders and academic press editors, who showed interest in this issue and inspired this book. As tribal identity is a contemporary controversy, the research would not have been possible without the help of present-day tribal leaders. I would like to thank citizens of the Cherokee Nation and others of the Five Tribes for their willingness to share their history, experiences, and insights with me. Citizens of the Poarch Band of Creek Indians and Eastern Band of Cherokee Indians also aided this work. Leaders of the MOWA Band of Choctaws and other state-recognized tribes were also extremely helpful to me in finishing this book. Archivists and other individuals working in the public history profession also showed a great willingness to follow through on requests for documents, and with other help in my research. I would also like to thank David E. Wilkins and Bruce Duthu for some early insights on conceptualizing the larger project. Arlinda Locklear read and offered critiques of a chapter on Indian gaming. Other scholars who spoke with me also proved extremely important to this work. The three anonymous reviewers for the University of Oklahoma Press aided the final product immensely with their insights and critiques: they have made this a much better book. Finally, acquisitions editor Alessandra Jacobi Tamulevich was a guiding light from the first day and a steady rock in helping me finish this project. I will always be grateful I met her years ago and completed this work under her direction.

Here in Utah, so far away from the Cherokee Nation and other Indian peoples involved in this book, colleagues at Southern Utah University aided my work immensely. Provost Brad Cook, Dean James McDonald, and former department chair Curt Bostick were always supportive, providing leave time so I could progress with my research and writing. Other colleagues here also helped with informal discussions of the larger issues involved in this study. My wife, Gia DeGiovanni Miller, helped perhaps more than any other person; daily talks with her in our kitchen or in our backyard helped me sharpen my arguments and clarify some of the grayer issues involved in this study. I will always be grateful to my mother Penny Miller Rothman, my father Charles Miller, and my stepmother Laurie Miller for their support of my career, and to Gia's folks, Dee and Bette DeGiovanni, for their help with the grandkids here in Cedar City. Finally, my children Delaney, Regan, and Gage were an inspiration and reminder of the real reasons we are working and moving the scholarship forward; they remind me that everyone needs a secure home and community to thrive.

CLAIMING TRIBAL IDENTITY

Introduction

In the spring of 1980 a newly established Indian group in Georgia published an issue of its newspaper with this enticing invitation: "The Southeastern Cherokee Confederacy, Inc. is accepting new members with 1/16th or more Indian heritage. You do not have to be Cherokee to be accepted in the nation." The group noted that it sought to "get back what belongs to the Red Man" and that obtaining federal tribal recognition was a major goal for the coming year. Individuals who chanced upon this paper may have been surprised to see an Indian tribe advertising for new members. They may have been perplexed that this group said it was "Cherokee" but did not require Cherokee ancestry to join. They might have been even more surprised had they learned what had transpired during the heady days of the 1970s. Under its chief, William "Rattlesnake" Jackson, the Southeastern Cherokee Confederacy had secured a proclamation from the governor of Georgia in 1976 granting it state tribal recognition. It had established various clans and bands, and the press regularly covered the new tribe's activities, excited that Indians were once again appearing in the state perhaps most associated with the forced removal of Indian peoples on the Trail of Tears during the early nineteenth century. The Southeastern Cherokee Confederacy ultimately would have more than a thousand members scattered across twenty-eight states, with the most active branch in Oregon.

A related group headquartered nearby, the Lower Muskogee Creek Tribe, was even more successful than Rattlesnake Jackson's organization.

With an official proclamation in 1973 from Georgia governor Jimmy Carter recognizing it as a tribe and its land as a "reservation," the Lower Muskogee band developed a tract it named the Tama Reservation into a fully functioning residential reservation during the 1970s. Here newly arrived members moved onto tribe-owned lands and began living a vision of Indian life they called "the Dream of the Creeks." At Tama Reservation the group reconstructed a tribal village and dance grounds, and established a modern recording studio where members produced Indian-themed country-and-western music to sell to visitors. As the 1980s progressed, both the Southeastern Cherokee Confederacy and the Tama Creeks submitted unsuccessful petitions to the Bureau of Indian Affairs (BIA) for federal tribal recognition.[1]

While interesting in its own right, the rise of new Indian organizations in Georgia was not an isolated phenomenon. Throughout the Southeast, people involved in dozens of similar entities were coming forward to reclaim their aboriginal identity and indigenous rights, and to demand access to scarce federal resources. In a few decades, starting in the 1970s, several hundred groups with names invoking Cherokees, Chickasaws, Creeks, Choctaws, and Seminoles had formed all over the United States. As time progressed, these peoples' fairly recent origins were largely forgotten. Few non-Indians in Georgia, and certainly few people involved with them in faraway corners of the country, were aware that they were not tribes of antiquity. With state recognition and a firm place on Georgia's Indian commission, the Lower Muskogee Creek Tribe was well on its way to full acceptance as an Indian tribe. Not surprisingly, however, these groups set off alarms in some quarters. Government officials and leaders of the Five Tribes of Oklahoma and related reservation tribes in the Southeast, such as the Mississippi Band of Choctaws and Eastern Band of Cherokee Indians, were concerned. They knew about the circumstances of the births of these new tribes, and they asked questions. Who were these people claiming to be related to them? Why had they never heard of these supposed Creek and Cherokee "tribes" that had somehow managed to avoid removal and were still living in the Southeast? Why was their traditional archenemy, the state of Georgia, recognizing Indian tribes at all? In time the Cherokee Nation would create a group, the Fraudulent Indian Task Force, to educate the public about these organizations and to expose their members for what tribal leaders felt they were: charlatans posing as Cherokees or other Indians for personal and financial gain.

Decades after the creation of the Southeastern Cherokee Confederacy, I began to meet and talk with individuals who were members of other recently created Indian groups and newly state-recognized tribes. About ten years ago, I attended an academic conference where I was asked to a dinner with other graduate students, most of whom studied some aspect of American Indian history or culture. One of my associates (I will call him James) was an individual I had known in various contexts for several years. At the dinner James told everyone that he was a member of a Cherokee tribe from one of the southeastern states. Since I was completing research on what became my first book, *Forgotten Tribes: Unrecognized Indians and the Federal Acknowledgment Process*, I knew that this "Cherokee" group was not universally accepted as a legitimate, long-standing entity, despite having state recognition. In fact, this band was often singled out by the Cherokee Nation of Oklahoma as a primary example of a fraudulent group masquerading as an Indian tribe in modern America. In chats with friends and associates it had not been uncommon to hear statements like this one: "James doesn't look Indian but you know *he is Cherokee*." James had been treated as a Native American in the academic and social contexts in which I had been present; no one had questioned his ethnic identity. It would have been highly impolite to raise the issue at all. At this dinner, however, I began to wonder. Was I the only one among these scholars who knew that James's group was not federally recognized? There are 566 Indian tribes, bands, and Alaska Native villages recognized by the BIA, and no one could be expected to know the name of every one. Was I the only person there aware that the Cherokee Nation and the related Eastern Band of Cherokee Indians did not accept James's tribe as legitimate, despite the claim that they were blood relatives? There seemed to be either ignorance about the existence of these groups and their members' claims to a Cherokee identity, or there was an unspoken secret about Native identity lingering around the dinner table. I realized then that this aspect of Indian identity and publicly declared ethnicity was a largely unexplored subject. I knew, however, that delving into the issue was fraught with potential minefields, both practical and theoretical. Because the subject concerns modern identity politics, personal ethnic identity, and definitions of Indian tribes and peoples, I had to approach it with sensitivity and professionalism.[2]

DEFINING NATIVES AND TRIBES

In 1969 noted Sioux writer and scholar Vine Deloria, Jr., challenged his contemporaries to rethink Native-white relations, remarking, "Before the white man can relate to others he must forego the pleasure of defining them."[3] Today we are witnessing efforts by the Cherokee Nation and its Fraudulent Indian Task Force, and by similar organizations, to reclaim from the government the "pleasure of defining" themselves. Increasingly Five Tribes members are exerting their power to determine who is, and what entities are, authentically Cherokee, Chickasaw, Creek, Choctaw, and Seminole. This book centers upon very public debates about tribal identity and recognition, and on more subtle discourses about tribal "authenticity" and individual claims to Native heritage involving the Five Tribes of Oklahoma and dozens of once or presently unrecognized communities in the Southeast. It is, at its core, about the modern politics of Indian identity and authenticity as revealed in ongoing battles about what groups and individuals can legitimately claim to be "Indian." The arenas where the struggles and debates play out are diverse, yet the most important conflicts are enacted within the BIA's Federal Acknowledgment Process (FAP) and in state capitals like Atlanta and Montgomery, where legislators have been avidly extending recognition to Indian-identifying enclaves, often with little concern for the wishes of the Cherokee Nation and other recognized tribes. In concerted political and public relations campaigns, Cherokee and other leaders are utilizing their power to influence, shape, and sometimes determine the outcomes of tribal acknowledgment cases. Long-recognized tribes more and more are demanding the sovereign right to define themselves and say which people can claim to be their "blood brothers." In the modern era of tribal sovereignty and self-determination it seems fitting that nations like the Choctaws and Creeks have a large say in legitimating and recognizing kindred peoples—or not.

Because of their position in the federal system, however, Native peoples must turn to an outside arbiter, the federal government, and to a seemingly non-Native regimen, the Federal Acknowledgment

Process, to determine which groups are legitimate Indian tribes. Almost all the existing scholarship on federal tribal recognition focuses upon a well-considered critique that it is essentially a nonindigenous process, decided by non-Indians using non-Native models of tribalism. To many critics the government process reveals the continuing truth that Indian tribes represent a quintessential "Other" political form, constructed by whites to facilitate colonial domination of aboriginal peoples or to fit Hollywood-derived images of how Indian societies function and how indigenous peoples live.[4] Much of what has been written on the larger issue of Indian identity and images has regarded non-Native definitions, social constructions, and bureaucratic institutions that work to constrain and reduce the Indian population. These valuable studies tend to point to the central quandary of indigenous identity: Indians are the only ethnic group that is expected to remain in a primordial state if its members are to be perceived as real and authentic. Indians are the only people expected to perform cultural difference to be seen as authentic communities able to exercise sovereignty.[5]

What is often lost in the critiques of the Federal Acknowledgment Process is the fact the leaders of the Five Tribes and other Indian nations do not see it as an entirely foreign, nonaboriginal regimen. They were actively engaged in its creation during the 1970s, and they continue to support the process because they view it as the best method available to determine which groups are viable indigenous nations today. By supporting the government process, Five Tribes leaders are engaging in an ongoing Native project that seeks new ways to define their peoples using both precontact, "traditional" measures and criteria borrowed from the dominant, Euro-American society. Ventures that seek to delineate and measure "Indianness" and "tribes" are no less troublesome from the tribal perspective. However, how Native leaders perceive unrecognized individuals and groups is important to understanding modern Indian identity. The Five Tribes and related groups have exerted their sovereignty by extending government relations to formerly unrecognized tribes in the Southeast. They have also chosen to withhold recognition to groups they feel are inauthentic. While they support the process of the Bureau of Indian Affairs, tribal leaders use their own definitions and "ways of seeing" when making these decisions. Their criteria generally represent a complex mixture of indigenous and non-Indian notions of ethnicity and authenticity.

The Five Tribes and other long-recognized Native nations have always been actively engaged in tribal acknowledgment debates. Today they have important reasons for remaining involved. Recognition politics involving established tribes, unrecognized communities, and non-Indians exposes the fundamental truth about ethnic and racial identities: they are constantly evolving and negotiated.

CULTURAL APPROPRIATIONS AND OPTIONAL INDIANS

During a congressional hearing on tribal acknowledgment reform in 1995, legendary Cherokee Nation principal chief Wilma Mankiller gave an impassioned presentation, arguing that Cherokees, more than any other American Indian people, were under assault from hundreds of groups that were appropriating and stealing her people's identity, parading in public in stereotypical Plains Indian garb, and hurting her people's reputation in the process. Chief Mankiller implied that these groups were making Cherokees a laughingstock.[6] She adamantly opposed any weakening of the stringent BIA recognition process since it seemed to guard against Indian imposters and other wannabe groups. Mankiller's fear about the widespread appropriation of her people's cultural identity represents one of the most important reasons she and other Indian leaders have entered tribal acknowledgment politics. They support the BIA's Federal Acknowledgment Process because they feel it protects their rights and identity as members of aboriginal nations. Mankiller and others view the widespread appropriation of their tribal names and distortion of their cultures as some of the greatest dangers facing their nations as they struggle to survive and exert sovereignty in America today. They believe that the recognition of dubious Indian-claiming communities might erode respect for Native nations and ultimately endanger tribal sovereignty itself. In recent years the Cherokees have persuaded the other Five Tribes nations to become involved in their crusade against these perceived fraudulent tribes. Their effort to stop the unauthorized use of their tribal names and identities is part of a larger trend that includes Native leaders demanding an end to Indian sports mascots and other non-Indian appropriations of Native cultures. Chief Mankiller and her associates ultimately have insisted that only citizens of their nations can legitimately claim to be Creek, Cherokee, Choctaw, Chickasaw, or Seminole.

Figure 1. Principal chief Wilma Mankiller, Cherokee National Capitol rededication, Tahlequah, Oklahoma, October 12, 1991. (Photograph by C. R. Cowen, courtesy of Oklahoma Historical Society)

The Cherokee-led crusade to protect their tribal identities can best be viewed as an Indian-led effort to establish and police a formal ethnic and political boundary line against potential fraudulent interlopers. Increasingly, tribal leaders across the nation are arguing that only citizens of treaty-based, federally recognized tribes (or groups recognized through the BIA's process after 1978) be able to claim to be Indian in most public contexts. While it may seem logical that the Cherokee Nation should determine who is Cherokee, the reality is not so simple. The Cherokees' formal boundary-drawing has created intense conflict because it often runs counter to the way people view their individual identity. It seems to challenge the American tradition of choice regarding one's ethnicity, and perhaps the grand tradition of personal reinvention. It also clearly runs counter to the ethnic revolution spawned during the 1960s. Most of the controversial "Cherokee" and other "tribes" decried by Chief Mankiller emerged in the 1970s, labeled the "Decade of the Ethnics" by popular writer Michael Novak. During this decade it was in vogue to claim an ethnic identity, and Americans widely celebrated the country's rich ethnic and racial mosaic. The old "melting pot" model was discarded, and few mourned its passing, yet the new tolerance and respect for all things ethnic manifested itself in ways not inherently advantageous to the Cherokees, Creeks, and other tribes.[7] The result was a bewildering array of groups and individuals choosing or asserting an Indian identity. A climate of tolerance emerged, and many who had once believed that they "knew what an Indian was" realized that it was no longer quite so clear. There were many ways of seeing and defining Native Americans but there was no consensus on what it meant to be Indian in modern America.

Various ways of defining and seeing American Indian people began to conflict in the early 1970s. By this time scholars such as Fredrik Barth had popularized the notion in academia that ethnic groups were not ancient entities bound by birth, race, and custom, but living, evolving organisms held together and separated from others by social boundaries. The boundary lines could include traditional markers of difference such as language, foods, or physical traits that anyone could see, but they also could encompass very fuzzy or invisible concepts such as senses of history, notions of "us and them," and feelings of belonging—beliefs and emotions that could be recently created or even false. Other academics challenged the concept of race itself, a formidable boundary that was once viewed as objective scientific reality and incontrovertible biological fact. If ethnic groups were malleable, Eric Hobsbawm and Terence Ranger convincingly demonstrated that their seemingly bedrock traditions often were socially constructed, that although appearing ancient and resolute, they could be manipulated, changed, and even invented. With Barth and other social constructionists they refuted deeply held conceptions of racial and ethnic groups as grounded, stable entities.

This theoretical stance, however, was not popular among tribal leaders who viewed the academic questioning as a real threat to their status in American society. It seemed dangerously close to a slippery slope, one leading others to question their distinctiveness. It could open the possibility that almost anyone who thought they were "part Indian" could claim that heritage. For established Indian leaders, activists like Ward Churchill would soon set what appeared to be a tight political trap: anyone who challenged their Native heritage by demanding "Western" forms of proof was accused of being a racist agent of colonialism by demanding such proof. Activists were the "real Indians" by rejecting supposed nonaboriginal forms of identification, and tribal leaders were "Uncle Tomahawks," "Apples," or "white Indians" for playing the white people's game.

Scholars detailed the phenomenon of the 1970s of assimilated, third- and fourth-generation white ethnics such as Greek or Polish Americans becoming what sociologist Mary Waters called "Optional Ethnics," donning an ethnic label that was often described as pliable, situational, and portable. This "dime store ethnicity" was deemed cheap and plastic. It meant that a formerly "white bread" American could identify from a list of ancestors, choosing identifiers, such as "Cherokee" or "Italian," that the individual found appealing or valuable. Anthropologist Circe Sturm gave the label "ethnic switchers" to individuals who newly identified themselves as Cherokee. The US Census revealed fantastic rates of increase for the country's self-identified Native American population. Various state and federal agencies loosened their eligibility requirements for Indian programs, and the waters were becoming muddy. There were limits on the available "ethnic options," however, especially when they infringed on tribal domains. Resentment arose in many Native communities: these "dime store" ethnic switchers had never experienced the costs of being Native American. They had never suffered the racial profiling, educational deprivation, and grinding poverty most Native peoples knew all too well. These suddenly proud Natives had crossed an invisible symbolic boundary, but many did not know they had crossed a forbidden line.[8]

Much of both the public and tribal skepticism about these groups centers upon the issue of choice. There is a sense that members of unrecognized groups came about their ethnicity through a conscious decision rather than traditional ways people become members of ethnic or racial communities—birth, socialization, and geography. While this belief is hardly correct in the case of many state-recognized tribes in the Southeast, the sentiment permeates acknowledgment debates. To citizens of treaty-based recognized tribes such as the Creek Nation of Oklahoma, at its core Creek identity is a community identity. The nation decides who is included, and the claims of entities like the Lower Muskogee Creek Tribe to their identity seem to run counter to the Creek Nation's right to decide who their citizens are. To the recognized tribes, the appearance of groups like the Lower Muskogee Creek Tribe seems just another, if extreme, example of white or black Americans making claims on their heritage. As they view the Indian hobbyists of the early twentieth century who dressed up as Native Americans and attempted to preserve "real" Indian ways they believed existing Natives had lost—and as they view the white New Age "shamans" of today—tribes see these so-called new tribes as just another case of people claiming their heritage while purposefully disengaging themselves from real Indians who might judge their bona fides. Instead of deferring to the power of Indians to judge their authenticity (most members of state-recognized and unrecognized tribes cannot meet enrollment criteria of the established tribes) they instead claim the right to define themselves, a claim that to many is cultural imperialism at its most extreme. When some claimants cannot meet the criteria in the BIA's acknowledgment process (a process that is supported by the established tribes themselves), and when it is clear that the tribe they claim will not claim them, these entities often go to a non-Indian source that is overtly political, Congress, to gain acknowledgment. Members of unrecognized and state-recognized groups claim that they are disjointed parts of historical tribes and thus have a right to recognition on their own, using their own rules for membership. In general, leaders of the Creek, Cherokee, and other nations of Oklahoma reject this position, feeling that these groups must be accepted by the established Five Tribes nations. When the unrecognized groups go forward anyway, this seems to them the worst form of cultural imperialism imaginable.[9]

INTERETHNIC COMPETITION

Ethnic self-identification is highly personal and seemingly innocuous on many levels. However, when a person's self-proclaimed heritage infringes upon valuable resources such as Indian-only funds and tribal sovereignty itself, a form of interethnic competition emerges. As sociologist Joane Nagel notes, all societies place limits on which groups and individuals can claim potentially valuable ethnic statuses. Despite serious problems with policing the ethnic and racial boundaries, Cherokee and Creek leaders have long demanded that Indian-claiming organizations provide proof of their racial and cultural heritage. They have demanded documentation because, in general, treaty-based tribes do not consider the newly emerged Indian enclaves and recently state-recognized tribes to be "really Indian." The issue is not an internal Indian squabble. To tribal leaders these Indian bands, despite their names, are nonindigenous, ethnic competitors for a host of scarce resources. Self-described Cherokee "full-bloods" and cultural conservatives have come to demand proof of bloodlines and living culture; to them being Indian is largely a genetic essence, based in the blood, or grounded in the lived experience of kinship, culture, and community. To this, generic ethnically defined individuals argue that they are Indian because they say they are—various government agencies have their own definitions of indigenousness. Confusing the matter is the fact that there are three often-conflicting definitions at play: American Indians are the only people defined as an ethnic group, a racial group, and by reference to membership in a recognized tribe (politically). Many individuals do not comprehend the distinctions. Because of the confusion, the Five Tribes and others came to demand citizenship in a federally recognized tribe as the gold standard for Indian identification. It is vital that a claimed Creek or Cherokee group or individual find acceptance among the people claimed if they are to be seen as truly legitimate. Much of the discourse in tribal recognition politics has to do with the limits placed on groups and individuals as they seek acceptance as Cherokees, Choctaws, or other groups. Bloodlines, race, and tribal sovereignty all play roles.[10]

Anyone following tribal identity politics, whether by reading articles in newspapers, attending congressional hearings on tribal recognition, or talking with people involved in the debates, will quickly become aware that terms like "bona fide," "real," and "authentic" infuse the discourse and debates. As historian Philip Deloria and others correctly point out, such concepts are problematic—achieving a state of so-called authenticity is an illusive quest. Terms such as "real" and "authentic" cannot be adequately defined because there is no general consensus about the attributes necessary to claim these states; there certainly is no consensus on what traits and attributes are needed to be authentically Indian or tribal.[11] However, for individuals using these words and concepts, it is also apparent that they possess meaning and power. People who say "she's *not really Indian*" or "the Eastern Band is a *bona fide tribe*" seem to know what they mean. Today's tribal recognition debates can be best seen as a conversation between insiders and outsiders over what it means to be Indian in the United States in the twenty-first century. The debates can be viewed as dialectic, as dialogue between those who have status and those who do not. As Elizabeth Bird has concluded, what is perceived as "authentic" is often less a matter of historical accuracy than about who has the power to say what is real, yet somehow a sense of authenticity can emerge when Native people have the power to define "Indianness" themselves, no matter how the labels are derived.[12]

TRIBAL ACKNOWLEDGMENT IN THE SOUTHEAST

Debates over recognizing new tribes began during what I call the southeastern Indian renaissance of the years following World War II: a flowering of Indian culture, tribal organizations, and pride in Native identity that also included demands for access to federal Indian programs, the creation of state Indian commissions, and compensation for lands illegally taken in preceding generations. This renaissance set the stage for subsequent tribal acknowledgment politics involving the Five Tribes and related groups. The postwar years provided a much more welcoming climate for Native peoples in the Southeast: economic growth opened the region to the outside world, the civil rights movement eventually broke down social and political barriers, and the overall decline in racism encouraged isolated Native groups to more strongly assert an Indian identity. The federal government's "War on Poverty" initiative in the sixties that had fairly liberal eligibility requirements for Indian-identified programs provided a clear incentive structure for claiming an indigenous heritage.

These developments undoubtedly were good for the region's Indian people. However, there was a troublesome side to the southeastern Indian renaissance. From the perspective of the established Five Tribes and other recognized tribes, newly state-recognized "tribes" and their demands were threatening. Concerned leaders of the Five Tribes and other recognized tribes were intimately involved with the major developments that led to the BIA's Federal Acknowledgment Process in 1978. Together with eastern and southern tribes, both federally recognized and unrecognized, they helped create the 1978 rules. BIA acknowledgment criteria were thus what Poarch Band of Creek Indians leader Eddie Tullis calls a "negotiated settlement" between the established tribes and contenders.[13] When the rules were formalized and in place, all parties were optimistic about a fair, evidence-based process for outside groups to gain entry into the family of federally sanctioned tribes. Leaders of the Five Tribes and others saw a rigorous, fact-based procedure that could determine which groups were real tribes and which were not.

The Federal Acknowledgment Process clearly was a successful exercise by long-recognized tribes in boundary creation. Because they had helped craft the rules using both indigenous notions and Euro-American legal concepts, they would support its rigorous requirements in the future. Tribes would help police the boundaries by lobbying against tribes like the Lumbees that they felt were seeking to bypass the BIA's valid procedures. Because the majority of new tribal groups in the Southeast claimed some relation to the Creeks, Chickasaws, Cherokees, Choctaws, and Seminoles, the matter was personal to Five Nations leaders—and their interest was intense. The southeastern Indian renaissance established the social and economic context for the rise of new Indian tribes in the region, and the Federal Acknowledgment Process seemed to offer a solution to the problem of deciding which groups were worthy, surviving Indian enclaves eligible to establish a government-to-government relationship with the United States.

In 1992 anthropologist J. Anthony Paredes presciently stated that the Southeast would prove a major testing ground for what constitutes an American Indian tribe under US law.[14] The blurry racial and cultural lines of surviving indigenous groups in the region meant that which groups were "still Indian" was in no way clear or undisputed. While subsequent recognition battles in Congress and elsewhere have proved that Paredes was correct, surprisingly few scholars have heeded his call to deeply examine Indian-identifying communities in the region for what they can reveal about notions of Indian existence and tribal survival. Almost all existing works on formerly or currently unrecognized Indian communities in the Southeast generally accept the aboriginal identity and self-proclaimed tribal origins of groups under review. There are several logical reasons for the trend. The most basic is revealed in a comment from noted historian James Axtell to a reporter for the *Boston Globe* that "you don't make an academic specialty out of denying tribes." As pitfalls may accompany raising the possibility that some well-known Indian communities may not be long-standing aboriginal peoples, there is very little academic work on the topic. Few social scientists deeply analyze why the legitimacy of some groups (and not others) is questioned. Books and articles on the Federal Acknowledgment Process likewise largely avoid examining potentially dubious or wannabe groups, instead focusing on the functioning of the process itself or the experience of seemingly unambiguous Native communities harmed by it.[15]

Studies that deal with federal tribes and their participation in acknowledgment politics tend toward several schools of thought. The first was articulated in the 1970s by iconoclastic political scientist Vine Deloria, Jr., popular author of such enduring works as *Custer Died for Your Sins: An Indian Manifesto*. Having helped tribes like the Tiguas of Texas secure federal acknowledgment, Deloria portrayed the presently recognized tribes as "the haves" who were selfishly refusing to share with their less fortunate unrecognized Indian kin. To Deloria and others, raw economics lies at the heart of tribal support of government definitions of Indianness such as those laid out in the Federal Acknowledgment Process. A host of scholars—many of whom, like Deloria, have aided petitioning tribes—support the "small pie" theory. They believe that government definitions of Indians and tribes are simply part of the old colonial order, set to "divide and conquer" Native peoples. These scholars see these government definitions as overreliant on nonindigenous models of tribalism, blood quantum, government rolls and censuses. Many of them call upon tribes and Native peoples to undertake decolonization projects, imploring Indian leaders to pursue a new acknowledgment agenda, one that is more inclusive and less based on national imperatives and Western epistemologies of race, history, empiricism, and science. The most accepted scholarly position, which has been called the "liberal-inclusive" model for identifying tribes and Indian individuals, implies that the vast majority of unrecognized Indian groups and individuals are worthy of acknowledgment. This acknowledgement is not forthcoming, they say, due to a host of factors, including federal neglect, inadequate Euro-American recordkeeping, racism, and opposition from established tribes. Scholars who take this position find it shameful that marginal, unacknowledged aboriginal peoples are languishing today. Certain individuals within this loosely defined ideological school argue that officials should rely not on the current restrictive policy, but upon self-identification, community acceptance, and state recognition.[16]

For a host of reasons, presently recognized tribes such as the Creek Nation and the Mississippi Band of Choctaw Indians have never accepted scholarly, liberal-inclusive models or self-proclaimed identity as valid ways of defining Indian peoples or tribes. While most academics have called for a more inclusive acknowledgment policy, few scholars besides anthropologist Bruce Miller have delved into the problematic nature of defining exactly which peoples are "indigenous" as a national and global phenomenon. Theoretical examinations of the problems inherent in various federal ethnic and racial identification policies undoubtedly have much merit. However, serious consequences follow from relying upon self-identification and other liberal-inclusive definitions for determining which groups and individuals qualify for the rights and benefits accruing to indigenous Americans. While admitting that measuring ethnicity can sometimes be ludicrous, sociologist Joane Nagel concludes that the whole enterprise "is by no means capricious . . . calculating authenticity turns out to be deadly serious in many cases where individual and community resources hang in the balance."[17] The Five Tribes and related tribes such as the Florida Seminoles would agree: decisions on who to include or exclude have major consequences, affecting issues as diverse as Native American health care, land claims, scholarships, tribal survival, and sovereignty itself.

TRIBES ACTING IN UNEXPECTED WAYS

In existing writings about federally recognized tribes and their engagement with tribal acknowledgment politics, a palpable theme is clear:

presently recognized nations are not acting in the "Indian way" when they refuse to acknowledge their less fortunate Indian relatives and share with them. To many writers, federally recognized tribal leaders are so ensconced in the hegemonic colonial order that they are not even aware that they are replicating and reinforcing its inequities. According to this line, because the Five Tribes and related groups like the Mississippi Band of Choctaws and Eastern Band of Cherokees have embraced nonindigenous notions of "being Indian" and tribal citizenship using federal censuses such as the Dawes Rolls and blood quantum they are not being authentic. Some critics charge that modern tribes like the Choctaw Nation have rejected aboriginal notions and conceptions of Indian social organization and nationhood. This thinking, however, seems to me to once again reinforce stereotypes about Indians as largely unchanging, primordial societies. The fact that the Creek and Cherokee Nations have evolved and adopted European notions of citizenship and nationhood is somehow held against them in tribal acknowledgment debates. We hear echoes of the "Noble Savage" idea once again. In other contexts when tribes have demanded a say in controlling their cultural property and identities—by protesting Indian sports mascots or the marketing of cars and clothing with their tribal names, or by arguing that studios should hire real Indians as actors—these actions are applauded. However, when these occur in tribal recognition contexts, the tribes are viewed as greedy or racist. The unspoken theme is that tribes are not acting in the "traditional" Indian way.[18]

In 2004, when the Cherokee Nation passed a resolution defining marriage as an act between one man and one woman, many parties were shocked that Cherokees would support the federal Defense of Marriage Act, a bill largely backed by conservatives. Much like the common feeling about the Five Tribes' position on state-recognized tribes, popular reactions to the Cherokee stance on this marriage law flowed from stereotyped images of how Indians act and think. The position challenged deeply imbedded cultural misrepresentations that all "traditional" indigenous societies are inclusive, open to alternative sexualities, and welcoming of outsiders. Because supposed "traditional" Native societies have been offered as radical alternatives to conventional American culture, this creates impossible expectations for modern tribal peoples as they struggle to adapt to today's political and social realities. With their cultures seen as frozen in time, the more tribes deviate from popular representations, the more they are seen as inauthentic. To the degree that they are seen as assimilated (or colonized and enveloped in the hegemonic order), they are also seen as inauthentic, corrupted, and polluted. The supreme irony is that when recognized tribes demand empirical data to prove tribal authenticity, critics charge that they are not being authentically indigenous by doing so.[19]

The sentiment that established tribes that oppose unrecognized communities are somehow not acting in the "Indian way" is logical and understandable. Many unrecognized groups are the quintessential "underdogs": they lack status, have been oppressed as nonwhite peoples, and are poor. Both recognized and unrecognized Indians have faced the same struggles to survive and the same anti-Indian government policies. Many sympathetic parties ask: Why do the established groups not reject the "divide and conquer" government agenda and work together with tribes that currently are not federally recognized? While this position seems to have moral clarity, it oversimplifies the discourse in many ways. The Five Tribes and related federal tribes have evolved, yet their changes do not make them less Indian, especially when they use available resources to battle against perceived threats. As historian Clara Sue Kidwell has found, tribes such as the Choctaws have created governments that are like large corporations or state governments. Similar to nation-states, the Creek Nation and others have established procedures for regulating citizenship. They have largely individualized and formalized membership, and the process has largely shorn their nations of traditional requirements for belonging, such as clans, residence, and ceremonial participation. Does the fact that the Cherokee Nation is acting like an "all-American" government or corporate entity, and hiring lobbyists to protect its financial empire, make it a less aboriginal entity? Its efforts clearly do not fit the image of what aboriginal tribes are perceived to be, yet the Cherokee Nation is no less Indian for using resources to exert power in matters of great concern. While constrained by the very nature of federal tribal recognition (only the US government can confer this status), the Five Tribes and others are working within set parameters to control their destiny. Even though the methods and criteria employed are hardly precontact, these are their modern ways of operating as Cherokee, Creek, Seminole, Chickasaw, and Choctaw Nations today.[20]

A basic fact underlies the official Five Tribes position: tribal leaders in Oklahoma and their allies in the Southeast doubt the legitimacy of most groups seeking federal acknowledgment today. Accusations against the Five Tribes, namely that they are greedy and do not want to share the pie, are oversimplified and distort the issue. It is apparent that the Oklahoma tribal leaders truly believe that most groups in the Southeast are not real Indian tribes or long-standing indigenous communities by any definition. Much like their non-Indian counterparts, tribal skeptics feel that these groups cannot prove their indigenous ancestry or demonstrate that they are historical aboriginal communities. Further, they lack aboriginal cultural forms that could prove they are real tribes. From the vantage of the Five Tribes and their associates, the vast majority of these groups are claiming an Indian identity for benefits it is perceived it will bring: money, access to social services, and pride in ethnicity (and, conversely, escape from blackness), among others.

ISSUES AND COMMUNITY HISTORIES

This book provides several detailed community histories of Indian-identifying groups in the Southeast as a way to illuminate what established tribes view as bona fide, legitimate Indian communities. Intricate details about specific groups seeking official recognition are vital to an understanding of the truly murky realities involved in decisions about whether groups and individuals are "authentic" Indians and tribes. What is often lost in debates about the significant problems with the tribal acknowledgment process is awareness of the underlying assumption accepted by most parties: that it is historical reality that some legitimate Indian tribes were accidently or maliciously left out of the federal relationship. The BIA process was based on the idea that scholarly and legal evidence would be enough to determine which groups were surviving Indian tribes and which were not. However, few groups in the Southeast resemble average notions of what an Indian "tribe" looks like. As sociologists note, individuals carry around a mental image of what a "model" ethnic group member looks like, and there is dissonance when the "real thing" does not match the model. The case studies in this work should provide a mental picture of groups that have won acceptance as authentic tribes and a different picture of communities that have failed to attain acceptance of their aboriginal identities.

In the 1930s and early 1940s, Office of Indian Affairs staffers and a few inquisitive anthropologists like Frank Speck of the University of Pennsylvania became aware that a small group of Creek Indians, apparently highly mixed with people of European blood, still existed in southern Alabama, concentrated near a small railroad station called Poarch. They went to investigate. At the same time, a female school-teacher in rural Louisiana reached out to the Indian Office, hoping to open a school for a small band of apparently full-blood Choctaw Indians eking out an existence near Jena, Louisiana. Organized later as the Poarch Band of Creek Indians and the Jena Band of Choctaw Indians, these two small remnant Native populations would be two of only three Indian groups in the Southeast able to secure acknowledgment through the BIA's Federal Acknowledgment Process to date. The reasons why they were able to convince bureaucrats—and, importantly, other Choctaws and Creeks—of their authenticity and tribal survival is the subject of this book's chapter 3. About sixty miles west of the Poarch enclave is the homeland of the MOWA Band of Choctaw Indians. Since at least the 1830s their ancestors have lived in a swampy and wooded corner of rural Alabama. At the same time that the Poarch Creeks came to the attention of government agents and scholars, the MOWA group, known erroneously as "Cajans," also caught the attention of outsiders, who were curious about their history, exotic appearance, and seemingly obscure origins. Like the Poarch Band, the MOWA people are of admittedly mixed heritage—European, Native American, and African—yet they have not won universal acceptance as Native, much less as Choctaw. Their claimed relatives, the Choctaws, Cherokees, and Creeks, have generally opposed their tribal aspirations, and have rejected their indigenous identity and use of the Choctaw name. To the east of the MOWA community, in rural Georgia, the Lower Muskogee Creek Tribe has also failed to gain outside acknowledgment that it is a remnant Creek tribe. The complex racial, cultural, historical, political, and evidentiary reasons for the failure of these two groups to secure federal recognition are explored in chapter 4.

In a larger sense, the history of these once forgotten and obscure groups sheds some light on the use of the term "tribe." Scholars grapple with the issue of how to use words to describe whole groups of indigenous peoples. For lack of better alternatives we are often forced to utilize the term "tribe"—I will use it where I deem it appropriate—but the word can conjure stereotypical images and cause problems. One reason is that it seems apparent that once a group calls itself a "tribe," it often becomes one by sheer force of will. A "tribe" becomes a tribe because it has labeled itself one, and because writers have subsequently and repeatedly used whatever tribal name the group gave itself. We may all think we know what is meant when we say "tribe," but dialogue and a more in-depth examination are warranted, encouraging people to question their assumptions about groups called tribes today. Both the Lower Muskogee Creek Tribe and the MOWA Band of Choctaws labeled themselves tribes in the 1970s but others still hotly contest their claims. While these two groups have valid reasons for claiming an Indian heritage, opponents have well-reasoned arguments for challenging this identity.

If the MOWA and Lower Muskogee groups complicate our under-standings of Indian tribes in the Southeast, the work of the Cherokee Nation's Fraudulent Indian Task Force has exposed the major impli-cations of the widespread, uncritical acceptance of self-proclaimed Indians and potentially dubious tribes. According to Five Tribes offi-cials, the situation has reached epidemic proportions: over two hundred groups claim to be Cherokee alone, and almost 30 percent of all groups currently seeking federal tribal status claim to be Cherokee, Chickasaw, Creek, Choctaw, or Seminole. The sheer number of these entities and the scope of their activities engender questions regarding whether the existence of obviously wannabe tribes has been overstated as a reason for maintaining the rigid federal recognition standards. Using the Internet for self-promotion and aided by public ignorance of their questionable characteristics, self-proclaimed Cherokee and other tribes have been emboldened in recent years. While scholars and other insiders generally scoff at them, these groups have paraded as Cherokees, Creeks, and other federally recognized groups, and have won acceptance. They have received federal Indian education funds while individual members have received jobs as Native Americans. Members market their artwork as Indian-made. The more unscrupulous have presented themselves as shamans, Indian sexual gurus, and peyote priests. The most revolting, Malcolm "Thunderbird" Webber, even sold expensive memberships in his "tribe" to naïve and impoverished undocumented immigrants who hoped these cards would secure them residency status. To experts on Indian affairs, the actions of these groups and individuals may appear ludicrous, but they have gotten away with their schemes. Few average Americans know the difference between "the Southern Cherokees" and the real Cherokee Nation. As the Five Tribes leaders view the problem, educating the public about the actions of fraudulent "Indians" and stopping their activities are important endeavors. Deciding whether these groups are legitimate is no trivial matter.

Financial matters certainly affect tribal acknowledgment cases. Money enters the picture in the form of Indian gaming. It also emerges when a group with over fifty thousand members like the Lumbee Tribe of North Carolina attempts to secure a piece of the federal Indian funding pie. The final chapter of this book explores the brute financial concerns that cloud what should be ethical and moral decisions over acknowledging forgotten Indian enclaves. It details the debates that have ensued over the potential costs of recognizing the Lumbee Tribe and the MOWA Band of Choctaw Indians. Ironically it was a tribe from the region, the Seminole Tribe of Florida, that pioneered today's Indian gaming industry, an enterprise that more than any single factor has thwarted the tribal aspirations of the region's surviving unrecognized Indian enclaves. Depending on one's viewpoint, Indian casinos either have been a positive trend or an extremely negative development in tribal recognition politics. The Lumbees and the MOWA Band certainly would argue that the Indian gambling industry has derailed their once promising efforts to secure federal tribal status via an act of Congress. Casino money has made their neighbors the Eastern Band of Cherokees, the Poarch Band of Creek Indians, and the Mississippi Band of Choctaw Indians extremely powerful, well-heeled opponents. The millions they have earned through gambling have granted them access to power on Capitol Hill. They have hired lobbyists to fight the Lumbee and MOWA organizations, potential federally recognized tribes they see as significant threats to their gambling monopolies in North Carolina, Mississippi, and Alabama. To the Lumbees and MOWA Choctaws, tribal casinos have been the kiss of death to their aspirations for federal status. Indian gambling has interjected a financial motive for tribal opposition to their hopes and dreams of winning unqualified acceptance of their Indian identity. After decades in the struggle, MOWA Band chief Wilford "Longhair" Taylor has concluded: "It's no longer a matter of red; it's a matter of green."[21]

UNRECOGNIZED VOICES, UNCOMFORTABLE QUESTIONS

In early 2010 a friend told me about a video I needed to see to under-stand how the Five Tribes' campaign against state-recognized tribes and allegations that some groups are "fraudulent tribes" affects people in those groups. At the beginning of the amateur video, a lean, clean-cut man in his early thirties approaches a microphone at a University of Oklahoma symposium on tribal economic development. The scene is nothing if not mundane: a formal conference hall setting, one of countless such meetings held annually across the country. The man introduces himself as Cedric Sunray, an enrolled member of the MOWA Band of Choctaw Indians of Alabama. With his young daugh-ter standing at his side, Sunray starts out by politely posing a ques-tion to one of the featured panel speakers, Phillip Martin, the legendary former chairman of the Mississippi Band of Choctaw Indi-ans, revered in many quarters for having led his once-impoverished tribe in one of the most remarkable, if improbable, Native economic development success stories of the twentieth century. I find myself lulled as Sunray starts out by calmly telling Martin that his people, the MOWA Choctaws, have attended Indian schools such as Bacone and Haskell, and have made up a long-standing Native community in southern Alabama since time immemorial. The tone soon turns decidedly ugly, however, as Sunray holds up a letter he says was written by Martin, one saying that the MOWA people are not Choctaw but a bunch of "mulattoes." Sunray demands to know why Martin is attacking the Native heritage of his people. He asks why the Mississippi Choctaw leader has paid millions of dollars to disgraced lobbyist Jack Abramoff to slander and impugn the Choctaw identity of his people, an impov-erished group that hardly has the resources to fight back at all. At this point the moderator steps in, telling Sunray that this is a sym-posium on economic development, not a forum for political issues. The moderator demands that he show some respect.

Sunray, an intelligent and athletic man who teaches Native lan-guages in eastern Oklahoma, has vowed to personally confront tribal leaders and members of the Cherokee Nation's Fraudulent Indian Task Force who attack his people's heritage and identity. A self-described kid of the streets who was raised in housing projects in Florida, Sunray is not easily intimidated. At this symposium he characteristically refuses to back down. As Sunray continues to challenge Phillip Martin over his alleged past actions, the moderator calls for security. Martin sits impassively at the table in the front of hall, his silence hiding his thoughts on the subject, perhaps betraying his position of power and authority at the meeting. As the video winds down we see Sunray being unceremoniously escorted out of the hall by several large men, but not before he manages to go around to tables, dropping off packets of information on the MOWA Band and other state-recognized tribes in the Southeast. Finally the panel participants and a visibly relieved audience settle down, happy that the conference can return to the less controversial matters at hand.

Cedric Sunray is not a popular man in some areas of eastern Oklahoma. While his tactics may upset many, the emotions that give rise to these confrontations are widespread among members of tribal communities that are not federally recognized. Although an employee of a federally recognized tribe can quite easily place a group on a "fraudulent" tribes list, the implications of this action affect members of these communities profoundly. The allegations can be quite personal and hurtful. Supported by many in the scholarly community, spokespersons for state-recognized tribes and other nonrecognized Indian groups challenge others to recognize and validate alternative ways of seeing and accepting aboriginal communities. Because assertions and claims to Native identity and status are part of a dialogue—albeit one with vast power disparities—unacknowledged leaders are locked in an ongoing quest to have established parties recognize their indigenousness. Sunray and others have generally taken what they see as the moral high road. As a matter of justice and acknowledgement of past colonialism and culturally imperialistic policies, the federal government and established recognized tribes should widely acknowledge groups that have maintained a historical aboriginal identity. Scholars and leaders of state-recognized tribes rightly point to the historical and political reasons that many unrecognized tribes lack concrete, written proof of their tribal heritage. Native peoples in the Southeast faced the first waves of colonization in the early decades of the sixteenth century. Given the long time span since then, it seems unreasonable to many that groups have to produce firm documentation of their historical existence. Due to the very nature of their unrecognized status, groups were passed over and therefore lack treaties, reservations, and government rolls that are now often demanded to establish tribal identities. To many experts and members of left-out groups, it seems outrageous to ask for these types of federal and other government records to prove tribal identity. If groups had these records they would be recognized. They are now caught in a catch-22, unrecognized yet forced to provide the sort of records possessed by recognized groups to prove they are real tribes.

THE STAKES

In many ways the discourse involving the Cherokee Nation and other tribes in the Southeast about what is a viable Indian tribe is part of a struggle between Natives and non-Natives about who should have the power to acknowledge, understand, and ultimately represent the Cherokees, Choctaws, and other tribal people in the United States today. The Five Tribes' position and how it is perceived reveals much about their ways of seeing indigenousness and also how non-Indians (scholars, politicians, and the general public) view Indian peoples.

Ever since tribal leaders became aware of the activities of non-reservation groups and pan-tribal Indian organizations in the late 1960s, they have voiced fears about an anti-tribal backlash, fueled in part by the demands of nontraditional Indian voices. Dozens of newspaper articles and television shows focusing on what producers see as the recognition of dubious "tribes" motivated by casino wealth and other potential benefits make clear that tribal anxieties about the erosion of tribal sovereignty is neither paranoid nor delusional. New images of rich casino Indians who do not "need" federal benefits have attached to unambiguous groups like the Seminoles of Florida, and scholars see these new stereotypes as potential threats to tribal sovereignty. Imagine how significant the danger must seem to tribal spokespersons if the general public views most tribes in East as undeserving, assimilated, wannabe opportunists.[22] In this light, tribes have valid reasons for insisting that hopeful groups go through the BIA's Federal Acknowledgment Process, with its perceived rigor and science, in preference to alternatives that most parties acknowledge are inherently political (congressional recognition) or biased (recognition via federal courts). While memories of the failed tribal termination era of the Cold War are starting to fade, those cognizant of the historical oscillations of federal Indian policy will remember that change is constant, that the American predisposition to want to envelop and assimilate tribal nations is still here, just out of sight. The winds of change might usher in a newfound, if really old and timeworn, solution to the perceived "Indian problem" and anomalous state of Indians in the federal system. Tribal leaders recognize that a real danger exists if people perceive Indians as assimilated and entirely self-sufficient, no longer needing federal aid and "ready" again to be terminated and join the American mainstream.

The Five Tribes' engagement with tribal acknowledgment issues reveals not only how they perceive Indian identity today but also the webs of interdependency and common interests shared by federal officials in Washington and tribal nations based in Tahlequah, Oklahoma, and Poarch, Alabama. The Five Tribes' position clearly betrays larger fears about culture change, anti-tribal backlash, and racial amalgamation. It also reveals a deeply protective urge to defend their tribal heritage and identity. Their response to unrecognized and state-recognized tribes is inextricably entwined with the non-Native political environment. The federally recognized tribes of eastern Oklahoma are enmeshed in a political and bureaucratic structure in which they are neither independent nor otherwise free to act. Although lacking full empowerment, tribal leaders know that their relationship with the federal government itself is the source of their power. They share with the government in Washington a common interest in protecting this status and guarding against potential fraudulent interlopers. The Five Tribes support the BIA's Federal Acknowledgment Process. This book explains the reasons why.

CHAPTER 1

Indian Renaissance in the Southeast

In 1980 the *Baton Rouge State Times* ran a front-page story describing a modern Indian "attack" perpetuated by the ironically named Indian Angels. Part of the Red Power movement, formed in the wake of the Indian occupation of Alcatraz in 1969, the pan-tribal organization was described by the press as "angry" and "militant." Whether one agreed with their tactics or not, the Indian Angels were certainly causing a stir in the Bayou State. According to the *State Times* article, Indian Angel protesters wearing war paint and headdresses had descended upon the governor's mansion with a list of demands. Yelling, "You can tell the governor he doesn't want a Wounded Knee in Louisiana!" and threatening to take scalps, they demanded that Native concerns be heard. They were noticed, though opinions about the protest varied.

While many whites were excited by the appearance of Indian activists in their midst, the generally conservative rural tribes of the state were appalled by the Indian Angels' tactics. They felt that the group's vocal, confrontational style was not at all the "Indian way." Probably unbeknownst to most Louisianans at the time, the Indian Angels were part of a larger Indian groundswell in the southeastern states. At the most basic level, groups like the Indian Angels were alerting local government leaders that Native Americans still existed in the region and that they had needs that were unfulfilled. They also gave notice that there were potential problems associated with forgotten, generally unrecognized Native communities scattered across the southern states.[1]

The Indian Angels' protest in Louisiana's capital capped a momentous era: the southeastern Indian renaissance that began developing after World War II. In the 1960s and 1970s especially, slumbering Native enclaves seemed to awaken, and Indian culture and identity flowered, as reflected in the growth of tribal organizations, economic development projects, and a desire by once-invisible groups to demonstrate their pride in Indian heritage and to preserve, reintroduce, or import indigenous cultural traditions. For isolated Native Americans these were exciting times. The renaissance they helped foster proved central to the continuing survival of Indian cultures in the region, especially for those Native people off-reservation, who had been submerged and forgotten within the popularly perceived black-and-white society of the South. The revival had a more troubling side, however, spawning contentious issues that continue to trouble intertribal and Indian-government relations in the region to the present day. It provided the context and inspiration for the appearance of questionable Indian groups and tribes that served to undermine the aspirations of long-suffering Native communities, ones struggling mightily to preserve their identities and reignite the traditions of their ancestors while gaining acceptance in the larger national community.

The transformations of these years were immense. Southeastern Indians entered the period almost invisible in local and national affairs and ended it as significant forces in each. An Indian alive in Louisiana in 1940 would scarcely believe the changes the next decades would unfurl. By the 1970s, southern Indians had emerged from their second-class citizenship of the Jim Crow era, gaining civil rights and a voice in local politics. They had established formal tribal governments that provided a host of services, joined in intertribal organizations, and become fixtures in local politics. Throughout the Southeast, powwows and other Indian celebrations became anticipated annual events. Once-scorned peoples were now celebrated citizens. By the 1980s, some southeastern Indian enclaves had secured state recognition, and a few had achieved federal acknowledgment. The privileged federally recognized tribes enjoyed a status that allowed them to exercise sovereignty and pursue self-determination in various areas of tribal life. All gained the simple but important public recognition that they were surviving Indian peoples in a region long thought to be devoid of Indians.

SURVIVING AS INDIAN IN THE JIM CROW SOUTH

After the removal era initiated officially in 1830 and the Seminole
Wars of the 1840s, most Americans had the misperception that no
Indians remained in the Southeast. Small communities of Indians
persisted, however. Largely hidden in isolated pockets of their former
homelands, southeastern Indians struggled to survive, both physically
and culturally, in the harsh social and political climate of the nineteenth-
century South. The groups that remained found refuge in generally
undesired places: mountain hollows, swamps, coastal marshes, and
pine-barrens were their homes. The survivors varied considerably in
community composition, ethnic makeup, and retention of aboriginal
culture. There were remnants of the once-powerful Five Tribes that
lived scattered about their former homelands, such as the Eastern
Band of Cherokees in North Carolina, the Mississippi Band of Choctaw
Indians, and the Seminoles of Florida. These groups possessed various
forms of traditional culture and were generally acknowledged as Indians,
both at the local and national level. Before the 1960s, the Mississippi
Choctaws, the Eastern Band of Cherokees, and the Seminoles and
Miccosukees of Florida had secured federal tribal recognition and
small reservations that served as homelands for their peoples. Small
tribes such as the Chitimachas and Coushattas of Louisiana had also
managed to secure federal recognition by this time. Despite federal
acknowledgment, most of the reservation tribes in the region faced
efforts by non-Indians to challenge their status. Most communities
had intermarried with non-Indians and faced challenges to their racial
status as Indians—local and state politicians repeatedly questioned
their tribal acknowledgment and tried to break up their reservations.
Another class of Indians consisted of lesser-known tribal groups that
survived on state-sponsored reservations, such as Virginia's Pamunkey
and Mattaponi Tribes, the Catawba of South Carolina, and the Alabama-
Coushattas of Texas. The latter two tribes have had on-and-off relations
with the federal government but are currently federally recognized.
While the state-recognized tribes generally lacked the protections of
their federally recognized kin, as land-based groups these tribes were
widely acknowledged as Native Americans despite some challenges
as to their "racial purity." A third class of southeastern indigenous
peoples consisted of refugee multiracial communities tucked away in
remote, marginal lands throughout the Southeast. The Lumbees and

related groups in North and South Carolina are the most well-known of these groups, but others include the MOWA Choctaw community of Alabama and the Houma Indians west of New Orleans. These Native groups generally have been accepted as Indian, but questions about their tribal origins and true genetic composition have long clouded their histories and identities. The fact that these groups often lack abundant traits associated with aboriginal culture also has prompted non-Indians to question their Native identities. People like the Lumbee, however, have retained an unwavering sense that they are descendants of the aboriginal peoples of the Southeast and have struggled valiantly to challenge those questioning their heritage. There is a final class of people identified today as Indians who survived in the Southeast. Dozens of groups once known by racist names like Redbones and Brass Ankles live dispersed throughout most of the Southeast. Historically they claimed some Native American ancestry, but never possessed a concrete, purely Indian tribal identity. Some of their descendants nonetheless took part in the southeastern Indian renaissance of the postwar years.[2]

Almost all the Native groups that survived in the region did so by retreating to undesirable areas, lands that provided a marginal subsistence lifestyle and left them a legacy of poverty. These haunts nonetheless proved a protected space to maintain their indigenous identity. Like Indians elsewhere, southeastern Indians were rural people, isolated not by formal reservations, as in the American West, but by a host of factors including racial discrimination, poverty, and personal choice. With the exception of the few reservation groups, southeastern Indian enclaves rarely exhibited community characteristics associated with western Indian tribes. Lacking federal reservations, they did not own lands in common. Lacking a relationship with the federal government, they did not have formal tribal structures such as rolls and elected chiefs or councils. As anthropologist J. Anthony Paredes notes, an individual looking for popularly envisioned "tribes," "chiefs," and "Indian villages" will rarely find them among the piney woods and bayous of the Southeast. Centuries of cultural contact and assimilation have left most groups bereft of cultural traits that are clearly aboriginal or Native, a reality that also adds to the invisibility of many southeastern Indian communities. The central fact about persisting Indian enclaves in the Southeast is that they survived by assimilating most of the cultural and economic modes of their non-Native neighbors.[3]

With the exception of multiracial, light-skinned Indian descendants who could pass as rural whites, Indians had a striking uniformity of experience in the post–Civil War Southeast. As nonwhites in a biracial, largely black-and-white world, Native-identified communities felt the sting of Jim Crow segregation and racism throughout the region by the beginning of the twentieth century. From the Pamunkey and Mattaponi Tribes in Virginia to the Alabama-Coushattas of Texas, Indians faced discrimination and lessened economic opportunities in the dark years prior to World War II. The system buttressing white supremacy was all-encompassing, including the realms of social relations, public accommodations, education, and the workplace. As historian Edward Ayers notes, the "New South" of the turn of the century saw little change in race relations and was an extremely violent place, with homicide rates among the highest in the world. In the volatile and racially stratified society, nonwhites had to "know their place"—it was a matter of survival. Until the major changes wrought by World War II, few had the power or ability to resist the system.[4]

Wherever small pockets of Native peoples persisted, they occupied an intermediate position in the racial hierarchy, squarely between whites and African Americans. A long history of interaction, intermarriage, pseudoscientific racial theories, and folklore left Native Americans above African Americans but clearly below the dominant whites. Southerners knew well romantic stories of Indians such as Creek leader William Weatherford (Red Eagle) who fought valiant, if doomed, wars for their beloved homeland before acknowledging their people's inevitable slide into disappearance from the southern scene. This warrior tradition led most southern whites to elevate Indians above their African American neighbors. As racial segregationist Ben Tillman noted in the late nineteenth century, "[W]e all respect the Indians because they were too brave to ever consent to be made slaves while negroes have submitted to slavery and seemed to thrive on it."[5] Despite the respect shown to past Indian warriors and civilizations, the in-between status of surviving Indian groups confounded the black–white color line in both practical and theoretical ways. As a nonwhite minority, southeastern Indians experienced segregation and racism to varying degrees depending on locality. Residential separateness meant that in intimate settings, most Indian people associated primarily with other Indians. Near New Orleans, Houma Indian houses lay on one side of the bayous while African

American and white homes were on the other, the muddy water serving as a physical and symbolic barrier between the groups. Indian children were socialized to know which places were "Indian" and thus safe, and which were not. In the Lumbee stronghold of Robeson County, North Carolina, some towns were "Indian towns" while others were the domain of whites and blacks. Local practices determined the limits of interchange in public places, especially in larger towns dominated by whites. It was widely known in rural North Carolina that Saturday afternoons were reserved as time the Indians could come to town. In places like Jena, Louisiana, Choctaws simply stayed out of town most of the time as its Jim Crow segregation served to remind that whites lumped them into the colored category. Segregation was often formal and institutionalized, but could be informal, by long-standing custom. Houma Indians were forced to sit in separate sections of local theaters and in the cordoned-off "Indian section" of Catholic churches. Even after the church railing was taken down by the 1960s, Bruce Duthu recalls that the tradition remained—few Indians strayed from the old segregated quadrant. In Robeson County, Lumbees could not eat in restaurants, sit in "whites only" waiting rooms, or get a soda at the drug store. As Ruth Locklear recalls, her parents rarely took her to these places, protecting her and her siblings from the effects of institutionalized racism.[6]

Although elevated above African Americans in the racial hierarchy, Indians still found themselves near the bottom of the socioeconomic ladder. Despite being among the first inhabitants of their regions, few possessed recognized legal title to their lands, and timber companies and other large enterprises gradually chipped away at the Indian land base. A fair number of Lumbees owned farms, yet most were reduced to tenant farming or sharecropping by the late nineteenth century. Chronic debt and poverty was the common condition of North Carolina Indians. Male members of groups like the MOWA Choctaws that had retreated to once undesired piney woods found work in the timber industry, gaining a reputation as first-rate lumbermen and turpentine workers. The Jena Choctaws became virtually attached to a local white land-owning family's estate, while the nearby Houma Indians lived a freer life off the bounty of southern Louisiana's bayous and the Gulf of Mexico. Houmas generally worked as trappers, fishers, shrimpers, and subsistence farmers at the turn of the century.[7]

During the Jim Crow era, large social and political forces also worked
to deny Indians their basic right to self-definition. Native peoples faced
constant pressures to force them into the larger "black" or "colored"
category, with all the incumbent disadvantages. Their existence as a
third "race" in the largely dichotomous, black and white South challenged the seemingly clear-cut racial order of the region. Dozens of
communities were known in local parlance by a bewildering array
of largely pejorative labels, many of them somewhat generic: Red
Bones, Brass Ankles, Melungeons, Creoles, Free Jacks, Yellow Ham-
mers, Red Niggers, and Guineas. Other names were more locally
specific: Louisiana had its Sabines, Alabama its Cajans, and North
Carolina its Croatans, shortened to "Cro." All these labels implied
that the communities were some mixture of Indian, black, and white,
often with traditions of shipwrecked pirates or lost Portuguese or
Spanish sailors thrown in for good measure. Scholars followed this
tradition, labeling these groups "tri-racial isolates," "little races," "racial
islands," or the more offensive "racial orphans," "American outcasts,"
and "WIN Tribe" (for White-Indian-Negro). The position of the dominant sociological and anthropological schools of the 1940s through
the early 1970s can be summed up by Brewton Berry in his widely read
Almost White: "These are all 'reluctant Indians'—Nanticokes, Chickahominy, Lumbee. Most of them would doubtless prefer to be white.
But since that goal is beyond their reach, they will settle for Indian. It
is better to be red than black—even an off-shade of red."[8] The economics
of this reluctance to confirm their Indian identity is revealed in several
examples. In one North Carolina town, businesses had to provide three
separate facilities for the three "racial' groups in their midst. As chemical plants began to dot the ports north of Mobile, Alabama, factory
owners simply refused to hire local "Cajans" (modern MOWA Choctaws)
because doing so would force them to provide another set of bathrooms,
locker rooms and other facilities.[9]

Added to southeastern Indian group identity problems, many faced
long-standing difficulty establishing or proving to skeptical outsiders
a concrete, historical tribal identity. Although in some cases it was a
logical product of centuries of colonial contact and disruptions, for
individuals more familiar with western tribes the fact that many of
these groups did not know their ancestral tribe was baffling and
seemed to point to a dubious claim to Indian heritage. For reservation
tribes like the Mississippi Choctaws and Florida Seminoles indigenous

identity was ironclad and never questioned. Others, however, had only vague and often undocumented traditions tying them to the Cherokees, Choctaws, Creeks or other well-known southeastern tribes. Most commonly, nonreservation Indians in the Southeast were known generically as "Indians" by their neighbors and even sometimes among themselves. Some, like a community studied by Louisiana State University student Mary Van Rheenan in northwestern Louisiana, had traditionally been known as Spanish or Mexican, yet had by the 1970s more often identified as Native American.[10]

The manner in which Indians have been recorded, tracked, and identified has also worked against establishing concrete tribal identities. Lacking a relationship with the federal government, these groups do not possess associated reservation records, tribal rolls, and recorded blood degrees that often help modern tribes prove their indigenousness. The work of U.S. census takers also clouds the waters. Until 1960, when self-identification became the rule, the Census Bureau instructed enumerators to use their own judgment to identify the supposed race of residents. This was most often based on the testimony of respondents or the visual judgment of the census taker. Neither was scientific, and this was hardly foolproof, yet these records would prove important for groups trying to establish tribal recognition. Added to the confusion was the general absence of local knowledge about historic tribes and tribal names, and the oft-cited comment that many Native claimants "did not look Indian." All these factors worked against consistent racial classification of Indians as reflected in the U.S. Census. A common scenario would find an individual listed as "free person of color" prior to the Civil War and afterward as "Indian," "black," or "mulatto," depending on the decade. All the while the black–white lenses of the society continually pushed Indian individuals into the "black" or "colored" category, most often against their wills. At the same time, lighter-skinned Indians, especially those who had moved away from their home regions, felt the pull to "pass" as white, and deny their indigenous roots.[11]

As pride in Indian ancestry increased following World War II, many groups with disparaging local monikers or ambiguous tribal origins worked to establish formal names of their own choosing. Groups in the Southeast generally derived their names from two sources: local geographic place-names and names of historic tribes indigenous to their homelands. Some combined the two trends. In

North Carolina the modern Haliwa-Saponi Tribe took their name by combining the names of the two counties where they lived, Halifax and Warren, while attaching the name of a tribe indigenous to the area. The MOWA Choctaw similarly created their name by combining "Mobile" and "Washington"—the names of Alabama counties where most live—with the name of the tribe indigenous to their homeland. The Lumbees derived their name from the nearby Lumber River, while the Waccamaw Siouan Tribe created their name from a local lake and the language likely spoken by indigenous groups in the region. Others took their names partly from names of nearby non-Indian communities—such is the case with the Poarch Band of Creek Indians, the Clifton Choctaws, and the Jena Band of Choctaws. Many took their names from the Five Tribes, a fact that became a major issue of contention, as will be discussed in subsequent chapters of this book. Whether intended by their originators or purely coincidental, many of the postwar tribal names have what some describe as an "Indian sound" to them, something else that causes suspicion about their identities in some quarters.[12]

A major result of their social and physical isolation and in-between racial status was the marked occurrence of endogamy among southeastern Indian enclaves. Members of local groups, whether the Houmas in Louisiana or the MOWA Choctaws in Alabama, tended to marry within the group. Community members often shared locally recognized "Indian names," such as Oxendine, Locklear, and Brayboy in Robeson County, North Carolina, and Pierite and Barby in Marksville, Louisiana. Near Houma, Louisiana, where some French names were shared by Indians and non-Indian Cajuns, a short conversation often included a question about where one was from. The answer "Dulac" or "Montegut" quickly established that the individual was Indian. In some localities, like Mobile and Washington Counties in Alabama, certain family lines were associated with darker complexions, darker hair, and other "Indian-looking" traits, with these individuals subject to greater prejudice at times, even among Indians themselves.[13]

It is surprising to many modern observers that southeastern Indians rigidly maintained the "color line" separating them from African Americans, avoiding social contact, proscribing intermarriage, and having prejudicial beliefs. Especially among groups whose acceptance as Indian was questioned, maintaining in-group marriage and avoiding contact with African Americans was seen as essential to maintaining their status above local blacks. This was particularly salient when acknowledging that even federally recognized tribes like the Mississippi Choctaws experienced local pressures to deny their unique status and lump them in with local African Americans.[14] Throughout the Southeast, Indian traditions and social practice were fairly uniform: a Houma or other Indian who married an African American was excluded from the community. Marriages with whites were not similarly proscribed, and in some cases were encouraged. Local whites generally maintained prohibitions against such unions, however, which further promoted endogamy. If social prohibitions against contact with African Americans were strong at the family level, they were institutionalized with the Lumbees in education. After fighting to secure their own Indian schools in the late nineteenth century the group established formal "Blood Committees" to ensure that no blacks gained admittance, an occurrence that could have eroded the status of their schools. It is difficult for many modern observers to understand the Indian position. However, it is easy to forget the racial climate prevalent in the turn-of-the-century South.[15] In this environment, southeastern Indian groups vigilantly worked to distance themselves from African Americans, seeing their status as Indians as a valuable deterrent to white efforts to force them into the "black" category.

Wherever an isolated Indian enclave existed, the twin institutions of southeastern Indians were found: an Indian church and school. Because most groups lacked formal reservations and associated institutions, churches and schools served as the physical, spiritual, and intellectual anchors of most Native communities. Both institutions grew from Indians' desire to control their own facilities and counter their exclusion from white schools and churches. They also clearly reflect Indians' refusal to attend African American institutions. Indian churches were heavily influenced by surrounding Anglo-American culture, with the vast majority of surviving Indian groups in the region absorbing the Christian traditions of their neighbors. As with their white neighbors, Native churches served as centers of local communities, places of everyday socializing, kinship bonding, and training of leadership. In largely undocumented processes, southeastern groups like the Lumbees, Poarch Creeks, and Alabama-Coushattas adopted the beliefs of the Methodists, Baptists, Presbyterians, and other Protestant denominations in the region. The Houmas of southern Louisiana proved an exception; they assimilated the Roman Catholicism of their

Figure 2. Children and teacher at Indian School, Houma, Louisiana, 1930s. (Photograph courtesy of State Library of Louisiana, Louisiana Collection)

Cajun neighbors. For most southeastern Indian enclaves, the religious adoption was so complete that by the early twentieth century little clearly identifiable aboriginal spirituality remained. Groups like the MOWA Choctaws of southern Alabama built their own churches, such as Reeds Chapel, that doubled as school buildings, run by missionaries sent by Protestant denominations. Even today, Reeds Chapel and similar buildings serve as points of pride and symbols of the Indian community. Because they were designated "Indian churches," for people like the MOWA Choctaw whose heritage was often challenged these churches remain important signifiers of Indian identity and valuable confirmation of indigenous heritage.[16]

All Indian schools have likewise served as anchors of Native communities, and like Indian churches formed as a result of both pressures from within and outside local Native American communities. From the reservation tribes of Virginia to the scattered Indians of Louisiana, Jim Crow segregation resulted in the exclusion of Indian people from white schools, and this, with Indian refusal to be lumped in with local blacks, led to the creation of Indian schools. In various places throughout the Southeast, a unique system of separate white, black, and Indian schools existed. The most noteworthy example of this phenomenon occurred in the mid-1880s in North Carolina. The Lumbees succeeded in having a state congressman designate them "Croatan Indians," a status that enabled the state to establish a separate school system, ultimately up to the college level, for Indian children. Native schools were far inferior to their white counterparts, however. Their very existence and the struggles that went into their creation and maintenance meant that they were nonetheless important signifiers of Indian identity and strongly valued as such. Prior to World War II, high school and post-secondary education was generally unattainable for Indian youths, especially members of groups not federally recognized. However, some individuals did gain admittance to Indian high schools and colleges such as the BIA school in Cherokee, North Carolina, and Bacone College in Oklahoma.[17]

The strange tripartite Jim Crow educational system was created by default, for purely racist reasons, yet the separate all-Indian schools grew to become extremely important to southeastern Native people. Lumbee schools generally were under Indian control, with respected community leaders forming committees that raised funds, selected teachers (who were often Indians), and controlled who gained admittance. This last fact led to the "Blood Committees" that jealously guarded entry, excluding any individual with a trace of known African ancestry.[18] The state of North Carolina ultimately created an institution of higher learning, the Croatan Normal School, to train Indian teachers. This school grew into the modern University of North Carolina at Pembroke, the first such Indian institution in the United States. It is difficult to overstate the importance of the Indian-led educational system in North Carolina. Over time local schools served as centers of Indian communities, confirming Native identity and fostering future leaders. The university at Pembroke, built and funded through generations of effort and sacrifice, served as the central training ground for Lumbee professionals and leaders during the twentieth century, and was also a point of pride for all of the state's Indian communities, many of whom sent youth to study there. Men and women educated at Pembroke became leaders in the post–World War II Indian renaissance in the Southeast.[19]

WATERSHED: THE WORLD WAR II ERA

The war that started in faraway Europe in 1939 forever ended the isolation of southeastern Indians, with their military service and employment sparking new demands for equality and opportunity once the conflict ended in 1945. The war led to the southeastern Indian renaissance indirectly, as returning veterans and war industry workers came to demand an end to their second-class status. A group of Lumbee veterans forced the state legislature to return the franchise to the people of Pembroke in electing town officials. Under a previous law, backed by the white minority, the governor appointed the town mayor and others. Veterans were among the Lumbees who faced down a Ku Klux Klan rally in 1958 (discussed later in this chapter), and other Native veterans throughout the Southeast utilized the GI Bill to further their education. Arnold Battise, an Alabama Coushatta from Texas, who had grown up speaking only his native language, attended the University of Houston, becoming the first of his people to earn a law degree. Returning Lumbee veterans were turned away from the University of North Carolina, however. The school did not accept Indians, an indignity that fired their later activism. For many southeastern Indian veterans, serving in the war had exposed them for the first time to the world beyond the Southeast. Many became acquainted for the first time with Indians from other areas, contacts that would prove valuable in coming decades. The war experiences of veterans proved central to southeastern Indians' mobilization and demands after the conflict.[20]

Defense work also shattered the insular world of southeastern tribes. Thousands moved to urban areas, taking employment in war-related industries in places like Baltimore, Mobile, and New Orleans. Houmas and MOWA Choctaws found work in shipyards and petrochemical plants. Many Lumbee families moved to Baltimore, concentrating in such numbers that their local neighborhood was known as "the reservation." The government's postwar relocation program also sent thousands of federally recognized Indians to urban areas, some as far away as Chicago and San Francisco. The effect of this mass migration was multiple: individuals gained exposure to the larger world, improved their economic prospects, and escaped from localized anti-Indian racism. But contrary to academic predictions of the era, urbanization did not lead to the demise of local Indian communities. As Lumbee Herbert Locklear told a local paper in 1970: "I've never heard our people refer to Baltimore as home"—Lumbees still thought of the swamps and piney woods of North Carolina as home.[21]

The war and its immediate aftermath also set in motion economic changes that sparked a revival among southeastern Indian communities, as the old agriculture-based economy was replaced by a growing industrial sector, complete with factories and mills. The Southeast was soon crisscrossed with modern highways and telephone lines, and dotted with airports, and these transportation and communications networks ended the isolation of the region's Indians. Groups like the MOWA Choctaws had once been separated from nearby Mobile by transportation and social barriers. Now they were exhilarated by the freedoms of the city, available within an hour's reach. The industrial and technological transformations opening once-languishing Indian enclaves to the outside world also ignited a newfound hope among southern progressives for political and social change. Forward-thinking politicians and civic leaders called for a truly new "post-racial South," one of both industrial development and improved racial relations.

This thinking somewhat unintentionally aided the southeastern Indian renaissance: politicians could support Indian causes with little cost, and at the same time demonstrate the regional change of heart.[22]

POSTWAR LAND CLAIMS AND TRIBAL ORGANIZING

Shortly after World War II, Congress created the landmark Indian Claims Commission, in part at the urging of the newly founded National Congress of American Indians (NCAI) and other Native advocacy groups, to settle outstanding claims by tribes against the U.S. government. Groups and individuals supported the commission for highly different reasons: tribes wanted justice and to use the funds to support tribal programs, while conservatives hoped the tribunal would help end the government's commitment to Indians and lead to their integration as equal citizens. Although intended to promote the ultimate termination of existing tribes, the commission had the unintended consequence of helping revive forgotten tribes in the Southeast, as it sparked interest among local Indians in past land losses and potential monetary compensation for illegal land seizures. It also illuminated the need for formal tribal organizations to pursue lawsuits. Southeastern Indians had sporadically sought to share in land claims judgments in the past, particularly several involving the Cherokees, yet the new commission promoted a more lasting interest in using the courts to secure compensation for lands lost in preceding decades.[23]

Local interest in potential land claims came in two waves, with the first occurring shortly after the creation of the commission in 1946. In this era, the efforts of Calvin McGhee and his organization, the Creek Nation East of the Mississippi, are most noteworthy. The act that created the commission allowed any "identifiable group of Indians" to bring claims, opening the possibility for traditionally unrecognized tribes and individuals to come forward.[24] After hearing of the tribunal, McGhee, a farmer and a Creek descendant with a limited education, began traveling the area around his home near Atmore, Alabama, to sign up other potentially eligible Creek descendants. Often described as "the blue-eyed Indian chief," McGhee organized several thousand Creek descendants into the Creek Nation East of the Mississippi in 1950, then hired a local attorney to pursue a land claims case. Traveling the Southeast, often dressed in full headdress and other Indian regalia, Chief McGhee almost singlehandedly spurred interest in all things Native American in the region through his efforts. His work had several long-term impacts. In pursuing the claim, commission judges determined that McGhee's organization was an "identifiable Indian group," a determination providing validation of its Indian identity. The commission ruling also allowed the Eastern Creeks to share in several multimillion-dollar awards to the larger Muscogee (Creek) Nation of Oklahoma. In the process, influential Muskogee chief Waldo Emerson "Dode" McIntosh acknowledged the identity and worthiness of the Eastern Creeks to share in the judgments. McGhee's group ultimately morphed into the Poarch Band of Creek Indians, one of the only southeastern tribes to secure federal acknowledgment in the modern era. The rolls of Creek descendants established in conjunction with the Indian Claims Commission activity, however, created much confusion about Indian and tribal identity in the region, and several groups splintered from the original Poarch-centered organization, groups few believed were long-standing tribal entities. Beginning with a 1962 award of $3.9 million, local newspapers in Alabama, Florida, and Georgia advertised for eligible claimants. In the end, over seven thousand Eastern Creek descendants shared in several awards with over thirty-four thousand Creeks of the Muscogee Nation in Oklahoma.[25]

A second wave of court cases occurred in the early 1970s, spurred by publicity surrounding several successful East Coast Indian suits. Native groups were encouraged to organize and bring suit under an obscure federal law, the 1790 Indian Trade and Intercourse Act, that federal courts had interpreted as protecting all tribes, including groups not federally recognized, from illegal land transactions by any agent except the federal government. Native groups saw that they needed effective tribal organizations to pursue claims under this law. In the bayou country of southern Louisiana, a Houma man, Tom Dion, heard of the possibility of pursuing claims for rich oilfields stolen from his ancestors, and went door-to-door enlisting support for this idea. Dion's activity ultimately led to the formation of the modern United Houma Nation.[26] Others used the threat of a suit to have their federal relationship restored. Following the lead of the Mashantucket Pequot of Connecticut, the Catawbas of South Carolina utilized a land claims suit as leverage to secure federal restoration of their tribal status.

Over time, the Native American Rights Fund (NARF) helped groups such as the Tunica-Biloxi Tribe and Pamunkey Tribe pursue cases under the 1790 law.

Overall land claims activity proved a mixed blessing for southeastern Indians, particularly those unrecognized by the federal government. For groups like the Poarch Band of Creeks and the United Houma Nation, interest in monetary compensation helped develop their modern tribal governments. For the Houmas and others, however, it also led to the public perception that they were only interested in being Indian for the "check in the mail." It also created powerful enemies that have included large petroleum companies, landowner groups, municipal governments, and state lawmakers—forces with vested interests in denying their tribal identity.[27]

While many southeastern tribes were just organizing in the 1940s and 1950s, the federal government was doing its best to "get out of the Indian business," a common phrase it used in conjunction with the termination policy of the era. During this time even the recognized tribes of the Southeast, including the Catawbas, Coushattas of Louisiana, and the Alabama-Coushattas of Texas found their relationship with Washington terminated. As such it is no surprise that lawmakers were in no mood to acknowledge new relationships with local tribes with no previous federal agreements. In 1950, for example, the Wide Awake Indian Council (today's Waccamaw-Siouan Tribe) of North Carolina secured powerful allies, including several congressmen, Association of American Indian Affairs president Oliver La Farge, and lawyer Felix Cohen, to produce a bill to recognize the tribe and create a reservation for it. Termination supporters in Congress and opposition from the BIA stymied this effort. In mid-decade Lumbee leaders had better luck, although their success has since placed the group in an anomalous position vis-à-vis other American Indian groups. After intense lobbying, in 1956 Congress passed a bill stating that "the Indians now residing in Robeson and adjoining counties of North Carolina . . . [are hereby] designated as Lumbee Indians of North Carolina." However, in light of the prevailing termination-minded sentiment of the era, the Senate added language stating, "Nothing in this Act shall make such Indians eligible for any services performed by the United States for Indians because of their status as Indians." Thereafter the North Carolina people have had a unique and intermediate status in Indian affairs. They were, however, the only group in the Southeast during the 1950s to secure any form of acknowledgment of their Indian identity from federal officials.[28]

THE FORGOTTEN CIVIL RIGHTS MOVEMENT

Just as Indians are often written out of nineteenth-century southern history, especially after the removal era, they are rarely, if ever, mentioned in standard accounts of the civil rights movement. While securing the rights of Native Americans was somewhat peripheral to the larger African American struggle, the era's battles for equality and rights affected southeastern Indians and provided context for much of the southeastern Indian renaissance. Like blacks, the region's Native peoples were influenced by the economic, technological, and societal changes that had led to the civil rights movement, and they shared with their African American neighbors the same desire to end Jim Crow segregation, have a political voice and power, and gain equal economic opportunities. They were also greatly influenced by the African American rights movement. Interviews with tribal leaders make clear, however, that they had their own, often-conflicting goals when they entered the battle for civil rights.[29]

Unlike African Americans, most Native groups were too small to exert effective pressure in local or state politics based on the ballot box alone. They also differed from their black neighbors in that many local tribes pushed for land rights and to have their sovereignty restored, so a sense of separatism rather than integration was central to many. Because most were nonreservation peoples, they generally could exercise the franchise in local and statewide elections, despite widespread discrimination and racial hostility aimed mainly at blacks, but they faced similar economic barriers. In 1931, an Indian Office investigator noted that the Alabama-Coushattas of East Texas could vote so long as they, like all local residents, paid a poll tax, yet as with other minorities, the cost often prohibited them from exercising this basic civil right. Many groups had to rely upon the paternalistic kindness of local white patrons for whatever freedoms and rights they enjoyed. The large Lumbee and Houma groups were exceptions to this: both used their sheer numbers and political organizing to gain rights and resources for their home communities during the late 1960s and 1970s. In Robeson County, Gerald Sider and Karen Blu detailed the numerous voter registration drives and other efforts that the Lumbees used to elect Indian leaders to offices in local school boards and sheriff's departments. With the way paved by African Americans and locally powerful Indian groups such as the Houmas and Lumbees, and by federal civil rights legislation, particularly the Voting Rights Act of 1965, southeastern Indians gained full political rights by the late 1960s. Some, such as Mississippi Choctaw leader Phillip Martin and Poarch Creek chiefs Calvin McGhee and Eddie Tullis, became not only locally powerful politicians but also effectively able to assert pressure in both state and national affairs.[30]

Encouraged by the political atmosphere of the era and by the wartime service of many of their members, a group of Lumbees famously faced down the Ku Klux Klan during the civil rights movement in 1958, an event that helped spark the larger Indian civil rights struggle and which lives on in Lumbee memory. In January of that year the KKK announced a cross burning in the town of Maxton, North Carolina. This was in response to an Indian woman dating a white man and news that an Indian family had moved to an all-white neighborhood in the area. When KKK members arrived at the arranged site on the evening of January 18, they found themselves surrounded by hundreds of angry and armed Lumbees firing their weapons into the air. When an Indian shot out the main lightbulb illuminating the rally, the Klan members fled to the waiting arms of state troopers who were supposedly on the scene to maintain law and order. The turn of events made national news. The sheriff arrested the Klan leaders, who were later convicted for inciting a riot. The Lumbees were justifiably proud of their stand against the Klan—it proved they would not be intimidated and reinforced their image as fighting Indians. Other Southeastern tribes in their pursuit of equal rights also faced threats from the KKK and other white supremacists, which stifled the newfound assertion of rights among some, while spurring the pursuit of equality among others. If the Lumbees fought violence with violence (or at least the threat of it), others like the Mississippi Choctaws reached out to Washington, seeing the administrations of John F. Kennedy and Lyndon Johnson as allies in their struggles for equal rights. In the early 1960s the chairman of the Mississippi Choctaws, Robert Ben, asked for aid from Johnson's White House after a local Klansman bombed a church operated by the Mennonites, a group trying to empower local Indians and blacks to break from debt peonage and stand up to local whites. It is often forgotten that Mississippi Choctaw reservation lands were near Philadelphia, Mississippi, site of the infamous killing of three civil rights workers during the Freedom Summer of 1964.[31]

The previous examples underscore the real dangers and obstacles faced by Indians when demanding civil rights, and partially explain why local leaders often distanced themselves from the larger African American movement. Southern Indians faced a potential erosion of their status if associating too closely with blacks, and many clearly shared the racial assumptions of the white majority. Houma leader Kirby Verret adds another reason Indians often remained apart from the larger civil rights movement. He felt that his relatively small group would be swallowed by the black-dominated movement, and, as lands claims activity indicate, Native peoples had treaty rights and other concerns that set them apart from the greater movement.[32]

As is widely known, integration of public schools was the centerpiece of the African American civil rights movement. This is also the realm that most clearly separates the African American from the Indian movement. Southeastern Indians generally opposed school integration for a number of interlocking reasons. Although inferior to white institutions, Indian schools were central to local communities such as Dulac, Louisiana, and Reeds Chapel, Alabama. Through Indian schools, parents participated in committees, chose teachers who were often Indians themselves, and held fund-raisers central to their continuing education. Within the schools' walls, children had an insular, protected space to get an education, while the structures often doubled as places for other community activities. Integration promised to tear these institutions apart. Indian schools had a psychological importance that was often unseen to outsiders. They served to identify and confirm the indigenous identity of local communities, many of whom faced long-standing doubts about their racial composition. The potential demise of these schools threatened to thrust Indian communities into the realm of the "colored" community, a fate long opposed by Indians from Virginia to Louisiana.

As a result, tearing down the "separate but equal" public school system was anathema to most Indian leaders. Kirby Verret recalls being taught a chant: "Five, six, seven, eight! We don't want to integrate!" At approximately the same time as the landmark Supreme Court desegregation decision, *Brown v. Board of Education* (1954), the Poarch Creek

Indian trustees opposed admitting blacks to their schools. They ultimately received a written promise from a Creek Indian woman who had raised the issue not to attempt to enroll her "mulatto" children. The Lumbee fight against school desegregation provides the best example of this phenomenon that was baffling to whites outside the region. Following the *Brown* case, civil rights groups as early as 1958 were threatening suit to force the all-Indian and white schools in Robeson County, including Pembroke State University, to admit blacks—over heated opposition from Indian leaders.[33] The threats met foot-dragging and outcry among local Indians. In 1969, although schools such as those serving the Four Holes Indian Community of South Carolina and Lumbees in North Carolina were under court order to integrate, the latter vowed a showdown in Robeson County. The next year the *New York Times* reported that over five hundred Lumbee students were using the famous sit-in tactic. Instead of using it to integrate schools, they held their sit-in' at their old Indian school to stop its integration. In one incident angry Indian parents threatened with knives and hatchets black teachers who had been appointed to the Indian school. Some Lumbees soon formed a group, Independent Americans for Progress, in part to fight desegregation. When plans emerged to bus Indian students to local schools and have blacks bussed to Indian facilities, the group filed suit in federal court for an injunction. In 1971 thirty-five Lumbee parents blocked the doors of a local school to prevent bussing from proceeding, and the school closed for a time. However, the pressure and conflicts forced the North Carolina group to concede. Other southeastern groups saw the best alternative as equal, integrated education. In the mid-1960s Houma parents took an alternate path from the Lumbees, winning a court order that mandated their access to all-white public schools. The effect was immediate and profound. Groups denied an education or barred from high school soon witnessed marked rises in education levels. Bruce Duthu, a Houma Indian, entered high school in the wake of these battles. With encouragement from a local aid worker from the North, he entered Dartmouth and then Loyola Law School, on his way to becoming a respected attorney and Indian educator. The Lumbees gained a reputation as the "Indian intelligentsia," with Pembroke State University turning out large numbers of doctors, lawyers, educators, and other professionals. Young educated southeastern Indians became leaders in both pan-Indian circles and regional politics.[34]

As historian Theda Perdue and anthropologist Jack Campisi have noted separately, the closing of all-Indian schools created a crisis for southeastern Indians. When institutions like the East Carolina Indian School in Sampson County, North Carolina, locked its doors, a symbol of Indian pride, independence, and identity was closed as well. Despite the negative publicity surrounding integration, some silver lining soon appeared. The loss of schools prompted many groups to establish formal tribal entities in place of old boards of education and related committees. Old school buildings such as those of the Haliwa-Saponi and Waccamaw-Siouan Tribes were converted into tribal headquarters, facilities that still serve their communities. Today in places like Montegut, Louisiana, the old Indian school stands as a mute symbol of a bygone era and the changes that have ensued.[35]

Southeastern Indians also were able to profit from national civil rights legislation, particularly the Civil Rights Act of 1964. The new federal law banned discrimination in hiring and public accommodations, superseding the Jim Crow segregation laws that pervaded the Southeast. The workplace clauses of the Civil Rights Act opened jobs to Indians in the region's burgeoning industrial economy. In the bustling chemical plants along the Tombigbee River north of Mobile, Alabama, plant managers had refused to hire local Indians, supposedly because it would force them to provide a third set of bathrooms and other facilities, as there were two already for blacks and whites. Now MOWA Choctaws were able to secure positions in local plants, with some rising to managerial posts. When B. F. Goodrich opened a tennis shoe plant in Robeson County, North Carolina, in the 1960s, it employed many Indians. Having access to jobs did not solve the lingering problems associated with the Jim Crow past, however. Kirby Verret vividly remembers an incident from the 1960s. Many Houma men, including his father, worked at the Delta Iron Works pipe-wrapping plant. When the company planned a major party at the new civic auditorium in the city of Houma, the mayor refused to allow Indians inside the facility. Aware of publicity surrounding similar events in the civil rights movement, Lewis Chaisson led a strike of Indian workers that shut down the plant. When threats did not return the Indian men to work, the company president decided to hold the event elsewhere. As Verret recalls, "It was a good feeling to see us stand up for what's right."[36]

Four years after the Civil Rights Act was passed, Helen Maynor Scheirbeck, a Lumbee leader and educator from North Carolina, was influential in prodding Senator Sam Ervin (D-N.C.) to helping pass the landmark Indian Civil Rights Act of 1968. Although controversial among some tribes, the law helped to bring Native citizens within the protections of the larger constitutional framework.[37]

The greater civil rights movement had a profound and positive impact on southeastern Indians. Leaders such as Kirby Verret and Helen Gindrat, both Houmas, have acknowledged being inspired by the African American movement. MOWA Choctaw leader Galas Weaver provides a telling example. A high school baseball star, Weaver attended Bacone College in Oklahoma on an athletic scholarship and later the University of Redlands in California. On the West Coast, he recalls, he became aware of the work and successes of the local NAACP. He later kept abreast of the work of Martin Luther King, Jr., while working in Alabama's capital, Montgomery. Like many other southeastern Indian leaders, Weaver came to believe that, with their larger numbers and assertiveness, African Americans "had it better" than Indians in the Southeast. He saw how the NAACP chapter in his county was successfully running black candidates, and he followed its lead, running for both the local school board and chair of the Democratic Party local committee. He became the first Indian to win these posts. Weaver and others also learned the value of local courts, successfully suing a plant that had passed over a worthy Indian man for promotion. Weaver saw the black movement as teaching his people to use their numbers and voting power to influence politicians to work for them. While benefiting from the larger waves of change, eventually many Native leaders came to see that Indians had to forge their own way. As W. J. Strickland, a Lumbee, argued: "We have to participate either with the whites or with the blacks, and you know what happens in that type of situation. You don't have any voice when decisions are made."[38] By the early 1970s southeastern leaders began pursuing a distinctively Native path.

THE RISING POPULARITY OF
NATIVE AMERICANS IN THE 1960S

Surrounded by Indian place-names, southerners have always been fascinated with Native Americans and their nineteenth-century past, especially when it is infused with family traditions of Cherokee ancestors. By the 1960s, interest in the romantic and tragic tale of the removal of the Five Tribes and potential Cherokee ancestors increased exponentially, negative associations diminished, and newfound pride in Indian progenitors and Native ways took their place. As a result thousands of individuals and dozens of communities increasingly asserted their Indian identity as the decade proceeded. While wannabe Indians and tribes certainly emerged in these years, the overall impact was positive, and an Indian renaissance was in full bloom by the early 1970s. Long-standing tribes reemerged, false ones were born, and all over the nation non-Indians sought connection with Native cultures more alluring and exotic than their own.

Older Indians recalled a less favorable racial climate. Houma Indian Tom Dion noted: "You see in this Parish, being Indian was so disadvantageous at one time . . . some of the Indians now don't really want to be called Indians."[39] Generally there was an awakening of interest in all things Indian in the region, however, with major newspapers like the *Atlanta Constitution* running significant stories on Indians "coming out of the closet" as Native Americans. A Louisiana woman captures the general feeling among white Southerners: "I came from New Orleans. We didn't have very many Indians there, but I have always felt close to them. As Mr. Strickland said, 'You were here first.' Everyone else here is an immigrant, and to me to get closer to our American Indians is to get closer to America. I feel that I love our land, and our country, but I really feel that our American Indians love our land more than anyone else."[40] In the late sixties and early seventies, Native-themed works such as Dee Brown's *Bury My Heart at Wounded Knee* and Vine Deloria, Jr.'s *Custer Died for Your Sins* became best sellers. Some groups, such as the Eastern Band of Cherokees and Alabama-Coushattas, opened tourist ventures to capitalize on the Indian craze.[41] The U.S. counterculture soon seized upon the Indian as a symbol of everything that decadent imperialist America was not, and existing southeastern Indian enclaves were affected by all of this.

The more accepting social climate of the sixties had immediate impact in terms of individual assertions of Native identity and in tribal organizing. After the Census Bureau allowed people to self-identify their race for the first time, the number of Indians counted on the census tripled between 1960 and 1990, with southeastern states like

Alabama counting over 100 percent increases. Louisiana's reported Indian population jumped 65 percent between 1980 and 1990. Surprising to many westerners, North Carolina soon boasted over one hundred thousand Native Americans, making it the leader in eastern states and nationally as well. Robeson County, North Carolina, had the sixth largest Indian population of any county in the United States.[42]

BECOMING VISIBLE AS INDIAN IN THE SOUTHEAST

The trend of "coming out" as Native American had actually started decades earlier. Because of their long obscurity and assimilation levels, some nonreservation Native groups in the Southeast took steps beginning in the 1930s to increase their visibility as Indians, often appropriating the visible symbols of more well-known Plains Indians in the process, such as donning feathered headdresses, beaded necklaces, and shell-and-bone breastplates. Most often local white communities were supportive. As Deborah Root remarks in her book *Cannibal Culture*, all parties realized that "cultural difference can be bought and sold in the marketplace."[43] Several reservation tribes, particularly the Eastern Band of Cherokees of North Carolina and the Alabama-Coushattas of Texas, were leaders in this effort, establishing profitable tourist industries. During the first half of the twentieth century the Eastern Band, located near the popular Great Smoky Mountains National Park, became, as their historian John Finger and others have noted, the quintessential "tourist Indians," operating crafts shops, having individuals working the streets "chiefing," and producing a well-known historical drama. Following their lead, the Indian Office hired Ella Deloria, an anthropologist who had worked with Franz Boaz (and aunt of Vine Deloria, Jr.), to write a drama detailing the history of the Lumbee people. Called *The Life-Story of a People*, the pageant focused on Lumbee educational achievements and service in the armed forces. It opened in 1940 in Robeson County, North Carolina, to great reviews, although it only ran a brief time. The Lumbees followed with an Indian fair the next year.

Years later, under the auspices of the Texas Indian Commission, the Alabama-Coushatta Tribe pursued a much more ambitious tourism program. In the early 1970s, with state and federal grants, the small woodland tribe built a 1,500-seat amphitheater, developed a drama called *Beyond the Sundown* modeled on the Eastern Cherokees' *Unto These Hills*, and developed a tribal museum complex complete with a living Indian display—with individuals modeling their culture for tourists. Despite criticism that this venture was turning tribe members into living museum pieces, the effort did markedly increase the average standard of living on the isolated reservation and raised the tribe's visibility in the state.[44]

Tribes throughout the region also developed programs to revive or stabilize traditional crafts that members could utilize to provide economic development for their people. Although often unspoken, another reason for these efforts was that they helped reinforce indigenous status. Most Americans still maintain notions of pristine, precontact cultures against which they measure modern groups. After centuries of contact with Euro-American society, however, few Indians, especially nonreservation groups, retained many cultural forms that could be positively traced to aboriginal traditions. Virtually every community worked to maintain traditional arts and crafts that did remain. Most also introduced older forms that had disappeared, many learning them from scholarly works or museums. Tribal leaders were often quoted as saying that these efforts were vital to the continued survival of their peoples, and groups became known for their crafts: the Alabama-Coushattas for intricate pine-needle baskets, the Catawbas for pottery, the Houmas for palmetto baskets, fans, blow guns, and cypress moss dolls. The Ma-Chis Creeks of Alabama made necklaces and other jewelry from chinaberry seeds. Tribal museums and gift shops were established to market these crafts. Some artisans found opportunities on the powwow circuit, setting up booths to sell their wares.[45]

Southeastern Indians, like those nationally, also struggled to preserve native languages, an effort that became particularly urgent in the postwar period. For Native Americans and non-Indians, the possession of a living, indigenous language often is seen as vital to cultural survival and an irrefutable marker of indigenous identity. However, with the exception of reservation tribes such as the Eastern Band of Cherokees, Mississippi Band of Choctaws, Miccosukees, and Seminoles, few Indian groups in the Southeast today possess speakers of Native languages, and those that do, sadly, have few. The Jena Choctaws of Louisiana are one of the only southeastern Native groups that had

significant speakers of their language in the 1990s. Anthropologist
George Roth notes that several others had native speakers into the
1930s and 1940s: the Chitimachas, Tunica-Biloxis, and Catawbas. Pio-
neering linguists Albert S. Gatschet and James O. Dorsey from the 1880s
through the early twentieth century found individuals in Louisiana
that still spoke Ofo, Tunica, Biloxi, and Choctaw in the Indian communities at Marksville and in St. Tammany Parrish on the north
shore of Lake Pontchartrain. The experience of the Catawbas reveals
the uphill battle that tribes face today in maintaining their ancient
tongues. In 1959 only one man spoke Catawba fluently, and he was a
non-Catawba Indian from Long Island who had learned it from the
last Catawba speaker, Chief Samuel Blue, shortly before Blue died.
Afterward several tribal members still knew tribal chants and legends
in Catawba but regretted not learning the language in their youth.
As linguist Emanuel Drechsel has found, many other southeastern
Indian communities, even those that had lost their native languages,
continued speaking a Native lingua franca, which scholars call Mobilian
Trade Jargon. Many of the surviving Native American–identified songs
and traditions of these groups are maintained in this idiom. Overall
the trend has been toward the extinction of Southeastern native languages. The descendants of the Powhatan Confederacy of Virginia
have lost their languages. All the recognized tribes of Alabama lack a
Native language. The Lumbees and other long-assimilated groups in
the Carolinas have spoken English as their native tongue for so long
that they do not even agree about what their ancestral tongues were.
In light of these realities, many tribes with knowledge of their Indian
languages, either through elders or linguistic works, have established
programs to teach these languages to their youth, with varying degrees
of success. Some are using the most up-to-date technology to preserve
ancient tongues. In 2010 the Chitimacha Tribe partnered with a com-
puter software firm, known most for selling language software to tourists
and business personnel, to develop a program to teach youths the
Chitimacha tongue, which had apparently expired when the last fluent
speaker died in 1940. Tribal leaders used hundreds of hours of surviving wax-cylinder recordings of Chief Ben Paul and field notes taken
by linguist Morris Swadesh in 1934. Although the odds are long for
reviving the Chitimacha language, the Louisiana tribe is fortunate to
have recordings. Those without them are bereft of reestablishing
this important marker of Indian tribal heritage.[46]

THE RISE OF THE POWWOW IN THE SOUTHEAST

As anthropologists Jack Campisi, Hiram Gregory, and others have noted, the powwow became by far the most visible and culturally significant institution introduced in the region following World War II. Derived from Plains Indian traditions in Oklahoma, the colorful powwow spread across the country for a variety of reasons. It was particularly important for groups that had lost most elements of Indian culture. Its role was noted by anthropologist Patricia Lerch when she concluded on a North Carolina tribe, "The powwow became an essential annual event in the Waccamaw community . . . powwows replaced the Indian school as the key Indian institution, reinvigorating and infusing new energy into the participants."[47] For some groups, including the small tribes of Louisiana, powwows eventually replaced traditional Indian ball games and dances at annual gatherings. For the majority of groups that lacked even Indian-origin games and songs, the powwow became even more important and served two somewhat unrelated purposes. It raised a group's visibility as Native American, and it served as a forum for intergroup communication and other socializing. Clearly not indigenous to the Southeastern ceremonial complex, the powwow was a purely imported, and somewhat invented, pan-Indian phenomenon. Its various "traditions" were not traditional to regional tribes.

Helen Rountree notes that the Chickahominy of Virginia were holding a fall festival in the mid-1950s. I have found references to Alabama-Coushatta "powwows" in East Texas during the 1930s. The Haliwa-Saponi Tribe was the first in North Carolina to hold a powwow, in 1965, with the Lumbees and Waccamaw Siouan Tribe soon following suit. During the 1970s and 1980s virtually every state-recognized tribe in the Southeast was sponsoring some form of Indian festival, whether called a powwow or not. Staged at tribal headquarters, local parks, and later casino grounds, the events served to bring together Indians from the region and across the nation in what became known as the "powwow circuit." On the circuit individuals exchanged gossip, renewed friendships, and kept abreast of larger Indian concerns. These networks and connections were particularly important to non–federally recognized tribes like the Houmas. Houma singing and drumming groups such as the Bayou Healers, Bayou Eagles, and Oumas Connection Drum Corps traveled to various celebrations, including the Cherokee National

Holiday event, where they found public acknowledgment of their indigenous heritage from other Indian tribes.[48]

Powwows also fostered ethnogenesis and ethnic renaissance, as Indian youths learned both traditional tribal culture and Native traditions from other peoples. They continue to be extremely important to Indian groups today. Usually held over weekends, powwows begin with some form of "Grand Entry" followed by a blessing ceremony, various dancing contests (in categories such as fancy, grass, traditional, and straight), and drumming competitions. Foods such as venison, turkey, roast corn, squash, sofke, and Indian fry bread are available for purchase. The Tunica-Biloxi Powwow is representative. In 2003 it drew dancers and drummers from Oklahoma and the southeastern states vying for $27,000 in prize money. The event was capped with a performance by the group Keith Secola and the Wild Band of Indians. Most powwows also include speeches by tribal leaders and some include the introduction of "tribal princess" competition winners. Whether doing traditional southeastern dances such as the Stomp Dance or Plains forms such as the Gourd Dance, powwow devotees become immersed in a syncretic, vibrant, evolving cultural milieu. For Todd Johnston, a MOWA Choctaw, powwow dancing has become central to his life and his sense of being Indian, as it has for many other Native men, whether the forms he partakes in are traditional or not. While "Indian princess" contests strike some as purely artificial, girls who participate must learn tribal history and wear tribal dress in order to represent their people.[49]

SOUTHERN RED POWER?

Southeastern Indian communities had a complicated, often conflicted, relationship with Red Power activists of the 1960s and 1970s. Their long separation from African Americans and their association of Red Power with Black Power played a part, as did the general conservatism of group leaders. Most established tribal communities distanced themselves from Red Power protests. However, whether they took part in high-profile militant activities or not, members of most southern Indian communities awakened to the possibility of change through tribal organizing and intertribal unity.

Two organizations stand out as clear examples of the Red Power movement in the region: the Indian Angels of Louisiana and the

Tuscarora Movement of North Carolina. The Baton Rouge–based
Indian Angels traced origins from the 1969 takeover of Alcatraz by
the "Indians of All Tribes," an event generally acknowledged as a
catalyst in the Red Power movement. After hearing of the occupation, Louisiana Indians formed Indian Angels to provide aid and
moral support for Indian activists in San Francisco. A largely urban
entity with multitribal membership, the Angels were led over time by
several women, Dawn Breaker, Sun Dawn, and Sarah Peralta, a self-
proclaimed "half-blood" from New Orleans, who was its most vocal and
controversial member. After its formation in 1969 the group sponsored
the state's first-known powwow in 1970, an event that included a full-
dress parade down Baton Rouge streets to the state capitol, a strategy
meeting, and speeches by a representative of the governor, Poarch
Creek chief Houston McGhee, local tribal chiefs such as Joseph Pierite
of the Tunica-Biloxi Tribe, and representatives of the National Congress of American Indians and the BIA.

Anthropologist Pete Gregory was involved in some Indian Angels
dealings, and recalls that they plugged into the anti–Vietnam War
movement, passing out "Make Love, Not War" cards and other antiestablishment paraphernalia. For some younger local Indians these
gestures struck a chord. Although not involved in the Indian Angels,
Kirby Verret recalls feeling that, because Indian youth were poor and
uneducated, local white-dominated draft boards tended to induct
Indian kids and not their own. Also active in the state was Claude
Medford, a young college student of Choctaw ancestry, who worked
with National Indian Youth Council leader Clyde Warrior. Medford
married a Coushatta from Louisiana, further establishing links between
national activists and local Indians. It was Medford who encouraged
Joseph Pierite to travel with him to New Mexico, where the chief met
Vine Deloria, Jr., and other national Indian leaders.

Nationally, the largely urban-based Red Power movement, with
which Indian Angels was loosely associated, soon caused friction both
for its tactics, such as the angry protest at the Louisiana governor's
mansion described earlier, and the fact that its membership was
overtly pan-tribal. In Louisiana, many involved in Indian Angels were
from tribes outside the state or were individuals with unknown tribal
ancestry. Bruce Duthu, who was a teen at the time, recalls his people
asking, "Who are these folks?" Most Houma Indians, he says, thought
the group was composed of wannabes or, as they would say, "New
Age" or "Born Again" Indians. Duthu remembers, "Peralta claimed

to be 1/3 Apache . . . how is that possible?" His conclusions regarding
the Indian Angnels organization and tactics are fairly typical for the
region. Duthu remembers feeling that the Indian Angels adoption
of American Indian Movement (AIM) militancy "was not at all the
'Indian Way.'" Especially appalling to many traditional Houma leaders
was Peralta's common tactic of shouting down officials—to them the
lack of respect showed that she was not a "real Indian."[50] Despite
questions as to the Indian Angels' authenticity, the group was important to Indian mobilization in Louisiana. It set up a chapter under
Tom Dion in the Houmas' traditional parishes and at Marksville
under Joseph Pierite. Helen Gindrat credited the organization with
helping her Houma people organize as a tribe and pursue federal
aid. By organizing powwows, wearing Plains Indian clothing in public,
and taking stereotypical Indian-sounding names such as Sun Dawn,
the group certainly raised the visibility of Indians in the state. As Sarah
Peralta had always worked closely with the Coalition of Eastern Native
Americans (CENA), a large pan-tribal group created in the early 1970s,
the Indian Angels ultimately was absorbed in this entity.[51]

The majority of Southeastern tribes were based in rural areas and
their leaders and community values were conservative. They eschewed
the tactics of AIM and other Red Power activists, preferring instead
to work in more low-key ways for change in their home communities
and the larger national arena. Tribes like the Alabama-Coushattas of
Texas, whose membership was overwhelmingly Presbyterian, believed
that the Red Power movement was overtly anti-Christian, which turned
them away from it. Having little if any remaining indigenous spirituality, few felt an appeal to return to traditional Native religions. Many
tribal leaders also came from the Christian ministry, a fact that affected
their distance from the Red Power movement. Lumbee leadership came
largely from Protestant denominations and ministers. In Louisiana, Kirby
Verret, one of the United Houma Nation's important chairmen, was an
ordained Methodist minister. In light of their backgrounds, leaders
like Verret and their activism were more in line with Martin Luther
King, Jr.'s Christian-based, nonviolent strategy than with Red Power.[52]

The Tuscarora Movement among the Lumbees provides one of the
best examples of the growing militancy among southeastern Indians
during the early seventies. In 1970 Carnell Locklear and others formed
the East Carolina Indian Organization, in part to resist the integration
of Indian schools. Claiming descent from the Tuscarora Indians that

once inhabited North Carolina (a claim contested by others) they soon formed their own tribal entity known as the East Carolina Tuscarora Indian Organization. Whereas the Lumbee majority preferred to use the legal system and more staid tactics, the Tuscarora group, which drew its membership from poorer, rural Indians residing in and around Prospect, North Carolina, took a more aggressive approach. Carnell Locklear used the rhetoric of Red Power, telling a reporter, "We are a new kind of warrior—we won't take 'no' for an answer. We come prepared to give our lives."[53] Like in Louisiana, established Lumbee leaders were appalled by this type of language and tensions predictably rose between them and the new Tuscarora group. Friction increased after AIM set up a local branch office in 1972, further linking the Tuscarora faction and national militants. In spring of 1973 the Lumbee stronghold of Robeson County was rocked by several events that were blamed on the Tuscarora group. In March the historic Old Main building of the once all-Indian Pembroke State University mysteriously burned to the ground. At the same time barns and other structures were set ablaze throughout the region, many owned by white farmers and businessmen and women. Many Lumbees believed that the militants were behind these actions. Howard Brooks, known as the most militant of the Tuscarora leaders, sought access to the Prospect Elementary School to discuss ways to combat integration of the all-Indian institution. After they were denied free admission by the all-Lumbee Indian school board, 150–200 Tuscaroras gathered near the school to attend a rally that included Vernon Bellecourt, national director of AIM, and Golden Frinks, black activist and field secretary of the Southern Christian Leadership Conference. The press had quoted Brooks as saying "we may need a Wounded Knee here in Robeson County," and tensions ran high. Local sheriffs, armed deputies, and state troopers in riot gear lined the road to stem potential violence. When the police moved to break up the rally, a scuffle broke out. Fifty-eight Tuscaroras, including Brooks, were arrested, and many were injured in what one Indian labeled a "police riot." Brooks was later convicted of inciting a riot and sent to prison.[54]

Around the same time, Tuscaroras held a mass rally in Pembroke, dubbed by the press a "Red Power" event, where they called for a boycott of businesses that refused to hire Indians. During this era the Tuscarora group also advocated for an all-Lumbee bank (something that eventually came to fruition), and an all-Indian shopping center.

Later in 1973 more militant Tuscaroras under Brooks organized a mass march on the state capitol demanding their rights as Native Americans. They also led a large motorcade of followers through the streets of Lumberton—honking horns, they ran red lights and smashed store windows. Also that year some Tuscaroras took part in an AIM march on Washington, DC, and AIM's occupation of the BIA headquarters. They stole truckloads of important papers and documents, bringing them back to Robeson County. Ultimately the division between the more militant, generally rural and poorer Tuscaroras and the larger Lumbee establishment based in Pembroke proved too great to bridge. The newly formed group soon broke from the larger Lumbee Tribe and sought federal recognition separately.[55]

Although not formally part of the Tuscarora Movement, Native scholar David Wilkins and his experience provide a window into the spirit of the sixties sweeping the Southeast. A self-described military brat, Wilkins had Lumbee parents from North Carolina but was largely raised outside the region. In 1968, when he was thirteen, his family moved back to Pembroke. He recalls being surprised at the racial climate of the local high school, which was approximately 98 percent Indian. Immediately upon his starting school there, other Lumbees told him not to associate with the only African American in his class. Robeson County was tri-racial, divided almost equally between Indian, blacks, and whites, and he recalls thinking: "Why aren't we forging alliances? They [other Indians] had been treated just like blacks and they don't associate?" After high school Wilkins attended nearby Pembroke State University, where he first began reading *Custer Died for Your Sins* and works by the likes of Dee Brown and N. Scott Momaday, which fired his desire to learn more about Native cultures. Wilkins hitchhiked up the coast in the early 1970s, seeking to find like-minded Indians, and he ended up working on the activist Iroquois paper *Akwesasne Notes*. He vividly recalls when the Iroquois-associated group White Roots of Peace came to his hometown, since he had his first sweat lodge experience then and became enthralled with Native spirituality. Wilkins soon met Maryland AIM chapter member George Whitewolf, who invited him to the Standing Rock Sioux Reservation in North Dakota. Here he met other like-minded Indians and became immersed in activist politics. Wanting nothing more than to take to the protest trail, Wilkins nonetheless heeded his parents' advice and returned to North Carolina to graduate from college. After that, he worked for the urban Indian group Guilford Native American Association before being hired by the United Indians of America, a Lumbee-dominated group under Helen Maynor Scheirbeck that was helping Indians in Virginia and elsewhere in the East research their histories. Through Scheirbeck, Wilkins became acquainted with Vine Deloria, Jr. The Sioux scholar became his mentor as Wilkins entered graduate school at the University of Arizona, and he went on to a distinguished career in academia.[56] Like many activists of his generations, Wilkins ultimately used his pen and scholarship to push for Native rights.

FROM TERMINATION TO SELF-DETERMINATION: FEDERAL POLICY INCENTIVES

As sociologist Joane Nagel has so convincingly argued, federal Indian policies often have provided an incentive structure or underlying motivation for tribal activity. This was certainly true in the case of the southeastern Indian renaissance. More than other minority groups, Native peoples are acutely aware of and affected by the ebb and flow of federal policies originating in Washington. Along with federal legislation, programs of the White House and federal agencies often have determined the economic and political destiny of reservation tribes, with decisions too frequently made without consulting Indians themselves. This all changed in the 1960s and culminated in the landmark Indian Self-Determination and Education Assistance Act of 1975, a law that sought to return power to tribal governments. Whereas unrecognized southeastern Indians had long been pursuing their rights, federal policies and their dictates most often had stymied these efforts. The elections of Democratic president John F. Kennedy and his successor Lyndon B. Johnson marked a significant change in emphasis. Kennedy essentially terminated the federal termination policy of the preceding decade, and his successor Johnson made Indians a part of his "War on Poverty" and other Great Society programs. The 1960s saw federal policy makers turning their attention to eastern and non–federally recognized Indian tribes for the first time in history.[57]

It is hard to overstate the positive impact of the new pro-tribal programs on struggling southeastern Indian communities. Johnson's administration began to see the problems of all off-reservation Indians, terminated, urban, and non–federally recognized, in the same light. A 1967 presidential task force emphasized the surprising fact that over ninety thousand Indians still lived east of the Mississippi, with social and economic problems often greater than their well-known western counterparts. The "War on Poverty" had discovered southeastern Indians. The government set off to remedy the entrenched "culture of poverty" that enveloped them and other forgotten Americans.[58]

Millions of dollars in federal aid began pouring into the hands of non–federally recognized tribes in the region. By the late 1960s and early 1970s most such groups had established programs in health, education, social welfare, housing, and job training. The Office of Economic Opportunity provided community development grants. The Department of Health, Education, and Welfare established an Office of Indian Education that was crucial to local Native educational advances. VISTA sent workers. Tribes used Department of Labor funds to run programs under the Comprehensive Employment and Training Act (CETA) and subsequent Job Training Partnership Act. The federal Office of Native American Programs helped fund tribal governments. The Commerce Department's Economic Development Administration helped groups build tribal centers. All of these federal programs were outside the traditional monopoly held by the BIA and the Indian Health Service. They did not adhere to the generally strict eligibility requirements of those two bodies, providing services as generic anti-poverty measures. The Jena Choctaws provide a typical example of how tribes not federally recognized used nontraditional funding sources for community development. Under its chief Jerry Jackson the tribal council secured a Department of Housing and Urban Development grant, using it to purchase three acres and construct a tribal center, which soon became the locus of group activity. In Alabama the MOWA Band of Choctaws secured an Administration for Native Americans grant, then used this tribal-status-clarification funding to pay its employees for the first time. They ultimately were able to pay upwards of twenty employees, including their chief. This development was significant, as it allowed these individuals to devote their full time and energy to the tribe. Using volunteer labor and various federal moneys, the Lumbees established one of the most significant non-BIA tribal programs of the era, the Lumbee Regional Development Association (LRDA). Chartered as a nonprofit corporation in 1968, the organization had a board of directors, advisory council, and steering committee, a structure that evolved into the Lumbee's modern tribal government. Beyond providing leadership, the LRDA conducted studies aimed at establishing programs to improve Lumbee health, education, and economic prospects. It also served as an advocacy group, with the ultimate goal of Lumbee self-determination and empowerment.[59] Together these various non-BIA funding sources proved central to community development and tribal organizing, providing impoverished southeastern Indians the seed money needed to launch modern tribal programs.

LEGAL AID AND ADVOCACY GROUPS DISCOVER SOUTHEASTERN INDIANS

By the early 1970s national Indian advocacy groups and individuals interested in promoting Native sovereignty finally discovered that tens of thousands of indigenous people still lived in the East. They realized that forgotten eastern Native communities needed help in securing rights denied their peoples for generations. More than any other factor, national Native rights organizations helped mobilize isolated Indian groups in the region, aiding them in creating tribal governments, social programs, and economic ventures that together enabled southern groups to emerge from the shadows. Although legal aid and advocacy programs tended to originate outside the South, they gained firm footing in states such as North Carolina and Louisiana.

The central galvanizing event that set 1970s organizing into motion occurred a decade before. In 1961 the NCAI and the Anthropology Department of the University of Chicago sponsored the American Indian Chicago Conference, calling together Native leaders and youths from across the country to discuss Indian problems and propose sweeping changes in federal Indian policy. Once isolated groups like the Houmas sent individuals like Helen Gindrat, who recalls being energized by finding out that other Indians shared the same hopes and problems of her people. She came home determined to organize the Houma as a tribe. Over 450 delegates from ninety tribes attended the weeklong event. Its landmark "Declaration of Indian Purpose" is often credited with sparking the Indian activism of the decade. The Chicago conference also helped ignite a revival among southeastern Indians. Like their national counterparts, southeastern Indians wanted an end to termination, the creation of new federal programs for Native peoples, and legal protection of indigenous culture and rights. Exposed to other Indian groups for the first time, future leaders like Gindrat returned home pledging to press for the rights of their indigenous peoples. While a positive event for people like the Houmas, the Chicago conference exposed, for the first time, fissures that would widen in the national Indian community. The conference was riven with distrust. Traditional leaders were wary of more-assimilated men and women in the NCAI. Younger Indians distrusted older leaders who seemed too conservative for their tastes. Importantly, as historian Thomas Cowger concludes, western tribes distrusted most eastern groups, peoples that they had no previously dealings with. A fundamental rift between the well-established western reservation tribes and generally unrecognized eastern groups had been exposed and would prove long-lasting.[60]

Among legal activists, Vine Deloria, Jr., did more than any single individual during these years to expose the plight of eastern Indians. Appointed executive director of the NCAI in 1964, Deloria battled to make the national group more inclusive, especially by admitting forgotten eastern tribes. According to his friend and student David Wilkins, Deloria became interested in southeastern groups through the work of his aunt Ella Deloria, who had aided the Lumbees in the 1940s. Having some non-Indian ancestry himself, Deloria did not care so much about the racial issues that often clouded southeastern Indian politics. To him recognizing the sovereignty of forgotten tribes was what mattered. Through his work at the NCAI and later as world-renowned scholar and writer, Deloria was a consistent advocate for underdog tribes, turning his powerful intellect and biting criticism toward the BIA's acknowledgment process and its tribal supporters, parties he believed were killing legitimate Indian tribes through bureaucratic entanglements.[61]

In the early 1970s Deloria and others created the Institute for the Development of Indian Law, which proved important to the southeastern Indian renaissance. Although often accused of "hunting" tribes and "creating" others out of thin air, the institute was central in educating languishing local Indian communities of their rights. With young Kiowa attorney Kirke Kickingbird and Ernest C. "Chuck" Downs in the trenches researching and writing about "lost" groups, Deloria's institute awakened the nation to their existence. The institute established a tribal locator service to find and aid isolated communities. It published a journal that highlighted unrecognized southeastern communities such as the Tunica-Biloxis and Houmas. It was no coincidence that Downs, who was also the research editor for the American Indian Policy Review Commission's 1976 report on unrecognized Indians, did much of the research for the Tunica-Biloxi Tribe, which secured acknowledgment through the BIA process in 1981, the third group to do so.[62]

There were several other legal aid organizations that were vital to individual Indian communities in the seventies. The Native American Rights Fund (NARF) and its partner, the Pine Tree Legal Services, under Tom Tureen, worked to revive southeastern communities. More than any single entity, NARF, a nonprofit corporation founded in 1970, allowed impoverished Indian enclaves to pursue their rights through the courts and helped produce much of the historical and legal research southern tribes used in the Federal Acknowledgment Process. With top-notch attorneys such as Arlinda Locklear, Lumbee, NARF worked on acknowledgment petitions for the two southeastern tribes that secured federal recognition within the first decade of the BIA process: the Poarch Band of Creek Indians and Tunica-Biloxi Tribe. It also aided groups like the United Houma Nation still languishing in the process. In one case a southeastern tribe created its own legal program. In the 1980s the Lumbee Tribe formed the Lumber River Legal Services, hiring its own attorneys and other professionals to work toward tribal recognition and other issues.[63]

A host of scholars turned their attention to local Indian communities in the 1970s as well. Anthropologists and historians such as Tony Paredes, Karen Blu, Gerald Sider, and Pete Gregory began studying surviving tribes of the Southeast, and their scholarship proved vital to groups in the region. Although anthropologists such as John R. Swanton and Frank Speck had previously investigated southeastern Indian enclaves, it was not until the 1970s that scholars widely made them the subjects of inquiry. In many ways it was the Indian revival that inspired this. Forgotten southeastern groups realized they needed empirical evidence to back their land claims and tribal recognition efforts, and they turned to scholars at nearby universities for help. While working at Florida State University, Tony Paredes was asked to aid the Poarch Creeks. In Louisiana, Pete Gregory, an anthropologist at Northwestern State University in Natchitoches, was approached to help many local groups. Gregory's experience provides an example of the serendipitous ways local scholars became entwined with local Indians and how relationships often grew into lifelong partnerships. Gregory had been a graduate student at Louisiana State University in Baton Rouge, and recalls his mentor there receiving a phone call in the mid-1970s from the nearby Tunica-Biloxi Tribe asking for help documenting artifacts then being unearthed. Gregory was sent, and his study of modern southeastern Indians so began. "I was hooked," he says. Like many anthropologists of his generation, Gregory was part of a growing subfield of applied anthropology, using his skills to aid an indigenous group with current problems. Often called "action anthropologists," many in the field were criticized for forsaking standards of scientific objectivity, but Gregory and others did not care. They felt they were doing important work, putting their skills to use for Indians who had been denied their identity and legal rights for generations. Together the scholarship of Paredes, Gregory, and others was of great value to southeastern Indians, particularly those without federal acknowledgment. While not always documenting exact tribal origins or confirming long-standing tribal oral traditions, their work formed the basis of the first significant scholarship on many surviving southeastern groups.[64]

The National Congress of American Indians also aided southeastern communities, although its meetings would serve as a battleground for contention regarding Native authenticity. Under Vine Deloria, Jr., the NCAI pushed a few struggling southeastern tribes into the spotlight for the first time, and the experience of the Tunica-Biloxi Tribe of Louisiana provides perhaps the most dramatic example. In the mid-1960s, Joseph Pierite was the chief of the isolated tribe. Although largely uneducated, Pierite had a literate friend write to Deloria, executive director of the NCAI. They became friends, and Deloria helped Pierite's tribe secure membership in the NCAI in 1967. The organization paid for Pierite and Claude Medford, Jr., to attend its annual meeting in Albuquerque in 1969, where the chief gave a heartfelt speech, noting in part: "It is the desire of the Tunica Tribe that they receive federal recognition since backing of this type would give some form of dignity to their people. With every passing year more of their land is taken, their religion repressed, and their culture ridiculed."[65] The NCAI responded, passing a resolution vowing to aid the Tunica-Biloxis and other Louisiana groups in their pursuit of federal

Figure 3. Joe Pierite of the Tunica Biloxi Tribe playing stickball, 1950s. (Photograph courtesy of State Library of Louisiana, Louisiana Collection)

recognition. After the Tunica-Biloxis secured membership, the Lumbees and Haliwa-Saponis both received membership in 1981, and the MOWA Choctaws were admitted later. Several southeastern Indian leaders became active in the organization. Chickahominy chief Oliver Adkins was involved for several decades, and Poarch Creek chairman Eddie Tullis was chosen vice president of the Southeast Region. Overall, membership in the NCAI has meant recognition by other Indians, but while the organization could provide important validation of a tribe's authenticity, it could also take it away. NCAI support of the Lumbees has vacillated widely. Several Lumbees were granted individual membership in the 1960s only to have these memberships later revoked, and in 1974 a Lumbee delegation attended the NCAI Annual Convention seeking support, only to encounter acerbic questioning of their racial origins and authenticity as Indians. The General Assembly eventually opted to oppose their recognition, leading to accusation by Vine Deloria, by then former director, that the NCAI leaders were pawns of the federal establishment.[66]

National religious groups also reached out to struggling southeastern tribes. During the 1970s and 1980s the National Indian Lutheran Board, the American Friends Service Committee (AFSC), and the Mennonite Church came south. In conjunction with the BIA, the Indian Lutheran Board held workshops in Louisiana to help groups prepare tribal recognition petitions. The Mennonites sent Greg Bowman and Janel Curry-Roper, who conducted invaluable unpaid research in the 1970s for Louisiana groups including the Clifton Choctaw Tribe, the Apache-Choctaw Community of Ebarb, and the Houmas. The AFSC successfully lobbied for the restoration of the Alabama-Coushatta Tribe of Texas in the 1980s. Together individual activists such as Deloria, legal groups like NARF, and church organizations worked to expose the plight of southern Indian communities. Their unpaid work often provided the spark these groups needed to reignite their people's long struggle for recognition in the region.[67]

PAN-INDIAN AND INTERTRIBAL ORGANIZATIONS

In the early 1970s two intertribal organizations formed that proved vital in helping local Indian groups find their voice and develop tribal organizations, the Coalition of Eastern Native Americans and the United

South and Eastern Tribes (USET). W. J. Strickland was an important figure in grassroots tribal organizing, and his group CENA was born in the wake of the first Eastern Indian Conference, sponsored by NARF in Washington, DC, in 1972. Under Strickland's dynamic leadership the coalition was the single most important force in helping disorganized and isolated southeastern Indian communities establish functioning tribal governments. Wherever Strickland and CENA went, new tribal organizations sprang to life. Formalized governments helped local groups more effectively compete for grants available to Indian communities and moneys provided for impoverished groups in general. Prior to this time, most southeastern Indian communities, if they were organized at all, operated only at the local level. One of CENA's strengths was its fostering of solidarity: Strickland preached that isolated groups should think in both pan-Indian and national terms. To help tribes organize, CENA sponsored seminars in Indian strongholds like Pembroke, North Carolina. Such Indian communities were typically small and adrift from the mainstream, and Strickland tried to have their leaders see politics in broader terms. As he told conference attendees in Louisiana in 1973: "The Coalition believes that ethnic identity is valuable and one of the most powerful mechanisms by which communities can fight poverty and degradation."[68] In this regard Strickland tried to locate and organize as many groups as possible, seeing strength in numbers. In a few short years CENA became the largest intertribal entity representing primarily unrecognized or state-recognized tribes in the eastern United States. It set up an office in the nation's capital to function, as Strickland told an Indian group, "as your Indian voice in Washington."[69] The coalition soon grew to have over twenty-five employees, and it mobilized over fifty eastern Indian communities, encouraging them to take pride in their racial and ethnic identity. Strickland's work engendered media attention and Native American–directed activity throughout the region. Part of the appeal was letting groups know that they were not alone or forgotten. As Strickland told one audience: "We Indians know who we are and know where we are going. There are 250,000 Indians east of the Mississippi River who are concerned about you and your community."[70] To most southeastern Indian groups whose identity was constantly questioned, Strickland's rhetoric and help was truly inspiring.

CENA and other organizations were the first to educate southeastern Indians about the need to research their histories to prove their identity to outsiders. As Strickland informed groups like the Rappahannocks of Virginia, they would need to formalize many things about their tribes. They would have to find and maintain historical documents, keep modern records, and maintain up-to-date tribal rolls, bureaucratic necessities generally foreign to most tribes not federally recognized. In the same era, the Lumbees started an "Indian Information Project" within the United Indians of America to similarly aid southeastern tribes in proving their identity. Under Helen Maynor Scheirbeck it hired young scholars like David Wilkins to research the obscure histories of many southeastern tribes. Wilkins's work on several Virginia tribes helped them secure state recognition during this era.[71]

STATE TRIBAL RECOGNITION AND STATE INDIAN COMMISSIONS

The 1970s witnessed a new phenomenon in American Indian affairs: state governments actively recognizing tribes within their borders and creating agencies to serve them. The drive to acknowledge state tribes occurred in many eastern states, but was centered in the Southeast. In 1970, Virginia, South Carolina, and Texas already had long-standing, if fluctuating, relationships with small tribes within their jurisdictions. However, by the close of the decade a largely unnoticed movement had occurred: almost all the southeastern states had established Indian commissions to aid their Native citizens, and most had recognized tribes within their borders. Commissions were created at the prompting of local Indian leaders because they felt Natives needed better representation in state government. The Tar Heel State was first, creating its North Carolina Commission on Indian Affairs in 1971. Louisiana followed suit in 1972. Alabama, Florida, and Georgia also established Indian-oriented offices during the decade. Although largely unnoticed at the time, state recognition would prove more valuable than local legislators or tribal leaders ever imagined. It would provide not only the intended acknowledgment that Indian communities still existed in these states, eligibility for token state programs for Indians, and a forum for Indian concerns, but also, seemingly, recognition that groups were bona fide Indian tribes. This recognition would ultimately open doors to a host of Indian-oriented funds and affirmative action programs that had not often been considered by local legislators when voting for recognition bills.[72]

The early history of the Alabama and Louisiana Indian commissions provides a good introduction to the politics involved with such institutions. Both states established formal commissions at the height of public interest in Native Americans. During the 1970s, when many southern journalists were proclaiming a "post-racial South," Democratic governors George Wallace of Alabama and Edwin Edwards of Louisiana gained minority support and public relations points by backing racial and ethnic causes. Creating an Indian commission was a relatively painless way for each leader to show his state's new direction in race relations. The career of George Wallace offers perhaps the most striking example of a change of heart. Infamous for his 1963 inaugural speech in which he vowed to uphold Jim Crow ("Segregation now! Segregation tomorrow! Segregation forever!"), Wallace was shot and paralyzed during his 1972 presidential campaign. The governor publicly repented soon after at Martin Luther King, Jr.'s old church in Montgomery, renouncing his segregationist views and going on to gain many African American supporters. Wallace also became an advocate for Native Americans, partly through his personal relations with Poarch Creek chairman Eddie Tullis. In the early 1970s Wallace wrote a letter supporting the transfer of the Creeks' old Indian school to the band, the first step toward their eventual federal recognition.

In reviewing records from this era, it is clear that these were exciting years for Indian affairs in the Southeast. Governors in Alabama and surrounding states went on a spree, declaring "Native American Days" and proudly competing with other politicians to show support for Indian causes. Largely oblivious to the implications, governors began recognizing local groups as tribes by proclamation and decree, and state legislators soon began doing the same by statute. In 1973 future U.S. president Jimmy Carter, as governor of Georgia, issued a proclamation recognizing and commending the Lower Muskogee Creek Tribe for preserving Creek culture in the state. Southern citizens who once called for removal of southeastern Indians were now proud to recognize and promote their existence. Showing how far they had come, the author of a book on the "First Alabamans" was clearly tickled that the "Mims Act," a law that created the state's first Indian commission in 1979, had been sponsored by a descendant of one of the survivors of the Fort Mims Massacre of 1813, the most deadly Indian massacre in the state's history. Wounds were healing. It is clear from surviving correspondence that many southerners felt they could support the "First Americans," especially in mind of the rising demands of blacks. As one Texas man put it: "Our American Negroes protest and riot but I do not believe they have suffered nearly as much as the Indians."[73] Because many southern whites believed that they had Indian blood, their support for Indian causes was personal, and it was certainly more palatable than getting behind other civil rights issues.

Although the benefits that states provided were largely symbolic, some tangible economic and social advantages flowed from state tribal acknowledgment. The Coushatta Tribe of Louisiana was aided by the state commission in having its federal recognition restored in 1973, as was the Jena Band of Choctaws in its recognition bid in the late 1980s and early 1990s. The Louisiana Indian commission and other state bodies served as clearinghouses for a host of grants, including state education funds for Indians, Community Services Block Grants, energy assistance programs, and scholarships for Native children. The commission directed a Louisiana Indian Housing Authority and in 1975 sponsored the first study of the state's elderly Indians, pointing to problems in social and economic realms. In North Carolina, the state commission published a newsletter, *Indian Times*, and Alabama and Louisiana's agencies also produced newsletters that kept local Indians abreast of issues of concern. At their own initiative, local leaders formed the Inter-Tribal Council of Louisiana in 1975, a Native American–directed organization that worked closely with the state Indian agency, and helped tribes gain and administer CETA and other grants. Although led by non-Indians at first, the Alabama and Louisiana commissions and intertribal groups soon came to be run by Indians themselves. In Alabama, men such as Eddie Tullis and Galas Weaver became important forces. In Louisiana, Ernest Sickey, Coushatta, and later Diana Williamson, Chitimacha, came to prominence directing the state commission, gaining valuable leadership and administrative skills in the process. With the advent of Indian gaming in the late 1980s and early 1990s, state Indian commissions often served as facilitators and mediators in the process of forming state-tribal gaming compacts.[74]

Largely unnoticed in the scholarly literature on American Indian politics, the growth of state Indian commissions was an important phenomenon. By the end of the twentieth century, the southern Native American political landscape had changed dramatically, with seven states in the region having formal Indian commissions or offices. There were forty-nine state-recognized tribes and other Native entities in the Southeast. In comparison, the region had just ten federally recognized tribes, some of which also had state recognition. Virginia had no federally recognized tribes but eight state-recognized groups, including the Chickahominy Tribe, Mattaponi Tribe, and Pamunkey Tribe. South Carolina had the federally recognized Catawba Tribe, as well as ten state-recognized groups, including the Pee Dee Indian Tribe, the Waccamaw Indian People, the Eastern Cherokee, the Southern Iroquois and United Tribes of South Carolina, the Natchez Tribe, and the Piedmont American Indian Association Lower Eastern Cherokee Nation.[75] North Carolina also had ten state-recognized tribes, including the Haliwa-Saponi Tribe, the Lumbee Tribe, the Occaneechi Band of the Saponi Nation, and the Waccamaw-Siouan Tribe.[76] Georgia had three state-recognized tribes: the Cherokee of Georgia, the Georgia Tribe of Eastern Cherokees, and the Lower Muskogee Creek Tribe. The Alabama Indian Affairs Commission recognized eight groups, including the Echota Cherokee Tribe, the Ma-Chis Lower Creek Indian Tribe, the MOWA Band of Choctaws, the Star Clan of Muscogee Creeks, and Cher-O-Creek Intra Tribal Indians.[77] Mississippi and Florida were exceptions, having no state-recognized tribes, although Florida had a state commission serving its federally recognized tribes. Louisiana had ten state-recognized tribes, including the Adai Caddo Tribe, the Choctaw-Apache Community of Ebarb, the Clifton Choctaw Tribe, the United Houma Nation, the Isle Jean Charles Band, and Louisiana Choctaw Tribe.[78] The majority of these groups were pursuing federal tribal recognition. Tennessee had a state commission serving formally affiliated tribal groups that were not officially recognized. Texas once had the most comprehensive state Indian commission in the country, serving the Alabama-Coushattas and Tigua Indians, but this was terminated in 1989.[79]

Much as with federal tribal acknowledgment, state recognition has been plagued by questions of authenticity, particularly battles over how to define bona fide Indian groups worthy of state and local aid. In retrospect, gubernatorial proclamations and acts recognizing the contributions of local Indians seem naïve. They opened a Pandora's box of issues never foreseen. Many state proclamations of the 1970s

seem to have involved little research into the history or composition
of groups seeking recognition. While many Indian bands were well
known and accepted as remnant tribes, others appear to have been
of more recent origin. Indian organizations came forward, having
newly established tribal entities, and then often approached local
politicians to support their recognition efforts. Many people in Alabama took Indian-sounding names, such as Running Deer or Big
Eagle, secured letters of support from local business and civic leaders,
and then came before state legislative committees dressed in stereotypical Indian clothing to make themselves appear more Indian than
they may have been. Groups that could not meet the federal acknowledgment criteria (that most long-recognized tribes accept) passed
through this feeble process. The innocent years and honeymoon
period quickly ended, however. Tribes with stronger claims to Indianness came to demand more strict criteria for recognizing additional
tribes. As Houma leader Helen Gindrat argued before other tribal
leaders on the Louisiana Board of Indian Commissioners in 1981:
"We have to get a set of criteria together for state recognition; now we
have 'resolutions' . . . the state does not care one way or the other about
that."[80] Some states such as Georgia continued to rely on ad hoc legislative bills, but others such as North Carolina and Alabama developed
recognition criteria modeled upon the BIA's Federal Acknowledgment
Process. These states established Indian-directed committees to make
acknowledgment decisions.[81]

The formal recognition rules, intended to create uniformity, only
fueled intertribal animosity in many states. Increased scrutiny led
to questioning of group identity and history, furthering discord. In
Louisiana an almost caste-like division developed between simple
"state-recognized tribes," acknowledged by non-Indian politicians,
and those admitted to the earlier-formed Inter-Tribal Council, a group
composed of long-standing, well-identified state and federal tribes.
For example, when the Clifton Choctaws petitioned the Inter-Tribal
Council for membership in 1991, the others closed ranks against
them. According to Tunica-Biloxi chief Eli Barbry, the Clifton group
had not provided evidence of their existence as a tribal government.
Chitimacha chairman Ralph Darden, Jena Choctaw chief Jerry Jackson,
and Coushatta chief Lovelin Poncho concurred that that Clifton Choctaws had not proven that they were a viable tribe according to the eight
criteria the council had established. The debates among local tribes

on state-recognition status almost exactly mirror the larger federal acknowledgment debates. As Jeanette Campos, director of the Inter-Tribal Council, stated at a meeting: "It has become very popular to claim Indian identity . . . because people tend to feel there are a lot of benefits wrapped into the package of being Indian." Helen Gindrat agreed, adding, "Anyone can walk in and say 'I'm Indian' and they can't find documents to back them up, nor are they able to say what tribe they belong to. . . . [We need standards so that we can keep] protecting ourselves on a state recognition basis." As in debates about federal recognition, Inter-Tribal Council leaders often met angry resistance to their efforts. Threatening a lawsuit, a man named David Barnett wrote to them in 1982, complaining that "the classification committee is gross discrimination," adding, "I know I am an Indian, full blood Creek, that's something you cannot take away from me, no matter what proposal you pass."[82] When the North Carolina commission denied the application of the Occaneechi Band of the Saponi Nation for lack of evidence, the band did pursue a lawsuit. According to the commission's executive director, Gregory Richardson, an administrative law judge ruled for the band after the commission's attorney missed a filing deadline.[83]

Receiving state tribal recognition opened many doors for small southeastern tribes, and validated their identity as indigenous Americans. For many Indian communities that had been identified and studied for generations, state-recognized status was long-awaited justice and well deserved. However, for some, state recognition essentially inaugurated their public existence as tribes. The Ma-Chis Creeks of Alabama provide an example. The Ma-Chis Creeks, like most Southeastern tribes, incorporated as a nonprofit, doing so in 1982. Its small membership of 284 was headquartered at the town of New Brockton in southeastern Alabama. The group's leader was Penny Wright, described often as a dynamic and well-connected individual. BIA researchers who spent months researching the Ma-Chis Creeks found no reference to the tribe or any Indian enclave in the area prior to the group's incorporation. A late 1970s canvass of surviving Indians in the state, sponsored by students at Florida State University, did not mention the group, and there were no references to a Creek or other Indian community in the New Brockton area in local histories, newspapers, or any other records. A local historian had never heard of there being an Indian group in the county. While their invisibility does not preclude historic tribal existence, the Ma-Chis's reasoning, while fairly typical, leaves much to doubt. According to their self-produced history, Ma-Chis ancestors hid for years in a local cave and that is a major reason they do not appear in any records. The group provided neither historical nor archaeological evidence to back its claim. Despite their apparent recent origins, state recognition soon led to the Ma-Chis appearing regularly in local newspapers and at local Indian-oriented events. They received Indian education grants, were invited to give presentations on Native American history at local schools, and were granted coveted membership in the NCAI. Their experience provides an important, although often unrecognized fact about state tribal acknowledgment: it can create tribes that did not exist before. Few people realize the frequently significant distinctions between well-established and unquestioned federally recognized tribes and some that possess state-recognized status. While many state-recognized tribes are widely accepted as legitimate Indian communities, many are not. State recognition likewise caused confusion among officials dealing with Indian peoples. Employees at large federal agencies such as the Public Health Service have become confused as to whether state recognition is the same as federal status.[84]

State recognition is far inferior to federal recognition. However, a few tribes, such as the Alabama-Coushattas, the Mattaponis, the Pamunkeys, and the MOWA Choctaws, have developed functioning reservations and tribal programs with only state recognition. The latter group provides a rare example of a non–federally recognized tribe with a well-developed state reservation. Located a few miles northwest of the Mobile-area town of Mt. Vernon, Alabama, the MOWA Reservation is set in a piney woods area a few miles off a major highway, U.S. 43. On the way to tribal headquarters, visitors pass several housing complexes administered by the tribal housing authority. The largest, named after MOWA historian Jacqueline Matte, has approximately twenty-five modest but well-kept brick homes, built through various federal and private loan and grant programs. The tribal headquarters is a neat wood-and-shingle building, with turquoise and red trim, surrounded by a sea of green grass. Athletics fields named after MOWA leader Galas Weaver are to its north. The tribal headquarters houses a health clinic, tribal offices, and meeting rooms. Nearby an old Indian school building is home to a developing tribal museum. While the MOWA Band does not have federal recognition and BIA services, the reservation has a neat, clean appearance, paved roads, and paved parking lots. Few non-Indians realize that this is not a federal reservation, and many who do feel that it appears more prosperous.

State recognition has proved a mixed blessing for many southeastern Indian groups. It has clearly placed them in an anomalous status vis-à-vis other Indian tribes and non-Indian neighbors. On one hand, state Indian commissions provide largely token services and programs for tribes that pale in comparison to those available to federally recognized tribes, and the constitutionality of state recognition itself is in doubt. State largesse is often a thin reed on which to lean. State legislatures dealing with budget crises have cut Indian programs. In the case of the once-significant Texas Indian Commission, in 1983 the state attorney general ruled that the institution was unconstitutional under the Texas constitution, a ruling leading to its demise. Many positive developments flow from state recognition, however. State status makes tribes eligible for many Indian-oriented (but non-BIA) social, educational, and economic programs at both the state and federal levels. Members of state-recognized tribes are eligible for many affirmative action programs for minorities, can apply for graduate schools and employment as Indians, and can market arts and crafts as Native American–made. Finally, state recognition has provided an important, if largely psychological benefit. When questioned, individuals can take out a state tribal identification card to prove their authenticity as Indian people.[85]

NATIVE GRAVES AND REPATRIATION ISSUES

In 1968 Leonard Charrier, an employee at the Angola State Penitentiary north of Baton Rouge, working in secret with a rudimentary metal detector, unearthed a cache of French and Indian artifacts dating from early colonial times, a find unparalleled for the period and region. After the find was publicized, the artifacts were dubbed the "Tunica Treasure" for the fact that they had been found in the Tunica Hills of Louisiana and because they comprised a priceless collection. The artifacts included beads, muskets, pottery, and, significantly, the remains of over one hundred Tunica Indians. The "treasure" and its finder were soon embroiled in a lasting controversy: the Native graves and repatriation issue had arrived in the Southeast. The conflict over the Tunica Treasure first centered on the fact that

Charrier was not trained in archaeology and had never received government clearance to undertake the dig, but it soon moved to who owned the artifacts. The so-called treasure ultimately found its way to Harvard's Peabody Museum, where its existence became a point of controversy with the newly organizing Tunica-Biloxi Tribe, whose members were angry that their ancestors' graves were awaiting study and potential display. The Tunicas secured a legal aid group and threatened suit if the remains were not returned to the tribe. They found an ally in Louisiana's attorney general who also wanted the Tunica Treasure returned to the state. After securing federal recognition in 1981, the Tunica Biloxi Tribe finally had the remains repatriated, one of the largest single returns up until that time, an event that helped influence the subsequent Native American Graves Protection and Repatriation Act of 1990 (NAGPRA). The tribe ultimately built a large modern museum to house the artifacts. While the Tunicas had the issue thrust upon them, other southeastern Indians soon became voluntarily involved with this important cause. In states such as Alabama, once devoid of a public Native American presence, state-recognized groups such as the Eastern Echota Tribe began lobbying local elected officials, demanding they protect Native graves and sites. In response the state passed laws and a constitutional amendment preventing the looting and desecration of indigenous graves.[86]

While the Tunica-Biloxis plowed new ground, NAGPRA would prove important to southeastern Indians, especially unrecognized tribes, on several levels. Protecting ancestral graves became a rallying point, encouraging individual Indians to come together for a common cause. For many people, grave destruction and desecration was an extremely emotional issue. Individuals who may have been generally passive jumped into action when called to save grave sites threatened with destruction. Unrecognized groups had an issue tribal members could unite around. A good example occurred in 1998 in New Orleans. That year the United Houma Nation held a formal protest rally at the Texaco Building to publicize the company's digging up thirty skeletons of their ancestors while it was constructing a gas plant in the region around Houma. The group ultimately succeeded, with the company returning the remains to the Houmas. On the negative side, involvement with NAGPRA has caused some friction with non-Indians that may hinder federal recognition goals. In some cases non-Indian officials have resented having to deal with numerous Indian-identified entities that they have never heard of before, and may have feared giving them a status that might bolster their demands. Overall, NAGPRA and related local laws have been beneficial to southeastern Indian groups, recognized and unrecognized alike. For state-recognized tribes like the Biloxi-Chitimacha Confederation of Muskogee Indians of Louisiana, the federal statute has provided them with a forum, placated their concerns, and led to some validation of their identity. Although only mandating that officials locate and consult with federally recognized tribes or lineal descendants, under NAGPRA local museums and other sources often consult with nearby state-recognized and unrecognized Indian communities to ascertain tribal groups affiliated with discovered remains and funerary objects. These groups feel empowered by being consulted, and they often use these contacts and related correspondence as proof of their tribal validity.[87]

ENTERING THE NATIONAL ARENA

By the mid-1970s, southeastern Indians had emerged from the shadows of national Indian affairs. The American Indian Policy Review Commission (AIPRC) and its reports did more than any other development to expose the concerns of southeastern Indians to the larger world. Unrecognized and terminated Indians played an unusually large role in the AIPRC proceedings, especially those hailing from southern states. The commission's work clearly introduced the region's forgotten Natives to the country, but in doing so it spawned acrimonious debates that have yet to be resolved. The Federal Acknowledgment Process that came in its wake became the essential testing ground for tribal authenticity in the Southeast and elsewhere.

On a February day in 1973 AIM militants seized the small hamlet of Wounded Knee on the Pine Ridge Reservation of South Dakota, the site of an infamous massacre of Native Americans in 1890. The seizure prompted Congress to create the AIPRC to inquire into the problems of Native peoples that had led to the era's increasing Indian militancy, culminating in the AIM takeover of Wounded Knee. The commission's work and findings would directly impact the Southeast. Although the AIPRC had lofty aspirations, seeking no less than a second Meriam Report that would lead to a complete overhaul of federal Indian policy, much as the Meriam Report had in 1928, one

of its few lasting impacts was the creation of the Federal Acknowledgment Process in 1978.[88]

The commission, aimed at examining all major Indian problems,
had various task forces, including one on terminated and unrecognized Indians. More than any time in modern history eastern Natives,
particularly non–federally recognized tribes, were fully represented.
The Lumbees, being the largest group and generally best educated,
were particularly prominent. Adolph Dial, a longtime educator at
Pembroke State University, served as one of five Indian commissioners
of the AIPRC itself. Lumbee attorney and leader Jo Jo Hunt was a
chair of Task Force Ten on non–federally recognized and terminated
tribes. Helen Maynor Scheirbeck was also actively involved. Vine Deloria,
Jr., Chuck Downs, and Pete Gregory, all veterans of southeastern Indian
organizing, played roles on the commission. Men like Tom Tureen
and Kirke Kickingbird who focused their work on the region also
were active in the AIPRC. During the mid-1970s the commission held
meetings in several locations in the Southeast: Baton Rouge and
Dulac, Louisiana, and Pembroke, North Carolina. At these hearings,
representatives of the Houmas and Lumbees presented the problems
they faced so that the commissioners could report back to Congress.
The commission compiled statistics and conducted research on unrecognized southeastern Indian groups. In 1976 and 1977 the AIPRC
published its findings, including a significant volume on terminated
and non–federally recognized tribes. The reports forcefully advocated
for eastern communities and all unrecognized groups. As the commission concluded: "Tribes which have been overlooked, forgotten,
or ignored must be recognized as possessing their full rights as
tribes."[89] The AIPRC reports highlighted for the first time the very
existence of tribes left out of the federal fold, with significant case
studies of southeastern groups such as the Tunica-Biloxis, Lumbees,
Haliwas, and Waccamaw Siouans. The commissioners called for an
independent congressional office to decide on federal acknowledgment cases. Transcripts of meetings reveal that participants like Tom
Dion were deeply appreciative that other Indians and the federal
government were taking an interest in their welfare. Commissioner
Dial found these hearings an eye-opening experience. He and others
realized, for the first time, the striking uniformity of experience and
concerns all southeastern Indians shared.[90]

During the same era, the 1970s, increasing Indian land claims spurred non-Indians—federal policy makers and average citizens—to see the need for consistent standards for recognizing new tribes. After a federal judge ruled that the Penobscot and Passamaquoddy Tribes could pursue a tribal lands claim although they were not recognized by the federal government, southeastern groups like the Tunica-Biloxis brought suit under the Indian Trade and Intercourse Act of 1790 for thousands of acres in their home region. Throughout the Southeast, groups like the Houmas, Tunica-Biloxis, and Lumbees began pursuing legislation that would formally recognize their tribal status, with some using threatened land claims suits as leverage.[91] Because tribal status affected these suits, the BIA and other federal agencies began meeting to discuss formal tribal recognition procedures to bring clarity to the situation.

At the same time, the NCAI began discussing similar ways to create consistent and fair acknowledgment procedures, an essential step in determining which groups were bona fide Indians worthy of qualifying for indigenous programs. Seeing the success of eastern and southern groups in securing grants and pursuing land claims, reservation leaders saw a potential sea change in Indian politics. The NCAI's executive director, Chuck Trimble, called a special conference on federal tribal recognition. Sponsored by Trimble's group and the United South and Eastern Tribes (USET), the recognition council was held in Nashville in 1978. Representatives of unrecognized tribes and CENA were invited to attend. Poarch Creek leader Eddie Tullis was very active at the event, presenting the voice of tribes present that were not federally recognized. Although Chuck Downs noted that the NCAI and USET were not known for supporting non–federally recognized groups, he found a spirit of peace and goodwill at the conference. The NCAI ended up adopting principles on tribal acknowledgment, calling for concrete ethnological, historical, and political evidence as criteria. Significantly, tribal leaders rejected the AIPRC's earlier proposal for creating an independent tribal acknowledgment commission. However, the AIPRC's plan spawned several bills to this effect, and the commission supported allowing the BIA, an agency dominated by members of recognized tribes, to make tribal recognition determinations. In 1978 the BIA established its Federal Acknowledgment Process and published a list of seven mandatory criteria that hopeful groups needed to meet to

secure federal tribal acknowledgment. It also established a small office
to handle forthcoming applications.[92]

Southeastern Indians had been intimately involved with a host of
issues alerting the nation that a formal federal acknowledgment process was needed in order to process claims by nonrecognized Indian
groups. They had helped create an Indian renaissance that in part
forced the government to standardize its once ad hoc and inconsistent
tribal recognition procedures, a nonpolicy that had left them outside
the fold. Not surprisingly, having led the crusade, the Tunica-Biloxi
Tribe and Poarch Band of Creek Indians were among the first to submit
petitions, and they were among the first tribes to gain status under
the new rules. In 1978, as the BIA published its first list of federally
recognized entities eligible for services, lines were being drawn and
hardened with many not knowing what was happening.[93]

A NEW INDIAN RESERVATION ON THE BLOCK:
SOME EFFECTS OF FEDERAL RECOGNITION

For most southeastern tribes, securing federal tribal status was the
ultimate goal and logical outgrowth of the cultural and economic
awakenings of the postwar years. The effect of federal acknowledgment
on long-neglected southeastern Indian communities was nothing short
of staggering for some tribes. The development of the once-impoverished
Poarch Band of Creek Indians near Atmore, Alabama, provides a case
in point. After the band secured federal acknowledgment through
the BIA process in 1984, the Department of the Interior took its 231-
acre land base into trust. This status exempted Poarch Creek lands
from local and state taxes and regulations. Although the learning
curve was steep, soon the tribe began exercising self-government on
its tribal lands, with a formal government that possessed the powers
of taxation, law enforcement, citizenship decisions, and a court system.
In time the Poarch Band built a sprawling government complex to
house these offices. As a federally recognized tribe, the Poarch Creek
possessed all the government powers of other tribal governments. Its
tribal council enacted laws, and its court system handled civil and
criminal cases involving tribal members on Creek lands. With recognition the Creeks were eligible to apply for Indian-only programs for

federal tribes, including contracting with the Indian Health Service to open a health center, a development that provided comprehensive health services to members. The band developed its own police force, recreation department, and employment and training center. Just as important was the tribe's business development. Aided by government grants and exemptions from local regulations, the Poarch Creeks built a Best Western motel, the Creek Indian Catfish Junction restaurant, and a bar-lounge. It developed its own industrial base, with the Muskogee Metalworks, Red Eagle Paint Company, and Perdido Farms, the latter a thousand-acre operation that involved fish farming and growing shiitake mushrooms. Through a BIA program the band operated its own radio station as well.[94]

By far the most important economic activity the Poarch Band of Creek Indians established was a highly lucrative gaming empire. The band got in on the first wave of Indian gaming, and by the early 1990s its various bingo-related ventures were multimillion dollar enterprises, aided by tribal land located near Interstate 65. As the only federally recognized tribe in the state, the band was exempt from Alabama anti-gaming laws, enabling it to operate large casino complexes. By 2009 the Poarch Creeks owned three large gaming halls, one near tribal headquarters at Atmore, and two near the capital of Montgomery. Tribal advertising claimed that the three casinos paid out in excess of $2 billion in winnings annually. The largest facility, Wind Creek Casino at Atmore, consisted of a 225,000-square-foot gaming hall and a seventeen-story, 236-room luxury hotel. The tribe used funds produced by its gaming ventures to fund social and economic programs for members. The once impoverished and shunned people were running businesses that served as a major economic engine for the surrounding non-Indian communities. All told, the changes for the Poach Creeks were phenomenal. Their success was something most unrecognized tribes hoped to emulate.[95]

SOUTHEASTERN INDIANS MEET THE FEDERAL ACKNOWLEDGMENT PROCESS

Federal tribal acknowledgment became what all southeastern tribes desired. However, it separated groups into dichotomous categories, "federally recognized" and "unrecognized." When the BIA regulations were published in 1978, the small office charged with making acknowledgment recommendations established a locator project to find eastern and southern tribes left out of the fold. At that time over forty groups centered east of the Mississippi had expressed interest in securing status.[96] The Federal Acknowledgment Process and the later Office of Federal Acknowledgment (OFA) became the essential testing ground for Indian authenticity in the nation. Southeastern groups like the Lumbees and Tunica-Biloxis had been central to the creation of the BIA process, and most supported its criteria and stated goals in 1978. The BIA recognition process would serve as the lens through which all Indians would be judged in subsequent years.

As the lines hardened among peoples who had once generally shared the same federal status as unrecognized, terminated, or ambiguously served Indians, a caste-like system developed in the Southeast. In Alabama, Louisiana, and North Carolina, federally recognized tribes, including some only recently recognized through the BIA, turned a cold shoulder toward their state-recognized neighbors. In Virginia state-recognized tribes with reservations remained aloof from Native groups with no land base, fearing a diminution of their own status. All over the United States leaders of federally recognized tribes and the BIA that served them expressed concerns over the potential costs of providing for newly recognized tribes. Residents of southeastern states unaccustomed to Indian reservations and baffled by their intricacies and exemptions expressed uneasiness about some claims of "new tribes" and "new Indians." Land claims caused conflict, and potential hunting and fishing rights did too, but these were nothing compared to the issues involved when Indian casinos popped up in the region after 1988. Federal tribal recognition had long been a goal of southeastern Indian groups, but it would be harder and harder to secure in the years after Indian gaming arrived.[97]

A SOUTHERN INDIAN RENAISSANCE

The post–World War II years were times of immense change for southeastern Indians. Whether federally recognized or not, they had entered the war years enveloped in a social world marked by Jim Crow segregation and daily reminders of their second-class status. Economically they were at the periphery of the southern economy, generally struggling as rural workers at the bottom rung. Most were unrecognized by the federal government, while those that were acknowledged rarely appeared in standard histories of Native Americans, and few officials thought of them when decisions were formulated for Indians in the nation's capital. The changes during the forty years after World War II would have made even the most optimistic Indian alive in 1945 awestruck. For starters, legal segregation ended and Indians were admitted to integrated public schools. Being Indian became something valued, both to Indians themselves and to whites and African Americans in the Southeast. Indian enclaves that once had been isolated and generally powerless now established viable tribal governments, many with state and federal sanction, and began providing services and exercising true governmental power and sovereignty. Regional tribes reached out to each other and to national Native groups, forging intertribal alliances and creating powerful national tribal organizations that served the interests of Indians. Groups that retained elements of traditional cultural proudly displayed them via increasingly popular powwows, regional fairs, and museums. Those that had lost indigenous culture revived extinct forms while importing pan-Indian, particularly Plains Indian–style, dances and ceremonies. Southeastern tribes emerged by the 1980s as a force with which to reckon in local politics, regional economics, and national Indian affairs. Some well-known tribes gained federal recognition, others remained in status limbo, and still others found themselves branded frauds and wannabes. When the Florida Seminoles pioneered Indian gaming in the 1980s, a new, lucrative yet divisive economic and cultural phenomenon had arrived. More than any other development in the postwar years Indian gaming would shape the history and politics of Indian authenticity in the Southeast.

CHAPTER 2

The Genesis of a Conflict

*The Five Tribes and the Birth of the
Federal Acknowledgment Process*

The early 1970s were heady days for the Five Tribes of Oklahoma. Congress passed an act in October 1970 allowing the Oklahoma-based tribes to elect their principal chiefs for the first time since the beginning of the century. The Five Tribes and their eastern relatives, such as the Mississippi Band of Choctaws, were operating tribal businesses and pursuing self-determination after decades of relative slumber. By mid-decade all of the five had held referendums creating new constitutions that established formal governments and citizenship requirements. They began building tribal enterprises such as the Cherokee Nation Industries. The Cherokee Nation established the Tsa-La-Gi Cultural Center as a focal point of tribal identity and pride. Under new federal laws the tribes were running their own programs, contracting for federal moneys, and establishing their own tribal welfare, job training, and health care programs. As Choctaw historian Valerie Lambert notes, these years witnessed a true tribal reawakening. The Choctaws, Creeks, and others embarked upon an intensive period of nation building, and people were excited at the real tribal sovereignty and self-determination these newly robust nations were able to exert. For the first time since they had been forcefully dissolved in 1906 with the coming of Oklahoma statehood, the Five Tribes were functioning governments again. People looked forward to a future in which they could rule their own destinies.

At the same time that these positive developments made the future so bright, tribal leaders were also becoming increasingly aware of several potential problems, ones that would gain importance in time. Census data and everyday experience told tribal leaders that thousands of individuals around the country were claiming a Cherokee, Choctaw, Creek, and less often Chickasaw and Seminole identity, accessing funds meant for Indians. The office of Cherokee Nation principal chief W. W. Keeler was looking into the problem, inquiring about well-known imposters like Sylvester Long ("Chief Buffalo Child Long Lance") and discussing general ways to police individuals selling "Native American" art, to make sure that Cherokee artisans were protected. An old story, it was apparent that both fraudulent and well-meaning (if ill-informed) individuals increasingly were taking a tribal identity and hurting Five Tribes citizens in the process. Elected to replace retiring Chief Keeler in 1975, new Cherokee principal chief, Ross Swimmer, began to acquire information on surviving Indian groups in the Southeast, trying to research tribal entities that were coming forward that were previously unknown to his people. The Cherokee Nation found its offices dealing with several new tribes in Tennessee claiming to be Cherokee, an assertion Chief Swimmer's sovereign nation found annoying and offensive at the same time. It seemed a group calling itself "the Far-away Cherokees" was serving as "tribal spokesman," consulting on sensitive Cherokee issues such as Trail of Tears commemorations. Other groups were forming tribes and attempting to gain recognition from state officials. At a moment when the Five Tribes were reformulating tribal citizenship and exerting tribal sovereignty, these unauthorized entities were troublesome.[1] The newly invigorated Five Tribes and related eastern reservation groups had certainly benefited from the Indian renaissance, pan-Indian activism, and the pro-Indian social climate of the era, but they also were running headlong into new groups and recently awakened "Indian" individuals that also benefited from these positive trends.

Just as the Five Tribes and others were formalizing their tribal governments and running their own programs, legal aid groups were helping nonrecognized tribes do the same: the two were on a collision course. One result was the Federal Acknowledgment Process, established within the BIA in 1978. Its rigorous criteria and evaluation process reflected the desires of the Five Tribes and many other reservation tribes to have a stringent regimen, one that protected their rights, economic resources, and overall ability to define "Indians" and "tribes." Throughout these debates pulsed questions of "authenticity" and being "real" or "bona fide" Indians and tribes. While academics and unrecognized groups questioned the ability of any party to accurately define "Indian" and "tribe," as a practical political and cultural matter tribes and their federal allies groped toward a way to measure and define these highly problematic terms. By 1978 leaders of federally recognized tribes felt they had found the answer in the new Federal Acknowledgment Process, with many unrecognized groups agreeing that finally a way had been found to determine what groups were "real" tribes.

MY GREAT-GRANDMOTHER WAS A CHEROKEE PRINCESS

Some tribes have had their identity and culture stolen and appropriated much more than others. In his landmark 1969 work *Custer Died for Your Sins*, Vine Deloria, Jr., identified the phenomenon:

> During my years as Executive Director of the National Congress of American Indians it was a rare day when some white didn't visit my office and proudly proclaim that he or she was of Indian descent. Cherokee was the most popular tribe of their choice and many placed the Cherokees anywhere from Maine to Washington State. Mohawk, Sioux, and Chippewa were next in popularity. Occasionally I would be told about some mythical tribe from lower Pennsylvania, Virginia, or Massachusetts which had spawned the white standing before me. . . . I eventually came to understand their need to identify partially as Indian and did not resent them. . . . All but one person I met who claimed Indian blood claimed it on their grandmother's side. I once did a projection backward and discovered that evidently most tribes were entirely female for the first three hundred years of white occupation. No one, it seemed, wanted to claim a male Indian as forebear.[2]

Deloria was writing at the end of the 1960s, a decade that witnessed a flowering of interest in Indians, when the phenomenon of white people claiming an Indian identity was at one of its historical peaks. It is often assumed that in the past people hid their indigenous heritage, that it was disadvantageous to "be Indian," but this belief is incorrect. As the Five Tribes and others know all too well, there have always been reasons for whites and African Americans to claim to be Cherokee, Creek, or Choctaw.[3]

More than most American Indian tribes, the Five Tribes have faced imposters and schemers trying to claim tribal membership for personal gain. While the phenomenon of *groups* claiming Cherokee or other tribal identity is a relatively modern phenomenon, the phenomenon of individuals who fabricate a genealogical relationship with the Cherokees and other tribes has a long and checkered past. The Cherokee Nation faced this problem as early as the first decades of the nineteenth century. In 1828 the *Cherokee Phoenix*, in a piece titled "An Imitation Indian," reported: "A person made his appearance in the city on Thursday last, dressed in the costume of an Indian, and calling himself 'Gen. William Ross,' which is engraved upon an apparently silver breast plate. He says his father is Daniel Ross, who is the Chief of the Cherokee Indians, and that he is an authorized agent of the nation." According to the article, this man was dressed in a black wig, "a gown of wide-stripped calico," and had beads around his neck. The appearance of "General Ross" prompted Daniel Ross, his purported father, to write to the press: "I have no knowledge of who this vile wretch can be, and I believe he has no connexion whatever with the Cherokees, and certainly not with me, or family. . . . Should this imposter gain credence with the credulous, so that they become loserers by his acquaintance, I can have no sort of objection (by way of atonement) to the hanging of this 'General W. Ross,' if merited." As this exchange shows, at an early date the Cherokees were experiencing problems with dubious claimants, with hanging deemed by at least one as an appropriate punishment.[4]

The Five Tribes also have had to guard against interlopers seeking to gain entry in their formal rolls. Almost immediately after their forced removal to Indian Territory, the Cherokees, Chickasaws, Choctaws, Creeks, and Seminoles found whites pushing onto tribal lands. Many whites married tribal members to gain entry, seeking access to the nations' coveted farmlands, mineral resources, and business enterprises. Others simply squatted on Indian lands and then claimed that the tribes were not protecting their interests as white men on U.S. soil. Federal officials and the Five Tribes did their best to evict these lawless individuals but the tide was generally against them. Squatters and intermarried whites were threats, but, as noted historian Angie Debo concludes, "The most troublesome of the intruders were those who had advanced some fantastic claim to citizenship, and who loudly demanded every privilege enjoyed by the Indians."[5] The Choctaws and others had a long-standing custom of admitting inter-married whites. However, after the Civil War the intentions of these individuals came under increasing scrutiny, causing alarm in some quarters over their growing numbers and right to share in the tribal estate. By this time the tribes also were sensitive to having govern-ment agents force individuals and groups onto tribal rolls. As early as 1866 punitive post–Civil War treaties mandated that the formerly slave-holding tribes give citizenship to the freed slaves, a move still controversial today. The treaties also forced tribes like the Cherokee Nation to give lands and rights to the unrelated Delawares and Shaw-nees. The tribal governments began to respond. An 1875 Choctaw law, for example, required intermarried white men to swear allegiance to the nation, pay a fee, and have a witness testify as to their moral character. Significantly, an individual who abandoned his Indian wife forfeited citizenship rights. The issue reached its highpoint on the eve of Oklahoma statehood. Through concerted political and legal wrangling, the Five Tribes had won exemption from the Dawes Act of 1887, a federal law designed to dissolve tribal governments and pave the way for citizenship for Indians. Its main instrument was allotment: the Dawes Act mandated that individual Indians receive homesteads carved from the tribal land base, and it was expected that after a waiting period, landownership would lead to U.S. citizen-ship. Despite winning exemption from the law, the Five Tribes soon felt the tide turn, and allotment was forced upon them in the 1890s. Congress seized the power to create final rolls for the nations, and the Dawes Commission, under former U.S. senator Henry L. Dawes, retired architect of the earlier allotment legislation, was charged with determining who qualified for membership. With this maneuver the federal government usurped the Five Tribes' fundamental right to determine their citizenship requirements.[6]

During the Dawes Commission proceedings, government agents were deluged with dubious and grasping white and black claimants hoping to grab a share of the varied tribal resources. Tribal citizenship was potentially lucrative: the Five Tribes owned some of the most valu-able lands remaining in the Great Plains. Small-population tribes like the Chickasaws, with their rich farmlands, grazing tracts, and mineral lands, were inviting targets for schemers and charlatans. The Dawes

Commission employed hundreds of clerks, surveyors, and appraisers to allot lands and determine who could share in the tribal assets. The Five Tribes created citizenship committees with knowledge of family relations to guard the gates. It was during this era that the Choctaws experienced their first encounter with eastern claimants, as thousands of individuals from Mississippi, some with valid claims and some without, hired attorneys to gain Choctaw lands. The Cherokee Nation also was alerted to relations left behind decades earlier. In the early 1880s the Eastern Band's tribal council tried to share in the Cherokee Nation's annuity payments, prompting the federal government to establish an agency in North Carolina for them. The government also empowered an agent to take a census of all Cherokees living east of the Mississippi. The final roll listed 2,956 Cherokees still living in the Southeast, with the majority concentrated around today's Eastern Cherokee reservation in western North Carolina, but hundreds of others were scattered in surrounding states, many of whom the North Carolina group insisted were non-Indians. These actions and a failed federal court effort to share in funds pursued by the Eastern Cherokees ultimately set the stage for the incorporation of the modern Eastern Band of Cherokee Indians as a separate tribe. Besides the Cherokees, other tribes and their leaders felt besieged as thousands came forward to claim a share of tribal resources. Douglas Johnston, Chickasaw tribal governor, believed that the issue of fraudulent citizenship claims was the number one problem facing the Chickasaws and Choctaws in 1900. In a few short years, hopefuls had hired more than three hundred attorneys to pursue citizenship in the Five Tribes, and lawyers for the Five Tribes could do little more than file perfunctory briefs denying the claimants' rights to citizenship. Those people who entered tribal rolls by legal maneuver were called "court citizens" by the Indians. Dawes Commission chairman Tams Bixby estimated that only one in ten claimants placed on the Chickasaw and Choctaw rolls by the courts were entitled to citizenship. In the end thousands of fraudulent claims were granted over the objections of the leaders of the Five Tribes—thousands of people became new tribal citizens. These dubious enrollees, with rights secured, often then led the charge to destroy the tribal governments and Indian way of life. Through this tumultuous, fraudulent process, the claims were so substantial that the Cherokees ended up running out of land for real Cherokee people.[7]

Would-be Cherokees, Chickasaws, Choctaws, Creeks, and Seminoles were at first always seeking personal profit. At the turn of the century this meant land or access to other tribal assets. As the agricultural economy waned, however, new wannabe Cherokees and Creek individuals emerged, seeking a connection to these peoples for entirely different reasons. After the rich tribal lands were gone, other ways to benefit emerged. Sylvester Long was perhaps the most famous example of a Cherokee Indian imposter in the early twentieth century. Born of white and Lumbee parents in North Carolina in 1890, Long went west at the age of thirteen, joining a "Wild West" show where he worked as a "Cherokee Indian," and learned the language from a Cherokee man. In 1909 Sylvester again claimed he was Cherokee, likely because of his language fluency and because it was a well-known tribe purportedly related to the Lumbee Indians, to gain admittance to Carlisle Indian Industrial School. For Long, gaining entry into the Indian school provided proof of his assumed Cherokee identity. Though he enrolled as a Cherokee and spoke the language, Cherokee students were indignant, even protesting his claims to the school superintendent, a man who felt compassion for Long and gave him the name "Long Lance" to help legitimate his claims. Still, Long failed to gain acceptance among his Cherokee cohorts, who called him the "Cherokee Nigger." A star athlete, Long became fast friends with his running mate, Jim Thorpe, the legendary future Olympian and football hero, and he went on to graduate as head of the class of 1912. Long was later adopted into the Canadian Blood tribe under the name Chief Buffalo Child Long Lance and he went on to fame as a journalist and author, writing on Indian themes for popular magazines. He even starred in silent films, becoming the toast of New York City high society for a time. According to biographer Donald B. Smith, Long's appearance is what got him by: to most Americans he looked like the "Noble Savage" of popular stereotype. Long's fraud and assumed identity took their toll, however, and he had to distance himself from his family back in North Carolina lest his true identity be discovered. Long ended up committing suicide in 1932, lonely and detached from his home and community.[8]

Perhaps the most famous yet still often unacknowledged Cherokee imposter was Iron Eyes Cody. A veteran of over one hundred Hollywood films in which he starred alongside the likes of John Wayne, Gary Cooper, Bob Hope, and Steve McQueen, Iron Eyes Cody achieved iconic status as both a Native American and environmental symbol in the early 1970s as star of a public service advertisement for the Keep America Beautiful campaign. Few Americans alive then can forget the image of a buckskin-clad Cody paddling a birch-bark canoe past belching smokestacks, landing on a litter-strewn bank, and weeping after someone tosses a bag of trash at his feet from a passing car. The "crying Indian" pained at the degradation of the earth struck a chord with Americans. Few realized, however, that this actor, likely the most identifiable Indian of the century, was not an Indian at all. In a fiction-filled autobiography, Iron Eyes Cody claimed to have a Cherokee father and Cree mother. He invented a fantastic childhood, complete with a story of being born "Little Eagle" and raised on a Cherokee farm in Oklahoma by his father, "Thomas Long Plume," a man who supposedly had ridden in Buffalo Bill's Wild West Show. Shortly before Cody's death in 1999, a film scholar wrote an often-overlooked piece for the *New Orleans Times-Picayune* in which she exposed his life of fraud. In the article, backed by interviews with Cody's half-sister and research in local archives, the author revealed Cody's true identity. He was actually born Espera DeCorti to Italian immigrants in Louisiana and lived an itinerant, impoverished childhood before migrating to California and reinventing himself as Iron Eyes Cody. Like many other imposters he parlayed his dark features and Roman nose, helped by constant wearing of Indian clothing and braided wig, into an assumed identity.

In some ways Iron Eyes was a second coming of Sylvester Long, but his assumption of an Indian identity was in some ways more ambiguous. Cody's identity was kept a secret for a long time mainly because many Native Americans respected him and the way he lived his life. Over the years Cody gave away much of his earnings to Indian causes, and he married an Indian woman, Bertha Parker Cody, a great-niece of Seneca chief and Civil War hero Ely Parker, and adopted two Indian children. Well-known Indian actors Lois Red Elk and Jay Silverheels knew about Cody's true past but kept it secret, feeling it would do more harm than good to expose him. To many Cody seemed to embody all that was good about being Native American. He had lived his life as an Indian and helped project a positive image. As Kathleen Whitaker, a friend and curator of the Southwest Museum remarked on his true heritage: "What difference does it make? Iron Eyes brought forth the true essence of what being American Indian is all about." Many people, including Indians, to this day refuse to admit that Cody was not really Native. As Russell Thornton, a well-respected

Cherokee academic, put it, Iron Eyes fit a time-worn image: "He looked like what white America thought Indians should look like . . . he was acceptable as an Indian."[9]

Likely the most improbable Cherokee imposter was white supremacist Asa Carter, whose 1976 book *The Education of Little Tree* became a best seller, reaching the number-one position on the *New York Times* nonfiction list in 1991. He wrote under the pen name Forrest Carter, and claimed to have been orphaned at a young age and raised by Cherokee grandparents in the Appalachian Mountains. *The Education of Little Tree* relates the importance of family to Indian life and centers on the need to live in harmony with nature, and it was hailed by scholars as an accurate depiction of Indian youth and values. Rennard Strickland praised the book using New Age references, hailing its mystical and universal values such as caring for the earth and nurturing youth. Carter's work was used in Native American Studies courses as well. Its importance was questioned, however, when writers gradually began to reveal that Asa Carter, former speechwriter for Alabama's George Wallace, and Forrest Carter, the supposed Cherokee orphan, were one and the same. As journalist John J. Miller notes, Asa Carter was likely the man who penned Wallace's infamous lines "Segregation now! Segregation tomorrow! Segregation forever!" during the dark days of the civil rights movement. He was a leader of the KKK and Northern Alabama White Citizens' Council. Despite Carter's ideology, like a long line of people before him the author had no qualms about assuming a Cherokee identity for personal profit, and *The Education of Little Tree*, despite being a fabrication replete with stereotypes about Indians as natural ecologists and primitives, struck a chord with white audiences. Many Native American studies courses still use the book in their classes, albeit with an eye toward examining the work critically rather than romantically.[10]

EVOLVING TOWARD AN INDIAN NATION-STATE

Beginning in 1830 the Five Tribes signed removal treaties and began the long process of emigrating from the Southeast to Indian Territory and reestablishing their tribal governments in the West. The infamous Trail of Tears took the lives of perhaps one-quarter of the Cherokees, and certainly thousands of Choctaws, Creeks, Chickasaws, and Seminoles. At journey's end, the tribes settled on lands in eastern Oklahoma. Leaders like John Ross of the Cherokee Nation and Roley and Chilly McIntosh of the Creek Nation attempted to heal old wounds, and eventually succeeded in reuniting their peoples and forging new governments. In Indian Territory a golden age ensued. During a remarkably short period of time, the Cherokees, Creeks, Choctaws, Chickasaws, and Seminoles ratified new constitutions, created social and educational institutions, and brought prosperity once again to their peoples. As Angie Debo writes, by the late nineteenth century each tribe had a constitutional government with an executive branch, legislature, and judicial body. The tribes created their own small "Indian republics," complete with tribal school systems and business enterprises. They were largely Christian and had made so much progress that whites began calling them "the Five Civilized Tribes" to contrast them with their Plains Indian neighbors. The Indian governments continued a process started earlier in the Southeast. During the eighteenth century, these peoples had pursued state formation— European colonialism had prompted the Choctaws and others to create more cohesive sociopolitical units—and in short order a larger national identity formed. Choctaw, Chickasaw, and Cherokee states took form, usurping power from the towns and smaller communities, and these new states became official bureaucratic and political centers of emerging national communities. One by one these tribal states adopted the tenets of the American society around them. Clans were divested of their governmental and legal powers, women were disenfranchised, and African Americans were excluded from citizenship. Indian "blood" increasingly buttressed this process, adopted as a medium for belonging and citizenship. The Five Tribes accepted mainstream American notions of race and nation, defining their nations largely as collectives tied by blood and kinship to a superorganism with a unique biological and cultural essence. As Native scholar Clara Sue Kidwell finds for the Choctaws, the peoples eventually transitioned from societies based on communal land ownership, kinship, language, and cultural traditions, to "political, corporate national entities."[11]

The Five Tribes became leaders in efforts to formally define citizenship and police their boundaries during the nineteenth century. In 1824 the Cherokee Nation passed its first miscegenation law, while its 1827 constitution prohibited blacks from holding office. The Cherokees and others were gradually incorporating American notions of race and citizenship. As Circe Sturm writes, "[T]hey also understood that the racial hierarchy of the United States placed them somewhere between African Americans and whites in status. They realized that they too were racialized others . . . and if they were not careful to establish their own social and political uniqueness, then they might be subjected to the same harsh treatment as African Americans."[12] During the mid-nineteenth century the Choctaws passed laws forbidding trespassers from settling within their nation, and they also had laws controlling white immigration in general and intermarriage. The Dawes Commission enrollment procedures furthered the tribes' immersion in racialized thinking. The final rolls, completed in 1906, divided the "Five Civilized Tribes" into citizens along racial lines—each enrollee was listed as a citizen by Indian "blood," freedman, or intermarried white. Where once notions of citizenship rested on family and community, citizenship now was a matter of formal governmental rolls.[13]

All the Five Tribes' progress at nation building came to an abrupt end during the 1890s. Several federal laws provided for the allotment of tribal lands to individuals, and the 1898 Curtis Act, sponsored by Charles Curtis of Kansas, a member of the Kaw Tribe, provided for the termination of tribal government. The once effective and proud Five Tribes' courts and legislatures were dissolved and their powers taken over by white institutions. Though the tribes were slated for termination in 1906, an act of that year allowed some aspects of tribal administration to continue in order to conclude tribal business and dispose of tribal assets. In a sad process, each of the Five Tribes went about their last elections in the early 1900s, selecting men like Pleasant Porter and Green McCurtain who were "mixed-bloods" from the elite class.[14] Of course, the people did not disappear, but their governments began a long period of invisibility and slumber. After Oklahoma statehood in 1907, the principal chiefs of the Five Tribes were made presidential appointees.[15]

LOST TRIBES AND INCONSISTENT TRIBAL ACKNOWLEDGMENT POLICY

Although Congress dissolved the Five Tribes' governments exercising its plenary (absolute) power over Indian affairs, a doctrine that is hotly debated today, their status as "recognized," sovereign governments rested on firm ground: treaties. The Cherokees, Choctaws, Creeks, Chickasaws, and Seminoles possessed treaties executed between their leaders and federal officials, though as their leaders would learn in the 1960s not every southeastern tribal community was similarly endowed. Acknowledgment of nations such as the Five Tribes was unassailable, but after the mass removal west many remnant communities remained in the Southeast whose legal status was ambiguous. Some, like the Mississippi Band of Choctaws and the Eastern Band of Cherokees, would secure federal tribal acknowledgment prior to the southeastern Indian renaissance, yet even these would have their status challenged repeatedly during the twentieth century. Others would have to wait through the ebbs and flows of federal Indian policy for their chance at sovereignty and self-determination.

Treaty acknowledgment is the absolute standard for tribal recognition. In the first hundred years of U.S. history approximately 370 federal treaties were made with Indian nations. These peace agreements acknowledged the indigenous nations' governmental sovereignty and their possession of lands. Significantly they also appropriated tribal lands, ultimately about two billion acres, leaving tribes with about 140 million acres. In 1785 and 1786 the Choctaws, Cherokees, and Chickasaws signed treaties at Hopewell Plantation in South Carolina, and several dozen treaties followed. The Cherokee Treaty of 1785 (the first Treaty of Hopewell) is reflective of the general pattern. Four federal treaty negotiators met with thirty-seven Cherokee headmen and warriors on the banks of the Keowee River, and here the Cherokee delegates signed a document declaring perpetual peace and friendship with the United States and acknowledging that the tribe was under the protection of the federal government. The treaty also dealt with matters such as prisoner exchange, the prohibition of intruders upon tribal lands, and extradition of non-Cherokee criminals hiding among the Cherokee. The first Treaty of Hopewell also set the formal boundaries of the Cherokee Nation, an agreement that would be broken many times. The treaties made with the Five Tribes recognized their inherent right to govern their internal affairs, with the federal government agreeing to respect their national boundaries. Although president Andrew Jackson would infamously call them a "farce," treaties were negotiated by the tribes from a position of relative power. As Vine Deloria and Clifford Lytle conclude: "Congress was not conducting a sham procedure when it considered and ratified Indian treaties; it really was dealing with an entirely foreign political entity and this entity possessed then and partially possesses today some elements in itself that have not been and cannot be subsumed under any federal law." In later parlance these treaties established a "government-to-government" or "nation-to-nation" relationship between the Indian tribes and the federal government.[16]

It is well known that the Cherokee Nation was central to evolving legal and political definitions of Indian tribes during the nineteenth century. As legal scholar William Quinn, Jr., and anthropologist Bruce Miller note, in the formative years of federal Indian policy what constituted an "Indian tribe" was largely taken for granted. The Commerce Clause of the Constitution (that grants Congress exclusive authority over dealings with Indian tribes) and the Trade and Intercourse Acts speak of "tribes" but leave them undefined. However, it is clear that federal officials generally viewed tribes as sovereign political entities: self-sufficient, independent, and self-governing. This aboriginal sovereignty was seen as predating white settlement. Indians were not incorporated into the body politic but lived outside formal U.S. and state jurisdiction, loyal and tied by blood and culture to their tribal communities. In the late eighteenth century, U.S. officials had little difficulty distinguishing between people of European heritage and Native Americans, based on ancestry and way of life, which likely explains the laissez-faire attitude toward defining aboriginal tribes. The common belief that Indians were a "vanishing race" also played a role in this. It seemed that the "noble" Indians and their "archaic" tribal forms were rapidly nearing extinction.[17] As the white population expanded and came to abut and surround eastern tribes protected by treaties, the issue of having Indian tribes within the larger American nation came to a head in Georgia.

During the 1820s the Cherokee Nation worked to formalize its tribal government, aware that white settlement would soon engulf the Cherokee people. The stage was set for a test of U.S. commitment to tribal sovereignty. Despite ratified federal treaties guaranteeing Cherokees the right to reside in northern Georgia, the state of Georgia unilaterally extended its laws and jurisdiction over the Cherokee Nation. There followed a series of U.S. Supreme Court decisions that would prove central to federal definitions of what constituted a tribe. The Cherokee Nation hired some of the country's best attorneys, including

William Wirt, former U.S. attorney general, to fight the state of Georgia in federal court. In the Supreme Court case *Cherokee Nation v. Georgia* (1831), the tribe argued that it was a foreign nation and thus the Supreme Court had original jurisdiction to hear its case against Georgia. The Supreme Court threw out the case, however, rejecting the Cherokee position. Chief Justice John Marshall concluded that the Cherokee Nation was not a foreign state but a "domestic dependent nation" under the ultimate authority of the central government. In the tribe's second case, *Worcester v. Georgia* (1832), Chief Justice Marshall, an old Federalist interested in expanding federal power over the states, ruled that the treaties negotiated between the United States and the Cherokees recognized the tribe's right to self-government and obligated the United States to protect its rights. Here the court began defining "tribes," saying that they were "a distinct community, occupying their own territory . . . in which the laws of Georgia can have no force." In these decisions that became known as the Cherokee cases, Marshall also declared that Indians remained in a state of pupilage, stating that their relationship to the federal government resembled that of a "ward" to the ward's "guardian." In light of this language, it is not surprising that federal courts spent the subsequent decades dealing with the implications of the so-called ward status, trying to determine the limits of federal paternalistic power over their charges. Courts would deal with questions of when to lift the dependent status from individuals and rule on how to remove restrictions to enable Indians and their lands to integrate fully into non-Indian American society. The Cherokee decisions established the two competing thrusts of federal policy that would affect tribal acknowledgment in subsequent decades. On one hand, Indians were treated as dependents of a paternal government, a negative state that would work against recognizing tribes. On the other, Marshall had acknowledged inherent tribal sovereignty, a fact that made tribal status worth retaining and achieving in subsequent decades.[18]

After the Five Tribes and others chose removal to the West over complete assimilation, federal officials changed tactics many times to deal with the quandary of having nondisappearing Native nations within U.S. borders. After the Civil War, officials turned their attention to finally solving "the Indian Problem" and integrating the tribes into the mainstream. As ward status is generally considered a handicap, they were more concerned with ending this status of Indians during this era rather than initiating new relationships with tribes not previously acknowledged. With Congress's unilateral declaration in 1871 that it would no longer engage in new treaties with Indian nations or acknowledge them, a further door to tribal recognition was closed, but this did not stop government officials from engaging in formal agreements with tribes. Presidents, through executive orders, created numerous reservations and other entities until Congress ended this procedure in 1919. During this era reservations became a target, seen by federal officials as isolated places that promoted the retention of uncivilized customs and barbaric tribal entities. Allotment as provided for in the 1887 Dawes Act was the congressional remedy to the problem. As Teddy Roosevelt famously predicted, the law would be "a mighty pulverizing engine to break up the tribal mass." From 1880–1930, a period David Wilkins calls the "Era of Allotment, Americanization, and Acculturation," there was an increasing emphasis on controlling definitions of Indians to limit service population under treaty obligations and to open lands to white settlement. A remarkably diverse group of non-Indians, including Democrats and Republicans, industrialists, philanthropists, and pious missionaries, came to agree that erasing Indian tribes and Indian identity would be the best solution to "the Indian Problem." Federal policy subsequently came to endorse ending communal land tenure in favor of private property, educational immersion in boarding schools, granting eventual U.S. citizenship, destroying tribes as legal entities, and ultimately replacing traditional cultural norms, such as indigenous marriage practices, religious ceremonies and beliefs, and traditional social organization, with Euro-American forms.[19]

During this era, federal courts were concerned with defining which groups and individuals were no longer Indian, in order to take their lands or to integrate them under state jurisdiction. As already noted, the Dawes Commission proceedings were fraught with conflict over deciding who qualified as tribal citizens. Federal officials increasingly moved toward blood quantum to limit benefits, and federal courts heard several cases that touched upon tribal existence and whether individual Indians were still federal wards. Overall the court language reveals the federal inclination to terminate tribes and assimilate Indians into the mainstream. It also reveals that for non-Indians, determining "who was Indian" was no longer simple or clear-cut. In a case involving the Taos Pueblo people, *U.S. v. Joseph* (1876), the Supreme Court tried to remove trust restrictions on the tribe by declaring that they were not a tribe according to the definition of an earlier law, noting, "They are Indians only in features, complexion, and a few of their habits; in all other respects they are superior to all but a few of the civilized Indian tribes of the country." At the time, social scientists generally viewed tribes as premodern governmental forms on an evolutionary scale crowned by Western constitutional governments. In a subsequent case also involving the Pueblos, however, the court reversed its earlier ruling, bringing the people under federal power, saying that their cultural advancement had not progressed sufficiently to remove the stigma of wardship. At the same time the United States was "freeing" the Five Civilized Tribes from federal supervision, it was still trying to determine whether other groups needed federal ward status and protection. In the 1925 Supreme Court case *U.S. v. Candelaria*, the justices reaffirmed the dependent status of the Pueblos. Using a combination of cultural and racial rationales, the court said: "They are plainly within the spirit and, in our opinion, fairly within the words 'any tribe of Indians.' Although sedentary, industrious and disposed to peace, they are Indians in race, customs, domestic government, always have lived in isolated communities, and are a simple, uninformed people, ill-prepared to cope with the intelligence and greed of other races." This statement rather succinctly encapsulates the racial and cultural thinking of the era.[20]

In total, this era reflected the traditional white American hostility toward Indian tribes existing within the country's borders. It was dominated by congressmen, federal courts, and Office of Indian Affairs officials trying to terminate tribes, end government obligations to Indian individuals, and force tribal peoples to become fully assimilated citizens of the United States. In this social and political climate it made little sense to begin new relationships with tribes that had never fallen under federal jurisdiction. However, we also see the judiciary attempting to provide working definitions of the people to whom federal Indian law and policy applied. Officials were trying to determine what wardship or trusteeship meant in real-world terms. The federal government fumbled toward definitions of "Indian" and "tribe" that still affect tribal acknowledgment discourse today. The key judicial definition of an Indian tribe, used later in the landmark Mashpee Indian land claims case of the 1970s, came in *Montoya v. U.S.* (1900). This case involved a New Mexico plaintiff's claims for compensation arising from an Apache raid years earlier. In its decision, the Supreme Court laid down a definition of "tribe" by saying, "By a 'tribe' we understand a body of Indians of the same or similar race, united in a community under one leadership or government, and inhabiting a particular though sometimes ill-defined territory." It was this statement that would be central to definitions of tribes used by courts and many modern tribal officials in later years.[21]

THE INDIAN NEW DEAL AND THE QUESTION OF TRIBAL EXISTENCE

The Great Depression, which began in 1929, touched off the modern era of tribal acknowledgment policy and debates that would impact the Five Tribes and other reservation peoples for decades. The work of federal New Deal officials established both the first concrete tribal recognition criteria and the Indian Reorganization Act of 1934, a law that placed Indian tribes on firmer footing. After his election in 1932, Democratic president Franklin Delano Roosevelt appointed John Collier as commissioner of Indian Affairs. A social worker from Georgia, Collier was a well-known Indian advocate who promised to forcefully pursue change in Washington. The Indian Reorganization Act and related Oklahoma Indian Welfare Act formally ended allotment, forced off-reservation schooling, and other measures aimed at forced acculturation. Although scholars have critiqued the Indian New Deal on several grounds, including that it imposed Western-style governments on tribal groups and ultimately supported full assimilation, it nonetheless proved a watershed for formerly unrecognized tribes and terminated nations like the Five Tribes of Oklahoma. It not only gave Indians hope by promoting their values and cultures, it also set the institutional framework for tribal governments that would increase their power and influence in coming decades. The law ultimately promoted the preservation of Indian identity, and spurred pan-Indian mobilization and political activity, factors that proved central to the rise of unrecognized tribes in the 1960s. At the time, however, many influential leaders of the Five Tribes were vocal opponents of Collier's new program, including Creek businessman Joseph Brunner and Alice Lee Jemison, a part Seneca-Cherokee. The Five Tribes, torn between assimilationists and more traditional Indians, generally did not take advantage of the Indian New Deal programs, although three Creek towns did organize under the New Deal laws. The era's emphasis on, and introduction of, nonindigenous governmental forms such as written constitutions and written laws, elected representatives, and ultimately the adoption of these governments by the majority of reservation tribes and the internalization of these forms would also affect the debates about unrecognized tribes in the 1970s.[22]

With the new emphasis on reorganizing tribes, Office of Indian Affairs and Department of Interior lawyers found themselves attempting to figure out which Indian communities could organize under the Indian Reorganization Act. The Solicitor's Office of the Interior Department ultimately played a major role in establishing precedents later utilized in federal acknowledgment decisions. Led by solicitor Nathan Margold, a former U.S. assistant attorney and NAACP lawyer, and Felix Cohen, a Harvard- and Columbia-educated attorney, the office established factors its employees were to use when deciding whether certain groups could organize under the New Deal law. Later called the "Cohen Criteria," these became the basic blueprint for the BIA Federal Acknowledgment Process. Important distinctions were made at this time based on lawyers' readings of past policy and Indian law. As Cohen noted, the government could not acknowledge mere social groups or societies that had no existence as governments. Also, the office believed it could not recognize tribes that had become extinct and then reemerged: it acknowledged only sovereign status that had existed unbroken since time immemorial. Immediately at issue, however, were the provisions in the Indian Reorganization Act that allowed all persons of Indian descent residing on a reservation then under federal jurisdiction or persons of "one-half or more Indian blood" to organize new Western-style governments. As discussed elsewhere, the blood provision would prove troublesome for many groups like the Poarch Creeks and Lumbees that attempted to achieve aid under the bill. According to Cohen, in determining whether a group constituted a "tribe" or "band" within the meaning of the law, his office looked at factors such as whether the group in question had treaty relations with the federal government, whether it had been denominated a tribe by congress or by executive order, whether it had been treated as a tribe or band by other Indians, and whether it had collective rights in lands or funds. The office also inquired about whether the group in question had exercised political authority over its members through a tribal council or other governmental form. Cohen noted that his office also looked to other factors such as special appropriations and the social solidarity of a group to determine whether it was a tribe; they also gave great weight to historical and ethnological factors when determining tribal existence. To make his point on this latter statement, Cohen outlined a complex case involving the Muscogee (Creek) Nation of Oklahoma. Here several tribal towns applied successfully to organize under the Oklahoma Indian Welfare Act separate from the larger Creek Nation. Relying on historical data and an anthropological report compiled by Morris Opler, the Solicitor's Office determined that the Creek Nation was traditionally organized as a confederacy of town and tribes, and because these towns continued their tribal governmental and clan traditions they could organize as separate governments.[23]

As Cohen noted, the term "tribe" was used in different contexts and came to take on different meanings. It was used in an ethnological sense when describing communities of similar culture, origins, and language, but it was also used in an entirely political context. Even today many individuals fail to grasp this distinction, causing much hair-splitting, confusion, and conflict. In one example, ethnological tribes with long histories, such as the Delawares and Shawnees, were forcibly combined with the Cherokee Nation after the Civil War, with decades of conflict ensuing when these peoples attempted to separate from the larger tribal body. In other cases, ethnological tribes of roughly the same size, such as the Walla Wallas, Cayuses, and Umatillas, were combined into one political unit by bureaucrats, placed on the same reservation, and given an entirely new name, here "the Confederated Tribes of the Umatilla Reservation of Oregon." This group was one politically sovereign "tribe" composed of three unrelated ethnic groups. In a final scenario, the separation of groups associated with the removal of the Five Tribes from the Southeast led to their later recognition as federally recognized, political tribes: the Eastern Band of Cherokee Indians, the Mississippi Band of Choctaws, and the Miccosukee and Seminole Tribes of Florida.[24]

The Indian New Deal was truly a remarkable turnaround in federal policy, with at least twenty-one tribes recognized during this era. As the example of the Creek towns attests, it also raised a concern for many large, diverse tribes: the potential for smaller communities, using federal procedures, to fissure from the main body. Such was the case with the Keetoowah Band of Cherokees in Oklahoma. During the 1930s leaders of this long-standing tribal organization attempted to organize a tribal government separate from the Cherokee Nation. The Solicitor's Office determined that the Keetoowahs were largely "full-blood" conservative Cherokees, but also that they were a secret society and not a band or tribe able to organize under the law. The Keetoowah Band kept battling, however, and ultimately was able to organize as a separate tribal entity shortly after World War II.[25]

The Indian New Deal provided the first signs of a change in federal recognition policy. The Office of Indian Affairs was affirmatively acknowledging government responsibility for neglected Indian tribes. Although pro-tribal policies would soon be swept aside after World War II, the era laid the groundwork for tribal rebirth and Indian cultural revival, and it saw the first formal acknowledgment procedures, all significant to later southeastern Indian history. With the Indian New Deal we see federal officials groping toward a coherent definition of "tribe" and "Indian," an endeavor that would increase in importance in coming decades.

POSTWAR LAND CLAIMS AND TERMINATION SCHEMES

If the New Deal era opened a window for some small, forgotten tribes to gain acknowledgment, the termination era that followed World War II closed it. During the early 1950s Congress passed a resolution calling for the eventual termination of many tribes. The government also established its relocation program designed to help reservation Indians move to cities, where it was hoped they would improve their economic lives and assimilate into the mainstream. Thousands of Choctaws, Creeks, and Cherokees in Oklahoma, Mississippi, and North Carolina moved to cities where they became an established presence. Many small tribes in the Southeast fell victim to the misguided termination policy while the government was in no mood to initiate new relationships with tribes lacking federal recognition. The Five Tribes, now officially terminated, struggled through this anti-tribal era, with one tribe, the Choctaws, having a faction that pursued full tribal termination, believing it would free tribal leaders to better handle and control the remaining Choctaw assets. The Mississippi Band of Choctaws found its very sovereign existence challenged again. Survivors would never forget this period when their dependence on the national political winds and congressional will imperiled the future of their people. While many leaders of the Five Tribes were central to tribal opposition to the termination agenda, the shadow of this misdirected project would hang heavily over the future. No matter how strong their gains in the coming decades, leaders would always fear a return to the termination era.[26]

The opening salvo in the termination era was a seemingly beneficent federal forum, the Indian Claims Commission (ICC). A quite diverse group of whites and Indians supported the claims tribunal designed to provide monetary compensation for Indian groups that had been swindled and defrauded in land transactions in decades past. Natives and liberals cheered the commission for providing some degree of justice for the First Americans, and conservatives supported the claims process thinking it would finally end lingering federal commitment to the tribes. As many historians have concluded, the commission's positive aims were clouded by its central role in the termination program. As previously discussed, it provided the impetus for many small southeastern Indian groups to reorganize, helping set the stage for the tribal and Indian renaissance of the 1960s and 1970s. This alerted the Five Tribes of the very existence of surviving Indians in the Southeast, and led to conflicts and competition as these groups intervened in existing claims or pursued their own actions for lands claimed by the Oklahoma tribes. During the era, each of the Five Tribes filed lands claims with the commission. Within a few years the Alabama-Coushattas of Texas and a group calling itself the Biloxi Indians, Consolidated Band of Pascagoula, Mobilian and Biloxi, had filed claims for lost southeastern lands. As recalled by longtime Poarch Band of Creek Indians chairman Eddie Tullis, the Creek Nation East of the Mississippi, founded by legendary chief Calvin McGhee, represented a real financial threat to the Creek Nation of Oklahoma. They intervened in the existing Creek Nation claim and ultimately shared in its multimillion-dollar judgment. As Tullis puts it, his people met opposition from the Oklahoma tribe "because they accepted the BIA position that all Creeks were removed to Oklahoma [during the 1800s]."[27] This was not an issue isolated to Oklahoma and the Southeast, it should be noted. As Bruce Miller has found, lands claims heightened tensions between official reservation tribes and landless, unrecognized tribes throughout the Pacific Northwest. Soon the Cherokees of Oklahoma under appointed principal chiefs J. B. Milam and W. W. Keeler found their land claim challenged by a group calling itself the Old Settler Cherokees. Descendants of the first group of Cherokees to emigrate west of the Mississippi prior to the Trail of Tears, some of the Old Settler Cherokees filed suit with the ICC separate from the larger Cherokee Tribe. The Department of the Interior solicitor ultimately determined that this entity had been incorporated into the larger Cherokee Nation in the 1830s and was precluded from filing suit independently.[28]

The Indian Claims Commission led to two major developments germane to tribal acknowledgment politics. The act that created the commission allowed any "recognized tribe, band or *other identifiable group of American Indians*" [emphasis added] to bring a claim. This ambiguous phrase led, once again, to practical and theoretical questions: What is an Indian tribe? What is an identifiable Indian group? In several legal briefs, Solicitor's Office attorneys ultimately took a liberal approach, allowing any group of descendants who could prove their descent from known Indian ancestors, no matter how recently created, to pursue litigation. As revealed in greater detail elsewhere, some descendant organizations such as the Creek Nation East of the Mississippi came to believe, erroneously, that the ICC suits granted them federal tribal recognition. The claims proceedings also led to the first major academic questioning of the concept of tribe. As Christian McMillan has noted, the ICC's work led to the birth of the interdisciplinary field of ethnohistory. Luminaries like Nancy O. Lurie and Alfred Kroeber were hired to work in the practical legal context, called to make academic, scientific conclusions on a claimant's "aboriginal territory," tribal descent, and "aboriginal occupancy." Few had been involved in legal adversarial proceedings and the experience challenged them to reexamine their terminology and methodology. These scholars began to question whether the terms they had been using were valid. How was one to determine a tribe's aboriginal territory, exclusive use of lands, and true community composition in centuries past when no written records existed? For the first time many academics began to openly question the whole conception of "tribes." Once widely viewed as a premodern evolutionary stage in political organization, tribes were largely a recent phenomenon scholars more and more came to believe, a product of colonialism itself. As Kroeber, an anthropologist from the University of California, Berkeley, argued in a 1955 piece, "It was White contact, pressure, or administration that converted most American Indian nations or nationalities into 'tribes,' that is to say 'tribal status.' It was we Caucasians who again and again rolled a number of related obscure bands or minute villages into the larger package of 'tribe,' which we then putatively endowed with sovereign power and territorial ownership which the native nationality had mostly never even claimed."[29] In addition to its leading to academic questioning of scholarly concepts, ICC activity made leaders of the Five Tribes aware of the existence of tribal descendants in their former homelands. The demands of various Creek, Choctaw, Seminole, and other groups for tribal recognition and claims moneys made established leaders very concerned.[30]

Despite the federal termination agenda, several southeastern tribes did gain forms of acknowledgment during this era. As discussed elsewhere the Lumbees achieved federal legislation in 1956 declaring them "Lumbee Indians"; this law did not provide federal tribal recognition, however, and specifically denied them access to federal Indian services. In a rare twist, ICC activity led to the federal recognition of the Florida Seminoles. As Harry Kersey notes, the Seminole descendants who avoided removal by hiding in the Everglades in the nineteenth century hired an attorney in 1949 to file a land claims case on their behalf. The larger Seminole Nation of Oklahoma filed its own suit at the same time and also a motion to dismiss the Florida band's claims, arguing it had the sole right to bring suit. The legal wrangling ultimately led to the Florida Seminole Tribe gaining federal recognition in its own right in 1957. The government then approved a constitution and charter for the tribe. The Florida Seminoles would go on to use this status to pioneer Indian gaming. That same year the related Miccosukees gained state recognition as the Everglades Miccosukee General Council, and they secured federal recognition in their own right in 1962.[31]

Despite these exceptions, most of the small tribes of the Southeast found their status under attack during the 1950s. BIA officials took steps to terminate the government's relationship with the Coushatta Tribe of Elton, Louisiana, and the Catawba Tribe of South Carolina. The Alabama-Coushatta Tribe of Texas was officially terminated by legislation in the same decade. The fiscally conservative belt-tightening that spurred the termination agenda also led states like California to hold hearings to determine "who is an Indian" in preparation for ending services. Old ideas of measuring Indianness by blood quantum were still prevalent, even among some Native Americans. As Jane

Penn, a resident of the Morongo Reservation in California surmised, "I would say a person who is half could be either one, but when you get to less than half you are more one than you are of the other." In the mid-1950s a federal bill was pending to limit benefits to only Indians of more than one-half "Indian blood." Although not terminated during these years, two remnant federally recognized tribes, the Mississippi Band of Choctaws and Eastern Band of Cherokees, faced repeated efforts by state and other local officials to challenge their federal status. Overall, the Five Tribes, the few recognized related remnant tribes in the South, and all reservation peoples became sensitive to potential tribal termination during these dark years. This experience would make them later fear a return to those days and affect their position in dealing with dozens of unrecognized tribes.[32]

THE PAN-INDIAN CHALLENGE

It has been widely noted that instead of promoting full Indian assimilation, federal programs to terminate tribes and relocate Indian individuals to urban areas promoted a pan-Indian response and unity aimed at fighting the disastrous policies. As was typical in Native affairs, urban Indians and various tribal members came to see the commonalities they shared as "Indians" in a larger ethnic sense. A new identity thus emerged as Indian, apart yet existing side by side with individual tribal identities. By the mid-1960s approximately one-half of all Natives lived off reservations or had no major connections to one, with many not receiving Indian-oriented services usually provided on or near reservations. As such, a little-known result of the 1950s federal initiatives of termination and relocation was that they served to place the majority of Indians in a position strikingly similar to unrecognized Indian enclaves scattered throughout the nation. A presidential task force created under Lyndon B. Johnson concluded as much, classifying relocated, terminated, and unrecognized Indians in the same category as perhaps the most impoverished and underserved Indians in America. The White House was alerted to this population in part from the landmark American Indian Chicago Conference of 1961, sponsored by anthropologist Sol Tax, the NCAI, and the University of Chicago. As previously noted, its "Declaration of Indian Purpose" was a siren for major change in Indian policy. Dozens of members of unacknowledged eastern groups joined their western reservation kin in a week of meetings to discuss Native problems and solutions. Importantly, the Chicago meeting spawned the National Indian Youth Council (NIYC), many of whose members were alienated college students with little connection to reservation or tribal communities. NIYC leaders were more militant than those of the NCAI and were often contemptuous of them, calling the NCAI heads "Uncle Tomahawks" or "Indian Bureau Indians." They attempted to connect or reconnect with traditionalists, whom they greatly respected. The NIYC would be a forerunner of the Red Power movement, speaking a language of "identity crisis," alienation, and "marginalization."[33]

The supposed "Uncle Tomahawks" included the leadership of the Five Tribes, and the Chicago conference and subsequent NIYC rhetoric alerted the more-conservative Five Tribes leaders of potential challenges to their rule from nonreservation groups and youth activists. Nine representatives of the Five Tribes attended the Chicago conference, including Cherokee principal chief W. W. Keeler. Raised in Bartlesville, Oklahoma, and noted to be one-sixteenth Cherokee, Keeler had graduated from the University of Kansas and ultimately advanced to CEO of Phillips Petroleum. In 1949 President Harry Truman appointed Keeler principal chief and he went on to become one of the nation's leading Indian leaders. By most accounts Chief Keeler spent a great deal of his own money and unpaid time advancing the causes of his people. Chief Keeler was concerned enough about the groundswell at the University of Chicago to send Cherokee attorney Earl Boyd Pierce to survey the planning stages of the conference, convinced that Sol Tax and other organizers were "reds," subversives in league with communists. Pierce, who was highly influential in tribal affairs during the 1960s and 1970s, had grown up in a Southern Baptist home, going on to work at the Justice Department where he had come to idolize J. Edgar Hoover, a staunch anticommunist involved in the McCarthy era witch hunts. Both Pierce and Keeler came to see campus radicals, civil rights activists, and organizations such as the NIYC as threats to the American way of life and democracy. The chief's office began compiling a list of subversives, and the list grew to include liberals in the BIA and activist actor Marlon Brando. At the Annual Convention of the NCAI in 1965, Pierce introduced a resolution calling on members to affirm their undying loyalty to America and promising that the NCAI would expel any member who was found to be a member of a subversive organization, a call clearly aimed at the NIYC and those associated with the liberal Carnegie project then underway in eastern Oklahoma. After the Chicago conference, Keeler told the press that he had met Russians who had been inspired by the rhetoric and communal spirit exhibited at the Chicago meeting. His office began compiling data on what they referred to as "militant Native American groups."[34]

As a sponsor of the Chicago conference, the NCAI was highly important in calling for an end to termination and a return to tribal self-determination and sovereignty. The group was founded in Denver in 1944, and its leaders, such as D'Arcy McNickle, were closely associated with the BIA. Like the earlier pan-Indian organization, the Society of American Indians, its leadership was drawn largely from the professional class. The Five Tribes were highly involved in early NCAI activities, with judge Napoleon B. Johnson, a Cherokee, its first president. During the early 1960s Chief Keeler had been very influential in the NCAI and in advising President Kennedy and President Johnson. As Hazel Hertzberg has found, the goal of the NCAI was to represent the nation's tribes in the broadest sense and to pursue collective goals by lobbying Congress and by other political means. Membership was restricted to persons of "Indian ancestry," with individual and group memberships offered. Group memberships were extended to "any Indian tribe, band, or community." As Hertzberg concludes, the influence of eastern tribes on the NCAI was largely negligible in its early years. The Indian congress came to be dominated by the Plains tribes and Oklahoma groups, many of whom had highly educated and fairly acculturated leaders. Besides lobbying Congress, the NCAI held its Annual Conference, published the *NCAI Sentinel,* and came to offer a collective voice in politics for Indian concerns.[35]

The pan-Indian spirit ultimately touched small, isolated eastern and southern Indian communities. As detailed earlier, the southeastern Indian renaissance was indebted to the work of Indian and non-Indian organizers who had spent years mobilizing struggling, forgotten Indians adrift in the largely black–white racial world of the Southeast. Free legal aid given by Vine Deloria's Center for the Development of Indian Law and by the Ford Foundation–backed Native American Rights Fund under John Echohawk, a Pawnee from Oklahoma, helped the kinship-based and isolated eastern enclaves create formal governmental

structures for the first time. Deloria's legal center also canvassed the
Southeast searching for groups in need of aid. He and applied anthropologists like Pete Gregory in Louisiana had a passion for actually
helping, not just studying, Indian groups. Although they were accused
of "hunting" for Indians and "resurrecting tribes" that were not really
tribes, Gregory and the others went on with their work.[36]

As previously detailed, Lumbee leader W. J. Strickland's Coalition of
Eastern Native Americans (CENA), founded after the first Eastern Indian
Conference, sponsored by the Center for the Development of Indian
Law in Boston in 1970, was instrumental in organizing scattered groups
into tribal entities and helping them secure federal grant moneys. By
mid-decade several religious groups were also aiding struggling area
tribes. The only people not pleased about the Indian organization
inspired by CENA and other groups were the established tribes in the
western states. By 1973, CENA already was clashing with the National
Tribal Chairmen's Association (NTCA) over who was the legitimate
voice of indigenous America. The seeming meteoric rise in the number
of tribes east of the Mississippi and their demands caused alarm among
leaders of western reservation tribes (many of whom shared the widespread belief that Indians had disappeared from the East) and the
few federally recognized tribes in the East. Their concerns rested on
two pillars. First, many reservation leaders doubted the authenticity
of these seemingly "new tribes" and resented these seemingly new-
born Indians claiming indigenous rights and funding. Second, many
distrusted the youth-directed, intertribal and pan-Indian emphasis
of groups like CENA, AIM, and others. David Wilkins recalls that most
non-Indians were nervous about the patent militancy of these groups.
In Louisiana, most conservative rural Indian leaders detested the
media-driven protests of the Red Power group, the Indian Angels,
closely aligned with CENA. The development of a rival group to CENA,
the United South and Eastern Tribes (USET), reveals the growing
schism. USET formed in 1969 when representatives of the Eastern Band
of Cherokees, the Mississippi Band of Choctaws, and the Seminoles and
Miccosukees of Florida, met at Cherokee, North Carolina, to discuss
common aims. Adopting the motto "Strength in Unity," these federally recognized tribes ultimately created the nonprofit USET to pursue common issues when dealing with the federal government. Early
on, USET worked with the Center for the Development of Indian Law
and CENA, but soon parted ways. With individuals like Eddie Tullis of

the Poarch Creeks, the organization became a fierce defender of the sovereignty and rights of federally acknowledged tribes alone. It doggedly opposed groups such as the Lumbees that pursued legislative recognition outside the Federal Acknowledgment Process.[37]

INDIAN PROGRAMS EXPAND

In April 1964 president Lyndon B. Johnson stepped onto the rotting porch of a coal miner's shack in Inez, Kentucky, and declared war on poverty. Riding a wave of prosperity, the Texas Democrat had initiated an optimistic domestic agenda to create a "Great Society," and he made aiding impoverished Native peoples a part of that. Keen observers of the political winds, Johnson and his secretary of the interior, Stewart Udall, appointed under Kennedy, sensed a rising public concern for Indians. They were responding to individuals like Mrs. Emil Bardach, who wrote to Udall, "One hears so much about the unfortunate plight of the First Americans . . . the Indians . . . that one wonders why this should be so in our land of plenty." They also were responding to what eminent historian Francis Paul Prucha calls the pervasive "white guilt" of the era, summed up by another constituent's letter to Udall: "Our crimes against the American Indian are a severe blot on our national honor." The Great Society planners set out to make amends. Johnson's "War on Poverty" spawned a host of new federal programs and agencies that helped foster community renewal among languishing Indian enclaves in the Southeast and elsewhere. Importantly, a host of development-related antipoverty programs were available to Native groups, many of which did not have the more stringent BIA and Indian Health Service policies for eligibility. A prime example was the important Indian Education Act of the early 1970s that allowed any tribe, band, or other Native organization, even terminated tribes or those recognized only by the state government, to take advantage of its programs. Dozens of non-BIA federal programs became available to impoverished tribal communities. Where once "being Indian" was a liability in many cases, conjuring images among whites of being uncivilized, immoral, backward, and racially deficient, it was now increasingly advantageous to come forward to access the new Johnson administration programs. While the majority of funds from these new programs went to federally recognized reservation communities, established tribes more and more came to see off-reservation groups as competitors vying for limited federal Indian moneys. The organizations aided by the 1960s programs also were seen as challenges to traditional tribal leadership.[38]

The various "War on Poverty" programs could be used by reservation tribes for their own ends, but the Community Action Programs, sponsored by the large Office of Economic Opportunity (OEO) under Sargent Shriver, a Kennedy family in-law, was seen by many tribal leaders as a threat to their power and authority. Created in 1964, the OEO also included the Job Corps and Volunteers in Service to America (VISTA), yet the Community Action Programs lay at its heart. Targeting the grassroots, the Community Action Programs were designed to empower communities locked in a culture of poverty by training leaders, establishing programs, and ultimately helping community members break their dependency on traditional welfare sources and government agencies. While these programs were available to any impoverished group, many unrecognized tribal communities such as the Pascua Yaquis in Arizona used the federal program to develop functioning reservations.[39] As the OEO was not directed by the BIA with its formal definitions of tribal eligibility, its actions were a direct challenge to established tribal leaders and BIA bureaucrats. Oklahomans for Indian Opportunity (OIO) and its relationship to Choctaw principal chief Harry Belvin is a prime example. A U.S. senator from Oklahoma, Fred Harris, and his wife LaDonna, a member of the Comanche Tribe, founded the OIO with OEO funds to mobilize average communities. The Harrises and Harry Belvin represented striking contrasts in leadership profiles. Young and attractive, Fred and LaDonna Harris were high-profile media darlings of the antiwar movement and minority causes. Belvin, in his sixties, had been appointed Choctaw chief by Harry Truman in 1948, pursued an increasingly unpopular effort to officially terminate the tribal government, and was seen as out of touch with the concerns of his people and the larger social currents of the 1960s. While Belvin was on the board of directors of the OIO, he became estranged from the organization and from Fred and LaDonna Harris. As the OIO organized grassroots programs and groups, Belvin saw their efforts as a direct challenge to his leadership. In public he charged that the community leaders were antigovernment militants who were fostering hatred and disillusionment with traditional leaders.[40]

The "War on Poverty" programs helped break the BIA's control of the nation's Indian programs. The Johnson administration made Native concerns a top priority and essentially ended the termination policy. The federal Indian pendulum was swinging once again. By the mid-1970s, the BIA was providing only about 40 percent of all Indian-related social services to Native Americans. Federal programs run through the Economic Development Administration, HUD, HEW, Department of Labor, and Department of Agriculture were of increasing importance to all tribal communities. However, these entities had widely varying qualifications for eligibility, often accepting state recognition or a group's self-proclaimed Indian status as valid for accessing funding. Established tribal leaders like Belvin and Keeler watched with growing concern as dozens of Indian groups, aided by non-BIA funds, were growing in stature and power at the national level.[41]

THE COUNTERCULTURE AND EMERGENT "TRIBES"

In December 1967, the popular magazine *Life* ran a special edition called "The Return of the Red Man," detailing what the authors saw as an astonishing fact, the "vanishing red man" had not, in fact, vanished. Native Americans had instead resurged with a vengeance. As detailed by *Life*, Indian culture, art, and lifestyles were riding a wave of popularity. In places like San Francisco and New York City, hippie "tribes" were forming, with members of these so-called new tribes living in makeshift communes and attempting to create an alternate culture based, in part, on rock music, communal ethos, drug use, and a sense of antiestablishment purpose, but also partly on a nostalgic vision of Indian life. As the writers noted, "The hippie discovery [of Indians] is most in evidence. Viewing the dispossessed Indians as America's original dropout, and convinced that he has deeper spiritual values than the rest of society, hippies have taken to wearing his costume and horning in on his customs." "Indian" clothing such as beads and breechclouts became chic among counterculture youth. Popular bands such as Jefferson Airplane and Big Brother and the Holding Company used Indian images to promote their concerts. Geronimo and Sitting Bull became iconic symbols. It was not just the counterculture, however, that had discovered the Native. In the Southeast other people were reconnecting with the Indian past and present. Articles such as a 1969 piece in the *Washington Post*, "The Amherst Cherokee: Virginia's Lost Tribe," publicized once-forgotten Indian groups in the region. The media attention and popular culture encouraged people to come out of the woodwork as Indians or to try to experience Native culture themselves. Every generation or two experiences an "Indian fad" but the sixties one was larger and had more of an impact than others.[42]

The 1960s and early 1970s witnessed an exponential rise in popular interest in Native American culture, history, and spirituality, a development that would lead to outright ethnic fraud and cultural appropriation to a degree previously unseen. A convergence of forces resulted in the phenomenon. Rising affluence and greater college attendance among youth coupled with the unpopular Vietnam War spawned the large countercultural movement of which the new "tribes" were a part. Besides the Native-enamored hippies, ecologists, members of the New Left and the feminist movement, and even civil rights activists saw a kindred spirit in their vision of Native American culture. During the early 1970s a slew of movies such as *Soldier Blue* and *Little Big Man* used Native themes to indict American imperialism and militarism. As Frederick Dockstader, director of the Museum of the American Indian in New York, wisely observed, this Indian fad, like all before it, was a white movement, created by Anglo-Americans and manipulated by non-Indians for their own reasons. However, Native peoples also played a role. Popular critic and writer Vine Deloria, Jr., in *We Talk, You Listen* proffered the Indian tribe as the logical model for future American social organization. It is not surprising many non-Indians, disillusioned with their own society, took him to heart. While most Indian-inspired communes never claimed to be Native American tribes, some groups did cross the line, forming tribes that aspired to be or become Native American. Rolling Thunder, a self-identified Shoshone, would say that "[h]ippies are the reincarnation of the traditional Indians who have fallen" and go on to create a tribal movement open to people of non-Indian heritage. Public figures like Rolling Thunder began to intone that anyone could become "Indian." Jamake Highwater, author of the wildly popular, *The Primal Mind*, speaking for all others who were told they didn't "look Indian," argued for self-definition: "I am an Indian only because I say I am an Indian" was his public conclusion. Others would widely challenge whether Highwater, born Gregory Markopoulos, was really Indian. The federal census soon reflected the Indian fad in raw data. Beginning in 1960 enumeration procedures allowed individuals rather than census takers to mark their own "race." The result was a phenomenal rise in the number of Indians. Largely stemming from this self-identification rather than natural increase, between 1970 and 1980 the number of Indians counted in the census increased from 792,730 to 1,366,676, an increase of 72.4 percent. By 1990 the Indian census count had tripled since 1960. Many western Indians were surprised to see that North Carolina was ranked fifth among the states in total Indian population in 1970, behind Oklahoma, Arizona, California, and New Mexico. Russell Thornton notes the phenomenon of "Census Cherokees": people who self-identified on the census as Cherokee but who were not enrolled and were not associated with tribal communities. Between 1970 and 1980 the census count of Cherokees more than doubled. Cherokees thus became the nation's second largest tribe in 1980, yet only about one-third of them were enrolled in the three federally recognized Cherokee tribes.[43]

Many of these individuals undoubtedly had first become enamored of Indian life through Boy Scouts and related programs. Twentieth-century Americans were steeped in a culture that offered numerous opportunities to "play Indian." At summer camps and in suburban Boy Scout and Girl Scout troops, young Americans could form "tribes." At school every child could learn "Native" arts and crafts. As many scholars have found, these activities could blur the lines between non-Indians and Indians, between what was real and what was play, and in time led to still greater confusion regarding what an Indian tribe was and who was "authentically" Indian. As historian Clyde Ellis has found, some white hobbyists and reenactors would have the audacity to claim that they were "more real" than the Indians themselves.

The twentieth-century phenomenon of non-Indians mimicking Indians began with wealthy naturalist Ernest Thompson Seton. In 1902 he created the League of Woodcraft Indians youth organization, establishing its first camp on his estate in rural Connecticut. Here boys could shed their overcivilized lives and get back to nature and wilderness. Like other anti-modernists, Seton believed that if young men could learn Indian ways, it would serve as an antidote to an effete, urban-industrial America. At Woodcraft Indian camps, young males became immersed in Seton's Plains Indian–style version of Indianness. They lived in tipis, dressed in leather, fringe, and feathers, and earned "coups," honors that gained young men leadership titles such as "sachem" and "sagamore." Seton crossed the nation, establishing "tribes" where non-Indians would learn Indian lore, Native "spirituality," and practice Indian-style self-government, complete with tribal councils and chiefs. Under the sway of Seton, his friends Luther and Charlotte Gulick established the Camp Fire Girls, based on many of the same Indian-centered themes as the Woodcraft Indians. Camp Fire Girls participants took "Indian" names, braided their hair, created fringed "Indian" dresses, and earned "coups" by perfecting domestic arts and crafts associated with Indian "maidens." Influenced by Seton and Wild West shows, the Boy Scouts of America (founded in 1910) also contained a strong play-Indian element. At Boy Scout camps boys learned "Indian" lore, slept in tipis, and reveled in the community spirit of the campfire circle. The YMCA Indian Guides program also involved the giving of "Indian" names and had Indian themes permeating its activities. It was begun in 1926 to foster father-son bonding, and a YMCA "Indian Maiden" program followed in the 1950s. Over decades, thousands of non-Indian children learned to value American Indian culture, at least in the stereotypical "Noble Savage" vein, through these summer activities. For generations of Americans, these adolescent forays into Indianness were simply fun, yet for a fringe element they undoubtedly smoothed the transition into an assumed tribal identity or made it easier to claim an Indian identity if they had some family lore about Native ancestry. In an odd scenario, coming full circle, some eastern descendants of Creeks in the 1970s, trying to revitalize cultural forms, would invite local Boy Scout troops to teach them Indian arts, lore, and ceremonies.[44]

By the 1970s self-styled medicine men and shamans had started appearing, called by Native critics "plastic medicine men" and "white shamans," and taking the cultural borrowing, imitation, and appropriation to a new level, further blurring the lines between Indian and non-Indian. Like others who "played Indian," the "white shamans" sought to connect to an idealized Indian past to fill a spiritual void. Seeking an "authentic experience" unavailable in the homogenized, urban American cultural scene, "plastic medicine men," as the label implies, were fake. They believed they could learn Indian spirituality, even perfect it, and teach it to followers, even though they lacked Indian ancestry. By the 1980s these individuals would argue that one could "go Indian" purely by adopting perceived "real" Indian lifestyles and culture. Indianness could be a "state of mind" to these "mental Indians"; some, who had been "Indians in a past life," ran seminars for profit, benefiting from the general public's ignorance of Native America. As Deborah Root finds, in coming years, some New Age devotees would claim that they were the true heirs to aboriginal spirituality: squalid reservations were too debased to count. Much of this experimentation was individualistic and about "self-discovery"; however, some individuals went on to form communities of a sort. Sun Bear, a self-identified Chippewa, founded the "Bear Tribe," which Dagmar Wernitznig describes as mainly composed of "Indianized" whites who purchased self-help books and Indian-themed products, and felt connected to like-minded folks through faux sweat lodges and other ceremonies. While perhaps innocuous at the individual level, the "white shamans" were certainly blurring the lines of tribalism, confusing and distorting the term "tribe" and forgetting its significance to Indian communities and to federal Indian law.[45]

The seeming explosion in the number of self-proclaimed Indians both baffled and concerned many tribal leaders. As Val Cordova, spokesman for the All Indian Pueblo Council, remarked in 1973, "All of a sudden in the last five or six years everybody is proud to be Indian." Activist singer Buffy St. Marie, a Cree, was more bemused than angry about these folks, yet she felt that Native people, not others, should benefit from the "Indian fad." During the early 1970s the Five Tribes in particular were swamped with applications from people seeking to identify with real tribal communities. As discussed elsewhere, those who could not get on the rolls had the option of joining dozens of Cherokee-named tribes springing up around the nation. As Tony Paredes put it, "In the 1970s, the tribes saw the proliferation of one of the country's most fantastic arrays of 'Indian wannabe' groups, most with only the most tenuous of claim to authenticity as tribes."[46] Besides the patently false tribal groups, the developments of the previous decades had led to the creation of a dizzying range of Indian enclaves and Indian-claiming individuals that did not closely resemble their reservation counterparts. Years of cultural intermingling, high intermarriage rates, government cultural suppression, and assimilation programs had made the very questions "who is Indian?" and "what is an Indian tribe?" no longer so clear. Instead of erasing Indians, the previous termination and relocation policies had made it more difficult to positively identify them. Federal bureaucrats and Indians themselves began to call for a consistent definition of "Indian" for federal and other purposes. Vine Deloria, Jr., argued that Congress should provide a standard definition of an Indian tribe because "almost every area of political and property rights is affected by the [current] nebulous definitions." As Jim Wolfe, the editor of the *Muscogee Nation News* argued in later years: "Perhaps the federal government should demand a blood quantum minimum for Indian identification purposes. Having traces of Indian blood isn't the same as being Indian."

So the 1960s developments helped set the stage for a crisis in Indian affairs over tribal acknowledgment and defining "Indian." As Joane Nagel has found, the decade witnessed a sea change in matters of ethnicity. Where once "melting pot" theory and assimilation discourses were hegemonic notions in the United States, now public pride in all things racial and ethnic emerged. Ethnicity became a valuable commodity, source of political power, and identity marker. It thus became more contested and regulated.[47]

SELF-DETERMINATION AGAIN

Though the Five Tribes had been officially terminated in 1906, they had carried on under presidentially appointed chiefs, who to varying degrees were supported by elected councils. The tribes also had an organization, the Inter-Tribal Council of the Five Civilized Tribes (founded in 1949) to work toward common ends. Prompted by tribal demand, in 1970 Congress passed a law allowing the tribes to once again elect their principal chiefs. Within a few years the Creeks elected Claude Cox, the Choctaws elected Harry J. W. Belvin, the Chickasaws elected Overton James, the Seminoles elected Floyd Harjo, and the Cherokees elected longtime appointee W. W. Keeler. They then pursued ambitious nation-building programs. Within a decade the Five Tribes were once again major economic and political forces in Oklahoma and major actors in national Indian affairs and would increasingly exert the era's hallmarks: tribal sovereignty and self-determination. In his inaugural address in 1971 Keeler cheered the return of the management of tribal affairs to the Cherokee people and looked forward to an era of renewed self-determination.[48]

The Five Tribes' efforts were part of a larger movement often labeled by scholars the "era of self-determination." As sociologist Stephen

Cornell has found, a number of factors converged in the early 1970s to foster a "return of the Native" to the national political arena: the proliferation of national pan-Indian lobbying groups like the NCAI, the pursuit of treaty-based litigation, the demands of Red Power activists, and a liberal consensus that white America should aid minorities. These all coalesced to produce a new wave of pro-Indian legislation and court decisions. As Vine Deloria, Jr., and Clifford Lytle conclude, during these years "tribes felt so confident in their talents" that they pressured federal officials for more power to run their own programs. The crowning achievement was the Indian Education and Self-Determination Act of 1975, a watershed law that greatly enhanced tribal power to contract for, administer, and control reservation programs. Tribes began to run their own programs and to operate more and more in the non-Indian political and economic world.[49] The tribal unit increasingly became central to the exertion of sovereignty and national political power.

During the next decade all of the Five Tribes nations reestablished formal governments, in the vein of their earlier constitutional governmental forms. In 1979 the Creek Nation adopted a new constitution that created a three-branch government. An executive branch contained the offices of principal chief and second chief, a legislative branch contained a unicameral body called the National Council, and a judicial branch handled cases involving Creeks on tribal lands. The other tribes did likewise. The Five Tribes built modern tribal office centers, some, like the Keeler Complex in Tahlequah, named for longtime chiefs. In addition to tribal offices, these complexes often housed BIA branches, tribal housing authorities, and Indian Health Service clinics. The Choctaws, Creeks, and others soon opened and largely ran their own hospitals, and provided a host of social welfare and educational programs for their people.[50]

The chiefs and their supporters elected in the first wave of self-determination tended to be conservative in their politics. Many had already been in office for years as appointees. Creek principal chief Claude Cox created a tribal political party that was closely aligned with the Republic Party and President Nixon. Cox soon found himself sued by rival Allen Harjo. Supported by the Institute for the Development of Indian Law, Harjo charged the longtime leader of conspiring to make himself the sole embodiment of the Creek government. Harjo and others wanted to restore the 1867 Creek Constitution that they felt better represented traditional Creek government. They also charged

Chief Cox with failing to bring housing programs and other services to the people. Cherokee leader W. W. Keeler also was closely aligned with the administration of Richard Nixon, who was well known for opposing radicals and speaking for the so-called silent majority of working-class, conservative Americans when he was swept into the White House in 1968. Nixon and Chief Keeler were close, and the Cherokee chief (in association with Phillips Petroleum) was convicted of giving Nixon illegal campaign contributions.[51]

After 1970, in the heady years of tribal nation rebuilding, the Five Tribes nations established formal membership requirements virtually identical to each other. Their governments allowed individuals who could prove they were a lineal descendant of an Indian "by blood" on the 1906 "Final Rolls of the Citizens and Freedmen of the Five Civilized Tribes" (Dawes Rolls) to enroll. The tribes established professionally staffed enrollment offices that were often very busy places. Following the lead of the BIA, the Five Tribes created procedures that required individuals to provide documentary proof to establish tribal citizenship. Applicants had to first obtain a Certificate of Degree of Indian Blood (CDIB), or "white card" issued by the BIA. They also were required to provide original state-certified birth and death records of all ancestors lineally connected to a citizen on the Dawes Rolls. If verified, the applicant would then be admitted into the tribe. The Choctaw Nation, for example, then issued a tribal membership card and a photo ID. Even if the member did not reside in the tribal service area or have any social connection to it, they could vote in tribal elections at age eighteen. There was no blood quantum minimum so some members had small fractions of "Indian blood" yet were full citizens of the Five Tribes.[52] Although blood degree was noted on records, the Five Tribes decided not to use blood quantum for membership because, with their traditional high rates of outmarriage to nontribal members, using blood percentages would have resulted in a clear path to tribal extinction for most of these tribes.[53]

The tribes also pursued highly successful business ventures, often using the revenues to finance cultural and social programs. As early as 1961, the Cherokee Nation was awarded $15 million in a lands claim suit, and Chief Keeler and Earl Boyd Pierce led a successful effort to have the surplus retained by the tribe after per capita payments. They used the $2 million left over to fund the Cherokee cultural center called Tsa-La-Gi near Tahlequah, housing a museum and an amphitheater that staged a pageant called "The Trail of Tears." By the 1980s the Choctaw Nation had become a major employer in Oklahoma, with several manufacturing plants and a ranch. The remaining recognized Five Tribes remnants in the Southeast, the Eastern Band of Cherokees, the Mississippi Choctaws, and the Florida Seminoles, likewise developed successful economic enterprises over time. The Choctaws, like the other Five Tribes, ultimately came to resemble "large multinational corporations," according to Clara Sue Kidwell, with gaming enterprises helping the nation employ more than 3,500 people with an annual payroll of over $38.5 million by the late 1990s. Earlier that decade Creek Nation principal chief Bill Fife estimated that his nation's economic impact on the state was approximately $280 million annually. Whether or not these tribes were like corporations, they certainly matched the model and legal construction of an Indian "tribe." Possessing treaties and tribal lands, the Five Tribes once again began exercising the sovereign powers inherent in such bodies, including having formal offices, holding elections, setting policy, regulating property, and determining citizenship rules. As Valerie Lambert notes, her Choctaw people comprised a highly diverse group, divided by race, color, class, and residence, yet the new formalized government had a homogenizing effect on the tribe—citizenship in the nation unified them. The rising power of the Five Tribes and related reservation tribes would impact the Federal Acknowledgment Process beginning in the mid-1970s.[54]

UNRECOGNIZED INDIANS STILL HAVE RIGHTS

As previously detailed, a host of Native-oriented legal organizations were created in the early 1970s that aided both federally recognized and unrecognized tribal communities across the country. The Indian Claims Commission had alerted established treaty tribes like the Creek Nation of the existence of living relatives in the Southeast, but during the 1970s a host of cases pursued under an obscure federal Indian law alerted the rest of the country about the existence of Native entities living in traditionally "non-Indian" areas. Now these groups were of concern not only to treaty-based tribes that had competing claims, but also to BIA officials, non-Indian towns, and other interest groups. For Indians federal courts became the new battleground

for indigenous rights, and actions by unrecognized tribes in the eastern
and southern states certainly played a part in the trend. Tom Tureen,
a lawyer working for Pine Tree Legal Services, an organization affiliated with NARF, was central to the new legalism of neglected eastern
tribes. In the early 1970s Tureen discovered the obscure 1790 Indian
Trade and Intercourse Act and used it to pursue lands claims for
groups once believed to lack rights. The law provided that only the
federal government could enter into land agreements or treaties
with Indian nations. It had been part of a larger effort by Congress to
secure supremacy in Indian affairs vis-à-vis the states and local citizens,
but the Founding Fathers could little have envisioned the effects it
would have two centuries later. With the aid of Tureen and NARF,
at least twenty eastern and southern tribes, including the Tunica-
Biloxis, Narragansetts, and Mashantucket Pequots, pursued lands
claims for over 11 million acres. Energized by the land claims work,
as early as September 1975 the Tunica-Biloxis of Louisiana sought
legislative recognition of their people as a tribe. Some of these groups,
most notably the Pequots, would leverage these claims into formal
tribal acknowledgment. Several of the Trade and Intercourse Act cases
proved central to national tribal acknowledgment debates. Actions
pursued by the Penobscots, Passamaquoddy Indians, and Mashpee
Wampanoags in the eastern United States played a part. Treaty rights
fishing cases pursued by several unrecognized tribes in Washington
State also alerted recognized tribes and BIA officials to the need for
more consistent formal procedures for recognizing Indian communities left outside the fold. Suddenly it became clear to Cherokee,
Creek, and other leaders that there were obscure groups in their
former homelands in the Southeast claiming to be Cherokee, Choctaw, Creek, and Seminole, and that these entities had some legal
rights as well.[55]

A 1972 land claims case pursued by the Penobscot and Passamaquoddy Indians of Maine was the first major action notifying the
Eastern Seaboard, including federal bureaucrats in Washington, of
the dormant rights possessed by local Indians. With legal aid from
NARF, the two tribes, living on state reservations, pursued a claim
under the 1790 law for compensation for the illegal taking of lands
that amounted to approximately two-thirds of the state of Maine.
The tribes also sued the Interior Department for failing to protect
their rights. The Maine tribes argued that a 1794 agreement between

Figure 4. Chief Elijah Barbre of the Tunica Biloxi Indians, Avoyelles Parish, Louisiana, 1930s. (Photograph courtesy of State Library of Louisiana, Louisiana Collection)

their ancestors and the state was invalid under the 1790 Intercourse Act that mandated that only Congress could deal in Native lands. In a ruling that shocked local non-Indians, a district court ruled that though the Maine tribes were not recognized by federal treaty in 1794, the intercourse law was intended to apply to all tribes, regardless of their federal status. Suddenly all parties were aware that non–federally recognized tribes had rights and would pursue them, often at great cost and disruption to non-Indians.[56] Around the same time, a federal court judge in Washington State ruled that several tribes there, both federally recognized and not, still possessed treaty rights to fish in their "usual and accustomed places" under mid-nineteenth-century treaties. Local non-Indian fishers were in an uproar that the judge gave the tribes up to half the annual salmon catch in the region. A subsequent land claims case involving the non–federally recognized Mashpee Indians of Massachusetts convinced many parties that some form of acknowledgment standards needed to be created. As James Clifford and Jack Campisi have vividly documented, the local jury had trouble seeing the Mashpee group, many of whom were multiracial and almost completely acculturated, as an "Indian tribe." Watching the Mashpees lose their land claims because the local jury did not feel they were still an Indian tribe, most unacknowledged Indians were convinced that the courts were ill equipped to deal with complex tribal acknowledgment issues involving race, ethnicity, and political organization. In each of these cases "tribal existence" was a threshold issue. These groups, although not acknowledged by the federal government at the time, could pursue their tribal rights so long as they still existed as a tribal community as divined through the use of decisions such as the *Montoya* case of 1901. Now a chorus of parties, from recognized tribes to local sportsmen's groups, began to demand a coherent policy to help the courts maneuver these complex waters.[57]

INDIAN ACTIVISTS, RED POWER, AND AN INDIAN COMMISSION

Red Power and other youth-driven Indian movements have justly been credited with many of the gains won by Indians after 1960, yet they had a contentious relationship with tribal leaders, being seen by them more as a threat than as an ally. Many leaders of the Five Tribes actively opposed Red Power groups and their media-oriented activities. The appointed principal chiefs of the Five Tribes, conservative and set in their ways, had come to associate off-reservation organizations, entities that included unrecognized tribes, as a direct challenge to their leadership and standing in the Indian community. They had come to associate all off-reservation, not officially recognized Indian entities with problems and controversies, which would affect their stance toward acknowledging new tribes.

The famous Red Power protests of Alcatraz, the Trail of Broken Treaties, and the occupation of Wounded Knee had their own, lesser-known counterparts, some taking place in the Southeast and Oklahoma, and some organized under the name of the American Indian Movement (AIM). Founded in 1968 by largely urban, off-reservation Indians in Minneapolis, iconoclastic AIM often championed the rights of nontraditional Indians. As the protest spirit swept the country, federally appointed chiefs of the Five Tribes and leaders of many southeastern reservation tribes grew wary of unofficial, unrecognized groups that increasingly attacked the legitimacy, vision, and conservatism of older established tribal leaders. Elected chiefs too decried tactics used by Red Power youths and activists, saying that they were not acting in the "Indian way." The very term "Red Power," a direct allusion to the militant Black Power movement, was unappealing to many southern Indian leaders, who were more conservative in their politics and racial views than many younger men and women. There may have been racialized fears as well: publications of the Black Panther Party courted Indians as "natural allies" in the fight against "the Establishment." The Tuscarora Movement of North Carolina provides a good example of the conflict between established leaders and militants. In 1973 what began as a protest in North Carolina in support of AIM's occupation of Wounded Knee led to violence and store damage as local Tuscaroras (a part of the Lumbee group) protested voting discrimination, lack of recognition, and control of Indian education. A widely circulated UPI photo showed the Tuscaroras and their supporters, some of whom were African Americans, raising a fist, the widely recognized Black Power symbol. Other tribal youth began to publicly challenge the programs sponsored by their tribal leaders. For example, during a 1970 protest, Gerald Wilkinson, a college-educated Cherokee, rejected

Cherokee tourist-oriented ventures, saying, "We weren't meant to be a tourist attraction for the master race—we don't use the language of the New Left, but that doesn't mean we're not militant."[58]

Historians often write about Indians as if they were not part of the larger national currents swirling around them, and this is certainly the case with Native Americans during the Cold War. This period of anticommunist hysteria that extended far beyond McCarthyism affected the Five Tribes leadership just as it influenced the general population. As Daniel Cobb notes, the Cherokees were embroiled in a "culture war" at the time, divided left and right. Appointed principal chief W. W. Keeler and his close supporter Cherokee general counsel Earl Boyd Pierce, both Republicans and supporters of conservative values and causes, believed that "action anthropologists," leftist Red Power youths, and other "outside agitators" were stirring up trouble among their people. One source of friction was the work of Sol Tax, the prominent University of Chicago anthropologist and organizer of the Chicago Indian Conference, and his student Robert K. Thomas, a Cherokee anthropologist. Under a Carnegie Corporation grant, Thomas came to northeastern Oklahoma in 1963 as part of a four-year literacy program intended to empower the impoverished and isolated traditional Cherokee communities. Thomas became a vocal opponent of established tribal government, arguing that Indian reservations were "internal colonies" that needed to secure liberation from colonial policies, of which the established tribal governments were a part. Well-known National Indian Youth Council founder Clyde Warrior, a Ponca from Oklahoma, was also involved with Thomas's program for a while. Around the same time, the Five County Cherokee Association, the Four Mothers and Seven Clans Societies, and more traditionalist Keetoowahs were challenging the authority of Keeler, an appointee with few ties to more traditional elements of the tribe, to speak for them, and called for more democratically oriented government. To Thomas and other activist scholars it was clear that the more conservative "full-bloods" were disconnected from the largely educated, "mixed-blood" elites like Pierce and Keeler. Criticism soon followed in the local and regional press, leading to further discord. Critics charged that Keeler was essentially a "white man" who was out of touch with rank-and-file tribal members. It was not just Keeler who was sensitive to charges of not being really Indian. All of the Five Tribes, with their history of white intermarriage and assimilation, were placed under the lens. The feeling of defensiveness was so pervasive that noted historian W. David Baird would feel compelled to write an article supporting them, titled "Are the Five Civilized Tribes of Oklahoma 'Real' Indians?" Much of the acrimony revolved around Keeler and Pierce's decision to use the surplus claims money to build the Cherokee cultural center. The Keetoowahs and others claimed that the center's amphitheater and pageant were a waste of tribal money and largely a pet project of the mixed-blood elites.[59] At the same time, Keeler and other Five Tribes leaders increasingly found themselves under attack in activist publications such as *Akwesasne Notes*. The Inter-Tribal Council of the Five Civilized Tribes spent part of their 1974 meeting discussing ways to counter AIM's planned registration drive in Oklahoma and rally at Claremore Indian Hospital. The battle lines were hardening between the generally conservative Oklahoma tribal leaders and young iconoclasts.[60]

The Original Cherokee Community Organization (OCCO), aided by the Thomas's Carnegie project, became a potent challenger to the formal tribal governments as well. Described in the local and regional press as a "full-blood" group from the hills of northeastern Oklahoma, this mid-1960s organization grew from the uproar surrounding John Chewie, a Cherokee arrested in 1966 for shooting a deer out of season. Many tribal leaders and most white Oklahomans were truly shocked when several hundred armed Indians appeared at the courthouse in Jay, Oklahoma, on Chewie's trial day to show support and to send a not-so-subtle message to court officials. Coverage of the militant protest went outside the state, and the Chewie case inspired a Memphis-based white civil rights attorney to form the OCCO in 1967. After its establishment the OCCO promptly filed suit, challenging the whole basis for the tribal government under Chief Keeler. The chief was quoted saying that the OCCO was led by a white man and was "just another case of outsiders trying to direct the Indian . . . telling Indian people to be militant and carry guns."[61] Rearguard challenges like this were not limited to the Cherokee Nation. Longtime Choctaw chief Harry Belvin was also attacked by an unofficial entity. In the late 1960s Charles Brown, described in the press as a "full-blood," organized the Oklahoma City Council of Choctaws. This group played upon Belvin's increasingly unpopular attempt to terminate the tribe and directly challenged his right to lead the people. The Oklahoma City group published a newsletter directly questioning the formal government embodied by Belvin. An unintended consequence of grassroots questioning of tribal government, however, was that conservative leaders more and more took a jaundiced view of all unrecognized Indian organizations.[62]

While reformers were attacking entrenched tribal governments, other activists placed the BIA in their sights. The agency was in constant turmoil during the 1960s and early 1970s, and, like conservative Five Tribes leaders, BIA bureaucrats grew soured of off-reservation, pan-Indian activist groups, a feeling that would bleed into their positions regarding recognizing new Indian tribes in coming years. Attacks by reformers and Red Power activists on John O. Crow make this point. Crow, a Cherokee from Oklahoma and a former pro football player, served as deputy commissioner of Indian affairs during the 1960s and again in the early 1970s. President Nixon had appointed Crow deputy commissioner under Louis Bruce, a committed reformer from the St. Regis Mohawk Reservation in New York, but Crow and Bruce soon came to loggerheads. Critics called Crow "one-quarter Cherokee and three-quarters bureaucrat," a public slur questioning his Indian identity and his commitment to change. Youth activists argued that he had been appointed deputy to stymie Bruce's efforts to overhaul the much-maligned agency. The conservative Cherokee became the figurehead for entrenched bureaucracy that activists charged was stifling Indian self-rule and self-determination. In one well-publicized incident Russell Means, the Oglala Sioux activist, led several dozen AIM and NIYC members in an attempted "citizen's arrest" of Crow. Popular among the youth, Bruce attempted to hire young reform-minded people like Ernie Stevens, an Oneida from Wisconsin, to counter Crow and longtime employees like Wilma Victor, a Choctaw from Oklahoma, whom activists called "the living symbol of the Old Guard approach." As tensions increased, in November 1972 the Trail of Broken Treaties caravan seized control of the BIA offices, occupied it for a time, and almost completely ruined the building. Afterward Crow and Bruce exchanged words over the direction of the bureau, and Bruce ultimately was forced out.[63] The John O. Crow controversy revealed the deep rifts then existing between Red Power activists and conservative supporters of the status quo.

In a more basic sense, as historian Hazel Hertzberg has found, the rise in pan-Indian groups like AIM led to more widespread questioning of Indian identity, especially because these entities were not associated with reservation communities. Many had a fair number of self-identified Indians, but non-Indians tended to be granted membership as long as they embraced the group's ways of thinking and vision of real Indian culture. As anthropologist Edward Spicer notes, by the late 1960s Indians throughout the United States were increasingly linked by networks of pan-tribal organizations, urban Indian centers, boarding schools, and intermarriage, which strengthened a growing "ethnic Indian" identity. That term, "ethnic Indian," could seem threatening to established tribal leaders while muddying the waters regarding who was an Indian and what constituted an Indian tribe or community.[64]

The Red Power movement also engendered a congressional commission that troubled the leaders of the Five Tribes and others over its membership and recommendations. After the famous AIM occupation of Wounded Knee in 1973 (which the NCAI denounced), concerned congressmen and congresswomen created the American Indian Policy Review Commission (AIPRC) with hopes of gleaning the causes of Indian unrest. The commission was the brainchild of U.S. senator James Abourezk, a non-Indian who had been raised on the Rosebud Sioux Reservation of South Dakota. According to the commission's backers, it would be the first such government commission to actually listen to Indians. It had eleven commissioners: six members of Congress and five Indians. The five Native members were Ada Deer, a Menominee who had recently helped her people gain restoration of their tribal status; Louis Bruce, the controversial Mohawk-Sioux former BIA commissioner previously mentioned; Lumbee educator Adolph Dial; Jake White Crow, an Oklahoma Quapaw/Seneca; and John Borbridge, an Alaska Tlingit. Ernest Stevens, an Oneida ally of Bruce and a fellow reformer, was chosen director. Because the commission was prompted by activity coming from off-reservation groups and pan-Indian entities, concerns of these sub-groups of Indians, including non–federally recognized tribes, were of great importance to the commissioners, most of whom represented this category themselves. Eastern, terminated, unrecognized, and urban Indians were perhaps overrepresented. A task force was created on terminated and non–federally recognized tribes, and another centered on urban and rural nonreservation Indians. The activist Pine Tree Legal Services provided volunteers, as did the Lumbee Regional Development Association. Three Lumbees took part: Dial, Helen Maynor Scheirbeck, who served

as chairwoman of the Indian Education Task Force, and Jo Jo Hunt, who
served as chairwoman of the task force on terminated and non–federally
recognized tribes. Joining Hunt on this important latter task force were
John Stevens, a Passamaquoddy from Maine, and R. Bojorcas, from the
terminated Klamath Tribe. As previously noted, the commission held
meetings in Pembroke, Baton Rouge, and at various unrecognized
tribal communities in Louisiana, helping to promote interest among
local Indians in national affairs. The high profile of these nontraditional
Indians and their association with radicalism, coupled with the fact
that they were not from the West, formed a major problem for many
reservation leaders. The National Tribal Chairmen's Association,
established during the Nixon administration and composed of more
traditional, conservative reservation leaders, filed suit in 1975 over
the selection of the Indian commissioners.[65]

The NTCA's suit reflected the growing schism between federal
tribes and off-reservation entities then so prevalently highlighted in
the media. In conjunction with the suit the NTCA passed a resolution
stating, in part: "The land based Federally recognized Indian Tribes
are not properly, if at all, represented by the Commission as presently
constituted." The NTCA argued that of the five Indian commissioners,
only one truly represented traditional tribes. Many members of the
NCAI also opposed the selection of the Indian commissioners. The
Inter-Tribal Council of the Five Tribes under president B. Frank Belvin,
a Choctaw and brother of principal chief Harry Belvin, passed a resolution strongly supporting the NTCA actions and lobbied members
of Congress in this effort. The All Indian Pueblo Council and USET
also passed resolutions against the selection of "nontraditional" Indian
commissioners. Overall these tribal leaders felt that off-reservation,
terminated, and nonrecognized groups who "were not among the
mainstream" of Indians were overly represented in the commission.
More established tribes questioned the race and cultural integrity of
most of these groups. Jonathan Taylor, longtime chief of the Eastern
Band of Cherokees, who was highly involved in the hearings of the
commission, noted, "All of a sudden, Indians are climbing out of every
crack." His implication: most of these individuals were not really Indians.
In what should have been a watershed development in Indian-directed
policy, the AIPRC proved disappointing to say the least. Its work certainly
put forgotten eastern tribes on the map, but conflict over commission

power and positions was one of the major reasons for its ultimate failure. As an NCAI report noted in 1977: "One of the principal reasons for opposition to the AIPRC among some tribal leaders was the fact that it would study and recommend actions for the recognition of non–federally recognized groups and the delivery of federal funds and services to them." The power of Lumbee commissioners was particularly troublesome to many members of the NCAI.[66]

The AIPRC compiled statistics and conducted research on unrecognized southeastern Indian groups. One of its few successes was prompting the BIA to finally create formal procedures for recognizing tribes that had been left outside federal protection. In 1977 the commission published its findings, including a significant volume on terminated and non–federally recognized tribes. The reports came out forcefully for the rights of eastern communities and all unrecognized groups. As the task force on unrecognized tribes concluded, "Tribes which have been overlooked, forgotten, or ignored must be recognized as possessing their full rights as tribes."[67] The commissioners called for an independent congressional office to decide on federal acknowledgment cases.[68] They reported, "In almost every case, the Indian heritage of every group seeking recognition is undeniable," but many established tribes were not so sure.[69] The task force on unrecognized tribes seemed to support using self-identification for groups seeking status. Reservation tribes, well aware of historically fluctuating federal funding and support, took notice of the AIPRC report that there were at least 133 unrecognized Indian communities, with a total population of over 111,728. They took notice that the commissioners seemed to feel each deserved federal support and status.

A subsequent meeting of the NCAI a year later was riven with controversy. Reservation leaders, associating the eastern groups with militant, urban Indian extremists, expressed outrage that new entities like CENA had gained funds intended for real Indians via the Comprehensive Employment and Training Act, HUD's Office of Native American Programs, and, most important, the Indian Education Act. Many tribal leaders were angered at what they saw as former director Vine Deloria's "more the merrier" approach to serving and recognizing new tribes. Regardless of one's political bent, all parties involved were now educated about the potential number of non–federally serviced Indians and the lack of consistent standards for determining which individuals and groups were eligible for Indian funds and programs. Many commented on the general arbitrariness of past acknowledgment decisions, and some observers believed this inconsistency posed a threat to the continuing status, self-government, and ultimately the sovereignty of all existing tribes. Even tribes that did not support the aspirations of unrecognized groups saw the need for a consistent procedure for recognizing Indian tribes and for defining "Indians" for federal purposes.[70]

The Five Tribes and related tribes in the Southeast were centrally involved in many of the task forces of the American Indian Policy Review Commission, but they were determined to not let what they saw as the commission's militancy and liberal approach guide the future of Indian affairs, including its calls for widespread recognition of neglected tribes. Sensing the political winds shifting, the more conservative tribal leaders feared a white backlash against their recent political and legal gains should the commission's work be seen as representing the dominant view of American Indians. In the end congressman Lloyd Meeds (D-Wash.), AIPRC's cochair, published a hundred-page dissent criticizing his own commission's findings, calling them "one-sided advocacy" and charging that they sought to "convert a romantic political notion into a legal doctrine." A host of white-dominated entities, including the National Association of Counties, wrote to the commission expressing fear and outrage over its support of tribal sovereignty and rights, positions that could affect issues as diverse as fishing rights, zoning, tax bases, and police jurisdiction. One Washington State man wrote: "They want to integrate the Negroes and segregate the Indians . . . why can't we do away with the reservation and all be Americans with equal rights?" Comments like these certainly reminded Five Tribes and other peoples that the sentiments that spawned the fairly recent termination policy were still around. Haunting the debates about recognizing tribes was the specter of a white backlash.[71] One concerned person was Claude Cox, principal chief of the Creek Nation. A former president of a local union of the International Brotherhood of Electrical Workers, Cox had experiences with unrecognized tribes through the Eastern Creek claims litigation. In 1977 Chief Cox wrote to Ernest Stevens about the commission's reports, expressing support for its work generally, but saying that its task force proposals were "too lax" on tribal recognition policy. Cox worried that indiscriminate recognition of new tribes would lead to fraud and undermine the finest traditions underpinning the federal-tribal relationship. He warned that new recognition should not be accomplished in a "haphazard manner that's going to recognize some illegitimate so-called government."[72]

A NATIONAL CONFERENCE ON RECOGNITION

The American Indian Policy Review Commission's conclusions on tribal recognition policy alerted both the BIA and its constituents to the threats posed by a potential flood of new tribes eligible for federal Indian programs controlled by the BIA and the Indian Health Service. The controversies surrounding the commission and the general southeastern Indian renaissance led to a series of recognition-related bills and proposals that the Five Tribes and the majority of other recognized tribes vehemently opposed. The Lumbee people continued to spur the drive for greater access to federal Indian funds. During the mid-1970s the North Carolina people were pursuing legislation that would grant them full tribal status. Oklahoma tribes that included the Absentee Shawnee Tribe passed resolutions against such action. U.S. senator Robert Morgan (D-N.C.) went on to introduce legislation that would grant federal recognition to any tribe, including the Lumbees, presently recognized by their state governments, but this bill was adamantly opposed by the Department of the Interior and many recognized tribes.[73] At the same time Senator Abourezk, keeping his promises, pursued legislation to create a formal, congressionally authorized federal tribal acknowledgment process. Quickly making their way through Congress, these bills mirrored the demands found within the activist-oriented AIPRC. One would establish a separate office within the Interior Department to decide acknowledgement cases, to avoid the apparent conflict of interest in having the BIA make such decisions. These bills established fairly liberal criteria for acknowledgment: a group need only prove it had been identified as "Indian" since 1934 (not since historical times, the standard in the 1978 regulations), that it had maintained political authority over its members, and that it possessed one other attribute selected from a list, such as having some form of surviving aboriginal culture, past collective rights in resources, or recognition by other Indians. If an unrecognized tribe could prove it had once possessed treaties or other formal relations with the federal government, it was then up to the government to shoulder the burden of proving that the group had not continued to exist since the date of the treaty or other document. In one bill, the government would pay for the group to be processed. At meetings with the BIA, Abourezk's Senate select committee made it clear that they would proceed with their legislation, with or without BIA approval. The Indian Office and its tribal constituency clearly risked losing control over defining groups served by the agency.[74]

Fear of the liberal Abourezk legislation prompted the NCAI and its tribal base to place tribal acknowledgment policy as top priority in 1977, when it met in Dallas. Members had been watching the activities of unacknowledged and off-reservation groups with suspicion and trepidation. Many scholars, most recently Annette Jaimes and Ward Churchill, have emphasized that federal policies have imposed racial and other nonindigenous structural definitions on indigenous peoples with an aim toward defining them out of existence. While this is certainly true when traced back to aboriginal forms and conceptions, as Native cultures have evolved, tribes themselves have been increasingly involved in policing and defining who they are. This is clearly seen in the NCAI dialogue over the criteria to utilize when recognizing new tribes. The Five Tribes and leaders from the Eastern Creeks, Eastern Cherokees, Mississippi Choctaws, and Seminoles were well represented in the hierarchy of the NCAI during these debates. As previously noted, a rift had opened between conservative reservation leaders and activist off-reservation groups. The 1977 NCAI convention agenda made it clear that its leaders felt that former NCAI executive director Vine Deloria, Jr., and other parties were out to paint the NCAI as a pawn of the BIA, refusing to share with their "less fortunate Indian brothers." It was certainly correct that Deloria represented what NCAI historian Thomas Cowger calls a passing of the torch to a newer, more educated generation. Deloria sought to unite all aboriginal peoples—urban and reservation-based, militant and conservative, recognized and un-recognized—into a larger, more powerful Indian interest group. The NCAI was, in fact, the first major Native-led group to mobilize Indians as a nontribal ethnic interest group, and it is credited with pushing for the Indian Claims Commission and ending termination. However, the intervening Red Power actions and rise in organizations representing nonreservation perspectives had taken their toll on pan-Indian unity. The criteria the NCAI ultimately developed that were included in the BIA process reflected a compromise between recognized tribes and unacknowledged contenders. As Eddie Tullis concludes, the BIA's Federal Acknowledgment Process was "a negotiated settlement." He believes that if Native leaders had failed to establish formal, agreed upon procedures, then Congress would have taken over.[75]

During the 1977 and 1978 debates, tribal leaders demanded the power to determine or at least be consulted about which groups received the federal seal of approval and joined their ranks. Non–federally recognized tribal leaders also agreed that Indian people should determine who was Indian.[76] The issue was complicated, however. Federal tribal acknowledgement is a formal act whereby the federal government acknowledges that a government-to-government relationship exists between it and a tribal body. Individual tribes cannot extend federal recognition in a formal sense. What they can do is influence decisions and in this case maintain control over decisions through their power within the BIA. By this time most of the agency's employees, including the highest post, were Indians. In these often-heated debates, it was clear that tribal positions crossed the ideological spectrum yet a fairly conservative agenda grew out of the formal meetings. An official publication of the NCAI reflected on the growing schism between tribes and non–federally recognized "urban Indians" who had disrupted NCAI conventions in 1969, 1970, and 1971, and damaged convention facilities in the process. Particularly memorable to the leaders of the Five Tribes was the 1973 NCAI conference in Tulsa, which was disrupted by a group of Cherokee members of AIM who took over a meeting, charging that Cherokee principal chief Keeler's use of the tribe's claims money was inappropriate and that he and others had also misused other funds. After a tense two-and-a-half-hour dialogue the NCAI passed a resolution asking the Solicitor's Office to inquire into these allegations. Beyond tensions between NCAI leaders and militants, delegates expressed cultural, racial, and sovereignty-related concerns. An NCAI writer frankly admitted that some leaders opposed groups, especially on the East Coast, on racial and cultural grounds, believing they were too admixed with African Americans or whites, and too far removed from traditional Native American culture to be recognized as Indians. The NCAI meeting agenda noted, additionally that "tribal leaders associated with federally-recognized tribes are increasingly expressing objection to what they see as greater and greater dispersing of federal funds, appropriated by Congress for Indians, going to questionably-Indian groups, programs, and individuals." Despite one attendee's argument that recognizing tribes had the potential to increase the political base of all tribes, the prevailing sentiment was fear of a diminution of federal funding. While encouraged by the recent Menominee restoration bill and an earlier Tigua recognition act, the NCAI believed additional tribal restorations would mean less federal funding for others. Jonathan Taylor was against the restoration effort on principal, believing the terminated tribes had willingly given up their status and now should not be reinstated. The NCAI also expressed concerns over efforts by the Yaqui Indians of Mexico and Native Hawaiians to secure federal status and benefits via Congress. The official program also noted the controversies over the "Lumbee Movement" and CENA's work to secure rights for eastern tribes.[77]

As Indian people debated how best to approach the touchy issue of tribal acknowledgment, the specter of an anti-tribal backlash continued to loom. The high-profile land claims cases pursued largely by non–federally recognized tribes in the East and the fishing rights cases brought by many seemingly assimilated Indians in Washington State had the remarkable effect of uniting a wide array of groups against tribal treaty rights. Especially in regions with little historic Native presence, locals were shocked that remnant tribes were demanding the right to hunt and fish without regard to state game laws, to create reservations exempt from local taxation, and to access sacred lands, many of which were public parklands. These demands made for some strange alliances. Groups as diverse as the Sierra Club, the Friends of the Earth, conservative "citizens' rights" leagues, the Puget Sound Gillnetter's Association, sportsmen's clubs, game wardens' associations, East Coast beach towns, and real estate agents, all joined a chorus to oppose the demands of forgotten Indian enclaves. Members of Congress received angry letters from constituents dismayed at the militancy of Indians, whom some referred to as "Super Citizens." As one man wrote to the secretary of the interior, Cecil Andrus, in 1977: "Indians are the best treated people on the face of the earth . . . paid to be born, raised, educated, and even buried!" Because Washington State was the center of much of the turmoil, it is no surprise that John Cunningham, a congressman from the state, introduced legislation during this era to abrogate federal treaty obligations to Indian peoples, a right Congress theoretically possesses under early federal court rulings and other precedents. Records of debates of this era show that tribal leaders clearly feared white backlash should they proceed too liberally on the recognition issue. Members of Congress warned tribal leaders of the growing anti-Native sentiment too.[78]

Endeavoring to receive tribal input, the BIA helped organize a meeting on acknowledgment policy. With financial support from the BIA, the tribal base represented by the NCAI held a "National Conference on Tribal Recognition" at the Opryland Hotel in Nashville in late March 1978. The conference was held in Tennessee so unrecognized eastern groups could more easily attend, and CENA and USET helped cohost. Approximately 350 tribal delegates came, including many members of non–federally recognized tribes. As head of CENA, longtime Poarch Band of Creek Indians chairman Eddie Tullis was a delegate and recalls that the Five Tribes and southeastern nations were well represented at the conference as at other debates about tribal recognition during the era. Phillip Martin, chairman of the Mississippi Band of Choctaw Indians, and delegates from the Five Tribes, Eastern Band of Cherokees, and Florida Seminoles attended the Nashville conference. All sides agreed with government reports that found that past acknowledgment policy had been arbitrary, inconsistent, and unfair, and most observers came to agree that a consistent and uniform policy was in order. However, as Joane Nagel has noted, whites increasingly viewed Indian ethnicity as a choice, especially in the case of people not living on reservations. Native Americans make up the only ethnic or racial group forced to prove its identity. The response of recognized tribal leaders, especially those from the West, reveals that it is not only non-Indians who question the identity of indigenous groups. Reflecting the general skepticism, most leaders expressed doubts about the long-term Native credentials of new, contending Indian groups. NCAI president Veronica Murdock, a Mohave Indian from Arizona, told the unacknowledged Indians: "I think we cannot get caught up in . . . the long lost relative concept, because we do not know you, we do not know you so you must let us know who you are. From my reservation we know who we are. . . . I think we would like explicit information, explicit documentation." Tribal leaders had clearly become sensitive to criticism of their position. Attending as head of the Center for Indian Law, Sam Deloria remarked: "It's been very easy in this emotional and difficult discussion that has gone on about ten years now, really, to put all of those people and their

leaders who point out problems with recognition policy or who are conservative in terms of policy in a class of greedy racists."[79]

Although financial concerns were apparent, many leaders expressed
their feelings in cultural terms. The conservative NCAI had admitted
unrecognized tribes in the past. By this time the NCAI had approximately twenty-one members from non–federally recognized tribes, with
membership granted through convention resolutions, mostly by using
what Vine Deloria, Jr., would call visual and "common sense" criteria:
if at first glance it looks like a tribe, then acknowledge it. Weighing
in, the NTCA argued against any form of pure self-identification. The
tribal chairs demanded evidence of treaties or language, ceremonies,
and other cultural criteria before they would certify a group as a bona
fide tribe. This position was mirrored in a 1975 statement by the NCAI
president: "Our stand must not exclude consideration of the many
small tribes that have retained their cultures, their languages, and their
governments against overwhelming forces to destroy them." Most were
opposed to legislative tribal recognition that leaders saw as too influenced by politics. Claude Cox, principal Creek chief, told Poarch Creek
leader Eddie Tullis that he would oppose the Poarch Creeks if they
pursued legislation. The Creek Nation was particularly concerned that
a new tribal acknowledgment program would encourage local splinter
tribes and communities to form in Oklahoma, breaking ties with the
larger Creek government. This was no idle concern. In subsequent
years a small segment of the enrolled Muscogee Creek population
formed a group, the Yuchi Tribal Organization, and unsuccessfully
petitioned for federal acknowledgment as a separate tribe. Cox and
the leaders of the Eastern Band of Cherokees, the Florida Seminoles,
and the Mississippi Band of Choctaws came to demand rigorous procedures to prove whether claimants were legitimate tribes. As Tullis
remembers, these leaders told him they would accept the Poarch
group as a bona fide tribe only if they could produce documentation
proving they were one.[80] Speaking for the NCAI, Leonard Tomaskin,
chair of the Yakima Nation, summed up the tribal position, saying
that recognized tribes "should say who their brothers are." The NCAI,
with support from the unacknowledged tribes present, ultimately
agreed upon twelve principles to guide recognition decisions. The
group came to demand what they termed "ethnological, historical,
legal, and political evidence" that a group was a functioning tribe.
The NCAI then lobbied forcefully against the various acknowledgment

bills wending their way through Congress. Eventually congress deferred to the tribes and the BIA, allowing them to create the Federal Acknowledgment Process within the bureau.[81]

ACADEMIC QUESTIONING OF THE CONCEPT "TRIBE"

The events of the seventies had forced all parties, non-Indians and tribal officials alike, to once again attempt to define "tribe," a term that on the surface seemed so clear, yet upon further analysis was difficult to delineate. Few realize that there are several conceptions of the term "tribe" at war with each other. There are popular, often stereotypical visualizations of the concept, and there are legal conceptions, political conceptions, and ethnological frameworks and constructions as well. While the various views of "tribe" share many factors, significant differences exist. The fact that few Americans are aware of the distinctions has proven highly problematic in federal tribal recognition debates.

Traditionally ethnologists, federal jurists, and most policy makers have viewed tribes in terms of being primordial. They have always been contrasted with modernity. Non-Indians have viewed Native tribes as having essential primordial traits, passed down unchanged from the distant past, including aboriginal language, simple modes of living (tipis, wigwams, longhouses), traditional culture, and racial purity. Early scholars treated tribes as a premodern form of political organization, locating them between simple band organization and modern nation-states. In economic terms, people envisioned tribes as nomadic hunter-gatherers or simple agriculturalists, their subsistence strategies contrasted with modern industrial society. Aboriginal groups have been recognized only to the degree that they have resembled ancestral populations. As Bruce Miller finds, indigenous peoples were constructed as backward-looking and primitive, wishing only to preserve ancestral lands and cultures against the tide of modernity. In this they were doomed, yet they could not envision fundamental change. Early ethnologists (structuralists) created laundry lists of traits against which to measure aboriginal groups and tribes. A post–World War II effort by India to catalog groups on its "Schedule of Backward Tribes" provides a lens into traditional thinking about tribes in North America. According to the government of India, tribal people were people who lived far from "civilization." They were of a minority race, spoke a dialect, were animistic, carried on primitive activities, and were nomadic. Tribes went naked or semi-naked, liked to drink and dance, and had low levels of literacy, simple technology, and were declining in population. These characteristics contained some elements of truth but were shot through with stereotypical notions of aboriginal communities. The very notion of primordial identity implied that true tribes were of great antiquity, that their real origins were shrouded in the unwritten historical past. As court cases previously discussed show, federal judges and bureaucrats in the United States have followed these notions when making and interpreting policy. Groups having lost essential aboriginal traits were no longer viable Native American tribes and thus were on the road to disappearance, assimilated into what was seen as the great American "melting pot."[82] By the 1970s, academics had moved beyond early notions of "tribes" and "Indianness," yet these earlier beliefs remained strong in the popular consciousness.

If social scientists rejected simplistic notions of tribes, real-world concerns compelled others to construct a workable definition of Indian communities for federal purposes, and some structural characteristics were necessary. Against this endeavor, however, were scholars of the social constructionist school, who questioned the very conception of tribes and well-bounded, delineated ethnic groups. To these academics, ethnicity and ethnic groups, including Indian tribes, were socially constructed, situational, and constantly evolving, especially in response to contact with the dominant society. Their mantra was that all groups evolve, preserving traits, reviving others, and constructing new traditions to meet the needs of the present. Ethnicity is plastic and fluid, and it can be used as a tool to access scarce resources in the larger nation-state. Postmodernists and post-structuralists challenged base assumptions of earlier eras. Efforts to be "objective," to quantify Indianness through blood quantum or other traits, were doomed to fail. Groups had traits, but attempting to create laundry lists to measure and delineate them was folly, and so influential academics came to advocate self-identification for ethnicity and race. A person's ethnic or racial identification was so situational and personal that it was better to let the individual define his or her own affiliation. This viewpoint seemed like common sense to most unrecognized tribes and their academic backers, and the U.S. Census would follow their lead.[83] As previously noted, it had become widely accepted by academics that the conception of an American Indian tribe (embedded in Indian law and federal policy) was the product of Native contact with colonial society. Like in Africa and Asia, imperialism and colonialism of Western governments forced indigenous groups to formalize political structures to better deal with them, effectively creating tribes. To most scholars, the entity we call a "tribe" is not aboriginal in form. Many scholars came to conclude that tribes are "ethnographic fictions," created by scholars for ease in studying and describing Native peoples.[84]

These positions, while theoretically valid, were untenable in the political realm. Any group could claim to be an Indian tribe and define its own membership, but should they then automatically secure recognition by the federal government? To groups with a stake in the outcome, the position that legitimated all self-proclaimed tribes—or those that had state proclamations declaring them tribes—was ludicrous. The stakeholder parties were forced to come up with a way to define a tribe for federal purposes. The scholarly position most reflected in the final BIA rules was articulated by Fredrick Barth, Edward Holland Spicer, and others of a school of thought on "enduring peoples;" it represented a mode of analysis that became the dominant paradigm for studying ethnicity in the mid-1970s. These thinkers recognized that language, a sacred homeland, a common race, and religion did bind groups together as a people, yet peoples could endure without any of these traits so long as they maintained a cultural sense of being a "people" apart from others. Academics of this school focused upon social "boundaries" maintained between ethnic groups and others. These boundaries could include language or isolated residence, but they also could encompass less visible symbols, philosophical frameworks, senses of history, and common values. So long as a group maintained a sense of being apart, if an "us and them" dichotomy existed between it and the larger society, then the group would endure as a separate people and could be identified as such. Both insiders and outsiders would agree that the group in question was an identifiable enclave.[85] In many ways, the Barth-Spicer school is reflected in the final rules for acknowledgment. The BIA would hire anthropologists and ethnohistorians, and look for whether a group had been identified by outsiders and insiders as Indian, that it had maintained a distinct community viewed as separate, and that it had had a continuous succession of its own leaders since precontact times. The entity could be mixed within a larger non-Indian community but be recognized only so long as it maintained a separate tribal identity. The one nod to traditional ways of recognizing Indianness was the requirement for ancestry. All but the most abstract theoreticians acknowledged that a tribe had to have Indian ancestry to be recognized. Having an Indian blood degree, surviving identifiable aboriginal culture, and maintaining isolated tribal villages were not required for federal tribal acknowledgment, but as future findings would reveal these traits would be seen as good evidence of the survival of a historical Indian tribe. The final federal conception of "tribe" would represent a complicated mixture of social science criteria, legal precedent, and past bureaucratic policy. In many ways the 1978 rules would be based on the Cohen criteria and court cases such as *Montoya*, criteria rooted in past policies and discarded views of tribes patterned on existing, Western-based reservation tribes. However, scholars working for the BIA would use the Barth-influenced insights to attempt to measure and judge the criteria established.[86]

While as Vine Deloria, Jr., and Clifford Lytle have so poignantly noted, "tribes" are both white creations and modern political forms, they have certainly gained salience in federal and tribal life. They have become, as Joane Nagel, notes "political organisms" with deep resonance for modern Indian identity. Tribal sovereignty and most Indian rights flow from the legal concept of tribe. As the courts have held, the status is a political status, not an ethnic or racial one, embedded in the Constitution, judicial history, treaties, and a host of federal acts. The concept of tribe cannot be discarded or deconstructed out of existence or divested of any true meaning. It is used by modern Indians to describe a political body, as well as a people, set apart and contrasted against the nation-state. To Indian peoples, being a member of a tribe means not only an attachment to a sacred landscape and sense of belonging to a unique people, but also membership or citizenship in a legal-political body. At the same moment academics were questioning the entire construct of "tribe," Indians were investing it with more importance and meaning, fighting ever harder for tribal existence in modern America.[87]

THE FEDERAL ACKNOWLEDGMENT PROCESS

Bud Shapard, a BIA employee who with others was charged with writing the initial regulations, recalls that most Indians he knew, including well-connected ones within his own agency, did not want to create a new tribal recognition platform at all. He remembers that most Indians "felt these groups really did not exist culturally" and did not want to begin recognizing new tribes. Married to a Ft. Sill Apache woman at the time he helped write the regulations, Shapard notes that many Oklahoma tribal leaders were against the whole process on principal. However, they would say "if it [has] to be done, then let's have it remain in-house," in other words kept within the BIA.[88]

In debates over what criteria to use, many of the traditional ways of identifying Native peoples were contemplated but rejected. The simple reason that many unrecognized groups lacked these traits or the absence of long-term federal relationships made quantifying them impossible. Academics, who would continue to do much to question the concept of tribe itself and the fairness of the Federal Acknowledgment Process in coming years, were largely absent from the final debates and rule-making. Blood quantum, a measure used by the majority of tribes at the time for membership and by federal officials for a host of Indian eligibility requirements, was demanded by some parties but ultimately rejected. Federal rolls that measured blood degree had not generally been kept for these new contending groups, ruling out this common, if flawed, way of measuring Indianness. Physical appearance or phenotype, while used by most outsiders when judging whether someone or some group is "really Indian" likewise was ruled out. Using physical features was patently racist and clearly unreliable as an indicator of Indian ancestry. Many conservative tribal organizations such as the NTCA and non-Indians demanded that groups still practice some form of identifiable aboriginal culture. These parties felt that if groups petitioning to be recognized were still really Indian tribes, they logically would still have a Native language and traditional religion, practice aboriginal crafts, and maintain Native ceremonies or other traditions. Some parties believed that "real" tribes would live in isolated villages or communities set apart from their black and white neighbors. Ultimately the BIA rejected these demands as untenable. The reality was that many eastern, southern, and West Coast groups had, over time, became fairly assimilated into non-Indian culture and society. They simply did not maintain cultural or community traits associated with stereotypical Indian life or tribes. On the advice of its attorneys, the BIA fell back upon established agency precedent, the Indian New Deal "Cohen criteria," and definitions found in several court cases when drafting regulations. It also incorporated social science criteria into its formulation of "tribe."[89]

Records of this era reveal that the BIA clearly feared the potential cost of what it saw as a possible flood of groups seeking status, an increase in service population that would drain its already precarious budget. Government service employees also agreed with recognized tribes that acknowledgment cases should be wisely considered. Final rulings should be unassailable to protect the sovereignty and meaning of recognition for existing tribes. To correct the widely believed arbitrariness of past policy, the new regulations presented a uniform set of procedures all groups would follow. The final criteria thus reflected the bureau's views and tribal arguments that recognition rules must be fairly conceived but petitions closely vetted and analyzed to protect the interest of the BIA, tribes, and other parties affected by new acknowledgments. The regulations finalized in 1978 required that groups meet each of seven criteria in order to secure tribal acknowledgment. Failure to meet one criterion would exclude a group from recognition. To paraphrase, with my emphasis added, a group had to prove "with a reasonable likelihood" of the facts that (a) it had been *identified* historically and continuously as Indian (this was later changed to *identified since 1900*); (b) that a substantial (later predominant) portion of its members comprised a *community*, distinct from others, since first contact with non-Indians; and (c) that the petitioner had maintained *political influence* or authority over its members as an autonomous entity from historical times to the present. The group also had to (d) provide its present *governing document*, including its membership criteria, (e) prove that its membership *descends from a historical Indian tribe* or from historical tribes that combined and functioned as a single autonomous political entity from historical times to present, (f) show that its membership is composed principally of persons who are *not members of another acknowledged tribe*, and finally (g) show that it is not subject to congressional legislation expressly *terminating the tribe* or the federal relationship. As discussed later, the federal government, at the urging of recognized tribes and others, essentially demanded written evidence to substantiate these. Over time, four criteria would prove the most important and difficult to establish: the majority of groups that have failed in the BIA acknowledgment process could not prove (a), (b), (c), and (e), outside identification, community existence, political authority, and descent from a historic tribe. In total, the criteria were much more comprehensive than the Abourezk bills, and certainly a far cry from various proposals to recognize all state-recognized tribes or all long-standing, self-identified Indian communities. However, as Eddie Tullis concludes and the record confirms, the new rules were a negotiated settlement between the various concerned parties. When the new regulations went into effect in late 1978, forty groups were already in line to petition for federal tribal status.[90]

At the time all parties seemed pleased with the new acknowledgment system. In time, however, it would become one of the most criticized and controversial federal Indian identification programs. Demands of the BIA staff, legal challenges, Indian gaming, and other factors made the production of petitions, the government's analysis of them, and the time and cost of passing through the process clearly beyond the level contemplated by anyone in 1978. The rigor of the process and the support it received from the recognized tribes meant, however, that federal tribal recognition would become the highest, least assailable form of Indian recognition available to unrecognized peoples. It would also remain the only form of recognition enabling a group to exercise sovereignty and self-determination, and so almost all groups would seek it. Federal tribal recognition is truly the gold standard of Indian identification. The value of federal acknowledgment has meant that the process would be the battleground upon which most issues of Indian authenticity would be played out in coming decades. The BIA claimed its process would be an objective, scholarly, and nonpolitical way to determine which groups were tribes within the meaning of federal Indian law, a position many parties would hotly contest in subsequent years. The new "in-house" process would largely supersede other avenues for acknowledgment. Congress and federal courts, the other branches that could confer status, largely deferred to the Indian agency and its claimed expertise. With Congress having bowed to the BIA, there would be no statutory definition of "Indians" or "tribes" eligible for federal Indian services. The BIA regulations would become the de facto threshold for unassailable Indianness in America. Acting for its constituency and internal bureaucratic needs, the BIA had maintained hegemony and ultimate decision-making power—it set the terms of discourse unacknowledged tribes would have to speak to achieve federal status. Each of the groups detailed in subsequent chapters would in some way have to comport with the demands of the BIA regimen.[91]

The new acknowledgment process offered opportunities and potential difficulties for dozens of Indian groups seeking to gain acceptance and self-determination. It gave forgotten groups the chance for equality and rights as Native Americans, yet it also created a new dichotomy in Indian affairs: federally recognized tribes versus unrecognized groups. As Francis Paul Prucha notes, the publishing of the acknowledgment rules witnessed the first use of the phrase "government-to-government relationship," a term that would become ubiquitous when describing the federal-tribal relationship. The 1978 regulations also spawned the first published list of recognized tribes. This list would become increasingly important, with individuals looking to it to delineate groups eligible for most federal Indian programs and to judge their authenticity.[92]

In the end, the creation of the regulations fits squarely within larger trends of the 1970s, the decade that began the "era of self-determination" for tribes. The BIA's Federal Acknowledgment Process was a negotiated act of self-determination, in that tribes helped establish rules for inclusion in the class that defined them as political bodies. While the essential act of political recognition is a bilateral act between the United States and a previously unrecognized tribe and cannot be accomplished by any pan-Indian group like the NCAI, the fact that government officials consulted tribes is important. In past eras, "the Great Father" and his offspring the BIA would simply have measured the federal self-interest, perhaps the legal and moral rights of the contenders, and acted accordingly and unilaterally. The fact that recognized tribes were central to the creation of the final criteria reflects the growing power and influence of tribal nations during the era of self-determination and sovereignty. Through their influence in the BIA and in Congress, tribes and their power in this arena would grow. In coming years non-Indians would continue to seek input from recognized leaders who would lobby Congress, testify on Capitol Hill, and use gaming money, their moral authority, and the media to continue to demand a voice in saying which groups could join the federal fold.

CHAPTER 3

Vetted Tribes

The Poarch Band of Creek Indians and the
Jena Band of Choctaw Indians

On the Gulf Coastal Plain, which dominates much of the South, are two surviving Indian communities, separated by almost three hundred miles, that avoided the Trail of Tears. In southern Alabama, at the former railroad switch at Poarch, is a small Native enclave composed of descendants of "Friendly Creeks" who fought on the side of Andrew Jackson during the War of 1812. Historically described as a "mixed race" group of Indian and European ancestry, the Poarch Creeks have remained fairly close to the lands of their ancestors since the early nineteenth century, and much is known about their history. Far to the west, in central Louisiana near the small town of Jena, is another remnant Indian community, this one composed of descendants of Choctaw Indians who avoided removal. For generations these people were known primarily as a "full-blood" Choctaw community, isolated from their relatives by hundreds of miles and decades of time. While the Alabama Creeks' history is fairly well documented, the facts surrounding the Jena Band's journey from the Choctaw homeland in Mississippi to the environs of Jena remain largely lost to history. As Indian peoples in the Southeast, the two groups shared many of the same historical experiences, but these culminated in one in the late twentieth century: after decades of struggle, the Jena and Poarch Indian enclaves gained tribal acknowledgment through the BIA's Federal Acknowledgment Process.

Since the creation of the BIA recognition process in 1978, only three groups from the Southeast have secured federal recognition: the Tunica-Biloxi Tribe of Louisiana, and the Poarch and Jena Bands.

The latter two are the only indigenous enclaves associated with the Five Tribes that have passed through the grueling process and are now widely accepted as surviving tribes by local non-Indians and other Native American peoples, most importantly the related Mississippi Band of Choctaw Indians and the Creek and Choctaw Nations of Oklahoma. While the Jena Band and Poarch Creeks are deservedly recognized today, they are considered "bona fide" Indian tribes for very different reasons. Historically the bands possessed very different community profiles. They diverged sharply in retention of tribal culture, Native language survival, degree of Indian ancestry, and physical appearance, yet each was accepted as a viable remnant of the Creek and Choctaw Nations. In some ways, by embracing these tribes, Indian leaders followed the largely nonindigenous logic of the Office of Federal Acknowledgment, but in other ways tribal leaders utilized indigenous ways of seeing and accepting other Indian peoples. The community and historical profiles of the Poarch Band of Creek Indians and the Jena Band of Choctaw Indians show what other Native groups and officials of the BIA's acknowledgment branch consider necessary to gain federal acknowledgment.

THE POARCH BAND OF CREEK INDIANS OF ALABAMA

The Poarch Band of Creek Indians secured federal recognition through the Federal Acknowledgment Process in 1984. Currently the band has approximately 2,300 members, many of whom reside on the tribe's several-hundred-acre reservation located near the small town of Poarch, some sixty miles northeast of Mobile, Alabama. Prior to its federal acknowledgment the band won acceptance from other Indians as a legitimate tribe; however, it used largely nonindigenous forms of evidence. Government treaties, federal censuses, land records, and other documentation ultimately persuaded other tribes and government agents that the small enclave at Poarch was a remnant of the mighty Creek Nation, one that had managed to avoid removal to Indian Territory in the 1830s.[1]

The Genesis of the Southwestern Alabama Creek Community

Historical evidence shows that ancestors of the Poarch Band of Creeks originally lived in the Upper Creek towns on the Coosa and Tallapoosa

Rivers near modern Montgomery, Alabama. The Poarch Creek ancestors were mainly classed as "mixed-bloods," men and women born
from unions between British traders and Creek women. They mostly
had the surnames Weatherford, McGillivray, Durant, McGhee, Moniac,
Cornell, Gibson, Colbert, and Rolin. Although it would be convenient
to describe these families as acculturated, in actuality the degree of
Creek or European culture varied within families and individuals.
What is evident is that the more acquisitive families among the Upper
Creek towns experienced repeated and continuing conflicts with
their kin in the late eighteenth century, prompting the McGhees,
Moniacs, and others to petition the Creek National Council for per-
mission to settle to the southwest, on the margin of traditional Creek
national boundaries. During this era ancestors of the Poarch Band
began to congregate along the lower Alabama, Tombigbee, and Tensaw
Rivers, just north and east of Mobile. Some of the residents of the
small enclave at Tensaw eventually migrated to the frontier area near
the headwaters of the Perdido River, the modern boundary between
western Florida and southern Alabama.[2]

Soon after the Creek-European migrants arrived in southern Alabama the Creek Civil War erupted, forcing the residents to choose sides.
The Creek Indian fighting was inextricably entwined with the larger
War of 1812, where Creek militants fought as allies of the British against
the United States. Encouraged by Shawnee leader Tecumseh, who had
Creek lineage, the majority of the Upper Creek towns from which
the Tensaw community hailed joined the militant faction of Creeks
known as the Red Sticks, who fought in alliance with the British.[3] In
part because of their earlier separation from their Upper Creek
kin, ancestors of the Poarch Band sided with the Americans; they were
known as "Friendly Creeks" thereafter. The most important event of the
Creek Civil War for later Poarch Band history was the Fort Mims Massacre. In the summer of 1813 some of the mixed-blood Creeks led by
William Weatherford (Red Eagle) took part in the Red Sticks' massacre
of whites at Fort Mims, located just to the west of modern Atmore. While
a great victory for the Red Sticks, the event soon brought the wrath of
Andrew Jackson's Tennessee Militia upon the Creek Nation. The next
year Jackson's forces smashed the Red Sticks at Horseshoe Bend on
March 27. Soon after, both sides sued for peace. A punitive agreement
known as the Treaty of Fort Jackson followed. With the treaty, the Creeks,
including the "friendly" southern faction that had aided the Americans,
were forced to surrender millions of acres of land.[4]

While the Treaty of Fort Jackson was a betrayal, it would prove highly important to the modern Poarch Band's efforts to prove their tribal identity. The document contained a section providing that every "Friendly Creek" warrior "shall be entitled to a reservation of land" of one square mile. It further noted that abandonment of the tracts in question would result in the lands reverting to the United States. Several famous multiracial leaders, such as William Weatherford and his descendants, chose lands under the treaty and ultimately established fairly successful antebellum plantations. They remained behind as their Creek relatives removed to Indian Territory, and they gradually assimilated into American society. Other mixed-race families did not assimilate, however. One man in particular, Lynn McGhee, described by Indian agent Benjamin Hawkins in 1797 as "a half-breed in the savannahs . . . who is of an excellent character, speaks English well," was the key progenitor of the Poarch Band. Under the Treaty of Fort Jackson, Lynn McGhee was granted 640 acres for his aid to Andrew Jackson during the Creek Civil War. Against long odds, his family and several others managed to retain some of these lands as white settlers engulfed the region after the Creek removal west.[5]

With the Creek Treaty of 1832 and subsequent military roundups, the vast majority of Creeks were forcibly exiled west of the Mississippi, leaving the ancestors of the Poarch Creeks behind in Alabama. The treaty contained provisions enabling individual Creek citizens to remain in the Southeast, take up homesteads, and accept citizenship in the territory. A census taken in conjunction with the treaty listed thirty members of the Tensaw "half-blood" community who stayed behind, their appearance on the census showing that these individuals were still regarded as part of the Creek Nation at that time. Life was not easy for the mixed-race families who remained in southern Alabama. Poarch Creek ancestors Lynn McGhee, Sam Moniac, Semoice, and others fought to keep their lands against grasping settlers who used various legal and political maneuvers to try to seize their estates. The depredations of the Creek War and subsequent land losses, trying for men like McGhee, would ultimately leave a rather clear paper trail detailing the existence of the Poarch Band's ancestors and their community. Local and federal depositions were taken in regard to Creek property losses, and these list many Poarch Creek ancestors, while probate inventories also listed their estates in due course. Fairly well-heeled for an Indian of the day, Sam Moniac lobbied Congress in 1816 to pass an "Act of Relief" for losses he suffered when his and others' "[p]lantations were laid waste." That same year a Mississippi Territory census lists many Poarch ancestors. Lynn McGhee, Semoice, Samuel Smith, and their heirs ultimately persuaded Congress to pass special acts for their relief in 1836 and 1852. Court records found within the docket of the 1852 case *William Weatherford v. Weatherford,* involving the heirs of William, Jr., the son of famous Creek leader William Weatherford, Sr., detailed key elements of the Poarch Creek history back to the Creek Civil War. Rare among unrecognized Indian communities, the Friendly Creeks' participation as American allies in the Creek Civil War, combined with their financial resources and the access to white political institutions this enabled, resulted in the appearance of Poarch Band ancestors in many records of the early- and mid-nineteenth century.[6]

A Tribal Land Base in Escambia County, Alabama

The modern Poarch Band of Creek Indians lives in an area of Escambia County in a region of rolling hills of pine and oak on the Gulf Coast Plain. In the era of Alabama statehood (achieved in 1819) the region around Poarch was a frontier, heavily timbered and rather isolated from the busy port town of Mobile to the southwest. It was during this era that some wealthier, lighter-skinned Creeks managed to retain some of the rich bottomlands near Tensaw. Their history gradually diverged from their darker-skinned, "Indian-looking" brethren. Although the movement is not fully documented, Poarch ancestors gradually were forced out of the fertile bottomlands to rougher country to the east. The multiracial families ultimately selected four sections of land under the Treaty of Fort Jackson. These tracts were occupied by several family groups, and the communally held lands promoted group cohesion while serving as centers of Creek settlement. Significantly several of the "reserves" were subject to federal trust restrictions. During the late nineteenth century four settlements or hamlets grew up on these lands, comprising a combination of individual homesteads, squatter farms, and Indian trust lands. The three that survive today historically were known as "Head of Perdido," "Poarch Switch," and "Hog Fork."[7] The "McGhee Reserve," a 240-acre tract at the head of Perdido Creek served as the nucleus of the most important community. Family members began to patent homesteads near these Indian grants. In 1854 the first Creek homestead was filed near the "Reserve," followed by almost twenty others in coming years. Tight-knit communities formed at the four Indian enclaves. Records show that group members served as witnesses for each other when filing homesteads. It was during this era until the turn of the century that the local mixed-race Creeks engaged in what the BIA described as "an extraordinary high degree of inter-marriage . . . within a relatively small geographical area." Inmarriage is a clear sign of community cohesion. At the same time, tribal ethnologist Tony Paredes notes, individual members and families were fissuring off from the main settlements and integrating into non-Indian society, a process that tended to concentrate the more "Indian" members in terms of physical features and culture. The high rate of intermarriage led BIA researchers to conclude that by the early 1870s "marriages of the Escambia County group became very localized, i.e., drawn solely from the immediate area" of closely clustered, interrelated hamlets.[8]

Despite having a tribal land base and farms, ancestors of the Poarch Band struggled for economic survival throughout the nineteenth century. Most were small, subsistence-level farmers and sharecroppers, supplementing their diets with game and fish from nearby open lands. With the coming of the railroads and the beginnings of a burgeoning timber industry, the ancestral Creeks' way of life was ending. During the 1890s timber operations increasingly took up public lands, nonwhite settlement increased, and the ancestors of the Poarch Band more and more were pushed into local and migrant wage labor. Like the nearby MOWA Choctaws, band members became known for their expertise in timbering and turpentine work. In the face of their growing poverty and social isolation, descendants of Lynn McGhee and the others still resided on the Indian lands. By virtue of this fact, title to these lands was still held in trust by the United States.[9]

THE ALABAMA CREEKS IN THE ERA OF JIM CROW

As with Indians nationally, the beginning of the twentieth century was a low point in the history of the southern Alabama Creeks. Elders of the band recall this as a time when whites were "hard on the Indians."[10] Southern Native Americans like those near Atmore faced increased segregation under the various local and state Jim Crow laws, and informal discrimination in most areas of social life. Much like other

Figure 5. Children in front of school, Poarch Band of Creek Indians, Alabama. (Photograph courtesy of Alabama Department of Archives and History)

groups in the Southeast, the overt discrimination served to hinder the Poarch Band's economic progress, yet at the same time it promoted internal cohesion and Indian identity. Racism certainly served to promote outmigration, as the lighter-skinned Creeks left the area to pass as white in nearby areas. It also encouraged increased inmarriage and local identification of those who remained. A 1912 photo hanging in the Poarch Band's cultural center, labeled "Hog Fork School," shows mostly dark-skinned, black-haired children who could not have easily passed as white if they had wanted. Both internally and externally, the boundary between band members and non-Indians was hardened during this period. As African Americans labored at the bottom of the racial hierarchy, local Creeks worked to maintain social and legal boundaries between themselves and blacks. Even so, observers noted that group members seemed to exhibit little pride in their Indian ancestry, seeing it as a stigma or possibly taking it for granted. Tony Paredes noted that elders said people back then did not like the word "Indian," as it was a pejorative, and if they expressed pride at all, it was in being Creek rather than the generic "Indian."[11]

The existence of Indian enclaves was anomalous in the biracial South, and as elsewhere the ancestors of the Poarch Creeks occupied a third position in the area around where they lived, somewhere in the social and political hierarchy between black and white. With their varying physical appearance, group members moved uneasily through the complicated racial and legal etiquette of turn-of-the-century Alabama. Local Indians could serve on juries but could not attend well-funded white churches. They could marry whites legally but not attend school with them. Their segregated schools were classified at the state level with those of whites.[12] Indians later interviewed by Paredes recalled, with bitterness, the indignities suffered in everyday life. In a timber trespass suit brought by the government for the local Creeks, a white man had no qualms testifying that as a race the local Indians were "worthless," "very low," and of "questionable character . . . the virtues of the noble Red Man are confined almost exclusively to works of fiction."[13] Tribal member Gail Thrower recalls elders telling how the darker Indians were forced to sit on the curb, not allowed a place at the local drugstore's all-white lunch counter. Others were forced to sit in the "colored" balcony of theaters and to use "colored" examination rooms at local doctors' offices. As a result, Thrower notes that most "just doctored themselves" and were more determined that locals acknowledge them as Indians rather than "colored."[14]

More than other forms of discrimination, band members viewed the
inferior "Indian" schools as an obstacle to progress. By 1900, several all-
Indian schools operated among the Poarch Band settlements.[15] Early
pupils had to pay their way, but by 1917–1919 the county was paying
teachers' salaries. By the early 1930s, local Episcopal missionaries
prompted the school board to establish a consolidated Indian school
at the McGhee grant at Poarch, which provided education to the sixth
grade. The consolidated institution further melded the various Creek-
identified communities together. As is so often the case with obscure
southern Indian groups, it was private non-Indian entities rather
than the federal Indian Office that came to the aid of the Poarch
Creeks, helping them survive, and in the process providing records
of their existence and heritage.[16]

Episcopal Missionaries and Tentative
Contacts with the Indian Office

In the early 1930s, in the midst of the Great Depression, an Episcopal
missionary couple, Edgar Van W. Edwards and his wife (the latter
listed in records simply as "Mrs. Edwards"), began working to aid the
Poarch-area community in both spiritual and temporal matters, helping
to build schools and to obtain medical care. It was also during this
era that competing sects such as the Holiness Movement also began
building institutions that served as focal points for community life.
Identified in institutional records and locally as "Indian churches,"
the Episcopal and other institutions provided a form of outside validation of the ethnicity of the isolated group. For several years the
Reverend Edgar Edwards campaigned to have the BIA come to the
rescue of the band, writing a series of letters that entered the public
record. In this correspondence, Edwards identified Fred Walker,
"Uncle" Alex Rolin, and Will McGhee as recent "Chiefs." Noting that
the government tracts were played out and "would grow nothing,"
the missionary wanted short-term, nonmonetary aid. Giving insights
into the local racial situation he warned: "I do not think it wise to
give them money or anything outright, [which] the white people will
get from them."[17]

With the initiation of the Indian New Deal in 1934, commissioner of Indian affairs John Collier sent Samuel Thompson, supervisor of Indian education, to investigate several Alabama Indian groups. This included the first federal investigation of the Poarch Band. While the focus of Thompson's study of the nearby MOWA Choctaws (whom he called Cajans) was determining their racial makeup, he did not question the heritage of the Poarch area Indians. Upon investigating, Thompson and other BIA officials determined that the Escambia County group exhibited little sign of admixture with "Negro blood," a fact that apparently would taint their chances for Indian aid. The agent was able to confirm their Indian trust lands, which had recently been given in fee simple to Creek descendants. Subsequent BIA investigations as late as 1938 concluded that the Poarch ancestors were "well above local Negroes" and that the thrust of federal involvement should concentrate on making the local school district provide adequate schools, not creating situations that would cause the local Creeks to lose their independence and self-respect. The Wheeler-Howard Act of 1934 (Indian Reorganization Act) that initiated Indian reform required that groups seeking aid prove at least one-half Indian blood quantum if they were not residing on federal reservations. As such, Thompson concluded: "There is no doubt but that these people are of Indian blood, but unless the Wheeler-Howard Act liberalizes things, I do not see that there is anything we can do for them." Commissioner Collier shut the door on federal aid, concluding that there was simply no money for them at that time.[18]

THE CREEKS' *BROWN V. BOARD OF EDUCATION*

Much as with other unrecognized Indian communities in the Southeast, the Alabama Creeks' efforts to improve their education in local schools served as a springboard to modern political mobilization and pride in Indianness. The basic issue was the substandard Indian consolidated school at Poarch and the fact that the county school board refused to provide bus transportation for Creek children to attend white secondary school in Atmore, a distance of approximately ten miles. As a result few children got beyond a sixth-grade education. The battle for better schools introduced the most significant Creek leader of the early recognition era: Calvin McGhee. A descendant of band founder Lynn McGhee and son of Lee McGhee, a prominent church leader from Hog Fork, Calvin McGhee was born in 1903 and was described in press reports at the time as an uneducated, dirt-poor farmer. In the course of education-focused organizing and later land claims efforts, McGhee became enthralled by his people's forgotten history and comprehensively researched larger Creek history and culture. A tireless and charismatic promoter of southeastern Indians, it was McGhee who enlisted the aid of two local attorneys, Hugh Rozelle and C. Lenoir Thompson, in the school fight. McGhee organized a group that met with local officials and the Alabama governor. At the same time, a Creek man named Jack Daugherty, in an act of civil disobedience, stood in front of a school bus and refused to budge unless his children were allowed to board. The school board offered Calvin McGhee a compromise of providing his and other "lighter-skinned" children bus transportation, which he refused. A subsequent suit, *Annie R. Walker, et al. v. O. C. Weaver, et al.*, was settled out of court. C. Lenoir Thompson proudly informed McGhee that Escambia County had relented, agreeing to provide a local grammar school "as fit as for whites" and provide bus service for secondary schools. Over half a decade before the landmark African American school desegregation case *Brown v. Board of Education* (1954), the Poarch Creek case was as important to modern group history, improving education and just as importantly instilling pride in racial identity.[19]

LAND CLAIMS AND POARCH CREEK IDENTITY

In the late 1940s a local teacher, hired in the wake of the school battle, told Calvin McGhee about a national forum called the Indian Claims Commission (ICC) that could aid McGhee's group in securing funds for lands taken from their ancestors illegally in past decades. Lawyers Rozelle and Thompson soon were on board, and the band filed suit. The claims case pursued by the Eastern Creeks would further promote group solidarity and community organizing, a phenomenon not particular to the Poarch Creeks. In 1950 with McGhee at the lead, local Indians formed the Perdido Friendly Creek Indian Band of Alabama and Northwest Florida to pursue the claim. The name was soon changed to the easier to say Creek Nation East of the Mississippi. McGhee traveled widely to locate and enlist all descendants who might share in the award. Gail Thrower recalls that her people had to prove that they were entitled to share in the judgment as Creek Indians. As she

Figure 6. Calvin McGhee (*left*), chief of the Poarch Band of Creek Indians, with president John F. Kennedy, 1961. (Photograph courtesy of Alabama Department of Archives and History)

remembers, when McGhee would travel to Washington he would often encounter the sentiment that "there's no Indians left in Alabama," so to counter this McGhee decided "he'd give 'em Indians; McGhee would find the darkest-looking Indians and line them up!" He would then have them dress up in Plains Indians costumes—essentially giving whites the stereotype they had come to expect. While officials of the Federal Acknowledgment Process generally look with disapproval upon claims-related activities of modern tribes as proof that a tribe exists, in the case of the Poarch Band, the BIA noted positively that these actions were fundamental evidence of group identity, acknowledgment that they were Creek Indians, and proof of community functioning and political leadership during the 1950s and 1960s. Even so, many groups who would later be denied recognition by the BIA, particularly in Washington State, would be surprised by the conclusion of the federal researcher in this case: "According to one member . . . land claims had been the sole purpose of the organization for 15 to 20 years."[20]

Finding that the Muscogee (Creek) Tribe of Oklahoma had previously filed suit, the Eastern Creeks sought to intervene. According to Eddie Tullis, the longtime Poarch chairman, the Muscogee Nation was not pleased by this development. At first the Indian Claims Commission dismissed them, ruling the Eastern claimants were not an identifiable Indian group under the act. Upon appeal the Eastern Creeks won the right to intervene as the entity "Creeks East of the Mississippi," a group of approximately seven thousand centered at Poarch but much larger than the local community of approximately three hundred. Any documented Creek descendant, no matter where they lived or how they lived, was eligible to share in the funds.[21] Thousands came forward for the rumored "Indian money"; groups formed using their acknowledgment by the ICC as leverage for future tribal status claims. According to Paredes, the claims activity led to a great revival of interest in Indian identity in the region. Individuals contacted by McGhee and others felt a sense of validation of their Indianness, and unfortunately a sense of entitlement to secure full federal benefits. Paredes recalls a local joke at the time: "There used to be three races of people around here: white, Indian, and colored; now there's only two: Indian and colored." It was not until 1972 that individual members of the various Creek organizations received a modest sum of $112.13 each. As a Branch of Acknowledgment historian noted, the case aided the group more significantly, providing thousands of pages of records and proof of their Creek ancestry. Besides Calvin McGhee, younger leaders such as Buford Rolin and Eddie Tullis gained experience working for the tribe on the case, providing something else of inestimable value: a strong organization identified externally as Creek Indian.[22]

THE POARCH BAND IN THE GREAT SOCIETY AND BEYOND

Calvin McGhee and the other Creek leaders had a vision that was never restricted to land claims and school issues alone, and during the 1960s and 1970s the Poarch Creeks developed tribal programs under various federal "War on Poverty" programs that greatly aided community members. These efforts also enhanced tribal organization, a fact that would prove central to their subsequent recognition efforts. The programs themselves, administered by the Creek tribal organization, provided tangible services and benefits that together fostered loyalty and dependence upon the newly created entity.

In 1971 the local group organized as a formal nonprofit called the Creeks East of the Mississippi. By the late 1970s the organization was administering programs covering a wide spectrum of needs, from a Head Start branch to employment training. Children were served under a grant from the Department of Education's Title IV Indian Education program. The Department of Health and Human Services and its arm, the Administration for Native Americans (ANA), provided funds to hire tribal members such as Buford Rolin and Gail Thrower, offering wages for the first time for tribal endeavors and offices. The ANA also gave funds under its Status Clarification Grant program, moneys that went into the Poarch Band's tribal acknowledgment efforts.[23]

Cultural Survival, Revitalization, and Importation

Led again by Chief McGhee, members of the Poarch Band, who scholars as early as Frank Speck (in 1941) described as being almost devoid of surviving Creek cultural traditions, embarked on a sustained movement to revive and import indigenous traditions to their community near Atmore, Alabama. By most accounts McGhee was a master at playing Indian for non-Indian audiences. Affectionately known as the Indian chief "with the blue eyes," McGhee had no qualms about donning Plains-style feathered headdresses and making buckskin outfits for public gatherings. His identity and pride was no act, however, and McGhee, like dozens of other forgotten southeastern Indian individuals, attended the landmark Chicago Indian Conference in 1961. McGhee was prominent enough or shrewd enough to be among the delegation that presented John F. Kennedy with the conference's "Declaration of Indian Purpose." Below a picture of McGhee with President Kennedy, an Associated Press reporter noted that the Creek chief, in presenting the document, had told how his people had aided Andrew Jackson in the Indian wars of the South, further cementing his peoples' image as "friendly Indians."[24]

In 1971, the Creek Nation East of the Mississippi held its first Thanksgiving powwow at the tribal area near Poarch, an event held annually since then and one that would become the group's primary moneymaker prior to recognition. At the powwow, members and invited Indian individuals sold indigenous crafts, artwork, fry bread, hominy, Indian corn, and other Native-oriented foods. Girls competed for the chance to be crowned "Indian Princess" while Native dance troops entertained. The annual powwow served multiple overlapping purposes for the band. It raised revenue, no doubt, but also heightened the group's profile locally and nationally as Indians. This recognition provided intrinsic value to Creek youths, and, as Paredes notes, it would prove valuable as the group marketed its Indianness prior to the advent of the Indian gaming industry.[25]

A host of scholars who have studied surviving southeastern Indian groups conclude that few if any of these peoples possess cultures that do not bear the mark of significant contact with nonindigenous societies. Even the most "traditional," such as the Seminoles of Florida, whom Nancy O. Lurie describes as "Contact-Traditional," were significantly altered from precolonial days by the time pioneer "salvage" ethnologists described their cultural traits and created laundry lists that have since become benchmarks for defining aboriginal culture in the region. To many more traditional, reservation-based groups, having surviving Indian cultural traits is extremely important to proving authenticity, although they are not required for acknowledgment via the BIA process. The existence of surviving Indian cultural traits is highly persuasive to most observers in proving that a group still exists as a viable tribal community.[26]

Various scholars, including Frank Speck (who visited the group briefly in 1941), noted that the Poarch Creeks still maintained some humble elements of traditional culture. Of course, the lack of precontact items and elements of culture was entirely logical, as southeastern Indian economies had long evolved and older ways had become obsolete. Speck did find that the Poarch Creeks still made sofke (an indigenous corn soup that they called Lazy Jack), Indian baskets, crossbows, and cane blowguns, and noted that a form of fish trap and a turkey pen from older days still survived. He found that the area's Indians still maintained curing practices and a dance known locally as "the Breakdown" that likely derived from the traditional

Stomp Dance of the Southeast. Speck concluded that the people had long-forgotten Creek clan organization. Tony Paredes later concluded that the group's ancestors were largely acculturated by the late nineteenth century, living on individual farms, and engaging in wage work, having become largely Christian. The last native speakers of Creek likely died out in the early twentieth century, though a few elders in the early 1970s could recall simple phrases and words of the Muscogee language.[27]

Over time the Poarch Indians revived Creek cultural traditions while importing nonlocal traditions as part of the larger, pan-Indian powwow movement. All over the Southeast during the 1960s and 1970s groups were reviving and reintroducing long-lost (if ever existing) tribal traits as part of cultural revitalization efforts and powwow activities. Calvin McGhee started the practice, inviting members of the nearby Mississippi Band of Choctaws and Oklahoma Creeks to teach southeastern traditions to the people. The Poarch Creeks established dance troupes, with dancers often wearing fancy Plains-style outfits. While some Poarch members disapproved of these actions, many saw the introduction of non-Creek elements as essential to raising the community's profile and to gaining outside acknowledgment that they were surviving Indians in Alabama.[28] To uninitiate politicians and non-Indian local supporters, these apparently primordial practices and traits indicate Indian identity. More skeptical tribal leaders and government investigators tend to give these outward accoutrements little weight when judging a group's authenticity. Others often hold these seemingly invented displays against groups. Beyond their intrinsic cultural value and economic benefits, the Poarch Creek cultural activities ultimately had little impact on their tribal acknowledgment, warranting little mention in the BIA documentation.[29]

FORMALIZATION OF THE POARCH CREEK TRIBAL ORGANIZATION

When the Creek Nation East of the Mississippi incorporated in 1971 it represented what the BIA termed a "dual constituency," having one segment who were members of the local Poarch community and another that comprised the wider claims descendants, who Paredes and other scholars believed did not in any one locale constitute a viable, coherent community. By 1973 conflicts arose over whether to use the ICC award funds for community projects, an option popular with Buford Rolin and the Creeks at Poarch, or whether to disperse the money on an individual, per capita basis.[30]

During the early 1970s the death of Calvin McGhee, who many Creeks said "was the Creek government," and the activities of rival Creek descendant groups such as the Principal Creek Nation East of the Mississippi, based at nearby Florala, Alabama, led to a major consolidation and formalization of the Creek tribal organization based at Poarch. According to both Tony Paredes and Gail Thrower, the tribe made a conscious effort to limit membership to those living in the Poarch area or to those related to these core individuals. This approach contrasted sharply with the United Houma Nation of Louisiana who erroneously believed there was "strength in numbers" and opened their rolls to thousands of descendants. Gradually the Poarch tribal council took on the roles formerly held by Calvin McGhee alone, and it replaced nonresident Creek descendants on the council with local individuals. What emerged was a more cohesive, recognizable tribal entity within the parameters that would be set later, in 1978, by the BIA.[31]

CHAIRMAN EDDIE TULLIS AND INDIAN POLITICS

Prior to the formal establishment of the BIA recognition process, Poarch Creek leader Eddie Tullis was highly involved in the political events leading to its creation. Living in Walnut Hill, a town just across the Florida border from Atmore, Alabama, Tullis was elected tribal chairman after the tenure of Calvin McGhee's hand-picked successor, his son Houston McGhee. Tullis would become the central figure in securing federal acknowledgment for his people. During the 1970s, Tullis worked at a Monsanto chemical plant full-time while keeping a full schedule also working for the tribe. The new chief was a striking contrast to Calvin McGhee. Tullis made no effort to "play Indian" to the masses. He kept his hair short, in a crew-cut, and never dressed in stereotypical Indian fashion. Tullis was also fairly outspoken, even aggressive, and so was viewed by some as not having the traditional Indian leadership style related to the ethic of harmony and its emphasis on consensus decision making. Tullis is described by a fellow tribal member as very determined in working to get what he wanted, someone "who would not stop till he got us recognition." Unlike many tribal leaders, Tullis was also a political conservative, joining the Escambia County Young Republicans. Here he chanced to meet Alabama political legend George Wallace, infamous for his diehard support for Jim Crow segregation and for his subsequent campaigns for president beginning in 1968. It was through this connection that the Poarch Band first entered national tribal recognition politics. Tullis and others had secured the aid of Tom Tureen, pioneer advocate for unrecognized tribes, and the legal aid group NARF. In 1975 Wallace wrote the BIA requesting that a tract of land encompassing the tribal school and community center at Poarch be taken into trust as a reservation. The group also was on record as having filed one of the era's first petitions for acknowledgment that year. This was in the days leading up to the formal Federal Acknowledgment Process, so the BIA deferred acting on the case until it had formalized procedures.[32]

Undaunted, Tullis took part in several key developments involving acknowledgment politics in the early and mid-1970s. He was part of the Boston convention in 1971 that spawned the Coalition of Eastern Native Americans (CENA), and it was through Tullis's activity that the Poarch group secured coveted membership in the NCAI. By the early 1980s Tullis was serving as vice president for the NCAI Southeast Region and as chairman of the NCAI Census Committee. By his own account, Tullis was central to devising the BIA acknowledgment regulations, noting, "In 1975, we started a campaign through the National Congress of American Indians to create a procedure by which the tribes could attain recognition." He would prove one of the staunchest defenders of the BIA process in years to come. Rarely taking a day off work, Tullis was proud of the political contacts and good relations his people maintained with Alabama governors, congressional delegations, and local politicians, contacts that would serve his people well after securing recognition.[33]

Into the Federal Acknowledgment Process (1978–1984)

As described above, in the Federal Acknowledgment Process established in 1978, the government created seven key criteria that unrecognized Indian groups had to meet in order to secure federal tribal status. Government social scientists judged cases (and each of the seven criteria) using the standard "reasonable likelihood." In other words, was it more likely than not that the facts presented were true? The

Poarch Creeks rather easily established their identity according to the four criteria generally most difficult to meet: demonstrating long-standing identification as Indians, descent from a historical tribe, historical community, and political leadership. Their success cannot be explained primarily because they achieved status in the first years of the process, before the BIA regimen became more burdensome. Like subsequent successful petitioners, the Poarch group proved it was a viable Indian tribe because it possessed the kinds of records that government and tribal leaders look for when recognizing tribes within the federal process.

OUTSIDE IDENTIFICATION AS CREEK INDIANS

The majority of remnant southeastern Indian groups have trouble locating identifiable tribal ancestors, but this would not prove the case for the Poarch Band. Compared to many southeastern groups who have obscure tribal origins, the Poarch Band had ample written evidence and a long-standing oral tradition establishing their indigenous ancestry and, more importantly, their Creek Indian roots. Beginning in the late eighteenth century, outside agents described *by name* key Poarch Creek ancestors such as Sam Moniac, Semoice, Lynn McGhee, and others. The band's ancestral community at Tensaw was enumerated as a town within the Creek Confederacy during the early nineteenth century. Some benefits accrued to Lynn McGhee and the others for siding with the United States in the War of 1812. Legal depositions of Poarch Creek ancestors and the special acts of Congress and memorials of the 1830s noted specifically that men such as Lynn McGhee and Semoice were "Friendly Creeks" and rewarded them with Indian homesteads.[34]

After migrating to southern Alabama, the BIA noted approvingly, the Poarch Creek ancestors had continued to live within an eighteen-mile radius of their ancestral community, a fact that made their whereabouts and identity easier to document over time. Band members appear on the Creek Census of 1832, and several members applied for membership and were accepted in the Creek Nation for purposes of land allotment related to the Dawes Commission activities in Indian Territory in the late nineteenth century. In connection with Eastern Cherokee land claims in 1907, special commissioner Guion Miller took testimony from dozens of local Creeks. Though they were rejected as non-Cherokee, Miller's records unambiguously identify the group as Creek descendants. The federal General Land Office initiated a timber trespass suit, *United States v. Carney Mill Company* (1912), because a local lumber company had illegally cut trust-protected Indian lands associated with the Lynn McGhee tract. This case alone generated pages of depositions that served as further proof of the Poarch group's identity as Indians and details about the functioning of their community. Indian mission and public school records followed, clearly identifying the Poarch-area schools and churches as "Indian."[35]

Most importantly, modern Native groups and federal Indian programs continued to recognize the Poarch Band as a viable Indian group. The NCAI admitted the group into membership, the Indian Claims Commission recognized the band, CENA accepted them, and the group was deemed eligible for aid from NARF, the ANA, and other Indian-oriented entities. The Alabama governor and congressional delegation supported their cause. Through Buford Rolin, who once resided in Florida, the band secured support from leaders of the Seminoles and Miccosukees. Having the formal support of related tribes is often crucial to a group's federal recognition hopes. As Eddie Tullis notes, the Poarch group ultimately gained support from many tribes and individuals, including the large Creek Nation of Oklahoma. Tullis and other leaders had met Claude Cox, principal chief of the Creek Nation, several times in the context of land claims litigation. Although Cox had opposed the Eastern Creeks at first, he came to the position that if the eastern groups could prove that they were still viable Indian communities, using concrete documentation, then his tribe would support their position. Phillip Martin, chairman of the Mississippi Band of Choctaws, took a similar stance. Both Cox and Martin obtained copies of the Poarch Band's petition and had staff members examine it for veracity. Tullis says many petitioners underestimate the value of personal contacts, such as those he had developed. He had become friendly with Martin, and leaders of the Miccosukees and Florida Seminoles, as well as the Eastern Cherokees. Tullis also became close to influential national leaders such as Cherokee John O. Crow, assistant commissioner of Indian affairs in the early 1970s, and Buffalo Tiger, a Seminole leader. As his people moved through the slow BIA regimen, Tullis notes, "Once we got Phillip Martin to say he supported us, then it was easier for us to continue to insist the BIA accelerate the process for us." Finally, in 1983, the Creek Nation of Oklahoma recognized the group, entering into a "government-to-government" relationship with the Alabama band. Creek Nation principal chief Claude Cox advocated that the Poarch Creeks secure acknowledgment, stating in his letter of support that the group forms "a distinct and separate band of Muscogee (Creek) Indians . . . [and] has . . . since . . . 1832."[36]

PROVING ABORIGINAL RACIAL ANCESTRY

Proving racial identity by reference to federal censuses and other records "acceptable to the assistant secretary of Indian affairs" is the most troublesome criterion for southeastern groups engaged in the Federal Acknowledgment Process. The Poarch Creeks' experience trying to use nonindigenous records to establish their historical Indian identity sheds light on the complexities of racial identification in the Southeast as it pertains to tribal acknowledgment. In many ways the modern group at Poarch was advantaged because of the socioeconomic class of many of its key ancestors.

Southerners historically have had a love–hate relationship with indigenous peoples. After ensuring the mass removal of Indians in the early nineteenth century, white Alabamans proceeded to name over 350 places after them, including the state, named for the Alabama Indians who once inhabited the region. The fact that the Poarch Creeks descended from the state's most famous tribe and some well-known Creek leaders such as William Weatherford (Red Eagle) undoubtedly aided retention of tribal memory about their origins, and this certainly enabled local non-Indian acceptance of the group. The example of Weatherford proves an interesting case in point. The child of non-Indian trader Charles Weatherford and his Creek wife Sehoy (Marchland Tate), William Weatherford grew up in a bicultural world among his matrilineal relatives. Like many of his class, he owned a plantation and many African slaves, and he was economically assimilating into American culture, but he sided with the Red Stick faction in the Creek War and led the massacre of whites and other Indians at Fort Mims in 1813. In a famous legend handed down in Alabama, rather than risk the complete destruction of his people after the massacre and his faction's defeat at Horseshoe Bend, Weatherford voluntarily walked into Andrew Jackson's camp and surrendered, saying: "I am in your power, do with me what you please." An impressed Jackson offered an olive branch. In return Weatherford reportedly rejected his old Indian ways, saying, "There was a time, when I had a chance. I have none, now—even hope is ended! Once I could animate warriors; but I cannot animate the dead. Their bones are bleaching on the plains." In this tale Weatherford accepted the fate of his race and renounced his indigenous family and heritage. He ultimately married a white woman and was accepted into Alabama planter society.[37]

Men like Weatherford were embraced as a memory, surviving as legendary Indian foes vanquished by frontier Alabamans. As early as the 1840s, whites had a sense of admiration for the great chiefs and warriors, and pictures of them adorned many inns and taverns throughout Alabama. A 1930s *Mobile Press Register* article on the Poarch group reveals that notions of the "Noble Savage" persisted and likely added to the collective memory of their existence. The reporter noted he had found a "remnant tribe" of a "fading race" of once "fierce warriors" who descended from William Weatherford. The article concluded: "Today though pathetic in their humble garb and humble appearance, these once great warriors and their stoic features [are] radiant with friendship. . . . These Indian families live, hunt, and cultivate the woods and streams that once echoed to the war-whoops of their fore fathers." Clearly their famous and historically noble ancestors helped ensure the continuing visibility of the small remnant at Poarch. The fact that their Creek ancestors also possessed plantations, slaves, and other forms of wealth aided their descendants. They appeared repeatedly in probate records, court cases, and other records as a result.[38]

Unlike many other southeastern groups, including the Lumbees and nearby MOWA Choctaws, the Poarch Creeks had no significant African American intermarriage to taint their motives for seeking to be recognized as Indians. Several scholars suggest a negative connection between African ancestry (whether certain or not) and acceptance of a given group as Native American. As discussed earlier, color consciousness pervades the membership of the Five Tribes, who through long association with southern white culture and the institution of slavery generally have accepted Indian-white admixtures while rejecting Indian-black ones. The experience of the Poarch Band seems to support this conclusion. Products solely of Indian-white intermarriage as far back as the eighteenth century, band members found a rather easy acceptance within the ranks of the national Indian community, with little overt challenge to their identity and claims to Indianness. Unlike they did with other groups, the BIA never questioned the Poarch group's motives for claiming an Indian identity, despite clear similarities between their history and institutions and those of other southeastern groups turned down in the acknowledgment process.[39]

After a long period of neglect, ethnologists, government scholars, and sociologists began to investigate surviving Indian groups in the Southeast at the beginning of the twentieth century. With many groups such as the MOWA Choctaws racial origins were a major question, but the Poarch Creeks faced no such inquiries in this early scholarship. The key government investigator, Samuel Thompson, who visited the group in 1934, confirmed through oral tradition and written documentation that the Poarch group was of Creek descent. Also coming for the Office of Indian Affairs was noted anthropologist Frank Speck, who in 1941 validated the group's Creek ancestry and community. Following their lead, foundational works on surviving eastern Indian groups and supposed "Tri-Racial Isolates," particularly studies by Harlen Gilbert and Brewton Berry, did not question the Creek Indian origins and tribal descent of the Poarch Band. Berry, in particular, who made a name focusing on the ambiguity of southeastern groups, concluded that the Poarch area people, like the Pamunkeys and Mattaponis of Virginia, "are all strongly suspected of having little Indian blood, and have retained almost nothing of their ancient language and customs— but [possess] an unbroken thread which binds them to the past, and they cling tenaciously to their tribal identity, and guard their old Indian names as priceless possessions."[40] From Berry's work to Paredes's in-depth ethnological studies of the group beginning in the late 1960s, scholars left no doubt that the Poarch group descended from Creek ancestors, a key requirement for federal recognition.

GENEALOGY AND PROOF OF DESCENT FROM CREEK INDIAN ANCESTORS

Most parties agree that Native groups seeking recognition must prove that they descend from Indians, and, importantly, from historical named tribes indigenous to the United States. Today Native American peoples seeking to preserve their identity and status amid growing threats cling to their bloodlines as a primary determinant of membership.

Some tribes maintain blood quantum, such as one-quarter proven blood degree from their tribe. Even so-called purely "descendancy" tribes such as the Five Tribes with no blood quantum requirement jealously guard some proven, documentary link by blood to distant ancestors. More than any single BIA requirement, however, this criterion has proven troublesome for southeastern groups because of its reliance on non-Indian records and the confused (and confusing) nature of surviving documents. The pan-tribal composition of many remnant groups also plays a role. Of the markers of Indianness, the requirement of proving an unbroken bloodline from a historic tribe has stymied the recognition of many unacknowledged southeastern groups. This was a strong point for the Poarch Band of Creek Indians, however. Genealogical documentation is at once the most "objective" criterion, yet the most misused and stultifying. If "community" and "political authority" are inherently slippery concepts, proving you have records of Indian ancestry seems to the uninitiated the most concrete of requirements. In the course of reviewing decisions of the Branch of Acknowledgment (Office of Federal Acknowledgment), it is clear that if a group possesses documented tribal-specific ancestry, BIA officials will glide over ambiguities inherent in the other criteria. Here the Poarch Band had an airtight case proving their descent from Creek ancestors in the distant past.

The BIA tells petitioners that although oral tradition can corroborate ancestral ties, government-produced records, whether federal censuses or Indian rolls, are the best form of evidence of descent from a historical tribe. The Poarch Creeks were fortunate in possessing many of these records, particularly in comparison to many other obscure southeastern groups. As the BIA reported: "Virtually all of the Band's 1,470 members can document descendancy from the historic Creek Nation."[41] That said, a review of the Poach Creek records reveals racial ambiguity as reported in federal census, ambiguity and inconsistencies common to the records of most unacknowledged southeastern tribes. In the course of compiling their case, Gail Thrower, Tony Paredes, and a BIA genealogist made ancestry charts of approximately one dozen key families. Since these derived from the identifiably mixed-blood Creeks of the Tensaw region, the parties researched these families forward, confirming that they continued to live in clustered enclaves and to be identified (if not always consistently) as Indian. The 1860 U.S. Census listed these core families as Indian—significant because the census did not have this designation as a formal category until 1870. Because the government researchers definitely identified these core ancestors as mixed Creek-white families, they made allowances for inconsistencies in the written record, a decision they would not make for groups that do not have such unambiguous early identification. In 1870 and 1880, for example, some Poarch Creek ancestors appear as "Indian," some as "White," and some as "Mulatto"—the range of labels even appears within some family groups. The BIA concluded, however, that after 1900 the census identification as "Indian" is more consistent—several families were included on special Indian census schedules as Creeks in 1910. The majority of members were qualified to share in the Indian Claims Commission judgment award, and formal BIA rolls were taken confirming their Creek ancestry in the process. The band then used individuals listed as "Indian" in several censuses (1870, 1900, 1910) as the baseline roll for the modern tribe, labeling any person listed in these censuses as Indian as "full-blood" for enrollment purposes. The band then instituted a one-quarter blood quantum for current membership. In the end, compared to many southeastern groups, the Poarch Band had an unusual depth of federal records identifying its Creek ancestry.[42]

PROVING POLITICAL AUTHORITY AND COMMUNITY COHESION

Unlike some urban and dispersed unacknowledged Indian groups, the southern Alabama Creeks faced little doubt that they occupied a historical, ethnically identified community at Poarch. The more problematic reality was that the band had to find evidence showing that they possessed tribal or community leadership since the founding of their ancestral hamlets in the mid-nineteenth century. Having tribal or community leaders was a basic and natural attribute of historical Indian tribes. Under federal Indian law, Native Americans possess special status as members of tribal polities, not as ethnic or racial minorities. As such, the BIA requirement that would-be tribes have a political organization and recognized leaders is elemental. In modern times, however, after even reservation tribes have had their tribal powers usurped or entwined within other political jurisdictions, this requirement vexes most groups in the Federal Acknowledgment Process. Tribal leaders and government bureaucrats are cognizant of the evolved and compromised nature of tribal government and political leadership, and the experience of the Poarch Band proves a case in point.

Despite the significance of tribal recognition and the controversies surrounding it, scholars have paid surprisingly little attention to the actual research required to prove tribal identity in the federal process, knowledge that is central to understanding the much-maligned process and why it receives widespread tribal support. The Poarch group's lead scholarly investigator, Tony Paredes, notes that doing the research needed to make it through the acknowledgment regimen is not glamorous. It is extremely tedious, time-consuming work. In Paredes and Gail Thrower, his Poarch Creek research assistant in Alabama, the group had one of the best teams working in the Federal Acknowledgment Process. Thrower has one the strongest grasps of the complexities of the acknowledgment rules of any tribal member I have interviewed. Many groups are not so fortunate to have such individuals. A few examples of how Thrower and Paredes proved tribal community and political functioning should shed light on the level of evidence needed to secure federal tribal status.

Authenticating that a group is a valid surviving tribe requires years of dedicated teamwork by paid and unpaid community members and scholarly experts. With a grant from the ANA, the Poarch group hired Paredes and Thrower to work in tandem to find evidence of the long-standing tribal existence of the band. NARF, the Lutheran Church, and others aided the effort as well. As Paredes knew, proving the existence of a "tribal" community under certain political leaders would be very troublesome, as few records would list the group as a "tribe." The Poarch Creeks simply did not look like a tribe to local whites and likely did not identify themselves with that term either. There were no formal political organizations such as a tribal council, and the group had no named leaders such as a chief or even a town mayor. The research team, however, was able to find notes from anthropologist Speck, Indian Office agents, and local missionaries that named men such as Fred Walker, Frazier McGhee, and Will McGhee as being "peace makers," "chiefs," or spiritual leaders from the late nineteenth century until Calvin McGhee became band leader in the late 1940s. Oral testimony and statements taken from group members confirmed that these men and others controlled group behavior and led community functions. As Paredes notes, proving "control" was often as basic as finding individuals who recalled that "old 'so-and-so' would not let those boys use knives in a fight" or that men like Fred Walker would enforce community standards as to what was "proper" behavior among youth. These are actions the BIA looks for when determining tribes' historic political bases. It is clear, however, from examining the BIA's determination in the Poarch Creek case that the tribe was not put to the rigorous tests of proving political leadership, as was the case with many other groups. This was because the band had clearly established that it had Creek ancestors and lived in tight-knit, almost exclusively Indian hamlets. The Branch of Acknowledgment logically assumed that political leadership had existed, or accepted this as factual, even when assertions were not ironclad, because other aspects of the Poarch Creek petition were so strong and irrefutable.[43]

Beyond the mere existence of a small community around Poarch, the BIA wanted some evidence of socializing and working together—and that the people saw themselves as a community beyond simply living in close proximity. Gail Thrower recounts how she set about proving community ties for 1880–1920, a period that has proven highly problematic for most southeastern groups, mainly because of the paucity of documentation during these years. As Thrower recalls, "[W]e assumed they'd be 'federal' and bureaucratic—it's the government and I knew they'd require tons of paperwork." She had a hunch that the government would not just accept her people's word for it, so when the acknowledgment team of George Roth (anthropologist), Bud Shapard (chief), and Lynn McMillon (genealogist) arrived, she asked point blank: "So how are we supposed to play this game?" Thrower feels that many other groups simply "play dumb" and hope that the BIA will treat them nicely. As she found, playing the game required more than oral stories and traditions. To prove that her ancestors comprised a community that regularly interacted, Thrower went to the local courthouse. A court case involving the people would likely have left a paper trail, and Thrower had long heard that one of her ancestors, John Rolin, had killed a man named Will Colbert around 1904. Even though no one at the courthouse had heard of the case, a clerk directed her down to the musty basement. After days of sifting through old boxes, Thrower was elated when she finally found a box containing records of the case. It confirmed that John Rolin had in fact killed Will Colbert and was taken to trial. Court records showed that many of the witnesses were from the Poarch community, demonstrating the ties between them. As Rolin was approximately sixty-five years old at the date of the trial and had lived around Poarch his whole life, the records showed that the community stretched back to the 1840s. Thrower found a newspaper article that revealed that the Poarch hamlet petitioned the governor and successfully got him to pardon Rolin because Will Colbert was a scourge to the group and "needed kill'n." Together these records proved that the community certainly existed in 1904–1905, and had social ties and community mores at that time, but also that it stretched back to the mid-nineteenth century.[44] Thrower recalls today that her first thought had been that the BIA "would not get any more Indians than they had to." Therefore she had tried to provide multiple, overlapping types of evidence of her community's historical existence. To Thrower, the work was tedious but also exciting. She and her husband Robert Thrower would stay up nights until 1:00 A.M. with records spread all over their bed, trying to find the exact document to prove a certain point. It was like trying to solve a puzzle. Tony Paredes's anthropological work also was central. Thrower worked closely with Paredes who was based at Florida State University. He would find an apparently significant fact in a source such as the Episcopal church records and call Thrower, asking her to put on her coat and go find things like an old headstone to confirm what the records said. She then would take a photo of names on the marker and send it to Paredes in Florida. Thrower knew that the easier it was for the BIA to understand her group's history, the easier it would be for the Poarch Creeks to achieve success. She got out old censuses and maps, and charted the residences of community members to show that they lived in close proximity. She made ancestry charts of the core families to show the unbroken chain of kinship between these households. In the end, Thrower was so masterful at this tedious research that the BIA offered her a job.[45]

Tribal Acknowledgment, 1984

The Poarch Band of Creek Indians was among the first groups to secure acknowledgment through the BIA process, achieving this status in June 1984.[46] (The Tunica-Biloxis were first, in 1981.) Always keen to public relations and political considerations, the group held a celebration powwow, inviting longtime Alabama congressman Jack Edwards to announce the momentous event. Governor George Wallace phoned in his congratulations as well. A tract of 229.51 acres were soon taken into trust and labeled the Poarch Band of Creek Indian Reservation. At that moment, a lucrative bingo contract had already been signed with a Texas firm. The group had a fairly clear-cut case for acknowledgment and passed rather smoothly through the process. Compared to the history of the Jena Band of Choctaws that follows, theirs was a case based primarily on government documentation. The Poarch Creeks were now the only recognized tribe in the state of Alabama, with the Mississippi Band of Choctaws their nearest federally recognized tribal neighbors. The group finally had outside validation. Gail Thrower says, "It was personal for me; I didn't care if we didn't get a dime because it made people recognize us as Indians."[47] They also had a valuable asset. Leaders in the Federal Acknowledgment Process, the Poarch Band would soon be leaders in protecting their hard-won status and federal benefits against potential interlopers.

THE JENA BAND OF CHOCTAW INDIANS OF LOUISIANA

The Jena Band of Choctaw Indians was recognized through the Federal Acknowledgment Process in 1995, making it and the Poarch Creeks the only two southeastern groups with ties to the Five Tribes that have secured status through the BIA since the inception of its process in 1978. Currently the Choctaw band has 241 members and a sixty-three acre reservation consisting of several parcels in Grant and LaSalle Parishes in central Louisiana. The Jena group has a strikingly different community profile than its Poarch Creek neighbor. Like them it convinced other Indians and government officials that it was a legitimate Indian tribe, but the types of evidence the Jena Choctaws presented provide a strong contrast to the records used by the Poarch Band to establish its identity.[48]

THE ORIGINS OF THE JENA BAND IN CENTRAL LOUISIANA

The Jena Band of Choctaws share one attribute common to groups that have failed to convince outsiders of their tribal authenticity: their exact origins are shrouded in mystery. Jena Choctaw oral tradition told that their band originated from several groups of Choctaws that were reported roaming in central Louisiana in the early nineteenth century. These people ended up settling near Catahoula Lake, a large body of water east of modern Alexandria, along a stream called Trout Creek. They were later joined by Choctaws who had defected from the mass of Trail of Tears migrants moving through the area after 1830. The group's original petition for acknowledgment submitted in 1985 argued logically that the Jena Band had originated from groups of these "wandering Choctaws." This was seemingly corroborated by early Louisiana travelers such as John Sibley, William Dunbar, C. C. Robin, Henry Marie Brackenridge, and others who noted numerous hunting parties of Choctaws in central Louisiana. It was also supported by the fact that several migration trails traversed the modern Jena area.[49]

A truism about the Federal Acknowledgment Process, like all historically based inquiries or legal proceedings, is that commonsense assumptions can be deceiving. The Jena Band's apparently likely origins seem to bear this out. As the band hired researchers and underwent BIA analysis, scholars found indications pointing to more recent origins of the band. No links were found directly connecting the modern group's ancestors with the various wandering bands mentioned in nineteenth-century sources. Instead the band's researchers found written testimony given before the 1902 Dawes Commission, census records, and a brief ethnography by pioneer linguist Albert Gatschet (1886), all indicating that the band had coalesced between 1870 and 1880 from several family groups who had migrated to LaSalle Parish, Louisiana, from Mississippi, and not earlier as previously believed. Testifying before the Dawes Commission, John Allen (Hatubbee), who was between seventy and eighty years old, stated that he had been born in Scott County, Mississippi, and that he only had lived in Louisiana for fifteen years. Using U.S. Census records, genealogist Sharon Sholars Brown and an anonymous Branch of Acknowledgment genealogist confirmed latter origins. Ancestors of the band do not show up on censuses of Catahoula Parrish in 1870 but do appear in 1880, apparently indicating that the Louisiana band formed between those years. (Catahoula Parish was divided to create LaSalle Parish in 1910). Read together with Choctaw oral testimony before the Dawes Commission and as told to Gatschet, the census documents seem to confirm that the band originated from several 1870s Choctaw migrant families from Scott and Newton Counties in Mississippi and not among earlier immigrants as the band and existing published works had suggested. According to scholars Hiram Gregory and Brian Klopotek, the new evidence forced living Jena Choctaws to reevaluate their origin beliefs, with most coming to accept the new evidence as fact. In a rare meeting of the minds between tribal researchers and BIA scholars, both sides agreed that the details of the Jena Band's manner of forming a community in central Louisiana might never be known. As the BIA historian concluded: "Their exact date of arrival, route of migration, and place of origin remain obscure"—and so they likely will remain in the foreseeable future.[50]

The Economic Life of the Early Jena Choctaw Community

Available documentation provides a fairly concrete picture of the economic activities of the Jena Band of Choctaws during the first decades of its ancestral community. For reasons still obscure, progenitors of the Jena Choctaws came to reside on plantations owned by the Bowie and Whatley families near Manifest and Eden, Louisiana, respectively. These communities are near Jena, the county seat of LaSalle Parish, a rural hub that grew into a regional commercial center beginning in the 1880s. While oral tradition recalls that the Indians once lived in the forests by traditional means, most modern scholars doubt this, as the region was fairly well settled by whites by the time the Jena ancestors arrived in the 1870s. What is clear is that a form of paternalism and dependency developed between the local landowning families and the Jena Band's ancestors. The inequalities are apparent as the local whites referred to the two groups as the "Bowie Indians" and the "Whatley Indians." Whatley store ledgers and census data reveal that the Choctaws worked largely as sharecroppers, domestics, and day laborers. Most purchased goods on credit from the local Whatley store while growing fruits and vegetables in family gardens. Band members augmented their diet with fish and game taken from the local woodlands. Several men tanned deerskins and a few women made baskets for sale. Available records from the late nineteenth and early twentieth century reveal a trend common among southeastern Indian groups. Band members gradually discarded traditional subsistence practices and items of material culture that accompanied them, such as hunting weapons and mortars and pestles for grinding grain. They replaced them with items more easily purchased and obtained from local stores.[51]

INTERMARRIAGE, TRADITIONAL RELIGION, AND LANGUAGE

Like most remnant southeastern Indian enclaves, the Jena Band was extremely isolated from non-Native society until World War II. Separation stemmed both from social and legal discrimination and from self-imposed isolation. The segregation of the Jena Choctaws would have profound impacts on the group's subsequent recognition battles, leaving them with ample markers of continuing indigenous heritage, including high Choctaw blood quantum, surviving traditional religion, and language retention. In their research the Jena Band scholars and BIA employees identified ten core ancestral families. In 1880s-era records, progenitors of the Jena Band possessed the surnames Allen, Gibson, Lewis, Jackson, and several others. Traced through time, the 1900 U.S. Census for LaSalle Parish showed eight Choctaw households under family heads Joe Allen, Thomas Tell (Williams), Victoria Wilson (Williams), Samuel Gibson, Emily Batice, Willis Berry, John Allen, and Henan Allen. Two families of Lewises lived in nearby Catahoula Parish under family heads William Lewis and Mary Lewis. Significantly, most of the Jena ancestors also maintained Choctaw names. While confusing to latter researchers, the fact that John Allen also went by Hatubbee, Sam Gibson by Machantubbee, and Willis Berry by Ahlapintubbee, presented strong and compelling evidence of the group's lack of assimilation at the beginning of the twentieth century. Encouraged by federal officials, several families removed to Oklahoma between 1902 and 1916. Although this was almost the death nail for the community, the group was saved by the migration of the Lewis clan ("Bowie Indians") from Manifest, Catahoula Parish, to the Jena area in 1917. From choice and racial discrimination, these families intermarried almost exclusively with each other, to the point that the Jena Band was essentially one large extended Native family, overwhelmingly bearing the surnames Lewis and Jackson. Until the late 1950s when intermarriage with whites began, approximately 85 percent of all marriages recorded in the Jena Choctaw community were between members of the band. The net effect was that local whites did not challenge their race. In 1932 the LaSalle Parish School Board

Figure 7. Choctaw Indian boys, Jena, Louisiana, 1950s. (Photograph courtesy Louisiana State Library, Louisiana Collection)

superintendent wrote that "there are about fifteen full-blooded Choctaw Indian children in this Parish . . . they will not, and should not, attend our negro schools." In their recognition petition the band could claim that in 1940 the band consisted of 84 percent full-bloods. The rate of full-bloods was 18 percent as late as 1980. when the band asserted that an additional 46 percent were half-blood or higher.[52]

Although not required by the BIA, the retention of traditional, clearly aboriginal religious practices and beliefs is highly persuasive evidence for securing tribal and non-Indian support in acknowledgment efforts. Allowed uncommon access because she aided the band's recognition research, PhD student Marilyn Watt found that the band still maintained pre-Christian spiritual beliefs well into the 1980s. Members believed in a form of spirit called Konacosha who took the form of a little man. "Little People" such as this could be harmful or beneficial. They also could bestow the gift of curing, a traditional form of medicine still found among the Jena elders. Members believed that witches lived among the community with evil spirits or little "Devil Men" to do their bidding. Taking the form of whirlwinds, balls of orange fire, or owls, the witches and evil spirits were often blamed for harm befalling individuals in the community. Manifestations of the dead could come in the form of cold gusts of wind, a ghostly voice, or animal guise. While the band's embrace of Christianity weakened these traditional beliefs, Watt noted that they were still strong among elders, who cited them as fact. They were cited as almost-fact among Choctaws in their thirties and forties. Watt ultimately concluded: "What was particularly striking in the Jena Choctaw community was the prevalence of such distinctive beliefs in the community today [1986]. They were not regarded merely as interesting or even bizarre stories to be related to someone unfamiliar to the community."[53]

The lack of interest in the band by local Christian denominations resulted in the Jena Choctaws retaining other religious customs much later than many other southeastern Indian enclaves. Racism and economics also played a role. Several sources note that local white churches did not welcome the small Choctaw group to take Communion. As a result, the group was largely unchurched until the 1930s, maintaining its own local burial customs and its own White Rock Indian Cemetery. The BAR anthropologists determined that group members maintained mourning practices such as refusing to cut their hair or to remarry until one year after the death of a loved one. Traditional marriage ceremonies overseen by Choctaw leaders were maintained from a combination of exclusion from Christian churches and from the high cost of obtaining a marriage license from the state.[54]

Of all the factors in the Jena Band's favor, its retention of an unusually high degree of fluency in the Choctaw language was paramount. No other marker of ethnicity is more persuasive to both Indians and non-Indians alike of the existence of a living aboriginal community. As the related Mississippi Band of Choctaw noted in their endorsement resolution in favor of the Jena group, the interlocking family ties and social isolation from non-Indians encouraged the Jena Choctaw retention of the Bogue Chitto dialect of Choctaw, common on the reservation in Mississippi. At a time when many other southeastern Indian remnant groups were perilously close to losing any trace of their native tongues, Jena Choctaw testimonies before the Dawes Commission in Muskogee, Indian Territory, in 1902 revealed that most applicants spoke no English, forcing the commissioners to conduct most business through an interpreter. Office of Indian Affairs correspondence written in conjunction with federal educational aid during the 1930s demonstrated that the Jena Indians still were largely monolingual in Choctaw. In fact, the entire impetus for funding education was the fact that a local teacher was shocked that the Jena Choctaw children had limited capabilities in English. While several reservation communities in the Southeast, such as the Eastern Band of Cherokees of North Carolina, the Seminoles and Miccosukees of Florida, and the Mississippi Band of Choctaws, maintained significant numbers of native speakers into the 1990s, among unrecognized groups, only the Jena Band of Choctaws could claim the same. In Louisiana anthropologist Pete Gregory found that only the Jena Band and the Coushattas could be considered still having native speakers in the early 1990s. At the time of the band's recognition in the mid-1990s, the BIA anthropologist found that eleven of the twenty-three Choctaws he interviewed were fluent in Choctaw or had been fluent as youths and could still understand the language. There was one elder who was entirely monolingual in Choctaw. At that date, this level of language retention was highly unusual even among reservation-based tribes in the American West. It was almost unheard of among unrecognized communities.[55]

SOCIAL AND EDUCATIONAL DISCRIMINATION
IN JIM CROW LOUISIANA

The ill effects of Jim Crow segregation and other forms of institutional racism figure less prominently in the oral tradition of Jena Choctaws than in most southeastern Indian communities. This fact seems to stem from the extreme social and geographic isolation of the Indian community and the small size of the group during the height of segregation in the South. No widely used pejorative terms like "Sabine," "Cro," or "Cajan" attached to the tiny group near Jena, although group members do remember that local whites viewed them as untrustworthy, thieving people. Group oral tradition recounts how local sheriffs would harass group members when they came to Jena on Saturdays to socialize and shop. The Jena group was so small, overlooked, and dependent on paternalistic white land owners that the parish governments provided no Indian schools for group members, institutions that served as social cores of other southeastern Indian communities and provided them some measure of outside validation of their Indian heritage. It is clear, however, that locals never questioned the Indian identity of the Jena Choctaws. They were simply segregated in rural isolation, a fact that promoted retention of aboriginal cultural elements while strengthening internal cohesion among group members.[56]

During the New Deal era of the 1930s the small Jena Band came to the attention of both the Office of Indian Affairs and local school officials. Beginning in 1929 Choctaw leader Bill Lewis had pushed the local school board to create a summer literacy program for Choctaw children. A few years later a local schoolteacher, Mattie Pennick, became interested in the Choctaw children's educational deprivation after seeing several swimming in a creek on a school day. Upon inquiry, Pennick was shocked to find the children could not speak English and became determined to do something to help them. The "Pennick Indian School" that operated at several locations between 1932 and 1938 was funded by the Indian Office through tuition payments for Choctaw children in attendance. Federal involvement with the Jena Band's education prompted several government letters and other correspondence later validating the Indian heritage of the local Choctaws. In letters between Edna Groves, superintendent of Indian education at Cherokee, North Carolina, and Mississippi Band of Choctaw Agency superintendent A. C. Hector, these federal agents repeatedly refer to the Jena "Indian families" while noting that they "are Choctaw and speak the language." At the same time, local Indian advocates caused a brief stir of activity in the Bayou State, which prompted local journalists and Indian agents to search Louisiana for so-called "lost Indians." Whereas other 1930s-era federal investigations by Roy Nash and Ruth Underhill emphasized the racial ambiguity, problems in proving tribal origins, and lack of proof of blood degree of other Louisiana Indian groups, agents involved with the Jena Choctaws exhibited no such doubts or questions about them. The various reports on the Jena people never questioned their Choctaw heritage.

Two other Louisiana groups did receive similar educational assistance to that given to the short-lived Pennick Indian School. The Coushattas near Elton and the Chitimachas near Charenton both had federal Indian schools, with BIA officials pointing to this fact in providing formal recognition for these tribes in 1972 and 1917 respectively. The Jena Choctaws' educational assistance abruptly was ended amid allegation of fraud committed by Mattie Pennick. The termination of the school led, however, to the most significant federal activity related to the Jena Band in the twentieth century prior to federal acknowledgment in 1994.[57]

A Mid-Twentieth-Century Indian Removal Plan

With the failure of local education at Jena, A. C. Hector, superintendent of the Mississippi Choctaw Agency, planned to remove the two core Jena Choctaw families to the Pearl River section of the Mississippi Choctaw Reservation. No other remnant southeastern Indian community was so unambiguously associated with a recognized tribe that federal officials considered removing it to a federal reservation. In 1938, J. M. Stewart, director of lands for the federal government, expressed no objections to the planned move. William Beatty, the noted education director of the BIA, remarked that the removal idea was "an excellent one." On July 11, 1938, acting commissioner of Indian affairs William Zimmerman gave his approval for the plan. Correspondence indicates that the Jackson family was in favor of relocating to Mississippi. When A. C. Hector left his post later in 1938, the new superintendent, L. W. Page, at Philadelphia, Mississippi, was not in favor of the approved plan. In closing the Jena Choctaw case, he noted: "We should delay

Figure 8. Choctaw students with teacher (*left*) and mother (*second from right*), Pennick Indian School, LaSalle Parish, Louisiana, 1930s. (Photograph courtesy Louisiana State Library, Louisiana Collection)

transferring any Louisiana Indians into Mississippi until the Mississippi Indians have been cared for." The flurry of federal interest in the Jena Band thus subsided, and the group quietly slipped from public consciousness as the country entered World War II.[58]

MODERNIZATION AND ASSIMILATION, 1945–1974

As with most Native American communities, World War II and the immediate postwar era would prove a watershed for the once-isolated Jena Choctaw group. Members were exposed to the larger world and sought greater economic and social opportunities outside the Jena area. Forces outside Louisiana were also promoting greater integration of small ethnic enclaves such as the Jena Band. A basic starting point was public education. For reasons still unclear, in the mid-1940s the local school board admitted Choctaw children to white facilities for the first time. In the same era the majority of Choctaw families moved to "town," meaning that they settled inside Jena proper. These trends ended their geographic isolation from non-Indians, as they now lived side by side with whites and went to school with non-Choctaws. The Jena group was responding both to economic forces and to desires among individual members for social and financial betterment. The Whatleys began selling off their estate, while other farmers turned to mechanized harvesting procedures, each pushing Choctaws off the land. Many Choctaw men had served in World War II and were dissatisfied with life upon returning to central Louisiana. They increasingly left for the oil fields or for nonagricultural work in nearby Alexandria. At the same time, most members became Christian, with many joining the Nazarene Church. As they had no "Indian church," religion further promoted integration. The first Christian burial of a Jena Choctaw was recorded in 1937, and traditional practices soon ebbed. These forces together led to significant levels of assimilation into the white community. After 1959 no new marriages were between Choctaw members. Although elders still promoted marriage between Choctaw couples, the group's tiny size and Christian and other taboos about marrying cousins soon put an end to intra-group unions. Mixed marriages and educational levels in turn precipitated a decline in the prevalence of Choctaw language use in homes.[59]

The Jena Choctaw group did not disintegrate during this era as with many other unrecognized groups. Family ties and mutual needs promoted social solidarity even as forces of modernization and integration promoted the opposite. Judging from statistics from the 1980s and 1990s when conditions had improved, group members were poorer than other residents of the Jena community. Only one-third of members had high school degrees and virtually none attended college. Unemployment was above local averages and most Jena Choctaws lived in substandard housing. The majority of Choctaws had to rent because they were unable to obtain home loans. A study found that 90 percent of members reported alcoholism as a leading social problem in the community. Because many members lived within walking distance, Jena Choctaws pulled together to help the disadvantaged. Social and financial commitments served to ease the continuing problems of poverty that still plagued the group even as some members assimilated into the larger, non-Indian world.[60]

REVITALIZATION AND FORMAL ORGANIZATION, 1960–1974

In a truly complex interplay of seemingly contradictory impulses, during the 1960s and early 1970s several younger, educated Jena Choctaw leaders emerged, using their education and organizational skills to gain advantages for the band, and succeeded in part by appealing to their ancestors' traditional poverty and aboriginal culture. Discussed earlier, Louisiana was rocked by Red Power protests, pan-Indian organizing, potential land claims, the African American civil rights movement, and other forces originating outside the state. Vine Deloria, Jr., the American Indian Law Center, NARF, and other legal-oriented forces were entering Louisiana to try to help the isolated communities organize and promote their legal rights through land claims and other avenues. As was common among Louisiana groups such as the Houmas, who had traditionally avoided association with African Americans in the biracial South, the Jena Choctaws remained aloof from larger civil rights struggles. Researcher Marilyn Watt found that the Jena elders wanted no part in the public antics of the Louisiana Red Power forces such as the Indian Angels—their rural and conservative heritage was too strong. One Choctaw man remarked that he wanted nothing to do with those "out-of-state Indians" he characterized as mixed-race, Plains-style wannabes, who were "part of that bunch of communists who took over Alcatraz."[61]

Because of their traditional conservative leanings, the Jena Band largely was absent from the key stirrings of reform in Louisiana Indian affairs. Even so, once established, the younger Jena Choctaw leaders were quick to seize the benefits of newly created Indian forums and Indian aid programs emanating outside traditional Indian channels. In response to Native demands, the state of Louisiana created the Governor's Commission on Indian Affairs in 1972 to serve as a liaison between the state and local tribes. In the same era, Indian activism far from Louisiana and public sentiment spawned a host of Indian funding programs outside the BIA and its orbit.[62] Because the Jena Band's last traditional leader, William Lewis, had died in 1968, the Governor's Commission on Indian Affairs took the initiative to organize the Jena Band of Choctaw Indians in 1974, first holding a meeting at the local courthouse. Outsiders helped the band write a formal constitution and articles of incorporation that provided for the election of a new five-member council and chair, all foreign to the traditional, kinship-based organization of the Jena Choctaws. While traditional leadership flowed to the eldest male, the new council (by conscious decision of the band) was young and educated and not selected by seniority. Jerry Don Jackson recalls that he and his younger cohorts were almost militant, getting together and trying to figure out how to "keep the tribe going." The young Choctaws were driven by the fact that they were "just as good" as the nearby recognized Coushattas who were receiving federal aid. State recognition followed in 1974 with a formal state resolution, but anthropologist Pete Gregory characterized the state declaration as symbolic, certainly not based on formal research. The band held an "Indian Day" that year to celebrate, inviting members of the Oklahoma Choctaws and Mississippi Band to attend.[63]

Like with the Poarch Band of Creeks, the new Jena tribal organization and leadership provided tangible benefits to tribal members, a fact that promoted allegiance and dependence upon the new institution. In 1974 Jerry Jackson was elected the first chairman, although he was soon replaced by Clyde Jackson, who would be the group's most visible leader in the next few decades. At age forty-four Mary Jackson was the oldest council member. The new tribal organization had formal membership requirements that mirrored traditional regulations under BIA governments. For membership, Jena Choctaws had to prove one-quarter Choctaw blood quantum from an ancestor listed on federal censuses of 1880, 1890, and 1910. At this point economic development and tribal cohesion were the major forces driving tribal leaders. With a HUD grant, the Jena Band completed a tribal center. With its tennis courts, pool tables, and small offices, the center soon became the locus of the tribal community. Jena parents gained a Title IV Indian education grant to start a successful program. The tribe began providing free haircuts, tutoring, school supplies, and Choctaw-language classes for its youth. The band also provided a CETA job training program, limited health and dental care, and drug abstinence programs. The Mississippi Band of Choctaws subcontracted an ANA grant in1981 that helped the Jena Band run its tribal offices and pursue its recognition petition research. In 1984 Clyde Jackson became the executive director of the governor's Indian commission. He was replaced as tribal chairman by Jerry Jackson, who would serve in this role from 1986 through the group's federal acknowledgment in 1994. These leaders and others on the council would spearhead the Jena Band's lengthy battle to secure recognition.[64]

INTO THE FEDERAL ACKNOWLEDGMENT PROCESS

Despite having what Bud Shapard, former head of the Branch of Acknowledgment, called one of the clearest cases for recognition he

had ever seen, the Jena Band of Choctaws struggled for over a decade
to secure federal tribal status. The BIA anthropologist who interviewed
group members found that prior to formal organization of the group
most Jena Choctaws had not seen themselves as a "tribe." They viewed
themselves as Indians almost by default. Motivations for seeking formal
recognition, like most communities, varied considerably among individuals. Clyde Jackson wanted to assert his ethnic pride and obtain
outside validation that his people were Native Americans on equal par
with other Native peoples. Others saw recognition as a vehicle for
funding. As Jerry Jackson recalls, a letter he received from the BIA
confirming his eligibility for Indian scholarships based on his full-
degree Choctaw blood made him start thinking about getting benefits
for his people that others like the Oklahoma Choctaws were receiving
as tribes. As Jackson's experience reveals, Jena Choctaw leaders were
moving toward a more formal, sovereignty-based approach in their
dealings with outsiders. Clyde Jackson summed up his thinking: "In
thirty years [one] of the things that I have had to overcome . . . it's
making these people see, look they're not just dealing with me, they
are dealing with a tribal government; I represent that government."
With Clyde and Jerry Jackson at the lead, the Jena Band of Choctaws
was active in Louisiana Indian politics outside its specific acknowledgment struggle.[65]

Garnering outside help from the Association on American Indian
Affairs and winning a federal ANA grant, the Jena Band began researching its acknowledgment petition in 1979, unwittingly entering a process
described by its creator in later years as "arduous" and by knowledgeable
observers as "lengthy, cumbersome, and expensive." After submitting
a completed petition in 1985, tribal leaders received an "obvious defi-
ciency" letter from the government, informing them about the problems
with their petition and issues that would need to be addressed to secure
acknowledgment. After hiring a professional genealogist and outside
anthropologists, the Jena Choctaws eventually submitted a 570-page
document within a few years and waited for what members thought
would be automatic recognition. Optimism sprang in part because the
nearby Tunica-Biloxi Tribe had rather easily secured acknowledgment
in September 1981 with what its scholars Pete Gregory and Vine Deloria, Jr., had viewed as a model case that the Jena people also felt they
possessed. The Tunica-Biloxi Tribe's ease of success unfortunately would

not be the case for the Jena Choctaws, despite the fact that they possessed more visible markers of aboriginal heritage than their neighbors.[66]

THE JENA BAND'S LEGISLATIVE RESTORATION ATTEMPT

Like the vast majority of groups impatient with the BIA, the Jena Band attempted to circumvent the process by appealing to their congressional delegation for a quicker remedy: legislative recognition. Unfortunately the band experienced the sting of rejection despite its rather unambiguous case for recognition. As discussed elsewhere, by the time their restoration and recognition bill came before Congress in 1990, forces had hardened against any group attempting to bypass the BIA process. Their experience provides a prime example of factors working against groups seeking congressional recognition, even ones with clear Native American heritage.

Through the governor's commission and the Inter-Tribal Council of Louisiana, Clyde Jackson and others had made valuable contacts that the uninitiated would have thought made for clear sailing for the acknowledgment bill on Capitol Hill. Although Indian gaming had entered the picture when the Chitimachas opened their bingo parlor in 1988, the obvious Indian identity of the Jena Choctaws overcame any financial concerns over their recognition from nearby tribes. They ultimately secured the highly important support of all the federally recognized tribes in Louisiana: the Tunica-Biloxi Tribe, the Chitimacha Tribe, and the Coushatta Tribe. More significantly the Mississippi Band of Choctaws under powerful chairman Phillip Martin issued a resolution supporting the Jena Band, stating that he and his council "[h]ave no doubt they are descendants of the Mississippi Band of Choctaws," possessing tribal surnames and speaking their language.[67] The group gained the valuable aid of Bud Shapard, former head of the BIA acknowledgment office, and longtime Louisiana senator J. Bennett Johnston was the major sponsor of the Jena bill in Congress. Though in 1988 he had cautioned against extending legislative recognition to any group, citing the Clifton Choctaw community in his warning, Louisiana governor Buddy Roemer came to heartily endorse the Jena Band. In his statement, the governor said he supported the Jena Choctaws because they had such strong documentary evidence and had agreed not to pursue land claims against the state. The Louisiana State congress passed resolutions in favor of the band while the state Indian commission lobbied for the Jena group as well.[68]

The Jena Band ultimately failed in its attempt to secure a legislative remedy—but not for the reasons that other groups generally have not succeeded. The Jena group failed more from poor timing and the BIA's fear of setting a bad precedent than any doubts about their authenticity. The group's supporters wisely took the position that they were really having their status "restored" rather than recognized for the first time. They made this argument based on the BIA's approval of the band's 1937 removal plan to Mississippi, an act the band believed recognized them as an Indian community. In arguing his case before Hawaii senator and Indian advocate Daniel Inouye in 1990, Jena chairman Jerry Jackson stated that his band was already recognized, saying, "We fell through the cracks of bureaucracy," which left "a legacy of suffering and poverty."[69] Jackson supported his case by emphasizing that the band's 150 members would cost the government little to service. He also noted that releasing them from the Federal Acknowledgment Process and its research burden (paid largely through federal grants) would save the government well over $100,000. The BIA strongly opposed the bill, however, correctly arguing that 1930s contacts did not constitute formal recognition of the Jena group as a tribe. It also incorrectly feared that the group might have ceased to exist as a coherent body after the 1930s. Despite the BIA opposition, legislators tend to look at other factors when deciding a case. Showing the commonsense approach generally taken by members of congress, in hearings on the Jena Bill, looking at Jerry Jackson, Senator Inouye asked Bud Shapard rhetorically: "History would seem to indicate that, notwithstanding the semantics or the technicalities, the man sitting at the witness table is a Native American, is that correct?" Because Jackson's Native ancestry was so apparent, Inouye told the band he would recommend their bill's passage in the strongest terms. The Jena bill made it through both houses of Congress only to be pocket-vetoed by the president, George H. W. Bush, in 1992.[70]

MEETING THE CRITERIA

In analyzing the Jena Band's submitted documentation, the BIA historian concluded, in an extremely rare statement in the annals of the Federal Acknowledgment Process: "No one has denied the Indian identity of the petitioner."[71] While outside studies of many other regional groups such as the MOWA Choctaws and Lumbees often centered on their racial mixture and ambiguity, the BIA correctly concluded that the Indian, and more importantly Choctaw, identity of the Jena group was never in question. Federal censuses, viewed by the BIA as among the best forms of documentation, clearly listed the Jena ancestors in 1900 and 1910, and in earlier censuses as Indian or Choctaw (or both). A special Indian schedule for LaSalle Parish listed the ancestors of the Jena Choctaws as "Full Blood Choctaw." Highly important in proving identity were the efforts of the Jena Band's ancestors to secure enrollment and allotments in the Choctaw Nation of Indian Territory in the early twentieth century.[72]

In 1902 all of the Jena Choctaw families with the exception of the two Lewis families in Catahoula Parish applied for inclusion on the final rolls of the Choctaw Nation. In 1893 Congress established the Commission to the Five Civilized Tribes, more popularly known as the "Dawes Commission" after its chairman, senator Henry L. Dawes of Massachusetts, to enter into agreements with the tribes in preparation for the final dissolution of tribal governments and allotment of their communal lands to individuals and families. The commission's work raised a question about Choctaw and other tribal citizens who had remained behind in the South and what rights they still maintained to share in the lands and resources of their parent tribes. In the Choctaw case, the Treaty of Dancing Rabbit Creek (1830) contained Article 14, a provision that allowed tribal members to remain in Mississippi so long as they took allotments and agreed to live under state law. As later government reports confirmed, thousands had remained in the East, particularly in the states of Mississippi, Alabama, and Louisiana. The Curtis Act of 1898 authorized the Dawes Commission to determine who among these could share in the proceeds of its work. It posted circulars, had notices printed in newspapers, and made trips to Mississippi to locate eligible individuals. As interpreted by the commission, those who could prove their ancestry and agreed to remove to Indian Territory within six months could share in the dissolution proceedings.

The commission was flooded with requests, the majority being fraudulent. Government agents determined that the commission could not adequately determine who had made a "good faith effort" to comply with the 1830 treaty because of a lack of records stemming from the negligence and fraud of the Office of Indian Affairs agent in charge of allotting lands in the Southeast. Commissioners ultimately concluded that full-bloods, determined by visual inspection and oral testimony, were exempt from having to provide documentation to prove their heritage. Mixed-bloods would have to provide written records. According to tribal tradition and surviving historical writings, Jena Choctaw families under elders John Allen Sr., Samuel Gibson, and Willis Jackson traveled on foot to Muskogee, Indian Territory, in 1902 to make their applications. Ultimately, based on testimony and the apparent Indian ancestry of the group, the Dawes Commission determined that twenty-two of the twenty-seven were "full-blood" Mississippi Choctaw Indians eligible to secure allotments if they removed to Oklahoma within six months. Of the group, only four, under family heads Ida Umber and Emily Batice, chose to trek to Indian Territory. Because of the short notice, the long distance, and reports of problems in Indian Territory, the rest of the Jena group remained in central Louisiana.[73] Possessing Dawes Commission records listing blood quantum and tribal identification proved important, however. Although perhaps not reflective of the reality of bloodlines and actual percentage of Choctaw ancestry, to government officials federally produced rolls are sacrosanct, used to determine the Certificate of Degree of Indian Blood (CDIB) and overall eligibility for Indian programs. Among remnant southeastern tribes, only the Jena Band possessed records of their blood degree approaching this high level as defined by the BAR regulations.

For the rest of the twentieth century, the Branch of Acknowledgment determined that the Jena Choctaws possessed other sufficient documentation of their Indian identity. The 1930s federal records provided "high evidence" of their Choctaw identity during that era. Researchers found sporadic local newspaper articles from the late 1930s, 1940s, and 1950s that identified the Jena community as an Indian entity. Surprisingly few academic studies were made during the twentieth century on their group. However, in light of the scholarly emphasis that persisted until the early 1970s on apparently ambiguous "tri-racial isolates" it is clear that the Jena Band's lack of ambiguity led to its lack of appeal to scholars. The Louisiana Choctaws simply did not fit the theoretical model they were pursuing. The activity surrounding the Jena Band's formal organization in 1974 and its tribal visibility thereafter proved sufficient evidence to the BIA that the tribe was identified as Indian for the rest of the century.[74]

Proving Historical Community and Political Leadership

As the Jena Band was an offshoot of the Mississippi Choctaw people who refused to remove to Oklahoma after 1830, it had to prove that its members had lived in a distinct community from the middle of the nineteenth century until 1994, the date it secured a positive decision from the BIA. In terms of proving "community," it is apparent that the Jena Band benefited somewhat from going through the government process in the years after its first decade, the decade in which the Poarch Band was reviewed. On the negative side, the Jena Band experienced a much longer wait, as the level of documentation required by the government dwarfed the data found in the earlier Poarch Creek case. Despite the band's high degree of surviving indigenous culture and government documentation of its Choctaw ancestry, the Jena Band languished over a decade in the bureaucratic process. Its only advantage came in going through the process after revised regulations were in place, especially as they regarded establishing "community" and "political authority," two of the most bedeviling criteria under the BIA rules.[75]

With revisions to the Federal Acknowledgment Process in 1994, the BIA set benchmarks for proving community existence and political authority. Upon showing that 50 percent of marriages were among community members, a group automatically established that it was a distinct community. If it proved that its membership resided within a small core geographic area, the group would also establish the existence of "community." If groups maintained unique cultural practices such as speaking a Native language, the same would hold. As proving the existence of tribal leaders or chiefs who exercised "authority" over members was the most ambiguous of the BIA criteria, the revised regulations now assumed that once a group had met its burden proving "community" up to a certain point in time, it automatically had proven the existence of political leadership as well.[76] In the Jena case, the BIA assistant secretary tended to rely on intermarriage rates when deciding in favor of the band. The BIA determined that from 1820 until 1950 at least 85 percent of marriages had been between band members. Although not required by the BIA regulations, the fact that the Jena group established that almost all of these individuals were "full-bloods" meant that the group could claim a high degree of Indian ancestry, which in government circles is a good indication of the existence of a close-knit Indian enclave. The Branch of Acknowledgment also noted favorably that since 1880 at least 50 percent of members had resided within twenty miles of Jena, and 72 percent had resided within thirty miles.[77]

Like the vast majority of groups seeking tribal acknowledgment through the BIA process, the Jena Choctaws would face more problems in confirming that their community had continued to exist after World War II. The trouble arose because postwar forces of modernization were dispersing the once-isolated rural enclave. It is also clear, however, that the BIA had markedly increased the level of detail it required approximately ten years after the Poarch Creeks had gone through the process. In the end, compared to their much larger neighbor, the United Houma Nation, the Jena Choctaw enclave's extremely small size, interlocking kinship ties, and location in the small town of Jena together made it easier for the BIA to overlook so-called gaps in the record and to recognize the community existence of the Choctaw enclave.

As the BIA noted, by the 1950s the ironclad markers of community ties, including housing clusters, intermarriage, and Choctaw language fluency had declined dramatically. After 1959 band members married almost exclusively white individuals, with children of these mixed families losing the ability to speak the Choctaw language. Although some members recalled that the white families involved were not happy about these unions, they also noted that gradually the white and Indian families came to embrace each other. Traditional marriage customs, religious beliefs, and burial customs also declined during this time, as the majority became Christians. Even so, the BIA determined that the band continued to use and maintain the exclusively Indian White Rock Cemetery, and the government researcher concluded that maintaining the cemetery was a central community activity. Through interviews and observations government agents determined that the group's 159 members regularly visited each other, kept track of each other via phone calls, and gathered at neighborhood homes to keep up with tribal goings-on. Group members continued to assist each other in times of need as well. The Branch of Acknowledgment ultimately determined that after World War II the majority continued to live in LaSalle, Grant, and Rapides Parishes in the vicinity of Jena (as 60 percent still did in 1994). While noting that simply living in close proximity does not prove community, the BIA researchers ultimately concluded that the group did maintain community ties from World War II to 1994, the date of acknowledgment. As the BIA anthropologist noted: "The children and grandchildren, whether residents of Jena or not, had a strong core community of all Indian parents, grandparents, aunts, and uncles, thus providing a 'home base' for families or individuals who had moved from the Jena area in search of jobs." This conclusion and the level of analysis differs markedly from the BIA's analysis of the United Houma Nation, a group with over seventeen thousand members, that faced palpable skepticism and intense scrutiny of its social relations, even though the vast majority of its members also lived in several adjacent parishes in southern Louisiana.[78]

Having met the benchmarks for community until 1950, the Jena Band did not have to undergo an intense analysis of its political functioning prior to that date. The BIA did find evidence, from oral tradition corroborated by interviews with local whites and several newspaper articles, that the band had formal chiefs before the 1960s. By tradition, the eldest male served as chief. The group maintained a list of men who had served as chief: John Allen (1850–1910), Sam Gibson (1910–1916), Bill Lewis (1917–1933), Will Jackson (1933–1950), and Chris Jackson (1950–1958). As noted by Choctaws and confirmed by a smattering of non-Indian sources, tribal chiefs had several functions within the community. Men like Bill Lewis enforced standards of conduct among Indian youths, in Lewis's case carrying a bullwhip and scaring the children into submission. Leaders officiated at weddings and funerals, and they also enforced mourning customs. Men such as Will Jackson led efforts to maintain the tribal cemetery and served as liaisons with the non-Indian community.[79]

Under the acknowledgment regulations, for the period after 1950, the band did have to prove that its leaders exercised significant functions within the community, a burden that has proven onerous and sometimes impossible for other southeastern tribes, such as the United Houma Nation. By the Jena Band's own account, traditional leadership was breaking down after the death of Chris Jackson in 1958, largely because of a major division between the Lewis and Jackson families. As with proving community existence, the Jena group benefited from its small size and interlocking kinship ties when proving political leadership. The BIA records tend to show that it accepted at more or less face value the assertions made by the band in regard to its political leadership. The government determined that the home of Chris and Alice Jackson (a traditional curer and midwife) served as the primary locus of community activities during the 1950s and 1960s. As noted, the group's last traditional eldest male leader died in 1968 and by most accounts he was not a very respected or influential individual. After 1974, a younger, elected council and chairperson replaced the earlier leadership structure. After that date, the Jena Band had clear evidence of its tribal political functioning, complete with tribal center, tribal council, meeting minutes, and outside state and local recognition of its leadership. Beyond the existence of the council, the acknowledgment team determined that the band's members had a strong interest in tribal politics—election participation was high. The tribe itself was important to band members, providing tangible leadership and benefits, facts that promoted allegiance to the body. In light of its evidence and commonsense judgments of the BIA staff, the Jena group had met its burden of proving that the majority of its members resided in a distinct Indian community under tribal leadership.[80]

DESCENT FROM A HISTORICAL TRIBE

The Jena Band had unimpeachable documentation of its Choctaw ancestry. It possessed government Indian rolls, Indian Office memoranda and letters, and federal censuses that showed that its ancestors were Choctaws—records the BIA deems "high evidence." The band also had an unusually high, proven blood quantum, with 50 percent showing that they were one-half or more Choctaw blood in 1990. One nongovernment scholar intimately knowledgeable of the bureau's process (and who prefers to remain anonymous) believes that the BIA should have required petitioners to have at least one-fourth blood quantum to secure recognition. He feels that this requirement would have limited the intense discord that has surrounded the process since its inception in 1978. While that was not mandated under the BIA regulations, this researcher (like many conservative Indians) believes that having this degree of Indian ancestry speaks volumes as to community relations and cohesion and points to the unambiguous existence of a viable Indian tribal enclave. High intermarriage rates among confirmed Indian individuals also tend to result in offspring that phenotypically "look Indian," avoiding the accusations and recriminations common in recognition politics that certain groups "don't look Indian to me." Although fraught with potential misconceptions, to many parties high Indian ancestry and visible appearance are commonsense markers of whether a group is "Indian" or not.[81]

As discussed previously, federal censuses from 1880, 1900, and 1910 unambiguously noted the Choctaw ancestry of the group's ancestors. Under its constitution, the Jena Band requires members to possess at least one-fourth Choctaw blood traced from ancestors listed on the above baseline documents. Most of the membership also descends from individuals listed as "full-blood" Mississippi Choctaws by the Dawes Commission. Unlike many other groups, such as the Poarch Band of Creeks who declared every ancestor listed on its baseline rolls as "full-blood" even if they were not, the Jena Band's recorded blood percentage is reflective of the reality of their Indian ancestry. As such, in a rare scenario, the BIA declared that 100 percent of the Jena membership could prove descent from individuals listed in federal censuses as Choctaws; 88 percent descended from "full-bloods" identified by the Dawes examiners. Photos included in the Jena Band's restoration petition before Congress leave little doubt that the group is of Indian descent. Together with the existing government records, the Jena Band had an extremely rare, entirely unambiguous pedigree. As assistant secretary for Indian affairs Ada Deer noted when proposing to acknowledge the band: "No one has denied the Indian identity of the petitioner."[82]

RECOGNITION COMES TO THOSE WHO WAIT

Jena Choctaw member Mary Jackson had a dream one night in 1995 that something joyful was about to happen. It came true the next morning when her daughter Cheryl Smith, a future tribal chairperson, called with the good news: the Jena Band finally had been recognized. As Cheryl recalled later: "When it came on the news that the Jena Choctaws had received recognition, it was like, I don't know, I was in a dream or something because I never, never thought—that we'd ever get it. It was just something too monumental for us few little people here to ever get." Though viewed by many as a panacea for the group's ills, it remained to be seen whether tribal recognition was the magic tonic that could undo a century of discrimination, poverty, and neglect, but for the moment the people were happy to have the simple acknowledgment that they were a bona fide Native people, "just as good" as their recognized neighbors.[83]

THE POARCH BAND OF CREEKS AND JENA BAND OF CHOCTAWS COMPARED

Very few groups from the southeastern United States who have petitioned for federal tribal acknowledgment have succeed in proving they are viable, surviving Indian tribes—exactly three since 1978. This has led to the perception that it is virtually impossible for presently unrecognized indigenous peoples from this region to establish a tribal identity using the rigorous regulations promulgated by the BIA and vociferously supported by tribal governments, including all of the Five Tribes of Oklahoma and related tribes such as the Mississippi Band of Choctaws and Eastern Band of Cherokees. The experience of the Jena Band of Choctaws and Poarch Band of Creeks proves this perception incorrect. Leaders of the Creek Nation, Choctaw Nation, Mississippi Band of Choctaws, and others supported both of these once-unrecognized Indian enclaves, but the support stemmed from these groups' possession of very different forms of proof. The Alabama Creeks had virtually no surviving elements of aboriginal culture and a fairly high intermarriage rate with whites, but they did possess a cache of written documentation proving they were who they said they were: descendants of Creek Indians who did not remove to Indian Territory in the 1830s. The Jena Band of Choctaws, on the other hand, could not prove exactly how their band originated but could show evidence that they were Indians and, more important to Choctaw people, that they were Choctaw Indians: people who still spoke the Choctaw language, intermarried with other Choctaw Indians, and maintained aboriginal religious traditions. Both clearly were surviving Indian communities in the aboriginal homelands of the Creek and Choctaw Nations. They were both fortunate in having evidence to prove it.

CHAPTER 4

Contested Tribes

The Lower Muskogee Creek Tribe and the
MOWA Band of Choctaw Indians

Galasneed Weaver sits on his lawn chair under an oak tree, patiently fielding questions, his calm, confident air betraying a lifetime of leadership in service to his people, the MOWA Band of Choctaw Indians. It is early October and the day is beautiful—warm and sunny. The wind carries a faint trace of coolness that provides relief from the long humid southwestern-Alabama summer that is only recently fading. Mr. Galas, as his community members lovingly call him, has a comfortable, middle-class home within sight of other MOWA Band members' homes in a traditionally Indian community about thirty miles north of the bustling port of Mobile. Mr. Galas is clearly a bit suspicious at first, but he quickly warms to me, and tells story after story detailing his battles to improve the lives of the MOWA people. At nearly eighty years old, Mr. Galas has seen the struggles and triumphs of his group play out before his eyes. Active in his local Baptist congregation at Reeds Chapel, Weaver recalls the day Baptist missionary B. Frank Belvin, a well-known Choctaw minister and brother of longtime Choctaw Nation chief Harry J. W. Belvin, encouraged him to accept a baseball scholarship and attend Bacone College, an institution founded for Indian students in Muskogee, Oklahoma. While attending Bacone, Weaver met the love of his life, "Miss Laretta," as she is locally known, a Cherokee from eastern Oklahoma. They married and after graduation returned to Weaver's home in southern Alabama, where both went on to distinguished careers in education. Laretta Weaver dedicated her life to Indian children while stealing precious moments to practice her art.

Mr. Galas became a high school principal and one of the most important leaders of his people, encouraging several generations of youths
to follow his path to Bacone and other institutions of higher learning
once thought beyond the reach of local Indian students.[1]

Although he has lived his whole life as an Indian and faced discrimination as an Indian, Mr. Galas is a member of a tribe that not
everyone accepts as legitimate, and some people think he is not even
an Indian at all. The BIA has concluded that the MOWA Band is really
a black–white "mulatto" people with little Native American ancestry.
Leaders of the nearby federally recognized Mississippi Band of Choctaw
have been overtly hostile to its aspirations, and the Cherokee Nation has
placed it on its "Fraudulent Indian Tribes" list. These fairly recent
developments truly trouble Mr. Galas. Although the MOWA Band of
Choctaw Indians is considered an Indian tribe by the state of Alabama
and many Native organizations, it is currently struggling to affirm its
identity as a surviving aboriginal people, with many forces and historical realities allied against this.

While there are dozens of state-recognized Native groups in the
Southeast, the histories of the MOWA Band and the nearby Lower
Muskogee Creek Tribe of Georgia provide important insights into the
reasons why certain groups have failed to win universal acceptance as
Indian tribes in America today. The Lower Muskogee group grew out
of the postwar Indian renaissance while the MOWA Band has very deep
roots in Southern soil, and although their histories are very different
both have failed to secure federal tribal acknowledgment. Critics
believe the Lower Muskogee Creek Tribe is a recently formed entity
with some verified Native ancestry. Their confirmed Creek heritage has
won the group some acceptance as a surviving Indian enclave. The
MOWA Band of Choctaw Indians, on the other hand, is a long-standing
community, although one whose Indian ancestry and exact tribal heritage are shrouded in mystery and controversy. Few Americans are
aware that not every group that calls itself a tribe is a long-standing,
historical entity. Few non-Indians also realize that today many recognized
tribes view contending groups on a continuum, from the truly bogus
to those that are worthy of federal acknowledgment. The MOWA Band
and Lower Muskogee Creek Tribe sit somewhere on the continuum,
not on the clearly fraudulent pole but also not completely on the accepted
end of the spectrum. The community profiles of both groups and the

historical documentation that exists about them reveal much about the complexities of claimed Indian identity in the Southeast.

THE LOWER MUSKOGEE CREEK TRIBE EAST OF THE MISSISSIPPI

ORIGINS

The Lower Muskogee Creek Tribe East of the Mississippi is based at the Tama Reservation outside the small town of Cairo in southwest Georgia. The tribe arose out of the work of the Indian Claims Commission of the post–World War II years. In 1950 Calvin McGhee, a largely uneducated, "dirt poor" farmer from the Creek community at Poarch, Alabama, heard about the claims tribunal and called a mass meeting at Poarch where participants formed the Perdido Friendly Creek Indian Band in order to pursue a potential claim. The next year the new group changed its name to the Creek Nation East of the Mississippi and established a formal twelve-member council. This entity would serve as the basis for all subsequent new Creek Indian groups and "tribes." In 1958 McGhee had a vision: he would unite all Creek descendants in the Southeast in an Indian-oriented political movement that stressed their land rights and pride in Native heritage. The movement would also support racial segregation, states' rights, and Republican President Dwight D. Eisenhower. As a political philosophy, McGhee believed there was strength in numbers, and the Creek leader took to the road to enlist support.[2] Later described as the Martin Luther King, Jr., of the Eastern Creeks, Chief McGhee (as he had become known) proved central to the southeastern Creek renaissance that followed. While doing genealogical work he and others located living descendants of Creek Indians who had refused to remove to Indian Territory, many of whom were unaware that they had Indian ancestry. From his base at Poarch, McGhee traveled widely, enlisting thousands of descendants to pursue a land claim, raising awareness that Creek Indians still existed in the Southeast. Numerous observers credit the Creek chief with starting the "Creek Movement" that spawned several groups, including the Lower Muskogee Creek Tribe of Georgia. As long-time Creek scholar Tony Paredes concludes, "If not for Cal McGhee there would be no Cairo group."[3]

McGhee soon found that the Muscogee (Creek) Nation of Oklahoma had previously filed a claim for over twenty-three million acres
illegally taken in Alabama under the Treaty of Fort Jackson. His group
nonetheless wanted to join the suit. The events that followed would
cause much confusion and generate feelings of legitimacy among all
the Creek descendants. After an initial denial, the claims court allowed
the Eastern Creeks to intervene, determining that they were an "identifiable" Indian group able to pursue the cause of action. The Indian
Claims Commission allowed groups of proven descendants to file under
Docket 21, while not specifically ruling on their tribal identity, a fact
not comprehended by most Creek plaintiffs at the time. The claims
work generated the first contact between the Eastern Creek descendants and the Oklahoma Creek government since the mid-nineteenth
century. According to longtime Poarch Creek chairman Eddie Tullis,
the Oklahoma Creeks opposed Chief McGhee's eastern group because
they accepted the BIA position that all Creeks had removed to Oklahoma in the nineteenth century. The Oklahoma Creeks also felt that
McGhee's people were trying to infringe on Oklahoma Creeks' money.
Because of the commission's ruling allowing them to intervene, however,
the Creek Nation of Oklahoma came around to accepting the eastern
relatives so long as they could prove their ancestral connection to the
nation.[4] In time, Waldo Emerson "Dode" McIntosh, principal chief of
the Creek Nation, became a major friend of McGhee's group, especially after he reconnected with Arthur Turner of Florala, Alabama, who
like the Oklahoma chief, was a direct descendant of chief William
McIntosh, Jr., a prominent Creek leader from the Revolutionary War
until the removal period. Dode McIntosh began attending reunions
with Turner and other long-lost family members in Alabama, using
these occasions to update Eastern Creeks on the claim's status. In
1970 Chief McIntosh invited Turner, Vivian Williamson, and several
other Eastern Creeks to a meeting in Oklahoma as his guests.[5] During
the 1950s and after advertisements were placed in local newspapers
seeking descendants for the class-action suit, eventually over seven thousand came forward to claim their share of the so-called "Indian money."
The BIA was charged with compiling a list and contacting individuals
descended from Creek Indians who had stayed in the Southeast after
the mass removal. Despite the importance of the claims case in spurring the reemergence of Eastern Creeks, the monetary return was
relatively paltry. The overall award of approximately $3.9 million was

substantial, but as it was spread among thousands of descendants, in 1972 each member received only $112.13, as previously mentioned. A later judgment provided several million more dollars divided among approximately thirteen thousand claimants. Many, like Bill Smith, an Eastern Creek dance leader, simply framed the un-cashed check for $112.13 as a symbol of pride and recognition of their Indian heritage.[6]

By all accounts Chief McGhee and his Creek Nation East of the Mississippi based at Poarch, Alabama, was the center of the Creek community and activity up until 1970, when he died of a heart attack while attending a funeral. By this time, fissures and factions that would characterize Eastern Creek politics already had emerged. Some members wanted to be leaders in their own right, while others disagreed as to how to disburse the claims money. Eddie Tullis echoes a common belief, recalling that it seemed that a number of groups had "just sprung up" at the time, mainly seeking "the Indian money." These individuals were derisively called "Docket 21 Indians."[7] As early as 1966 McGhee had faced a rear assault from a group seeking to go its own way, dissatisfied with his handling of the claims case. In 1969 Arthur Turner, energized and emboldened by his familial and personal relationship with Dode McIntosh began efforts to create his own tribe based in his hometown of Florala, Alabama, a small town just north of Pensacola, Florida, that was also relatively close to the future Lower Muskogee Creek Tribe's home base in Cairo, Georgia. Unlike some members of the southeastern Creek organizations, Turner had solid claims to being a Creek Indian. In his early sixties at the time, Turner had descended from Catherine McIntosh, a daughter of William McIntosh, Jr. Catherine had witnessed her father's murder in 1825 for signing a treaty that illegally ceded the Creek Nation's land. Thereafter she and several relatives moved, first to southern Alabama and then to Walton County in the panhandle of western Florida. Here Catherine and her descendants lived in a small rural community along the Shoal River, where the group continued the McIntosh pattern of intermarrying with whites and assimilating most aspects of the Anglo-American culture.[8] In 1969 Arthur Turner's group organized as the Principal Creek Nation and held its first powwow at Florala, with many Florida Creeks present. The first powwow ever held in the region, the Florala event was attended by Calvin McGhee, as well as individuals from nearby Pensacola, including Perlocca Linton, Vivian Williamson, and several others who had long been active in Creek activities. Dode McIntosh attended many of the

Principal Creek Nation's meetings and he soon appointed Arthur Turner his "town micco" or personal representative in the area. The "mother tribe" of the new Creek groups, the Principal Creek Nation gained Alabama state recognition in 1971. Future Lower Muskogee Creek tribal leaders Neal McCormick and John Wesley "Wes" Thomley were active in the new tribe, with McCormick listed as "vice chief" and Thomley as "medicine man." There was a degree of intermingling between members of the new Principal Creek Nation and the existing Indian community at Poarch. For example, current Poarch Band of Creek Indians chairman Buford Rolin was actively involved in Pensacola-area activities at the time.[9]

The Lower Muskogee Creek Tribe East of the Mississippi divided from Turner's new tribe in 1972. That year McCormick, his wife Peggy, Thomley, Thomley's wife Billie Ruth, Vivian Williamson, and others filed papers with the state of Georgia to incorporate under this name. The impetus for this action appears to have been political conflicts between these and other Creek leaders, and a growing division between the various Creek descendant organizations and the core Creek community at Poarch. McCormick reported that the primary cause was Arthur Turner stepping down as leader of the Florala group, and stated that he and Thomley did not accept Turner's hand-picked successor. After the death of the charismatic and energetic McGhee in 1970, leadership of the Creek Nation East of the Mississippi fell to his son Houston, a middle-aged carpet factory worker. Houston was described as an unassuming, behind-the-scenes leader, a striking contrast to his father. According to existing records, Houston and many Poarch Creeks were offended and concerned by the formation of the Principal Creek and Lower Muskogee Creek organizations, seeing them as an affront to the primacy of the Poarch community and as "Johnny-come-lately" Indians in general.[10] The division between the Poarch community and the others only widened over time. In 1984, after the Poarch Band received federal recognition, open conflict erupted over the disbursement of residual claims money, with Eddie Tullis intoning, "We've got to be sure these people who are running around saying these things are really Indians." To this Thomley responded, "Poarch up there thinks they are the only Creeks in Alabama and Northwest Florida."[11]

A central event in the history of the Eastern Creeks occurred in February of 1973. That year Houston McGhee called a meeting at Poarch to reunite the various factions, later sometimes called the Creek Unity

Conference. At this meeting a concord was reached: the Creek descendants agreed to form the "Tri-State Tribal Council," with Poarch-
based chief Houston McGhee as principal chief. At the conference
he appointed McCormick "chief of the Georgia Creeks" and Thomley
"chief of the Florida Creeks." Thomley's branch soon incorporated
under Florida law. The unity and amity proved short-lived, however, and
personal rivalries and animosity returned. McCormick and Thomley
had their own ambitions. Peggy McCormick also complained that it
seemed "everybody wants to be chief" and that too many were breaking
away to form their own tribes. As discussed elsewhere, the Poarch-
based Creeks were increasingly trying to distance themselves from the
other groups. Many in the Poarch group believed that it was the only
true Creek "community"—one that had lived as Creek Indians and
faced discrimination as Indians—and that it had a better chance at
federal recognition if it jettisoned the other groups. Within a year of
the unity conference the Poarch Band and the other Creek organizations began to cut ties.[12]

The dynamic leadership of Neal and Peggy McCormick and John
Wesley Thomley proved central to the continuing existence of the
Lower Muskogee Creek Tribe. Eddie Tullis recalls that all three had
"big personalities." Neal "Pappy" McCormick was the guiding force
behind the organization in its infancy. Hollywood casting could hardly
have created a more colorful, if improbable, Indian chief. Tall at approximately six foot, four, McCormick often wore a cowboy hat, vest, and a
pair of high-priced cowboy boots. Tony Paredes recalls that McCormick
was a "country-and-western version of an Indian chief." Although
McCormick seemed to be mixing cowboy and Indian images freely,
Eddie Tullis recalls that he "was a true Southern gentleman" and "a
real character." Born in 1909 into a sharecropping family in Wing, Alabama, Neal left a life of rural poverty for a chance at stardom, his musical
virtuosity providing his ticket out. From a family of musicians, McCormick
had learned to play all the family instruments by ear. According to a
biography written by his only daughter Juanealya, who performed with
her father, McCormick had Creek ancestry and grew up with this knowledge. After inventing an early form of the electric guitar, Neal formed
a band called the Hawaiian Troubadours. According to the biography,
McCormick passed as Hawaiian to hide his Indian ancestry in Jim Crow
Alabama, Florida, and Georgia, the states he most toured. Because Neal
and his first wife Nancy Jane were like parents to the traveling young

Figure 9. Chief Neal McCormick (*glasses*), Peggy McCormick (*left*), and their children, with Georgia governor Jimmy Carter (*center*) and unidentified official (*right*), 1973. (Photograph courtesy of Georgia Archives, Small Print Collection, spc 22-080)

band members, they affectionately called them Pappy and Mama. Trying to make it big, McCormick moved to Nashville, though he later returned home, operating a dance hall called the Barn Dance in Panama City, Florida, where his band regularly played. He also had a radio program, becoming a well-known local radio personality. Over the years the McCormick family lived in Pensacola, DeFuniak Springs, and Panama City, Florida, as well as Dothan, Headland, and Florala, Alabama. McCormick is most known for hiring a sixteen-year-old named Hank Williams (who also reportedly had Indian ancestry), giving the future country music legend his start. McCormick also created a four-sided, revolving steel guitar called "the contraption" that once was displayed at Roy Acuff's museum in Nashville. Over the years McCormick played guitar for the likes of Tex Ritter, Ray Price, Gene Autry, and Ernest Tubb. True fame eluded him, however, which perhaps played a role in his new gig as Indian chief.[13]

John Wesley Thomley was also a central figure in the early years of the Lower Muskogee Creek Tribe. In an affidavit, Thomley noted that he was born in Semice Springs, Monroe County, Alabama, on June 4, 1925, a great-great-grandson of John Semoice, a "Friendly Creek" granted land under the Treaty of Fort Jackson. He was raised in a farming community: the family grew much of its own food and slaughtered hogs and other animals. Thomley's father was a preacher who would often preach at the "Indian settlements" in Poarch. By the mid-1970s Thomley was a heavyset, middle-aged paper-mill worker in the Pensacola area. Though he had not been raised in Poarch, local Indians and scholars generally accepted his Indian ancestry. Eddie Tullis notes that "there was no doubt he was a Creek Indian."[14] According to Tony Paredes, who was also familiar with Thomley in the 1970s, "he looked Indian," and could prove he descended from Creek Indians who had settled Monroe County in the early nineteenth century. Thomley was active in early Creek affairs and was respected by the Poarch community, especially because he was the first to show up at a powwow wearing a genuine Creek outfit. Eddie Tullis recalls Thomley fondly, noting, "[He] was a good friend of mine."[15]

Peggy McCormick was by most accounts the real driving force behind the family and the new tribe. She and Neal divorced in the late 1970s and he moved back to the Pensacola area, leaving the tribe to her and the children. Afterward she became the undisputed leader of the organization. As a teen, Peggy, who was a powerful gospel singer, had performed with the McCormick Band where she became close to Neal, and they married when she was only sixteen. In later years she became an evangelical preacher of some skill. According to existing accounts, Peggy had difficulty proving her Indian ancestry, although Eddie Tullis believes that she "had more Indian in her" than Neal had in him. Peggy was prone to mysticism, believing she had a psychic connection to Mary Musgrove, a famous Creek woman of the eighteenth century. Peggy believed that Musgrove gave her powers to bestow Indian names and blessings on group members. She and other Lower Muskogee tribal members took part in Indian protests and got involved in state tribal issues, but were careful not to offend local whites—they often repudiated the activities of AIM, while stressing their loyalty and patriotism. In time, however, Peggy began demanding monetary compensation and the return of the "Old McIntosh Reservation" in Carroll County, Georgia, actions that engendered opposition from the local park at the site. Peggy McCormick, now Peggy Venable, is still active in tribal affairs, and by most accounts, so busy that she is hard to reach.[16]

There were other lower-level leaders of the group, some of whom later dropped out or formed their own tribes. The McCormick children, raised at the Tama Reservation, became leaders in their own right. At one point son Tommy was a clan chief, though he is currently a recording artist in Florida. Son Nealie, a police chief, is the current chair of the Georgia Council of American Indian Concerns. In the early 1970s Vivian Williamson was an active leader. She created her own organization in 1973, and was founder and "clan mother" of another new group, the Tukabatchee Clan, active around Pensacola in 1976. Perlocca Linton, who helped with Calvin McGhee's movement and later helped organize the Lower Muskogee Creek Tribe, by 1976 had formed her own tribe in Pensacola and was involved in a public relations battle with Eddie Tullis and other Creek leaders. Many other former leaders defected and formed their own organizations, a primary characteristic of the Eastern Creek groups.[17]

THE TAMA RESERVATION

As they embarked on their journey of ethnogenesis, the McCormicks dreamed of establishing a reservation for the new tribe. With their purchase of 102 acres in 1974 the group had a land base on which to build the dream. They named the tract the Tama Reservation, after a traditional Creek town, Tamalithi. The Tama Reservation became vital to the visibility of the group, giving the impression that they were an aboriginal community of long duration. What the reservation meant to the McCormicks was personal, but the term "reservation" has powerful connotations to average Americans, implying a political entity with a long-standing recognized history. People coming upon the Tama Reservation would rarely realize that the community was largely a reservation in name only, lacking federal status, exemption from local regulations, and other attributes associated with federally recognized enclaves. Shortly after signing the deed for their land, group members found archaeological remains and claimed that they were of Creek origin, seeking to establish an ancient link.[18] In 1976 the McCormicks secured a proclamation from the Georgia governor, George Busbee, acknowledging the site as a reservation, although exactly what that meant was ambiguous from the start. In 1974, both John Wesley Thomley and

Neal McCormick had made attempts to secure federal tribal recognition, actions that had failed to garner immediate attention. As an incorporated entity, however, they were eligible for a host of federal programs outside the BIA orbit. Early on, the McCormicks received an $85,000 grant through USET that was administered by Peggy McCormick. They used the money for arts and crafts training, though the Lower Muskogee organization was soon accused of mishandling funds, causing a permanent rift between the Tama group and USET.[19] The Lower Muskogees also secured a small Manpower Development and Training Act grant and enlisted VISTA volunteers to build structures at the site. With this aid and much labor, the group ultimately built a small community at Tama, and by 1977 thirty individuals lived on the land. The site included the homes of the Neal and Peggy McCormick's sizable family, a trading post, a "model Indian village," and a dance stadium, and it grew in population, ultimately housing over fifteen families. A sign out front welcomed visitors to "Tama Tribal Town" with images of a tribal fire, sun, and corn.[20]

Shortly after forming, the Lower Muskogee Creek Tribe had secured several forms of state recognition that would add to its public credibility. In 1973 Georgia governor Jimmy Carter signed a proclamation recognizing Neal and Peggy McCormick's group as a tribe and commending it for helping preserve Indian culture in the state, and the Georgia legislature followed later that year with its own recognition legislation. Carter's proclamation specifically noted that Neal was the great-great-grandson of Creek chief William McIntosh, seemingly affirming the current group's genealogical and symbolic relationship to an ancestral Creek past. In 1976 Governor Busbee again recognized the group as a tribe when he issued the proclamation declaring Tama a state Indian reservation. Neal McCormick was central to the efforts to create the Georgia State Commission on Indian Affairs as well, and he was appointed an early commissioner.[21] His daughter's biography of him contains many pictures of Chief McCormick in full headdress and fringed buckskin, with his Indian-dressed family members in tow: clearly the McCormicks had succeeded in becoming the public face of Indianness in the state in the 1970s. As with those organizing nearby groups such as the newly created Southeastern Cherokee Confederacy, Neal and Peggy's new roles gave them prestige. The majority of members of the rising tribes in the area were of poor or working-class backgrounds, and by claiming or rediscovering an Indian identity they found a sense of empowerment and even renown. All over the area formerly ordinary citizens gave themselves titles: principal chief, elder of the nation, chief-over-all-clans, war chief, tribal mother, chief council orator, among others.[22] Neal's daughter wrote that he "was elected as the Principal Chief of the Lower Creek Nation East of the Mississippi River. In this nation, this is *equal to being elected President of the United States* [emphasis added]." Neal received numerous honors and commendations from the Georgia senate and house on behalf of his efforts for Indians in general. As the state became enthused about the rediscovery of Indians in their midst, the McCormick family reaped benefits, becoming something of local celebrities in the process. The Lower Muskogee Creek organization was later removed or voluntarily left the state Indian commission, in part because of conflicts between the McCormicks and other groups. In one case the McCormicks charged that illegitimate Cherokee groups were cropping up, taking money intended for real Indians.[23] The tribe later secured new Georgia recognition legislation in 1993, over the vocal protests of Cherokee Nation principal chief Wilma Mankiller, representatives of the Creek Nation of Oklahoma, and the Florida Seminole and Miccosukee Tribes.

During the early and mid-1970s, Alabama, Georgia, and Florida were buzzing with Indian activity, groups were organizing powwows, newspaper articles regularly appeared highlighting local Native American activities, and news was spreading of educational and social welfare benefits available to Indians. The Lower Muskogee Creek organization at the Tama Reservation was one center of this activity. It served as the nexus for several dynamic individuals who were responsible for engineering various Cherokee-named groups in the region. Many soon-to-be chiefs of Cherokee tribes, such as Malcolm Webber, attended events at the Tama Reservation. Witnessing the energy at Tama, Webber formed his own tribe, called the Etowah Cherokee Nation, in nearby Quitman, Georgia, and went on to a strange career discussed in the next chapter.[24] William Jackson formed the most important entity, the Southeastern Cherokee Confederacy, based in his home in Albany, Georgia, a small town near Cairo. In 1976 Jackson, now calling himself Chief Jackson or Rattlesnake Jackson, formally organized the Southeastern Cherokee Confederacy with a set of by-laws. It later secured status as a nonprofit corporation under Georgia law. In December of 1976, Georgia governor Busbee "recognized" the group for its contribution to state culture. In subsequent years nine local governments in some way replicated the proclamation recognizing the efforts of Jackson's organization to preserve Cherokee culture and history in the state.[25] Showing the cross-fertilization going on at the time, Jackson's brother, Jim "Little Hawk" Jackson, later told a reporter: "It was the Lower Muscogee Tribe east of the Mississippi that got us going. Six or eight years ago at a Creek pow-wow in Cairo, we got organized."[26]

The Georgia senate bill recognizing the Lower Muskogee Tribe clearly noted its tourist value to the state, pointing to a major organizational thrust of the group at Tama. According to Bud Shapard, the primary creator of the BIA acknowledgment regulations, when he visited the McCormicks he thought their attempt to create an Indian tribe "was so bad it was funny; it was so obvious they put it together to bilk the government out of money." The Tama Reservation represented a unique mixture of 1970s communal spirit with Nashville-style commercialism, which was exciting or off-putting depending on one's viewpoint. As early as 1970 boosters in the small town of Florala, Alabama, had showed unbridled enthusiasm for the efforts of local Creeks such as Arthur Turner to revive an Indian tribe in their town. The local *Florala News* ran story after story on the new tribe. A December 10, 1970, article had a large photo showing Arthur Turner, H. M. Stewart, V. R. Stewart, and Loree Wallace holding spears and tomahawks and dressed in pan-Indian style costumes: full headdresses, fringed buckskin shirts, and moccasins. The writer excitedly noted that they had brought "to the annual Pow Wow Days in Florala an outstanding group of ceremonial dancers. They are always dressed in colorful costume and really liven things up with their rhythmic movements and dance to the beat of drums."[27] In 1977 the Lower Muskogee Tribe established a corporation to promote economic development. Talk of creating an "Indian Disneyland" was swirling around southwest Georgia and southeast Alabama at the time, and the Lower Muskogee Creeks purchased ten acres in 1980 near Hermosa Springs, Florida, for potential tourist development. The local Cairo, Georgia, newspaper and other town boosters offered enthusiastic support for the new reservation's efforts to create a historical, Indian-themed park at the site. In a typical occurrence, local business leaders were made "honorary members" and then, not surprisingly, tended to support the new tribes' economic aspirations. The same went for local politicians who became honorary tribal members, and then predictably supported the Creeks' political aspirations.[28]

During the 1960s countercultural communes sprang up across the country, with members often trying to create Native American–inspired institutions. Residents of New Mexico's famous New Buffalo Commune lived in tipis, grew Indian crops, and tried their best to live in "social harmony" in a stereotypically Indian vein. There was a clear identification with the oppressed, including African Americans, Vietnamese, and well-known Native leaders Geronimo and Crazy Horse. The McCormicks and their followers also had visions of creating a better society at Tama that was identified strongly with their oppressed real or imagined indigenous ancestors. Early on, Neal and Peggy announced what they referred to as the "Dream of the Creeks." It consisted of a McCormick-led effort to "induce Creeks to return to the lands of their forefathers."[29] To fund the dream, the Lower Muskogee Creeks held an annual powwow which had overtly profit-oriented characteristics: a fee was charged for entry, and the tribe had a monopoly on the sale of food and crafts on the site. With all the excitement around Indian issues at the time, the event was no small affair: the group claimed upwards of fifteen thousand attended annually. At the powwow the group had a booth where it solicited new members. Funds raised in this way were used to purchase the 102 acres at Tama, and the effort was so successful that the group paid off its mortgage in 1978. The Tama Reservation's growth was not unusual or inherently questionable. Other groups, including many that are currently federally recognized, conducted similar activities during the era.[30]

Compared to those organizing most other new tribes in the Southeast, Neal and Peggy McCormick and Wes Thomley were remarkably successful at Tama Reservation. Longtime show people and entrepreneurs, the McCormicks in a brief time established a base for their version of an Indian community: a theme park complete with amphitheater, "authentic" Indian village, chapel, camping sites, and nature trails. The McCormicks also effectively created a true community at the site, with a small residential population and a store. Tama Reservation currently has between fifteen and twenty families, mostly living in mobile homes on "tribal land" held by the organization, and an unpaid Pentecostal minister provides services at the chapel. Tama also has a powwow complex, several permanent homes, and a "living Creek village" with a dancing square, re-created summer and winter Creek dwellings, and a reconstructed Creek cooking house.[31]

INVENTED AND AMALGAMATED CULTURAL TRADITIONS AT TAMA

In addition to erecting physical structures, the McCormicks and their followers made a concerted effort to create a new amalgamated white–Indian culture at the Tama Reservation in the mid-1970s. Group members were based in the evangelical, rural southern white culture of the region, and they imported or manufactured various Creek and pan-Indian forms as needed. As Teresa Lofton, a sociologist who has studied the group extensively, has found, the Lower Muskogees represent a pure case of ethnogenesis. They created an ethnic group at Tama, identified themselves primarily in reference to their Creek ancestors, and engaged in a process of renewing tribal structures. Essentially they created a new ethnic community where none had existed previously. They also marketed the whole creation at the reservation, engaging in an old American tradition of "selling the Indian." As revealed in their seminal work *The Invention of Tradition*, Eric Hobsbawm and Terence Ranger first demonstrated how seemingly ancient cultural forms have often, in fact, been recently created and invented to serve the present needs of ethnic and social groups. As Hobsbawm noted, inventing traditions "is essentially a process of formalization and ritualization, characterized by reference to the past." The Lower Muskogee Tribe was certainly engaged in the invention of traditions at Tama. Similar to incidents detailed in the Hobsbawm and Ranger book, it is clear that few visitors knew just how modern and fabricated the Tama "traditions" were. Part of Neal and Peggy McCormick's "Dream of the Creeks" was not only to establish a home for the Creeks but also to reestablish "authentic" Indian culture that would induce pride in their heritage.[32]

The Lower Muskogee Creek Tribe's social construction of a new culture and identity raises important questions. If many group members sincerely believed they had Creek ancestry, even if it was not necessarily true, were they fraudulent in their efforts? At what point (if any) will their new tribal traditions become accepted and considered authentic? In time, will the fabricated nature of these traditions even matter?

Before the self-conscious project at Tama, Wes Thomley, the McCormicks, Arthur Turner, and members of the Poarch Creek community had developed a more organic, ceremonial "powwow" tribal culture in the region. Tony Paredes recalls that the Eastern Creeks, even those at Poarch, had lost virtually all elements of aboriginal Creek culture by this time and had to borrow and cobble together various Indian traditions

as they went along. They had Boy Scouts and other Indian lore enthu-
siasts help them learn Indian dances and develop "authentic" costumes.
As the Creek descendants did their best to introduce Indian costumes
and dancing, they melded them with regional traditions such as fiddling,
square dancing, and Grand Old Opry music. In one case Jacqueline
Linton Collins combined what the press called "Indian dancing" with
jazz styling. Thomley, Turner, and Calvin McGhee made sure to wear
colorful headdresses to "chief" for the cameras. Group members wore
all kinds of pan-Indian, Plains-style clothing and jewelry in public to
increase their visibility. Some women scandalized the more conservative
by wearing their version of "Indian maiden" outfits that consisted of
skimpy buckskin-fringed dresses and knee boots. Although these actions
are controversial today and lead to questions about authenticity, Eddie
Tullis, who was often teased for having a buzz-cut hairstyle, feels that
this activity was necessary to get the public's attention and to educate
them that Creek Indians still existed in the South.[33]

In many ways the Tama group was engaging in a timeworn tradition
of "playing Indian," with the twist of actually believing that they were
Native American. As Robert Berkhofer, Philip Deloria, S. Elizabeth Bird,
and others have detailed, Americans have long turned to Indian culture
as an antidote to the ills of a society perceived as being overcivilized:
industrial, urban, and capitalistic. Antimodernism is central to this cultural current, as disaffected Americans looked to the Native American
"Other" for a more peaceful, spiritual, nature-centered, and communal alternative to their own culture. Clyde Ellis has found that the
"Indian lore" movement of the twentieth century—exemplified by the
work of Ernest Thompson Seton, cofounder of the Boy Scouts of
America and creator of the Woodcraft Indian Movement, hobbyists
Reginald and Gladys Laubin, and others—likewise romantically conceived of ancient Indian cultures as having valuable attributes that could
teach overcivilized American children valuable traits such as generosity,
resourcefulness, and closeness to nature. Participation in Indian-oriented
events also offered an escape from everyday life. Undoubtedly individuals involved with the "Creek Movement" were steeped in a culture
where Boy Scouts, Indian Guides, and Campfire Girls were ubiquitous.[34]
Many were intimately directly connected with the Boy Scouts. In 1976
in the Pensacola area a group of people calling themselves the Tucka-
batchees created a dance group of not only local Indian descendants
but also many Eagle Scouts who learned Native traditions and dances

through the organization. It is clear from existing records that they also drew heavily from Hollywood and pulp fiction in their re-creation of Indian culture. This is not surprising since its members had lived through or come of age in the 1950s, the golden era of the Hollywood western with its stereotypical images of Native Americans. Similar to the Woodcraft Indians of an earlier time, the various Creek-named groups began to create tribes, new traditions, and Indian lore, and they also tried to live a version of Indian life as they envisioned it. They soon, as Philip Deloria said, "mimed white-created Indian Others back at white Americans."[35]

In 1976 and 1977 Georgia State University graduate student Amelia Bell Walker spent many weeks conducting fieldwork at Tama Reservation. She later reported that the group represented a dynamic cultural movement characterized by several component parts. Group members generally had a rural southern upbringing and came from working-class or lower-middle-class backgrounds. (According to Walker, several scholars in the early 1970s had noted this, even saying that a western Indian had visited the Mississippi Choctaws and joked, "Are you sure you guys aren't red-necks instead of redskins?")[36] One can feel confident that many observers felt the same about the Tama Creeks, who were from rural backgrounds, politically conservative, and generally adhered to fundamentalist Christian religions. They also were culturally oriented toward country music.[37] These traits were in keeping with the lifestyle of the McCormicks. Additionally, Peggy McCormick was a minister and charismatic preacher, and in this she was not alone: a high percentage of Eastern Creek leaders were evangelical preachers.[38] Peggy regularly held religious services at the Tama Reservation, complete with "old-time" gospel preaching, gospel singing, and "laying on of hands" healing. Because of the strong focus on evangelical, charismatic Christianity, group leaders expressed no interest in traditional Creek religion. In one case they expelled a man after he said he was not a Christian and after subsequent prayers to save his soul failed. Because the adoption of Indian ceremonies had been so recent, there was no syncretism of indigenous and Christian traditions apparent in the religious services so central to Tama life. In fact, group leaders publicly proclaimed that there were no pagan, non-Christian rites taking place on the reservation.[39] The group's approach to spirituality is apparent in something Peggy McCormick said at the time: "The religious ceremonies do not take away from our being Baptists or

Methodists. The religious ceremonies are about our Indian heritage. And whether we call Him 'Master of Breath' or Jehovah, He is God."[40]

As noted, Neal McCormick was a country-and-western singer and had played guitar with many of the era's great country artists, and residents of Tama were treated to professional performances by his band. Other southern cultural traditions carried on at Tama Reservation included bluegrass festivals, CB radio conventions, and religious camp revivals.[41] The darker side of 1970s rural southern culture was evident with the Lower Muskogee Creeks as well. As Philip Deloria states regarding other groups: "Many hobbyists reserved their cultural relativism and tolerance exclusively for Indian people, maintaining racist stances toward other groups."[42] Although most Lower Muskogees reveled in the Indian past and their perceived genetic connection to it, the same could not be said for their stance toward African Americans. Walker reported often hearing the term "nigger" on the site, and in 1976 a reporter quoted Peggy McCormick referring to a USET employee, who accused her of wrongdoing, as "a big, black, nigger-looking liar."[43] Like some white southerners, group members felt little sympathy for the African American civil rights movement. However, their reclamation of an Indian identity allowed people like Neal and Peggy McCormick to assume a minority identity, and they could and did speak as representatives of an oppressed minority that they often contrasted with the larger African American civil rights struggle. While arguing for his rights as a Native American, Neal told a reporter, "The black man is always complaining about his troubles, but the black man did not lose his land."[44] Sociologist Terry Lofton acknowledges that group members shared many of the racist beliefs of southern society, listened to country music, and spoke with thick accents, but argues that these facts alone did not mean they were not "real Indians." She notes that residents of the Eastern Cherokee Indian Reservation also share many of these traits. Lofton feels that the generally negative tone of the few academic studies on the group stems from an anti-southern bias in the scholarly world. Essentially she concludes that outsiders felt that the Lower Muskogee people looked like southern "rednecks" and this was somehow incompatible with "true" Indianness.[45]

In due course the Tama residents blended rural southern traditions with Creek cultural practices learned from books, pan-Indian groups, and media stereotypes. In this they were not alone: Tony Paredes reports that the Poarch Band was doing the same thing at the same time. All the southeastern Creek groups made efforts to appear "more Indian" in the pan-Indian, Hollywood fashion. Group members appropriated symbols of Indianness such as feathers, beadwork, fringed leather costumes, and silver and turquoise jewelry. They also began using various Muscogee words in ceremonies and speeches. The Lower Muskogee group at Tama created a tribal seal with a four-pointed star, with fire, sun, wheat, and corn in its points and a buffalo at its center. Upon enrolling, new members took Indian names, inserted between their first and last names. Wes Thomley went by "Long Pine" while Neal McCormick was "Tall Pine." Peggy "Morning Star" McCormick often bestowed new Indian names as a form of blessing. To look "more Indian," Walker noted, many women darkened their hair. The former red-headed Peggy O'Neal singing gospel with the McCormick family's band was so transformed to the raven-haired Peggy McCormick, tribal chairwoman at the Tama Reservation. When criticized for these actions and the lack of authenticity to Creek roots, Peggy said, "If the public wants feathers, we give them feathers . . . besides who wants to run around in moss skirts today?"[46]

Because the vast majority of members had not been raised in a vibrant Native American culture, establishing links to Indian ancestors, real or imagined, was of extreme symbolic importance. Neal McCormick tied himself to William McIntosh, Jr., the Creek leader executed for treason in 1825. True or not, it was widely circulated that McCormick was McIntosh's great-great-grandson. Likewise, as mentioned above, Peggy McCormick connected herself to eighteenth-century Creek "princess," Mary Musgrove, engaging in actions often associated with New Age adherents of the time. Because Peggy had difficulty proving her exact heritage, she claimed to have inherited supernatural prophetic powers from Musgrove.[47] Hobbyists and New Age devotees generally associate Indians with being close to the land and "one with nature," and a photo in Neal McCormick's biography has a picture of him clad in buckskin and beads with the caption, "Chief Neal McCormick communing with nature in the way of his ancestors." By establishing a reservation in southwest Georgia, in proximity to where William McIntosh, Jr., had lived, and claiming that the Tama site was an ancestral Creek village, the McCormicks were also establishing a symbolic connection to place. In this regard, they implied (and likely believed) that the spirits had brought them to return to the sites of their Creek forebears. The theme of "returning" to their homeland was ubiquitous in press articles

on the group and was promoted vigorously by the McCormicks. Revealing the blended nature of the new identity, however, the group's major
annual powwow was held on July 4, the most significant U.S. national
holiday. The group's essentially white, southern cultural heritage was
clearly evident in a 1976 article on their July powwow. Neal McCormick
was quoted: "I am sure we are the only tribe in the South celebrating
this day. All the chiefs went to Washington, D.C. not long ago . . . all
tribal chiefs were given a chance to celebrate the Bicentennial by the
government and nobody accepted but us."[48]

The overt commercialism of the Tama Reservation led many observers
to label the group inauthentic, "Indian frauds" and "instant Indians."
One called the group an "instant fake tribe." The McCormicks made
no bones about the moneymaking goals of the reservation. Tama had
a "rotunda" with bleacher seating around a concrete stage where the
McCormicks and other groups produced dances and performances
for guests and members. Powwows were also held, where the tribe and
hobbyists set up booths selling wares and foods of all kinds, including
fry bread, jewelry, and tribal T-shirts. At group functions the Lower
Muskogees also solicited new members and donations. The reservation ran the Light Feather Trading Post, where it sold Indian crafts,
groceries, postcards with photos of members dressed as Plains Indians,
and tribal bumper stickers. The McCormicks also operated the Tama
Recording Studio at the site, producing and selling records such as
"Indian Country," a song about the Trail of Tears written and sung by
the McCormick Indian Singers. Today the family continues to write,
record, and perform gospel music as the McCormicks. Lofton, who still
has close ties to Peggy McCormick and her family, agrees that the group
was creating an eclectic culture, essentially defining itself as it went
along, but she rejects the sentiment that it was doing this for primarily
commercial purposes. As she concludes, "Tribal members do not reclaim
Indian identity for the purposes of jobs, money, influence or social
status. They do it for the nonrational reasons that reflect family history,
individual experience and self-meanings." Playing Indian and attracting
tourists necessitates appealing to the Indian past, as the common Indian
image is a primeval one. In this light, Peggy McCormick never hid
her intentions. As she told a reporter in 1974, participating in Lower
Muskogee Creek activities was "like stepping back 200 years in history.
It makes us feel a part of our heritage and history."[49] To attract visitors, Peggy wrote a drama, *Sounds of the Swamp*, which ran during

Thanksgiving. She also wrote, produced, and recorded the songs that were played during the performance. The drama recounted Creek lore, the story of the Trail of Tears, the experience of Creek ancestors who hid in swamps to avoid removal, and the eventual return of the Creeks to Tama. Not surprising, Peggy and Neal were central characters in the drama, playing a young couple.[50]

Toward Recognition of the Group: Scholarship

In October 1978, Neal and Peggy McCormick and Wes Thomley signed a petition seeking recognition as an Indian tribe through the newly created Federal Acknowledgment Process. Like the nearby Poarch Creeks, the Lower Muskogee Creek Tribe was one of the first groups to submit documentation to the BIA. They sent a 246-page petition for acknowledgment, heavy on treaties and government documents detailing the Creek Nation *prior* to its removal to Oklahoma in 1836. It had little concrete evidence on Creek Indians in the Southeast after that date, the period of most importance in proving their case. Group advisors clearly had little knowledge of what would be required in the federal process. They provided no documents linking their group to the historic Creek Nation, and they presented little evidence that their ancestors ever lived as Indians or had inhabited an Indian community. The McCormicks, Thomley, and the others, understandably but erroneously believed that the confirmation by the Indian Claims Commission of some members' Creek ancestry, along with the recognition of their tribe and reservation by the state of Georgia, entitled them to federal tribal status, and that the federal government would quickly recognize them.[51] The McCormicks also surmised that the political connections they had made over the years would pave the way for federal recognition. The Lower Muskogee petition often referred to their "Friendly Creek" ancestry while distancing themselves from the controversial Red Power activities of the 1970s. Clearly leaders like Thomley believed that recognition was largely a political, rather than an evidentiary process—one that they could influence by contacting their members of Congress, referring to their personal friendship with Oklahoma Creek chief Dode McIntosh, and noting past state proclamations.[52]

To gain federal recognition and the support of recognized tribal leaders, the Lower Muskogee Creeks would need historical, anthropological, and genealogical evidence to support their contention that the Tama group was a viable, historic Indian tribe. Scholars who have studied the tribe, however, have not produced reports helpful to their tribal aspirations. As a result, members today are defensive about their identity and reticent to speak to researchers. Modern leaders, including Peggy McCormick (now Peggy Venable), have declined several requests to be interviewed for this book. All existing scholarship on the Lower Muskogee group has in some way questioned their identity and validity as a tribal community. Perhaps most damning is the work of Tony Paredes, the most noted authority on modern Eastern Creeks. In a published article Paredes concluded that "there are many more Creek descendants who gather at pow-wows and other meetings to proclaim their identity as Creek Indians. However, it is only at Poarch [Alabama] that historical forces welded many descendants of the McGhees, Manacs, and others into a unique social and geographic community of Creek Indians east of the Mississippi."[53] Legal scholar William Quinn, Jr., a former ethnohistorian at the Branch of Acknowledgment, was clearly referencing the Lower Muskogee Creek Tribe and similar groups when he described the "Southeast Syndrome," a phenomenon he characterized as "Indian descendant recruitment organizations" sprouting up all over the South after 1970, seeking members with supposed Indian ancestry, forming "tribes" and then petitioning for federal recognition. As previously noted, Walker, the scholar who spent perhaps the most time with the tribe in its heyday, concluded that the Lower Muskogee Creeks were "instant Indians." Most of the in-depth newspaper articles written on the McCormick group in the 1970s in some way questioned the legitimacy of the tribe.[54] One scholar who worked closely with several Creek groups at the time felt that they "did not have a case" for recognition as an Indian tribe. According to this scholar, after researching the group it was clear that they did not "have a social organization" historically.[55] Speaking of the Lower Muskogee Creek Tribe and similar organizations, Paredes concludes bluntly that "there is an ongoing, fascinating sociological phenomenon among certain Southerners seeking to establish an 'Indian' identity that borders on the fraudulent, if not the psychopathological."[56]

Beyond lacking recent scholarship confirming their tribal identity, the Lower Muskogee Creeks possessed few other forms of evidence that could attest to their long-standing existence as a surviving Indian community in Georgia. Their best claim rested on written proof of their Creek Indian ancestry, a form of evidence that many groups lack. Of the approximately one thousand members of the organization when it petitioned in 1978, approximately 38 percent could document their Creek ancestry to the satisfaction of the BIA; 24 percent had shared in the Docket 21 funds of 1972; and approximately 25 percent more had applied for a subsequent award that was pending in 1981. The smaller, related Principal Creek Nation under Arthur Turner proved to the BIA's satisfaction that 81 percent of its membership descended from Creeks who had refused to move west to Indian Territory. The McCormick organization, however, clearly had grown exponentially over time, expanding outward from the members involved in the claims activity. It did so by advertising in local newspapers and setting up booths at local Indian powwows and non-Native events where new members were actively encouraged to enroll. Tribal registrars did not vigorously verify ancestry, thus diluting the ancestral bloodlines. Its ability to document significant Creek descent, however, made the Lower Muskogee Creek Tribe somewhat rare among declined petitioning tribes in the Southeast, in that some group members could document their ancestral tribe with specificity.[57] Also rare was that other regional Indians generally accepted as fact that the McCormick group had Indian ancestry. It was the group's recent origins that made outsiders refuse to believe that the Lower Muskogee Creek Tribe was a legitimate Indian community.

The Lower Muskogees made conflicting arguments concerning the historical continuity of their tribal community. Early newspaper reports and comments by tribal leaders stated unambiguously that the tribe was created in 1972, that it was a "new tribe" that sought to unite all the Creek descendants in the Southeast. As revealed in testimonies of the era, group members often said they got together to reclaim their long-hidden Indian identity. A common belief was that they and their families always "knew" they were Indian but had hidden the fact due to a host of factors, including shame, racism, and plain lack of confirmation of their heritage. The BIA researchers concluded that a Creek identity may have been maintained within families or small clusters of families but that as a tribal organization the Lower Muskogee Creek Tribe did not evolve from an historical Indian community as did the Poarch Band of Creeks. The Lower Muskogee Creek Tribe, concluded the BIA, was created by disaffected leaders like Neal McCormick who separated from the claims-oriented Creeks based in Poarch, Alabama.[58]

Unlike with the Poarch Creek enclave, several factors pointed against the existence of a long-standing, historical tribal community at or near the Tama Reservation in Cairo, Georgia, or one that migrated there. There was virtually no intermarriage between group members prior to the group's creation in 1972. Pappy McCormick, Wesley Thomley, and the others did not produce, and the BIA did not find, any evidence that group ancestors had identified as Indian in the past, either in censuses, tax rolls, or similar documents, prior to signing up for "the Indian money" during the claims litigation. Similarly, none of the early scholarly studies on surviving Indian groups or mixed "racial islands" in the East referenced a Creek community in the Southeast other than the Poarch group, although these studies were clearly flawed. While accepting that the Lower Muskogee group possesses some Creek ancestry, Eddie Tullis and other Poarch Creeks believe that the Tama Reservation group does not comprise a "tribal operation."[59] What do the Poarch Creek Indian leaders mean by this term? One element that they feel points away from the existence of a long-standing indigenous enclave is that the Tama group has clearly had a fluctuating, unstable membership. Within a year of submitting their acknowledgment petition, the Lower Muskogee rolls ballooned from 1,000 to 1,700, something highly unlikely for an authentic ethnic community bound by kinship ties. Membership numbers swung widely up and down as new members signed up at will, with some staying on for years while others soon dropped out as their interest waned. The BIA found that over half of the members listed in 1981 had not been members in 1977.[60]

Several personal stories of one-time Lower Muskogee tribal members seem to confirm the voluntary and unstable nature of the group's membership. Rose Smith is a current and active tribal member. Born in the 1950s, Smith recalls that she was into drugs and alcohol until Neal and Peggy McCormick invited her and some friends to come out to the Tama Reservation. As she puts it, "I always knew in my heart that I was Indian"—her exposure to the Tama Reservation was like "reconnecting with my tribe." As to proving her ancestry, Smith notes: "I don't know my Indian blood percentage; my mother is my connection." However, she remarks that her mother will not admit to being Indian, even today, and her father has no Indian heritage. Smith's parents were never members of the Lower Muskogee Tribe. One of her sons also has not joined the tribe and thinks it "is a joke." After being involved with Tama for some time, Smith drifted away from the group for over thirty years until she had a stroke. She now works for the Tama group, answering phones and sending out promotional literature. Another member,

Wilma Trulock, seems to have become acquainted with the McCormick and Thomley organization in a similar manner. In the 1970s she came to know both Pappy and Peggy McCormick, and according to Trulock they told her that she "was supposed to be a Creek Indian; they traced my family members back." Trulock soon became a tribal officer and signed many of the group's important organizational documents in the 1970s and early 1980s. Running a store, however, she had little time to participate in cultural activities held at the Tama Reservation and left the tribe. She is no longer a member. It was not just rank-and-file individuals who left the McCormick organization, however. One-time leader Wesl Thomley quit the tribe in the late 1970s, and he soon formed a group, the Creeks East of the Mississippi, based at his home in Molino, Florida. This organization was denied acknowledgement at the same time as the Lower Muskogee Tribe. Thomley later reportedly enrolled with his one-time rivals the Poarch Band of Creek Indians. Arthur Turner, who started the Principal Creek Indian Nation as the first splinter tribe, also petitioned for federal acknowledgment on his own. Like its relatives Turner's Principal Creek Nation was denied, in 1985.[61]

As revealed by these facts, the Lower Muskogee Creek organization based at Tama Reservation lacked attributes widely accepted as characteristics of ethnic groups (or Indian tribes). The group had no historical existence prior to 1972. While the Tama Reservation people are not a purely "fake" or wannabe Indian group, mainly because many members do have Creek ancestry, the available evidence and statements from group members reveal that these individuals did not comprise a distinct Native American enclave historically. They hailed from assimilated families that had traditionally identified as white. Group members had never lived in an Indian community—in fact, they never claimed to have lived together prior to the formation of the McCormick group in the early 1970s. The Lower Muskogee people had Indian ancestry but no long-standing identity as a Native community. In this vein it is not surprising that the McCormick tribe had no common cultural traditions other than those of rural, white southerners from which the band's membership more significantly derived. Enrolled individuals shared no historical experiences, other than family traditions of having Creek or other Indian ancestry. Some did not even know they had Indian blood until they conducted genealogical research or were recruited to join the tribe. As a group, they shared little social or familial connections, a fact revealed in the lack of intermarriages between group members prior to formal organization of the Lower Muskogee Creek Tribe in 1972. However, many scholars note that an ethnic group possesses shared ancestry and history, or *a belief* in shared ancestry and history. As sociologist Joane Nagel has written, an ethnic group is "a community of people who see themselves as descended from common ancestors and whom others consider part of a distinctive community." In theory, individuals can undertake a process of tribalization, creating tribes as political entities that serve as focal points of their identities. The Lower Muskogee Creeks certainly possess a belief in shared ancestry and history, some possess confirmed Creek blood, and all share oral traditions tying them to the struggles of the Creek Indians. These facts raise intriguing questions: Is their *belief* in these things enough to make them a viable ethnic and tribal group today, especially because many now live together and have invented cultural traditions that they share? Now that they have existed for almost forty years, have they become, or are they becoming, a true ethnic Indian community? It is possible that their children may have, or may be, internalizing a racial identity and cultural identification as American Indians, an identity that will be passed on to their children, despite its problematic origins.[62]

What is certain is that the McCormick group failed to garner the support of existing tribes when it petitioned for federal recognition in 1978. From the start the Tama Reservation people faced hostility from leaders of the Creek Nation of Oklahoma, a constituency whose support was badly needed if they were to secure legitimacy in the eyes of both Native Americans and non-Indians. During the 1970s Creek Nation principal chief Claude Cox began closely following the developments of the eastern Creek-named groups, including the recognition efforts of the Lower Muskogee Creek Tribe and the related Principal Creek Nation. Cox was concerned enough about their actions to encourage the BIA to develop rigorous tribal recognition criteria in the mid-1970s. The Creek Nation of Oklahoma subsequently offered no support for these groups' tribal recognition efforts, and it later publicly supported the ruling against the Lower Muskogee organization. Terry Lofton reports that Oklahoma Creek leaders today do not accept the Tama people as a legitimate Indian tribe. When Creek Nation representatives have met members of the Georgia group the encounters have been tense. According to Tony Paredes, Wes Thomley admitted that the group he helped found was not, and had never been, an "Indian settlement" like the Poarch Creek community. In the end, the Tama Reservation group was seen as illegitimate, not only by white observers, but also, more importantly, by related Indian tribal communities.[63]

THE LOWER MUSKOGEE CREEK TRIBE TODAY

Despite failing to gain federal acknowledgment in 1981, the Lower Muskogee Creek Tribe and its Tama Tribal Town still exist today, engaging in many of the same activities that have become hallmarks of the group. A small core still lives at the site, while other active members drive to the reservation weekly to attend church services. Peggy McCormick (Venable) still lives on the reservation, frenetically traveling to Indian-oriented meetings and events in the state of Georgia. Her son, Nealie, named after his father, the police chief in the small Georgia town of Pelham, serves as chair of the Georgia Council of American Indian Concerns. In this capacity he is a high-profile advocate for Indian matters including grave repatriation and images of Native Americans.[64] Group leaders have generally given up any hope of ever securing federal recognition, and go about their lives rather quietly trying to re-create their vision of Creek Indian life in southwestern Georgia. The Tama Reservation still hosts busloads of schoolchildren on field trips from nearby Tallahassee, seeking to learn about Creek culture. Today long-time Poarch Creek leader Eddie Tullis is somewhat philosophical about the group. Though he laughs when the name is brought up, saying that the state recognition of the Tama Reservation is "a prime example that local politicians will do anything to get some publicity," he feels the group's efforts to host schoolchildren and teach about Indian culture is "better than nothing." As he views it, this seems apropos, seeing that "the understanding of America about Indians is still at the fourth-grade level." However, thinking about the Tama Reservation, Tullis feels "it's ironic that people don't know it's not real."[65]

THE BAFFLING CASE OF THE
MOWA BAND OF CHOCTAW INDIANS

If the Lower Muskogee Creek Tribe is a recently created organization, the MOWA Band of Choctaw Indians of southwestern Alabama has a long-standing identity as an Indian people, though its exact origins

are murky. Of currently non–federally recognized Native groups, the
MOWA Band is at once one of the most accepted and most controversial. To those seeking clear demarcations of Indian identity they
are baffling and even disturbing. When asked about the MOWA Band,
the former head of the Branch of Acknowledgment, Bud Shapard,
now one of the BIA process's harshest critics, remarks: "If any group
looked like a tribe and wasn't, it was them." All knowledgeable parties
agree that the MOWA Band of Choctaw Indians is unique, composed
of nonwhite people whose community has existed in an isolated area
approximately forty miles north Mobile since at least the 1830s. It is
their Indianness, particularly their claim to being a remnant Choctaw
tribe, that many individuals debate. The MOWA people have engendered heated opposition to their claims from nearby tribes such as
the Poarch Band of Creek Indians and the Mississippi Band of Choctaws,
as well as the Cherokee Nation of Oklahoma. They failed to gain acknowledgment through the Federal Acknowledgment Process in 1994. Certain
aspects of their history are well accepted, but important details, notably
their Choctaw (or other Indian) ancestry are not. Modern leaders like
Leon Taylor proudly note: "Today, I am Choctaw . . . tomorrow I will still
be Choctaw." [66] Many of his Indian contemporaries are not so sure.

GENERAL BACKGROUND

The modern MOWA Band of Choctaw Indians is based on a state-
recognized reservation several miles northwest of Mount Vernon, Alabama, a small town approximately thirty miles north of Mobile on the
Gulf Coast. The group took its name by combining the names of the
two counties where many enrolled members live: northern Mobile
County and southern Washington County. The MOWA people have
lived in a relatively small area, measuring approximately twenty miles
north to south and ten miles east to west, since at least the 1830s. In
the nineteenth century this land was generally considered undesirable,
comprising mainly hilly pine barrens, dense woodland thickets, and
swamps. Though isolated, the area was just west of the Tombigbee River,
a major travel artery in frontier Alabama. By 1840 it is accepted that
three core families, the Weavers, Byrds, and Reeds, settled on homesteads in this area. Although discussed at length elsewhere, these families
generally were classed as nonwhites, either as "free persons of color"
or black in the antebellum period, with certain individuals listed in

Figure 10. Kathy Wilkerson, Heather Snow (Wilkerson) and daughter Annslee, and Nicole Williams (Wilkerson), MOWA community members, early 2000s. (Photograph courtesy Cedric Sunray)

government documents as white. Socially they were not accepted by local whites, and because they were free the MOWA ancestors were set apart from the enslaved blacks of the area. In time the three families began to intermarry, eventually forming densely intertwined family bonds. Within several generations, virtually every MOWA individual descended from the Weaver, Byrd, and Reed clans.[67]

In the years following the Civil War the social lines between blacks and whites hardened. Jim Crow segregation and the increasingly dichotomous black–white racial climate of Alabama had the effect of isolating the MOWA people from both African Americans and whites. At approximately the same time that the MOWA ancestral community was coalescing, the once powerful Choctaw and Creek nations that inhabited the borderlands region the Weavers, Byrds, and Reeds homesteaded were removed to Indian Territory. Because they had European ancestry, the ancestors of the MOWA Band occupied a somewhat intermediate racial position between black and white. They generally refused to associate with freed blacks (freedmen), while not finding acceptance among whites. Individual whites and blacks did sometime marry into the group but group members always saw themselves as a people apart. The MOWA Band ancestors became a highly endogamous, isolated population in the years after the Civil War. As with many other multi-racial communities, the MOWA were culturally and economically indistinguishable from other poor, rural southern communities by this time. Sometime during the 1890s locals began calling the group "Cajans" because of a supposed resemblance to the Louisiana Cajun people. Racism helped bind the MOWA enclave closer together and helped produce a strong ethnic identity. As chief Wilford "Longhair" Taylor concludes, "Our people . . . are not white and never have been white. We have experienced extreme prejudice here in Alabama due to our marginal position in southern society."[68]

Like other nonwhite communities in the Southeast, the MOWA people were extremely impoverished. Some ancestors such as Daniel and Rose Reed owned land and businesses. However, through fraud and tax sales, group members had gradually lost most of their property by the early twentieth century. Their hard-won lands were now in the hands of timber companies and the powerful Boykin family. MOWA men generally worked in timber-related industries such as logging and turpentine production. This type of work was desirable because it engendered freedom of movement and schedule. MOWA men also preferred timbering to sharecropping cotton, an occupation closely associated with African Americans. In 1929 Laura Frances Murphy, a young missionary who lived with the group for several years, described their living standards: "I rented the only spare room in the community. It had four window openings with not even one pane of glass, and cracks between the wall planks so wide that it was necessary for me to dress under the shade of darkness. . . . One morning in the winter I awoke to find my bed covering frozen over as a result of rain that had fallen on the bed during the night. It was always necessary to keep my trunk in the center of the room to avoid it being damaged." Modern plumbing and running water were largely unknown. Some observers described the "Cajans" as more economically downtrodden than their black neighbors.[69]

Virtually all the MOWA people lived in small rural communities scattered about the piney woods in their core territory in Mobile and Washington Counties. Poor roads and social discrimination isolated these from the larger local towns of Chatom, McIntosh, Mount Vernon, and Citronelle. Group members seldom, if ever, traveled the relatively

short distance to Mobile, a scant forty miles. Locals could chart the
MOWA territory by drawing lines on a map: within the boundaries about
90 percent of residents were members of the community. Hamlets
such as Sims Chapel, Reeds Chapel, and Shady Grove were essentially
all-MOWA enclaves. Until the 1920s few outsiders ventured into this
world, and the people were generally suspicious of outsiders due to
the racism and economic deprivation they had suffered. They developed
a reputation as tough and unwelcoming to whites and blacks, further
isolating them from the outside world. Local historian Jacqueline Matte
recalls their reputation for violence. Before meeting her first MOWA
leader, Matte recalls hearing, "[D]on't mess with them or you'll get
knifed." Protestant denominations and churches did not penetrate
the MOWA area as they had with territories of larger groups such as the
Lumbees of North Carolina. Starting in 1921, however, the Southern
Baptist Church and the Methodist Episcopal Church sent several
missionaries to the area. Formal education and formal religion came
to the region for the first time. Several young female teachers served
Indian missions and ran schools. Their introduction of baseball proved
particularly popular. In time, the majority of people became Baptist,
with many others converting to Methodism or Catholicism. The new
Indian churches became important centers of MOWA life—people were
proud of their humble chapels and in time group members served as
church leaders and ministers. The designation of the churches as
"Indian" also was an important confirmation of their identity. Skeptics,
however, charged that the only reason the missionaries gave them the
name "Indian" was to flatter the MOWA people and gain their support.[70]

The group's educational history closely parallels that of other southeastern Indian groups like the Lumbee and Houma people. Until the
desegregation mandates of the civil rights era, MOWA children were
more educationally deprived than blacks. They refused to attend
"colored" schools or accept black teachers, while whites refused them
entry into their schools. Some members passed as white and their
children were allowed to enroll in white institutions, but the group
had an appallingly high illiteracy rate that hindered their economic
and social advancement. By the 1920s community leaders forced the
Washington and Mobile County school districts to provide a third school
system, one just for Indians. Even so, a missionary who served the community in the 1920s reported on the inadequate system: "For the more
ambitious there are poorly equipped one-room buildings in which

an underpaid teacher presides over all grades below the eighth." Until
the 1960s, high school education was denied the MOWA group. In
place of that, many men and women went to Bacone College, a Southern
Baptist Convention school for Indians, in Muskogee, Oklahoma. A few
students also attended the BIA-supported high school on the relatively
close Mississippi Choctaw Reservation. At these schools they met other
southeastern Indians, where some, like Galas Weaver, married members
of federally recognized tribes. Like with Indian churches, the acceptance of MOWA students into these Indian colleges and high schools
provided further outside acknowledgment of their Choctaw identity.[71]

During the 1960s the civil rights movement and the Indian renaissance
swept across the MOWA territory, bringing great changes. People became
more adamant about asserting their rights as a nonwhite minority and,
in particular, as Indians. Because of new civil rights laws, local chemical
companies were forced to open jobs to MOWA Choctaw men. Verma
Reed, a future tribal council chairman, got a job at a chemical factory
and stayed on for decades, retiring as a production supervisor in 2001.
Galas Weaver soon was elected to the local school board, and some
members saw their standard of living rise. During the 1960s MOWA
elder Roosevelt Weaver, the father-in-law of current chief Longhair
Taylor and longtime logger and hunting guide for the Boykin family,
recalled Eastern Creek chief Cal McGhee visiting the region, recruiting
MOWA claimants for his land case and nascent Indian political movement. As the racial climate improved, MOWA leaders increasingly
began to publicly assert their Indian and Choctaw identity.[72]

The MOWA Choctaw Tribe was formally organized in 1980 when
Framon Weaver, a businessman and budding entrepreneur, and other
leaders charted it as a nonprofit under Alabama law. Inspired by the
ongoing Indian renaissance and civil rights movement, Galas Weaver
and Framon Weaver soon became leaders in Alabama Indian affairs.
They and others immersed themselves in national organizations such
as the NCAI, the National Indian Education Association, and the Governors' Interstate Indian Council. As naming is essential to empowerment,
the group formally retired the old pejorative label "Cajan" and created
the new name: MOWA Band of Choctaw Indians. They made it clear
that they would not be known by any other name, and today they are
widely called MOWA Choctaws. The group received formal state recognition in 1979 through legislation sponsored by congressman J. E.
Turner and signed by pro-Indian governor Fob James. Galas Weaver

and other MOWA individuals were central to the creation of the Alabama Indian Affairs Commission in 1984. The MOWA Band was one
of the original five state-recognized tribes that also included the Poarch
Band of Creek Indians, the Star Clan of Muscogee Indians, the Echota
Cherokees, and the Jackson County Cherokees. As discussed earlier,
the MOWA Band created one of the nation's few functioning state
reservations, complete with tribal center, health clinic, legal services,
recreation facilities, tribal business enterprises, and two housing complexes on a 160-acre site. In 1980 the group held its first powwow, an
event that became increasingly popular in coming years. Because of
their Indian status, the MOWA group secured various grants for indigenous groups. They procured a HUD grant for community housing, a
federal Indian education grant that allowed Laretta Weaver to teach
Indian culture, languages, and history in the public schools, and an
Administration for Native Americans (ANA) grant to fund their recognition work. While poor by the standards of the country as a whole,
the MOWA Band under leaders like Framon and Galas Weaver became
a true success story. Creating a functioning tribal government that
provided social services and housing most importantly helped instill
a sense of pride among members of the once-isolated and downcast
people. Like the majority of other unrecognized southeastern Native
groups, the MOWA Band came to see that federal tribal acknowledgment was essential if they were to continue progressing with tribal
development. Under chief Framon Weaver, the band completed a
petition, filing it formally with the Branch of Acknowledgment and
Research in 1988.[73]

ENTERING THE FEDERAL ACKNOWLEDGMENT PROCESS

While suspicious of outsiders, who had generally been unkind, MOWA
members made important allies in the 1970s as the Indian renaissance
inspired them to open to the outside world. Group leaders felt certain
these friends would aid them in their quest for federal tribal acknowledgment. In the early 1980s MOWA Band leaders met Jacqueline Matte,
who would become a tireless researcher, writer, and advocate for her
adopted people. Using primarily volunteer labor, Matte spent countless
hours in local archives and courthouses trying to ferret out the murky
history of the MOWA group. Vine Deloria, Jr., one of the nation's best-
known Indian scholars, also became a great advocate. In 1999 he wrote

the forward to Matte's book on the group, *They Say the Wind is Red*, concluding that the MOWA Band members "have a typical profile of southeastern Indians" and admonishing readers to contact their members of Congress about acknowledging the group, saying: "[L]et's get this recognition problem solved once and for all."[74] In the early 1980s the MOWA group also secured the support of Poarch Band of Creek Indians leader Eddie Tullis who promised, "in the spirit of Indian brotherhood," to back their aspirations for tribal status. The MOWA Choctaw Band also gained admittance to the NCAI, an important acknowledgment of their status as bona fide Indians. While Framon Weaver was chief, Matte presided over a recognition committee that was charged with creating a petition for acknowledgment. Records show that the leaders were confident that their long-standing recognition as an isolated, Indian people would lead to the federal imprimatur. They submitted a fairly substantial petition to the BIA in 1988, complete with complex genealogical charts, documents that, unbeknownst to them at the time, would serve as the crux of contention in the group's case. Realizing the slow pace and costliness of the BIA process, MOWA leaders also gained the support of U.S. senator Richard Shelby and congressman Sonny Callahan, who introduced several congressional recognition bills beginning in 1987 to circumvent the BIA regimen. MOWA recognition legislation was passed by the Senate in 1994, bringing the group achingly close to a final resolution, but it failed to pass in the House. As detailed elsewhere, the MOWA Band has continued to pursue acknowledgment legislation.[75]

In trying to convince outsiders that they were a legitimate tribe, the MOWA people had several facts working in their favor. No one refuted the fact that the vast majority of their people had lived in an isolated, rural territory for over 150 years. This was no fly-by-night entity. The band had high intermarriage rates that pointed to dense social and kinship bonds that are hallmarks of ethnic groups. The MOWA Band clearly saw themselves as a unique people, and outsiders certainly did too. Although they had to rely on oral traditions to support many of their claims, the U.S. Census of 1910 for Mobile and Washington Counties had listed many ancestors, albeit for the first time, as Indians. Also, like some other Southeastern Indian groups, the MOWA people worshiped in all-Indian churches and attended Indian schools. Members had enrolled in Indian institutions such as Bacone College in eastern Oklahoma where they were accepted as Choctaws.[76]

THE MOWA ARGUMENT

It is difficult to condense the complex issues involved with the MOWA case. However, the MOWA Band of Choctaw Indians essentially argued that their people descended from Choctaws that escaped removal by retreating to the densely wooded frontier north of Mobile, finding refuge in the area's piney hills and swamps. They argued that Choctaw chiefs Piamingo Hometak, Hoshi Homa (Captain Red Bird), Tom Gibson (Eli-tubbee), Zadoc Brashears, Pierce Juzan, and other documented Choctaw leaders started their tribe. Supporting this contention, their communities are on lands ceded by the Choctaw Nation in 1805. The Choctaw trading post at St. Stephens, established at the start of the nineteenth century, is close by, several miles north on the Tombigbee River. The MOWA Band argued that the core community formed by the Weaver, Byrd, and Reed families clearly was established in their territory by the 1830s. The band acknowledged that the tribal origins of these families were diverse: they included not only Choctaw, but also Cherokee, Creek, and perhaps Chickasaw, Houma, and Apache Indians. (Geronimo's Chiricahua Apaches were incarcerated in nearby Mt. Vernon between 1887 and 1894.) They believed that over time residents of the Choctaw Six Towns who had refused to remove to Oklahoma had joined this enclave. The MOWA Band also admitted that their ancestral community had always had a multiracial character: the founding families were of European, African, and Indian origin. Over the years, people of English, French, Spanish, and African blood married into the core Choctaw community. Oral tradition told that after its founding, Choctaw and Creek men and women continued to marry into the group, although these individuals are largely untraceable. They were so unassimilated that they do not appear in local records, had only aboriginal names, or are known only by anglicized first names. To augment their case, the MOWA group found historic written correspondence from government Indian agents, travelers' reports, and newspaper articles noting that hundreds of Choctaws still inhabited the Mobile area well into the 1860s. The modern MOWA researchers logically concluded that these Choctaws were some of their ancestors. According to the MOWA tradition, these individuals were more traditional than those appearing in records. The men continued to live by hunting and fishing, while the women sold various items, including firewood, in Mobile. Today MOWA researchers and leaders truly believe that their people always comprised a Choctaw enclave: they proudly claim Choctaw chiefs such as Piamingo Hometak as their ancestors.[77]

In the Federal Acknowledgment Process virtually all the tribes that have been declined have failed to meet three important criteria. They have failed to prove with a reasonable likelihood that a predominate portion of the petitioning group constitutes a distinct community and has existed as a community from historical times until the present, that the group has maintained political influence or authority over its members from historical times until the present, and that the group consists of individuals who descend from one historical Indian tribe or from historical Indian tribes that combined.[78] The MOWA Band seemed to have an extremely strong case on its community and the related issue of political influence and authority. However, in a 1994 proposed finding, the Branch of Acknowledgment rejected the MOWA petition based on an expedited analysis of the last criterion, which can be focused upon if preliminary reviews lead researchers to believe that the group cannot establish its Indian ancestry and tribal descent. The BIA branch concluded that the core MOWA ancestors, the Weavers, Byrds, and Reeds, were not Native American. According to the government these families had a mixture of European and African ancestry. Significantly, leaders of local federally recognized tribes and the Five Tribes have accepted the BIA's genealogical work as being definitive as to the origins of the MOWA group. There is little debate that to be acknowledged a group must descend from Indian people and indigenous communities that possessed aboriginal sovereignty. The MOWA people cannot demonstrate to the BIA or to related recognized tribes that with a reasonable likelihood ("more likely than not") their founding community was a Choctaw tribal enclave, and this is the central problem with their claims for federal acknowledgment. It ultimately has stymied their acceptance as an authentic Indian community.[79]

At this point it is important to examine the burden of proof employed by the Office of Federal Acknowledgment (OFA). As discussed earlier, it is difficult for most groups to meet its thresholds. However, OFA standards are accepted by most tribal officials. Evidentiary issues, while extremely important to the process, are rarely examined in a systematic fashion by scholars of unrecognized tribes. As a legal concept, the government employs a "reasonable likelihood" standard: is it more likely than not (greater than 50 percent probability) that alleged facts are true? In practice, evaluators, whether federal bureaucrats or tribal officials, employ a form of "balancing test" when looking at the totality of evidence. In this light, no one piece of evidence can be separated from the entirety of the evidence as to whether a claimed tribe is in fact a group descended from a historic Indian community. Evaluators have to determine whether it is more probable than not that an alleged claim is true. Because of the significant issues and rights involved in acknowledging a tribe, presently recognized tribes and federal Indian officials will generally not accept oral traditions alone, especially traditions that are generations removed from the alleged event, when computing probabilities. They instead demand corroborating evidence such as federal Indian rolls, federal censuses, state and local government documents, and church and school records that point to an Indian identity for the group. As these sorts of documents were produced by non-Indians and since they deal largely with illiterate Indian or other nonwhite societies, the government's demand for written documentation is indeed onerous for non–federally recognized groups seeking this status. However, it is important to note that tribal and federal evaluators, if they are ethical, are not to look at single documents, or their absence, in isolation. In the eyes of Cherokee, Choctaw, and other leaders, the totality of the evidence has had the effect of working against the MOWA people's tribal claims.

There are a lot of misconceptions about the Federal Acknowledgment Process and eastern tribes. Many members of declined groups and many scholars too argue that their early contact with non-Indians, mixed racial nature, and historic record keeping, make it virtually impossible for multiracial eastern groups to gain acknowledgment. The record is full of claims that the process demands blood quantum, racial purity, and clear-cut aboriginal culture for groups to secure status. However, most of these accusations are not true. While many conservative eastern tribes such as the Seminoles and the Mississippi Band of Choctaws would require tribes to possess surviving Indian culture, this is not a requirement of the BIA regimen. Nor does the BIA have a blood quantum threshold. The entire basis of the Federal Acknowledgment Process is simple in theory: the federal government is acknowledging a historic Indian community (tribe) that has existed since first contact with whites and that possesses inherent aboriginal sovereignty. The purpose of acknowledgment is to right a historic wrong and acknowledge sovereignty-possessing Native groups left outside federal protections. By procedure, government evaluators are to take the unique history of eastern tribes into account, and in theory they are not looking for tribes in the Southeast that perfectly mirror their western, reservation-based relatives. OFA evaluators are supposed to take into account several facts about southeastern groups, the first being that since they have been unrecognized they of course will lack an isolated, insulated reservation that serves as a cultural homeland. Likewise unrecognized Eastern groups will lack a formal government inspired by federal Indian policy, and, finally, centuries of contact and lack of formal reservations will mean that eastern tribes will have married outside their groups to a high degree, especially as compared to western tribes.

Ideally BIA scholars and Indian leaders will find certain traits maintained by a hopeful tribe if it is to secure federal recognition. Again the often-overlooked starting point is that, in theory, the government is recognizing a historic tribe that possessed aboriginal sovereignty yet was never officially treated with or acknowledged in other manners. In this vein successful southern and eastern tribes ideally will live in rural communities. They will possess long-standing Indian-identified institutions such as churches and schools. Admitting that almost every remnant tribe (and federally recognized tribe) has extensively married outside the group, and married non-Indians, they still must establish descent from a Native American tribe. However, the tribal or at least Indian identity must predominate if a multiracial contending group is to make a compelling case that it is heir to a known historical tribe. To prove its case, a group must have some evidence that outsiders viewed it as an Indian community, some indication that the group always had an Indian and tribal identity, and evidence that this identity was primary or at least significant. In essence the group must be an Indian community and not some other community that had members who possessed some Native American ancestry. As most tribes view the matter, individuals of other races can marry into the indigenous group over time but these non-Indians must be assimilated into the Indian community or tribe. Even in groups that started out with many Indian ancestors, there may be a point where the group as a whole becomes so racially and culturally diverse and socially assimilated into the dominant society that its group identity is no longer predominately Indian. At that juncture many tribal and BIA evaluators believe that descendants can no longer make a viable case that they are heirs to a tribal group that possessed aboriginal sovereignty yet was not recognized as a tribe: there simply is no "Indian" community or tribe to recognize.

It is widely accepted that uncounted thousands of whites and blacks in the South have Indian ancestors, yet it is not often explicated generally how this historic process worked. As the historiography of the Five Tribes makes clear, general patterns existed. It was not uncommon for white male traders to marry into tribes like the Cherokees for the advantages and benefits this could bring (e.g., land, access to trade, sex partners). As these were matrilineal societies, the offspring of these marriages would have been drawn to the Cherokee orbit—they would assimilate into the Cherokee tribe and be Cherokee. However, half-white, half-Cherokee offspring would have relatives in white society, and they may have been sent to visit white family members, live with them, or to attend schools in white settlements. In this environment certain individuals may have been drawn into the Anglo-American orbit. They perhaps found spouses and work, and in the process would have slowly become assimilated into the dominant society. This is a primary way Indian ancestry entered southern white society (and in the process perhaps spawned "Cherokee princess" traditions as well). At this point two common scenarios emerge. First, some mixed Indian–white descendants who were already from prominent families may have been "whitened," because of wealth, and accepted into elite society. Their descendants kept a tradition of acknowledging Indian ancestry yet it could hardly be said that they or their relatives were an "Indian tribe." Second, and more importantly for tribal acknowledgment purposes, others likely were marginalized in the dominant society due to the racial climate and laws of the era. They were "half breeds," "mongrel races," and "mixed-bloods." These individuals and families may have gravitated to frontier areas or to mixed-race communities that were more welcoming of their heritage. They too kept traditions of their Indian lineage alive, yet the fact that they assimilated into existing, non-tribal (if also nonwhite) communities leads to the same conclusion as the white–Indian individuals mentioned: it could hardly be said that these mixed Indian, black, and white communities were tribes. Because of stereotypes, however, it is easier to view these impoverished, marginal enclaves as Indian. The basic facts pertinent to tribal recognition are the same: thousands of individuals left tribal communities in the nineteenth century, and their descendants cannot now make a convincing case to be aboriginal Indian tribes.[80]

While no one questions that the MOWA Band comprised a distinctive community and was a unique ethnic group in 1900, there are two major issues working against their acceptance as a tribal community. The first problem they faced was an existing body of literature on the group that in some way questioned their Indianness. While rarely acknowledged by various parties today as having an impact, these works have colored the Alabama group's case for decades. Beginning in the 1920s and continuing until the early 1970s, a series of academic studies and nonscholarly articles were produced that detailed the southern Alabama people. Many of these works were based in part on firsthand accounts. This was a significant period because these writings predate the Federal Acknowledgment Process. Many of these works also go back to an era before the Indian renaissance and revival of pride in Indian ancestry. As such, the motives of the writers and the statements of MOWA ancestors and local residents were not colored by the group's effort to gain federal status. They also were closer in time to the key era of the tribe's purported origins in the 1830s. These studies, however, were tainted by the racial thinking of the times. Their authors would certainly be surprised at their importance a half-century later. In regard to the modern MOWA Band's aspirations the question arises: do these studies accurately reflect the origins of the MOWA people in southern Alabama?

ISSUES OF ORIGINS AND COMMUNITY IN THE MOWA LITERATURE

The central problem for the MOWA Band of Choctaw Indians is the historical scholarly focus on the group's racial ambiguity. In general, more recent scholarly critics have discounted existing studies on the MOWA people for several reasons. Some note their racial bias, others challenge their use of discredited academic models, and many charge that the authors did not conduct actual research within the MOWA community. This last criticism also includes a claim that researchers based their conclusions on secondhand knowledge of earlier flawed reports or derived their findings from brief interviews of local whites, thus reflecting the racist views of people of the area who were biased against the MOWA enclave. At the core of the critique is that scholars of the MOWA people utilized a theoretical model that focused on the "tri-racial" nature of the group, not their Indianness.

No one debates that the MOWA people were often highlighted in sociological and anthropological literature that examined dozens of communities that were labeled "tri-racial isolates," "American isolates," "racial islands," "quasi-Indians," "mestizos," and "marginal peoples."

Scholars in this line sought to utilize these names to replace terms that had been rejected by the groups themselves, such as "Red Bones," "Brass Ankles," "Issues," and "Croatans." The MOWA community was included in all of the major works of this school—they were studied and labeled as "Cajans." One author considered the MOWA people perhaps the best example of the "tri-racial isolate" phenomenon. The authors of these works came from different disciplines and had somewhat varying academic agendas. Their findings, however, in totality, represent a challenge to the MOWA Band's aspirations, as they point away from a clear-cut, long-standing identity as Choctaws.[81]

The first academic study was by Horace Mann Bond, "Two Racial Islands in Alabama," published in the *American Journal of Sociology* in 1931. Bond was an African American professor at Fisk University in Nashville, Tennessee, who went on to become a noted leader in the administration of historically black colleges and universities in America. He earned a PhD from the University of Chicago with a dissertation on black education. He was the father of noted civil rights leader Julian Bond. It is clear that the elder Bond spent time visiting the MOWA community and another nearby "racial island," a "Creole of color" community in Baldwin County, Alabama. Unlike with authors of other works of the era, Bond's purpose was not to examine the tri-racial nature of the MOWA group per se, but to compare the "Cajans" and Creoles. He viewed both groups as examples of intermediate peoples, stuck between black and white societies, who exhibited characteristics of both "races." In the brief article, Bond concluded that contrary to prevailing wisdom the white blood of the "Cajans" did not elevate them above blacks. He described them in highly derogatory terms, perhaps resulting from the fact that Bond was a black man studying a group that he found would deny "the presence of any 'Negro taint.'" His essential conclusion was that the "Cajans" were a hybrid race, perpetually suspended between white and black societies by a lack of acceptance in the former and their own racist rejection of the latter.[82]

In the same era, Laura Frances Murphy published several minor works on the MOWA community. While not a leading scholar, Murphy could not be described as a casual acquaintance or passing observer of the MOWA people. A young woman missionary trained at the Methodist Scarritt College in Nashville, in 1929 she was sent by the mission board to teach and proselytize among the largely unchurched "Cajans." Murphy spent six years living with MOWA families while teaching at the Shady

Grove and Byrd settlements. She wrote a master's thesis in the Department of Sociology at Scarritt in 1935 entitled "The Cajans of Mobile County, Alabama," and an article in the *Missionary Voice* magazine in 1930, both of which emphasized the baffling racial origins of the group. In the latter work Murphy concluded: "The Indian Cajan group [is] a mixed race composed of varying combinations of Spanish, French, English, German, Russian, [and] Italian, with Mexican and American Indian predominating. Little is known of their history. They comprise a third racial group in Alabama, known among their own people as *the mixed race* [emphasis in original]." While noting that "Mexican" and "American Indian" ethnic heritage predominated in the group, Murphy did not highlight or state that any specific tribal group or aboriginal group dominated. She went on to note that each settlement had its own oral traditions and folklore to account for this unique racial mixture. Some attributed it to pirates who had married into the group. Others claimed that the mixture resulted from the fact that Apache women and local soldiers had started families while the Chiricahua Apaches were held at Mount Vernon.[83] Although Murphy's scholarly credentials do not match Bond's, she spent years among the group and based her theories on oral testimony from group members, so her conclusions as to their identity cannot be easily discounted. While she may have skewed her conclusions in the interest of presenting the group as a "tri-racial isolate," this seems unlikely. Murphy was not writing within this scholarly model; she also was serving an Indian mission and wrote about the Indian mission, a fact that would give her an interest in accentuating the Indian culture and traditions of the group rather than their lack. There was a lot of interest in Native Americans in the era in which Murphy wrote, a reality that would have led Murphy to accentuate the Alabama people's Indian heritage rather than the general lack of clear tribal identity and customs among the group.

In 1934 Carl Carmer published his well-known *Stars Fell on Alabama*, a best-selling work that contained a chapter on the "Cajans" of southern Alabama. A New Yorker with a master's degree from Harvard, Carmer had moved to the South to become a professor of English at the University of Alabama and spent time traveling the byways of the state in preparation for the book, which cemented his reputation as one of the most popular authors of the era. In *Stars Fell on Alabama*, Carmer reported spending two days inquiring into a commonly asked question: "Where do the Cajans come from?" He reported that no one really knew for sure, but that some "Cajans" and local whites said they came from pirates who intermarried with Spanish, Russians, French, English, and "Niggers." One man reported, "Long time ago wasn't no folks on them sand flats. . . . Them Cajans sprung up right out'n the ground. Some say they come from animals—coons and foxes and suchlike—but that ain't right. Just sprung up out'n the ground." Carmer reported speaking to a "Cajan" whose last name was Byrd, who said that the people all descended from a Captain Red Byrd who was a "Mexican Indian" who came to Mobile and married a Louisiana Cajun— and who was eight feet tall and covered all over with hair. A white farmer told the inquisitive author that the "Cajans" all descended from Daniel and Rose Reed, who were "colored folks." A "dark boy" told Carmer that they were "[f]rom French people that married Indians . . . and not from any niggers at all."[84]

During the Indian New Deal of the 1930s, Lena Byrd, a white school-teacher who had married Elvin Byrd, a member of the MOWA community, wrote to the Indian Office seeking aid for her husband's people. The office sent Samuel H. Thompson, supervisor of Indian education, on a trip to investigate potentially providing educational aid for several non–federally served groups in southern Alabama, including the Escambia County (Poarch) Creeks and the Creoles of Baldwin County. Under the Indian Reorganization Act, Thompson needed to ascertain whether it was feasible to determine blood quantum, because the act applied only to nonreservation Indians of one-half or more "Indian blood." Thompson's findings were not helpful to the MOWA group, either in proving the predominance of Choctaw blood or the existence of a functioning Choctaw community in Washington and Mobile Counties. The Indian education supervisor met with a host of locals, including Laura Frances Murphy and another missionary, white school administrators, and several MOWA individuals. Thompson found that the school laws of Alabama classed individuals as either white or colored and that, though few actually possessed black ancestry, the MOWA people were inevitably classed as colored. He concluded: "I might state also that no one seems to know where these people came from, and they do not know themselves." The MOWA people apparently had no accepted group name at the time. The missionaries told him it was best to call them "Cajans," while Thompson reported that several of the group told him they had not used that term prior to the missionaries' arrival. Thompson met Roy Lambert, a MOWA individual, who, he recalled, "told me frankly that he is a Cajan." Murphy informed the Indian investigator that the quantity of their Indian blood "is so remote that they cannot be counted as Indians." However, the assistant superintendent of the Mobile County schools reported that he did class some as Indians. Prior to leaving, Thompson was introduced to Thomas Byrd who was fifty-eight at the time, which would place his date of birth in the mid-1870s. Thompson noted that Byrd said he had lived all his life on forty acres of land inherited from his father. Thompson reported that Byrd "looks Indian" and that he said his family was of Choctaw blood but did not know where they originated or when. Despite this last statement, the overall theme of Thompson's brief report centered upon the ambiguity and uncertainty of the tribal origins and Indian blood of the Washington and Mobile County people. This contrasts significantly to his notes on the nearby Poarch Creeks from the same trip, whom he called Indians and stated were of obvious Indian blood.[85]

By the 1950s the concepts of "racial islands" and "tri-racial isolates" were becoming the dominant theoretical models that academics utilized when examining the once-obscure Indian groups remaining in the East. Revealing their focus, one early writer, William Harlen Gilbert, Jr., called these people "mixed outcasts from both the white and Negro castes of America." Labeled "Cajans" at the time, the MOWA group figured prominently in the era's scholarship that largely continued the racial ambiguity theme. Together a loose association of social scientists, who often consulted with each other, particularly Gilbert, Calvin Beale, Edward T. Price, and Brewton Berry, wrote several significant articles and one book on the so-called racial islands or tri-racial isolates. One author pointed to the MOWA group as a model of the phenomenon. Though challenged today, the studies on the MOWA people bear a more systematic analysis, especially in terms of whether their authors systematically ignored evidence of Choctaw heritage in favor of emphasizing the tri-racial nature of the group.[86]

The MOWA group appeared in the first of these studies, Gilbert's broad overview, "Mixed-Blood Racial Islands," published in 1946 in *Social Forces*. They subsequently were noted in Brewton Berry's *Almost White* (1963), a more popular account that undoubtedly reached a larger audience. Berry characterized the "Cajans" and others as racial "outcasts," "racial orphans," and "Indians by courtesy" or "quasi-Indians" who, as the book's title implied, wanted to be white but would settle for Indian. This type of language makes these works offensive and unpalatable today, a fact that has largely led to a general rejection of their conclusions in scholarly circles. Three articles of this genre presented fairly substantial studies on the MOWA people. Edward T. Price produced the first, "Mixed-Blood Populations of the Eastern United States," a PhD dissertation in geography from the University of California, Berkeley, in 1950. Price's committee included Carl Ortwin Sauer, a geographer of national reputation, and Paul Schuster Taylor, an economist, who with his wife Dorothea Lange had produced iconic work on the Dust Bowl refugees in California during the Great Depression. In his dissertation Price presented the "Cajans" as perhaps the group most fitting the "racial island" concept in the entire work. Contrasting the MOWA enclave with the nearby Escambia County (Poarch) Creeks who "are known as Indians," Price accentuated the ambiguous, tri-racial nature of the MOWA group. Like Berry, he wrote that they made every claim to whiteness over the alternatives. By this time, the term "Cajan" had clearly become a pejorative label, so Price inquired as to its origins. He had heard that a local state senator, L. W. McRae, had invented the term. After contacting the senator's son, Price confirmed to his satisfaction that the senator had in fact come up with the label in 1885 because he felt the MOWA people resembled the Louisiana Cajuns and wanted to "dignify" them with a name because they lacked one. It was several decades before academics again studied the MOWA enclave. In 1975 Auburn University professors Curtis T. Henson, Jr., and B. Eugene Griessman (a PhD graduate of Louisiana State University and later author of popular books on achieving success in life) published a study on the MOWA group in the scholarly journal *Phylon*. Griessman and Henson noted that they had spent over two years studying the group. They had found that the term "Indian" was not widely used by local whites and blacks when describing the enclave, and that some of the people even rejected its use. Griessman and Henson found that in the 1970 census only 183 of the 3,000-plus group identified as Indian, which they felt was consistent with their conclusion that members generally wanted to be considered white. The Auburn professors found that the group's history was unknown and that they even spoke of themselves as "a peculiar people." The last scholar to write on the "Cajans" as a "tri-racial isolate," was G. Harry Stopp, Jr., an LSU graduate student. Stopp produced a master's thesis on the MOWA, concluding that because they "never really tried to be anything but White" they would largely disappear as an identifiable group once

the civil rights movement and civil rights legislation opened opportunities for them to do so.[87]

Finally, several blood-type and genetic studies have attempted to
unravel the complexity of MOWA ethnic origins. In 1977, W. S. Pollitzer,
professor of anatomy at the University of North Carolina, Chapel
Hill, and several other scholars published a study of 324 MOWA individuals in the *American Journal of Physical Anthropology*. They utilized
generally discredited physical measurements, but they also took blood
samples. They determined that serological traits pointed to the conclusion that the group was approximately 70 percent white and 30
percent black, with very little Native American ancestry. In 2007 MOWA
chief Longhair Taylor took part in another study, the Human Geno-
graphic project of the National Geographic Society, as part of an increasingly popular trend of people using genetic testing to trace their ancestors
to the far corners of the globe. As reported by a local television station
doing the testing, Taylor's genes pointed to clear origins in western
Europe, not eastern Asia where Native Americans originated.[88]

Readers of these studies do not come away with an impression that
the MOWA enclave has had a strong, long-lasting Choctaw identity.
However, supporters of the band argue that these works are not valid.
MOWA advocates feel that they focus on somewhat rare "tri-racial groups"
composed of people of white, Indian, and black ancestry, with not
one of the major "racial" strains predominating. MOWA leaders and
their friends believe that this theoretical focus caused scholars to misread
or mistake the underlying Choctaw identity of the group as a whole.
The works proffered examples of peoples representing a complex amalgamation of three "races" at a time when few writers acknowledged
the possibility of multiple and overlapping racial and ethnic identities.
These scholars certainly would have had an incentive to accentuate
the tri-racial nature of these groups rather than focus upon a group's
Indian (or white or black) identity. This raises the possibility that these
scholars would slant the evidence toward this end. However, to the
MOWA Band's critics it seems unlikely that six scholars, many with
impressive academic training and who spent considerable time studying the MOWA group, and two other writers who investigated the group
seriously, would ignore the conventions of their disciplines and pro-
fessions, and in effect bury evidence of a strong Choctaw tribal identity
in Mobile and Washington Counties if it existed. To skeptics it seems
more probable that these scholars and observers wrote what their

informants essentially told them. Readers of these articles find scant if any support for a clear Choctaw tribal identity as early as 1929—at this date individuals would have been alive who intimately knew members of the founding generation of the MOWA Band. To many observers, the studies and publications published before the acknowledgment process point to the conclusion that the group was a mixed-race, multi-ethnic society, and that at some point the group rolled its identity into the package of "Cajun" and later "MOWA Choctaw."

PHENOTYPE: THE QUANDARY OF RACIAL PHYSICAL APPEARANCE

In his seminal study of the controversial 1970s Mashpee Wampanoag land claims case in Massachusetts, James Clifford detailed an often unspoken fact about the tribal recognition process: first appearances are extremely important. People often make up their minds about whether a group of people are "really Indians" based on their physical appearance. In the Mashpee case, Clifford observed, it was apparent that the jury did not believe that this mixed African American, white, and Indian group could possibly be a bona fide tribe worthy of regaining tribal lands. I recall getting a haircut in 2000 from a woman from Martha's Vineyard (an island near Mashpee), where a group known as the Gay Head Wampanoags resided. When we began discussing my academic work on tribal acknowledgment, she told me that when she was growing up in the 1960s the Gay Head Wampanoags were viewed as blacks who pretended to be Indians: "We used to call them the Wampa-Nigs," she said bluntly, a statement that echoes Clifford's findings. This same sentiment is found among non-Indians in the Mobile area about the MOWA Band of Choctaw Indians. Many parties believe they are really mulattos or African Americans trying to pass themselves off as Indians. In some ways, the BIA's negative findings against the group have compounded this image. A staunch critic of the Federal Acknowledgment Process that he helped establish, Bud Shapard nonetheless believes the bureau's genealogical work on the MOWA Band was "first-rate" and that it proves the MOWA "are black." Another scholar with much knowledge of the process, an enrolled member of one of the Five Tribes of Oklahoma who prefers to remain anonymous, agrees. Although the BIA does not rely on appearances or phenotype, it is clear that the subjectivity of perceived racial appearance leaks into the process, whether through historical studies, archaic record keeping, local conventional wisdom, or first impressions of modern observers. This issue has done nothing to help the MOWA people win universal acceptance as Indians. Their apparent "blackness" has clouded the people's motives for claiming an Indian identity.[89]

The unique racial appearance of the MOWA group was a major subject of concern to early observers. They were clearly considered nonwhite, but most observers were intrigued as to the source of their "exotic" appearance. Laura Frances Murphy's 1920s account was typical: "It was interesting to see the great variety of color and other physical characteristics of the members of the congregation, for the Indian Cajan has no typical physical characteristics. In one family it is not uncommon to find blonde, brunette, and Spanish-blonde types. . . . In *a race so young* as this [emphasis added] there is no typical height or weight. Both curly and straight hair are found in practically all families." Because of their African ancestry they were classed as colored in Jim Crow Alabama, yet most observers noted that black ancestry was not predominating. The distasteful racial discourse of the early reports reveals the subjectivity of judging supposed racial appearance. BIA investigator Samuel Thompson, writing in the 1930s, noted that Thomas Byrd "looks Indian," but that Herbert Taylor, who claimed to be Indian, "showed [his] colored blood very much." Because of the extreme racist environment of Alabama prior to the civil rights era, these observers concluded that this ambiguous group chose to accent its white or Indian ancestry to avoid association with the oppressed black minority. Edward Price determined that MOWA people aspired to be white, noting that they shunned darker group members who "might be considered as drawbacks to that end." He believed the average "Cajan" looked similar to urban "mixed negroes" in northern cities saying, "Neither could the Cajan match the bronze skin of the aboriginal North American Indian or his traditionally prominent racial features. . . . in general there are among the Cajans more characteristics reminding one of negroes than of Indians; kinky and curly hair, widening of the nostrils near the base of the nose, and thicker lips crop up with varying frequency. I have seen none who look strikingly like Indians." The appearance of any perceived African traits served to impugn the Indianness of the group. Tribal historian Jacqueline Matte, a longtime resident of Washington County, recalls local whites asking her: "So how's those kinky-headed Indians?"—a clear jab at their racial claims and appearance.[90] The implication of judgments on the MOWA group's appearance was that their darker complexions came from African ancestry, that they were really black but claimed to be Indian for social and political advantage.

Social scientists today do not accept race as a viable category to describe differences among *Homo sapiens*, but few scientists were of such opinion in the mid-twentieth century and the view was almost unknown among the general population when these studies were produced. Today most Americans continue to place great saliency on "race" as an important social reality, and being African American historically has been a social, economic, and political liability. This brings up an important point on the MOWA Band and other supposedly tri-racial groups of the Southeast. The racial order of Jim Crow Alabama clearly presented incentive for members of mixed Indian, white, and black communities to "pass" as white, and in the case of groups classed as "colored" like the MOWA, to "pass" as Indian. This has affected perceptions of the group's motives for asserting an Indian identity since the late nineteenth century. Because their appearance had long been in question, at the height of Jim Crow segregation the MOWA clearly had incentives to accentuate the Indian side of their ancestry. A few examples will illuminate this point, the first being a 1920 miscegenation case involving Percy Reed and Helen Corkins. Reed, an ancestor of today's MOWA Band, was taken to trial for marrying Corkins, a white woman, violating an Alabama statute prohibiting "a negro, or descendant of a negro within the third generation," from marrying a white person. His unsuccessful defense was that his ancestors, Daniel and Rose Reed, were not Negroes but instead of mixed white–Indian blood (the testimony offered was inconclusive as to the racial ancestry of Rose Reed). In a second instance, MOWA families used claims of Indian blood to force county funding of special Indian schools, thereby separating themselves from the stigmatized "Negro" educational system and society.[91] The fact that the MOWA Band has mixed Indian, white, and African blood has been important to their case. The African part has led to questions as to motives for claiming a Choctaw and other Indian identity. The ambiguous nature of their racial appearance, especially as it contains black ancestry, explains to non-experts the seemingly nonwhite appearance of the people—and further separates them from acceptance as an Indian community.

Problems of Using Official Records for
Racial Identification

The federal acknowledgment regulations require that a group must know the tribe from which it descends and prove, using written records and other evidence such as language or cultural traditions, that it does in fact descend from this aboriginal people. As shown earlier, the majority of recognized tribal leaders supported this rule when it was made in 1978. In the case of the MOWA Band, they clearly had long-standing oral tradition that they descended from Choctaw, Cherokee, and other southeastern tribes, and they believed that the Choctaw predominated. Proving descent or ancestry is one of the seven federal criteria, and because it necessitates detailed genealogical work it is perhaps the most difficult to meet. In the early 1980s Matte and volunteers such as MOWA community members Reva Lee Reed, Peter A. Rivers, and Mary Byrd Taylor set out on an arduous task to prove that MOWA Band ancestors were Choctaw. In this work the BIA and its tribal supporters believe the MOWA committee failed, a finding that has served to make the band questionable in the eyes of many outsiders.[92]

The inability of the MOWA people to procure written evidence backing their claims that their ancestral community was Choctaw was the second major factor working against MOWA recognition, and eventually the most important because it served as the basis for the acknowledgment office's denial of the group's petition. Because the BIA researchers felt the group likely could not prove its Choctaw ancestry, the Branch of Acknowledgment conducted an expedited review of its petition under the FAP's fifth criterion. That criterion requires a group to establish that it descends from a historical Indian tribe or an aggregate of individuals from historic Indian communities that functioned as a tribal community using evidence such as federal Indian rolls, federal censuses, state and local government records, church and school records, land records, wills, and marriage documents. The government ultimately concluded that the core MOWA ancestral families, the Weavers, Byrds, and Reeds, could not be verified as hailing from the Choctaws or from any other Indian nation. The government finding was complex but can be summarized as follows.[93]

The MOWA Band conducted an extensive series of oral histories about their people and their origins that pointed the way toward proving their heritage using non-Indian records. According to group oral traditions and writings produced by the band, Choctaw and other Indian ancestors hid out in the pinewoods and swamps of modern Mobile and Washington Counties, Alabama, to avoid removal. Well-known Choctaw leaders Piamingo Hometak and Tom Gibson were among these people, as were dozens of Indians who went only by Indian names, names that have been lost to time. The modern MOWA people believe that they logically descended from men listed on several Choctaw treaties and various nineteenth-century reports noting Choctaws in the Mobile area. However, upon intensive research, Matte and her MOWA team admitted that they could not document these assertions with specificity, it just seemed logical that if there were Choctaws noted in Mobile in the 1840s and 1850s that they were related to the MOWA group only forty miles away. Without specific linkages between these historic documents and the MOWA homeland, however, tribal researchers had to focus on several families and individuals for whom fairly extensive documentation existed for the antebellum period, an era that would be of utmost importance in their case. It was between 1810 and 1850, both sides agree, that the Reed, Weaver, and Byrd families began appearing in records of the MOWA group's core region. The tribe and BIA researchers ultimately concurred that these three family lines were the key progenitors of the modern MOWA people. Virtually all the group's members were proven to descend from several ancestors who settled in Washington and Mobile Counties in the early nineteenth century. The MOWA Band argued that the Reeds were Choctaw, white, and Creek, that the Weavers were of mixed Cherokee and European blood from North Carolina, and that the Byrds descended from Lemuel Byrd and his wife, who were Cherokees from North Carolina by way of Georgia.[94]

Proving with a "reasonable likelihood" that the founding community composed of the Reed, Weaver, and Byrd families had Choctaw and other Indian ancestry was central to the MOWA Band's case. A major obstacle in establishing this was existing antebellum documentation that employed ambiguous and inconsistent racial categories. Prior to the Civil War federal and state census records and county tax rolls listed members of the Reed and Weaver clans as "free persons of color." They were never designated as Choctaw or as Indian. Often modern scholars and nonprofessional researchers make the mistake of conflating this category with African ancestry alone. As several scholars have demonstrated, researchers generally see the terms "free person of color" and "mulatto" in antebellum records and read this to mean "individual of African descent." The work of Gary B. Mills, Jack Forbes, and others makes it clear that in many southern states prior to the Civil War, individuals of partial Indian ancestry who lived among whites and had no tribal relations often bore this designation. Modern researchers similarly conflate "mulatto" with African ancestry as well. The term "mulatto," which in modern times implies a person of black and white ancestry, was used in early U.S. history for mixed-blood Indians as well as persons of mixed black and white heritage. So the conclusion cannot be made that the Reeds and Weavers were black because they appeared as "mulatto" or "free persons of color" in existing documents. However, the record does not point to clear Indian ancestry either. These facts are important when examining the central yet confounding case of Daniel and Rose Reed, a couple who are acknowledged as important ancestors of the MOWA community.[95]

Rose Reed has figured prominently in MOWA oral tradition as the most important and venerated matriarch of the group. She lived to a robust age, dying at over ninety in 1877 or 1878. Passed from generation to generation, oral tradition holds that she was the daughter of George S. Gaines, the first factor (chief trader) of the Choctaw trading post at St. Stephens in 1804–1805 and a Choctaw woman named Kachiloke. The post at St. Stephens was just upriver from the MOWA Band's homeland in modern Washington and Mobile Counties. Existing records show only that Gaines was married to a white woman, Ann Gaines, a distant cousin who shared the same last name, Gaines, prior to the marriage. Her father, Young Gaines, was a prominent slaveholder in the region. George S. Gaines became one of the great white colonizers of lower Mississippi and Alabama as well. Significantly, yet understandably, he left no records of his supposed union with Kachiloke or a child named Rose by her. After finding that Rose and George S. Gaines were roughly the same age and that therefore the oral tradition that she was his daughter could not be true, the MOWA Band argued that it was Young Gaines, who at one point served as a Choctaw interpreter, who was the father of Rose. They believed that she was held as his slave, living in the plantation slave quarters after her mother Kachiloke emigrated west with the Choctaws while Rose was still a child. MOWA people argued that one of Gaines's cattle drovers, Daniel Reed married Rose while she was a slave and had several children by her. (They believe Reed was of partial Creek ancestry, though this has not been proven.)[96]

The first documents on Rose Reed appear in conjunction with her emancipation. Records show that Daniel Reed purchased the freedom of Rose and several of their children in the early nineteenth century. One of the first issues the MOWA group faced was explaining why Rose, the child of a white plantation owner and a Choctaw woman who later emigrated west with her people, was held in slavery, but the fact Rose was a slave does not prove she was of African ancestry. Indians were often enslaved during the colonial period although this practice had waned in the era when Rose lived. An 1818 act of the Alabama legislature in which it is written that Daniel Reed purchased Rose from Young Gaines is important as it is one of the first documents found detailing an ancestor of the MOWA community. As both George and Young Gaines were close associates of the Choctaws it also points to a MOWA connection with the tribe. At this point, the key issue was whether there was proof that Rose and Daniel Reed were of Native American ancestry, and more importantly of either Creek or Choctaw heritage as the MOWA Band claimed. The 1818 document describes Daniel as a "free male of colour" and Rose as a "mulatto slave" being manumitted from the possession of Young Gaines. Subsequently federal census records list Rose as mulatto in 1850 and 1860 and as white in 1870. While Forbes has shown that these designations could indicate possible Indian ancestry, the documents on their face do not specify Indian or tribe-specific heritage. Several pieces of testimony from descendants in the 1920 Percy Reed miscegenation case were contradictory as to Rose Reed's ancestry. The group's oral tradition also is contradictory as to Daniel's origins. Although the MOWA petition claimed he was part Creek from Spanish West Florida, his descendants' testimony, statements in censuses, and applications for the Eastern Cherokee Judgment (Guion Miller 1907) stated that Daniel Reed's birthplace was variously in Mississippi, Texas, Kentucky, and Mexico. This last location supports several other sources that point to his origins in the Spanish colonies. Daniel is said to have been born in approximately 1790—or as early as 1767. While his birthplace could have been in West Florida, which was under Spanish rule at the time, early-twentieth-century oral testimonies from relatives stated that he was part Spanish from either Jamaica, Santo Domingo (Dominican Republic), or Louisiana. An 1823 digest of Alabama laws listed him simply as a "free negro." Despite questions about Daniel Reed's and Rose Reed's origins, they were a fecund couple, producing children who served as the major Reed branch of the MOWA people. As such, this couple's racial origins are extremely important to the MOWA Band's case for acceptance as a Choctaw community.[97]

It is often alleged by MOWA leaders and by scholars such as Renee Cramer and Susan Greenbaum, both of whom researched the MOWA Band, that racism, including past racism as reflected in government records, has been a factor in the denial of federal recognition of the group. This allegation bears examination. It is well established that many Native Americans have a tendency to accept individuals of Indian and white unions while rejecting individuals of Indian- and African heritage. Years of struggle with the BIA and recognized tribes has led Wilford "Longhair" Taylor to conclude that the government will accept you if you are white and Indian, but if you are perceived as "black Indians" like his people it will be against you. Chief Taylor and several scholars believe that the MOWA Band's partial African heritage is a reason why other Indians will not accept them. There is a large body of literature on the subject by Jack Forbes, Circe Sturm, and others. There are examples of individuals working in the BIA who do not want to recognize the MOWA group and other supposedly "tri-racial" groups partially because they believe that they are essentially African Americans who for various historical reasons have chosen to accent the Indian side (real or alleged) of their ancestral chart over the black. More compelling is Jacqueline Matte and Renee Cramer's contention that historic racism, as reflected in official records and racial designations, is one of the primary obstacles prohibiting the MOWA Band's recognition today.[98] At the root of this accusation are the racial and legal categories discussed above, particularly the fact that individuals like Daniel and Rose Reed were listed as "free persons of color" or "mulattos" during their lifetimes and never as "Indian," "Creek," or "Choctaw." MOWA leaders truly believe their oral traditions that say that both ancestors were of Creek, Choctaw, white, and perhaps African ancestry. They want recognized tribal leaders and the BIA to accept their position and presume that the designations "free persons of color" and "mulatto" mean that they were Indian and white, not of white and African descent.

Unfortunately for the MOWA group, neither recognized tribal leaders nor the Office of Federal Acknowledgment will accept the listing of the Reeds and others as "free persons of color" and "mulattos" as proof

Figure 11. Chief Wilford "Longhair" Taylor of the MOWA Band of Choctaw Indians. (Photograph courtesy of Jacqueline Anderson Matte Research Collection, Doy Leale McCall Rare Book and Manuscript Library, University of South Alabama)

that they were Indian, much less specifically Choctaw and Creek Indians. One reason is that there are groups such as the "Freejacks" of Louisiana, with similar histories, that for various reasons have never claimed a concrete Indian identity.[99] In terms of whether the Reeds and other core MOWA ancestors were part of a tribal community in the early nineteenth century, the racial ambiguity has to be seen as part of the totality of their known life situations. Utilizing a "balancing test," looking at the evidence as to what is more probable or more likely than not, critics see the facts and evidence in the case of Rose and Daniel Reed as inconclusive as to Choctaw and Creek origins or lean toward the conclusion that it is more likely that they were not part of an Indian community. Even if the MOWA group's position as to Daniel and Rose Reed were true, Rose was clearly not part of the Choctaw Nation—she was half Choctaw and half white, and was living within the plantation culture of Alabama. The MOWA group's oral history acknowledged that Rose's Choctaw mother had emigrated west with her Choctaw band, leaving Rose behind with her white father to be raised by a slave woman in the slave quarters. If the MOWA position is true, Daniel Reed was clearly closely associated with the Gaines's plantation world as an employee of the Gaines family. As the BIA and its tribal supporters concluded, people of mixed ancestry could be fully assimilated into Indian society but it is clear that Daniel chose a partner from the slave community and had apparently become more attached to plantation society than to his reputed Creek community or to a Choctaw enclave in modern Mobile and Washington Counties, the existence of which remains undocumented and historically murky. Today the MOWA leaders truly believe the Reeds were associated with a Choctaw community that existed but, because of its unassimilated nature, does not appear in any written records. While this is possible, the federal government and many tribal leaders require more than possibility for acknowledgment purposes. The MOWA people were unable to refute the finding of the Office of Federal Acknowledgment, and they also were unable to produce compelling proof their ancestors retained any surviving Choctaw cultural forms such as language, arts, or religious traditions, attributes that would ameliorate the lack of written documents or the records that point away from tribal heritage.

The other two core kinship lines of the MOWA Band, the Weavers and Byrds, were related. A brief examination of the known history of these two families provides a glimpse into the difficulty of deciphering the ethnic composition and true nature of the founding MOWA community. Like with the Reed clan, existing nineteenth-century documentation does not list the Weavers and Byrds as Indians or as Choctaws. The MOWA Band has argued that the Weaver line descended from David Weaver, a Cherokee from Georgia, and his white wife, Linny. While a Dave Weaver did appear on the pre-removal Cherokee Henderson Roll of 1835, MOWA researchers were unable to procure evidence showing that this Dave Weaver was their ancestor. Supporting claims of Cherokee ancestry, however, in 1908 grandchildren of David and Linny Weaver attempted to share in Eastern Cherokee judgment funds with special commissioner Guion Miller. The applications were rejected for lack of evidence. The Weaver descendants' testimony reveals that they did not know the exact heritage or background of their grandfather. David and Linny Weaver had four children that all appear in early records of Alabama. The first, James, is noted as having been born around 1800 in Georgia, and later he married a former slave girl, Margarette (or Marguerite) who was born between 1810 and 1816 in Alabama.

She was described as a "light complexioned, blue-eyed mulatto" in a document stating that a James Johnston had emancipated her in Mobile County in 1824. David and Linny's daughter Edy was a maid in the home of Joel T. Rivers, a white man from Virginia. Rivers and Edy had children together, thereby starting the common Rivers line in the modern MOWA group. Son David Weaver, Jr., was the most significant for acknowledgment purposes. Even though the MOWA people believe he was of white and Cherokee ancestry, he was listed in censuses as a "free person of color," "mulatto," "black," and as "white" throughout his lifetime. According to the MOWA petition, David Weaver, Jr., married a woman named Cecile Weatherford, the daughter of famous Creek chief William Weatherford and Nancy Fisher, a Cherokee woman. As told in MOWA Band oral tradition, Nancy swam a river with baby Cecile on her back to escape a Creek massacre during the Creek War of 1813–1814. As tradition has it, Nancy Fisher and Cecile settled among the MOWA ancestral community. However, none of the records or literature on Chief Weatherford note that he was associated with Nancy Fisher or had a daughter Cecile by her. Even so, the fact that a noted MOWA ancestor had the Weatherford surname does seem to point to a Creek Indian connection. Cecile Weatherford is proven to have had a son by Jerome Chastang, a member of the free Creole of Color group descended from French Catholic and African individuals that lived in a hamlet called Chastangs in Mobile County, just south of the modern MOWA settlements. Many MOWA ancestors were associated with this mixed-race Creole of Color community.[100]

The fairly well documented Creole of Color community of Chastangs is important to the MOWA family tree. Cecile Weatherford was resident in this community by about 1830, she had a child by Jerome Chastang, and she later married David Weaver, Jr. Cecile was also related to another core MOWA ancestor, Lemuel Byrd, who also resided in Chastangs at the time. Byrd is a larger-than-life figure in MOWA oral tradition. Known by descendants as "Daddy Lem," he may have been the "Captain Red Byrd" frequently mentioned. He came from North Carolina by way of Georgia and settled in Mobile County on land he received for his service in the Seminole campaigns. He married a woman named Anna "Twy" Weaver and had several children by her, introducing the Byrd line into the MOWA community. MOWA traditions said they were of Cherokee origins, yet census records of 1850, 1860, and 1870 classified the family only as "mulatto." By 1905 a member of the presently recognized Mississippi Band of Choctaw Indians with the last name Laurendine, who lived in Chastangs, married into the MOWA group.[101]

By the mid-nineteenth century the Byrd, Reed, Rivers, and Weaver lines became highly endogamous. These families began to intermarry to the point that almost every member of the modern MOWA Band descends from at least one of the four families. A good example of this phenomenon is the marriage patterns of the eight children born to David Weaver, Jr., and Cecile Weatherford (Weaver): three of their daughters married sons of Daniel and Rose Reed; one daughter, Tobie, married a first cousin, Jesse Weaver; one son married a Byrd; and one son married a Rivers. Another son apparently took a spouse outside these families: records show that he married a woman by the name of Parnell, who was recorded as white. Only one son, Thomas, married a woman whose family name (and thus origins) is unknown. Described in records only as "Mary," this woman was listed in the 1870 census as black. Sometime in the latter nineteenth century the family of Alexander Brashears began to intermarry into the core group. He is important to further show the genealogical complexity. Brashears was a documented Choctaw who chose to remain in the East under terms of the removal Treaty of Dancing Rabbit Creek. By 1850 his multiracial family was resident in Mobile County near the Weavers. Brashears is counted as white on all federal censuses thereafter, although he had documented Choctaw ancestry. As mentioned above, the Mississippi Choctaw Laurendine family moved to Mobile County sometime after the Civil War and settled among the well-known Creole of Color community called Chastangs. It is documented that members of this line married into the Weaver, Reed, and Byrd families sometime around 1900.[102]

How these nineteenth-century ancestors of the MOWA people identified themselves is unknown. They are described in surviving documentation as "free person(s) of color," "mulatto," "black," and as "white." As historians know, these surviving official designations represent a mixture of an individual's self-reported "race" and also observations by outsiders. By 1900, however, the MOWA Band's ancestors were clearly identifying in public records as having partial Native ancestry. As previously noted, in 1908 several members applied to Guion Miller to receive judgment funds entitled to Cherokees Indians. Many grandchildren of Cecile Weatherford Weaver applied for Cherokee money claiming Creek ancestry (through Weatherford) or Cherokee (through Nancy Fisher), but these were rejected for lack of evidence.[103] As these applications were from grandchildren of founders of the known MOWA core community, they were close in time to the debated tribe's formation. The actual testimony reveals that these individuals had a clear reckoning of who their ancestors were, and that they had traditions of Cherokee and Creek ancestry. Shortly after, for the first time in their history, the 1910 federal census listed many MOWA Band ancestors as mixed-race Indian rather than "mulatto," "white," or "free persons of color." In Washington County a census marshal wrote a marginal note explaining his use of the "mixed" category: "These people entered as mixed are composed [of] Indian and Spanish. Some others mixed French, some with white and some with negro. (The prevailing habits are Indian). Called Cajuns." In Mobile County, however, they continued to be noted as "mulatto" or "Creole," though several known Mississippi Choctaws living in the area were noted as "Indian" in the same census. These facts reveal that the MOWA ancestors' Indian identity was becoming increasingly prominent, although clearly more ambiguous than nearby Mississippi Choctaws.[104]

INTERPRETING THE CONFUSED AND UNEVEN RECORD

How does one make sense of the MOWA ancestral community's complex, known and purported racial amalgamation? How does one interpret it, particularly in light of the MOWA Band's claims to being a historic Indian tribe, with a continuous history as a Choctaw community living on ancestral lands, with clear oral traditions of Choctaw Indian descent? The Mississippi Band of Choctaws had strong opinions on the matter. Testifying against the MOWA Band in 1991, chairman Phillip Martin weighed in:

> Attached is a study of the MOWA question which was carried out by an anthropologist on our staff. It demonstrates to me that without a doubt the members of the MOWA community had some Choctaw ancestors in the remote past. (Of the 30 first-generation Indian ancestors listed in the MOWA documentation, only 16 are identified as Choctaws, and of these, only one, Alexander Brashears, appeared on the Armstrong Roll of 1831, the listing of all Choctaw households east of the Mississippi compiled prior to the Removal to Indian Territory.) But *descendency to some fractional degree* by

some people does not make them an Indian tribe. There are *areas of culture and political relations* that more closely define a tribe, areas reflected to some extent in the current Bureau of Indian Affairs federal acknowledgment process. [emphasis added]

Cultural and political considerations were important to Chairman Martin and other Mississippi Choctaw leaders. Martin added that his tribe had only in the last twenty years become aware that there were people in the MOWA area claiming to be Choctaw. The chief stated flatly, "Our people could discern no Choctaw customs extant among the MOWA population at the time of our first contacts with them," and he added that the only traditional Choctaw customs now displayed had been taught to them by members of his tribe. Martin continued that though the MOWA claimed to speak the language, his group knew of none that were fluent in Choctaw.[105] Eddie Tullis, longtime chairman of the Poarch Band of Creek Indians, weighed in as well. The Poarch Band hired the director of the Bienville Historical Society, Johnnie Andrews, Jr., to analyze the MOWA petition. Andrews noted correctly that many of the group's petition claims to Indian ancestors and ties to tribal communities supposedly located at occupation sites of Kun-shak, High Hill, and Kuns-ly were never documented by the MOWA group, but based largely on oral statements over 100 years removed from the events. Essentially agreeing with the BIA, Andrews noted: "In dozens of instances . . . much alleged information presented remains undocumented. Oral history, family tradition, and 'it is said to have been . . .' can not be considered by any scholar to be primary source material. . . . These types of historical facts are important to us in light of no or little documentation, but we historians and genealogists are acutely cautioned of the possible high degree of error often involved in totally relying on such statements."[106] Echoing the perceptions of some Indian leaders, Eddie Tullis believes that the MOWA Band is essentially a mulatto enclave, although he adds, "I firmly believe there are Indian people there . . . I [just] don't feel it is a Choctaw tribe."[107] The Choctaw Nation of Oklahoma offered no official support of the MOWA. The Cherokee Nation's Fraudulent Indian Task Force lists the MOWA Band among groups it considers illegitimate. Leaders of the Eastern Band of Cherokee Indians have publicly challenged the authenticity of the MOWA Band as a tribe.

Scholars have taken the opposite tack: virtually all the academics who have detailed or mentioned the MOWA Band of Choctaw Indians since they began their long tribal recognition odyssey have accepted the group as an Indian tribe. They do so based on the fact that the group has a long history as an Indian-identifying community, displays community features typical of surviving non–federally recognized southeastern Indian enclaves, and has been recognized as Native American by such entities as the state of Alabama, the American Indian Policy Review Commission, and the NCAI. Most who have written about the band, however, have worked for the group and have a personal and professional investment in their case. Others, like Renee Cramer, have logically relied on earlier studies and state recognition when writing of the band as a historic tribal community. Because earlier studies in the "tri-racial isolate" school were so hurtful to the modern MOWA Band's aspirations, recent scholars have systematically rejected or ignored them as having any validity. Almost all modern academics who have taken a position on the group, including Vine Deloria, Jr., have taken the logical advocacy position that basically says: "They are Choctaw because they say they are Choctaw."

Whether the three core MOWA families, the Reeds, Weavers, and Byrds, comprised a Choctaw tribal enclave worthy of federal recognition is a question of fact within the power of the BIA to decide. Most related recognized tribes have accepted its genealogical work as definitive proof. Currently the genealogy both supports and contradicts the MOWA Band's oral history. Other than geographic location within traditional Choctaw lands, however, the MOWA group did not locate a single contemporaneous record saying its core ancestors were Choctaw. They did not find any written account showing that an Indian-identified community existed in their area shortly after the removal era. Existing records show that some ancestors were associated with antebellum plantations, where some were held as slaves and when freed listed as "mulatto" and "free person(s) of color." While these individuals could have been Indians, the absence of any evidence (other than oral tradition generations after the fact) means that the BIA and recognized related tribes will not assume that they were. To skeptics, these individuals' association with non-Indian economic and social institutions points away from an assumption that they were assimilated into a mixed Choctaw-Cherokee-Creek tribal community. To them, even if the Indian links alleged by the band are correct, the fact that two of the three core families are of claimed Cherokee, mixed-race descent, who emigrated outside the Cherokee homeland to the Alabama frontier and inter-married with a group with a high mixture of European and African ancestry does little to prove with a reasonable likelihood that a Choc-taw tribal community existed in the Mobile and Washington County area shortly after the removal period.

To more culturally conservative southeastern groups like the Eastern Band of Cherokees, Mississippi Band of Choctaws, and Seminoles, the complex genealogy only confirms that a group without significant surviving cultural traits (as early as the 1920s) cannot possibly consider itself an indigenous tribal people. In this case, to opponents of the MOWA Band, the fact that the MOWA group cannot provide substan-tial evidence that Choctaw or other Native culture survived in their community makes it more probable than not that whatever Indian individuals may have lived within the ancestral community likely were assimilated into a multiracial, English-speaking, non-Indian enclave. As revealed in the Guion Miller proceedings and other surviving records, children and grandchildren of these core ancestors as early as 1908 did not present what appeared to be a strong tribal identity or specific Choctaw community identity. The acknowledgment office documented with specificity the marriage patterns of the three core ancestral fami-lies. It concluded that members of these families did not marry an individual with recorded Choctaw ancestry until the late nineteenth century. The MOWA group was not able to refute this claim. MOWA opponents believe that the fact that the BIA could trace the ancestral charts and marriages and not find a substantial pattern of marriage with Choctaws (or even ambiguous individuals who could be claimed to have come from an undocumented Choctaw community) contravenes the assumption that these large family groups married into an existing remnant Choctaw community in Mobile and Washington Counties. To critics of the MOWA Band, it seems more probable that the Native individuals who married into the group were assimilated into a multi-racial, essentially non-Indian enclave.

REMAINING ENIGMA

The MOWA Band is not a wannabe, Johnny-come-lately Indian tribe. Its members are not delusional in thinking they are indigenous. The group's oral traditions that they are of Choctaw, Cherokee, and Creek descent and their later status as mixed Indian, white, and black people give credence to the argument that they are of Native American heritage. There is no doubt that the post–Civil War intermarriages with the Mississippi Choctaw Laurendine and Brashears families increased the Indian blood within the group. They are a nonwhite people who historically have had strong communities in a once-isolated region in southwestern Alabama. They have won state recognition as an Indian tribe, they have membership in the NCAI, and many scholars accept them as a surviving Indian community in the Southeast. Many of the band's members live on a reservation and live their lives culturally as Indians. The Bureau of Indian Affairs, however, has declined to acknowledge them as a tribe, and nearby tribes such as the Mississippi Band of Choctaws and Poarch Band of Creeks and other groups they claim as their relatives, including the Eastern Band of Cherokees, the Cherokee Nation, and the Choctaw Nation of Oklahoma, have either offered no formal endorsement or have vigorously opposed the MOWA Band's tribal aspirations, supporting the BIA findings against the people. These tribes and others accept that the MOWA people have some degree of mixed tribal ancestry but believe this fact does not entitle them to federal tribal recognition. There is little doubt, however, that historical forces have forged the MOWA into a people and even a "tribe" whose indigenous origins are much debated. They represent a confounding scenario to parties seeking easy answers when acknowledging tribes. Their story reveals the true complexities behind tribal recognition decisions and debates about Indian authenticity.

CONCLUSION

Neither the Lower Muskogee Creek Tribe nor the MOWA Band of Choctaw Indians is a completely bogus Indian tribe or entity. They both have reasons for insisting that they deserve tribal recognition and acknowledgment of their Indian identity. However, there are also compelling reasons why the government and other tribes vehemently challenge their claims. The Lower Muskogee group based at the Tama Reservation in Georgia has many members with documented Creek Indian ancestry. However, the tribe itself formed in the early 1970s when dozens of formerly unrelated individuals and families came together to establish a community to fulfill the McCormick family's "Dream of the Creeks," a wonderful dream of reestablishing a Creek presence in their former homeland in Georgia. Their lack of historical depth and lack of surviving cultural traits meant that few knowledgeable parties would accept the group as legitimate. The MOWA Choctaws, on the other hand, have a community in southern Alabama that is almost two hundred years old—their historical roots in southern soil run deep. Unlike the Lower Muskogee group, the MOWA Band cannot document its original tribal ancestry, however, and there lies the problem. Although having claimed Indian heritage for over a century, the fact that their ancestral community may have been composed primarily of a mixture of European and African individuals, with a small fraction of Indian ancestry added much later, clouds their chances of ever attaining widespread acknowledgment of their claimed Choctaw heritage.

CHAPTER 5

"Fraudulent Tribes" and "Fake Cherokees"

The Five Tribes and the Politics of Indian Authenticity

Troy Wayne Poteete vividly recalls the day he first became aware of the issue. A Cherokee Nation Supreme Court justice, Poteete was living in the small Arkansas River town of Webbers Falls in eastern Oklahoma when he heard that a group calling itself the Southern Cherokee Nation was coming to town. Its "chief," Gary Ridge, had big plans for the sleepy town on the edge of the historic Cherokee Nation. Ridge had found an investor willing to front $250,000 to purchase riverfront land as a site for the Southern Cherokee Nation's proposed riverboat casino that would be housed on an antebellum-style paddle wheeler floating in the Arkansas River. Poteete chaired the Cherokee, Creek, and Choctaw Riverbed Commission, which owned the Arkansas River bottom, and the actions of the so-called sovereign Southern Cherokee Nation disturbed him. The "tribe" was operating within sight of the real Cherokee Nation and seemed to have conned the local political establishment into supporting its plans. Poteete soon learned that Ridge's "tribe" had engaged in formal meetings with the town's mayor, and pictures of the event were posted prominently in the local paper. A search revealed that the Southern Cherokee group had a professionally designed website, a "government," formal membership requirements, and other attributes of an Indian nation. A lawyer, local historian, and descendant of the real southern Cherokee faction of the Civil War era, Poteete was appalled at the audacity of Gary Ridge's group. Its members were representing themselves as Cherokees right in the historic heartland of the Cherokee Nation—and seemingly getting away with it. Locals were clearly confused by Ridge's claims and schemes. Poteete believed that if a fraudulent group could operate here, his people were in real trouble. As he researched further, the judge became shocked at the depth and magnitude of the issue. Dozens of similar groups were masquerading as Cherokees from Georgia to Alaska. Vowing to fight these imposters, Poteete and others soon created the Fraudulent Indian Task Force to challenge what the Cherokee Nation saw as the whole-sale appropriation of its people's identity and culture.[1]

The establishment of the controversial Fraudulent Indian Task Force was the opening salvo of an ongoing Cherokee Nation–led battle to counter a host of individuals and groups that have claimed to be long-lost relatives of the Cherokee, Chickasaw, Choctaw, Creek, and Semi-nole Nations. These groups range from state-recognized tribes to clearly bogus wannabe tribes. Individuals who claim to be related to the Five Tribes likewise have varying degrees of validity. To Poteete and others, the Cherokee Nation's Fraudulent Indian Task Force is a vital voice defending tribal integrity and protecting citizenship. Task force members are trying to draw clear ethnic and political boundaries around their people. Many Cherokees and members of other recognized tribes do not see unrecognized, largely self-proclaimed "tribes" as legitimate, and because these entities take their tribal names, the issue is personal. Individuals like Poteete take offense to their claims to being kin.

The Cherokee Nation's campaign to expose these groups as fraudu-lent often leads to unpleasant encounters: people do not appreciate being labeled wannabes and imposters. However, Poteete and his allies feel the battle must be enjoined, and they get emotional when speak-ing on the topic. They believe their work is important because these groups' actions strike at the heart of important Indian issues: tribal sovereignty, who can claim to be Indian, and who has the power to decide. Cherokee Nation spokespersons and leaders of other tribes feel these groups are engaging in cultural appropriation, fraud, and cultural misrepresentation, and they are taking moneys intended for real Indians. Poteete and others believe they need to educate the public about these fraudulent entities, yet the task can seem daunting. The battlefield is wide, and the arenas are quite diverse. They include the BIA's Federal Acknowledgment Process, state capitols where uninformed legislators confer "tribal" status on would-be tribes, Indian powwows, art venues, and even local high schools.

Leaders of the Five Tribes and related remnant tribes in the South-east (the Mississippi Band of Choctaws, Eastern Band of Cherokees, and Poarch Band of Creeks) are endeavoring to set more clear-cut, publicly recognized, formal boundaries separating their sovereign nations from perceived interlopers who are muddying the waters and confusing the public about their identities. The clear boundary they seek is enrollment (citizenship) in a federally recognized tribe. As such, the Five Tribes are against state-recognition of Indian groups. They oppose self-identified individuals working professionally as Chero-kees, Creeks, or other Indians. They will not accept groups that seek to gain federal status by going through Congress. Only those who make it through the BIA's rigorous acknowledgment process will find acceptance as legitimate tribes. The standards of the Five Tribes leaders for legitimizing presently unacknowledged tribes are very much in line with government criteria embodied in the Federal Acknowl-edgment Process. This is not surprising, since recognized tribes were highly involved in drafting the criteria in 1978: the FAP regulations and other modern Indian identification policies represent an evolved, Indian definition of who qualifies for Indian status today. To many tribal citizens the current acknowledgment and identification regimens make perfect sense. They have valid and well-articulated reasons for supporting strict standards and concrete, well-bounded political defi-nitions for identifying Indians in modern America. Against them are individuals like Ward Churchill and others who have set what appears to be a strong ideological trap for non-Indians and tribal leaders in the identity wars: if someone challenges their credentials by requiring proof, he or she is accused of being racist or an agent of colonial oppres-sion. The non-enrolled Indian spokespersons often claim to refuse to provide "Western" nonaboriginal forms of proof as both strategic and theatrical protest. They are the true Natives, they seem to say, by refusing to play the government's game. Tribal spokespersons are aware of the hegemonic, often colonial-derived structures in which modern tribes operate. However, various issues and concerns have prompted the Five Tribes and related recognized tribes to support strict, empiri-cally based criteria for recognizing Indians and tribes. As Patti Jo King, a Cherokee scholar studying at the University of Oklahoma, puts it, "We need some type of boundary; all tribes were originally family groups and bands but we were forced into political lines; we need to

draw the line somewhere and we need to use the structure that's there."
Cherokees like King want the political boundary to include only those
who are enrolled in federally recognized tribes.[2]

NORTH, SOUTH, EAST, AND WEST:
TRIBES RECOGNIZE THE PROBLEM

As early as 1970, Five Tribes leaders such as Cherokee Nation principal
chief W. W. Keeler and Creek Nation principal chief Claude Cox were
concerned about the rise in the number of self-proclaimed Indian
groups, organizations, and individuals. To these chiefs, unauthorized
tribal groups and organizations seemed a direct threat to their authority.
Keeler and Earl Boyd Pierce, the Cherokee Nation attorney, long
associated these groups with Red Power activists like Clyde Warrior
and urban groups like AIM that were challenging the authority of tribal
governments. Activists had accused Keeler and other well-educated
appointed leaders of being "white men" and not responsive to the full-
blood, more traditional communities in eastern Oklahoma. Because
some unrecognized groups, by no means the majority, utilized militant
rhetoric and were aided by new Indian legal rights groups, Keeler,
Pierce, and other leaders of the Five Tribes saw all unrecognized groups—
and nontribal entities like AIM and the grassroots Original Cherokee
Community Organization—as radicals and threats to their leadership.[3] All over the Southeast, established tribes felt they were losing
control of their identity, and perhaps status, as groups seemed to be
sprouting up all over. By the mid-1970s, leaders began to take action.
In 1976, in response to the Creek renaissance then at high tide in Florida,
Alabama, and Georgia, Florida Seminole chief Howard Tommie
demanded that the Florida governor refrain from recognizing these organizations and legitimizing them. As he testified to the Florida Governor's
Council on Indian Affairs, "There happens to be Indian tribes cropping
up all over the state of Florida; I get a little worried if they say we're
going to serve other Indian constituents here that somebody is going to
say we're going to take part of the Seminole Tribe's money and give it to
them." In time the Seminole chief would be joined by leaders of the Five
Tribes as they began to see self-proclaimed tribes as a collective problem.[4]

    While Keeler and many other Five Tribes leaders dealt with unrecog-
nized groups more as a theoretical and potential threat, Keeler's
hand-picked successor Ross Swimmer had to deal with these groups

on a more practical level. A lawyer, banker, and Republican, Swimmer was appointed tribal attorney at the recommendation of Pierce upon his retirement in 1974. Although only in his thirties, Swimmer won election as principal chief in 1975 and soon became a major force in Cherokee tribal development and politics. In 1985 he would be selected by president Ronald Reagan to head the BIA. In the early 1980s the chief found himself dealing with groups claiming to speak for his people, although this was not his most pressing concern. In 1984 an entity calling itself the Far Away Cherokees, which had both Indian and non-Indian members, was representing the Cherokee people in an official capacity from its Memphis home, seeking to erect a monument commemorating victims of the Trail of Tears. The problem of self-proclaimed local "tribal representatives" with no authority to speak for the Five Tribes had emerged. It would grow.[5]

It was Swimmer's successor, principal chief Wilma Mankiller, who launched the Cherokee Nation's concerted effort to fight the phenomenon of so-called wannabe tribes and fraudulent Indian individuals in all their manifestations. Born in eastern Oklahoma but raised in the San Francisco Bay Area by relocated Cherokee parents, Mankiller was an activist in the Red Power movement. After returning home in the early 1970s, she became a well-respected community development leader in the Cherokee Nation. Over objections from conservatives who claimed that the Cherokees were not ready for a female (or Democrat) leader, Swimmer nonetheless selected Mankiller as his running mate in 1983. After Swimmer's resignation in 1985 to accept the post of assistant secretary of the interior for Indian affairs (head of the BIA), Mankiller became nationally known as the first woman to become chief of a major Native American tribe. She was elected in her own right as principal chief in 1985, with a central goal of protecting the resources and rights of her people against threats to tribal sovereignty. With her straight-talking, no-nonsense style, Mankiller and the tribal registrar, Lee Fleming, made opposition to questionable Indian groups one of their major concerns during her administration (1985–1995). Also working in the Cherokee registration department, Richard Allen, a Vietnam veteran and self-described full-blood, recalls that he and Fleming were deluged with claims from individuals and groups hoping to associate with the Cherokee name and tribe. For several years the three began to compile data on dubious Cherokee-named groups and to plan ways to combat them. It was in part from his experience dealing with the issue that Fleming was chosen to head the Branch of Acknowledgment and Research (later named the Office of Federal Acknowledgment [OFA]) in the late 1990s. Fleming would take his experiences with Cherokee wannabes and frauds to his new post as overseer of the acknowledgment process.[6]

Lee Fleming, Richard Allen, and others involved with Cherokee registration and cultural preservation, working with the encouragement of Chief Mankiller, began recording groups claiming to be Cherokee tribes. The results were astounding. According to their findings, over 269 separate groups stretching from Florida to Alaska claimed to be some form of long-lost Cherokee tribe, nation, clan, or band. An analysis of the 2007 OFA list of groups seeking to petition for federal acknowledgment shows that 68 of the 324 groups on the list have "Cherokee," "Chickasaw," "Creek," "Choctaw," or "Seminole" in their names. This represents approximately 21 percent of all organizations seeking federal acknowledgment. Reflecting the four cardinal directions, there is a Northern Cherokee Nation based in Columbia, Missouri; the Southern Cherokee Nation previously mentioned; a group that claims to be the Eastern Cherokees (not the federally recognized ones), from South Carolina; and the Western Cherokee Nation based in Paragould, Arkansas. There are several "Lost Cherokee" bands and tribes with apparently no direction. Some have names like the Cherokee-Powhatan Indian Association that combine two famous Indian tribes. Others take nature-themed, New Age–sounding titles like the Osprey Band of Free Cherokees. There are "tribes" with simply bizarre names, such as the Phoenician Cherokee II–Eagle Tribe of Sequoyah. While many enrolled Cherokees will smile and chuckle when discussing these entities, Cherokee Nation leaders thought the proliferation of these organizations, at the macro level, was no laughing matter. They led the charge against these groups, believing that they had no right to proclaim themselves Cherokees and get away with it. Mankiller's group soon enlisted the support of the leaders of the other Five Tribes and related recognized tribes in the Southeast, Indian nations that also were affected by the trend.[7]

IN-BETWEEN TRIBES:
THE PROBLEM OF STATE-RECOGNIZED TRIBES

Chief Mankiller's most pressing issue was trying to convince state governments to refrain from recognizing tribes, an activity Cherokee leaders believed was the prerogative only of the federal government. The major problem was that few Americans realized that there were different levels of "tribes," and Mankiller and the others wanted to make sure they did. At least a dozen states have a class of non–federally recognized Indian entities known as state-recognized Indian tribes. Little known, even in Indian Country, these entities have been acknowledged by laws passed by legislatures in Alabama, Georgia, Louisiana, and other states declaring them "Indian tribes." These groups vary widely in their histories, community composition, and general acceptance as legitimate Indian entities. At issue with these groups is that states have varying standards they employ when bestowing this often-valuable status. Mankiller's group realized the often-hidden fact that few, if any, state-recognized tribes have undergone the rigorous review of their histories and ancestry that groups recognized through the Federal Acknowledgment Process have experienced. According to leaders of the Five Tribes and other knowledgeable parties, the very existence of these ambiguously recognized Indian groups causes confusion in Indian affairs. To some observers, state recognition has provided a loophole for dubious groups and individuals to qualify for a host of valuable benefits and programs intended for Indian citizens.[8]

It is dangerous to group all state-recognized tribes in the same category. They vary considerably in their histories, community composition, and political functioning. On one end of the spectrum are the colonial era tribes of the Eastern Seaboard, such as Virginia's Mattaponis and Pamunkeys. They live on state reservations that the Commonwealth of Virginia set aside prior to the founding of the United States. Few knowledgeable parties take issue with these state reservation communities, although questions as to their racial composition, particularly African admixture, have swirled around them since the early nineteenth century. At the other extreme are certain groups that have secured state recognition since the 1960s. Often these "tribes" were able to convince well-connected state legislators to introduce bills declaring them tribes, the whole procedure essentially amounting to an honorary proclamation. Over time, to add gravitas to the procedure, several states have created Indian commissions that have criteria for acknowledging tribes, yet none of these state bodies force would-be tribes to submit detailed petitions for acknowledgment or undergo the rigorous vetting process required by the BIA. Members of state legislatures rarely have the time or expertise to wisely judge the cases before them in session.

In some cases group members dress up in stereotypical Indian garb and appear before the legislature to make their case. Oblivious to the complexities of the issue, state politicians are impressed with the seeming "Indian appearance" of the individuals placed before them. More often than not, the less "Indian-looking" members of the hopeful tribe are not along to testify. An egregious example of this process occurred in Arkansas. In 2005 a state congressman there introduced a bill to recognize a new tribe, the "Lost Cherokees of Arkansas." The problem was that this congressman also was the "chief" of the group in question. Groups hoping for state recognition typically have piles of letters of support from local businesses and governments touting the unique cultural and financial benefits that state status would confer on the new tribe and citizens of the local area. Even with groups with weak cases, unwitting state legislators, not wanting to seem against Native Americans (or happy to have "real live Indians" in their districts) often pass these seemingly innocuous pieces of legislation. While far inferior to federal status and once largely honorary, state recognition has come to give groups access to many local, state, and federal programs and grants, Indian scholarships, and other valuable programs. It also allows group members to market art as American Indian–made under federal statute.[9]

Led by the Cherokees, representatives of the Five Tribes and related federally recognized tribes increasingly have lobbied against state recognition of Indian tribes. Their position is based on legal, political, and moral grounds, stemming from a growing perception that what was once a largely symbolic or honorary designation has opened a Pandora's box of issues unforeseen by state legislators. The battle began in the early 1980s once recognized tribal leaders realized that southern states were increasingly acknowledging self-proclaimed Indian groups within their borders. These leaders quickly became aware of the complications wrought by state-recognized tribes, state Indian commissions, and non-enrolled Indian claimants. One catalyst was a historic meeting in 1984 between the Cherokee Nation and the Eastern Band of Cherokee Indians at the historic Red Clay Council Grounds in Tennessee. Here the two Cherokee tribes met for the first time in almost 150 years to discuss issues of mutual concern. The meeting created a lot of interest in the Southeast. Chief Swimmer received much correspondence from excited individuals, including a letter from a man calling himself Tomah. While thrilled about the historic meeting, Tomah questioned why he and other "Indian brothers" were not invited to attend. In the wake of the Red Clay Council, the Tennessee state legislature created the Tennessee Indian Affairs Commission. Cherokee-named groups, including the Etowah Cherokee Nation, the Tennessee Band of Cherokee, the Far Away Cherokee Association, and the Red Clay Band of the Southeastern Cherokee Confederacy, were founding members and dominated the new entity. The last group was associated with the Georgia-based entity described in chapter 4, the Southeastern Cherokee Confederacy, which gained state recognition in its founding year, 1975, but failed to secure federal acknowledgment in 1985. After learning that the leader of the Etowah group, Alvin O. Langdon, had been convicted of mail fraud and that others like the Far Away Cherokee group admitted non-Indians, Chief Swimmer wrote to the Tennessee governor expressing his concern over the criteria used to select members for the commission. The Cherokee Nation chief and the Eastern Band leaders were concerned enough to issue a 1984 "Joint Council Resolution" requesting that Tennessee "require that those appointed or elected members representing Indian America be members of federally recognized tribes." Swimmer also began acquiring data on surviving Indian groups in the Southeast, perplexed and concerned over the apparent reemergence in former Five Tribes homelands of Cherokee and other tribes that the Cherokee Nation and Eastern Band had never heard about.[10]

Known for her dogged protection of tribal sovereignty and desire to overturn stereotypes about Native people, Wilma Mankiller took the crusade against wannabe tribes to new heights after assuming her position as principal chief in 1985. Frustrated at the weekly complaints, headaches, and phone calls prompted by dubious groups, Mankiller had her staff compile a list of spurious groups, which the tribe then circulated. The list was potentially explosive because it flatly questioned the authenticity of groups it enumerated. Taking upon herself the often-unpleasant task of educating the public about wannabe tribes, in 1993 Chief Mankiller wrote to Georgia governor Zell Miller to express her opposition to the state's recent recognition of several Cherokee-named groups and the Lower Muskogee Creek Tribe discussed in chapter 4. She was joined in this battle by leaders of other federally recognized tribes such as the Miccosukees of Florida and some Oklahoma Creeks. As Tom Berryhill, described in the papers as a "full-blood" and former member of the Creek National Council, told a reporter: "They [state legislators] have not really looked into what is really an Indian. They

have [just] taken the word of a woman." That woman was Lower Muskogee chief Marian "Vonnie" McCormick, wife of Nealie McCormick,
the son of the group's founder Neal McCormick detailed previously.
As is typical in this discourse Chief McCormick countercharged that
greed had inspired Berryhill's comments, but she still wanted good
feelings between them, saying, "They're part of us and we're part of
them." Berryhill went on to state that the Georgia Creeks might possess
some Indian blood but were not "true Indians." To him the latter meant
belonging to a clan, having a ceremonial fire, speaking the language,
and practicing Creek traditions. Berryhill told the press: "These so-called
Indians are not Indians at all. I feel like there are a lot of wannabes
that want to jump on the bandwagon."[11] Just as Berryhill was accused
of being selfish and greedy, other tribal critics were accused of "not
acting in the Indian way" when they questioned these groups. As the
most visible activist, Chief Mankiller encountered the most angry
responses to her work. In one instance a woman named "Day Flower"
of the Pan American Indian Association wrote asking what gave Chief
Mankiller the right to determine who was Indian. Day Flower ended
her letter by calling Mankiller "an ugly person" and an "Old Hen."
Another individual, after being told by Chief Mankiller that the only
way he could join the Cherokee Nation was to prove his ancestors were
on the Dawes Rolls, indignantly replied: "I wish to tell you here and now
that I am 3/8 Cherokee and no person on this earth can change that!"[12]

As the years passed and recognized tribal members increasingly
experienced hassles and tense confrontations with individuals representing non–federally recognized tribes, the official position of the
Five Tribes hardened against state-recognized groups. Once again the
Cherokees, the people most negatively affected by the issue, led the way.
The Cherokee Nation and Eastern Band issued Joint Council Resolutions in 1988 and again ten years later in opposition to state recognition
and what they referred to as "fabricated Cherokee 'tribes.'" As the issue
spread, other Indian nations joined the effort. On May 21, 2009, the
Inter-Tribal Council of the Five Civilized Tribes passed a resolution
stating in part:

> Be it resolved, that the Inter-Tribal Council of the Five Civilized
> Tribes objects to the recognition of Indian heritage groups and
> cultural clubs by states as "state recognized tribes."

> Be it further resolved that the Inter-Tribal Council of the Five
> Civilized Tribes encourages the United States Congress to limit
> the expenditure of funding designed for American Indian and
> Native American nations, tribes, and bands to federally recog-
> nized nations, tribes and bands.

The resolution represented the high-water mark for tribal unity on
the issue and was signed by Bill Anoatubby, governor of the Chickasaw
Nation, principal chief A. D. Ellis (Muscogee Nation), principal chief
Gregory E. Pyle (Choctaw Nation), principal chief Kelly Haney (Seminole Nation), and principal chief Chad Smith (Cherokee Nation).[13]

In 2009, the state of Tennessee introduced a bill to recognize a
strangely conceived grand "Confederation of Tennessee Native Tribes,"
an entity that included a group calling itself the Remnant Yuchi Nation
(the Yuchis are part of the Creek Nation), and now the Muscogee (Creek)
Nation was alerted. The Tennessee confederation also included groups
called the Upper Cumberland Cherokees, the Chikamaka Band, the
Central Band of Cherokees, the Cherokee Wolf Clan, and the Tanasi
Council of the Far Away Cherokees. Cherokee Nation principal chief
Chad Smith sent out an urgent e-mail message to tribal citizens advocating they contact their congressional representatives in opposition
to the Tennessee bill. By this time, the Cherokee Nation had formulated a legal argument, supported by attorney general briefs from
Texas and Arkansas, that states lacked constitutional authority to recognize Indian tribes. The Creek Nation and Cherokee Nation also presented a moral argument, saying that Tennessee and Georgia, states
that had been perhaps the greatest advocates of the removal of the
Five Tribes, had no ethical right to "recognize" new groups today. In
arguing against the Tennessee legislation, Chief Smith also noted:
"Ancestors of the Cherokee Nation were forcibly removed from their
homes in Tennessee and the southeast to Indian Territory in 1838–39
and the Cherokee Nation contends that no Cherokee clans, bands,
tribes or nations were left behind or have continued to exist in Tennessee." The Creeks and Cherokees sent tribal representatives to fight the
pending Tennessee actions as well. Cherokee Richard Allen succeeded
in having the Cherokee groups removed from the legislation. This left
only the Yuchi group in the confederation. With Muskogee Nation
cultural preservation officer Joyce Bear lobbying against it, the Creek

Nation likewise succeeded in blocking the attempted state recognition of the "Remnant Yuchi Nation" of Tennessee.[14]

THE PROBLEM OF OPTIONAL ETHNICITY

The modern phenomenon of state-recognized tribes was only part of a larger problem of individuals appropriating tribal identities for personal gain. This was an old story. As previously discussed, individuals such as Sylvester Long (Buffalo Child Long Lance) and Iron Eyes Cody appropriated a Cherokee identity for professional advancement almost a hundred years ago. However, in the eyes of the leaders of the Five Tribes, the problem had grown exponentially since the 1970s and manifested itself in various venues. At its root is the phenomenon of individuals with no historic connection to the Five Tribes suddenly choosing to claim that they are Cherokee, Chickasaw, Choctaw, Creek, or Seminole. Called "optional ethnicity" by Harvard sociologist Mary Waters, or "ethnic shifting" or "ethnic shopping," the practice really started in the 1960s when individuals increasingly chose to identify with ethnic groups in their family trees that they perceived as more appealing than the generic "white" category. During this era some people viewed groups such as Italians and Greeks as warm, family-oriented, and colorful, and so to be Italian American or Greek American was better than being simply "white" (which implied blandness). As David Stowe so vividly puts it: "To the melanin-deprived . . . Whiteness describes not a culture but precisely the absence of culture; there seem[s] to be a kind of emptiness at the core of whiteness." While Waters does not discuss American Indians, the phenomenon could apply to thousands of previously labeled "white" Americans who chose to claim an Indian identity during the era. Not surprisingly, some of these individuals sought like-minded associates and formed "Cherokee" or other "tribes." These formerly disconnected individuals suddenly found a sense of belonging, complete with fictive (but perceived real) kinship ties, a romanticized yet seemingly sacred history, and tangible benefits of belonging to a sympathetic ethnic minority. To thousands of newly identified Creeks or Cherokees, the shift in identity was largely symbolic and even recreational in nature. Most joined these "tribes" by conscious choice—they were not associated with the historic and traditional institutions of the Creek or Cherokee peoples. Their experience as members of these new groups rarely displayed attributes associated with real ethnic communities. Most often individuals did not live in an ethnic community, practice a common religion, or speak an indigenous language. They rarely were born of parents hailing from the group, and few chose marriage partners from within the group. From the most jaded perspective, these individuals claimed an Indian identity for purely recreational purposes. Because they chose to join the "ethnic" group, having no long-term association with it, these folks had the option of claiming or discarding the ethnicity at will. They could don the ethnic tag if they wanted (depending on the situation and the perceived costs and benefits of doing so) and drop the identity just as easily. As Waters finds for other white ethnicities, these "optional" ethnic individuals felt few if any of the historic costs experienced by members of the group in question, such as discrimination, limited educational opportunities, or proscribed economic prospects. To tribal leaders and citizens raised in eastern Oklahoma, the newly proclaimed Cherokee and Creek Indians seemed to fit this description perfectly.[15]

Few of the generally white people who claim to be "part Cherokee" realize how they are perceived in Indian Country. Enrolled members of the Five Tribes have mixed reactions when they encounter self-proclaimed Cherokees, Chickasaws, Creeks, Seminoles, or Choctaws. On one end of the spectrum is Cherokee Nation councilman Jack Baker. An affable man in his fifties, Baker laughs when he thinks about the dozens of people who, after finding out he is Cherokee, inevitably tell him they too have a great-great-grandmother who was a Cherokee, and who go on to proclaim how proud they are of having the same heritage. Many tribal members are not amused by these white Indians, however, and simply do not say anything when they encounter the "Cherokee great-grandmother" phenomenon. Patti Jo King, an enrolled Cherokee doctoral student at the University of Oklahoma, and others are angry in these cases. King calls these supposed Cherokee relatives "just pathetic." Cherokee Nation policy analyst Richard Allen also gets visibly agitated when discussing what he calls "wannabe Cherokees." A self-described "identifiable" Indian, Allen has concluded: "People want to be Cherokee and I don't know why. That they see it as an elevation in status is funny to me. I did not have the ability to switch—I'm identifiable." As Allen's reaction reveals, he is dismayed by what he sees as white individuals "choosing" to switch to a supposed "elevated" Indian identity like the other white ethnics described by sociologist Mary

Waters. Both Allen and Patti Jo King note that they grew up as "Indian-looking" people with the incumbent discrimination that being non-white entails. To them, these "instant" Indians are claiming their people's identity without experiencing any of the costs historically associated with it. In particular, Allen believes that none of the groups claiming to be Indian in the Southeast today (with the exception of the Jena Choctaws) look Indian to him. He feels that members of unrecognized and state-recognized tribes look either white or part black. As Allen says, take away the stereotypical Indian garb that they often wear and they "would look like any other white or black guys in the building." Allen feels that because these folks did not grow up in an indigenous community, do not practice indigenous culture, and are not Indian in appearance, they have no right to claim to be Indian in modern America.[16]

THE TRAIL OF TEARS AND THE IMPLICATIONS
OF HISTORICAL MEMORY

Central to the identity of the Five Tribes of Oklahoma is the historical memory of their ancestors' suffering on the infamous Trail of Tears, the forced removal of the tribes from their southeastern homelands in the 1830s. Although death toll estimates vary, the Cherokees likely lost a quarter of their population, and the other tribes also lost considerable numbers. While the tragic experience of the Five Tribes figures prominently in romantic tales of antebellum southern history, to the Five Tribes the cultural memory of the death marches lives on in family and tribal oral tradition. Being a descendant of these brave souls provides a strong ethnic boundary marker. Few individuals who are proud to claim they had a Cherokee great-great-grandmother realize how the event affects how they are perceived by enrolled members and how proving a genealogical link to these families eases the path to acceptance into the fold. In her significant study of Cherokee identity, Circe Sturm interviewed a seventy-six-year-old fluent Cherokee speaker who told her: "For someone to be registered who's 1/2000 Cherokee, that's really splitting hairs. But you must remember that their ancestors came over on the Trail of Tears just the same as mine did or the equivalent. They suffered the same consequences and the same hardships and probably lost many of their relatives that way." Conversely individuals

Figure 12. Patti Jo King, Cherokee Nation citizen and scholar,
2012. (Photograph courtesy of
Patti Jo King)

who cannot prove that their ancestors suffered on the Trail of Tears
are not welcomed. Few nonmembers realize that tribal identity was
constructed, in part, in opposition to Anglo-American culture that was
intent on destroying their peoples and nations. Many whites who
choose to identify with a perceived Indian ancestor do not comprehend
the real difference between their experience and that of members of
Native communities. They in no way experienced the legal discrimination and racial violence directed against citizens of the Five Tribes. As
James Hamill argues in *Going Indian*, a 2006 study of Indian identity
in Oklahoma, non-Indians in the state are largely unaware of the fine
points of both tribal and pan-Indian ethnic identity in the region.
Most are oblivious to how local Indians have constructed a strong
symbolic boundary between themselves and the surrounding society.
Ethnic and tribal identity has been constructed in adversarial, Indian-
versus-white terms, the "us and them" dichotomy strengthened by oral
and family traditions based on a strong sense of shared experiences
of removal, forced assimilation, land loss, and allotment at the hands
of white Oklahomans. This private identity is defensively maintained,
if largely invisible to non-Indians.[17]

The implications of tribal historical memory are clearly evident in
modern debates about the authenticity and worthiness of many groups

that seek federal tribal recognition in the Southeast. As early as 1976, Creek, Miccosukee, and Seminole leaders opposed what they saw as Johnny-come-lately Indians popping up in Alabama, Georgia, and Florida. When the Florida groups sought state aid, the federally recognized tribes sprang into action. George Tiger, public relations officer for the Creek National Council in Oklahoma, openly challenged the identity of these groups in the press. Implicit in questions about whether the rising tribes were "really Indian" was the sentiment that they had not suffered for their identity and culture like the reservation-based Creeks, Seminoles, and Miccosukees. As chief Howard Tommie of the Florida Seminole Tribe noted: "Now everyone wants to be Indian, including these fly-by-night [Eastern Creek] Indians who never became Indian except to capitalize on federal funds." At the time, one reporter found that some Seminoles and Creeks in Oklahoma still held a grudge against the Eastern Creek descendants, because, even if they could prove their heritage, their ancestors had sided with Andrew Jackson in the Creek Wars and therefore had not endured the Trail of Tears with their kin.[18]

The issue of interlopers seeking to associate with the tragic Trail of Tears came to the fore as the sesquicentennial of the event approached in the 1980s. As chairman of the Trail of Tears Association, an organization that received Cherokee Nation funding, Jack Baker increasingly had to contend with various "Cherokee Nations" attempting to speak for his people on this painful and sensitive issue. The problem was particularly acute in southern states where interest was high yet where a certified Cherokee presence was generally absent. According to Baker, the existence of several local "Cherokee" groups caused much confusion. While they did their best to look Indian, dressing in buckskin, wearing fur, and putting beads and feathers in their hair, Baker feels that members of these entities cannot prove that they are Cherokee descendants. Even if they could prove their Indian blood, Baker echoes a common sentiment when he says that they are not true tribes, and so they have no right to represent the Cherokee Nation, especially in matters as sensitive as how to commemorate the Trail of Tears. To Baker these groups are an annoyance but he can understand their motivations. He thinks that these folks truly believe they are Cherokee: they have heard the family stories for so long that they think they are Indian. If Jack Baker is sympathetic, fellow Cherokee councilperson Cara Cowan Watts has no patience for these self-proclaimed tribes invoking her people's name on such sensitive matters. She notes: "Many of them are hostile and almost frantic about their claims of an Indian identity. Others just need to be educated and will often distance themselves from groups that are out there causing harm. I believe that most folks are in need of a personal identity and find the movie version of Native America more alluring than the reality of their family tree."[19] Richard Allen and Patti Jo King likewise have no patience for self-proclaimed Indians, whom they see as cultural interlopers seeking to associate themselves with Cherokee people yet who have not shared in the oppression experienced by the Cherokees. Allen notes that darker-skinned Indians did not always have an easy time in eastern Oklahoma. King agrees, noting that few whites realize just how she feels when they claim to be Cherokee. She thinks about her ancestors who endured the Trail of Tears, the theft of lands, boarding schools, and discrimination in Jim Crow Oklahoma at the hands of white people—and she sees white people before her claiming to be her kin. Overall the memory of the Trail of Tears remains strong and affects the reception that undocumented Indians receive among enrolled members. As Watts says: "My ancestors stood up and said they were Cherokees when others removed themselves from the tribe, giving up citizenship for themselves and their descendants."[20]

There are other related cultural and historical issues that make self-identified Indians and their actions a highly sensitive matter for citizens of the Five Tribes. As Richard Allen notes, dubious groups and individuals are constantly calling his office asking how to "hook up" with a tribal medicine man. Government agencies often inquire about the legitimacy of various groups seeking rights under the Native American Graves Protection and Repatriation Act. Prison officials call, confused by individuals claiming to be Cherokee in order to practice Native American religious rights. To Allen these people are both an annoyance and an affront to his people's way of life. As he notes, dubious entities and individuals do not possess community ties with his tribe, and they do not have Cherokee cultural knowledge. Allen echoes a common sentiment, saying that his people know their history, they know who their relatives are, and that these folks are strangers and unwelcome as such. "I wish they would just go away," Allen says in exasperation.[21] However, they have not gone away, and, as the Cherokee Nation has recognized, dubious Indian individuals and tribes have come to affect a wide array of Indian-related issues in America today.

QUESTIONABLE INDIANS IN THE ARTS

Some leaders of the Five Tribes have made policing who can market
art as "Native American" part of their crusade against what they refer
to as "fraudulent" Indians and tribes. Efforts to protect indigenous artists
and artisans from non-Indian interlopers date to the Indian Arts and
Crafts Act of 1935, part of the Indian New Deal under commissioner
of Indian affairs John Collier. With the law, for the first time a federal
statute prohibited non-Indians from selling arts and crafts as "Indian-
made." Like the larger Indian New Deal, the law was designed to promote Native American economic development. In 1990 Congress passed
a revised act to regulate the increasingly lucrative Indian art market that
experts estimated at the time at close to $1 billion annually. Member-
ship in a federally recognized tribe was the general threshold for marketing work as an Indian artist. However, the 1990 law allowed members
of state-recognized tribes to sell their wares as indigenous-made, a fact
that has displeased many leaders of the Five Tribes and added to the
simmering conflict between the two types of tribes.[22]

The 1990 Indian Arts and Crafts Act was widely supported by Indian
artists and tribal leaders, but it is not without its critics. Kay Walkingstick, a painter and self-identified Cherokee, provides a typical critique
of the efforts of recognized tribes and federal legislators to police and
define authenticity in the arts. Claiming that her ancestors refused
to sign the Dawes Rolls as a form of political protest, Walkingstick now
decries the fact that she and others have to prove they are Indian by
reference to federal rolls and formal tribal membership that are alien
to Native cultures. Similarly, multimedia artist Hulleah J. Tsinhnahjin-
nie, who identifies herself as Dine/Seminole/Muskogee, created a
piece entitled *Nobody's Pet Indian* for a 1993 exhibit, protesting the need
to have a government-imposed pedigree to market Indian art. The
work consisted of three photographs of the artist with her enrollment
number and bar codes printed across her face. Ward Churchill, who
has self-identified as Cherokee and Creek, similarly has protested government efforts to regulate authenticity by using enrollment. To Churchill
and others the government stamp of approval should been seen as a
stigma more than an honor. In a well-known essay, "Nobody's Pet
Poodle," he made an argument, heard since the 1960s, that the federal
arts law was insisting that Indians have "pedigrees" much like registered dogs do. A leading proponent of the self-identification school,

Churchill criticized recognized tribes for blindly aping racist federal membership requirements, excluding their Indian kin in the process. Artist Criss Smith, a Creek/Navajo living in Holbrook, Arizona, agrees that the federal laws are simply part of an ongoing tribal effort to further bureaucratize Indian affairs and usurp the rights of individuals to sell and market art as they see fit.[23]

Many parties reject these arguments, believing that far from being too restrictive, the 1990 Indian Arts and Crafts Act does not go far enough. They point to a 2009 study showing that at least 40 percent of works sold in the approximately $2 billion annual Native American arts and crafts industry was fake. They view efforts by self-identified Indian artists, who sell objects as diverse as jewelry, paintings, moccasins, dream-catchers, Kokopelli figurines, and religious "rites," as nothing less than cultural appropriation and theft. Seminole Tribe of Florida employee Pete Gallagher recalls becoming aware of the issue while surfing the Internet. "There were a lot of Indian sites and several large web page rings. But a lot of the information on these sites seemed suspicious to us. It was hard to tell authenticity . . . whether it was a legitimate American Indian tribe or entity or not. Many of these sites included shopping areas, gifts shops and the like and it was difficult to determine if they were fraudulent or not." As a result the Seminole Tribe created Indian Circle, the first website to link together home pages restricted to federally recognized tribes across the nation. According to tribal webmaster Dan McDonald, "This [will] ensure the authenticity, and keep out those entities that, for whatever reason, cannot qualify for federal recognition."[24]

The venues where non-Indians represent themselves as American Indians for profit are quite diverse. Beyond marketing art and other products on the Internet, it is common in the southeastern United States for non-Indians and members of unrecognized Indian groups to set up booths at powwows, to present Native American dances, and to otherwise represent American Indians at local events and commemorations. There are a few local Indian watchdog groups that have challenged these activities, but the assistant manager of Cahokia Mounds Historic Site near East St. Louis, Illinois, admitted that he allowed questionable "enthusiast" groups to participate in Indian-themed activities at his park because there simply were not enough Native Americans in the area to staff gatherings or to receive allocated state grants. Artist Criss Smith, who has lived and worked in the Southeast and who considers herself more in the "live and let live" tradition of Indian culture, still takes issue with individuals, whether enrolled in recognized tribes or not, selling art detached from its cultural meaning and significance. She reports that it is common for businesspeople to buy truckloads of real Indian art in Gallup, New Mexico, and fake objects from Asia, and transport them to Indian gatherings throughout the South, a practice she finds both fraudulent and reprehensible.[25]

Allegations of ethnic fraud also extend to the increasingly popular Native American music industry, and once again most of the accused imposters claim to be Cherokee. Beginning in the early 1970s when singer and actress Cher told the press that she was "1/16th Cherokee" and dressed as a flesh-exposed Indian "maiden" to boost the sales of her record "Half-Breed," recording artists have claimed Indian heritage for professional purposes. Artists as diverse as Johnny Cash and Wayne Newton have at various points claimed to be Cherokee and have closely identified with Native struggles. There is a current controversy raging over the Native American Music Awards or "Nammy Awards," which allow any artist who identifies as indigenous and works in the Native music genre to receive awards. Several Cherokee writers have accused artists such as Rita Coolidge and her group Walela, Douglas Blue Feather, and others of fraudulently claiming indigenous heritage to sell their works and infiltrate a category intended for Native Americans. While Coolidge and the others' authenticity is still debated, it is clear that some enrolled citizens of the Five Tribes are attempting to draw a boundary in popular music as well, using media "outing" as a means to ensure that only members of federally-recognized tribes can market their music as American Indian.[26]

On January 21, 2008, Chad Smith, principal chief of the Cherokee Nation of Oklahoma signed a tribal law, the Truth in Advertising for Native Art Act, to remedy what the Cherokee leaders saw as an epidemic of fraudulent artists and writers using the Cherokee name for profit. Smith, elected principal chief in 1999, is a descendant of Redbird Smith and other "traditionalist" members of the United Keetoowah Band. Prior to election his work as an attorney and legal scholar sensitized him to Cherokee identity issues. The Truth in Advertising Act was simply the most recent salvo in an identity war that had much longer roots in Oklahoma. Since the renewal of the Five Tribes' governments in the early 1970s they had instituted an arts and crafts training program, with an eye toward providing sustainable jobs for tribal members. Cherokee chief Wilma Mankiller took pains to open arts and crafts outlets for tribal artisans. However, ensuring "authenticity" was an ongoing concern. As early as 1973 the Five Tribes Foundation had instituted a seal of authenticity, concerned with shoddy and fake goods that it called a "drug" on the Indian market.[27] The 2008 Cherokee Nation law followed up on this concern. It was designed to curb what the Cherokee Nation saw as the widespread appropriation of Cherokee culture and identity by non-Indians and noncitizens. It applied to events held within the Cherokee Nation or sponsored by it. The tribal law closed what the Cherokees saw as the loophole in the 1990 Indian Arts and Crafts Act that allowed members of state-recognized tribes to market work as Native artists. The Truth in Advertising Act mandated that only members of federally recognized tribes could sell works as American Indian–made. As sponsor Cara Cowan Watts noted, "A line must be drawn to define Indian. Tribal citizenship is a reasonable definition." The tribal law also expanded on the federal definition of protected "art" to include not only arts and crafts but also written works and performance arts such as storytelling and music.[28]

Predictably the Cherokee law drew mixed responses. On the one hand, some observers charged the Cherokee Nation with racism, of being "identity police" by excluding non-enrolled individuals. Many people were surprised and saddened when the Cherokee Nation pulled works from the walls of the Cherokee Cultural Center in Tahlequah by well-known artist Murv Jacobs because, although he was known as a Cherokee artist, he was not enrolled in the tribe. Vendors who once had booths at the Cultural Center's art shows clearly were dismayed to find they were no longer welcomed. While non-enrolled artists were angered or dejected, many others welcomed the Cherokee efforts to draw clear ethnic boundaries. As Cherokee Nation web manager Tonia Williams told the press: "[F]or every dollar [fake Indians] receive, it's a dollar that doesn't go to a real Native American." Enrolled Cherokee artist Roger Cain responded in the same vein: "To me, if they are federally recognized they are the ones with the ancestors who stood up and said 'I'm Cherokee; I'm Keetoowah.' We have to honor our ancestors who did this." Suzanne Shown Harjo (Cheyenne/Creek), a prominent national Indian leader, also praises the Cherokee effort: "Someone has to step up and talk about these people, even if they are your friends. A lot of these con artists are very talented . . . at making a buck on someone else's identity." It bears mentioning that many state-recognized tribes are taking similar steps, demanding vendors show their state-issued tribal identity cards to sell their wares as Indian made.[29]

SPIRITUAL CHARLATANS, NEW AGE SHAMANS, AND RELIGIOUS APPROPRIATION

Few issues are as emotional or important to Native Americans as the appropriation of indigenous spirituality by non-Indian individuals seeking to profit from real or distorted American Indian culture. Once again the Cherokees have felt the brunt of the issue as charlatans of all stripes have claimed their tribal identity to peddle various forms of Indian indigenous spirituality to uninitiated individuals. Tribal members entwined in traditional Cherokee spiritual institutions such as the Keetoowah Nighthawk Society and the Cherokee Baptist churches are dismayed, and often angered, by the proliferation of white "shamans" and New Age Indian prophets trafficking in Native American traditions. While financial reward is the foremost motivation of vendors, followers partake in Indian-themed spiritual traditions for personal reasons, some seeking enlightenment, others searching for self-actualization. Few, however, have a true awareness of the time commitments required to immerse oneself within living indigenous traditions, and most do not realize how their spiritual forays affect living Native Americans.

Richard Allen recalls the day he first became aware that non-Indians were infiltrating his tribal traditions. Asked by Chief Mankiller to represent the tribe at a ceremony honoring Nez Perce prisoners of war who were exiled to Oklahoma in the nineteenth century, Allen was surprised to find a man he did not know introduced as Two Rabbits, a "Cherokee spiritual leader, pipe carrier, and member of the Bear Clan Medicine Society," sitting in an honored position at the head of the table. Allen had made a personal commitment to challenge people he thought were imposters so he confronted this man, and he recalls that Two Rabbits began to stammer, ultimately claiming that his great-great-grandmother was a Cherokee from Alabama, Tennessee, or Kentucky (he did not know precisely) and it was through her that he had been given the right to claim his titles. According to Allen the man's fraud was apparent. Real Cherokee people did not have special medicine clans, and they do not carry Plains-style medicine pipes. Overall, Allen was appalled that so blatant a fraud could infiltrate such an important ceremony. He soon found that this man was not unique. All over the country white so-called shamans and plastic medicine men were conning naive Americans, offering to conduct "ceremonies" for a price, experiences that mixed traditions from various tribes and even Eastern religious traditions into a strange hodge-podge of supposed spirituality.[30]

While individuals connected to their tribal communities can easily identify spiritual charlatans, other parties cannot, and the opportunities for fraud and misunderstandings are immense. Like with art, ersatz and authentic Native American spirituality is a multimillion-dollar industry. However, as Allen points out, real shamans would never charge for their services. Devoid of context and meaning, there are hundreds of websites selling all sorts of Native American religious artifices, natural materials, books, and "experiences" to an unsuspecting public. Leaders of the Cherokee Nation clearly are annoyed and concerned at the confusion that wannabe Native spirituality peddlers cause. Its tribal headquarters in Tahlequah regularly receives calls from prison officials inquiring whether a self-proclaimed Cherokee is eligible to conduct sweat lodge purification or other ceremonies generally only available to members of federally recognized tribes. Patti Jo King uses the Cherokee word for "thieves" to describe the folks peddling her people's secrets and traditions, and she calls their followers "spiritual orphans." King believes that millions of white Americans are simply seeking an earth-based tradition they find more deeply rewarding than the Christian traditions of their upbringing.[31] She sees a larger peril in the seemingly innocuous activities of spiritual seekers. As she notes: "These frauds are endangering to Native American people. We are a small minority and when our lifeways and belief systems are compromised we are in danger of losing them." Although she is clearly aware that culture changes over time, King sees a major threat in the work of New Age shamans. To her, they are incorporating disparate belief systems, including Eastern mysticism and real tribal traditions, into one pan-Indian, New Age stew, creating new, diluted forms far removed from traditional spiritual indigenous traditions. A danger lies in what she has actually seen: young urban Indians learning "Native religion" from these individuals. King and others are concerned that what is left of the ancient traditions is completely lost or distorted in the new rendering. She is not alone: as early as 1980 the Traditional Elders' Circle, a grassroots pan-Indian spiritual organization, passed a resolution warning gullible souls to stay clear of individuals who sell Indian ceremonial services.[32]

A prime example of an apparently non-Indian shaman leading followers into actions that verged on the illegal is the career of James Warren "Flaming Eagle" Mooney, a self-proclaimed Seminole "peyote priest" from the unlikely location of Sanpete County, Utah. The leader of a group called the Oklevueha Earthwalks Native American Church and an apparent member of the non–federally recognized Oklevueha Seminole Band of Oklahoma and Florida, Mooney was arrested in 2000 and charged with ten first-degree felony counts that included drug trafficking and racketeering. In a sheriff's raid on the group's six-acre compound, law enforcement officers seized ceremonial pipes and twelve thousand peyote buttons, the latter totaling thirty-three pounds, used in conjunction with Native American religious ceremonies. A 1994 federal law exempted members of federally recognized tribes from various state narcotics laws dealing with peyote as a hallucinogenic substance. In this vein leaders of the Native American Church were on record opposing Mooney and his largely non-Indian followers for tarnishing the church's reputation and raising the ire of opponents of the American Indian institution. According to Forrest Cuch (Ute), director of the Utah Division of Indian Affairs, Mooney's use of the drug was a defilement of a religious sacrament. It seemed to law enforcement officials and many adherents of the faith that the exception for using an otherwise federally banned substance should be only for members of federally recognized tribes who were also members of the Native American Church. However, the Utah Supreme Court later ruled in Mooney's favor, finding that limiting peyote use to members of federally recognized tribes would violate the equal protection clause of the Constitution. The potential now existed for non-Indians to use this loophole to join the organization, in part to engage in otherwise illegal drug use. In submitting a state law requiring that practitioners be members of federal tribes, Utah attorney general Mark Shurtleff stated: "If you're a Native American of a federally recognized tribe participating in the ritual, you will be protected. If you're a white, [wannabe] Indian who wants to deal drugs, then you'll be prosecuted." Mooney's case provides yet another example of a sacred Native American rite seemingly appropriated and misused by non-Indians. His case made national news, confirming to conservative individuals the slippery slope of allowing exemptions to federal drug laws: in this case, to non-Indians under Indian guise. It also potentially endangered the continuing religious traditions of the Native American Church.[33]

Even more disturbing are several cases where supposed Native American gurus used their false status for sexual gratification, sexual assault, or to peddle sexual practices anathema to many tribal leaders. To Chief Mankiller, in particular, these types of activities were perhaps the most appalling of the Cherokee frauds. A prime example is Harley Reagan. Calling himself "Swift Deer," Reagan appeared in a 1992 HBO documentary called *Real Sex*, purporting to be a Cherokee sex guru. Over protests from Chief Mankiller, the program aired. Scholar Deborah Root reports seeing the video on a motel-room television set, and she recalls being quite shocked to see a confident, bearded white man and his demure wife leading middle-aged couples in a seminar teaching "traditional" Native techniques to revive their sagging sex lives. Using smudge sticks, sacred drums, and a blackboard, the guru admonished participants to enter the natural world of purported Cherokee sex. As reported by journalist Susy Buchanan in a later 2002 article, "Sacred Orgasm," Reagan claimed not only to be Native American but also that the traditions taught were authentic Indian ways. Reagan stated that it was his grandmother, "Spotted Fawn," a Texas Cherokee medicine woman, who arranged for him as a fourteen-year-old boy to be initiated into the Native American traditions of fine love-making by an adult woman, "Phoenix Fire Woman." Whether harmful or not, the middle-aged couples engaged in the sex seminar seemed oblivious to questions of whether its teachers were truly Cherokees or whether the techniques were part of Cherokee tradition. While extreme, this New Age, for-profit seminar reveals the commodification, fabrication, and appropriation of the Cherokee name for dubious purposes. Seeing this program made Chief Mankiller more determined to attack these groups as frauds.[34]

THE IVORY TOWER: ACCUSATIONS OF ETHNIC FRAUD IN ACADEMIA

One of the most sensitive and potentially explosive areas where allegations of ethnic identity fraud plays out is in the ivory tower of academia. The Cherokee Nation Fraudulent Indian Task Force, AIM, and a small group of scholars and journalists are among the few voices currently challenging the largely unverified, self-proclaimed tribal affiliations of many well-known academics. As they clearly are the people most affected by the issue, the Cherokee Nation and the Eastern Band of Cherokees have led recent efforts to force individuals who are not enrolled in the three federally recognized Cherokee tribes to cease claiming to be "Cherokee" in public.

Ward Churchill is the most prominent individual accused of falsely claiming indigenous heritage for professional advancement. A nationally known and controversial activist, author, and university professor, Churchill has a devoted following in academic and leftist circles. His most substantial linkage to Indianness was his membership in the United Keetoowah Band of Cherokees, but according to published sources his story has changed. At various times he has claimed Cherokee, Creek, and Métis heritage. According to articles in the *National Review*, the *Rocky Mountain News*, and other publications, Churchill's army records list him simply as "Caucasian." He changed this to "American Indian" when applying for a lecture position in Native American Studies at the University of Colorado. His subsequent claimed tribal affiliations and racial heritage opened many doors, allowing Churchill to speak as a Native American and member of an oppressed minority in left-leaning academic and political circles. Though Churchill was a highly visible member of AIM, fellow members like Patti Jo King long suspected he was a fraud because of inconsistencies in his life story. Suzan Shown Harjo, former president of the NCAI, seconds King's assessment. Speaking of Churchill, she says: "You can spot these phony baloneys across the continent. Right away, I could tell he was a faker because he refused to talk about his family." Although close associates suspected something was amiss with Churchill, it was not until he published a piece on the al-Qaeda terrorist attacks of September 11, 2001, that others in the ivory tower questioned his long-standing claims. In the work, Churchill wrote that the victims of September 11 were not innocent, comparing them to Nazi technocrats and war criminal Adolf Eichmann, arguing that the terrorist attacks were the logical result of U.S. foreign policy toward the Middle East, that the chickens had come home to roost, as Malcolm X once put it regarding the assassination of John F. Kennedy. Public outcry soon led to a University of Colorado inquiry into Churchill's scholarship and ethnic claims, hearings that led to his dismissal. AIM publicly denounced the firebrand who was bringing unwanted, negative press to the group and its one-time member, and published primary documents on the Internet challenging Churchill's various claims. In one announcement AIM argued: "Ward Churchill has been masquerading as an Indian for years behind his dark glasses and beaded headband. He waves around an honorary membership card that at one time was issued to anyone by the Keetoowah Tribe of Oklahoma." The United Keetoowah Band later confirmed that it had in fact only issued him an "associate" or honorary membership, a status it also bestowed upon President Clinton around the same time (Clinton claims to be 1/8 Cherokee). It subsequently ceased issuing these cards. Journalists later attempted to out Churchill as an ethnic imposter, which was ironic, because he had previously published works denouncing others as Indian imposters. As Churchill wrote in a well-known piece on Indian sports mascots: "Think about the significance of charlatans like Carlos Castaneda and Jamake Highwater and Mary Summer Rain and Lynn Andrews churning out 'Indian' bestsellers, one after another, while Indians typically can't get into print." The sad irony of Churchill's words is that he not only denounced other authors as Indian frauds but also argued that appropriating Native identity in the sports arena (and by extrapolation in any context) was nothing short of "cultural genocide." Today many citizens of the Five Tribes deride Churchill as "king of the wannabes," saying that he cannot prove any Indian ancestry, much less Cherokee. While Churchill has stated that he refuses to enroll out of political protest, this statement rings hollow to many.[35]

Beyond Churchill, lesser-known but well-respected academics have also felt the sting of accusations and repercussions for claiming to be Cherokee while being unable to prove it by reference to enrollment. Most often these academics, like many Americans, possess family traditions saying that their ancestors were Indian, stories that they have parlayed into lucrative professional careers, allowing these individuals to speak for and about Native Americans. Andrea Smith is allegedly one such individual. From the San Francisco Bay Area, Smith earned her PhD from the University of California, Santa Cruz, in 2002. Receiving a dual appointment in the American Culture Program and the Women's Studies Department at the prestigious University of Michigan, Smith went on to publish books such as *Conquest: Sexual Violence and American Indian Genocide* while founding "INCITE!" a group working to end violence against women of color. Throughout her career, Smith has been referred to as both a "woman of color" and a "Cherokee." She has often been referenced as one of the few indigenous scholars working in the white-dominated feminist field. The only problem was that Cherokee scholars such as Patti Jo King, Richard Allen, and Steve Russell found out she was not enrolled in the tribe. According to Allen, he and King met with Smith at the University of Oklahoma campus and confronted her. At first she claimed that her mother was enrolled, but upon hearing of their research she admitted that she was not. According to Allen she agreed to stop claiming to be Cherokee. However, promotional materials still list her with the parenthetical "Cherokee" label.[36] Others, such as well-known American Indian studies professor and lawyer Jace Weaver and author Robert Conley, who was commissioned by the Cherokee Nation to write its history, have long claimed Cherokee as their ethnic identity and spoken for Native America, yet have been asked by activists to stop their public claims due to the fact that they are not formally enrolled in the Cherokee Nation. Weaver has stopped listing a Cherokee tribal affiliation on promotional literature.

As early as 1993, the Association of American Indian and Alaska Native Professors, concerned about the infiltration of "ethnic frauds" within their ranks, issued a statement calling for universities to demand proof of enrollment in federally or state-recognized tribes for eligibility in classifying and hiring Native American individuals in academia. As David Cornsilk, an admissions official at Bacone College, put it: "I don't believe in the right of self-identification. I believe that's an assault on the rights of the group." Despite these calls, it appears that self-identification is still the norm in higher education. The result of allowing individuals to largely self-identify as "Indians" in academia is that a fair percentage of scholars that identify themselves with a tribal name are not enrolled in federally recognized tribes.[37] As scholars Mary Annette Pember, Cornel Pewewardy and others are just beginning to study and publicize, unlike with undergraduate scholarship applications, few universities actually check a professor's background when he or she checks "Native American" as his or her race or claims a tribal affiliation on their application. As few individuals are aware of the distinctions between tribes (federally recognized, state-recognized, or simply self-proclaimed), there are individuals working in academia who are members of "tribes" that few knowledgeable parties consider legitimate. When an individual says he or she is a member of a "Cherokee" tribe in the Southeast, few of his or her colleagues realize that the group may not be a widely accepted tribal entity. This state of affairs results either from simple negligence, college administrators not wanting to inquire into a sensitive subject, professional courtesy, or because the potentially false applicants help universities fill various diversity goals. As Pember notes, following Ward Churchill, some scholars refuse to formally enroll in protest over federal efforts to control the definition of Native peoples. While acknowledging the theoretical position, many members of federally recognized tribes see these individuals primarily as "ethnic shoppers" choosing a formal, professional label that, put bluntly, is more advantageous to them personally. Steve Russell, a Texas trial court judge, associate professor of criminal justice at Indiana University, and enrolled citizen of the Cherokee Nation, writes: "Ward Churchill's case brings it up in our collective face, but most Indians in academia have had the problem of persons who 'self-identify' as Indian without anything to back up the identity beyond alleged family oral history. . . . In what sense is somebody Indian who has to hire a genealogist to find an ancestor? I'm not saying that an adult onset Indian cannot belatedly form tribal ties, but connection to a tribe for such people is the exception rather than the rule." Cherokee leaders Jack Baker and Troy Wayne Poteete likewise agree that academia, enveloped in "political correctness," has been too lax in uncritically accepting supposed "family tradition" and oral history as proven fact of tribal ties. Whatever the reason, it is clear at the academic professional level that few engaged in hiring check whether applicants are enrolled in tribes. As a result of this seeming win-win state of affairs played out between universities and self-identified Indian scholars, the only apparent losers are impoverished and disadvantaged American Indian individuals for whom most federal aid and affirmative action programs are intended to benefit. More and more, enrolled citizens of the Five Tribes are demanding that academics be required to show that they are enrolled in federally recognized tribes in order to claim Indian status at universities and other scholarly venues. Increasingly, traditionally Native American educational institutions such as Haskell Indian Nations University in Kansas are requiring membership in a federally recognized tribes or one-fourth-degree Indian blood for admission.[38]

DUBIOUS CHEROKEE TRIBES AND FEDERAL INDIAN EDUCATION PROGRAMS

Many federally recognized tribes oppose unacknowledged Indian groups and individuals because they have the potential to take scarce funds earmarked for impoverished Native Americans. A recent Arkansas case seems to confirm these fears. It involved an unrecognized Indian "tribe," well-meaning and cash-hungry local school administrators, and ignorant individuals who had long heard family stories that they had "Cherokee ancestors" in their family trees.

In 2005 Kathleen Wesho-Bauer and the American Indian Heritage Center, a watchdog group associated with the Cherokee Nation's Fraudulent Indian Task Force, alerted the federal Office of Indian Education about a potential fraud perpetuated by twenty-four Arkansas school districts. Even though the dubious activities likely were unintentional, the districts faced the daunting prospect of having to give back federal Indian education grants totaling $1,089,745. The funds were secured because a group called the Lost Cherokee Nation of Arkansas and Missouri had encouraged its members to fill out forms so that local school districts could qualify for federal Indian funds. Its leaders Dub Maxwell and Jim Davis went so far as to hold workshops at local school cafeterias to help students fill out forms. To drum up interest the group sent out a letter stating in part: "If your gggg-grandmother or your gggg-grandfather was of Native American Blood SO ARE YOU AND SO IS YOUR CHILD. You do not have to prove your Native American Blood for this program, so please fill out the following 506 form and return it to your school. PROOF OF INDIAN DESCENT IS NOT REQUIRED AND THERE IS NO PENALTY FOR COMPLETING THE 506 FORM [emphasis in original]." This group's lax requirements were not unusual. The Northern Cherokee Nation, also of Arkansas, tried to present a sheen of formality, though, requiring that documents submitted with an application be notarized. However, all that the Northern Cherokee group asked for was that the applicant write, for example, "mother told me when I was a little girl/boy that Grand-dad Smith was 1/2 Cherokee." No other data were required. In the case of the Lost Cherokee group, encouraged by the letter, thousands of white children signed up. The problem was that the federal program was reserved for children who were members of federally recognized or state-recognized tribes, and the Lost Cherokee group was not in either of these categories. Not surprisingly, the Russellville, Arkansas, school district saw its number of Native American children jump from 19 in 2002 to 751 in 2004, and nearby towns showed similar increases. The Lost Cherokee group saw its membership surge as well, and its coffers swelled with funds gained from the $30 membership fee it charged. The Lost Cherokee organization also made money by charging some districts a 5 percent "administration fee" for its services. The "tribe" was so successful in its efforts that David Waddell, a principal at one of the Arkansas high schools, bought a membership. Later embarrassed by the whole situation, Waddell told a local paper that he had just been thrilled to be acknowledged as Cherokee. If many of the fraud victims were embarrassed or amused by the entire scenario, the woman who blew the whistle on the fraud, Kathleen Wesho-Bauer, a Menominee and Potawatomi Indian, was not. She was angered that a program designed for poor Indian children was being pilfered by nonindigenous individuals. As she told the press: "We have treaty rights and have fought for these treaty rights and carried the burden in order to get rights; for someone who's lived in the mainstream and has had the benefits of being white all their lives to get in on what we have for our own children isn't right."[39] While the Lost Cherokee actions certainly were not morally sound, they reveal how unethical individuals can prey upon the public's ignorance of federal Indian programs and eligibility requirements, all in the name of profit.

THE STRANGE CASE OF MALCOLM "THUNDERBIRD" WEBBER

While the actions of dubious "tribes" and their leaders can range from the humorous to the morally questionable, the career of one longtime, self-proclaimed "Cherokee chief," Malcolm Webber, reveals how charades can turn criminal. The activities of Webber show how a con man and Indian guru can lead largely innocent followers into joining supposed tribes and supporting illegal activity in the process.

Webber first emerged in Indian affairs in the mid-1970s as the principal chief of a group calling itself the Etowah Cherokee Nation of Georgia. Within a short time, Webber began publishing two newspapers, the *Cherokee Nation Times* and the *Etowah Nation News*, and, like his associates the Southeastern Cherokee Confederacy, actively sought people to join his group, requiring little in terms of proof of ancestry. Although Webber claimed several tribal heritages, most sources determined that these statements were spurious. In time he led several interrelated Indian groups, including the United Lumbee Nation of North Carolina and America and the Kaweah Indian Nation. These entities were pioneers in the Federal Acknowledgment Process, losing their bids for federal recognition in 1985. While his Kaweah group was headquartered in Oatman, Arizona, a virtual ghost town on the Colorado River, Webber was convicted of several sex-related offenses involving two five-year-old girls. By 2007 he had reemerged into the national spotlight. The self-proclaimed "Grand Council Chief Thundercloud IV" made national news for selling Kaweah Indian Nation membership cards to as many as thirteen thousand unsuspecting undocumented Latin American immigrants in his hometown of Wichita, Kansas. According to court records, Webber, who had worked as a preacher, utilized networks of Hispanic churches and pastors to sell undocumented workers memberships in his tribe at charges ranging from $50 to $1,400. The victims believed that membership in an American Indian tribe could be used to secure Social Security cards. Sources estimated the fraud netted approximately $1.2 million. Webber's actions were so notorious that Jacqueline Johnson, NCAI executive director, felt compelled to respond for the nation's tribes, issuing a public statement that said, in part:

> Our members are very concerned by recent news stories of people claiming to be an Indian tribe for the purposes of exploiting a vulnerable group of people. . . . Fraud and impersonation is shameful. The actions of the groups in question not only exploit illegal immigrants, but also do a tremendous disservice to the legitimate tribal governments who are working hard to meet their governmental obligations to their citizens. Tribal citizenship in Indian Country is a serious process. Tribal membership cannot be bought or sold. We trust that the FBI investigation will handle this issue appropriately.

Webber, at the age of seventy, was found guilty of fraud and harboring illegal aliens, and he was sentenced to sixty months in prison. Other individuals have pursued their own illegal schemes, creating their own "tribes" and using their self-proclaimed "sovereign status" and "immunity" to issue driver's licenses and license plates. Others have claimed that their "tribal status" exempts them from paying taxes, recognizing federal and state laws, or even stopping for the police. These individuals, in one of the more unlikely "Indian tribe" scenarios, include former white supremacists and survivalists, who after going underground after the terrorist attacks of September 11, 2001, reappeared as Indian tribes to advance their racist, self-sufficiency, and antigovernment agendas. Many have utilized anticapitalist, antigovernment rhetoric to gain followers. Together the actions of Webber and others reveal just how serious the problem can become of allowing non-Indians to self-proclaim tribal status in America today. In these instances, the issue is not simply a tribal concern but a larger national problem.[40]

IDENTITY APPROPRIATION:
THE USE OF TRIBAL NAMES AND IMAGES

In an article on identity and naming, Cornel Pewewardy (Comanche/Kiowa) poignantly identifies the problem that the Five Tribes and others face: "Given the sacred nature of naming who we are and given the association of a name with our tribal identity as extended families, our struggle over names imposed on us by outsiders was a double tragedy; tribal people had lost control of this most fundamental of human processes, the self-determination of naming ourselves, of saying to the world, not asking, who we were."[41] The Cherokee Nation and other tribes' battle against the proliferation of self-proclaimed groups using their names can be seen as part of the larger struggle Pewewardy identifies. More than any other tribal group, the Cherokee people have been victims of the appropriation of their name. From Chrysler's Jeep Cherokee automobile to the Target retail chain's Cherokee clothing line, their tribal name is certainly the most readily recognizable tribal moniker in the United States. While some may argue that this appropriation is a positive thing, showing respect and veneration for the people, the leaders of the Five Tribes have gone on record against the related use of Indian images for sports mascots as an inappropriate use of their identity. Angela R. Riley, the director of the American Indian Studies Center at the University of California, Los Angeles, and other scholars increasingly are demanding that all Indian nations control the usages of their cultural property, including names and images.[42]

Because they have been victimized most often, the Cherokees in both Oklahoma and North Carolina have been leaders in opposing the indiscriminate use of their tribal names in various arenas. Tribal leaders have expressed concerns about the impact on the self-esteem of their children of non-Indians using tribal names and stylized or cartoon images as sports mascots. Some have even tried to trademark their tribal names and national seals and have fought others using similar names and seals, an overall effort that remains unresolved.[43] Both the Eastern Band and the Cherokee Nation in Oklahoma have voiced trepidation about the impact of self-proclaimed "Cherokee" tribes on public perceptions of their recognized tribes, their people, and their ultimate identity. In 1995 Wilma Mankiller testified before Congress, relating her people's dismay at losing control of the display of their tribal culture, their name, and public perceptions of the Cherokee people: "Unlike any other Native American tribe, the Cherokee Nation is experiencing an identity crisis. Who are these individuals who purport to be Cherokee? The Cherokee Nation [has] been embarrassed by groups such as 'The New Echota Cherokee Warriors' showing up at the National Congress of American Indians meetings dressed in stereotypical Hollywood garb—a tribe's sovereignty, reputation, and identity are at stake."[44] Mankiller's concerns were not merely theoretical or esoteric, but the result of common interactions tribal members experience among other Indian peoples. They suffer from a general stereotype, both among Indians and non-Indians, that the Cherokees, and perhaps all the Five Tribes, are assimilated and "white." There is a common perception that the Five Tribes are not "real Indians," with whatever vague notions that this phrase conjures. This belief prompted noted Five Tribes historian David Baird to write an article defending the fact that they were "real" Indians. Patti Jo King, who has spent much time among tribes such as the Mojaves and Lakotas in the American West, has lived with the stereotype. She recalls a full-blood Cherokee friend visiting her on a reservation and having the resident Lakotas not believe that her friend was really Cherokee because he was a full-blood and looked Indian. Hearing these things "gets old," she concludes. The actions of the "New Echota" group referenced by Mankiller do little to ameliorate the stereotype.[45]

The widespread use of the Cherokee name and distortion of their identity by hundreds of groups is a growing point of contention. Tribal leaders believe that the Internet and popular genealogical sites have exacerbated the problem. The Lumbees of North Carolina have faced the most consistent opposition to their recognition aspirations in part from their entanglement in the tribal name issue. Discussed elsewhere in greater detail in chapter 6, at issue is that the Lumbees once called themselves "the Cherokees of Robeson County," despite having little if any documentation to support a Cherokee link. Since 1913, leaders of the North Carolina–based Eastern Band of Cherokees have routinely opposed the Lumbees' effort to secure federal tribal recognition. In 2004, Michell Hicks, principal chief of the Eastern Band, testified against a Lumbee acknowledgment bill, saying, "We face a new threat to our separate identity; groups of people who claim, or have claimed Cherokee or other tribal affiliation whose legitimacy is doubtful at best."[46] Similarly, Eddie Tullis, as chairman of the Poarch Band of Creek Indians, has defended the BIA acknowledgment regimen and opposed easing its requirements, in part because it succeeded in denying tribal status to three Creek entities in the early 1980s, groups the Poarch Band believes cannot claim a legitimate relationship to the historic Creek Confederacy. Chairman Phillip Martin of the Mississippi Band of Choctaws likewise fought against a 1989 recognition bill pursued by the group he referred to as the "so-called MOWA Choctaws" and that he believed was inappropriately using the Choctaw name.[47]

INVASIONS OF SOVEREIGNTY

The most common argument that leaders of the Cherokee Nation and other recognized tribes make when lobbying against the acknowledgment of groups claiming a relation to their people is that these entities and individuals infringe on their most fundamental rights as sovereign Indian nations: to speak as tribal representatives, to serve as the sole tribal government, and to decide who can become citizens of their nations. To non-Indians the claims of hundreds of shadowy groups may seem harmless, but to tribal governments they literally strike at the heart of their existence as sovereign aboriginal nations. In 1988, Jonathan Taylor, the outspoken principal chief of the Eastern Band of Cherokees, testified before Congress to enlighten non-Indians on the issues:

> I'll tell this committee that there are only two Cherokee Tribes; one of them is in North Carolina and the other is in Oklahoma. If I had a dollar for every time I have heard that some stranger's great grandmother was a Cherokee Princess I would be a wealthy man. We have no problem with people taking pride in their ancestry,

however, in the same way that 500 people of Norwegian descent in
Minnesota cannot consider themselves to be a second "country"
of Norway, 500 people of Cherokee descent in Arkansas cannot
consider themselves "The Cherokee Tribe."[48]

Taylor's statement rather succinctly articulates his people's views on
the seemingly innocuous claims of many unrecognized entities. These
groups are not simply claiming Indian heritage, they are claiming to
be successors to the ancient and venerated Creek, Chickasaw, Choctaw,
Seminole, and Cherokee Nations. The modern Five Tribe governments
are the entities with status as aboriginal nations within the United States.
Like the majority of federally recognized tribes, the Five Tribes have
status based on solemn treaties agreed upon by their ancestral governments and federal officials. To the Eastern Band, Creek Nation, and
others it is presumptuous and absurd for groups like "the Southern
Cherokee Nation" or "the Remnant Yuchi Nation" to unilaterally claim
to be another Cherokee Nation or Creek Nation.

Despite the legal clarity of the Five Tribes' position, average Americans, including those claiming Indian status, do not comprehend fundamental aspects of Indian identity. They fail to understand that Indian
status for most federal programs and tribal status for exercising sovereignty is fundamentally a political status. Native Americans have special
rights as members of tribal polities, not because of their racial or ethnic
affiliation. As previously detailed, it is easy, and often a matter of self-
identification, for millions of individuals with real or perceived Indian
ancestry to claim to be Indian in a pan-Indian, pan-tribal sense in social
settings or on forms requiring ethnic or racial affiliation. These same
individuals, however, cannot enroll in federally recognized tribes because
they lack the necessary family connections or blood quantum required
by various tribes. On a mission to clear the confusion, Cherokee principal chief Chad Smith has repeated the following statement on various
occasions: "Heritage is different from citizenship. Many people with
genuine Indian heritage will never meet the qualifications to become
citizens in a federally recognized tribe. The Cherokee Nation does not
question anyone's claims of heritage or ancestry, but merely points
out the significant difference between claiming heritage and having citizenship."[49]

Most Americans truly are baffled when individuals with blond hair
and blue eyes say they are enrolled in the Cherokee Nation. How can

these "white Cherokees" with as little as 1/256th Indian blood be Indian? Most Americans fail to realize that one can be largely white in ancestry yet be enrolled in a federally recognized tribe. Membership in a tribe rather than physical "Indian appearance" is what is important for claiming to be Indian in modern America. According to the Five Tribes and related recognized tribes, as governmental and bureaucratic entities they fundamentally must view membership as a sovereignty issue. To these tribes, who belongs and who does not belong is not a matter taken lightly—it speaks to their right to define their own membership using their own criteria. To make the distinction more clearly, the Five Tribes have begun to emphasize using the term "tribal citizenship" rather than "membership" in everyday discourse. According to Tom Mooney, tribal archivist at the Cherokee Cultural Center, the tribal position makes sense. As he puts it: "Are you a 'member' of the United States or a 'citizen'?" Tribal Council member Cara Cowan Watts expounds on Mooney's conclusions, saying:

> Politically, I am Cherokee. I have citizenship in the Cherokee Nation. I am descended from the Dawes Rolls through both sides of my mother's family. Our citizenship is not a question of race. Our identity as Indian people is both a political identity and a racial identity [but] our programs, services, and citizenship are based on the political identity. In the case of Wannabes and frauds, we are defending our political identity as a classification based on treaty rights.[50]

Few Americans realize that belonging to an Indian nation rather than simple ancestry is what is important to claiming to be Cherokee, Creek, or Choctaw. As principal chief Chad Smith told me, many people saying they are Cherokee likely have some ancestry. However, their ancestors "expatriated from the nation" and renounced their tribal ties by failing to travel west on the Trail of Tears. The cost of that decision is that their descendants cannot now claim citizenship. Cherokee Nation Supreme Court justice Troy Wayne Poteete further emphasizes the often emotional, group and kinship nature of the issue, fine details often missed by non-Indians claiming Indian status. "Our issue is our ancestors had so little to pass on to us. We lost 90 percent of what we had. What they were able to pass on to us was a unique legal status, as well as a distinct culture and heritage."[51]

To Cherokees, Creeks, and others, belonging is more about being a part of a large, extended family and community rather than an individual's unsubstantiated claims. As Cherokee judge Steve Russell puts it, "My own position is that Indian identity is not about what you claim, but rather about who claims you."[52] Russell and others are not telling people they are not "part Indian," just that they are not part of the family. In many ways the tribal position makes sense. How many American families would embrace an outsider showing up to "join" the family without any proof of descent? The blood and family connection issue reared its ugly head in 2007 when the Cherokees, in a national referendum, voted to renounce the citizenship of thousands of descendants of Cherokee freedmen (men and women who had formerly been slaves owned by the Cherokees). In response, Diane Watson, a Democratic congresswoman from California, with support from the traditionally pro-Indian Congressional Black Caucus, introduced legislation seeking to cut hundreds of millions of dollars in funding from the Cherokee Nation and revoking its gaming rights. In editorials in Indian newspapers and on the Cherokee Nation's website, Chief Chad Smith responded that excluding nonblooded members was done as part of the Cherokee Nation's inherent right to define its own citizenship, and like most other Indian nations, the tribe chose to define it by blood. As he argued: "Cherokees chose to exclude non-Indians because of a sense of identity. Cherokees are Indians. They are the indigenous and aboriginal people of this land and there is a commonality of history, language, heritage and culture."[53]

THE FRAUDULENT INDIAN TASK FORCE AND RESPONSES FROM UNRECOGNIZED INDIANS

In 2008 Smith helped create the Fraudulent Indian Task Force, part of a larger effort to re-articulate Cherokee Nation citizenship rules. A somewhat informal group, it consisted of Richard Allen, Cara Cowan Watts, John Parris and Richard Osborn of the tribal Justice Department, Troy Wayne Poteete, Youth Business Loan Center councilor Teri Rhoades, Tonia Williams, and Jack Baker.[54] With Chief Smith at the helm, the Cherokee Nation, with growing support from the other Five Tribes nations and related recognized tribes, began to formalize its opposition. The task force worked to highlight not only clearly fake, fraudulent tribes, but also state-recognized tribes and individuals members believed were misrepresenting themselves as Indians. In 2008, using the Cherokee Nation's website as a base, the task force began posting documents as part of what members saw as their primary mission to educate the public on the issue. The "Wannabe Tribe List" probably was its most important, and most controversial, contribution, but the task force also collected data, formulated legal arguments, talked to the press, posted primary documents, and took to the road to lobby against state recognition of new tribes. There was a general feeling among members that with the Internet and its increasingly popular genealogical sites, the number of dubious Cherokee and other contending Native groups was growing. This sentiment, combined with sour dealings with blatantly fraudulent entities and charlatans, lent a sense of urgency and mission to their work.[55]

Task force members and allies have embarked on a crusade to educate the public on the issues involved in recognizing Indian tribes and legitimately claiming an individual tribal identity. They and other enrolled members of the Five Tribes and related federally recognized southeastern tribes want to make membership in a federally recognized tribe *the threshold* for all services, benefits, entitlement, and programs earmarked for Indian peoples. As they see it, enrollment should be the only basis for claiming to be Indian in America today.

As mentioned, this effort at creating formalized boundaries around Indian tribal identity has engendered heated and emotional responses from individuals whose legitimacy and heritage has been impugned. With identity such a personal issue, it is not surprising that people accused of being "wannabes" and groups accused of being "fraudulent tribes" have reacted to Cherokee accusations with a mixture of dismay and outrage. Individual responses have varied from this, however. Cherokee councilman Baker has found that when he questions groups that have no right to represent the Cherokee Nation about their actions, individuals tend to feel embarrassed, accept that they are not true Cherokees, and move on with their lives. The experience of Jack Hitt, a *New York Times* journalist, reveals something rarely discussed: many individuals enrolled in non–federally recognized tribes are insecure in their identities as Indians and worried that others will accuse them of fraud. In 2005 Hitt attended a powwow put on by the Cherokee Tribe of Northeast Alabama. Hitt spent most of his time there with a woman who had recently joined the tribe after a hiring a genealogist who had informed her that she was Indian. To Hitt she admitted to being "a completely new Indian." Hitt noted that almost all the members looked like "regular Alabama white folks" and thus "more than half my time with this tribe was spent dealing with their anxiety that I might make this observation." While this group's members may feel anxious about their public identities as Indians, it is too simplistic to view all non–federally recognized groups in the same light. Individuals who have lived their lives as Native Americans often erupt in anger and outrage when others question their heritage. Ward Churchill has allegedly threatened violence against those who questioned his identity. Members of the MOWA Band of Choctaws feel true indignation that the Fraudulent Indian Task Force has placed their people on its "Wannabe Tribe" list. Member Cedric Sunray has made it his mission to repudiate the Cherokee allegations at conferences and other public forums. As Sunray believes: "The Cherokee Task Force, which was formed to fight against 'non-federal' tribes and state recognition, is primarily made up of non-identifiable, non-Cherokee-speaking, extremely low-blood-quantum individuals. White Indians like Cara Cowan and Troy Poteete mistake race for culture, blood for community, and exclusion for strength."[56]

The task force's crusade has engendered an ugly, racialized discourse that is multifaceted. As Sunray's statements attest, members of the MOWA Band, historically a racially identified community of color, believe it is outrageous that phenotypically white individuals (even if they are enrolled) are saying that their people are wannabes and non-Indian. MOWA chief Wilford Taylor responded to the task force this way:

> It has come to my attention that two employees and one of your tribal council has made extremely negative comments about our tribal community. I was educated at Bacone College many years ago. I count numerous Cherokees as friends from my time spent there. Upon more recent visits, individuals that I had known as white while living in Oklahoma have suddenly become 'Cherokees.' These individuals seem to be the majority amongst your tribal enrollment. It is not us who needs to prove to you that we are Indian. In fact, I would say it is the opposite and it sounds like . . . these people are a chromosome away from wearing a hood.[57]

Because the Five Tribes base enrollment entirely on proving descent by blood—no matter how minute—from ancestors on the Dawes Rolls, groups like the MOWA Band and individuals who feel they are Indian but cannot prove it charge that the Cherokees are acting as "blood police" using outdated, racist policies to delineate true Indians from wannabes. Anthropologist Circe Sturm confirms that many Cherokees have fetishized blood as a measure of cultural and social belonging, when, in fact, blood alone rarely confirms such a relationship. Enrolled Cherokees and others that "do not appear Indian" yet who act as agents policing Indian authenticity rankle many. Critics charge that it is the members of the Fraudulent Task Force who feel insecure in their Indianness and therefore cling to their enrollment cards as proof of their identity. Because the Five Tribes rely on blood and blood symbolism as the defining attribute for inclusion, critics often compare them to racist organizations like the Ku Klux Klan. Artist Murv Jacobs, who has had his Cherokee identity challenged, calls the task force Kowan's Kulture Kommittee (KKK), alluding to its vocal spokesperson Cara Cowan. Seconding this, historian Robert J. Conley, who likewise had his ancestry questioned, notes, "If Cara Cowan and her cohorts have nothing better to do than be the Cherokee blood police, then they need to find some kind of lives for themselves." James Murray, a Tahlequah resident, perhaps sums up the critics' position best when he challenges the task force's accusation that groups are appropriating Cherokee identity, saying, "It is the Cherokee Nation appropriating discredited 18th and 19th century ideologies of 'citizenship by blood.' These concepts, retrieved from the ash heap of history, were learned from the white man. Nowhere do they exist in the traditional Cherokee worldview. These ideologies were learned from the white colonialists, but the 'white' Cherokee elite have learned these lessons well."[58]

FIVE TRIBES' SUPPORT OF THE FEDERAL ACKNOWLEDGMENT PROCESS

In studying the issue, it is clear that defending against "wannabe" Indians and fraudulent "tribes" cuts across party, generational, and residential lines within the Five Tribes and related remnant federally recognized tribes in the Southeast. Peoples most affected by the issue, from the Cherokee and Creek Nations in the west, to southeastern tribes such as the Eastern Band of Cherokee Indians, Mississippi Band of Choctaws, and Poarch Band of Creek Indians, consistently have lobbied against reforming the Federal Acknowledgment Process, against Congress acknowledging new tribes via legislation, and in some cases challenging self-styled Indians in public arenas. Conservative Republican leaders including W. W. Keeler, Claude Cox, Ross Swimmer, Chad Smith, and Eddie Tullis have been active in challenging perceived fraudulent tribes and individuals. Liberal Democrats such as Wilma Mankiller have also been vocal in their opposition. To AIM activist Patti Jo King, it is not a conservative or liberal issue, it is "a right and wrong issue"; it is not about money to her people but about "what is right." She and others have opposed fellow liberal activists such as Andrea Smith, not from politics or ideology, but from a deep-seated moral belief that non-Cherokees should not falsely claim to be Cherokee.[59]

At virtually every congressional hearing on bills to recognize new tribes in the Southeast or to reform the much-maligned Federal Acknowledgment Process, a representative from the Five Tribes and related tribes has been present to oppose the legislation. These tribes have been among the most ardent supporters of the BIA process, praising the Office of Federal Acknowledgment for its objective standards, thorough review, and efforts to protect the sanctity of the federal-tribal relationship. In essence, tribal leaders believe the stringent process protects federal tribes against fraudulent interlopers.[60] As Leon Jones, principal chief of the Eastern Band of Cherokee Indians testified in 1999:

> We hope the BAR [the Branch of Acknowledgment and Research] will always be very methodological because if they were not the consequences would be very serious. An example of this is the previous BAR petitioner group calling itself the Mowa Choctaw of Alabama. This group, among other things, claimed to be descendants of the Choctaw Treaty of Dancing Rabbit Creek. . . . After six months of genealogical research, the BAR found that the Mowa's claims were astonishingly flawed. . . .The Mowas were eventually denied recognition but had this extensive research not been undertaken, their fallacious claims would not have been discovered.[61]

It is almost certain that Chief Jones did not have personal knowledge of the MOWA group's genealogical charts, but he clearly has faith in the BIA's work. He and other leaders such as Poarch Band registrar

Gail Thrower accept the federal acknowledgment office's findings as gospel, believing they are methodologically sound and wisely considered. Thrower represents a common sentiment, acknowledging that the process is inherently bureaucratic and difficult, but believing that contending groups can make it through if they are "real" tribes.[62]

The fact that some non-Indians believe that the Five Tribes today are not "real Indians" also motivates leaders. Cherokee principal chiefs Chad Smith and Leon Jones consistently have expressed trepidation that the acknowledgment of dubious tribes would further the stereotype. They worry that the public association of new tribes with Indian casinos could engender a congressional backlash against tribal sovereignty, especially since gaming has introduced a host of controversies and ill will into debates. As Jones testified: "If tribal recognition is attained via any sort of inexact process, the very concept of a special and unique tribal, government-to-government relationship and tribal sovereignty is demeaned and diminished. There are already too many enemies of tribal government out there who want us destroyed. We cannot hand them any ammunition suggesting that our relationship with the United States is anything but solid and historical." Jones and others fear the long-term consequences of recognizing groups that have no distinction from surrounding non-Indian society, groups that have no tribal language, traditional songs and dances, or any racial distinctiveness. This is no idle fear, considering the power Congress has over Indian tribes. Tribal memories of the failed 1950s-era termination policy are deep. As Smith noted regarding the freedmen disenrollment, non-Indians and even other tribes "criticize us for being too inclusive" and "not having a blood quantum requirement," that is, that the Cherokee Nation is not Indian enough.[63] Smith's concerns are stoked by statements such as those made by Oklahoma Republican senator Tom Coburn in his 2004 race against Democratic rival Brad Carson, a Cherokee citizen. While speaking in the southwestern Oklahoma town of Altus, Senator Coburn referenced a battle over maintaining Five Tribes trust land, telling the audience that the Cherokee Nation only wanted to enroll new members to receive more federal funding. Saying that "the average Cherokee [blood] quantum is 1/512," Coburn exhorted, "Alright, listen, I know tribal issues; I was a congressman where most of the Indians are in this state. The problem is, most of them aren't Indians." Referencing the trust land controversy, Coburn concluded: "I mean this is a joke. . . . It is one thing for us to keep our obligations to recognized Native Americans, but it's a totally different thing for us to allow a primitive agreement with Native Americans to undermine Oklahoma's future and that's what they're talking about doing and it's big money."[64] As the senator's comments reveal, many members of the Five Tribes and related tribes have had experiences that make them understandably sensitive to issues of tribal recognition, debates about "who is a real Indian," and fears about the erosion of tribal sovereignty. Published records and my personal correspondence with members of the Five Tribes and related groups reveal that members have a deep-seated respect for the BIA's Office of Federal Acknowledgement, its staff, and its criteria that they believe do a fine job of determining which groups are authentic.

CLOSING THE CIRCLE

As witnessed from the preceding discourse, despite vocal complaints from those left outside the circle, many Five Tribes citizens and their governments view their efforts to set formal, empirical boundaries around tribal citizenship and tribal status as a necessary function of protecting an increasingly valuable and threatened Indian status, identity, and cultural heritage. As Patti Jo King poignantly puts it: "All tribes originally were family groups and bands. We were forced into political lines . . . [and as such] we need some type of boundary—we need to draw the line somewhere—and we use the structure [Dawes Rolls] that is there." As she insightfully notes, for people who can prove they are related to tribal ancestors, the Five Tribes are more inclusive than tribes using troublesome blood quantum requirements. As King's comments reveal, tribal leaders and activists are aware of the academic critiques, but their position is not a theoretical one. Their stance is fundamentally conservative and practical: they seek to draw clear boundaries to protect their tribal rights against interlopers and opponents of tribal sovereignty.[65]

The result of the troublesome interface of Cherokees and members of other recognized tribes with wannabe Indians and fraudulent tribes is that leaders of the former have come to vigorously support strict federal requirements for unrecognized groups to qualify as tribes and individuals to identify as Indians. From interviews with tribal leaders like Troy Poteete, Jack Baker, and Gail Thrower it is clear that members of currently recognized tribes have a genuine respect for the Federal Acknowledgment Process and tribes that have passed its rigorous review. Leaders like Eddie Tullis of the Poarch Creeks have testified in support of the process. Tullis stated: "We are just less convinced than certain critics that the FAP is as broken as some allege. These criteria have been in place since 1978, and are well accepted by most impartial archaeologists, historians, genealogists, and I might add, very definitely, as well by most tribes." Tullis believes groups that cannot meet the standards of the BIA are "not true tribal outfits."[66] Though entities languishing in the process or rejected by its strict rules would not agree with his assessment, support for the current Federal Acknowledgment Process by the Five Tribes and related tribes has been a potent force in maintaining the status quo. Tribes that "make it through" the detailed process are welcomed into the fold, while those that do not are scorned as wannabes. Recognized tribal leaders continue to insist that recognition through treaties and other historic federal agreements, or through the formal BIA process, is the absolute threshold to tribal status and Indian identity in America today.

CHAPTER 6

The Numbers Game

*The Lumbees, the MOWA Band,
and the Economics of Tribal Recognition*

On June 20, 1981, Eddie Tullis, the influential and out-spoken chairman of the Poarch Band of Creek Indians, wrote to the nearby MOWA Band of Choctaw Indians: "This letter is to formally ask your tribe, in the spirit of Indian brotherhood, [to] support our efforts for Federal Recognition. . . . We as Native Americans must work together to protect our rights. I assure you that if you assist us with our struggle . . . you can count on us to be there when your petition is ready for consideration by BAR." Three decades later, however, Tullis told me, "I don't feel [the MOWA Band] is a Choctaw tribe . . . it's not a tribal operation. They just cannot not stand to hear the truth. They have to accept they are not a legitimate tribe."

What had transpired between 1981 and 2010 to make the Creek leader come to such different conclusions about the authenticity of his MOWA neighbors? To MOWA Band leaders the answer is clear: the Poarch Creeks did in fact secure federal recognition in 1983 and thereafter opened a lucrative casino, a multimillion-dollar business that would suffer should the MOWA Band achieve federal status, especially because the MOWA group's land base is about as close to the major market of Mobile as the Poarch Creek Reservation is. Even though MOWA chief Framon Weaver dutifully did write a letter supporting his "Creek brothers," Poarch Band support for his tribe was not forthcoming. Today MOWA leader Todd Johnston calls Tullis "a snake" for double-crossing his people. Tullis insists he believes that there are

Indian people in the MOWA community, but that they are not a real tribe. He feels that most just want to open casinos and get rich.

Welcome to the world of modern tribal acknowledgment politics, where issues of authenticity bleed into talk about scarce resources, casino monopolies, and the perceived motives of groups involved. During the 1970s, when questioned about his identity, Lumbee educator and spokesman Adolph Dial would state simply: "We know our people . . . we've always been Indian." Before the rise of Indian casinos this pronouncement was often enough, but it is not enough in today's climate, where gaming-generated profits and other valuable resources are at stake.[1]

THE PROBLEM

Questions about who can qualify as an Indian and what is an "Indian tribe" have long been open to debate. Since the early twentieth century, outsiders have questioned the Indianness of many southern groups, including the MOWA Band of southern Alabama and the large and well-known Lumbee Tribe of coastal North Carolina. However, Indian gaming has exponentially elevated existing conflicts over the cultural and racial authenticity of most regional tribes, with the high-profile Lumbees and the well-known MOWA Band bearing the brunt of the current high-octane conflict. The perceived urgency to protect vital casino revenues has elevated the decades-long conflict between the federally recognized Eastern Band of Cherokee Indians of western North Carolina and the Lumbees. It also seems to have spawned the recent battle between the once allied MOWA Band and their presently recognized neighbors the Poarch Band of Creek Indians. Shared interest in protecting casino territories has attracted nearby recognized tribes like the Mississippi Band of Choctaw Indians, who, working through the influential pan-tribal group United South and Eastern Tribes (USET), have succeeded in having the entire regional organization of twenty-four federally recognized tribes present a solid front, guarding the gates to federal tribal recognition, the status that opens the door to Indian gaming in the United States. They have hired lobbyists, including the disgraced team of Jack Abramoff, to influence policy and to keep most other southeastern groups out of the fold.

Federally recognized tribes like the Poarch Band have positioned themselves as institutional gatekeepers: their lobbying activity, congressional testimony, and position as the only federally acknowledged area tribes have given them a clear position of power. Since the 1980s the recognized tribes have set the terms of debate while the non–federally recognized MOWA Band and Lumbee people have struggled on the defensive, trying to counter allegations against them while proving to increasingly skeptical lawmakers that they are genuine Indians worthy of securing acknowledgment. As anthropologists George Castile, Anthony Paredes, and others have noted, in modern Indian politics, the special federal-tribal relationship *is the central, valuable resource* that tribes possess. The status enables access to Indian-only federal programs that many established tribes feel large groups like the Lumbees threaten. More importantly, federal recognition acknowledges a group's sovereign right to open tribal casinos. In today's politics, the boundary line is federal tribal recognition. The "haves," the presently acknowledged tribes, have mobilized opposition to most newcomers that threaten to cross this clear dividing line. As Tullis's quotes reveal, before his people had the vaunted federal seal, they were willing to reach out to their fellow non–federally recognized kin, but they are no longer willing. As a sign of the times, in North Carolina and other states federally recognized tribes like the Eastern Band of Cherokees keep their distance from state Indian commissions composed of non–federally recognized tribes.[2]

Since the 1980s increasingly sophisticated, economically and politically powerful recognized tribes are proving skilled protectors of their most important economic niche, the Indian gaming industry that their sovereign status enables. They use their clout in Congress to safeguard their interests and demand that other groups go through the BIA acknowledgment process, a test that tribal leaders believe is the best to determine what is a "real" and "authentic" Indian tribe—and one that is increasingly difficult to pass. With the Lumbees and MOWA Choctaws it is clear what happens when Indian tribal identity becomes a valuable commodity. Suddenly all pretenses of social justice are swept out the door in the face of raw, economic competition over Indian gaming and federal, Indian-only funding. The struggle of the MOWA Band of Choctaw Indians and the Lumbee people to secure acknowledgment through Congress reveals how economic competition for scarce resources has entered the acknowledgment arena, making it more and more challenging for groups to secure the rights and financial aid that they feel they deserve as Indian-identifying people. Both the Lumbees and the MOWA Band have come tantalizingly close to crossing the federal finish line, yet opposition from other tribes has time and time again stymied their dreams.

LEGISLATIVE BACKGROUND

On multiple occasions during the 1990s and early 2000s the MOWA Band and the Lumbee Tribe fell just short of securing bills that would recognize them as federally acknowledged tribes. Of all non–federally recognized tribes, the Lumbees have the most impressive record of both state and congressional recognition of their Indianness. The Lumbees' acknowledgment as Indians dates from 1885. That year a state legislator and friend of the tribe, Hamilton McMillan, passed a bill designating the people as Croatan Indians, a name reflecting the group's oral traditions and McMillan's own conclusion that they descended from survivors of Sir Walter Raleigh's famous "Lost Colony of Roanoke," who intermarried with Indians of this tribe and ultimately moved inland to their present location in Robeson County. McMillan's law and the "Lost Colony" theory provided many immediate benefits to the ancestors of today's Lumbee people. They gave them a romantic history tying their people to both the first white settlers of America and to the aboriginal peoples of North Carolina, and also allowed them to establish their own Indian school system and otherwise distance themselves from African Americans at a time when whites were trying to lump all groups into the same "colored" category, during the rise of Jim Crow segregation. With an Indian minister named W. L. Moore at the lead, the group submitted a petition signed by forty-four men in 1888 to the Office of Indian Affairs, seeking federal moneys to run their new school system. This petition prompted what would be the first of many federal investigations into the status and origin of the North Carolina group. In response to the petition, commissioner of Indian affairs Thomas Jefferson Morgan declined to offer aid to the people, citing funding concerns and the fact that the United States had no treaty obligations toward them or other similarly situated "civilized tribes." Several other failed attempts to secure federal education and recognition followed. In 1911 and 1912 Angus W. McLean, a state senator who was soon to be governor, doggedly advocated for a federal education bill for the group that passed the U.S. Senate only to fail in the House of Representatives. In relation to these efforts, the Indian

Office commissioned several studies on the origins of the group, none of which questioned their racial identity as Indians. An important work by Indian Office employee O. M. McPherson in 1915 concluded that the group was composed of descendants of Hatteras Indians, survivors of the "Lost Colony," and Scots who had settled the Lumber River region in the eighteenth century. During this era, a sign of their acceptance as Indians, several tribal members were allowed to enroll in the Carlisle Indian School, perhaps the most famous Indian boarding school of the time. However, group leaders wanted more definitive acknowledgment of their Indian identity at the federal level. Beginning in 1924 Lumbee leader A. B. Locklear spearheaded a multiyear crusade to have Congress recognize his people as "Cherokee Indians" and thus allow them admittance to federal Indian boarding schools. While the secretary of the interior supported the bill in its infant stages, assimilation-oriented commissioner of Indian affairs Charles Burke opposed the legislation, citing old arguments that the group lacked a relationship with the federal government, was self-supporting, and did not live in tribal relations. Locklear's efforts to secure acknowledgment and aid for the group came up short.[3]

At the turn of the century the Lumbees had also embarked on a bewildering number of name changes, efforts prompted from inside and outside the Indian community. Beginning their public and legal existence as Croatan Indians, the group soon found local whites and blacks shortening that appellation to "Cro"—a not-so-subtle slur, implying that they were really "colored people"—"crows"—passing themselves as Indians. As Karen Blu, a noted authority on the tribe notes, the label "Cro" clearly shows that the people had not won universal acceptance as Indians in the early twentieth century. It was during this time, Lumbee historian Malinda Maynor Lowery finds, that there were people trying for the first time to force their oddly shaped history into the square pegs required to match federal and local white expectations of what tribes looked like in order to secure federal aid and outside recognition. Tribal leaders, realizing that the name "Croatan" not only led to a local racial slur but also perhaps was not the name of a historic Indian tribe (the basis of federal recognition), persuaded the state legislature to pass a 1911 bill changing their name to "the Indians of Robeson County," a purely geographic designation. In 1913, in an effort to link themselves to a historic tribe, Indian leaders had a state law passed fatefully redesignating them "the Cherokee Indians of Robeson County." This

Figure 13. Lumbee Indian members of Red Men's Lodge (Improved Order of Red Men), Robeson County, North Carolina, 1910. (Photograph courtesy of Monnie Sanderson and Native American Resource Center, University of North Carolina, Pembroke)

effort to meet outside expectations brought the ire of the Eastern Band of Cherokee Indians, who protested the law to no avail. For several decades the state college for Lumbees went by the name Cherokee Indian Normal School, rubbing more salt in the wound. Contention over the use of the Cherokee name would persist: as late as 1979 a group calling itself the Cherokee Indians of Robeson County was seeking tribal recognition under that name. In recent decades representatives of the Eastern Band of Cherokees have testified against Lumbee recognition, citing the ill-begotten use of their tribal name as one of the reasons for their opposition. The MOWA Band of Choctaw Indians have also faced problems over their use of what they believe is their ancestral tribal name. In 1991 Phillip Martin, the leader of the Mississippi Band of Choctaws, made an impression when he testified against a MOWA recognition bill, calling them "the so-called Mowa Choctaw" and saying that his people were angry that the MOWA people were "misrepresenting" the name "Choctaw."[4]

During the 1930s and again in the 1950s tenacious Lumbee leaders were successful in getting legislation before Congress to acknowledge their identity as Indians. A division within the leadership, however, severely hampered the overall tribal effort. One group of influential Lumbees, hailing mainly from the Oxendine and Lowry families, well-educated and progressive in their politics, had for decades pursued recognition of their people as Cherokee Indians. In 1932 they approached

John Collier, then executive secretary of the American Indian Defense Association, who agreed to support their efforts, noting in one report that they demonstrated "strong Indian characteristics." A U.S. senator representing the Lumbees, Josiah W. Bailey, introduced legislation that year to recognize the group as "Cherokee Indians," yet it ultimately was foiled by strong opposition from the commissioner of Indian affairs, C. J. Rhoades. The bill reemerged the next year, and it now designated the group "Cheraw Indians," based on the theories of respected Bureau of American Ethnology anthropologist John Reed Swanton. In a trend that would plague the group in future years, the Robeson County Indians soon divided over the new name. Joseph Brooks, James Chavis, and Buddy Graham led the lobbying effort for the newly christened "Cheraw faction" that supported Swanton's theory, organizing a formal business committee as a form of government for the people. The name debate grew even more complex. Because historic tribes like the Cheraws spoke languages of the Siouan linguistic family, secretary of the interior Harold L. Ickes, who supported the tribe's aspirations, advised that they change their name to incorporate "Siouan." In 1934 a new piece of legislation declaring the group the "Siouan Indians of the Lumber River" began making the rounds of Capitol Hill. At the insistence of Secretary Ickes, the bill identified the people as "Siouan Indians" but denied them rights accruing to federal tribes at the same time. Led by Reverend D. F. Lowery, a vocal political opponent of Joseph Brooks and Clifton Oxendine, the Cherokee faction rose in opposition to the new law and new name. Not surprisingly, although the Siouan bill passed the House, it failed to make it through the Senate.[5]

The Siouan faction did not give up, however. The group convinced the new commissioner of Indian Affairs, John Collier, who was spearheading the ambitious Indian New Deal under President Roosevelt, to send scholars to try to certify whether individual Lumbees were "one half or more" Indian blood able to organize under the Indian Reorganization Act of 1934. As discussed elsewhere in greater detail, the Indian Office sent a team (under anthropologist Carl Seltzer) to use then-accepted anthropometric measurements and other techniques to try to decipher which Lumbees had the requisite amount of Indian blood cursing through their veins. Seltzer's team eventually certified twenty-two of the approximately two hundred Indians who submitted to the demeaning tests as "one-half or more" Indian by blood. This group, later known as the "Original 22," gained the support of Collier, his legal expert Felix Cohen, and others in the Indian Office, and they were entitled to Indian preference and educational programs for Indians under the New Deal umbrella. Because they lacked a reservation and larger funding shortages, the "Original 22" were informed that they were not eligible for federal tribal status at that time. Federal officials, however, supported other development projects for the Lumbee people during the Depression. Having established the Siouan Indian Council, Joseph Brooks and the Siouan group ended up taking part in two federally backed programs, establishing the Red Banks Mutual Association and Pembroke Farms, both run by a non-Indian agency, the Farm Security Administration. These projects bought land for Indian farmers, helping them establish a cooperative system to break the cycle of poverty embedded in the sharecropping and tenant farming system. Of all the Farm Security Administration projects, the Red Banks Mutual Association was the most successful and long lasting, operating until 1968.[6]

The general dissatisfaction with the tribal name ultimately led to the Lumbee Act of 1956. In the early 1950s tribal leaders agreed to hold a referendum on a new tribal name, and it was then that the people voted to change their name to "Lumbee Indians," a more inclusive designation based on their location along the Lumber (Lumbee) River. In 1953 the state legislature passed a law designating the group the "Lumbee Indians." Leaders pursued a federal law several years later to further formalize this name. This effort led to a triumph of sorts: the Lumbee Act of 1956. This act designated the people the "Lumbee Indians of North Carolina," but, as it was passed at the height of the termination era, contained a clause demanded by the Bureau of Indian Affairs: "Nothing in this Act shall make such Indians eligible for any services performed by the United States for Indians because of their status as Indians and none of the statutes of the United States which affect Indians because of their status as Indians shall be applicable to the Lumbee Indians."[7] The Lumbees were thereafter uniquely situated among American Indian peoples: they were acknowledged as Indians by Congress yet were specifically prohibited from a federal-tribal relationship and programs for Indians emanating from the BIA. At the time most tribal leaders were happy, however. The bill provided what they had longed for—recognition of their people as Indians with a tribal name of their own. Discontent would soon arise, however.

Like the Lumbee people, the MOWA Choctaw group has significant forms of outside recognition of their indigenousness, although they do not have a federal law declaring them "Choctaw Indians." Beginning in the 1920s the Southern Baptist Convention established Indian mission schools among the ancestors of the MOWA Band. After decades of struggle and extreme social isolation, during the 1960s and 1970s MOWA leaders like Galas Weaver, Verma Reed, and Framon Weaver emerged as actors in modern Alabama politics, and in 1979 they succeeded in securing a state law recognizing the MOWA Band as a tribe of Indians. The Federal Acknowledgment Process had been created the year before, and the MOWA Band immediately began to develop a strategy to secure federal tribal status through the new procedures. While they created a committee to prepare their documentation, group leaders also approached Alabama members of Congress about helping secure legislation that could more quickly establish that they were a surviving Indian tribe. In 1987 chief Framon Weaver, a businessman and entrepreneur, persuaded U.S. senator Richard Shelby (R-Ala), a newly elected former lawyer from Tuscaloosa, to introduce recognition legislation. Shelby was committed to the group and after it failed to pass that year faithfully resubmitted the bill in subsequent sessions. The MOWA Band also hired a Mobile-based law firm with a Washington branch to represent and lobby for the group. They scraped together money to hire an applied anthropologist from the University of Arizona to study their people and confirm that they were an Indian group. Around this time, the MOWA Band was granted coveted membership in the National Congress of American Indians. It seemed the tide was turning in the MOWA people's direction. The 1991 Congress was, to date, the band's shining moment: with strong Indian supporter Daniel Inouye (D-Hawaii) as chairman, the Senate Select Committee on Indian Affairs approved Shelby's bill to recognize the MOWA Band as a tribe by an 11–2 vote. It then passed the full Senate by a voice vote. MOWA leaders like Galas Weaver were preparing for a huge victory party. Their hopes were dashed, however, when the House did not take up the legislation that session.[8]

MOWA leaders believed that their near-win in 1991 portended good things for the future— that they just needed to work harder to get their recognition bill through Congress in the next session—and they were almost correct. In 1994 MOWA legislation again passed the Senate. Everything changed later that year, however, when the BIA issued a preliminary negative finding on the MOWA's petition, a ruling that greatly decreased the band's chances of future success in Congress.

Several years later the Branch of Acknowledgment published its final negative ruling on the group. In its report, the federal government found that the MOWA group had failed to prove that its members had descended from Choctaws who avoided removal in the 1830s. More damning, it stated flatly that few of the MOWA people actually had Indian ancestry at all. The band filed a last-ditch appeal to an internal government appeals board, but this was denied in 1998. During the 1990s and after Senator Shelby, senator Jeff Sessions (R-Ala.) and members of Congress Sonny Callahan (a Republican representing Mobile), Earl Hilliard (a Democrat representing Birmingham), and Callahan's successor Jo Bonner (another Republican representing Mobile) introduced new bills to acknowledge the MOWA group. Chief Wilford Taylor spent the majority of his time working toward tribal recognition, but the tide had turned against the band. The BIA ruling had colored perceptions of the group. An aide to Senator Shelby admits that members of Congress with MOWA constituents submit bills for the MOWA people almost as a courtesy but that this legislation does not have much of a chance at passing. Even so, the band has continued to lobby for congressional recognition.[9]

While the MOWA Band has a BIA finding against it, all unrecognized tribes currently face great challenges to securing federal tribal recognition through Congress. Since the creation of the Federal Acknowledgment Process in 1978 a general consensus has formed in Congress that the BIA process is more fair, objective, and uniform in dealing with tribal acknowledgment cases than legislation. Even so, the Lumbee Tribe, with its unique status under the 1956 Lumbee Act, has its own seemingly compelling reasons for securing acknowledgment on Capitol Hill. Always a leader among nonfederal tribes, the Lumbee community and its advocates persuaded their congressional representative Charlie Rose, a Democrat, to introduce a bill in 1974 to remove the termination-era language from the 1956 law and therefore enable the group to possess the full powers and rights of federal tribes. The legislation did not pass but instead became swept into the larger debates and politics surrounding the creation of the BIA acknowledgment process itself. Although lacking federal tribal status, the Lumbee Tribe developed an impressive local organization during these years. Starting as a Great Society "War on Poverty" entity, the Lumbee Regional Development Association (LRDA) was chartered in 1968 to pursue economic, educational, and political projects for the people. The LRDA ultimately provided important social and legal services for the Lumbee community. While non-elected, LRDA leaders became the de facto government of the tribe. The association and related Lumber River Legal Services raised over $1 million to prepare the tribe's petition for the Federal Acknowledgment Process, and when completed the petition was the largest ever submitted to the government. Lumbees Cynthia Hunt-Locklear (Legal Services employee), and Julian Pierce (an important attorney who, tragically, was later murdered), prepared the documentation with anthropologist Jack Campisi and historian Wesley White, and the petition was submitted in 1987.[10] Like the MOWA Band, the Lumbees also pursued legislation while their petition was waiting review. The tribal team drew up a recognition bill that was introduced by their congressional backers in 1988. Its success was enhanced when, in 1989, Department of the Interior lawyers ruled that the Lumbees were ineligible to proceed through the Federal Acknowledgment Process: language in the 1956 Lumbee Act stated specifically that they were precluded from a federal-tribal relationship, a prohibition that disqualified a group from the BIA process. Unless this provision in the 1956 Lumbee Act was removed, congressional recognition was the Lumbees' only option. Much like the MOWA Band's bill, the Lumbee legislation came tantalizingly close to passing. In both 1991 and 1993 the bill made it through the House only to die in the Senate. It was during this time that the Lumbees' old adversary, the Eastern Band of Cherokees, reemerged, helping to kill the bill. Eastern Band principal chief Ed Taylor, a vocal and strident opponent of the Lumbees, testified that his people could not support the group unless they had met the stringent standards set by the BIA. During this time Arlinda Locklear emerged as the key Lumbee tribal acknowledgment advocate. A graduate of Duke University Law School, Locklear's commitment to Native issues led her to accept a position with the Native American Rights Fund, transferring to its Washington office to better learn the legislative process. She became the first Indian woman to argue before the U.S. Supreme Court. In 1988 gaining Lumbee recognition became one of her top two priorities and she worked tirelessly for her people on Capitol Hill. According to Locklear, it was archconservative North Carolina senator Jesse Helms who blocked the Lumbee bill each time it came close to passage, using various Senate rules procedures. "The Helms filibuster" would have to be overcome for the group to achieve status.[11]

Figure 14. Arlinda Locklear,
Lumbee citizen and lawyer.
(Photograph courtesy of
Arlinda Locklear)

For the Lumbees, the retirement of Senator Helms in 2003 seemed a wonderful opportunity. His Republican successor, Elizabeth Dole, made passing a Lumbee recognition bill a major priority during her first term. Within a few years the legislation once again cleared the House, only to die in the Senate. The election of Democratic candidate Barack Obama to the presidency in 2008 seemed a breakthrough: on the campaign trail Obama had courted the large Lumbee vote in the swing state of North Carolina. As a result, when Mike McIntyre, a Democrat from Lumberton known for his ability to work across the aisle, introduced another bill to recognize the Lumbees in 2009, most observers were shocked when the Bureau of Indian Affairs, the tribe's most serious traditional adversary, switched positions. A BIA representative actually testified for the bill. It took little insight to see that the group's chances had never been better. It had the bipartisan support of the state's two senators, Democrat Kay Hagan, who had defeated Dole in 2008, and Republican Richard Burr, plus the impassioned advocacy of Congressman McIntyre. At hearings on the bill, Lumbee chairman Jimmy Goins testified for his people. The legislation once again passed the House, garnering approximately 180 cosponsors from both parties.

Longtime advocates felt that the group's hundred-year crusade for acknowledgment was about to end. Once again, however, their hopes were dashed. At the close of 2010 the bill made it out of the Senate committee but was not taken up by the full Senate.[12]

PROBLEMS WITH ACKNOWLEDGMENT: DISPUTED ORIGINS AND INDIANNESS

Many observers believe that recognized tribes oppose both the MOWA Choctaws and Lumbees primarily for economic reasons, but other issues complicate the picture. Leaders of the Eastern Band of Cherokee and other opponents truly believe that the Alabama and North Carolina groups cannot document their tribal origins. These challengers often note that neither the MOWA Band nor the Lumbees had surviving aboriginal cultural traits that were recorded or documented over a hundred years ago. To them this is grounds enough to disqualify both groups as Indian tribes. Aiding the critics is the fact that the Federal Acknowledgment Process requires groups to document the historic tribe or tribes that they descend from and to provide written, genealogical records linking their ancestors to a known historic tribe. Leaders elected by the Poarch Creeks and Mississippi Band of Choctaws feel that the MOWA and Lumbee people cannot prove that they descend from a historic tribe and thus do not deserve recognition. To spokespersons of the two non–federally recognized groups, issues of Indian identity are not that clear-cut, however. As Cedric Sunray, a MOWA educator puts it: "People just don't like the gray area we represent."[13]

The disputed origins of the MOWA group have been detailed earlier. In essence, many other tribes, most vocally the Mississippi Band of Choctaws and the Poarch Creeks, believe that the band is non-Indian. Critics charge that the MOWA Band derives largely from an ancestral community that formed in the mid-nineteenth century northwest of Mobile that was composed mainly of families of European and African ancestry, with a small amount of Indian ancestry added in later decades of the century. Challengers believe that the MOWA people's ancestors chose to accentuate a largely contrived Choctaw and Cherokee identity, sometimes augmented with claims of Chiracahua Apache, Creek, and other Indian ancestry, to "pass" as Indian in the Jim Crow era. In other words, as a nonwhite, multiracial group, it was better to claim

Indian than to be labeled black. Some facts in the MOWA acknowledgment case seem to support the contention. Although the Choctaw
Nation at one point extended into the lands now occupied by the
MOWA community, the modern group has not been able to find
concrete documentation that these Choctaws lived among the MOWA
ancestral community. No existing historical reports describe the group's
core families as Indian or even part Indian. Instead surviving contemporary land records, censuses, and other documents detail origins
among European Americans and freed slaves. By the late nineteenth
century some ancestors of the MOWA people were claiming to be Indian
in the context of miscegenation cases, a stance that would avoid penal-
ties under the miscegenation laws of the time. To date the MOWA
Band has not found records pointing to a central Indian-identified
enclave. They have found no evidence that MOWA ancestors had
surviving, clearly identifiable aboriginal cultural traits such as Choctaw
language, religious observances, or clan organization. While this state
of affairs does not prove that the group is nonaboriginal, the Mississippi Band of Choctaws under their noted chief Phillip Martin has used
these facts against the MOWA group. As early as 1989, Martin in testimony at a congressional hearing referred to the group as the "so-called
MOWA Choctaws," a straightforward aspersion as to their Indian credentials. After commissioning an anthropologist to study the MOWA
Band, Chief Martin wrote to Senator Inouye opposing the group's
1991 recognition bill, saying that while the group had some Choctaw
ancestry, "descendency to some fractional degree by some people does
not make them an Indian tribe. There are areas of culture and political
relationships that more closely define a tribe." He went on to note that
when his people first became aware of the southern Alabama group
they "could discern no Choctaw customs" among the MOWA, and what
Choctaw customs they displayed later were learned from his people.[14]
As the closest federally recognized Choctaw group, Martin's comments
carry great weight, especially among other Indian tribes. These arguments also resonate with many non-Indians who believe that it is absurd
to be recognizing new groups that do not possess aboriginal traits.

Critics likewise believe that the Lumbees cannot prove they descend
from a historic indigenous tribe, yet an impressive group of scholars
support the Lumbees' position that they descend from the Cheraw
Indians and other eastern Carolina tribes that amalgamated with both
blacks and whites in the colonial era. Vine Deloria, Jr., and Jack Campisi

have publicly testified for the Lumbees that they likely descend from the Cheraw and related peoples of the colonial period. So have respected University of Chicago anthropologist Raymond Fogelson and Eastern Woodlands Indian culture expert William Sturtevant, former president of the American Anthropological Association and general editor of the Smithsonian's landmark *Handbook of North American Indians* series.[15] Other noted scholars who have published works on the Lumbees, such as Karen Blu, Gerald Sider, David Wilkins, and Malinda Maynor Lowery, likewise support the theory. The Cheraw hypothesis dates from the 1890s and grew from the efforts of the Robeson Indians to gain federal aid. The first scholarly work linking the Lumbees to the Cheraws appeared during this decade, written by James Mooney, a Bureau of American Ethnology scholar who worked under John Wesley Powell, the famous explorer of the Grand Canyon. Mooney and other government investigators made the logical conclusion that the modern Indian group residing in Robeson County, North Carolina, likely descended from Cheraw and other Indian peoples who retreated to the swamplands along Drowning Creek (today's Lumber River) during the eighteenth century to escape the ravages of disease, slave raids, and warfare in the wake of European colonization of coastal Carolina. According to Mooney and others, a refugee community formed on the Lumber River frontier that included not only the remnants of the decimated coastal tribes, but also escaped slaves, free blacks, and migrating whites. In coming to this conclusion Mooney and others were in many ways refuting the popular theory first promoted by Indian patron Hamilton McMillan that the group originated from survivors of Sir Walter Raleigh's "Lost Colony" of Roanoke who intermarried with Croatan Indians and migrated inland to the Lumber River sometime in the seventeenth century. Indian oral traditions and the fact that the Indians had common surnames found among the "Lost Colony" ship rosters tended to support the theory. According to Adolph Dial and Karen Blu, belief in the "Lost Colony" theory was still common among the Lumbees in the late 1960s and early 1970s.[16] John Reed Swanton, a Harvard-trained anthropologist employed at the Bureau of American Ethnology, also concluded that the group descended from the Cheraw. During the 1930s Swanton studied the Robeson County Indians and in his standard *The Indian Tribes of North America* put forward a theory as to their origins. In a section on the Keyauwee Indians, a Siouan-speaking tribe associated with the Cheraw, Swanton concluded that "some of their descendents are represented among the Robeson County Indians, often miscalled the Croatans." As to the Cheraws, whom Swanton believed had united with the Catawbas of South Carolina, "a part are [*sic*] undoubtedly represented among the Siouan Indians of the Lumber River." How did Swanton and the others come to this conclusion? Existing evidence suggests that he and others examined colonial maps and other sources and deduced that the modern Robeson County Indians had descended from the historic Indian tribes that were noted as living in the same region in the colonial period. While the Cheraw name had been lost by the group, it is clear that many Lumbees came to embrace the Cheraw theory by the 1930s. It is also clear that the name did not matter to many group members. They had been raised as Indians and the more specific name was embraced to satisfy the federal government.[17]

To most scholars the Lumbee position makes sense. Robeson County, a region of swamps and piney woods along the border of North and South Carolina was one of the last areas of the Carolinas to be settled by whites, making it a logical refuge for Indians and other peoples fleeing the southern plantation culture. Lumbee researchers located several colonial-era documents that supported their hypothesis. To link themselves to a historic tribe, the Lumbees had to trace the elusive movements of the Cheraw Tribe. Colonial records show that the tribe inhabited the border between Virginia and North Carolina around 1700, with documents saying the Cheraws migrated south to the Pee Dee River of South Carolina sometime between 1700 and 1737, when at least a segment joined the Catawba Nation. A 1725 map produced by John Herbert, the British Indian commissioner of the region, shows a "Wacomas" Indian village in the Drowning Creek (Lumber River) area. In 1753 the royal governor of North Carolina issued a proclamation identifying Drowning Creek as a frontier for Indians. As late as 1771 a South Carolina newspaper reported a Cheraw settlement on Drowning Creek. Jack Campisi has testified that the common Lumbee surnames of Locklear, Chavis, Sweat, and Dees were also common to the Cheraw tribe. Beginning in 1754, known Lumbee ancestors begin to appear in local land records. Men like John and Major Locklear are recorded as having received land patents that year in Prospect, a community that is today almost entirely Lumbee. In the 1760s men with the common Lumbee surnames of Lowrie, Chavis, Oxendine, Cumbos and others began to appear in local land records as well. In 1790, the first federal census clearly shows known Lumbee ancestral families like the Locklears, Chavises, Oxendines, Hammonds, Brookses, and Cumbos in Robeson County, listed generally as "free persons of color."[18]

In 2009, Michell Hicks, an accountant who in his late thirties became the youngest person ever elected principal chief of the Eastern Band of Cherokees, testified against the Lumbee origin theory, calling it "tenuous" and arguing that the group's claimed tribal affiliation and legitimacy is "doubtful at best." Bolstering his position is the fact that the Federal Acknowledgment Process requires all contending unrecognized groups to find written documents tying their ancestral community members, by name, to known historic Indian individuals who inhabited their region. Some Lumbee leaders and scholars admit that making such a formal link in this case would be next to impossible, although this would not be required for congressional acknowledgment legislation. Most scholars believe that the historical reality of the colonial era makes linking Native groups to written, European records such as censuses and land records highly unlikely. Even without written documentation, to them it is logical that a preliterate Indian society living on the frontier of white settlement would not appear in sources now required to prove their existence. The MOWA Band has faced many of the same challenges. As Chief Wilford Taylor argues, "Ironically enough, we can most persuasively prove our presence by our absence from all writing-based white institutions." Tribal spokesman Cedric Sunray seconds this position, saying: "If we had a middle-class white history like the Poarch Band of Creeks then we'd probably qualify." A common complaint is put forth by leaders of another non–federally acknowledged group, the Snohomish people of Washington State, who have testified that the government "demands proof [of ancestry] that you don't get from the Royal Family." In light of the valuable resources involved, however, opponents challenge the theoretical and philosophical position Chief Taylor articulates that the benefit of the doubt should go to unrecognized tribes. To leaders of recognized tribes their own position is akin to the royal family protecting the royal jewels by demanding proof of familial ties.[19]

The fact that the MOWA Band and Lumbee Tribe cannot definitively prove their origins leaves both open to identity politics and challenges to their authenticity. For the North Carolina group, opponents point to several facts they believe disqualify the Lumbees for federal acknowledgment as a historic Indian tribe. The first allegation is that the Lumbees have no records showing that their originating community was Indian much less specifically Cheraw. While the Lumbees can prove that their documented core community lived in the Lumber River area by 1790 on lands often still owned by descendants, existing records note only that these families were composed of "free persons of color" or white individuals. As argued, however, by Jack Forbes, a scholar with roots among the Chickahominy Indians (a group also affected by the issue), terms such as "free persons of color" and "mulatto" encompassed a wide range of individuals and do not preclude Indian ancestry. Prior to the Civil War the word "free" was the operative term. It was used to denote free blacks, free mulattos (black-white individuals and Indian-white persons), and also free Indian people. To the Lumbees and their supporters it is entirely logical that their ancestors, who were identified in written reports as Indians in the 1870s, were Indians in 1790 even if the records that exist from that year are imprecise as to their race. Besides the vague terms used to describe race in the eighteenth century, several other facts are used by opponents of the North Carolina group to challenge their authenticity and identity. As summarized by noted historian Theda Perdue, early histories of the people, apparently based on oral tradition and other sources, report that when first "discovered" by immigrating Scots-Irish in the early eighteenth century, the Lumbee ancestors were living just like their new white neighbors: they dressed like Europeans, spoke English exclusively, lived in log cabins, and tilled the soil like Europeans. The early histories note that the group at this time did not have any visible Indian cultural traits and had apparently assimilated the ways of their white neighbors.[20] One of the earliest records that refers to the ancestral Lumbee community was a 1754 report made for the colonial governor in preparation for the French and Indian War: "Drowning Creek on the head of Little Pedee, 50 families a mixt Crew, a lawless people filled the lands without patent or paying quit rents; shot a Surveyor for coming to view vacant lands being enclosed by great swamps . . . no arms stores or Indians in the county."[21] This report and the federal census of 1790 are extremely important to the controversy about the Lumbee people's origins. Almost all parties agree that the report above refers to the ancestral Lumbee community, but how the various sides interpret these few surviving words are often diametrically opposed. As Chief Hicks's comments reveal, his group does not consider these scraps of paper proof that the group was Indian. While the Lowry, Locklear, Chavis, Brooks, and Oxendine families listed on the 1790 census can definitely be linked to the modern Indian community, the census does not say specifically that the group was "Indian." These documents do not indicate a connection to a specific tribe, Cheraw or otherwise. They do reveal that there was an identifiable, distinct nonwhite community in the region, but the specific orientation of the enclave is lost to history. Why did the 1754 report state that there were no "Indians in the county"? It could be that the Lumbee ancestors were seen as "civilized" and because they were "mixt" with non-Indians, they were not seen as Native American. It could be that the canvassing was not thorough and missed Indian ancestors of the Lumbee. It also could be that there were no Indians in the Drowning Creek region. The records that survive do not state that there was an Indian tribe or community in the area, and to critics this makes all the difference.[22]

PURE POLITICS

While the scholarly community, many members of Congress, and certainly the Lumbee people themselves accept that the group originated with the Cheraws and other tribes, nearby tribes with much at stake will not take the logical leap. The formerly oral tradition–based tribes have become strict empiricists and demand written proof like the Office of Federal Acknowledgment does. With the Poarch Band of Creek Indians at the lead, regional recognized tribes have become staunch supporters of the BIA process, testifying against almost all recognition bills with the same basic argument: groups like the MOWA Choctaws and Lumbees should not be treated specially—they should be required to go through the process like everyone else. Testimony by Tim Martin, executive director of USET and member of the Poarch Band of Creeks, against a 2003 Lumbee recognition bill was typical: "We went through the process; I cannot in good conscience sit here and say [they are a tribe] and you should just take their word for it. . . . [We cannot support any group] that wishes to circumvent that system." The powerful USET has consistently opposed the Lumbees and other tribes seeking a legislative solution. The Eastern Band of Cherokees and the Poarch Creeks have also been firm defenders of the BIA regulations, regularly testifying against any attempts to lessen their strict requirements. The Eastern Band has always been able to count on the federally recognized Tulalip

Tribes of Washington, whose interests in West Coast fishing rights have led it to testify against the Lumbees seeking to use their clout in Congress to avoid the BIA process and create a seemingly bad precedent.[23] BIA representatives consistently testify against acknowledgment legislation. However, in a select few cases, such as noted above in the case of the Lumbee legislation of 2009 and in the case of the Lac Vieux Desert Band of Lake Superior Chippewa, BIA officials have supported tribes because they felt they had "high evidence" or were prohibited by law from going through the BIA process and thought that the congressional route would be most expeditious to give them status.[24]

To many observers the seemingly neutral position that the Lumbees and the MOWA Band should go through the Federal Acknowledgment Process to be fair to others is disingenuous at best. BIA and USET opposition to the Lumbees and the MOWA Band is likely influenced by common perceptions about the illegitimacy and potential costs of recognizing both groups. Few knowledgeable parties feel that the Lumbees will have an easy time in the channels of the BIA. One insider notes that the Oklahoma tribes are a powerful force in the Indian agency and that over time leaders of the Five Tribes and USET have maligned both the MOWA and Lumbees. The governments of the Five Tribes and related recognized tribes in the Southeast closely follow the cases of groups like the MOWA Band. On a more general level, former Branch of Acknowledgment anthropologist Steve Austin admits that the BIA "has a vested interest against recognizing tribes." It is clear that well placed members of the Five Tribes, whose tribal governments are against recognizing the Lumbees and the MOWA Band, have held positions of great influence in the BIA. Ross Swimmer, former principal chief of the Cherokee Nation was head of the agency during the Reagan administration in the 1980s. Hazel Elbert (Creek) served as acting assistant secretary of the interior for Indian affairs and at other posts during the 1990s and early 2000s, Neal McCaleb (Chickasaw), a Republican, was head of the agency in the early 2000s, and Lee Fleming (Cherokee) has been the longtime head of the Office of Federal Acknowledgment.[25]

While the proposition that the Lumbees should be required to go through the BIA process for recognition seems neutral, it hides real difficulties the group will likely experience. If the review of the large United Houma Nation of Louisiana is any indication, the larger Lumbee Tribe faces much travail ahead. The regulations were created with smaller tribes in mind, and in light of the BIA's findings against the United Houma Nation (with seventeen thousand members), the Lumbees (with fifty-five thousand) will likely experience many of the same challenges and obstacles to securing recognition. In particular their large size and multiple communities will make establishing community and political cohesion difficult. According to Arlinda Locklear, the USET position that her tribe must go through the BIA masks their underlying racial and economic motives for opposing the tribe. As she has concluded, "it's no longer PC" to say that it is about money or race anymore. Locklear notes that she has seen evidence that the BIA does not believe her people can make it through the process. The bureau plans to use an "expedited procedure" to review her people (like they did the MOWA Band) on one criterion alone, that of proving descent from a historic tribe, and then summarily reject her people's bid.[26]

While financial concerns loom large, other tribes challenge both the Lumbees and the MOWA Band on the basis of their motives for claiming an Indian identity. Much of the controversy comes down to race: members of tribes like the Eastern Band of Cherokees and Mississippi Choctaws sincerely believe that both state-recognized tribes are essentially composed of mulattos whose ancestors claimed to be Indian to escape the stigma of blackness in the Jim Crow South. Attorney and former BIA ethnohistorian William Quinn confirms that while he worked in the agency he observed individuals say racist comments about groups. A common complaint was that many unrecognized tribes were really African Americans pretending to be Indian. As Quinn notes, "Indians go by looks, and if a person looks half white and half Indian then they are okay, but if they look half black they will object." Working against both groups' acceptance as Native American is a now largely discredited body of literature on the so-called "tri-racial isolates" of the eastern United States produced generally by sociologists and ethnologists up until the 1970s, in which both the Lumbees and the MOWA Band (then called "Cajans") figured prominently. These works, discussed earlier in greater detail, essentially concluded that the Lumbees and others were "tri-racial" enclaves, communities of mixed white, African, and Indian ancestry that lacked Indian cultural traits but passed as "Indian." As Brewton Berry, the most popular writer of the school, concluded on the Lumbees and others: "Most of them would doubtless prefer to be white. But since that goal is beyond their reach, they will settle for Indian."[27] There clearly were historic advantages for claiming an Indian identity over African. As Ariela Gross notes, colonial-era newspapers are filled with advertisements for runaway slaves (noted as "mulattos") that state that the runaways in question likely will claim to be part Indian or part white as the reason for their freedom. Claiming to be Indian could have enabled such "mulattos" to vote prior to the Civil War and could have been used as a defense against anti-miscegenation laws up until the early twentieth century. Historians have found that it was common for mixed-race African Americans to claim Indian ancestors, perhaps as a way to link themselves to a proud, warrior tradition and to distance themselves from slavery. Interviews and research for this book reveal that many average members of federally recognized tribes like the Poarch Band of Creek Indians accept the Lumbees and MOWA Choctaws as fellow-Indians, but the official position of their tribal governments is that both the Alabama and North Carolina peoples are not Indians, unless proven within the confines of the BIA process. Many believe that the official position has an essential financial underpinning, but Arlinda Locklear feels that many Eastern Cherokees have "blatantly racist" reasons for opposing her people. According to Locklear, "[T]hey truly believe we are blacks masquerading as Indians; saying we must go through the Federal Acknowledgment Process is the PC way to say 'we just don't like these black people.'"[28]

In recent years Michell Hicks of the Eastern Band of Cherokees has testified against the Lumbees, referencing several genealogical studies to cast doubt on the tribal origins of the group. In 2009 testimony, likely written by the tribe's staff scholars, Chief Hicks drew data from several works by genealogists Paul Heinegg and Virginia Demarce that question the Indianness of the Lumbees. The two worked together on Heinegg's *Free African Americans of North Carolina, Virginia, and South Carolina*, a significant and deeply researched history (an earlier version won the Donald Lines Jacobus Award of the American Society of Genealogists). Demarce, a longtime staffer of the Office of Federal Acknowledgment with a PhD in history from Stanford University, has also published works on the origins of the Lumbees and Melungeons. While Demarce's work could be dismissed as biased, Michell Hicks reported that Heinegg was not affiliated with the Eastern Cherokee Band, neither did he work for the government. It appears that Heinegg's primary purpose was to trace the origins of free blacks whose modern descendants include such

luminaries as tennis greats Arthur Ashe and Althea Gibson, and former
NAACP president Benjamin Chavis. While used in a political setting,
his work cannot be dismissed out of hand. It contains a glowing
introduction by respected historian Ira Berlin, one of the foremost
authorities on African slavery and free blacks in the United States.
Berlin praises Heinegg for his over twenty years of intensive research
into the origins of free blacks in the Southeast. As noted by Hicks,
Heinegg used existing censuses, birth records, tax documents, and
other data, and he concluded that the vast majority of free "colored"
families of North Carolina can be traced to migrants from colonial
Virginia. As Heinegg noted, white indentured servants mixed and
socialized rather freely with African servants in the early colonial era.
He found that almost all the families noted as "free persons of color"
originated in unions between white women and black men. Social
ostracism and poverty led to a steady migration of these people to
frontier areas like Robeson County where they formed communities
noted in records as "mixt" or as mulatto enclaves. According to the
testimony of Hicks, Heinegg concluded that although these communities were mixed African and white, anthropologists helped them
establish an Indian identity in the twentieth century. Heinegg states
bluntly that the Lumbees are among the numerous "invented North
Carolina Indian tribes," a position supported by some in the BIA and
by Ira Berlin in the introduction to Heinegg's work.[29]

An issue related to genealogy is each group's phenotype or apparent
racial ancestry. In many ways the nonwhite physical features of the
MOWAs and Lumbees, such as darker skin and facial features stereotypical to the Indian "race," have favored both groups. While not required
in federal acknowledgment decisions, a group's appearance matters
significantly. Records from the late nineteenth century show that some
noted anthropologists used their "scientific" judgment to conclude that,
based on appearance, members of the Lumbee group were clearly of
the Indian race. The Smithsonian Institution contains a photo of a
Lumbee man labeled "Indian Man, Tribe: Croatan." John Reed Swanton provides the context for its origin. As he wrote in the early 1930s:
"My first encounter with a Robeson County Indian was in the office of
Mr. Mooney a few years before his death. He called me in on this occa-
sion, pointed to a tall swarthy individual standing near and asked me
if I did not clearly recognize the Indian features."[30] A similar scenario

played out among the MOWAs in the 1920s when the Baptist Church established Indian mission schools based partly on the Baptist observers' agreement that the group looked like it had partial Indian ancestry. How much a group "looks Indian" is still important. In materials submitted with its 1994 recognition legislation, the MOWA Band included notebooks with photographs of their people, many dressed in dance regalia, to impress the legislators that they looked Indian. This endeavor is not disingenuous or fraudulent, it is savvy when playing politics. The presently recognized Poarch Band of Creek Indians and their leader Calvin McGhee would find the darkest-skinned Indians in the community and dress them in war bonnets and buckskin when asking for help from members of Congress.[31] However, while Lumbees and MOWA Choctaws have been helped in the past by some people thinking that they looked Indian, this nonscientific basis for judging a group's authenticity is prone to error. Conclusions vary per individuals making the assessment based on appearance. I have often heard that both groups "do have Indian ancestry," but the debate was over where it came from or how much there was. Individual assessment based on looks can cut both ways. One woman I spoke with in Oklahoma, a member of the Comanche Tribe of the western part of the state who had apparently met many Lumbees through her professional work, told me, "They don't look Indian to me."[32] It takes little imagination to realize how these perceptions bleed into acknowledgment politics.

Today the MOWA Band's greatest challenge is the BIA's negative finding against them. Interviews for this book reveal that the bureau's final determination has entered popular discourse and to some extent scholarly discourse. It is more and more seen as definitive as to the non-Indian nature of the Alabama group. The government's issuing of press releases and short "final determinations" have the effect of oversimplifying the dense, complex nature of acknowledgment cases like that of the MOWA Band. An enrolled citizen of one of Oklahoma's Five Tribes with much knowledge of the BIA process feels that the BIA finding is conclusive proof that the MOWA group is non-Indian. Even Bud Shapard, a longtime critic of the process he helped create, states that the government's genealogical work on the MOWA proves that they are not who they say they are. As he concludes, "[A]lmost any other thing in the process can be interpreted but not genealogy."[33]

"IT'S NO LONGER A MATTER OF RED;
IT'S A MATTER OF GREEN"

Although it is no longer politically correct to argue against groups being recognized based on the potential costs, many opponents of the Lumbees and MOWA Choctaws have no qualms about sounding an alarm to warn of the financial consequences of passing legislation acknowledging them. In 1992 Poarch Creek Chief Eddie Tullis told a reporter: "Congress should be concerned about economics—they should be more concerned about meeting the needs of existing tribes . . . than creating new ones." The federal government has declined to acknowledge the Lumbee Indians since the 1890s based on financial costs. At every hearing in modern times, the Congressional Budget Office has proffered evidence on the potential costs to the U.S. taxpayer of providing Indian services to the large group. A related issue is the perceived need of groups like the Lumbees for federal aid. Beginning in the 1890s and reaching a crescendo in the 1956 Lumbee Act, federal officials challenged the wisdom of providing federal aid to eastern Indians, creating "wardship" and "dependency" in once "civilized" groups not under federal supervision. In eras before Indian tribal sovereignty was firmly acknowledged, many lawmakers feared the negative consequences of acknowledging federal trust responsibility in formerly independent Indian enclaves. These beliefs are still prevalent in the general public. Over the years the Lumbees in particular have developed a proud tradition and a reputation as an educated, powerful, and successful people, an image that often works against them in an arena where groups that are perceived as small, impoverished, and needy have a better chance of success. In 1994 congressman Craig Thomas said that he believed all tribal recognition legislation could lead to "disastrous" results should groups like the MOWA and Lumbees secure status not because of ancestry but because of their power and support among influential lawmakers. The common sentiment persists that Congress should refrain from recognizing enclaves that do not need help. In 1988 assistant secretary for Indian affairs and former principal chief of the Cherokee Nation Ross Swimmer argued against a bill to recognize the Lumbees, citing several reasons, including "the sheer economic impact" of bringing over thirty thousand individuals who are "a sophisticated, well-educated people" into the BIA orbit, an act that would erode their formerly "independent status" by creating a "pocket of paternalism" in Robeson County.[34]

While rhetoric about a tribe's "needs" and "costs" is rarely heard in hearings on bills for small groups such as the Jena Choctaws, it is at the forefront of debates about the Lumbee Tribe. It is no secret that many parties fear the economic consequences of recognizing the North Carolina group. With fifty-five thousand members now, the Lumbee would become one of the nation's largest federally recognized tribes. BIA officials feel that with natural population growth and the tribe having control over its own membership criteria, the current number will certainly grow markedly over the coming decades, increasing costs to service the group in ways perhaps not apparent today. One factor working against the Lumbees that has nothing to do with ancestry or legitimacy is policy makers' fear of unintended consequences of passing a tribal recognition bill. The issue is related to factors that favor the status quo in Congress. As political scientist Frank Baumgartner has noted, the existing lawmaking process tends to discourage change. The legislative process—with its powerful interest groups, lobbyists, committee chairs, and entrenched agencies—all serve to protect the status quo and serve as staunch institutional gate-keepers. Today the status quo is that the Lumbees and MOWAs are not federally recognized, and conventional wisdom on Capitol Hill holds that the best way to handle acknowledgment cases is the BIA process. Members of Congress, who are not expert on the issue and who are faced with hundreds of other pressing issues, tend to fall back upon the years of accumulated wisdom held by members of special interest groups, federal agencies, and powerful lobbying firms. Rather than risk unintended and potentially costly consequences of passing a tribal recognition law, most legislators would rather default to the status quo, a state of affairs that hurts the chances of groups like the Lumbees.[35]

Ever since the first debates about the rights of unrecognized tribes in the mid-1970s, Bud Shapard and other sources confirm, costs were a major concern of government officials. In 1978 the deputy secretary of Indian affairs fought a liberal congressional recognition bill, arguing that it would place the burden on the government of "acquiring additional groups to serve." If acquiring new groups is a general concern, "acquiring" the large Lumbee Tribe represents these parties' worst fear. In 1988 alarm over the prospect of recognizing the North Carolina people reached the surface. Testifying against a Lumbee bill, Ross Swimmer argued that the law would cost the federal government between $30 and $100 million per year. During the 1980s Reagan administration cutbacks, the sheer budgetary impact of providing services to the group struck a chord, with many parties opting for the conservative approach of retaining the status quo. At a hearing on the Lumbees' 2003 bill, the Congressional Budget Office reported that the legislation, if passed, would cost the government $430 million over 2004–2008. In debate, however, the deputy assistant secretary for Indian affairs testified that this estimate was far too low. She stated that providing federal services to the tribe's fifty-five thousand members would ultimately swallow 15–20 percent of the existing budget then going to recognized tribes. While these numbers are alarming, fears of unintended consequences of passing a Lumbee law also loom. One former Office of Federal Acknowledgment scholar admits that his office mates "cringe" when they contemplate acknowledging groups that potentially could loosen their membership rules after recognition and that in turn could make the BIA's service population "explode."[36]

Fear that groups like the Lumbees will one day open a casino complex also favors inaction. In several incarnations of the Lumbee recognition act, tribal leaders promised not to engage in gaming. However, enrolled Eastern Band of Cherokee businessman Jim Cooper echoes a common sentiment when he note that "the current leaders can say they don't want gaming but who's to say the next generation won't come along and say, those guys didn't know what they were doing. . . . 'Let's open a casino.'" Cooper's feelings are no idle concern—the record is filled with cases like the Tiguas and Alabama-Coushattas of Texas, who promised they would not engage in gaming, only to open casinos soon after securing tribal recognition.[37]

Opponents of both the Lumbees and the MOWA Band have made good use of a general concern among recognized tribes that their slices of the federal funding pie will be diminished should too many groups secure tribal status. Leaders like MOWA chief Wilford Taylor and Lumbee attorney Arlinda Locklear note that USET has used fears of federal funding to mount a concerted campaign against their peoples. They feel that three members, the Poarch Band, the Mississippi Choctaws, and the Eastern Band of Cherokees, have manipulated the entire organization to back their crusade to block the acknowledgment of the MOWA Band and Lumbee Tribe. In the early 1990s when the MOWA bill seemed destined to pass, Phillip Martin and others mobilized other tribes to contact their representatives and members of the Senate Committee on Indian Affairs to lobby against the legislation. Several years later when the MOWA bill again made it through the

Senate, Ada Deer, the respected Menominee leader and spokesperson for the BIA, sent out an urgent letter to House leaders, claiming the group was fraudulently claiming Indian ancestry and should not be acknowledged. Overall, concerns about losing scarce federal funding strike a deep chord. When USET members raise fears that federal Indian funding is precarious, memories of the Reagan years and budget cuts help to make their case. USET members have been particularly adept at manipulating the historic rift between western and eastern tribes, particularly the widespread belief among western reservation communities that the Lumbees "aren't real Indians" because they lack aboriginal culture and treaties. The BIA has supported and aided the USET efforts. As early as 1973 the assistant secretary for Indian affairs warned an audience at the NCAI Annual Convention in Tulsa that their scarce BIA resources were "in jeopardy" because of interlopers seeking access to funds that flow only to those with a special relationship with the federal government. BIA superintendents in western states have held meetings with recognized tribes where they have warned that the tribes will find their federal moneys significantly lessened if the large Lumbee tribe secures status. This has led to tribal resolutions and testimony against recognizing the North Carolina Lumbees from tribes like the West Coast Tulalip, Arizona's Tohono O'odham, and the Absentee Shawnee Tribe of Oklahoma that seem to have little historic connection to Lumbee people.[38]

Warning of the cost of recognizing groups like the Lumbees is not the only rhetoric heard. Statements about their lack of aboriginal traits, lack of federal treaties, and clouded origins emerge, yet these can mask economic roots. The rhetoric usually overlaps, with concerns reinforcing the status quo that controversial groups should not attain federal status via legislation. The opposition can prove potent. As Eastern Band of Cherokee chief Michell Hicks testified against a Lumbee bill in 2009: "Congress should not obligate enormous spending where the identification of the tribe is uncertain at best—the impact on appropriations to other tribes would be unprecedented in the history of acknowledgment." Echoing the fear of unintended consequences, Hicks added that the Lumbee Tribe was much larger than their stated membership of fifty-five thousand. His numbers showed that the size of the tribe was close to sixty-four thousand, with the cost of servicing the group more than $768 million over the coming four years. Congressman Doc Hastings (R-Wash.), the ranking Republican on the House committee that deals with Indian legislation, backed the Cherokee chief's position, warning other tribes that even with the figure of fifty-five thousand members, the cost of providing services to the Lumbees would diminish federal funding for other Indians, an issue increasingly important in the hard economic times of that year. The fact that this and earlier bills failed to pass bears testimony to the fact that concerns about the consequences of passing a law recognizing large groups like the Lumbees serve to enhance the status quo.[39]

INDIAN GAMING AND TRIBAL ACKNOWLEDGMENT LEGISLATION

Numerous observers have applauded the fact that Indian gaming has allowed tribes to exert true sovereignty. Moneys generated by tribal casinos have helped Native nations break free from federal dependence. Vast sums give some tribes political clout and access to federal power in Washington. While it is hard to argue that Indian gaming has not been a positive development for Native Americans overall, Lumbee attorney Arlinda Locklear calls the advent of Indian casinos "the kiss of death" for unrecognized tribes' hopes of securing tribal acknowledgment legislation today. As detailed in my book *Forgotten Tribes* and other works, the steady growth of the tribal gaming industry, especially as it has become linked in the popular mind with once-unrecognized tribes like the Mashantucket Pequots of Connecticut and their fabulously successful Foxwoods Casino complex, has had a significant negative impact on tribal acknowledgment politics. Opponents have challenged many groups on the grounds that they are inauthentic, that in order to enter the lucrative gaming arena they fooled the government into recognizing them. Since the early 1970s local cities and citizen groups have opposed eastern tribes, fearing land claims, loss of tax bases, and other financial costs associated with a newly recognized tribe. Land claims have clearly hurt groups like the MOWA Band and the United Houma Nation, bringing powerful business interests to bear against their aspirations. However, all other economic factors pale in comparison to the effects of Indian gaming. The valuable industry has apparently raised the stakes for any piece of tribal recognition legislation, arraying powerful forces against any group seeking status.[40]

The Indian gaming industry that has done so much damage to tribal acknowledgment politics in the Southeast arose in the very same region. Indian gaming had its inauspicious beginning with a small bingo parlor. In the 1970s the Florida Seminoles opened a modest bingo operation, which took in needed revenue for the tribe. At the time only two states, Nevada and New Jersey, had legalized gambling, and the Florida group hoped to use their sovereign status to bypass local anti-gaming laws. Within a short time area governments challenged the Seminole enterprise in court, with the issue finally settled in the landmark federal appeals court decision *Seminole Tribe of Florida v. Butterworth* (1981).[41] In this case the court ruled that unless a state completely prohibited gaming as a criminal activity then tribes could engage in almost unlimited gambling activities free from state interference. After years of conflict between tribes and local governments, a late 1980s Supreme Court decision arising in California supported the Seminole case's basic position. Public concern prompted Congress to enter the fray, however, and gaming tribes and other parties agreed to compromise with the passage of the Indian Gaming Regulatory Act of 1988. The law provided some federal oversight of the rapidly expanding Indian gambling industry, creating three classes of gaming: Class I (essentially social games), Class II (bingo and similar forms of games), and Class III (casino-style gambling, including blackjack and pari-mutuel betting), with the latter the greatest concern of non-Indians. As such, tribes were required to negotiate compacts with the states to operate "Las Vegas style" facilities. Around this time tribes established the National Indian Gaming Association, an organization that worked with government officials to regulate and protect the industry. To many observers Indian gambling seemed the coming of the "new buffalo," a vehicle Native nations could use to provide economic independence. Budget-conscious legislators promoted gaming as a means for tribes to become self-sufficient and free of government control. Few envisioned that it would impact tribal acknowledgment decisions.[42]

If the Florida Seminoles created the enterprise that would do so much to bedevil groups like the Lumbees and MOWA Choctaws, their relatives the Poarch Band of Creek Indians and their allies have been among the region's staunchest institutional gatekeepers, using all means at their disposal to prevent others from entering their increasingly lucrative gambling territories. Today in the states of Alabama, Mississippi, and North Carolina, only three tribes have federal status: the

Poarch Band, the Mississippi Band of Choctaws, and the Eastern Band of Cherokees. Only they can operate tribal casinos. A perusal of overlooked congressional hearings reveals that tribal rhetoric rarely mentions the casino issue, but few could deny that the underlying fear of losing their regional gaming monopolies motivates leaders of the Poarch Band and others to lobby Congress against groups like the MOWA Band and the Lumbees. Recognized tribes are only a recognition bill away from losing their stranglehold on Indian gaming in their home states. These tribes have found the usual assortment of allies in their efforts to block the Lumbees and the MOWA Band, with some surprising out-of-state forces backing them in their campaign.

By the early 2000s the Poarch Creeks, the Eastern Band of Cherokees, and the Mississippi Choctaws had built impressive gaming-related empires in the Southeast. As they had only secured federal status in 1983, the Poarch Band's development seemed almost miraculous. Residents of sleepy Atmore, Alabama, watched in genuine amazement as a small skyscraper and glitzy casino emerged in their rural southwest corner of the state. By 2010 the group was operating three gaming complexes, including several near the state capital in Montgomery. The Atmore facility included a seventeen-story hotel, several restaurants, and a 225,000-square-foot gambling hall. Tribal advertising claimed that its three resorts paid out over $2 billion to gamblers annually. Its facilities near Montgomery included a complex built on the Creek Nation's ancestral Hickory Grounds. The Poarch Band's decision to build here prompted angry outcry among Native leaders such as Suzan Shown Harjo.[43]

Neighbors to the west, the Mississippi Band of Choctaws, also created an impressive gaming empire. Building upon their renowned business acumen, the band entered into the high-stakes casino industry in the mid-1990s. Construction of what was billed as the region's first full-scale casino resort began then, with the thirty-five-thousand-square-foot Silver Star Hotel and Casino near its headquarters in Philadelphia, Mississippi. This $35.5 million facility was projected to employ over nine hundred individuals, with a combined $15 million annual payroll. By 2011 the Mississippi Band operated other hotel complexes as well, including the Pearl River Resort, Golden Moon Hotel and Casino, and Bok-Homa Casino, plus the Dancing Rabbit Golf Club. The Silver Star facility had by then expanded to ninety thousand square feet, with 2,500 slot machines, and over seventy tables offering craps, roulette, baccarat, and poker. The tribe's venues attracted well-known entertainers such as Merle Haggard and Alan Jackson. The Choctaws claimed that their casino businesses employed several thousand, making the tribe one of the top ten employers in the state of Mississippi.

The Eastern Band of Cherokee Indians likewise entered the casino world. Already well-known pioneers in the Indian tourism business, the Eastern Band transitioned rather smoothly into the new industry. They partnered with Harrah's, a company that operates major casinos in Las Vegas, Atlantic City, and New Orleans, building the fifteen-story Harrah's Cherokee Casino at the group's reservation in the Great Smoky Mountains. It included a 576-room four-star hotel, a fifteen-thousand-square-foot conference center, and gambling hall with slot machines, video poker, and other electronic games of chance. Its pavilion hosted top-name music acts.

The Cherokees and their kin increasingly found their tribal governments and programs dependent on these enterprises: by 2007 Indian gaming had grown into a $26 billion industry annually. Tribes like the Poarch Creeks had invested millions into these enterprises. To tribal leaders it did not seem unreasonable that they should protect them.[44] Gaming profits have affected more than intertribal relations, they have had negative implications within tribes themselves. At Cherokee, North Carolina, per capita payments have put pressure on tribal officials to limit enrollment. Jim Cooper, a prominent hotel owner and enrolled citizen, notes that casinos provide members between $8,000 and $10,000 in per capita payments annually. At reservations gambling profits fund essential tribal social services, provide operating revenues, and are used for additional educational benefits: at Poarch every citizen aged ten to twenty-five is eligible to receive a $30,000 education stipend. While it is hard to argue that these funds are not beneficial, Cooper laments that the per capita payments have put pressure on his tribe to limit enrollment. The current 1/16th blood quantum has excluded his daughter. As he puts it: "[F]or some purposes we want the tribe to be big, but when it comes to our tribal per capita payments we want the tribe to be small." Protecting their resources, gaming tribes across the country have been riven with bitter conflicts as estranged members attempt to return to the fold, only to be challenged and driven away. Competitors come not only from potential interlopers, but also from other interests such as riverboat casinos and state-sponsored gaming enterprises. Tribal leaders also fear that court challenges and political grandstanding may terminate their casino businesses. Leaders have developed a defensive position and almost siege mentality when it comes to protecting their gambling empires. Their desire to maintain gaming monopolies and clients eventually swept the southeastern tribes into one of the most notorious lobbying scandals in modern U.S. history.[45]

LOBBYING AND THE ACKNOWLEDGMENT PROCESS

"It boils down to politics and money," said MOWA Choctaw chief Wilford "Longhair" Taylor. His view is universally shared by members of other non–federally recognized tribes that have faced opposition to their recognition attempts. Big money has entered the tribal acknowledgment process, much to the chagrin of groups seeking status. According to Federal Acknowledgment Process creator Bud Shapard, this was not how the process was intended to function. As he recalls, "I was so naïve . . . casinos were not even thought of then. I believed a hometown historian could write up a twenty-page petition and a decision would be made . . . everyone would tell the truth and be honest." Unfortunately, gambling money has intruded upon the process. Increasingly cash-strapped tribes like the MOWA and Lumbees find it harder and harder to compete for recognition in today's political arena where lobbyists and other forces can make decisions that may trump authenticity and history.[46]

According to Robert G. Kaiser, a *Washington Post* reporter with over forty years' experience in the capital, lobbying and influence peddling have reached epidemic levels in Washington, corrupting the entire U.S. political system in ways unimaginable in the past. As he notes, "ethical rot" has set in among legislators. Taboos against bribery and law breaking are eroding as members of Congress are awash in millions in campaign contributions and perks of the job. There are certainly signs that that lobbying and big money have skewed the Federal Acknowledgment Process. Opponents of unrecognized tribes have infused millions of dollars into the BIA process, leading some bureau employees to admit that they have raised the bar on what is required of petitioners, for fear of being challenged or sued. Big casino money has enabled a select few petitioning groups to submit larger and more complex petitions, yet these documents have not led to a greater chance of success

in the increasingly legalistic and adversarial BIA process. Lumbee and
MOWA leaders likewise see a raising of the bar on what is required
to secure status via Congress. From the 1960s through the Mashantucket Pequots' 1983 recognition legislation, gaining tribal recognition legislation on Capitol Hill was a rather simple affair. Groups like
the Pascua Yaquis of Arizona had powerful legislators usher their bills
through Congress with little fanfare. However, with the 1987 effort of
the Alabama-Coushattas and Tiguas to achieve legislation, it was apparent
that gambling had forever raised the stakes for any acknowledgment
decision, a decidedly negative trend for hopeful tribes.[47]

The Mississippi Choctaws' efforts to protect their gaming monopoly
ultimately swept them and other tribes into one of the most notable
lobbying corruption scandals in modern political history. The infamous
Jack Abramoff scandal, involving the Mississippi Band of Choctaws
and other tribes, shows just how deeply gaming has strained tribal
acknowledgment politics, and in fact strained all intertribal relations
in the Southeast. The scandal was made public in 2004 when the *Washington Post* ran a series of articles revealing that "super lobbyist" Abramoff,
aged forty-six, and his partner Michael Scanlon, thirty-three, had bilked
four tribes, the Louisiana Coushattas, the Mississippi Choctaws, the
Agua Caliente Band of Mission Indians, and the Saginaw Chippewas,
of approximately $80 million since the election of Republican presi-
dent George W. Bush in 2001. A former leader of the College Republicans and Hollywood movie producer, Abramoff parlayed his conservative
credentials into a high-paid career in the nation's capital. He became
a well-heeled lobbyist for the Washington firm Greenberg Traurig, where
Scanlon also worked. Both touted their close ties to powerful House
Majority Leader Tom DeLay (R-Tex.) and leading Indian advocate
Senator Inouye, as well as links with the Bush administration, to convince
newly wealthy gaming tribes like the Mississippi Choctaws and Louisiana Coushattas to give millions to theoretically influence policy in
Washington. Abramoff was also a close associate of Ralph Reed, one-
time head of the Christian Coalition and another former College
Republican leader, who also aided the tribal lobbying effort. To the
somewhat naïve tribes green to Washington politics, the Indian gaming
industry seemed constantly under attack, and Abramoff fanned their
fears that their casinos and tribal sovereignty were in grave danger.
Soon the four tribes were each paying the lobbyists $180,000 per month.

Even by Washington standards this was a huge sum. Knowledgeable parties noted that a "good rate" for a lobbyist would be $40,000 per month. During the early George W. Bush years, tribes had quietly switched their political allegiance from the Democratic Party to the Republican Party, with the desire to protect Indian gaming a clear motivator. Even to jaded Washington insiders the sums paid by the Mississippi Choctaws and others were unconscionable. Scanlon alone received approximately $31 million from the four tribes, a sum comparable to moneys spent by large corporations during the same period to influence multiple issues. To many, the attitudes of Abramoff and his colleagues toward their tribal clients were also unconscionable: private e-mail messages reveal that he and Scanlon routinely referred to their Indian clients as "monkeys" and "idiots," while reveling in how much money they were plucking from their pockets. Abramoff ultimately was caught, pled guilty to tax evasion, conspiracy, and fraud, and spent several years in prison. Abramoff's friend Tom DeLay also completely fell from grace. He was forced to resign his office, and later, in a Texas court, was convicted of money laundering and then sentenced to three years in prison.[48]

Some of the Abramoff money was used to fight newly recognized tribes that sought to edge into the established groups' casino territories. The problem had to do with so-called "forum shopping" of newly acknowledged tribes who had the ability to locate their original reservations far from their actual tribal homelands. This fact sent a shiver of fear among established casino-running tribes and gave them another reason to oppose the recognition of groups in their states. The tiny Jena Band of Choctaw Indians of Louisiana was one group that felt the sting of the increasingly acrimonious casino-driven intertribal politics in the Southeast. As detailed previously, the Jena Band secured tribal status through the BIA process in 1995 with strong support from the related Mississippi Band of Choctaws and other nearby tribes. Relations turned sour, however, when the Jena group sought to create their initial reservation in more lucrative corners of Louisiana than their traditional village site in out-of-the-way Jena. In 2002 the tribe signed a compact with the Louisiana governor to secure a reservation and potential casino site near Vinton, Louisiana, a town on the Texas border. This would have made the Jena Band the front-runner in reaching the valuable Texas market, as the Coushatta-run nearest Indian casino was fifty-five miles from the state line, and the nearest riverboat casinos, operated by gambling giants Isle of Capri and Harrah's in Lake Charles, were twenty-five miles from the border. To win over the governor the Jena Band agreed to give the state 15.5 percent of its profits, a considerable advantage: the other Louisiana tribes paid nothing. The various gaming forces blocked this bid by the Jena Choctaws, yet the fact that newly acknowledged tribes could open a casino almost anywhere in the state raised fears among many parties in the region. Alarm over the thought of a gambling hall popping up in places that had no resident Indian tribes could be used to good effect by established gambling entities. Chief Phillip Martin of the Mississippi Band of Choctaws paid Abramoff to oppose the Jena group, and the Louisiana Coushattas gave Scanlon and Abramoff close to $30 million to stymie the casino plans of the Jena Choctaws and other tribes.[49]

The crusade to block casino expansion in Louisiana made for some strange bedfellows in the Jena Choctaw case, odd pairings that are also apparent in lobbying related to the Lumbees in North Carolina. The *Washington Post* reported that, through Abramoff, the gaming tribes gave Ralph Reed and evangelist James Dobson, the latter of the conservative Focus on the Family organization, up to $4 million to cause a frenzy over the potential expansion of casinos in Texas and Louisiana and the possible effect on the morals of residents there. The hypocrisy mounted as the Louisiana Coushattas spent millions to oppose the plans of their close relatives the Alabama-Coushattas of East Texas. The Abramoff associates drafted anti-Jena letters, opposing Jena casino plans, and provided them, ready for signing, to members of Congress who had also received campaign contributions from the established casino tribes. Encouraged by the casino-driven campaign, the Texas Baptist Christian Life Commission and the conservative Texas Eagle Forum rallied to the cause. Abramoff had his tribes (the ones he had bilked) give money to a group founded by Gale Norton prior to her selection by President Bush as secretary of the interior, head of the department that oversees the Bureau of Indian Affairs with its decisions on whether to grant tribes new reservation sites. This money led to access. Mississippi Choctaw chief Phillip Martin was given a meeting with the secretary to discuss his opposition to the Jenas and other issues during her tenure. MOWA Band leaders likewise believe that some of Chief Martin's moneys were used to lobby against the recognition of their people. The Jena Band hired their own lobbyist lawyer, however, a former chief of staff for several powerful Louisiana Republican members of Congress, with the cycle beginning again.[50]

The politics involved with the Lumbee Recognition Act debated in Congress between 2008 and 2010 provides a good example of the effects of casino money and lobbying on the acknowledgment process. Congressman Mike McIntyre (D-N.C.), a native of Lumberton in the Lumbee homeland and a graduate of the University of North Carolina, introduced several bills to recognize the Lumbees. Most tribal members lauded McIntyre for his firm commitment to their people and diligent work in trying to pass the legislation, and the bill seemed destined to pass: never before in their hundred-year struggle had the Lumbees had so much support. As mentioned earlier, longtime observers were surprised when a representative of the BIA testified *in favor* of the law. Seeking support from the large tribe in his bid to win the presidential election of 2008, eventual winner Barak Obama promised to support the Lumbee bid to secure acknowledgment legislation. It took prodding from Arlinda Locklear, but the BIA begrudgingly agreed to honor the pledge. Over one hundred members of Congress, from both parties, signed on as cosponsors of the bill. To overcome anticipated opposition, the tribal government agreed to a provision banning gambling. To address concerns over its financial impact, one version of the law had provisions for increasing the federal budget should the Lumbees come under the federal umbrella.[51]

Despite all the promise, the Lumbee Recognition Act again failed to pass. The group's recognition politics had long been Byzantine, but the defeat of the law had some surprising twists and turns, even compared to others in the annals of the tribe's struggles. According to several sources, the Eastern Band of Cherokee Indians was the primary obstacle to the Lumbee law. It succeeded in mobilizing its allies in USET to block the bill, using their substantial casino profits to lobby against their North Carolina neighbors. As Arlinda Locklear notes, the Eastern Cherokees rallied their close associates the Mississippi Choctaws and Poarch Creeks and together the three tribes seized control of USET for their purposes. Students of tribal acknowledgment know that the Eastern Cherokees and their lobbyist George Waters, a non-Indian based in Washington, have been leaders in lobbying for the interests of federally recognized tribes since the 1970s. By the time of the Lumbee debates of 2008–2010, the Cherokees had replaced Waters with lobbyist Wilson Pipestem (Osage and Otoe-Missouria), who reportedly is married to an enrolled member of the Eastern Band of Cherokees. According to Arlinda Locklear, she has heard that Pipestem is paid well for his services. Locklear has heard that the Eastern Band pays approximately $1 million each congressional session to block Lumbee acknowledgment legislation, with Pipestem receiving a bonus of $100,000 every time he successfully defends the Cherokees' gaming interests. In other contexts, scholars have noted how Indian gaming and various self-determination policies have given tribes true power in today's politics, and this fact is apparent in the tribal lobbying against the large Lumbee tribe. In 2009 the House of Representatives voted 240–179 in favor of a version of the Lumbee Act that ultimately failed in the Senate. Showing how tribes were influencing politics, most Democrats voted for the Lumbees, yet Democratic representative Stephanie Herseth-Sandlin from South Dakota, an individual who usually supported Indian legislation from a traditional "Indian state," voted against the bill. Dan Boren (D-Okla.), the representative from the district encompassing the Cherokee Nation opposed the bill, as did Heath Shuler (D-N.C.), the representative from the Eastern Band's home region. Tom Cole (R-Okla.), a member of the Chickasaw Nation, also opposed the Lumbee bill.[52]

Behind these votes is the often-hidden power of lobbyists. Both recognized tribes and their ambiguously acknowledged neighbors the Lumbees have used various lobbying strategies to access power and influence legislators. While the Lumbees, the MOWA Band, and other groups play the lobbying game as best they can, gaming money clearly has stacked the deck in favor of the United South and Eastern Tribes. Formed explicitly to protect the interests of federally recognized tribes, USET has helped foster strong, interlocking webs of relationships between its members and also provided links with lobbyists serving the member tribes. It holds conferences that influential politicians, lawyers, and tribal leaders attend. As the majority of USET members run gambling businesses, protecting this base is a foremost concern. A list of clients from the California law firm Sheppard Mullin reveals that this group represents many USET members and other gaming tribes across the nation. Lobbyists representing powerful interest groups have grown exponentially in number since the 1960s. As noted by political scientist Frank Baumgartner and his associates, in many congressional debates a small number of interest groups are the only parties influencing decisions on legislation. Only they have the specialized knowledge, resources, and plain staying power to affect the lawmaking process. With any piece of legislation there is a policy community that is central to its ultimate success or failure. It consists of the chair of the committee where the bill is introduced, lobbyists for the various interests involved, and representatives from federal or other agencies affected by the legislation. Since the 1980s senators John McCain (R-Ariz.), Daniel Inouye (D-Hawaii), and Ben Nighthorse Campbell (R-Colo.) have at times chaired the influential Senate Indian Affairs Committee and have provided valuable support for the interests of many unrecognized tribes. However, these groups have generally faced more opposition than support from the policy community involved with tribal acknowledgment. The lobbyists of the USET members coupled with testimony from BIA representatives make up a potent force against the passage of any tribal acknowledgment legislation. Another factor working against the Lumbees and the MOWA Band is the tendency of legislators to fall back upon the status quo rather than risk the consequences of change. Because law makers often have dozens of issues demanding their attention at any one time, the fears of the unintended consequences of passing a law such as a Lumbee or MOWA recognition act have the effect of favoring inaction.[53]

As the status quo is that the large Lumbee Tribe and the controversial MOWA Band are not currently federally recognized tribes, lobbyists for the Eastern Band of Cherokees, Poarch Creeks, and Mississippi Choctaws make the rounds each legislative cycle, following a circuit that has proven successful in the past to block their acknowledgment. Whether George Waters, Wilson Pipestem, or others, lobbyists for the USET group go to their other clients and ask for tribal resolutions against the Lumbees and others. They go to the secretary of the interior or BIA officials to voice their fears and concerns. When the Lumbee or MOWA legislation gained traction in the past, lobbyists have visited chairs of major Indian committees, such as senator Byron Dorgan (D-N.D.), to keep the bills from getting out of committee. With both the Lumbees and the MOWA Band, opponent tribes have hired scholars to conduct research and write briefs challenging the authenticity of these people as Indian tribes. In the early 1990s, for example, Poarch Creek chairman Eddie Tullis hired a local historian to write an essay arguing that the MOWA Band was not Choctaw, then had it printed in local Alabama news outlets and submitted to the Congressional Record. Mississippi Choctaw chief Phillip Martin likewise had a staff anthropologist write a report challenging the identity of the MOWA group, and this he submitted to Congress. Years later the leaders of the Eastern Band of Cherokees hired a scholar to challenge the Lumbees' identity, later using the research in prepared testimony before the Senate and House Indian affairs committees. Once prepared it is clear that tribal leaders use these reports over and over again in verbatim testimony against the two unacknowledged tribes.[54]

These tactics usually prove successful, but, as noted earlier, on several occasions the Lumbees and MOWA Choctaws have succeeded in getting their legislation out of committee and even passed by one house of Congress. When this has happened opponent tribes and officials of the BIA have made blocking their bills a major priority. In 1994, for example, when a MOWA bill made it out of committee and passed the full Senate, the head of the BIA, Ada Deer, sent an impassioned letter to the chairman of the House Subcommittee on Indian and Native Alaska Affairs, charging that the group's petition was fraudulent and incompetent. With this testimony, it is no surprise that House members fell back on the status quo and did not pass the law. In the Lumbees' case, tribal attorney Arlinda Locklear notes, several tactics have been used to block recognition. During the 1980s and 1990s powerful senator Jesse Helms used an arcane Senate rules procedure to put a hold on the bill. After Helms retired, a 2009 version of the law was blocked in a similar manner when congressmen representing the USET and Oklahoma tribes, senators Thad Cochran (R-MS), Jeff Session (R-AL), and Tom Coburn (R-OK), put holds on the legislation. Senator John Ensign (R-NV), representing the gaming interests of his home state, also put a hold on the bill.[55]

Of course the actions of their opponents anger the Lumbees and MOWAs, but they are severely restrained in their ability to counter the recognized tribes and their congressional allies. As Billy Hunt, a tribal asset manager for the Lumbee Tribe notes, federal rules mandate that grant money and other tribal funds cannot be used for lobbying purposes. Both groups can get small federal grants to research their tribal history for acknowledgment purposes, but in general they are handicapped in the acknowledgment arena. The Lumbee Tribe holds fundraisers such as golf tournaments and benefit dinners to raise money for their campaign, and many tribal members have donated generously to their people. The MOWA Band has used a traditional Indian way of incorporating allies into the fold by making people such as U.S. representative Jo Bonner "honorary Choctaws." Without significant money to spend, however, both groups often are forced to use moral arguments and their power as voting blocs to win supporters in Congress. As noted, Arlinda Locklear was the largely unpaid lawyer and lobbyist for the Lumbee Tribe from 1988 to 2010, and her tactics are perhaps typical of lobbyists for groups seeking legislative recognition. In the past the Lumbees created a "road show" for the tribe, traveling to western reservations in attempts to prove that the Lumbees are Indian people. On these excursions members like Ruth Locklear, the tribe's current enrollment officer, met with tribal representatives in South Dakota and elsewhere to dispel myths that they are "not real Indians." They also have invited other tribal leaders to visit Robeson County, where, both Arlinda and Ruth Locklear note, most are shocked to see that they *are* Indians. Lumbee leaders also make the rounds of Capitol Hill, arguing that recognizing their people is the "morally right thing to do." Many members of Congress, such as Nick Rahall (D-W.Va.), have taken up their cause, providing impassioned support for the Lumbee people in Washington, testifying that acknowledging them will end a century of injustice against the North Carolina group. A recollection of Ruth Locklear, however, reveals the sometimes arbitrary ways of Capitol Hill. She remembers visiting the office of a western congressman with a delegation of Lumbee teachers advocating that he support a tribal recognition bill sponsored by Charlie Rose. After noting how impressed he was that they were educated and cleanly dressed, the congressman remarked: "You know what? I like you Indians. In my state all our Indians are alcoholics and don't work. . . . I'll vote for it. . . . Rose needs a headache in his state just like I have!"[56]

It is widely acknowledged that few members of Congress have expertise on Indian issues, especially complicated recognition cases. When deciding to support a group, legislators have traditionally looked to several sources before committing their time and political capital. In the era before Indian gaming, tribes tended to have similar dossiers: most had files with letters of support from local business and civic leaders testifying to their moral character and economic value to the community. In the case of the MOWA Band and the Lumbee Tribe each has an impressive résumé attesting to the support it has in the local community, and this has in the past proved highly important. The MOWA group possesses letters from local churches, community service organizations, local governments, and even the Alabama governor supporting the cause. It has the seal of approval from the state legislature

that they are a tribe. Both groups have coveted membership in the
NCAI, the nation's largest pan-tribal group, and the MOWA Band has
the support of the federally recognized Tunica-Biloxi Tribe of Louisiana, while at various times the Lumbees have had the backing of the
Tunica-Biloxis, the United Keetoowah Band of Cherokees, the Seminoles of Florida, and others. Hearings on both Lumbee and MOWA
Choctaw recognition bills are replete with tribal rhetoric that was highly
effective in the past but is decreasingly effective today. Group members
have testified that their men have served their country in military
uniform and that their people are poor and struggling and thus
in need of government Indian aid. Members testify that they only
want federal funds to help their people become independent and
self-supporting, and that their primary motivation for seeking tribal
recognition is that it would validate their identity and provide a sense
of justice. Some have testified erroneously that they have evidence that
their "native language" was spoken in the twentieth century. The MOWA
Band has argued that their ancestors used bows and arrows, made dug-
out canoes, and practiced traditional hunting methods. Also working
in favor of groups like the MOWA Band and the Lumbees is the
potential economic benefit that would flow to the local region if they
secured federal status. It is clear that having a federally recognized
tribe is good for business, bringing increased tourism, thousands in
federal Indian aid, and the potential for free-trade industrial zones.
This has traditionally spoken loudly to the local business community,
and it is rare case where local chambers of commerce and other booster
groups do not support groups like the Lumbees. The Lumbee power
as a voting bloc also works in the people's favor. The MOWA Band
members too have used their power as voters to gain the support of
politicians in southwestern Alabama. As the record attests, these facts
have proven highly influential in the two tribes gaining support from
their local congressional delegations. However, in the calculus of whether
to support a bill, legislators hear other voices, especially those of gaming
lobbyists and anti-gambling forces that have changed the essential equa-
tion decidedly against unacknowledged tribes.[57]

INDIAN GAMING AND TRIBAL
ACKNOWLEDGMENT POLITICS

Indian gaming has turned every tribal acknowledgment bill into a
regionally, if not nationally, significant piece of legislation. Don Miller,

an attorney with NARF with over twenty-five years' experience in the field, notes that members of Congress tend to defer to state and local congressional delegations on Indian matters, seeing these issues as fairly unimportant or purely local in nature. When matters of national significance are involved, however, Miller feels it is an entirely different matter. Indian gaming has had this effect, vastly widening the circle of parties concerned about the implications of acknowledgment legislation.[58] The loud chorus of voices against the Lumbees, MOWAs, and others is diverse in origin and takes many forms, but it is highly organized. One part of the chorus is the Christian Right. In the Bible Belt states of Alabama and North Carolina, organized opposition to gambling and associated vices has deep roots. Fears center on the moral and social decay that opponents feel will follow the spread of Indian gaming. The Lumbee Tribe has certainly felt the full force of this movement. In 2004 evangelical groups lobbied to stop the Lumbee tribal acknowledgment law, worried that it would lead inevitably to the expansion of gambling in the Tar Heel State. At the forefront was the Christian Action League, a group formed to support Prohibition in the early twentieth century and still active in the twenty-first. The league published articles against Lumbee acknowledgment and sent documents to Congress opposing the group. In one piece, Mark Creech argued: "Our concern is that attempts to validate this group as a tribe will ultimately have broad and unintentional negative effects, via gambling, on all of North Carolina." In 2004 William J. Brooks, president of the North Carolina Family Policy Council, outlined to Congress what his group believed those negative consequences would be. He testified that a Lumbee casino would place a major gambling center within a short drive of all the state's major cities. This in turn would bring a host of ills associated with gaming, including gambling addiction, destruction of family finances, domestic violence, child abuse, rising divorce rates, embezzlement, theft, bankruptcy, and suicide. It would lead to organized crime and an overall rise in crime rates. The casino-operating Eastern Band of Cherokee Indians shared one belief with the Family Policy Council: a Lumbee casino along I-95, the major north–south highway on the Eastern Seaboard, would draw great numbers of gamblers and other tourists. A gaming expert testified that a future Lumbee casino could become a $1 billion a year enterprise. It clearly would siphon many of the approximately 3.3 million annual visitors away from Harrah's Cherokee Casino, the state's largest tourist draw, that is located in the fairly out-of-the-way western corner of the state. As previously noted, the Lumbees had promised not to gamble, but few interested parties believed their claim.[59]

It was not just the Lumbees who felt the effects of anti-gaming forces. Also in 2004, a host of Connecticut-based lobbyists and members of Congress called for a moratorium on all new acknowledgment decisions, mobilized over several controversial recognition decisions in their state. As representative Nancy Johnson (R-Conn.) testified: "Something has gone terribly wrong with the tribal acknowledgment process; it has become driven by casino money, big, big, bucks." Johnson's opinion was widely shared. Jeff Benedict, an outspoken opponent of unrecognized tribes, argued for his group the Connecticut Alliance against Casino Expansion that the entire BIA process was corrupt and said that the potential growth of gaming in his region was putting "the future of the state of Connecticut at risk."[60]

Indian gaming clearly has sparked a reemergence of the old "rich Indian" stereotype once widely associated with eastern Oklahoma Indians during the early oil boom of the early twentieth century. The new image links Indian tribes, especially recently recognized groups, with casinos, and the prevailing belief is that tribal recognition was "invented" so that big investors could find essentially assimilated groups and use them to open casinos and grow fabulously rich. The stereotype started on the East Coast as knowledge of the phenomenal success of the recently acknowledged Mashantucket Pequots' Foxwoods Casino in Connecticut spread. In 1987, the same year the landmark Supreme Court *Cabazon* case paved the way for the expansion of Indian casinos, the *New York Times* began running articles linking local unacknowledged groups with casinos. Most prominent was the Ramapough group of New Jersey whose home area was close to New York City and thus, if acknowledged, could destroy the established gaming centers of Atlantic City and Foxwoods. Articles noted that the Ramapoughs had hired a large gaming conglomerate to fund their acknowledgment bid, and rumors then circulated that the group had links with organized crime and a secret deal to share their future gaming profits with the Mafia. While this was juicy reading, the linkages did little to help Ramapough chances in the court of public opinion. Other groups that had spent decades pursuing recognition, many with state reservations, found their quests tainted by headlines like "Another Tribal Nation? Another Casino?," "Tribe Recognized as a Nation: Mohegans May Build State's 2d Casino," and "U.S. Denies Tribal Status, Foiling Plans for a Casino." Years later the Lumbees and the MOWA Choctaws faced headlines such as "North Carolina Group Says Lumbee Recognition Means Casino." Though they had pursued federal status long before Indian gaming came along, groups like the MOWA Band and the Lumbees certainly were damaged by the linkage. To many non-Indians, both groups became tarnished by a belief that they sought undeserved riches, a sentiment that undermined public support for the tribes. As David Wilkins and Anne McCulloch have noted, public support usually flows to Native groups perceived as impoverished victims of past U.S. policies and injustice, not ones seen as powerful or greedy. It certainly did not help the Lumbees, who were already widely perceived as one of the most powerful Indian groups in the country, to now be seen as potentially one of the wealthiest as well. Tribal leaders are forced now to spend a significant amount of time and energy refuting rumors that all they really want is to open a casino. As MOWA chief Wilford Taylor laments, "Gaming has really heated things up; people around here got jealous. People think we're all rich, driving big cars and smoking cigars."[61]

EASTERN INDIAN SUPPORT OF THE
FEDERAL ACKNOWLEDGMENT PROCESS

Southeastern tribes, through USET and other organizations, have presented a united front against groups like the Lumbees seeking acknowledgment legislation that would circumvent the BIA's acknowledgment process. USET members, especially the Eastern Band of Cherokees, have been strident in their attacks on groups that seek to use Congress to achieve tribal status. Their common argument is that granting the Lumbees or the MOWA Band legislative recognition would be unfair to other groups and would introduce the potential for fraud. While clearly economically motivated, the USET position does have validity that cannot be discounted out of hand. Those familiar with the congressional process know that the average member of Congress has little expertise on tribal acknowledgment issues. The congressional route is prone to manipulation and politics. A good example concerns the origins of the Lumbees and the MOWA Band. Congressional hearing testimony reveals that there has been some stretching of the truth with both tribes. Representatives from the Lumbees and the MOWA Choctaws have testified that they once had "native speakers" (a fact that would be good evidence of Indian identity), yet there is no existing documented evidence of this claim. The MOWA Band has provided legislators with lists of Choctaw individuals from the early nineteenth century, claiming these as ancestors, yet no clear link has been established tying these individuals to known MOWA ancestors from the era. How many legislators or other people have the expertise to identify the problems with these seemingly clear-cut claims? In another instance, a formal congressional report that accompanied a 2003 version of the Lumbee recognition legislation stated that the group could meet six of the seven BIA acknowledgment criteria, including descent from the Cheraw Tribe, when, as previously noted, this assertion is certainly debatable. While these few examples do not mean that either group is not a tribe or that their leaders are intentionally deceptive, they do point to the non-expert nature of congressional acknowledgment. These inconsistencies may stem from tribal advocates' desire to put their best foot forward, or perhaps to simplify the complicated nature of their cases, but they provide fodder for opponents' contention that the BIA process is superior—more objective and uniform—for deciding recognition cases.[62]

It is apparent that USET members like the Poarch Creeks and Eastern Band of Cherokees see the BIA acknowledgment process as the primary bulwark protecting them from association with other tribes, particularly state-recognized tribes of the Southeast. It protects their most valuable resource—federal acknowledgment itself—from a host of contenders in what they clearly see as a dangerous, competitive world. USET views one of its foremost missions as educating the public about the significant difference between federal and state entities. The status distinction is important, reflecting true historical differences between many groups, but it also engenders contention among groups. Indian gaming has only exacerbated the conflict. Both the Poarch Creeks and Eastern Cherokees have long-standing prickly histories with their state Indian commissions, with the Cherokees generally refusing to associate via the commission with their less prestigious state-recognized kin. MOWA Choctaw spokesman Cedric Sunray calls USET "the Big Boys Club" of Southeastern tribes, and in many ways it is just that, using its power to challenge bills put forward by Sunray's people and others.[63]

If USET is the "Big Boys Club," then passing the BIA acknowledgment process serves as the formal initiation ritual. To USET members, the

Lumbee and MOWA attempts to gain acknowledgment legislation smack at trying to gain entry through the back door. Tribal spokespersons have provided consistent testimony against the congressional acknowledgment procedure. In 2004 Tim Martin, executive director of USET, testified that "the BAR process [works] . . . Federal Recognition of Indian tribes is a formal act that acknowledges the sovereign status of a tribe and affirms the perpetual government-to-government relationship between the tribe and the United States. . . . it assures the tribe the dignity it deserves." That same year Michell Hicks, principal chief of the Eastern Band of Cherokee Indians, with Chad Smith, principal chief of the Cherokee Nation sitting nearby, argued vehemently against the passage of Lumbee acknowledgment legislation. As Hicks said, they wanted to present a united front that the bill would undermine "the integrity of our long government-to-government relationship," warning about would could happen "[if] politics and emotions take over rather than facts about tribal identity." As Hicks concluded, "Folks, this is all about identity."[64]

In his quest to have the Lumbees go through the Federal Acknowledgment Process, Hicks had a North Carolina congressman sponsor a 2004 bill that would remove the language from the 1956 Lumbee Act that prevented them from availing themselves of the BIA process. The new bill to require the Lumbees to submit a new petition and undergo the rigorous BIA system was cosponsored by congressman Brad Carson (D-Okla.), a member of the Cherokee Nation. While the Cherokee position was seemingly neutral and principled, it perhaps belied the Cherokees' true feelings regarding the authenticity of the Lumbees. In the same session the Eastern Cherokee chief challenged the tribal status of the Lumbees, arguing they had no treaty with the U.S. government like his tribe did, had never possessed a reservation, and had claimed so many names that they had, at best, a confused identity. Hicks also noted that the group was not culturally Indian: "They do not speak an Indian language . . . they possess no traditional Indian customs, such as dances, songs or tribal religions." Clearly Hicks and others would not be celebrating should the Lumbees pass the BIA process, but they do not think the group can make it through. As such, the bill requiring the Lumbees to go through the BIA process is unsatisfactory to the Lumbees. Like their opponents, some Lumbee leaders believe they will have a difficult time with the BIA criteria. Arlinda Locklear believes the BIA is biased against her people: "The BIA has [long] been gunning for the Lumbees," she notes. Similarly MOWA chief Longhair Taylor and his friends feel that the Office of Federal Acknowledgment did not provide a fair forum for his people. They believe that its head Lee Fleming, a former tribal enrollment officer of the Cherokee Nation under principal chief Wilma Mankiller, is patently against their people. Many individuals, including Chief Taylor, believe that Fleming was placed in the OFA at the Cherokee Nation's request after having proven his skills leading Mankiller's crusade against unrecognized tribes in the Southeast. Chief Taylor and others believe that unrecognized groups like the Lumbees have no friend in the Office of Federal Acknowledgment.[65]

RECENT DEVELOPMENTS

In 2009 the Lumbee tribal government grew increasingly frustrated that its acknowledgment legislation had failed to get through Congress, and it decided to join forces with a gaming firm from Las Vegas. At the time many tribal officials felt that Arlinda Locklear's approach was not working. Billy Hunt asserts, "She had worn out her welcome in Washington." Hunt and others believed that Locklear's appeals to justice, that passing their bill "was the right thing to do," was anemic in the face of foes like the Eastern Cherokees who "would come in the next day and say 'here's $25,000 for your campaign, now you need to make this vote.'" As such, when Las Vegas gaming consultants Lewin International approached the Lumbee tribal council with an offer, it seemed logical to listen carefully. Tribal chairman Jimmy Goins, a middle-aged Vietnam veteran and insurance company owner, and a segment of the tribal council entered into hushed discussions with Lewin without informing Arlinda Locklear and others. Goins soon hired the firm, which agreed to front money to lobby for the tribe in return for the exclusive right to run casinos for the Lumbees and a percentage of all future gaming profits. According to Hunt, he and others believed that the Lumbees could not compete with the Eastern Cherokees, who were spending millions to oppose his people. Lewin International's pitch that the firm could get the people recognized and "that it wouldn't cost the tribe a dime" sounded good. Others note that the gaming firm came on strong, promising to "make you all million-aires." Lewin also claimed that the firm had close connections with Harry Reid (D-Nev.), the powerful Senate Majority Leader, who could neutralized his state's consistent opposition to other gaming interests. Goins's hiring of Lewin International led to what Arlinda Locklear calls "a parting" between her and the tribe she had served for over twenty years. It also led to a major rift within the tribe, as supporters stood up for Locklear, eventually forcing Lewin to back out. A major problem with the tactic of hiring the Las Vegas gaming consultant was that the bill then working through Congress had a provision banning gambling. Lumbee officials had promised that they had no intention of opening casinos. Arlinda Locklear had drafted the anti-gaming clause at the request of the chairman of the House Natural Resources Committee, who had told her he could not get the bill out of committee without a gaming ban. With these agreements, the legislation passed the House, a major accomplishment, and was awaiting consideration in the Senate when the Lewin scandal broke. It now appeared that tribal leaders had a secret plan to double-cross legislators. They had, as local reporter Mike Hixenbau notes, "poisoned the bill" by their contact with the gaming firm. Not surprisingly the law failed to pass. To many this seemed like just another example of tribal leaders shooting themselves in the foot just as they were about to achieve the Lumbees' long-awaited goal. The tribe soon had a new chairman, Purnell Sweat, a longtime public school and government education administrator, and under Sweat the tribe hired Anderson Tuell, an Indian-owned lobbying and law firm based in Washington. While they dropped the Las Vegas gaming consultant, Lumbee leaders still believed that the tribe needed to enter the world of paid lobbyists if they were to succeed on Capitol Hill.[66]

The tribe's hiring of Anderson Tuell reveals the increasingly complex links between former Department of the Interior officials, BIA employees, and lobbying firms involved in tribal acknowledgment politics. As I noted in my 2004 book *Forgotten Tribes*, a "tribal recognition industry" has developed that shows no sign of going out of business. Social scientists, always facing a tough job market, find fairly lucrative careers with the Office of Federal Acknowledgment, but their salaries pale in comparison to other professionals involved in tribal recognition politics. Over time a clear link has been made between former BIA officials, tribal lobbyists, gaming firms, and other parties. As Bud Shapard, drafter of the government regulations notes, tribal recognition has become big business, quite contrary to the aims of the parties in the late 1970s. Several examples will help make this point. The Indian-owned Anderson

Tuell has intricate ties to the Bureau of Indian Affairs and acknowledgment policy that its founders parlayed into a lucrative law practice and lobbying firm. When the Lumbee Tribe hired the firm it was buying access to individuals enmeshed in the tribal acknowledgment process, with one associate linked to some high-profile controversies that occurred during assistant secretary Kevin Gover's tumultuous years as head of the BIA. Lead partner Michael J. Anderson, is an enrolled citizen of the Muscogee (Creek) Nation of Oklahoma and former deputy assistant secretary for Indian affairs under President Clinton. A graduate of Georgetown University Law School, Anderson served as a tribal planner for his people and then executive director of the NCAI, where he helped establish the NCAI-NIGA Gaming Task Force. Anderson then was appointed general counsel for the Senate Indian Affairs Committee under Senator Inouye. His work here led to Anderson's appointment by President Clinton to serve as associate solicitor for Indian affairs in the Interior Department before being selected as deputy assistant secretary for Indian affairs under Kevin Gover. Anderson's partner, Loretta A. Tuell, is a member of the Nez Perce Tribe and graduate of UCLA's Law School. She served as chief council for the Senate Indian Affairs Committee before being promoted to serve several Indian-related posts, including director of the Office of American Indian Trust and acting director of the Office of Tribal Services within the BIA, an office that includes the Office of Federal Acknowledgment. Like others before them, the team entered government employment before segueing into much more lucrative careers in the private sector of Indian law and lobbying.[67]

The BIA rules were created to take the politics out of tribal acknowledgment decisions but developments during the Clinton administration while Anderson and Tuell worked under Kevin Gover cast serious doubts about the claimed objective and scientific nature of the acknowledgment process. Michael Anderson was a close professional associate of Gover, who as assistant secretary during most of the Clinton administration, was perhaps the most controversial individual ever in this position in terms of tribal acknowledgment politics. A member of the Oklahoma Pawnee Tribe and one-time lawyer for an Albuquerque law firm involved in Indian gaming, Gover had served as lawyer for the Golden Hill Paugussetts of Connecticut and as a fund-raiser for Clinton before the president appointed him to head the BIA. In this position Gover took the unprecedented step of reopening the acknowledgment case of the Paugussetts, who had earlier received a negative initial BIA ruling. He also reversed the negative initial findings on the Schaghticoke Tribal Nation and several Pequot groups in Connecticut. The latter groups had casino plans backed by Donald Trump and others. Gover also overruled the negative findings of OFA staff on the West Coast Chinooks, another group with which he had close personal and perhaps professional ties. Gover left his post in early January 2001 in the last months of the Clinton administration and soon joined the powerful Washington law firm of Steptoe and Johnson, a firm closely tied to the Clinton White House. A former partner in the firm was none other than Bruce Babbitt, secretary of the interior during much of the Clinton era. After he left office, Gover was dogged by a congressional inquiry and constant allegations that he had acted inappropriately in his acknowledgment decisions. Several knowledgeable parties said off the record that his acts were clear examples of how gaming money and politics have infiltrated the acknowledgment process, resulting in money corrupting the BIA's work and leading to at least initial recognition determinations for several groups. The outspoken Bud Shapard points to a case decided under Gover where "a tribe was clearly recognized because a casino sponsored it; it spent several million dollars and said 'let's get this recognition done'"—and the government obliged. With his boss departed, Michael J. Anderson came to the forefront of several contentious acknowledgment decisions. Now acting director of Indian affairs, Anderson sat in his car on his last day of office, signing several favorable acknowledgment decisions against the advice of his staff. One group affected was the Nipmuc Tribe of Massachusetts, which allegedly had casino and legal ties to Gover. The Nipmucs were later turned down after Gover's initial positive ruling. When newly elected president George W. Bush entered office, one of his first acts was to have his new assistant secretary for Indian affairs, Neal McCaleb, a Chickasaw from Oklahoma, freeze the controversial decisions of Gover and Anderson. Most of the groups entangled in the scandal were later denied recognition. Despite all the controversy, the experience clearly paid: Anderson proudly touted his recognition work and Indian gaming expertise in promotional literature to gain new clients, and Gover resumed his Indian law work. Many former OFA employees have likewise left government jobs to work for unrecognized tribes or for newly acknowledged groups.[68]

In 2012 the Lumbee Tribe is attempting to pass a version of its 2009 tribal acknowledgment bill. Leaders hope that paying a lobbyist with close ties to the process will end their century-long struggle to gain the full tribal status they believe is due their people. They have the support of the Obama administration and their members of Congress. However, their tribal opponents the Eastern Cherokees, Poarch Creeks, and Mississippi Choctaws show no sign of giving up their battle to block the North Carolina group. They will travel again to Washington when the new Lumbee bill is debated, putting forth the same arguments from decades past: the group should be forced to go through the BIA process like everyone else. They will also say that the group is not a "true Indian tribe" and, if recognized, will cost taxpayers hundreds of millions of misspent dollars. The MOWA Band of Choctaw likewise will have legislators introduce new bills to recognize them as an American Indian tribe. However, unlike the Lumbees, the momentum is clearly against the MOWA Band. The BIA's final negative determination has entered the public discourse and severely curtails the band's ability to prove that they are a bona fide Indian tribe worthy of recognition outside the established administrative process.

BRUTE ECONOMIC FORCES

Many critics chastise tribes like the Eastern Band of Cherokees and Poarch Band of Creek Indians for not acting in the "Indian way" by refusing to accept their less fortunate kin into the fold. This rhetoric seems to echo old stereotypes about Indians, as if modern tribal governments, acting out of self-interest to protect their economic resources, are somehow less Indian by doing so. Working to defend their economic lifeblood, governments in USET have stymied bills that would recognize tribes like the MOWA Band and the Lumbees, groups that they feel should not be permitted to bypass the BIA process by going through Congress. As revealed in their words, recognized tribal leaders care deeply about preserving indigenous culture. They also fight hard to protect their hard-won sovereign status in the United States, status that could be eroded should a perception develop that recently acknowledged tribes are bogus entities created to make a fortune through legal loopholes in the Indian gaming industry. However, few battles over recognition have been as bitter as the ones involving the Lumbees and the MOWA Band, where something more than culture or tribal integrity is clearly at stake.

As is apparent from the rancorous discourse and large sums spent by USET members fighting both the Lumbees and MOWAs, tribal acknowledgment politics is a messy affair. Is the opposition purely motivated by financial concerns? Some parties believe it is. Others think the issue is too intermixed with cultural and racial concerns to isolate one factor. Eastern Band of Cherokee citizen Jim Cooper feels it is his tribal government's concern over federal dollars and Indian gaming competition that leads it to fight their North Carolina neighbors. Lumbee Billy Hunt agrees, saying that his many Eastern Cherokee friends accept the Lumbees as real Indians but that it is the Eastern Cherokee government, with its officials who "are not one bit concerned with culture," that opposes his people. In Alabama, MOWA Band chief Wilford Taylor concurs, believing that his tribe's once-allied but currently poor relationship with its Creek neighbors proves that "it's no longer a matter of red; it's a matter of green." However, some knowledgeable observers think this conclusion is too simplistic. As Arlinda Locklear sees it, many members of the Eastern Band of Cherokee Indians "just don't think we are Indians" and therefore support their tribal position. While acknowledging her opponents' financial motivations, Locklear feels that race is the "number one factor" in tribal opposition to her people. NARF attorney Don Miller seconds this. His twenty-five years working in Indian law have led him to believe that "the primary reason recognized tribes oppose the Lumbees is they say they are not 'real Indians' . . . it's really racism at work." Overall it seems highly unlikely that the Eastern Cherokees, Mississippi Choctaws, and Poarch Creeks would spend the time and resources, however, opposing groups like the Lumbees and the MOWA Band at this level if valuable economic resources were not at stake. It seems doubtful that if the Lumbees were a small band of two hundred they would have faced such concerted attacks on their recognition aspirations. It seems even less likely that if local tribes did not have gaming monopolies to protect that they would spend hundreds of thousands of dollars and countless employee hours finding arguments against groups like the MOWA Band. Unfortunately for the elusive search for the truth, big casino money has entered the picture, and the desire of the 1970s that unacknowledged eastern tribes should receive an unbiased chance to prove their heritage is the ultimate casualty.[69]

Conclusion

More than forty years have passed since the southeastern Indian renaissance encouraged thousands of individuals who might have previously passed as white to proudly proclaim their Cherokee or other Indian ancestry. Dozens of tribes have formed in the Southeast, some evolving out of centuries-old communities, others seemingly out of thin air. Most states in the region have "state-recognized tribes" that hold powwows, give aid to their members, and provide a tangible presence in a region once thought devoid of Native American people. Raw census data tell the tale in dry numbers: states like Alabama have seen their American Indian populations more than double in several decades. Few could argue that the spirit of ethnic Indian pride has not been a good development in the region: everyone seems to benefit. Long-standing communities such as the Lumbee Tribe and the MOWA Band can raise their children in a social environment where they can be proud of their Native heritage. Grants aid not only Indian groups but also the larger communities where they are located. Youth receive scholarships and a hope for a better future than their parents had. Groups like the Poarch Band of Creeks have achieved federal recognition, and their new reservations serve as hubs for economic development in rural corners of the Southeast. Some have opened Indian casinos that have become major tourist draws while providing valuable income and services for tribal members. As this book has shown, however, the Five Tribes and well-established reservation groups like the Mississippi Band of Choctaws have seen a darker side of the Indian wave.

The discourse of tribal leaders in Tahlequah, Oklahoma, and Poarch, Alabama, about which groups are legitimate Indian tribes reveals much about how modern Indians view indigenous peoples and nations in the United States today. While personally important to tribal leaders like Chad Smith and Eddie Tullis, the battles waged by the Five Tribes and their allies have significant policy implications. Tribes' endeavors to protect their identities promise to become even more important in coming decades. Since the 1960s experts on American Indian affairs have been asking: Who is an Indian? What is an Indian tribe worthy of exercising sovereignty in an increasingly complex, postindustrial society? While the questions are now decades old, defining Indians will only become more complex and clouded in coming years, as Native Americans marry outside their group at rates much higher than other ethnic groups, and as the vast majority of identified Native Americans do not reside on isolated reservations as they did over a century ago. Most are not "full-bloods" who speak a native language and carry on ancient aboriginal traditions. Few practice the pastoral or agricultural pursuits of their forebears. Many have college degrees and work in modern occupations. They may "look" Indian or not, but they increasingly blend in and are invisible. If the questions "Who is an Indian?" and "What is an American Indian tribe?" were problematic in the 1960s, they are even more difficult today.

Tribal leaders like Cara Cowan Watts are aware of the challenges of deciphering and delineating Native identity, but she and her compatriots believe they have a simple answer: only verified citizens of federally recognized Indian tribes can legitimately claim to be Indian. This book has shown the ways her Cherokee Nation is trying to police the racial and ethnic boundary. It has created a task force to expose groups it sees as fraudulent, lobbied legislators against recognizing new state tribes, and tried to expose ethnic imposters in realms as diverse as academia, Hollywood, and the Native American Church. The Cherokee Nation opposes Congress recognizing tribes, believing that the average legislator lacks the expertise to determine which groups are real and which are bogus. It believes that a few groups in the Southeast, like the Jena Band of Choctaws, are legitimate tribes, but that there are very few other viable Indian tribes still remaining in the Southeast.

Ideally, leaders of the Five Tribes would exercise their sovereignty and be the governments that recognize groups that claim to be their blood kin. However, political and legal realities intervene: only the federal government can recognize that a "government-to-government" relationship exists between it and forgotten Indian communities scattered about the country. As such, the Five Tribes and other reservation groups helped establish the Federal Acknowledgment Process within the BIA in 1978 to determine which groups were still living indigenous communities. Some tribal leaders wanted only groups with surviving cultural traits, tight-knit communities, and strong bloodlines to achieve the stamp of approval. However, as a nod to social science and past bureaucratic policy, all parties agreed that legal, historical, and anthropological factors could also suffice and that the new BIA process could determine what groups were extant Indian tribal communities. Native leaders such as Creek Nation principal chief Claude Cox came to demand written proof that groups were real Indians. Scholars like Vine Deloria, Jr., wanted a more visual, commonsense approach, but tribal leaders would have none of that: too many valuable resources were at stake. In debates about identifying Native peoples activists like Ward Churchill set what appeared to be a perfect trap: if others challenged their identity by requiring "Western" forms of proof, these skeptics were labeled racists or agents of colonial oppression—the activists were "more Indian" by rejecting Western-style evidence as proof of authenticity. Individuals with something to lose, however, do not give up their assets on the word of unknown individuals. The BIA and its tribal supporters ultimately demanded that groups provide tangible proof that they were still Indian and that they have descended from tribes indigenous to American soil. To tribal leaders, only groups that have strong evidence and pass through the rigorous BIA regimen are accepted as bona fide tribes. As revealed in this book, people like the Poarch Creeks had such proof but it was hardly in the form recognizable to the lay person: congressional acts, government Indian land grants, and treaty provisions. Most of the Alabama Creeks had intermarried with whites, and few had any recognizable aboriginal cultural traits remaining, but other Indians accepted them as a bona fide Indian tribe. The Jena Band of Choctaws also possessed many of the traits of their Eastern Creek neighbors: they lived in an isolated, rural environment, and they had government records saying they were Choctaw Indians. However, their cache of government documents in no way reached the level of those of the Poarch Creeks. In the end the Jena group was accepted as Indian by all observers for the reasons Native peoples were once easily recognized as Indian: they had members with a high Indian blood quantum, they "looked" Indian. Many still spoke the ancient Choctaw language. Even more so than the Poarch Creeks the Jena Band's cultural evidence spoke volumes as to their survival as indigenous Americans.

Not every group, even those with long-standing histories as Indians, has the evidence to convince skeptical tribes and non-Indians that they are legitimate. The MOWA Band of Choctaw Indians and the Lower Muskogee Creek Tribe are examples. Both failed to secure acknowledgment through the BIA, and both failed to demonstrate to critics that they were authentic remnant Choctaw and Creek communities. However, the reasons they were not accepted as federally recognized tribes (despite having state recognition) are quite different. The Creek group had close ties to the Poarch community, having been encouraged to come forward as Indians to share in claims money. It had many members who had government confirmation that they were descendants of Creek Indians who had refused to emigrate to Indian Territory in the nineteenth century. Leaders Neal and Peggy McCormick even established a small residential reservation where the people began living as Native Americans and were accepted in the region as Indian peoples. The only problem as concerned federal officials and tribal representatives was that the Lower Muskogee Creek Tribe was a recent invention: it had not evolved out of an existing enclave like the Poarch Creeks had. The community that formed at its Tama Reservation had no historical antecedents, members generally had not known each other previously, no historical leadership had existed, and other than Creek ancestry the group exhibited few if any traits generally associated with viable ethnic communities or aboriginal tribes. The MOWA Band, by contrast, did exhibit many traits characteristic of ethnic enclaves. However, like their Lower Muskogee Creek neighbors, they are currently considered a fake Indian tribe by Cherokee Nation leaders and by related groups like the Mississippi Choctaws and Poarch Creeks. While the Lower Creek people generally were considered "white" (despite some proven Indian ancestry), the MOWA group has a long history as a nonwhite racial enclave. For perhaps two hundred years the community has existed in rural Alabama, set apart from its black and white neighbors by physical space and social distance. It possesses most of the traits of southern Indian communities: it is generally poor and isolated, and it has Indian churches and Indian leaders who serve the community. Local governments have provided Indian schools to the MOWA people, and they have attended Indian colleges out of state.

The group has state tribal recognition. Despite all of this, many doubt that they are a real tribe. As Bud Shapard remarks, "If any group looked like a tribe and wasn't, it was them." What the MOWA Band lacks is written proof that it is Choctaw, and to opponents this makes all the difference. As of today the group has not been able to produce a single document that states that its original ancestors were of Choctaw or any other Indian heritage. It is true that a few Choctaws and other Indians married into the community decades after its founding and that group members had an Indian identity by at least 1900. However, to critics this ancestry does not prove the current group descends from an aboriginal Indian tribe or community. Skeptics charge that the evidence hardly points to the conclusion that the enclave was founded as a Choctaw community. While there may be historical reasons why the MOWA ancestors do not appear in records as "Choctaw" or "Indian" during the formative period, challengers will not accept the possibility that they were Native as proof for federal recognition. People as diverse as BIA critic Shapard and supporter Eddie Tullis have seen the BIA findings on the group's genealogy and have concluded the same thing: the MOWA Band is essentially a "mulatto" or "black" community that chose to claim an Indian identity to escape the stigma of blackness in the U.S. South. Others have made similar conclusions as to the Indian identity of the Lumbee Tribe of North Carolina.

Many leaders of the Five Tribes and their federally recognized kin genuinely feel that the MOWA group, the Lumbees, and other-state recognized tribes are not real Indians and not bona fide Indian tribes. However, they commit significant tribal resources to fighting these groups for another reason: economics. If acknowledged, the Lumbees would be among the ten largest tribes in the country, and opponents believe it would drain significant federal resources from their people. Gaming has complicated the picture. Local reservation tribes have joined forces to oppose congressional recognition of the Lumbees, the MOWA Band, and all groups seeking to pursue federal recognition through this constitutional, if often discredited, avenue. Raw economics drives the opposition, but as shown here, opponents are aided by historical deficiencies in many groups' cases for acknowledgment.

Critics have accused Native leaders of not acting in the "Indian way" when they oppose recognizing new tribes. They charge that tribal leaders are the "haves" who are refusing to share resources with their less fortunate indigenous kin, having accepted the government's traditional restrictive and nonindigenous models for defining Indians and tribes. Members of unrecognized and state-recognized Indian tribes are hurt and angered by the efforts of the Five Tribes and others to police Indian identity. Many, like Galas Weaver, have lived their entire lives as Native Americans, and are shocked that individuals who appear white, like Office of Federal Acknowledgment director and enrolled Cherokee Lee Fleming, tell them that they are not Indian people. Many scholars believe that groups like Weaver's MOWA Choctaws should secure federal acknowledgment, that but for accidents of history and documentation that logically does not exist, they would be included on the list of federally recognized tribal communities. Men like Eastern Cherokee principal chief Michell Hicks have scars gained in the wars trying to police and control Indian identity. It is not pleasant to challenge a person's long-standing ethnic and racial identity. However, Hicks and others feel that the effort to control access to Cherokee, Chickasaw, Choctaw, Seminole, and Creek identity is of utmost importance. It affects issues as diverse as BIA funding and program development and maintenance, Indian Health Service moneys, tribal identity, cultural property, and, not least, Indian gaming. It is no surprise that the Five Tribes, longtime leaders in remaining Native while assimilating nonindigenous ways, are leading the crusade to define Native peoples in the United States today. They are demanding the power to say who is Indian, rather than having the "white man" do it for them.

Abbreviations

Bartlett Collection	Dewey F. Bartlett Collection, Carl Albert Center, Monnet Hall, University of Oklahoma, Norman
BAR	Branch of Acknowledgment and Research (now Office of Federal Acknowledgment), Bureau of Indian Affairs, Department of the Interior Building, Washington, D.C.
	HF History Files
BIA	Bureau of Indian Affairs
Callahan Papers	Sonny Callahan Papers, University Archives, University of South Alabama, Mobile
Diamond Papers	Tom Diamond, Personal Papers, Law Offices of Diamond, Rash, Gordon, and Jackson, El Paso, Texas
Dardar Files	Personal Files of Brenda Dardar, Chief of United Houma Nation, Raceland, Louisiana
FITF	Fraudulent Indian Task Force, Office Files, Cherokee Nation Headquarters, Tahlequah, Oklahoma
GCIA	Records of the Governors Commission of Indian Affairs, Louisiana State Archives, Baton Rouge

ITC	Institute of Texan Cultures, San Antonio, Texas
Keeler Papers	W. W. Keeler Papers, Cherokee Cultural Center, Tahlequah, Oklahoma
LBJ Library	Lyndon Baines Johnson Presidential Library, Austin, Texas
Mankiller Papers	Wilma Mankiller Papers, Western History Collections, Monnet Hall, University of Oklahoma, Norman
Matte Papers	Jacqueline Matte Papers, Department of Archives, University of South Alabama, Mobile
Morris Udall Papers	Morris Udall Papers, Special Collections, Main Library, University of Arizona, Tucson
NAB	National Archives Building, Washington, D.C.
NACP	National Archives–College Park, Maryland
NCCIA	Records of North Carolina Commission on Indian Affairs, Office of the Governor, Raleigh
NSU	Northeastern State University, Special Collections, Tahlequah, Oklahoma
OFA	Office of Federal Acknowledgment (formerly Branch of Acknowledgment and Research), Department of the Interior Building, Washington, D.C.

	HF	History Files
	JBCI	Jena Band of Choctaw Indian Files
	KIN	Kaweah Indian Nation Files
	LMCT	Lower Muskogee Creek Tribe Files
	LT	Lumbee Tribe Files
	MBCI	MOWA Band of Choctaw Indian Files
	PBCI	Poarch Band of Creek Indian Files
	PCN	Principal Creek Nation Files
	SECC	Southeastern Cherokee Confederacy Files
	TB	Tunica Biloxi Tribe Files
	UHN	United Houma Nation Files

OHS	Oklahoma Historical Society, Oklahoma City
Rhodes Papers	John Rhodes Papers, Special Collections, Hayden Library, Arizona State University, Phoenix

Steed Collection	Tom Steed Collection, Carl Albert Center, Monnet Hall, University of Oklahoma, Norman
Steiger Papers	Sam Steiger Papers, Department of Archives and Manuscripts, Cline Library, Northern Arizona University, Flagstaff
Swimmer Papers	Ross Swimmer Papers, Cherokee Cultural Center, Tahlequah, Oklahoma
TIC	Records of the Texas Indian Commission, Texas State Archives, Austin
Tyler Papers	S. Lyman Tyler Papers, Special Collections, Marriott Library, University of Utah, Salt Lake City
Udall Papers	Stewart Lee Udall Papers, Special Collections, Main Library, University of Arizona, Tucson
White Papers	Richard C. White Papers, Sonnichsen Special Collections, University of Texas–El Paso

Notes

INTRODUCTION

1. "History and Goals," *Southeastern Cherokee Confederacy News*, March 1980; BAR, "Genealogical Report: Southeastern Cherokee Confederacy (SECC)," 61, SECC, OFA; Frederick Ferguson to Neal McCormick, 26 April 1977, HF, OFA; Lower Muskogee Creek Tribe (LMCT), "Petition," April 1979; and Hazel Elbert, "Recommendation for Final Determination: LMCT," 17 September 1981, LMCT, OFA.

2. Department of the Interior, "Indian Entities Recognized and Eligible to Receive Services," *Federal Register* 75, no. 190, October 1, 2010, 60810; Department of the Interior, Indian Affairs, http://www.indianaffairs.gov (accessed 20 May 2012); Friedman, "The Past in the Future," 837–59; Green, *Issues in Native American Cultural Identity*.

3. Deloria, quoted in Roediger, *Wages of Whiteness*, 93. Increasingly scholars and tribal leaders are demanding the power to control cultural representations. See Troy Johnson, "Foreword," in Jolivette, *Cultural Representations*, ix; Cornell, "Discovered Identities," 111.

4. Berkhofer, *White Man's Indian*, xvi. See, for example, Blu, "Region and Recognition"; Campisi and Starna, "Why Does It Take So Long?"; Cramer, *Cash, Color, and Colonialism*; Field, "Complicities and Collaborations"; Grabowski, "Coiled Intent"; Greenbaum, "In Search of Lost Tribes," and "What's in a Label?"; Klopotek, *Recognition Odysseys*; McCulloch and Wilkins, "Constructing Nations within States"; M. Miller, *Forgotten Tribes*; Paschal, "The Imprimatur of Recognition"; Porter, "In Search of Recognition"; Rafert, *The Miami Indians of Indiana*; Starna, "Public Ethnohistory"; Tolley, *Quest for Tribal Acknowledgment*; Weatherhead, "What Is an 'Indian Tribe'?"; and Wilkins, "Breaking into the Intergovernmental Matrix."

5. Churchill, "The Tragedy and the Travesty"; Jaimes, *The State of Native America* and "American Indian Identification/Eligibility Policy"; Goldberg-Ambrose, "Of Native Americans."

6. Testimony of Wilma Mankiller, Senate, Committee on Indian Affairs, *Federal Recognition*, 13 July 1995, 211–16.

7. Novak, *The Rise of the Unmeltable Ethnics*; Halter, *Shopping for Ethnicity*, 5–10.

8. Barth, *Ethnic Group Boundaries*; Hobsbawm and Ranger, *The Invention of Tradition*; Albers and James, "On the Dialectics of Ethnicity"; Atkinson, "The Evolution of Ethnicity"; Castile and Kushner, *Persistent Peoples*; Clifton, "Avocation Medicine Men," and *The Invented Indian*; Cohen, *The Symbolic Construction of Community*; Harmon, *Indians in the Making*; Henry, *Ethnicity in the Americas*; Mauzé, *Present Is Past*; McCall and Simmons, *Identities and Interactions*; McIlwraith, "The Problem of Imported Culture"; Moermon, "Being Lue"; Rose, "The Great Pretenders"; Royce, *Ethnic Identity*; Sider, *Lumbee Indian Histories*; Spicer and Thompson, *Plural Society in the Southwest*; Suttles, *The Social Construction of Communities*; Weibel-Orlando, *Indian Country, L.A.*; Wray, *Not Quite White*; Sturm, personal communication with author; Waters, *Ethnic Options*.

9. P. Deloria, *Playing Indian*, 171–75.

10. Nagel, *American Indian Ethnic Renewal* and "False Faces"; Waters, "Multiple Ethnicities," 23–31; Snipp, *American Indians*.

11. P. Deloria, *Playing Indian*, 100–101; Lawrence, *"Real" Indians and Others*; B. Miller, *Invisible Indigenes*; Raibmon, *Authentic Indians*; Barker, *Native Acts*.

12. Bird, "Introduction," 9, in *Dressing in Feathers*.

13. Eddie Tullis, interview by author.

14. Paredes, "Introduction," 5, in *Indians of the Southeastern United States*.

15. Axtell quoted in Ellen Barry, "It's a War of Genealogies," *Boston Globe*, 12 December 2000, http://cache.boston.com/globe/nation/packages/gaming/part3.htm (accessed 17 May 2011); M. Miller, *Forgotten Tribes*; Cramer, *Cash, Color, and Colonialism*; Klopotek, *Recognition Odysseys*; Tolley, *Quest for Tribal Acknowledgment*. For the few works that have questioned Indian-identifying groups, see: Clifton, *The Invented Indian*; Quinn, "Public Ethnohistory?," "Southeastern Indians," and "The Southeast Syndrome"; Paredes, "Indigenous Renascence."

16. See, for example, Klopotek, *Recognition Odysseys*; Barker, *Native Acts*; Kauanui, *Hawaiian Blood*; Steinman, "Settler Colonial Power." For Deloria's criticism and other critiques of the Federal Acknowledgment Process, see Senate, Select Committee on Indian Affairs, *Federal Recognition of the Lumbee*, 12 August 1988.

17. Nagel, "False Faces," 95; B. Miller, *Invisible Indigenes*; Lawrence, *"Real" Indians and Others*; Pewewardy, "Will the 'Real' Indians Please Stand Up?"

18. Jaimes, *The State of Native America*; Churchill, "The Tragedy and the Travesty." For an excellent study of the general issue of cultural expectations, Indians, and modernity, see P. Deloria, *Indians in Unexpected Places*.

19. Barker, *Native Acts*, 195–97, 240; Deloria, *Indians in Unexpected Places*.

20. Kidwell, *The Choctaws in Oklahoma*, vii. Also see Lambert, *Choctaw Nation*; Sturm, *Blood Politics*.

21. Chief Wilford "Longhair" Taylor quoted in "MOWA Indians Seek Callahan's Help," undated clipping, folder "Mowa Choctaw BIA Recognition," Callahan Papers.

22. Cattelino, *High Stakes*, 166–99.

CHAPTER 1

1. "Indian Delegation Presents Petition," *(Baton Rouge) State Times*, 15 December 1980; Bruce Duthu, interview by author; Hiram Gregory, interview by author.

2. Finger, *Cherokee Americans*, 9–10; Kersey, *An Assumption of Sovereignty*, 140–41; Memorandum, "Validity of the North Carolina Statute of April 5, 1947 relating to the Eastern Band of Cherokee Indians," 29 August 1947, Department of the Interior, *Opinions of the Solicitor*, 1464; Memorandum, "Request for Restoration of Bureau Services to the Louisiana Coushatta Indians," 13 June 1973, HF, OFA; "Coushatta Victory," *Indian Affairs*, July 1973, 3; *United States v. John*, 437 U.S. 634 (1978), 634–54; "Ruling Endangers Choctaws," *Indian Affairs*, May 1975, 6; "Report to Accompany H.R. 1344," 16 December 1985, box 1990/1-41, folder 2, TIC; M. Miller, *Forgotten Tribes*, ch. 6, "From Playing Indian to Playing Slots"; Hook, *The Alabama-Coushatta Indians*; Shuck-Hall, *Journey to the West*; Rountree, "Indian Virginians," 10, 14–17; "The Catawbas—Hail and Farewell," *Indian Affairs*, August 1959, 1–2; Hudson, *The Catawba Nation*, 47–53, 86–88; Swanton, *Indians of the Southeastern United States*, 81; Brewton Berry, *Almost White*; Pete Gregory, interview by author; Peterson, *The Indians in the Old South*.

3. J. Anthony Paredes, interview by author. For contact and cultural change, see Axtell, *The Indians' New South* and Merrell, *The Indians' New World*.

4. Ayers, *Promise of the New South*, 155; Daniel, "Passers and Pluralists," 91.

5. Tillman quoted in Martin, "My Grandmother Was a Cherokee Princess," 139; "A Brief History of the Indians of Escambia County," 1920s newspaper clipping, box 4, fd. "Creek," Matte Papers.

6. Kirby Verret, interview by author; Helen Gindrat, interview by author; "Houma and Tunica Face Tough Recognition Fight," undated newspaper clipping, Dardar Files; Bruce Duthu, interview by author; Lumbee River Legal Services (LRLS), "Lumbee Petition," Vol. I, 132; Ruth Locklear, interview by author.

7. Usner, *American Indians in the Lower Mississippi Valley*; LRLS, "Lumbee Petition," Vol. I, 133–35; Richard Stoeffle, "Rapid Ethnographic Assessment,

Mowa Band," no boxes, folder 21002, Callahan Papers; BAR, "Anthropological Report: JBCI"; "A History of the Jena Band," *Neka-Camon*, December 1991; BAR, "Historical Report: JBCI," 29; Verret, interview by author.

8. Griessman, "The American Isolates," 693–95; Gregory, interview by author; Reggie Billiot, interview by author; "'Sabines' Segregated Because of Their Names," *San Francisco Chronicle*, 18 September 1964; Fischer, "History and Current Status," 212–35; Berry, *Almost White*, 9–27, quoted 161.

9. Weaver, interview by author; LRLS, "Lumbee Petition," Vol. I, 120–36.

10. Van Rheenen, "Can You Tell Me Who My People Are?," 1, 4, 120.

11. LRLS, "Lumbee Petition," Vol. I, 120–21; Maria Root, "Within, Between, and Beyond Race," 3, 5; Terry P. Wilson, "Blood Quantum: Native American Mixed Bloods," 111; Daniel, "Passers and Pluralists," 91; *U.S. Census Schedules—Terrebonne Parish*, 1860 and 1900; BAR, "Anthropological Report: UHN," 30; Poll Tax Records, Washington County (AL) 1892, box 9, folder "Poll Tax," Matte Papers.

12. Jacqueline Matte, interview by author; Ruth Locklear, interview by author; Lerch, *Waccamaw Legacy*.

13. LRLS, "Lumbee Petition," Vol. I, 32; Oakley, *Keeping the Circle*, 38–39; Verret, interview by author; Duthu, interview by author; Brenda Dardar, interview by author; Todd Johnston, interview by author.

14. Phillip Martin to Lyndon B. Johnson, 13 April 1965, box "Indian Affairs/Ex IN/A-Z," folder "IN/C," LBJ Library; Verret, interview by author; Weaver, interview by author; LRLS, "Lumbee Petition," Vol. I, 30–36.

15. Winston, "The Relationship of the Whites to the Negroes," 313; Chafe, *Remembering Jim Crow*, 1–3, 50–55, 205–9.

16. "The Indians in Polk County, Texas," *Frontier Times*, 30–31; "Doctor Retires after 37 Years," *Houston Post*, 25 April 1937, both in Vertical Files, ITC; Weaver, interview by author; "Mowa Children Write about Reeds Chapel," undated newspaper clipping, no boxes, folder "Mowa Choctaw BIA," Callahan Papers.

17. LRLS, "Lumbee Petition," Vol. I, 30–36; Rountree, "Indian Virginians," 11–12; Weaver, interview by author; Johnston, interview by author; "Association Aids Lumbees," *Indian Affairs*, December 1960; Evans, "The North Carolina Lumbees," 54–55.

18. LRLS, "Lumbee Petition," Vol. I, 30–35, 50; Oakley, *Keeping the Circle*, 25–27.

19. Blu, *The Lumbee Problem*, 21–22; Perdue, *Native Carolinians*, 50.

20. LRLS, "Lumbee Petition," Vol. I, 92, 100; "New Lawyer Also Indian," *San Antonio News*, 21 July 1972; Blu, *The Lumbee Problem*, 86.

21. Locklear quoted in "They Work Here but Their Ties Are Elsewhere," *(Baltimore) Evening Sun*, 1 October 1970, published in *Awkwesasne Notes* 2, no.2 (March 1971), 34.

22. Oakley, *Keeping the Circle*, 9; Goldfield, *Black, White and Southern*, 204–10; Murphy, "The Cajans of Mobile County," 499; Weaver, interview by author.

23. William A. Brophy, "Summary of the Indian Claims Commission Act of 1946," box 64, folder "Indian Claims Commission Act of 1946," RG 48, NACP; "President Johnson's Indian Message to Congress: The Forgotten Americans," 6 March 1968, box 140, folder 4, Udall Papers; Cowger, *The National Congress of American Indians*, 151; Mowa Choctaws, "Legal Memorandum to Sonny Callahan," 20 January 1998, no boxes, folder "Mowa Recognition 1 of 2," Callahan Papers.

24. "Indians of California as 'Identifiable' Group of Indians," 17 March 1948, Solicitors Office, General Correspondence, box 64, folder "Indian Claims Commission Act 1946," RG 48, NACP.

25. Tom N. Tureen and NARF, "Eligibility of the Poarch Creek Band under the Indian Reorganization Act," 8 May 1975, PBCI, OFA; "Calvin McGhee, 70-year Old Chief of Creek Indians," *Awkwesasne Notes* 2 (no. 5), September 1970; Memorandum, Solicitor, "Discussing the Loyal Creek Claims," 24 May 1948, box 64, folder "(1946–49) Bureau of Indian Affairs Jan–June 1948," RG 48, NACP; BAR, "Final Determination against Acknowledgment, MaChis Lower Creek Indian Tribe of Alabama," 13 June 1998, 18–19, MaChis Lower Creek Files, OFA; C. Lenoir Thompson to Walter Jenkins, 12 August 1964, box "Indian Affairs/Ex In/AZ," folder "IN/C," LBJ Library.

26. Billiot, interview by author; "Houma Indians Seeking to Regain Former Lands," *Times-Picayune*, undated newspaper clipping, Dardar Files.

27. "Statement of Michael Anderson," on *H.R. 3671, The United Houma Nation Recognition and Land Claims Settlement Act*, 17 July 1996, UHN, OFA; Rountree, "Indian Virginians," 17; "Tunica-Biloxi Tribe Obtains Federal Recognition," *NARF Announcements* 7, no.3, 7; Pat Arnold, interview by author.

28. Philp, *Termination Revisited*; Lerch, *Waccamaw Legacy*, 78, 89, 115–16; House, Committee on Interior, *A Bill to Amend the Act Relating to the Lumbee Indians*, 22 January 1974, HF, OFA; LRLS, "Lumbee Petition," Vol. I, 96–98.

29. Lurie, "American Indian Renascence?," 307; Verret, interview by author.

30. Blu, *The Lumbee Problem*; Sider, *Living Indian Histories*; LRLS, "Lumbee Petition," Vol. I, 102; Berry, "The Alabama and Coushatta Indians," 20–23; "Nash Report on Visit to Texas," Vertical Files, ITC; Roth, "Federal Tribal Recognition in the South," 190; White, "Phillip Martin," 195–210.

31. "Hundreds of Armed Indians Break up N.C. Klan Rally," *Shreveport Times*, 19 January 1958; LRLS, "Lumbee Petition," Vol. I, 99–100; Robert Ben to Lyndon Johnson, 23 February 1966, box "Indian Affairs/EX IN/AZ," folder "IN/C," LBJ Library; Goldfield, *Black, White, and Southern*, 159.

32. Lurie, "An American Indian Renascence?," 307; Verret, interview by author.

33. Verret, interview by author; NARF, "Petition: PBCI," 85 (note 153); "Lumbee Indians in for School Showdown," *(Baltimore) Afro-American*, 5 April 1958.

34. "Indians Resist Integration in Triracial County in Carolina," *New York Times*, 13 September 1970, 40; LRLS, "Lumbee Petition," Vol. I, 104–5; Davis, *South Carolina's Blacks and Native Americans*, 15; Ruth Locklear, interview by author; "Sabines Segregated Because of Their Names," *San Francisco Chronicle*, Duthu, interview by author; Evans, "The North Carolina Lumbees," 67.

35. Perdue, *Native Carolinians*, 55; Campisi, "Resurgence and Recognition," 760; Lerch, "Indians of the Carolinas," 330–32; Tom Dion, Testimony before the American Indian Policy Review Commission (hereafter AIPRC), Hearing at Dulac, Louisiana, box 51, no folders, RG 220, NACP.

36. Weaver, interview by author; Evans, "The North Carolina Lumbees," 62; Verret, interview by author.

37. Clarkin, *Federal Indian Policy*, 263–64.

38. Gindrat, interview by author; "Indian Leader," undated newspaper clipping, Dardar Files; Weaver, interview by author; Transcript of Speech by W. J. Strickland, Coalition of Eastern Native Americans (CENA) meeting, Marksville, Louisiana, 1973, HF, OFA; Verret, interview by author.

39. Tom Dion, Testimony before AIPRC Hearing, Dulac, Louisiana, 1975/6, 69, box 51, no folders, RG 220, NACP.

40. Quote from "Mrs. Jean," Transcript, CENA Meeting, Marksville, Louisiana, 1973, HF, OFA; Duthu and Ojibway, "Future Light," 24–32; "We Are Here Forever," special issue, *Southern Exposure* 13, no. 6 (1985).

41. Finger, *Cherokee Americans*, 159–85; Beard-Moose, *Public Indians, Private Cherokees*; "Christian Faith on a Texas Indian Reservation," *Houston Chronicle*, 19 July 1975; M. Miller, *Forgotten Tribes*, ch. 6.

42. Thornton, *Cherokees*, 144–45, 170, 183; "A Look At the U.S. Census," *Akwesasne Notes* 5, no. 5 (Early Autumn 1973), 35; "Census Finds Many Claiming New Identity: Indian," *New York Times*, 5 March 1991; Ross, *American Indians in North Carolina*, 37.

43. Root, *Cannibal Culture*, 68.

44. Finger, *Cherokee Americans*, 99–101; "Pageant of the Robeson County Indians," 1940, in LRLS "Lumbee Petition," Vol. I, 89–91; Dempsey Henley to Dolph Briscoe, 11 July 1975, box "1990/1-34," folder "Tigua Housing/Misc." TIC; "Alabama-Coushattas Host Colorful Powwow," *On Campus* 17, no. 29 (30 April 1990), 4, in Vertical Files, ITC. See generally Johnson and Underiner, "Command Performances: Staging Native Americans at Tillicum Village," 44–61.

45. "LBJ Project Focuses on Indians' Problems," *On Campus* 17, no. 29 (30 April 1990), 4, in Vertical Files, ITC; Davis, *South Carolina's Blacks and Native Americans*, 10; BAR, "Summary Against Acknowledgment: MaChis Creeks," 28; Evelyn Truxilo, "Weaving History," *Louisiana Life*, July 1990, 104; Dardar, interview by author; "Saying Goodbye to a Dear Friend," *Talking Bayou: United Houma Nation Newsletter* 3, no. 4 (May 1999), 4.

46. BAR, "Final Determination for Acknowledgment: JBCI"; Roth, "Overview of Southeastern Indian Tribes,"183–84; Davis, *South Carolina's Blacks and Native Americans*, 11; Tunica-Biloxi Tribe, "Petition for Federal Acknowledgment," 53, TB, OFA; Drechsel, "Mobilian Jargon," 175–77; Larry Abramson, "Software Company Helps Revive 'Sleeping' Language," NPR, February 2, 2010, http://www.npr.org/ (accessed 2 February 2010); Lowery, *Lumbee Indians*, 4–6. Generally see Blu, *The Lumbee Problem*.

47. Lerch, *Waccamaw Legacy*, 117; Campisi, "Resurgence and Recognition," 763; Gregory, "Survival and Maintenance," 657–58.

48. Gregory, "Survival and Maintenance," 657–58; Rountree, "Indian Virginians," 22–24; Roth, "Overview of Southeastern Indian Tribes," 187; Lerch, "Indians of the Carolinas," 331; "Kalita's People," *Houston Chronicle*, 1963, in Vertical Files, ITC; LRLS, "Lumbee Petition," Vol. I, 89–91; "Bayou Healers and Bayou Eagles," *Talking Bayou* 3, no. 4 (May 1999), 5; "Bayou Healers Attend Cherokee National Holiday" *Talking Bayou* 3, no. 2 (October 1997), 2; Dardar, interview by author.

49. Campisi, "Resurgence and Recognition," 764; Tunica-Biloxi Powwow, flyer, 2003, in possession of author; "Feast for a Chief," *Texas Highways* 25, no. 11 (November 1978), 14; Poarch Band of Creek Indians Thanksgiving Day Powwow, flyer, no boxes, folder "Poarch Creek Indians-19," Callahan Papers; Johnston, interview by author; "Miss and Jr. Miss United Houma Nation Crowned," *Talking Bayou* 3, no. 4 (May 1999), 7.

50. "State Indian Tribes Will Meet In Dulac," 1969 newspaper article, and "Indian Meeting Unites Tribes," 1970s newspaper article, clippings file, GCIA; Gindrat, interview by author; Gregory, interview by author; Verret, interview by author.

51. Duthu, interview by author; Gregory, interview by author; "Indians," undated newspaper article, in Dardar Files.

52. Verret, interview by author; LRLS, "Lumbee Petition," Vol. I, 45–48, 93; Campisi, "Resurgence and Recognition," 761; "Christian Faith on a Texas Indian Reservation," *Houston Chronicle*, 19 July 1975.

53. Jeanette Henry, "North Carolina Indian Controversy," *Wassaja*, April/May 1973, 13; Locklear quoted in "We Are Here Forever," 89; David Wilkins, interview by author.

54. Sider, *Living Indian Histories*, 118–21.

55. Dennis L. Peterson to Miss Connee Brayboy, 6 March 1979, HF, OFA; LRLS, "Lumbee Petition," Vol. I, 104–8; Sider, *Lumbee Indian Histories*, 55–56; Blu, *The Lumbee Problem*, 75–76; Ruth Locklear, interview by author; Wilkins, interview by author.

56. Wilkins, interview by author.

57. Nagel, *American Indian Ethnic Renewal*, 114; Peroff, *Menominee Drums*; BIA News Release, "BIA Prepares for Implementation of Self-Determination

Act," 1975, box 113, folder 11, Tyler Papers; Clarkin, *Federal Indian Policy*, 118; "Address by Commissioner Robert L. Bennett," 18 October 1967, box 44, folder 4, Rhodes Papers.

58. "Report on Inter Agency Task Force on American Indians," 23 October 1967, box 20, folder "American Indians–1968," LBJ Library.

59. Governor's Commission on Indian Affairs, Annual Report, 1981–2, box "P 92-92," folder "Correspondence Jan 81-6/30/82," GCIA; "Indian Affairs Participation in Louisiana is Increasing," *Times-Picayune*, 11 July 1973; "The Jena Choctaw's Battle for Restoration," *Neka-Camon* 2, no. 4 (December 1991), 4; "Lumbee Indians of North Carolina," in AIPRC, *Report on Terminated and Nonfederally Recognized Indians*, 160–62; George Blue Spruce Jr. to Gov. Raul Castro, 22 January 1975 and Department of Labor, Memo: "Yaqui Indians' Eligibility under CETA," box 117, RG 220, NACP.

60. Lurie, "Report on the American Indian Chicago Conference"; Gindrat, interview by author; Cowger, *The National Congress of American Indians*, 133–40; Steiner, *The New Indians*, 36–37.

61. Cowger, *The National Congress of American Indians*, 148–49; Wilkins, interview by author.

62. Gregory, interview by author; Downs, "The Struggle of the Louisiana Tunica," 85; NARF, "Tunica Biloxi Petition," TB, OFA. See generally *American Indian Journal*.

63. Thomas Tureen, "Federal Recognition and the Passamaquoddy Decision," no date, box 277, folder "Recognition Tureen," RG 220, NACP; Senate, Select Committee, *Federal Acknowledgment Process*, 2 June 1980, 9; Wilkins, interview by author.

64. Paredes, interview by author; Gregory, interview by author. See Blu, *The Lumbee Problem*; Sider, *Lumbee Indian Histories*; and the various works of Gregory, Paredes, Speck, and Swanton cited in bibliography. Frank Porter was also central to the early study of eastern Indian communities. Porter, *Nonrecognized American Indian Tribes* and *Strategies for Survival*. Also see Stanton, "A Remnant Indian Community" and "Southern Louisiana Indian Survivors."

65. Pierite, quoted in NARF, "Tunica Biloxi Petition," 61, TB, OFA; Gregory, interview by author.

66. NCAI Resolution, RE: Tunica Biloxi Tribe, in NARF, "Tunica Biloxi Petition," TB, OFA; Perdue, *Native Carolinians*, 57; Rountree, "Indian Virginians," 25; NCAI, "34th Annual Convention," Report, HF, OFA.

67. Helen Grindrat to Greg Bowman, 21 April 1982, box "P 92-92," folder "Correspondence Jan 81 – 6/30/82," GCIA; Greg Bowman to M. Senaca, 16 January 1979, and Roland E. Johnson to Russell B. Long, 28 January 1978, UHN, OFA; Gregory, interview by author; Cindy Darcy, interview by author. Mennonites Bowman and Curry-Roper helped produce the first manuscript on the Houma Indians. See Bowman and Curry-Roper, *The Houma People*.

68. Wilkins, *American Indian Politics*, 215; "Tunicas Move toward Organization, Recognition," newspaper clipping, 12 August 1973, HF, OFA; W. J. Strickland, oral interview transcript, interviewer Lew Barton, 4 November 1974, Samuel Proctor Oral History Program, University of Florida, http://ufdc.ufl.edu/?b=UF00006827 (accessed 29 September 2012).

69. Strickland quoted in Transcript, CENA Meeting, Pembroke, North Carolina, 1974, HF, OFA.

70. Strickland quoted in "Tunicas Move toward Organization, Recognition," newspaper clipping, 12 August 1973, HF, OFA; Transcript, CENA Meeting, Pembroke, North Carolina, 1974, HF, OFA.

71. Transcript, CENA Meeting, Pembroke, North Carolina, 1974, HF, OFA; Rountree, *Pocahontas' People*, 245; Rountree, "Indian Virginians," 26; Wilkins, interview by author.

72. "State Reservations Subject to Muskie Bill," *Indian Affairs*, November 1969, 4; Paul Brooks to James B. Hunt, Jr., November 1999, NCCIA; BAR, "Anthropological Reports: LMCT," LMCT, OFA, 23; Weaver, interview by author. In 1967 nineteen states had established offices to study and report to the governor's office on Indian affairs. "Address by Commissioner Robert L. Bennett," 18 October 1967, box 44, folder 4, Rhodes Papers.

73. Texas man quoted, L. Tripp to Dear Sir, 16 June 1967, box "1967 RCW & General Legislation," folder "H.R. 10599–Tiwa Indian Bill," White Papers; Goldfield, *Black, White, and Southern*, 115; Bates, "Up from Obscurity," 95–98; Cromer, *Modern Indians in Alabama*, xv–xvi; *Proclamation*, signed by Jimmy Carter, in LMCT, "Petition for Acknowledgment," no date, LMTC, OFA; *An Act Relating to Washington County, Creating the Mowah Band of Choctaw Indian Commission, Act No. 79-228, Alabama Laws of the Legislature of Alabama*, vol. 1, in box 4, Matte Papers.

74. Marvin L. Franklin to Mr. Garrison, 27 June 1973, and Diana Williamson to J. Bennett Johnston, 25 September 1989, box 80, folder "40-23," US Senate Series, Johnston Papers; Patricia Schilling to Joan Nettles, 12 April 1982, and Governors Commission on Indian Affairs, Annual Report, 1981–2, box "P 92 92," folder "Correspondence Jan 81 – 6/30/82," GCIA; "The Elderly Indians of Louisiana and Their Needs," Office of Indian Affairs, 1 December 1975, GCIA; Perdue, *Native Carolinians*, 58; "Official Said to Have Removed Himself," *(Baton Rouge) State Times*, 30 August 1975; "Indian Gaming Commission Appointed," and "Introducing GCOIA Staff," *Neka-Camon* 1, no. 1 (June 1990), 1, 5; "Indians Enthusiastic about New Commission," *(Baton Rouge) State Times*, 12 July 1972; Pat Arnould, interview by author.

75. South Carolina Commission for Minority Affairs, Institute for Native American Affairs, http://www.state.sc.us/cma/nai_re.html (accessed 23 December 2009).

76. North Carolina Commission of Indian Affairs, Annual Report, 1998–1999, NCCIA; "State Recognized Tribes," 500 Nations, http://500nations.com/tribes/Tribes_States.asp (accessed 29 September 2012).

77. "State Recognized Tribes," 500 Nations, http://500nations.com/tribes/Tribes_States.asp (accessed 29 September 2012); Alabama Indian Affairs Commission, "Tribes Recognized by the State of Alabama," http://www.aiac.alabama.gov/tribes.aspx (accessed 29 September 2012).

78. Louisiana Governor's Office of Indian Affairs, "State Recognized Tribes," http://www.indianaffairs.com/tribes.htm (accessed 11 October 2008; site discontinued).

79. See Taylor, *The States*, and M. Miller, *Forgotten Tribes*, ch. 6. Virginia had no federally recognized tribes but eight state-recognized groups, including the Chickahominy Tribe, Chickahominy Indians Eastern Division, Mattaponi Indian Nation, Monacan Indian Tribe, Nansemond Indian Tribal Association, Pamunkey Nation, Rappahannock Tribe, and Upper Mattaponi Tribe. South Carolina had the federally recognized Catawba Tribe and five state-recognized tribes: the Beaver Creek Indians, Pee Dee Indian Tribe, Pee Dee Indian Nation of Upper South Carolina, Santee Indian Organization, and Waccamaw Indian People. It also had a category, "state-recognized groups," that included the Eastern Cherokee, Southern Iroquois and United Tribes of South Carolina; Natchez Tribe; Pee Dee Indian Tribe of Beaver Creek; Piedmont American Indian Association–Lower Eastern Cherokee Nation; and Wassamasaw Tribe of Varnerton Indians, for a total of ten state-affiliated groups. North Carolina also had ten state tribes: the Coharie Intra-Tribal Council, Cumberland County Association for Indian People, Guilford Native American Association, Haliwa-Saponi Tribe, Lumbee Tribe, Meherrin Indian Tribe, Metrolina Native American Association, Occaneechi Band of the Saponi Nation, Sappony (Indians of Person County), and Waccamaw-Siouan Tribe. Georgia had three state-recognized tribes: the Cherokee of Georgia, Georgia Tribe of Eastern Cherokees, and the Lower Muskogee Creek Tribe. The Alabama Indian Affairs Commission recognized eight groups: the Echota Cherokee Tribe, Cherokee Tribe of Northeast Alabama, Ma-Chis Lower Creek Indian Tribe, MOWA Band of Choctaws, Star Clan of Muskogee Creeks, Cher-O-Creek Intra-Tribal Indians, Piqua Shawnee Tribe, and United Cherokee Ani-Yun-Wiya Nation. Mississippi and Florida had no state-recognized tribes, although Florida had a state commission serving its federally recognized tribes. Louisiana had ten state-recognized tribes: the Adai Caddo Tribe, Biloxi-Chitimacha Confederation, Choctaw-Apache Community of Ebarb, Clifton Choctaw Tribe, Four Winds Tribe, Point-Au-Chien Tribe, United Houma Nation, Isle Jean Charles Band, Louisiana Choctaw Tribe, and Grand Caillou/Dulac Band. The majority of these groups were pursuing federal tribal recognition. Tennessee had a state commission with formally affiliated tribal groups that were not officially

recognized but that were served by it. Texas's once-significant Indian commission that served the Alabama-Coushattas and Tigua Indians was terminated in 1989.

80. Gindrat quoted in Transcript, Tribal Chairmen's Meeting, Clifton, Louisiana, 22 August 1981, box "P 92 92," folder "Finished Minutes," GCIA.

81. Tribal Acknowledgment Criteria, pamphlet, NCCIA; "Commission Meetings Address State Recognition," *Alabama Indian Advocate*, January/February 1982.

82. David Barnett to Whom It May Concern, 1982, and Meeting Minutes, Tribal Chairmen's Meeting, Clifton, Louisiana, Transcript, 22 August 1981, box "P 92-92," folder "Finished Minutes," GCIA; Campos and Gindrat, quoted in Inter-Tribal Council of Louisiana, Board of Directors Meeting, 11 February 1991, box 81, folder "41-8," US Senate Series, Johnston Papers; Gindrat, interview by author.

83. Gregory Richardson, interview by author.

84. BAR, Final Report against Acknowledgment of MaChis Creeks," 19–20; Dennis Peterson to Les Morris, Public Health Service, 1978, HF, OFA.

85. Jim Mattox to Charles D. Travis, 22 March 1983, box "1990/1-41," folder 5, TIC.

86. Calvin Trillin, "Louisiana—The Tunica Treasure," *New Yorker*, 27 July 1981, TB, OFA; Tunica-Biloxi Tribe of Louisiana, http://www.tunicabiloxi. org (accessed 7 December 2009); *Native American Graves and Repatriation Act, P.L. 101-601*; Gregory, interview by author; Fred G. Benton to John A. Shapard, 14 May 1981, TB, OFA; T. J. Hutto to Sonny Callahan, no boxes, folder "21002," Callahan Papers; "Native American Legacy," *Alabama Indian Advocate*, January/February, 1982, 4.

87. "May They Rest in Peace," *Talking Bayou* 3, no. 4 (6 May 1999); Holly Reckord to Rosalie Billiot, 4 March 1997, and Rosie Billiot to Ada Deer, 3 December 1996, UHN, OFA; James Ziedler, interview by author.

88. "Speech by Senator James Abourezk," 10 November 1975, box 227, no folder, RG 220, NACP; "News Release," Department of the Interior, 16 March 1973, box 58, folder 1 & 2, Rhodes Papers; Senate, Subcommittee on Interior, *Establishment of the American Indian Policy Review Commission, Hearings on S.J.R. 133*, 19 and 20 July 1973, 1; Anthony D. Brown, *New Directions in Federal Indian Policy*, 1–2.

89. Quoted from AIPRC, *Final Report*, 8; AIPRC, *Report on Terminated and Nonfederally Recognized Indians*, Kickingbird, "The AIPRC," 251; James Abourezk to Walter F. Mondale, 17 May 1977, letter in AIPRC, *Final Report*, inside cover; AIPRC, *Meetings*, 6–7 January and 4–5 February 1977, 22–23; "Notice of Hearing, Baton Rouge, Louisiana, AIPRC," 5 March 1976, box 119, no folders, RG 220, NACP; AIPRC, *Final Report Appendixes and Index, Vol. II*, 7, 13.

90. AIPRC, *Final Report*, 37–39; AIPRC, *Report on Terminated and Nonfederally Recognized Indians*, AIPRC, Transcript, Hearing Dulac Louisiana, RG 220, NACP.

91. *Passamaquoddy v. Morton* 528 F.2d 370 (1975), 371, 376; "Legal News," *Akwesasne Notes*, Late Spring 1972, 14; Thomas N. Tureen, "Federal Recognition and the *Passamaquoddy* Decision," no date, box 277, RG 220, NACP; "Briefing Report on Tunica-Biloxi, (LA) Litigation Request," September 1981, HF, BAR; Theodore Krenzke to J. Bennett Johnston, 21 April 1975, UHN, OFA; Theodore Krenzke, Brief, 23 October 1981, TB, OFA; House, Committee on Interior, *A Bill to Amend the Act relating to the Lumbee Indians*, 22 January 1974, box 105, folder 902, Steiger Papers; LRLS, "Lumbee Petition," Vol. II, 26–32.

92. "The National Congress of American Indians Declaration of Principles on Tribal Recognition," *American Indian Journal* 4, no. 5 (1978), 4; Charles E. Trimble to John Shapard, 10 March 1978, Testimony of Eddie Tullis, Transcript of NCAI Conference on Tribal Recognition, and Dennis L. Petersen, "Report of Meeting with Senate Select Committee," date illegible, HF, OFA. The NCAI maintains the position that its members have a *governmental interest* in the workings and potential reforms of the BIA process. NCAI, "Federal Recognition Task Force," http://www.ncai.org/ (accessed 20 May 2003).

93. "Procedures for Establishing that an American Indian Group Exists as an Indian Tribe," *Federal Register* 43, no. 106 (1 June 1978), 23744.

94. "Poarch Creek Indian Economic Development," and "Poarch Band of Creek Indians," pamphlet, folder "Poarch Creek Indians-19," Callahan Papers.

95. PCI Gaming Authority, http://www.pcigaming.com/coda/index.htm (accessed 29 September 2012).

96. Senate, Select Committee, *Oversight of the Federal Acknowledgment Process*, 21 July 1983, 7; "Locate and Identify," tribes list, HF, OFA.

97. Gregory, interview by author; Rountree, "Indian Virginians," 26; Forrest Gerard to Allan Campbell, 1 August 1979, HF, OFA.

CHAPTER 2

1. Wilma Mankiller, "Message from the Chief," *Cherokee County (Oklahoma) Chronicle*, 5 June 1986; File on Buffalo Child Long Lance, box 24, folder 195, and the Five Tribes Foundation, "Area Arts and Crafts Program Report," 30 June 1973, box 18, folder 153, Keeler Papers; "Cherokee Nation Looks to the Future," newspaper clipping, no date, W. W. Keeler, "Inaugural Address," 4 September 1971, Cherokee Nation, informational pamphlet, Vertical Files, SC, NSU; "Cherokee Chief Becomes Top Indian Official," *Indian Trader*, November 1985; Fixico, *Daily Life*, 212–13; Lambert, *Choctaw Nation*, 3.

2. V. Deloria, *Custer Died for Your Sins*, 10–11.

3. Hagan, "Full Blood, Mixed Blood," 309–26.

4. "An Imitation Indian," *Cherokee Phoenix*, 2 July 1828, and Notice, *Cherokee Phoenix*, 21 July 1828, transcriptions available from Hunter Library, Western Carolina University, http://www.wcu.edu/library/DigitalCollection/CherokeePhoenix/.

5. Debo, *And Still the Waters Run*, 12.

6. Debo, *The Rise and Fall of the Choctaw Republic*, 179–81; Debo, *And Still the Waters Run*, 23–27; Sturm, *Blood Politics*, 74–78.

7. Kidwell, *The Choctaws in Oklahoma*, 165–68; Debo, *The Rise and Fall of the Choctaw Republic*, 181–83; Mooney, *History, Myths, and Sacred Formulas*; Lovegrove, *A Nation in Transition*, 48–65; Debo, *And Still the Waters Run*, 31–39, 50–51; Chang, *The Color of the Land*, 73–105.

8. Smith, "From Sylvester Long to Chief Buffalo Child Long Lance," 185–202.

9. "Make-Believe Indian," *(Los Angeles) New Times*, 8 April 1999, http://www.newtimes.com/issues/1999-04-08/feature.html (accessed 24 November 2009; site discontinued); Angela Aleiss, "Native Son," *Times-Picayune*, 26 May 1996, transcription available from the Mail Archive, http://www.mail-archive.com/nativenews@mlists.net/msg01286.html (accessed 24 November 2009). See also Krech, *The Ecological Indian*.

10. Carter, *The Education of Little Tree*; John J. Miller, "Honest Injun? The Incidence of Fake Indians Is Almost Epidemic," *National Review Online*, http://www.nationalreview.com/flashback/miller200601271228.asp (accessed 24 November 2009); Wernitznig, *Going Native*, 8–9.

11. Thornton, *The Cherokees*, 74; Woodward, *The Cherokees*, 237–38; Wright, *Creeks and Seminoles*, 304–6; Foreman, *The Five Civilized Tribes*, 147–67, 215–16; Debo, *And Still the Waters Run*, 3–9; Lambert, *Choctaw Nation*, 49; Debo, *The Road to Disappearance*, 6–14, 84–85; Champagne, *Social Order and Political Change*, 1, 135–36, 185, 198, 205, 253; Perdue, *Cherokee Women*, 174–81; Boulware, *Deconstructing the Cherokee*, 10–31, 127–29, 179–82; Sturm, *Blood Politics*, 39–65, 204–10; Kidwell, *The Choctaws in Oklahoma*, vii.

12. Sturm, *Blood Politics*, 54–55.

13. Kidwell, *The Choctaws in Oklahoma*, 45; Faiman-Silva, *Choctaws at the Crossroads*, 200–201; Sturm, *Blood Politics*, 78–80; Lambert, *Choctaw Nation*, 47; Debo, *And Still the Waters Run*, 37.

14. Debo, *And Still the Waters Run*, 64–65; Denison, *Demanding the Cherokee Nation*, 238–41.

15. Conley, *The Cherokee Nation*, 20; Kidwell, *The Choctaws in Oklahomas*, xviii, 204.

16. V. Deloria and Lytle, *American Indians, American Justice*, 51, 61, 126; Indian Claims Commission, *Final Report*, 1; Michael J. Kelly, "Treaty with the Cherokee, Nov. 28, 1785," 285–86; Wilkins, *American Indian Politics*, 42–44.

17. Quinn, "Federal Acknowledgment: Authority, Judicial Interposition," 38; B. Miller, *Invisible Indigenes*, 133; Wilkins, *American Indian Politics*, 106; V. Deloria and Wilkins, *Tribes, Treaties*, 25; Lawrence, *"Real" Indians and Others*, 28–29. See generally Quinn, "Federal Acknowledgment of American Indian Tribes." As late as 1924 the Snyder Act continued the loose construction, applying the law to all Indians and tribes, yet not defining them. *Snyder Act*, 25 U.S.C.A. sec. 13.

18. *Cherokee Nation v. Georgia*, 30 U.S. (5 Pet.) I (1831); V. Deloria and Lytle, *American Indians, American Justice*, 30, 32; King, "Cherokees in the West," 358; *Worcester v. Georgia*, 31 US 51 (1832); Prucha, *The Great Father*, 76, 160, 194.

19. Roosevelt quoted in Wilkins, *American Indian Politics*, 110, 111; V. Deloria and Wilkins, *Tribes, Treaties*, 38; Hoxie, *A Final Promise* and "From Prison to Homeland."

20. *United States v. Joseph*, 94 U.S. 614 (1876), 616; *United States v. Sandoval* 231 U.S. 28 (1913); *United States v. Candelaria* 271 U.S. 432 (1926), 441–42; Lawrence, *'Real' Indians and Others*, 74; Harmon, "When Is an Indian"; B. Miller, *Invisible Indigenes*, 118.

21. *Montoya v. United States* 180 U.S. 261 (1901), 359.

22. *Act of June 18, 1934*, 25 USCA sec. 461 et seq (Indian Reorganization Act); Cohen, *Handbook of Federal Indian Law*, 271; Biolsie, *Organizing the Lakota*; Finger, *Cherokee Americans*, 89, 181–201; Innes, "Creeks in the West," 400; Wilkins, *American Indian Politics*, 114. See generally Lawrence J. Kelly, *The Assault on Assimilation*.

23. *Act of June 18, 1934*, 25 USCA sec. 461 et seq; Cohen, *Handbook of Federal Indian Law*, 271; Cohen, Memo to Commissioner of Indian Affairs, 8 April 1935, HF, OFA; Oscar L. Chapman to Mr. President, 22 August 1946, box 64, folder "Indian Claims Commission Act," RG 48, NACP.

24. *Cherokee Nation of Oklahoma v. Babbitt*, 117 F. 3d 1489 (D.C. Cir. 1997); Obermeyer, *Delaware Tribe in a Cherokee Nation*; "Federal Court Upholds Delaware Tribe's Recognition," *Delaware Indian News*, 27 December 2002; "Constitution and By-laws of the Confederated Tribes of the Umatilla Reservation in Oregon"; Cohen, *Handbook of Federal Indian Law*, 271. Also see Goldberg-Ambrose, "Of Native Americans."

25. Department of the Interior, "Memo: Keetoowah Organization as a Band, 29 July 1937," *Opinions of the Solicitor of the Department of the Interior*, 775; Nichols, "Indians in the Post-Termination Era," 84.

26. LaGrand, *Indian Metropolis*; Kidwell, "Termination of the Choctaws," 130–32; Wilkins, *American Indian Politics*, 114–15. See generally Fixico, *Termination and Relocation*, and Burt, *Tribalism in Crisis*.

27. Eddie Tullis, interview by author; Harry Rainbolt to Barbara Billiot, 1 May 1975, HF, OFA; Ross, *Index to the Decisions of the Indian Claims Commission*, 17, 20, 25; Pascagoula, Biloxi and Mobilian Consolidated Band of Indians,

"Petition to the Indian Claims Commission," no date, UHN, OFA; Doster, "The Creek Indians," in *American Indian Ethnohistory: Florida Indians*. See generally Rosenthal, *Their Day in Court*.

28. Mastin G. White, Solicitor, to A. Devitt Vanech, 10 June 1948, box 64, folder "1946–49, Bureau of Indian Affairs, Jan.–June 1948," RG 48, NACP; B. Miller, *Invisible Indigenes*.

29. Mastin G. White, Solicitor, to A. Devitt Vanech, 10 June 1948, and Memorandum, "Indians of California as 'Identifiable' Groups, 17 March 1948," box 64, folder "1946–49, Bureau of Indian Affairs, Jan.–June 1948," RG 48, NACP; Lower Creek Muscogee Tribe, "Petition for Recognition," October 1978, LCMT, OFA; Beals, "The Anthropologist as Expert Witness," 139; Lurie, "Problems, Opportunities, and Recommendations"; Kroeber and Kroeber, *Ishi in Four Centuries*; Kroeber, "Nature of the Land-Holding Group," 304.

30. Tullis, interview by author.

31. *An Act Relating to the Lumbee Indians of North Carolina*, 7 June 1956, 70 Stat. 254; Kersey, *An Assumption of Sovereignty*, 135–44.

32. Penn, quoted in "What Is An Indian?," California State Senate Committee on Indian Affairs, Hearing Transcript, 1954, box 113, folder 10, Tyler Papers; Commissioner of Indian Affairs to Chairman Jackson, 4 April 1974, and Acting Director, Office of Indian Services to Secretary of Interior, memorandum on Louisiana Coushatta Indians, 13 June 1973, HF, OFA; M. Miller, *Forgotten Tribes*, ch. 6.

33. "Report of the Inter-Agency Task Force on American Indians, 27 October 1967, box "Task Force Reports," folder "American Indians 1968," LBJ Library; Spicer, *A Short History*, 134; "News Briefs," *CILS Newsletter*, 14 June 1972; American Indian Chicago Conference, "Declaration of Indian Purpose: The Voice of the American Indian," 1961, box 35, folder "Declaration of Indian Purpose," RG 220, NACP; Gindrat, interview by author; Nagel, *American Indian Ethnic Renewal*, 158–78; Josephy, Nagel, and Johnson, *Red Power*.

34. W. W. Keeler, "If I Were Twenty-One Today," address, no date, Vertical Files, NSU; Cobb, "Devils in Disguise," 465–80; "Abolishment of Area Indian Office Is Suggested at Meet," *Muskogee Daily Phoenix*, 22 June 1961; "Militant Native American Groups," box 24, folder 200, Keeler Papers.

35. Hertzberg, *The Search for an American Indian Identity*, 290–92; Clarkin, *Federal Indian Policy*, 34; "Keeler Tells Congress About Indian Project," February 1961, clipping, Vertical Files, NSU; Cowger, *The National Congress of American Indians*, 30–48.

36. "Lawyers between Two Cultures," *NARF Announcements* 2, no. 1 (January 1973); Hiram Gregory, interview by author.

37. Transcript of CENA meeting, 1973, Pembroke, North Carolina, HF, OFA; "Eastern Native People Federate," *Akwesasne Notes* 5, no. 1 (1973); USET Web Page, "All About USET," and USET Resolution No. 2008: 042 "Restating

Position on Lumbee Recognition," http://www.usetinc.org/AboutUSETHistory.aspx (accessed 22 December 2009; site discontinued); Josephy, *Red Power,* 156–57; Wilkins, *American Indian Politics,* 215, 245; "National Indian Lutheran Board Proposal: Wampanoag Tribal Council of Gay Head," 31 October 1975, box 118, no folders, RG 220, NACP; "State Indian Tribes Will Meet in Dulac," clipping, 1969, HF, OFA; Bruce Duthu, interview by author.

38. Mrs. Emil Bardach to Stewart Udall, 15 January 1961, and second citation, Dorothy L. Wright, 16 January 1961, box 82, folder 2, Udall Papers; John F. Kennedy "The American Indian," address, box 113, folder 10, Tyler Papers; *Title IV, Indian Education Act, Pub. Law 92-318,* 23 June 1972, 86 Stat. 345; NCAI, "Federal Programs Available to Indian Communities," no box, folder 218, Diamond Papers. For many purposes membership in a federally recognized tribe is the basic requirement for Indian preference. *Preference in Employment,* 25 C.F.R. Part 1.2. See generally: Clarkin, *Federal Indian Policy.*

39. "A Summary of the Economic Opportunity Act of 1964," box 523, folder 523/15, Morris Udall Papers; Matusow, *The Unraveling of America,* 243–55; M. Miller, *Forgotten Tribes,* 98–103.

40. Kidwell, *The Choctaws,* 208–16.

41. "A Free Choice Program for American Indians," 23 December 1966, box 3, folder "1966 Task Force on Indians," LBJ Library; "The Forgotten Americans," 6 March 1968, box 138, folder 1, Udall Papers; Small Tribes Organization of Western Washington (STOWW), "Eligibility, Brief," RG 220, NACP; Officer, "The Bureau of Indian Affairs," 61–72.

42. Richman, "Return of the Red Man", special issue, *Life,* 1 December 1967; "The Amherst Cherokees: Virginia's Lost Tribe," *Washington Post,* 15 June 1969; "Indians of the Southeast: White Man's Record Makes Indians Wary," *Atlanta Constitution,* 17 April 1970. See also P. Deloria, *Playing Indian.*

43. Steiner, "The White Indians," *Akwesasne Notes* 8, no. 1 (Early Spring 1976), 38–40; "Five Indian Movies 'Not About Indians,'" *Akwesasne Notes* 3, no. 4 (May 1971); Jojola, "Absurd Reality II: Hollywood Goes to the Indians," 13; Vine Deloria, Jr., "'White Society' Is Breaking Down around Us," *Akwesasne Notes* 5, no. 1 (Early Winter 1973), 43; Jamake Highwater, quoted in Highwater, "Second Class Indians," *Akwesasne Notes* 15, no. 2 (Spring 1983), 15; Shanley, "The Indians America Loves to Love and Read," 26–51; Thornton, *The Cherokees,* 144–45, 170, 183; "A Look at the U.S. Census," *Akwesasne Notes* 5, no. 5 (Early Autumn 1973), 35; "Census Finds Many Claiming New Identity: Indian," *New York Times,* 5 March 1991.

44. Ellis, "More Real"; Van Slyk, *A Manufactured Wilderness,* 169–90; Root, *Cannibal Culture,* 93; "Indian Guides," http://www.ymca.net/adventureguides/ag-history.html (accessed 12 February 2010; site discontinued); Rayna Green, "The Tribe Called Wannabee," 30–55; Anthony Paredes, interview by author.

45. Sutler-Cohen, "(Dis) Locating Spiritual Knowledge," 43–53; Wallis, *Shamans/Neo-Shamans*, 49–78; Wernitznig, *Going Native or Going Naïve?*, ix, 12–19; Root, *Cannibal Culture*.

46. Cordova quoted in U.S. Congress, Senate, Subcommittee on Indian Affairs of the Committee on Interior and Insular Affairs, *Establishment of the American Indian Policy Review Commission*, 1973, 47; St. Marie quoted in "Outside Fashion," *Village Voice*, 31 July 1969; Paredes quoted in Bonney and Paredes "Introduction," *Anthropologists and Indians in the New South*, 4.

47. Leonard Hill to Area Directors, 24 January 1961, box 89, folder 4, Udall Papers; "Question: Who Is an Indian?" *Akwesasne Notes* 1, no. 5 (May 1969); Deloria quoted in "American Indian Policy Attacked," *Native Nevadan*, 6 May 1972; Wolfe quoted in "Supreme Court Doesn't Clear Air," *Muscogee Nation News*, March 1991, 2; Nagel, *American Indian Ethnic Renewal*, 23–30; Castile, "The Commodification."

48. Conley, *The Cherokee Nation*, 217; "Principal Chief of Creek Nation Seeks 5th Term," *Tulsa World*, 23 September 1987; W. W. Keeler, "Inaugural Address," 4 September 1971 and "Keeler Legacy Affects Cherokee," undated clipping, Vertical Files, NSU; Lambert, *The Choctaw Nation*.

49. *Indian Self-Determination and Education Assistance Act of 1975;* Cornell, *Return of the Native*, 4–8; V. Deloria and Lytle, *American Indians, American Justice*, 6.

50. Claude Cox, "State of the Muscogee (Creek Nation)," *Muscogee Nation News*, November/December 1982; Innes, "Creeks in the West," 400; Fixico, *Daily Life of Native Americans in the Twentieth Century*, 212–13; Conley, *The Cherokees*, 22; Muscogee Nation, Office of Public Relations and Communications, Information Booklet, Vertical Files, NSU.

51. "Creek," in Pritzer, *A Native American Encyclopedia*, 381; "Creek Election," *Muskogee Sunday Phoenix*, 10 August 1975; V. Deloria, *American Indian Policy in the Twentieth Century*, 144; Lewis and Jordan, *Creek Indian Medicine Ways*, 21–22; "Today in the News," *Deseret News*, August 1973, clippings file, box 113, folder 11 Tyler Papers.

52. "Frequently Requested Information" and "Certificate of Degree of Indian Blood Application," CDIB and Tribal Membership Department, Choctaw Tribe, Durant, Oklahoma; "Frequently Asked Questions," Cherokee Nation Registration Department, Cherokee National Headquarters, Tahlequah, Oklahoma.

53. Wilma Mankiller, "Message From the Chief," 22 May 1986, Vertical Files, NSU.

54. Gregory E. Pyle, to Choctaw Nation, 26 January 1998, and Choctaw Nation promotional pamphlet, Vertical Files, NSU; "The Creek Influence," *Tulsa World*, 6 May 1993; Kidwell, *The Choctaws*, 220–21; Lambert, *Choctaw Nation*, 12–17; Kidwell, "Choctaws in the West," 530–31; Pierce and Strickland, *The Cherokee People*, 54; Galloway and Kidwell, "Choctaw in the East," 517; Finger, *Cherokee Americans;* Kersey, *An Assumption of Sovereignty*.

55. STOWW, "Position Paper," no date, and Federal Regional Council of New England, to David W. Hays, 30 January 1975, box 277, RG 220, NACP; *United States v. Washington* 520 F.2d 676 (1975), 692–93; *Passamaquoddy v. Morton* 528 F.2d 370 (1975), 371–76; "Briefing Report on Tunica-Biloxi, (LA) Litigation Request," September 1981, HF, OFA; *Congressional Record-Senate, H.C.R. 240, to Recognize the Tunica-Biloxi Indian Community*, 3 September 1974, box 277, RG 220, NACP; *Mashpee Tribe v. New Seabury Corp.*, 592 F.2d 575 (1979); Congress, *An Act to Settle Certain Claims of the Mashantucket Pequot Indians, Public Law 98-134*, 18 October 1983, 97 Stat. 851.

56. *Passamaquoddy v. Morton* 528 F.2d 370 (1975), 371, 376; "The Maine Land Claims," *Akwesasne Notes* 9, no. 2 (Late Spring 1977), 20; Tureen, "Federal Recognition and the *Passamaquoddy* Decision," no date, box 277, RG 220, NACP; House, Committee on Interior, *Federal Recognition*, 10 August 1978, 23.

57. "Tribal Attorneys Assess Boldt Case," *Indian Voice*, August 1979; "Passamaquoddy Tribe Wins Decision," *American Indian Law Newsletter* 8, no. 2 (1978); *United States v. Washington* 520 F.2d 676 (1975), 692–93; *Mashpee Tribe v. New Seabury Corp.*, 592 F.2d 575 (1979); Clifford, *Predicaments of Culture*, 8–17, 278–319; Campisi, *Mashpee Indians*, 151–58; Jo Carillo, "Identity as Idiom: Mashpee Reconsidered," 43–45; National Wildlife Federation to John Cadwalader, 26 June 1975, box 33, no folders, RG 220, NACP.

58. Raymond Wilson, "Russell Means," in *The New Warriors*, 144–55; "Red Power, Black Power, Tuscarora Power," *Akwesasne Notes* 5, no. 3 (Early Summer) 1973, 42; "Look: Join the Caucus" pamphlet, box 65, RG 220, NACP; "Indian Rebirth," *The Black Panther Party*, 25 May 1969, box 65, RG 220, NACP; Wilkinson quoted in "Angry American Indian: Starting down the Protest Trail," *Time*, 7 February 1970.

59. Cobb, "Devils in Disguise," 465–70; "Cherokee Feud 5 Years Old," *Tulsa World*, 28 July 1966; "Cherokees Start Industrial Complex," 1 August 1966, *The Pictorial Press*, Vertical Files, NSU; Kidwell, *The Choctaws*, 211.

60. "What Makes an Indian Bank Indian," *Akwesasne Notes* 5, no. 6 (October 1973), 29; "Report on Quarterly Meeting of the Inter-Tribal Council of the Five Civilized Tribes," 11 October 1974, box 34, folder 4, Bartlett Collection; Baird, "Are the Five Civilized Tribes of Oklahoma 'Real' Indians?"

61. Steiner, *The New Indians*, 3–4; Collier, "The Theft of a Nation: Apologies to the Cherokees," *Ramparts*, no date (early 1970s), Vertical Files, NSU.

62. Kidwell, "Termination," in *Beyond Red Power*, 135–36; Lambert, *Choctaw Nation*; 61–71.

63. "It Isn't Easy to Change the B.I.A.," *Akwesasne Notes* 5, no. 1 (January 1973), 22; "Removal of Bruce Hinted, *Gallup Independent*, 10 October 1969; "Background in the Bureau of Indian Affairs Power Struggle," *Akwesasne Notes* 3, no. 7 (July/August 1971); "26 Indians Arrested in D.C. Protest," *Washington Post*, in *Akwesasne Notes* 3, no. 7 (September 1971); "Angry American Indian:

Starting down the Protest Trail," *Time*, 7 February 1970, 26; Cobb and Fowler, "Introduction," *Beyond Red Power*, x, xvi; "Nixon Finds New B.I.A. Commissioner," *Akwesasne Notes* 5, no. 5 (October 1973), 28–29.

64. Hertzberg, *The Search for an American Indian Identity*, 322; Spicer, *A Short History*, 144–46; Steiner, *The New Indians*, 300, x–xi.

65. Goldberg-Ambrose, "Of Native Americans," 1137; James Abourezk, "Speech by Senator James Abourezk for the National Council of American Indians," 10 November 1975, box 22, no folders, RG 220, NACP; "Indian Policy Review Committee Must Sort Priorities," *Minneapolis Tribune*, clipping, 1973, box 21, folder "Newspaper File," in RG 220, NACP; Senate, Committee on Interior, *Establishment of the AIPRC*, 19 July 1973; James Abourezk to Dear Friend, 18 April 1975, box 113, folder 8, Tyler Papers; "Ernie Stevens Wants to Win," *Talking Leaf* 40, no. 10 (November 1975), 1; AIPRC, *Report on Terminated and Nonfederally Recognized Indians*; James Abourezk to Dewey F. Bartlett, 18 March 1976, box 29, folder 25, Bartlett Collection; AIPRC, "Notice of Meetings, Louisiana," 5 March 1976, box 119, no folders, RG 220, NACP.

66. B. Frank Belvin Telegram to Senator James Abourezk, 27 March 1975, and NTCA Resolution, 18 March 1975, box 74, folder 4, Steed Collection; "News from the American Indian Policy Review Commission: NTCA Decision Reached," 27 February 1976, box 29, folder 14, Bartlett Collection; "American Indian Policy Review Commission Selects Task Forces," *Akwesasne Notes* 7, no. 3 (Late Summer 1975), 20; Taylor quoted in AIPRC, *Meetings of the AIPRC*, Nov. 19–23, 1976, 216; Transcript, 34th Annual Conference, NCAI, HF, OFA.

67. Quoted in AIPRC, *Final Report*, 8; AIPRC, *Report on Terminated and Nonfederally Recognized Indians*; Kickingbird, "The AIPRC: A Prospect for Future Change in Federal Indian Policy," 251; James Abourezk to Walter F. Mondale, 17 May 1977, letter inside AIPRC, *Final Report*; AIPRC, *Meetings of the AIPRC*, 6–7 January and 4–5 February 1976, 22–23; "Notice of Hearing, Baton Rouge, Louisiana, AIPRC," 5 March 1976, box 119, no folders, RG 220, NACP; AIPRC, *Final Report Appendixes and Index*, Vol. II, 7, 13.

68. AIPRC, *Final Report*, 37–39.

69. Quote from AIPRC, *Final Report*, 479; "Today's Challenge through Leadership," Report of the 34th Annual Convention, NCAI, Dallas, Texas, 19–23 September 1977, HF, OFA.

70. "Today's Challenge through Leadership," Report of the 34th Annual Convention, NCAI, Dallas, Texas, 19–23 September 1977, HF, OFA; AIPRC, *Final Report*, 467; AIPRC, *Report on Terminated and Nonfederally Recognized Indians*, 218; Anderson, "Federal Recognition," 7–19; Downs and Whitehead, "The Houma Indians," 2–22.

71. Brown, *New Directions*, 15; Meeds quoted in "Meeds Attacks Move for More Indian Power," in AIPRC, *Final Report*, vol. 2, 781; Fred Johnson to Chair,

27 April 1977, and Washington State man quoted, Lue Seil to AIPRC, 19 March 1977, in AIPRC, *Final Report*, vol. 2, 391–92, 422.

72. Claude Cox to Ernest Stevens, 25 April 1977, AIPRC, *Final Report*, vol. 2, 5; Daniel Edward Green, *The Creek People*, preface.

73. BIA, Memorandum on Federal Recognition Act, 12 July 1977, HF, OFA; Tom Steed to John L. Sloat, 20 November 1975, box 74, folder 4, Steed Papers; Floor Statement, Senator Robert Morgan, 1 August 1978, copy of *S. 2090*, 95th Cong., 2d, 1978, and Acting Assistant Secretary-Indian Affairs to Dewey Bartlett, 30 August 1978, in box 36, folder 2, Bartlett Papers; House, Committee on Interior, *A Bill relating to the Lumbee Indians*, 22 January 1974, box 105, folder 902, Steiger Papers.

74. Copy of *S. 2375*, 15 December 1977, 95th Cong., 1st sess., HF, OFA; Senate, Select Committee, *Recognition of Certain Indian Tribes*, 18 April 1978; Senate, Select Committee, *Bill to Establish an Administrative Procedure*, 15 December 1977; House, Committee on the Interior, *Federal Recognition*, 10 August 1978; Dennis L. Petersen, Report of a Meeting with Senate Select Committee on Indian Affairs, 20 December 1977, HF, OFA. The NTCA formally opposed the various recognition bills. House, Committee on Resources, *Federal Acknowledgment Process*, 10 August 1978, 37.

75. Jaimes, *The State of Native America*; Churchill, "The Crucible," 40–44; NCAI, Report on 34th Annual Convention, HF, OFA; Cowger, *The National Congress of American Indians*, 4–11; Tullis, interview by author.

76. Institute for the Development of Indian Law, "Report to the NCAI on Congress and Pending Legislation," 3 September 1978, box 119, folder 4, Tyler Papers.

77. NCAI, Report on 34th Annual Convention, Agenda, 19–23 September 1973, 8, HF, OFA; "The Shadow of W. W. Keeler . . . A Cherokee Watergate," *Akwesasne Notes* 7, no. 4 (Early Autumn 1975), 19; NCAI, "Transcript of National Conference on Recognition," 1978, HF, OFA; Getches, Wilkinson, and Williams, *Federal Indian Law*, 265; Downs, "A National Conference," 2.

78. "Washington State Officials Ignore Court Decision," *Akwesasne Notes* 8, no. 2 (Early Summer 1976); angry citizen quoted, Willie Clark to Cecil D. Andrus, 20 February 1977, box 16, folder 5, Domenici Papers; "The Confusing Spectre of White Backlash," *Akwesasne Notes* 9, no. 5 (December 1977); "Fishing Rights Turmoil," *Akwesasne Notes* 8, no. 4 (Early Autumn 1976); House, Committee on the Interior, *Bill: Native Americans Equal Opportunity Act*, 12 September 1977; NCAI, 34th Annual Convention Program, HF, OFA.

79. Charles Trimble to Hazel Elbert, no date (early 1970s), box 35, folder 10, Bartlett Collection; Acting Director, Office of Trust Responsibilities, to Assistant Secretary for Indian Affairs, 18 October 1977, HF, OFA; Murdock and Deloria quoted in Transcript, NCAI Conference, 1978; Bud Shapard to Robert W. Trepp, Creek Nation, no date (1978 era), HF, OFA; Tullis, interview

by author; Senate, Select Committee, *Recognition of Certain Indian Tribes*, 18 April 1978, 17–18.

80. David Lindgren to Chuck Trimble, 20 October 1975, HF, OFA; B. Miller, *Invisible Indigenes*, 96; Deloria quoted in House, Committee on Interior Affairs, *Federal Acknowledgment*, 8 July 1992, 104–5; NTCA Statement, House, Committee on Interior, *Federal Acknowledgment*, 10 August 1978, 154–56; NCAI president quoted in NCAI 34th Annual Convention Program, HF, OFA; BAR, "Proposed Finding against Federal Acknowledgment of the Yuchi Tribal Organization," *Federal Register*, 24 October 1995, 55406–7, https://www.federalregister.gov/articles/1995/10/24/95-26158/proposed-finding-against-federal-acknowledgment-of-the-yuchi-tribal-organization; Valerie Lambert, interview by author; Tullis, interview by author. Lambert was the BAR ethnohistorian who worked on the Yuchi case.

81. Tomaskin quoted in transcript of NCAI Conference on Tribal Recognition; twelve principles in Senate, Select Committee, *Recognition of Certain Indian Tribes*, 18 April 1978, 26, 37.

82. Lawrence, *"Real" Indians*, 1–2; B. Miller, *Invisible Indigenes*, 36–37, 53–55, 160–61.

83. Lawrence, *"Real" Indians*, 2–3; B. Miller, *Invisible Indigenes*, 38–39; Moerman, "Who Are the Lue?," 153–67.

84. See, for example, Albers and James, "On the Dialectics of Ethnicity"; Dole, "Tribes as the Autonomous Unit"; Helm, *Essays on the Problem of Tribe*; Fried, "The Myth of Tribe," *The Notion of Tribe*, and "On the Concept of Tribe"; Kroeber, "The Nature of the Land-Holding Group"; Lurie, "Problems, Opportunities." Some anthropologists weighed in late arguing against trying to create structural criteria: Theodore Krenzke to George J. Jennings, 12 January 1979, and Michael E. Melody to John A. Shapard, 21 August 1978, HF, OFA.

85. Barth, *Ethnic Group Boundaries*; Spicer and Thompson, *Plural Society*; Sheridan and Parezo, *Paths of Life*, xxv–xxix. The social constructionist school has become the dominant paradigm regarding the concept of tribe. See Campisi, "The Iroquois," *The Mashpee Indians*, and "The New England Tribes"; Clifford, *The Predicaments of Culture*; Greenberg, "Group Identities"; Hauptman, *Tribes and Tribulations*; Slagle, "Unfinished Justice"; Starna, "We'll All Be Together"; Weatherhead, "What Is an 'Indian Tribe'?," and Wilkins, "Breaking Into the Matrix."

86. McCulloch and Wilkins, "Constructing Nations."

87. Nagel, *American Indian Ethnic*, xxii, 12; V. Deloria and Lytle, *American Indians, American Justice*, 105.

88. John "Bud" Shapard, interview by author.

89. Ibid.; William Quinn Jr., interview by author; Senate, Select Committee, *Oversight of the Federal Acknowledgment Process*, 21 July 1983, 111–15; BAR, Briefing Paper, 24 April 1980, HF, OFA.

90. Denis L. Petersen to assistant secretary for Indian Affairs, 20 December 1977, HF, OFA; "Procedures for Establishing that an American Indian Group Exists as an Indian Tribe," *Federal Register* 43, no. 106 (1 June 1978), 23744; regulations later amended, "Mandatory Criteria for Federal Acknowledgment," sec. 83.7, 25 C.F.R. 262–65 (1 April 1997); Department of the Interior, news release, "Forty Indian Groups Petition," 27 October 1978, Tyler Papers.

91. Holly Reckord, interview by author; Shapard, interview by author; George Roth, interview by author. The majority of employees of the BIA are enrolled in federally recognized tribes. See Mazurek, *American Indian Law Deskbook*; Officer, "The Bureau of Indian Affairs."

92. Prucha, "A Historian Looks at Recent Indian Policy," presentation, American Indian Policy Conference, University of California at Los Angeles, 22 February, 1985; "Procedures for Establishing That an American Indian Group Exists as an Indian Tribe," *Federal Register* 43, no. 106 (1 June 1978), 23744.

CHAPTER 3

1. Deputy Assistant Secretary-Indian Affairs, Memorandum "Recommendation for Federal Acknowledgment of the Poarch Band," 29 December 1983, PBCI, OFA; "Poarch Creek Indians," Allindiancasinos.com, http://www. allindiancasinos.com/indian-tribes/alabama/192/poarch-creek-indians. html (accessed October 3, 2012) and "History of the Poarch Band of Creek Indians, State of Alabama Indian Affairs Commission, http://www.aiac.state .al.us/tribes_PoarchCreek.aspx (accessed 2 April 2011).

2. Wright, *Creeks and Seminoles*, 7; BAR, "Historical Report on the Poarch Band of Creeks (PBCI)," PBCI, OFA; NARF, "Petition for Federal Recognition: PBCI," 10 January 1980, 2–5, PBCI, OFA; Paredes, "Emergence of Contemporary Identity," 66.

3. Wright, *Creeks and Seminoles*, 161–72.

4. NARF, Memorandum: Eligibility of Poarch Creek Band under the Indian Reorganization Act, 8 May 1975, PBCI, OFA; BAR, "Historical Report: PBCI," 10–14; Wright, *Creeks and Seminoles*, 175–79; Michael D. Green, *Politics of Indian Removal*, 43–44.

5. BAR, "Historical Reports: PBCI," 4, 9, 13; Young, *Redskins, Ruffleshirts and Rednecks.*

6. NARF, "Petition," 15–21; BAR, "Historical Reports: PBCI," 17; Poarch Band, pamphlet, Tribal Headquarters, Poarch, Alabama; Paredes, "Back from Disappearance," 124; Paredes, "Emergence of Contemporary Identity," 66; *An Act for the Relief of Samuel Smith, Lynn MacGhee and Samoice, a Friendly Creek Indian,* Statute I, 6 Stat 677, 2 July 1836 and *An Act for the Relief of the Heirs of*

Semoice, a Friendly Creek Indian, ch. LXXXIV, 10 Stat 735, 16 August 1852, box 4, folder "Creek," Matte Papers.

7. Paredes, "Federal Recognition," 121; Paredes, "Back from Disappearance," 126.

8. BAR, "Historical Report: PBCI," 1, 31; BAR, "Anthropological Reports: PBCI," 10; NARF, Memo: Eligibility of Poarch Creek Band; Paredes, "Back from Disappearance," 128.

9. NARF, "Petition," 24; Paredes, "Federal Recognition," 121; Paredes, "Emergence of Contemporary Identity," 68.

10. Paredes, "Emergence of Contemporary Identity," 69.

11. 1912 photo, Poarch Band Creek Indians Cultural Center, Poarch, Alabama; Paredes, "Back from Disappearance," 132.

12. BAR, "Historical Reports: PBCI," 38.

13. Paredes, "Back from Disappearance," 134.

14. Gail Thrower, interview by author.

15. BAR, "Anthropological Report: PBCI," 26.

16. Gail Thrower, interview by author; Paredes, "Back from Disappearance," 132; BAR, "Anthropological Report: PBCI," 26.

17. Edgar Edwards to C. J. Rhoades, 10 September 1931, and Edgar Edwards "Report on Indian Work" (1936), box 4, folder "Creeks," Matte Papers; BAR, "Anthropological Report: PBCI," 26–27.

18. John Collier to Edgar Edwards, 21 April 1936, William Beatty to Theodora Wade, 27 May 1938, Samuel H. Thompson, Report on Trip to Alabama (1934), William Beatty to Edgar Edwards, 27 May 1938, box 4, folder "Creeks," Matte Papers.

19. BAR, "Historical Report: PBCI," 35–38; BAR, "Anthropological Reports: PBCI," 35–37; "History of Alabama Indian Communities: The Poarch Band of Creeks," *Alabama Indian Advocate* 1 no. 1 (May 1981), 2; "Calvin McGhee, 70-Year-Old Chief of Creek Indians," *Akwesasne Notes* 2, no. 5 (1970); "Chief Calvin W. McGhee Named to Atmore Hall of Fame," *Poarch Creek News* 23, no. 10 (October 2006); Eddie Tullis, interview by author; Paredes, "Federal Recognition," 69–71; Paredes, "The Emergence of Contemporary Identity," 71; Gail Thrower, interview by author; C. Lenoir Thompson to Calvin McGhee, 22 November 1949, PBCI Cultural Center.

20. Gail Thrower, interview by author; NARF, "Memorandum: Eligibility of Poarch"; BAR, "Historical Report: PBCI," 44–45; BAR, "Anthropological Report: PBCI," 38. McGhee also visited the nearby MOWA Band of Choctaw Indians in the claims mobilization. Weaver, interview by author.

21. Petition, *C. W. McGhee, Ruby Weatherford et al., before the Indian Claims Commission,* box 4, folder "Creeks," Matte Papers; Paredes, interview by author; BAR, "Anthropological Report: PBCI."

22. Tullis, interview by author; Paredes, interview by author; Paredes, "Emergence of Contemporary Identity," 72; Paredes, "Back from Disappearance," 136; BAR, "Historical Report: PBCI"; Gail Thrower, interview by author.

23. Gail Thrower, interview by author; Paredes, "Federal Recognition," 133–34; NARF, Memo: Eligibility of Poarch Creek Band.

24. Gail Thrower, interview by author; Speck, "Notes on the Social and Economic Conditions," 198; Paredes, "Back from Disappearance," 137; AP story [title not with article], 6 August 1962, PBCI Cultural Center.

25. BAR, "Historical Report: PBCI" 46; PBCI, "The Annual Poarch Band of Creek Indians Powwow," no boxes, folder "Poarch Creek Indians—19," Callahan Papers; Castile, "Commodification of Identity"; Paredes, interview by author.

26. Paredes, "Paradoxes of Modernism," 344–45.

27. Speck, "Notes on the Social and Economic Conditions," 198; Paredes, "Back from Disappearance," 127; BAR, "Anthropological Report: PBCI," 20.

28. Robert Thrower, interview by author; Gail Thrower, interview by author.

29. BAR, "Anthropological Report: PBCI."

30. BAR, "Anthropological Report: PBCI," 37–39; NARF, "Petition," 33–41.

31. NARF, "Petition," 33–41; Gail Thrower, interview by author; Paredes, interview by author; NARF, "Petition," 60–62; BAR, "Historical Report on the Lower Muskogee Creek Tribe-East of the Mississippi, Inc.," 1981, LMCT, OFA.

32. Tullis, interview by author; Gail Thrower, interview by author; Thomas N. Tureen to Morris Thompson, 15 May 1975, PBCI, OFA; Eddie Tullis to John A. Shapard, 14 November 1978, and Briefing Paper on Poarch Band, 27 April 1982, HF, OFA.

33. "Government Relationship to Tribes Seen as Critical Issue," *Alabama Indian Advocate* 1, no. 1 (May 1981), 2; NARF, "Petition," 67; Tullis, interview by author.

34. BAR, "Anthropological Report: PBCI," 5–10; NARF, "Petition," 11–23.

35. Deputy Assistant Secretary–Indian Affairs, Recommendation for Acknowledgment, PBCI, 29 December 1983, PBCI, OFA; BAR "Anthropological Report: PBCI," 10–15; NARF, "Petition," 11–24.

36. Tullis, interview by author; "John O. Crow Appointed Deputy Commissioner," Department of the Interior News Release, 23 July 1971, http://www.bia.gov/cs/groups/public/documents/text/idc-021599.pdf (accessed 3 October 2012); Paredes, "Federal Recognition," 132; NARF, Memo: Eligibility of Poarch Band; Deputy Assistant Secretary–Indian Affairs, "Recommendation: Proposed Finding for Federal Acknowledgment of the Poarch Band," 29 December 1983, PBCI, OFA.

37. Weatherford quoted in Frank, *Creeks and Southerners*, 121–22.

38. "Social Conditions in Alabama as Seen by Travelers," 3–23, and *Mobile-Press Register*, (1930s), box 4, fd. "Creek," Matte Papers; NARF, "Petition," 10–22.

39. See, for example, BAR, "Historical Report: United Houma Nation," UHN, OFA; Wilkins, speech on Black-Indian relations, in author's possession; Sturm, *Blood Politics*.

40. Samuel H. Thompson, Supervisor of Indian Education, "Report of Trip to Mobile County, Washington County, and Escambia County" (1934), box 4, Matte Papers; Brewton Berry, *Almost White*, 33; Gilbert, "Memorandum Concerning the Characteristics," 438; Price, "Mixed-Blood Populations," 50, 54–55. See also Price, "A Geographic Analysis," 144–45.

41. "Procedure for Establishing That an American Indian Group Exists as an Indian Tribe," *Federal Register* 43, no. 106 (1 June 1978), 23, 743; Deputy Assistant Secretary–Indian Affairs, Recommendation for Acknowledgment, PBCI, 29 December 1983, PBCI, OFA.

42. BAR, "Anthropological Reports: PBCI," "Genealogical Reports: PBCI."

43. BAR, "Anthropological Report: PBCI," 32–33; Gail Thrower, interview by author; Paredes, interview by author; McClurken, interview by author.

44. Gail Thrower, interview by author.

45. Gail Thrower, interview by author; Paredes, interview by author.

46. Final Determination for Federal Acknowledgment of the Poarch Band of Creeks, *Federal Register* 49, no. 113, 11 June 1984, 24083.

47. Tullis, interview by author; Paredes, "Federal Recognition," 135–36; Gail Thrower, interview by author.

48. OFA, "Petitioners by State," 29 October 1999, http://www.doi.gov/bia/bar/indexz.htm (accessed 6 April 2000; page discontinued); "Jena Band of Choctaw Indians, Brief Historical Summary," Jena Band of Choctaw Indians, http://www.jenachoctaw.org/history.html (accessed 6 April 2011); "Proclaiming Certain Lands as a Reservation for the Jena Band of Choctaw Indians of Louisiana," *Federal Register* 72, no, 62 (2 April 2007), 15711–13.

49. BAR, "Summary under the Criteria: Jena Band of Choctaw Indians (JBCI)," 1994; Gregory, interview by author; Ernest C. Downs to Les Gay, 23 February 1978, HF, OFA; Klopotek, "The Long Outwaiting," 209–14; Dunbar, *Life, Letters, and Papers*, 209–10; Robin, *Voyage to Louisiana*, 188; Brackenridge, *Views of Louisiana*, 83; Sibley, "Historical Sketches"; Watt, "Federal Indian Policy," 39–44; Kniffen, Gregory, and Stokes, *The Historic Indian Tribes*.

50. BAR, "Historical Report: JBCI," 1; BAR, "Genealogical Report: JBCI"; BAR, "Historical Indian Tribes in Louisiana," 38, no date, UHN, OFA; Watt, "Federal Indian Policy," 87–92; Sharon Sholars Brown, "The Jena Choctaw," 181; Gregory, interview by author; Klopotek, "The Long Outwaiting," 214.

51. BAR, "Anthropological Report: JBCI"; "A History of the Jena Band," *Neka-Camon*, December 1991; Watt, "Federal Indian Policy," 66–67, 117; BAR, "Historical Report: JBCI," 29.

52. Parish Superintendent quoted in E. E. Richardson to John Overton, 10 May 1932, box "C.C.F. 1907–1939," folder "68776-31-800 pt 1," RG 75, NAB;

BAR, "Summary under the Criteria: JBCI," 1994; BAR, "Historical Report: JBCI," 16–18; BAR, "Genealogical Report: JBCI," 1–2; Senate, Committee on Indian Affairs, *Confirming the Federal Relationship, Jena Band*, 30 June 1993, 1; Senate, Select Committee, *Federal Recognition Mowa Band . . . Jena Band*, 28 March 1990, 268–70.

53. Watt, "Federal Indian Policy," 220–23.

54. BAR, Summary, Proposed Finding for Acknowledgment, Jena Band, 27 September 1994; BAR, "Anthropological Report: JBCI," BAR, "Historical Report: JBCI," 30; BAR, Summary, Proposed Finding; Watt, "Federal Indian Policy," 113–14.

55. Mississippi Band of Choctaw Indians (MBCI), "Resolution CHO-66-90," 20 February 1990, box 81, folder 41–47, Johnston Papers; Edna Groves to J. C. McCaskill, 12 December 1937, in Jena Band of Choctaw Indians, "Petition for Restoration," no box, no folders, GCIA; BAR, "Anthropological Report: JBCI," Gregory, "The Louisiana Tribes: Entering Hard Times," 167, 178–79; Drechsel and Maukuakane-Drechsel, "An Ethnohistory of 19th Century Louisiana Indians," 73.

56. BAR, "Anthropological Report: JBCI," 5–6.

57. "A History of Jena Band," *Neka-Camon*, December 1991; BAR, "Historical Report: JBCI," 30–38; Edna Groves to J. C. MaCaskill, 12 December 1937, A. C. Hector to Paul L. Fickinger, 15 December 1937, in JBCI "Petition for Restoration," GCIA; E. J. Armstrong to A.C. Hector, 24 June 1936, and Shapard testimony, Senate, Select Committee, *Recognition of Mowa Band . . . Jena Band*, 28 March 1990, 279, 260; John Collier to Caroline Dorman, 6 September 1935 and "Lost Indians of Louisiana to Be Sought," undated newspaper clipping, in Dorman Collection, NWSU; Roy Nash, "The Indians of Louisiana in 1931," HF, BAR; Ruth Underhill to Frank Speck, 22 October 1938, in Downs and Whitehead, "The Houma Indians," 13–14; A. C. Hector to Commissioner of Indian Affairs, 6 July 1937, and Ruth Underhill, "Report on a Visit to Indian Groups in Louisiana, Oct. 15–25, 1938," BIA, Central Classified Files, 1907–39, General Services, folder "68776-31-800. Pt 2," RG 75, NAB.

58. J. M. Steward to Education Division, 8 January 1938, A. C. Hector to Paul L. Fickinger, 15 December 1937, Edna Groves to J. C. MaCaskill, 12 December 1937, in JBCI, "Petition for Restoration," GCIA; William Zimmerman to L. W. Page, 11 July 1938, box 80, folder 40-23, Johnston Papers; L. W. Page to Commissioner of Indian Affairs, 22 July 1938, in JBCI, "Petition for Restoration," GCIA.

59. BAR, "Summary, Proposed Finding: JBCI"; BAR, "Historical Report: JBCI," 39; Watt, "Federal Indian Policy," 132–33, 154.

60. BAR, "Anthropological Report: JBCI," 11–12, 24–25; JBCI, "Petition for Restoration," GCIA; BAR, "Summary under the Criteria: JBCI," 1994.

61. Watt, "Federal Indian Policy," 169; Verret, interview by author.

62. "Annual Report, 1981–2," box P92-92, no folders, GCIA; Watt, "Federal Indian Policy" 168.

63. Gregory, interview by author; BAR, "Genealogical Report: JBCI," 2–3; Watt, "Federal Indian Policy," 176.

64. BAR, "Anthropological Report: JBCI," 17–23; BAR "Genealogical Report: JBCI," 5; BAR, "Summary under the Criteria: JBCI," 1994; JBCI, "Report of Activities," in "Annual Report, 1981–2," no boxes, GCIA; Gregory, "Jena Band," 9.

65. Bud Shapard to Jerry Jackson, 25 February 1989, box 80, folder 40-23, Johnston Papers; BAR, "Anthropological Report: JBCI," 17–22; James D. Hale to Sam Jackson, 25 April 1968, in JBCI, "Petition for Restoration," GCIA; Meeting Minutes, Board of Commissioners on Indian Affairs, 29 December 1983, box P92-92, folder "Finished Minutes," GCIA.

66. J. Bennett Johnston, testimony, Senate, Select Committee, *Recognition of Mowa Band . . . Jena Band,* 28 March 1990, 41; John Shapard to Jerry Jackson, 25 February 1990, box 80, folder 40-23, Johnston Papers; Gregory, "The Louisiana Tribes," 165; Gregory, interview by author; Watt, "Federal Indian Policy," 181–85, 201; OFA, "Petitioners by State," 29 October 1999, http://www.doi.gov/bia/bar/indexz.htm (accessed 6 April 2000; page discontinued); "Louisiana Choctaws Seek Federal Recognition," *Indian Affairs,* Fall 1979.

67. "Work Begins on Indian Reservation," *Baton Rouge Morning Advocate,* 16 March 1988; Chitimacha Tribal Resolution "CH-TC #2-90," 25 January 1990, Tunica-Biloxi Tribal Resolution #03-90, 7 January 1990, MBCI "Resolution CHO-66-90," 20 February 1990, box 81, folder 41-7, Johnston Papers.

68. "Jena Band of Choctaws Hosts Governor's group," newspaper clipping, in "Annual Report, 1987–8," no folders, GCIA; Buddy Roemer to J. Bennett Johnston, 27 October 1988, box 80, folder 40-23, Johnston Papers; Buddy Roemer to J. Bennett Johnston, 27 November 1989, Senate, Select Committee, *Recognition Mowa Band . . . Jena Band,* 77; "Annual Report, 1987–8," no folders, GCIA.

69. Jerry Jackson, testimony, Senate, Select Committee, *Recognition Mowa Band . . . Jena Band,* 28 March 1990, 45.

70. Daniel Inouye, testimony, Senate, Select Committee, *Recognition Mowa Band . . . Jena Band,* 28 March 1990, 1, 46–47; Eddie Brown to Senate Select Committee, 30 April 1990, box 80, folder 40-23, Johnston Papers; "Opening Statement of Hon. Bill Richardson," House, Committee on Natural Resources, Subcommittee on Native American Affairs, *Jena Band Confirmation Act,* 22 July 1993.

71. BAR, "Summary under the Criteria: JBCI"; BAR, "Historical Report: JBCI," 14.

72. Thirteenth Census of the U.S., Department of Commerce and Labor, 1910 Indian Population schedule, in Senate, Select Committee, *Recognition Mowa Band . . . Jena Band,* 28 March 1990, 272.

73. Ibid.; BAR, "Historical Report: JBCI," 19–25; Tams Bixby to Willis Jackson, 4 May 1903, Certificate "FULLBLOOD MISSISSIPPI CHOCTAW INDIANS," Willis Jackson and family, in JBCI, "Petition for Restoration," GCIA; Gregory, "Jena Band," 5; Debo, *The Rise and Fall of the Choctaw Republic*, 272–76; Lambert, *Choctaw Nation*, 47–50. See generally Debo, *And Still the Waters Run*.

74. BAR, "Summary under the Criteria: JBCI"; BAR, "Historical Report: JBCI," 40–43.

75. Department of the Interior, Notice of Receipt of Petition, Jena Band of Choctaw Indians, 27 February 1979, HF, BAR.

76. *Procedures*, C.F.R. Part 83 (1997); BAR, "Acknowledgment Guidelines," http://www.doi.gov/bia/bar/arguide.html (accessed 6 April 2000; page discontinued).

77. BAR, "Summary under the Criteria: JBCI."

78. BAR, "Historical Report: JBCI," 39–40; BAR, "Summary under the Criteria: JBCI"; BAR, "Anthropological Report: JBCI," 11–12, 24–25; M. Miller, *Forgotten Tribes*, ch. 5; quote from BAR, "Genealogical Report: JBCI," 14.

79. BAR, "Anthropological Report: JBCI," 7, 15–16, 19–20.

80. BAR, "Anthropological Report: JBCI," 1–2, 11–20, 24–25; photo, plaque in Tribal Office, Traditional Leadership, box 80, folder 40-24, Johnston Papers.

81. Interviewee's name withheld by request; Blood Quantum pie charts, Senate, Select Committee, *Recognition Mowa Band . . . Jena Band*, 28 March 1990, 268–69; BAR, "Genealogical Report: JBCI."

82. Deer quoted in BAR, "Summary under the Criteria: JBCI"; BAR, "Genealogical Report: JBCI," 1–2; JBCI, "Petition," GCIA; "Background on H.R. 2366," House, Committee on Natural Resources, Subcommittee on Native American Affairs, *Jena Band Confirmation Act*, 22 July 1992, 12.

83. Smith quoted in Klopotek, "The Long Outwaiting," 268.

CHAPTER 4

1. Weaver, interview by author.

2. Poarch Band of Creek Indians (PBCI) "Petition for Federal Recognition," 10 January 1980, 30–32, 81–83, PBCI, OFA; "Indians Would Organize for Political Work," *(Burlington, N.C.) Times-News*, 31 January 1958; Paredes, interview by author.

3. Lofton, "Reclaiming an American Indian Identity," 444.

4. Petition, "The Creek Nation East of the Mississippi, before the Indian Claims Commission," in box 4, Matte Papers; Tullis, interview by author.

5. BAR, "Anthropological Report on the Lower Muskogee Creek Tribe," 4, LMCT, OFA.

6. "Indians Finally to Be Paid Off," *Sarasota Journal*, 12 August 1963; "Creek Pow-Wow Is Held," *Tuscaloosa News*, 26 November 1976; PBCI, "Petition," 30–32, 59; "Eastern Creeks Paid for Land Taken Almost 175 Years Ago," *St. Petersburg Times*, 17 January 1987.

7. Tullis, interview by author; Paredes, interview by author; "Creek Chief Dies at 70," *Tuscaloosa News*, 11 June 1970.

8. PBCI, "Petition," 83; BAR, "Anthropological Report: LMCT," 4; Acting Deputy Assistant Secretary-Indian Affairs, "Recommendation for Proposed Finding against Federal Acknowledgment of the Principle Creek Nation (PCN)," 8 June 1985, PCN, OFA; BAR, "Anthropological Report: PCN," PCN, OFA, 12; Wright, *Creeks and Seminoles*, 238–39; Frank, *Creeks and Southerners*, 111.

9. BAR, "Anthropological Report: LMCT," 3–4; Tullis, interview by author; BAR, "Anthropological Report: PCN," 16–39; "Creek Indian Nation Pow-Wows on Beautiful Lake Jackson," *DeFuniak Herald*, 8 June 1972; Paredes, interview by author.

10. Articles of Incorporation, 23 February 1973, in LMCT, "Petition," 2; BAR, "Anthropological Report: LMCT," 3; Paredes, interview by author.

11. "Indians at Odds over Federal Money," *Gadsden Times*, 24 December 1984.

12. Houston L. McGhee, to Whom it May Concern, appointing McCormick and Thomley chiefs, 16 February 1973, in LMCT, "Petition"; Paredes, "The Emergence of Contemporary Eastern Creek Indian Identity," 75–76; Paredes, interview by author; Tullis, interview by author.

13. Tullis, interview by author; Paredes interview by author; Sutton, *The Man behind the Scenes*, 1–5, 17, 23, 59; Duncan, *Alabama Curiosities*, 111; "Neal 'Pappy' McCormick," Florida Folklife Program, Florida Division of Historical Resources, http://www.flheritage.com/preservation/folklife/ (accessed 22 February 2010.)

14. John Wesley Thomley, affidavit, 4 October 1978, in LMCT, "Petition," 223; "Creek Tribes Split in Fight for Funds" and "Creek Chief Dresses for TV," *Tampa Times*, 19 October 1976, available at "Series of Articles from the Tampa Times Newsaper," http://southernhistory.us/TampaTimes.htm (accessed 24 February 2010); Tullis, interview by author; "Creek Indians in Protest Ride," *Sarasota Herald-Tribune*, 9 May 1978.

15. Paredes, interview by author; Tullis, interview by author.

16. Rose Smith, interview by author; Sutton, *The Man behind the Scenes*, 139; Paredes, interview by author; BAR, "Anthropological Report: LMCT," 7; Lower Muskogee Creek Heritage Home Page, http://muskogee-heritage.tripod.com (accessed 22 February 2010).

17. BAR, "Anthropological Report: LMCT," 9; "Creek Tribes Split in Fight for Funds," *Tampa Times*, 19 October 1976, available at "Series of Articles from the Tampa Times Newsaper," http://southernhistory.us/TampaTimes.htm (accessed 24 February 2010).

18. "Creeks Return to Tama," undated newspaper clipping in Sutton, *The Man behind the Scenes*, 127; LMCT, "Petition."

19. "Indian Funds Are Sometimes Mispent," *Tampa Times*, 20 October 1976, available at "Series of Articles from the Tampa Times Newsaper," http://southernhistory.us/TampaTimes.htm (accessed 24 February 2010).

20. State of Georgia, *Proclamation*, 12 November 1976, signed by George Busbee, in LMCT, "Petition"; BAR, "Anthropological Report: LMCT," 5–6.

21. State of Georgia, *Proclamation*, 15 March 1973, signed by Jimmy Carter; State of Georgia, *Proclamation*, 12 November 1976, signed by George Busbee; Georgia State Senate, *A Resolution Recognizing the Muskogee-Creek Indian Tribe East of the Mississippi River*, 16 March 1973; Georgia House of Representatives, *A Resolution Recognizing the Muskogee-Creek Indian Tribe East of the Mississippi River*, 8 March 1973—all in LMCT "Petition"; BAR, "Anthropological Report: LMCT," 21; "Indians Angry," *Rome News-Tribune*, 27 September 1977; "40 Groups Are Seeking Recognition as Indians," *(Charleston, S.C.) News and Courier*, 11 July 1977.

22. BAR, "Ethnohistorical Report: LMCT," 42; "Group Aims to Preserve Indian Heritage," *Sarasota Herald-Tribune*, 15 July 1980.

23. Sutton, *The Man behind the Scenes*, 108, 112–21; BAR, "Anthropological Report: LMCT," 5–6.

24. BAR, "Ethnohistorical Report on the Southeastern Cherokee Confederacy, Inc. (SECC), et al.," 15–16, SECC, OFA.

25. Shapard, interview by author; "History and Goals of Our Nation," *Southeastern Cherokee Confederacy News*, March 1980; City of Sarasota Proclamation, 15 January 1981, in SECC, "Petition for Recognition," SECC, OFA.

26. "He Shouts Out Heritage," *Valdosta Daily Times*, reprinted in *Southeastern Cherokee Confederacy News*, March 1980.

27. Shapard, interview by author; "Creeks Seek Ways to Finance Council," *Florala News*, 10 December 1970.

28. BAR, "Anthropological Report: LMCT," 5–6; Paredes, interview by author; BAR, "Anthropological Report: PCN," 17; "Recreation of Old Indian Village Near Cairo Could Be a Significant Feature!," undated newspaper clipping, in Sutton, *The Man behind the Scenes*, 126.

29. State of Georgia, *Proclamation*, signed by Jimmy Carter, 15 March 1973, in LMCT, "Petition."

30. P. Deloria, *Playing Indian*, 155–60; "Creek Indian Nation Pow-Wows on Beautiful Lake Jackson," *DeFuniak Herald*, 8 June 1972; "Georgia News Briefs," *Rome News-Tribune*, 12 June 1973; LMCT, "Petition."

31. "There is a Need," advertisement for Lower Muskogee Creek Indian Tribe, no date, printed in Sutton, *The Man behind the Scenes*, 124–25; Smith, interview by author.

32. Quoted from Eric Hobsbawm, *The Invention of Tradition*, "Introduction: Inventing Traditions," 4; Meyer and Royer, *Selling the Indian*, xi–xiii; Lofton, "Reclaiming an American Indian Identity,"13–14; Walker, "Instant Indians," 16.

33. Paredes, interview by author; "Creek Indian Nation Pow-Wows on Beautiful Lake Jackson," *DeFuniak Herald*, 8 June 1972; Tullis, interview by author.

34. Berkhofer, *The White Man's Indian*; Bird, "Introduction," 3, 10; Hutchinson, *The Indian Craze*, 4; P. Deloria, *Playing Indian*, 101, 121–27; Ellis, "More Real," 4, 6–9.

35. P. Deloria, *Playing Indian*, 147; "Creek Tribes Split in Fight for Funds," *Tampa Times*, 19 October 1976, available at "Series of Articles from the Tampa Times Newsaper," http://southernhistory.us/TampaTimes.htm (accessed 24 February 2010).

36. Quoted in Walker, "Instant Indians," 17; Ellsworth and Dysart, "West Florida's Forgotten People: The Creek Indians," 430–33; Walker, "Instant Indians," 17.

37. Walker, "Instant Indians," 15, 18; "Creek Indian Nation's Rebirth Proclaimed by Descendants, *Tampa Times*, 18 October 1976, available at "Series of Articles from the Tampa Times Newsaper," http://www.southernhistory.us/TampaTimes/htm (accessed 24 February 2010).

38. "Indians Would Organize for Political Work," *Times-News*, 31 January 1958; "Creek Indian Nation's Rebirth Proclaimed by Descendants, *Tampa Times*, 18 October 1976, available at "Series of Articles from the Tampa Times Newspaper," http://www.southernhistory.us/TampaTimes/htm (accessed 24 February 2010).

39. Walker, "Instant Indians," 15, 18.

40. "Creek Indian Descendants Highlight 7th Happening," undated newspaper clipping, in Sutton, *The Man behind the Scenes*, 131.

41. "Creeks Meet Again: Indians Powwow on Ancient Tribal Land near Cairo," undated newspaper clipping in Sutton, *The Man behind the Scenes*, 130; Walker, "Instant Indians,"18.

42. P. Deloria, *Playing Indian*, 146.

43. "Indian Funds Are Sometimes Misspent, *Tampa Times*, 20 October 1976, available at "Series of Articles from the Tampa Times Newsaper," http://www.southernhistory.us/TampaTimes/htm (accessed 24 February 2010); Walker, "Instant Indians," 18.

44. Quoted in "Pow-Wow Marks July 4," undated newspaper clipping, in Sutton, *The Man behind the Scenes*, 129.

45. Lofton, interview by author.

46. Cited in Walker, "Instant Indians," 15, 18–19; Tribal Seal, photocopy in LMCT, "Petition"; "Creeks Return to Tama" and "Creeks Meet Again: Indians Powwow on Ancient Tribal Land Near Cairo," undated newspaper clippings in Sutton, *The Man behind the Scenes*, 127, 130.

47. Sutton, *The Man behind the Scenes,* 110; State of Georgia, *Proclamation,* 1973, signed by Jimmy Carter, in LMCT, "Petition"; Walker, "Instant Indians," 19. Other Creek descendants expressed similar sentiments of just feeling something "deep inside" that they were Indian. "Creek Indians Revive, Rich, Hidden Heritage," *Ocala Star-Banner,* 16 September 1984.

48. Quoted in "Pow-Wow Marks July 4," "Lower Creek Indian Village of Eufaula Antedates 1733," and "Creek Indian Descendants Highlight 7th Happening," undated newspaper clippings in Sutton, *The Man behind the Scenes,* 129–33; "2nd Pow Wow Held," *Thomasville Times-Enterprise,* 9 July 1974.

49. Quoted in "2nd Pow Wow Held," *Thomasville Times-Enterprise,* 9 July 1974; Walker, "Instant Indians," 15–17, 20–21; Lofton, interview by author; Lofton, "Reclaiming an American Indian Identity," 483.

50. Walker, "Instant Indians," 20.

51. Neal McCormick to Assistant Secretary-Indian Affairs, transmitting Petition, October 1978, LMCT, OFA; Foreman, *The Five Civilized Tribes,* 152; Director, Office of Indian Services, "Recommendation for Final Determination That the Lower Muskogee Creek Tribe . . . Does Not Exist as an Indian Tribe," 17 September 1981, LMCT, OFA; "Locate and Notify" list (1978 era), HF, OFA; Frederick Ferguson, Solicitor, to Neal McCormick, 26 April 1977, HF, OFA.

52. Wesley Thomley to Marvin L. Franklin, 21 March 1973, in LMCT Files, OFA.

53. Paredes, "Back from Disappearance: The Alabama Creek Indian Community," 139. See similar statements in Paredes, "The Emergence," 74, Paredes, "Paradoxes of Modernism," 343, Paredes, "Some Creeks Stayed," 698; Paredes, interview by author.

54. See: "Creek Indian Nation's Rebirth Proclaimed by Descendants," *Tampa Times,* 18 October 1976, available at "Series of Articles from the Tampa Times Newsaper," http://www.southernhistory.us/TampaTimes/htm (accessed 24 February 2010).

55. Quinn, "Southeast Syndrome," 147, 149, 151; Walker, "Instant Indians," 15–26; interview, name withheld at request of interviewee.

56. Paredes, "Paradoxes of Modernism," 342.

57. Deputy Assistant Secretary-Indian Affairs, "Recommendation for Proposed Finding against Federal Acknowledgment: PCN," 8 June 1984; Theodore Krenzke, "Recommendation for Final Determination: LMCT," 17 September 1981, and Acting Deputy Commissioner, "Recommendation for Proposed Finding: LMCT," 29 January 1981, LMCT, OFA.

58. Neal McCormick to House, Committee on Interior, letter in House, Committee on Interior, *Federal Recognition,* 10 August 1978; LMCT, "Petition," LMCT, OFA.

59. "Recommendation for Final Determination: LMCT," LMCT, OFA. Gilbert provided an early overview of what he called the "larger" mixed-blood racial islands in the eastern United States. He details the current MOWA Choctaw group of Alabama and the nearby "Creoles." He does not mention the Poarch Creeks by name, only noting that Alabama has "Creeks" in a class of additional groups "no less worthy of notice." Gilbert, "Memorandum concerning the Characteristics of the Larger Mixed-Blood Racial Islands," 447. The more significant work by Edward T. Price surveyed "White-Negro-Indian" groups in the eastern states. It does not mention Creek groups or show a group in southwest Georgia or southern Alabama beyond the MOWA group. This is likely because of his focus on African American admixture. Price, "A Geographic Analysis," 138–55. Similarly Horace Bond's earlier study "Two Racial Islands in Alabama" focuses on the Creoles and ancestral MOWA group. Because of his focus on African ancestry he also does not mention the Poarch Creeks. Bond, "Two Racial Islands in Alabama," 552–67. The lack of inclusion of any possible ancestral groups related to the Lower Muskogee Creek organization may stem from the fact these groups were considered white or Indian–white and thus not of interest to the researcher. See also Berry, *Almost White*; Griessman, editor, "The American Isolates"; Paredes and Lenihan, "Native American Population," 45–56. Frank Speck, the foremost scholar of isolated eastern Indian groups in the mid-twentieth century, studied the Poarch Creeks but makes no mention of the LMCT or other bands in Georgia. Speck, "Notes on the Social and Economic Conditions," 194–98. Government investigations in the 1930s of potential surviving Indian groups in the Southeast, particularly one conducted by Samuel H. Thompson, visited the MOWA community and Poarch community but did not include the ancestors of the LMCT or related groups. Samuel H. Thompson, "Report on Visit to Southern Alabama," box 4, Matte Papers; Tullis, interview by author.

60. BAR, "Recommendation and Summary of Evidence . . . against Federal Acknowledgment of the LMCT," 29 January 1981, LMCT, OFA; BAR, "Genealogical Report: LMCT," 13.

61. Smith, interview by author; Wilma Trulock, interview by author; BIA, "Creeks East of the Mississippi," Clarification Notice, *Federal Register* 47, no. 66, Tuesday April 8, 1982, Notices, 14783–84; Acting Deputy Assistant Secretary-Indian Affairs, "Recommendation and Summary of Evidence for Proposed Finding against Federal Acknowledgment," PCN, 8 June 1985, PCN, OFA; Lofton, interview by author.

62. Nagel, *American Indian Ethnic Renewal*, 9; Bryant and LaFramboise, "The Racial Identity and Cultural Orientation of Lumbee American Indian High School Students," 87; Royce, *Ethnic Identity*, 22. For intermarriage rates within an ethnic group as an indicator of group cohesion, see Waters, *Ethnic Options*, 102–13.

63. Claude Cox to Ernest Stevens, 25 April 1977, AIPRC, *Final Report, Appendices*, Vol. II, 5; Director, Office of Indian Services, "Recommendation for Final Determination" on LMCT, 17 September 1981; Lofton, "Reclaiming an American Indian Identity," 320; Paredes, interview by author.

64. "Sites of Ancient Culture Could be Destroyed," *Macon Telegraph*, 5 November 2003; "Indian Skull Will Rejoin Tribe," *Atlanta Journal and Constitution*, 11 November 1999.

65. Tullis, interview by author; BIA, "Final Determination That the Lower Muskogee Creek Tribe-East of the Mississippi Does Not Exist as an Indian Tribe," *Federal Register* 46, no. 203, October 21, 1981, 51652; Smith, interview by author.

66. Taylor quoted in Matte, *They Say the Wind*, 163; Shapard, interview by author; Johnnie Andrews Jr., "Origins of the Mowa Band of Choctaws: A Critique" (report commissioned by PBCI), 1991, box 4, Matte Papers; Phillip Martin to Senator Daniel Inouye, 1991, in Senate, Select Committee on Indian Affairs, *Federal Recognition of the Mowa Band of Choctaw Indians*, 26 June 1991, 244; BAR, "Summary under the Criteria and Evidence for Proposed Finding against Federal Acknowledgment of the MOWA Band of Choctaw Indians (MBCI)," 16 December 1994, MBCI, OFA. After the MOWA appeal was denied the finding became final in 1999.

67. MOWA Band, "Historical Report on the Mowa Band," 20 August 1984, box 4, and Poll Tax Records, Washington, County, Alabama, 1892, box 9, Matte Papers; BAR, "Proposed Finding: MBCI."

68. Wilford Longhair Taylor to Cherokee Nation of Oklahoma, 8 September 2006, MOWA Band Headquarters, Mt. Vernon, Alabama; BAR, "Technical Reports: MBCI," 21–23, 43, 47–56. For racial ideology, see Fields, "Slavery, Race and Ideology."

69. Murphy, "The Cajans of Mobile County," 499; BAR, "Technical Reports: MBCI," 34–37; Weaver, interview by author; Matte, *They Say the Wind Is Red*, 107–8; "Of Turpentine, Timber and Chemical Plants," *Mobile Press-Register*, 18 December 2001, http://www.al.com/ (accessed 8 September 2008); Bond, "Two Racial Islands in Alabama," 563.

70. Price, "Mixed-Blood Populations of the Eastern United States," 50; Matte, *They Say the Wind Is Red*, 111–20; "Missionary Recalls MOWA Days," (*Mobile*) *Daily Press*, 12 October 1994; Greissman and Henson, "An Ethnic Island in Alabama," 105; Matte, interview by author.

71. Obra Rogers, "Among the Cajuns of Alabama," *Trained Lay Worker*, 2, no. 5 (December 1929), 1; Griessman and Henson, "An Ethnic Island in Alabama," 103–5; quote from Murphy, "The Cajans of Mobile County," 500; Edward B. Freeman to Rev. Elbert Isbell, 11 March 1981, no box, folder "MBCI: Response to MOWA Band of Choctaw Indians to Dec. 16, 1994," Callahan Papers; "Mix Appeal Dismissed," newspaper clipping, 1962, box 4, Matte Papers;

Samuel H. Thompson, Report on Trip to Alabama, "Mobile County," 1934, box 4, Matte Papers; Weaver, interview by author; Todd Johnston, interview by author.

72. Weaver, interview by author; "Of Turpentine," *Mobile Press-Register*, 18 December 2001; oral interview, Roosevelt Weaver, 16 August 1983, Mowa Choctaw Oral History Collection, tape 5, University Archives, University of South Alabama.

73. *Act No. 79-228, Creating "Mowah Band of Choctaw Indian Commission," Alabama Laws of the Legislature of Alabama, Organizational Session, 1979, Vol. I,* 350; Weaver, interview by author; Senate, Select Committee, *Recognition of MOWA Band of Choctaw Indians,* 28 March 1990, 124–27; Matte, *They Say the Wind Is Red,* 144, 150–52; "Mowa Choctaw Indian Spring Festival, *Alabama Indian Advocate,* May 1981, 2; "Committee Meeting Addresses State Recognition," *Alabama Indian Advocate* 1, no. 6 (January/February 1982), 1.

74. Deloria quoted in Matte, *They Say the Wind Is Red,* 11; Matte, interview by author.

75. BAR, "Proposed Finding: MBCI," 5; Senate, Select Committee, *Recognition of the MOWA Band of Choctaw Indians,* 28 March 1990, *Federal Recognition of the MOWA Band of Choctaw Indians, Hearing on S. 362,* 26 June 1991; House, Committee on Interior, *Federal Acknowledgment of Various Indian Groups, Hearing on HR 2349 et al,* 8 July 1992 ; Sonny Callahan to Framon Weaver, 27 December 1990, no box, folder "21002 Mowa Band of Choctaw Indians, 1990," Callahan Papers; Davis, interview by author.

76. Stoeffle, interview by author.

77. MOWA Band, "Preliminary Petition/Historical Report," box 4, Matte Papers; MOWA Band, "The Five Points: Critique of BAR Technical Report," Jacqueline A. Matte personal files, Birmingham, Alabama; Stockel, *Shame and Endurance,* 69–99; Douglas L. McCoy, Memorandum on "S. 362: MOWA Band of Choctaw Recognition Act," 12 July 1991, box 4 Matte Papers; Matte, interview by author; Wilford "Longhair" Taylor, interview by author.

78. 25 C.F.R. § 83.7.

79. BAR, "Proposed Finding: MBCI"; Tullis, interview by author; Cherokee Nation, FITF Files, Tahlequah, Oklahoma; Phillip Martin to Daniel K. Inouye, 12 July 1991, box 8, Matte Papers.

80. Perdue, "A Sprightly Lover," 165–71; Logan and Ousley, "Hypergamy, Quantum, and Reproductive Success," 184–85.

81. For a good summary, see Griessman, editor, "The American Isolates," 693. Also: Parenton and Pellegrin, "The Sabines," 48–54.

82. Bond, "Two Racial Islands in Alabama," 555–65.

83. Murphy, "The Cajans of Mobile County," 498; Rogers, "Among the Cajuns of Alabama," 1; Thompson, Report on Trip to Southern Alabama, 1934, box 4, Matte Papers.

84. Carmer, *The Stars Fell on Alabama*, 256–62; long citation from Matte, *They Say the Wind Is Red*, 19.

85. Thompson, report of trip to Alabama, box 4, Matte Papers.

86. Gilbert, "Memorandum concerning the Characteristics of the Larger Mixed-Blood Racial Islands," 438.

87. Berry, *Almost White*, 9, 15–16, 90, 136; Griessman and Henson, "The History and Social Topography of an Ethnic Island in Alabama," 102; Stopp, "On Mixed-Racial Isolates," 344; Price, "Mixed-Blood Populations of the Eastern United States," 50, 54–55; Price, "A Geographic Analysis of White-Negro-Indian Racial Mixtures," 144–45.

88. Pollitzer, "The Cajuns of Southern Alabama," 1–6. Pollitzer had earlier printed a similar yet preliminary report also concluding that the "Cajans" had little Indian ancestry, as reflected in his analysis of blood samples. Pollitzer, "The Physical Anthropology and Genetics of Marginal People in the Southeastern United States," 730.

89. Clifford, *The Predicaments of Culture*, 285–90; interviewees' names withheld by request when discussing sensitive subject; Shapard, interview by author. Jack Campisi later furthered the examination of the Mashpee in *The Mashpee Indians: Tribe on Trial.*

90. Murphy, "The Cajans of Mobile County," 498; Thompson, Report on Trip to Alabama, 5; Price, "Mixed-Blood Populations of the Eastern United States," 51, 56–57; Matte, interview by author.

91. Transcript of the Record, Circuit Court of Washington County, Alabama, *In the Cause of Percy Reed*, 18 October 1920, box 8, Matte Papers; MOWA Band, "Timeline for Choctaw Indians in Alabama From 1813–2003," Jacqueline A. Matte personal files; BAR, "Technical Reports: MBCI," 44–45; T. B Pearson, Superintendent of Education, Washington County, interview transcript, 17 June 1985, box 9 Matte Collection. See generally Pascoe, "Miscegenation Law."

92. Matte, *They Say the Wind Is Red*, 155.

93. Under a 1994 reform the Branch of Acknowledgment and Research instituted the expedited procedure intended to speed the process; it ultimately did not aid the Mow Band. 25 C.F.R. § 83; BAR, "Proposed Finding: MBCI"; Virginia DeMarce, interview by author.

94. MOWA Band, "The Five Points"; BAR, "Technical Reports: MBCI."

95. Census extracts of Monroe, Mobile and Washington Counties listed MOWA ancestors as mulatto, white, and colored; some were listed as black. Extract 1850 Census, Monroe County, Alabama; Extract 1860 Census, Monroe County, Alabama; Extract Census, 1850 Mobile County, Alabama—all in unprocessed collection, MOWA Choctaw Cultural Museum, MOWA Reservation, Mt. Vernon, Alabama; Mills cited in MOWA Band, "The Five Points," 34; Forbes, *Africans and Native Americans*, 3–4, 89–99, 240.

96. BAR, "Technical Reports: MBCI," 30–33, 42–46.

97. BAR, "Technical Reports: MBCI," 6, 30, 33, 42–44, 46; Wright, *The Only Land They Knew*, 281.

98. Cramer, *Cash, Color, and Colonialism*; Greenbaum, "What's In A Label?" 107–9; Matte, interview by author; Matte, "Extinction by Reclassification," 168, 180; Taylor, interview by author; Sturm, *Blood Politics*; William Quinn, Jr., interview by author; Shapard, interview by author. Other interviewees' names withheld by request.

99. Posey, "Origin, Development," 177–92.

100. BAR, "Technical Reports: MBCI," 52–61, 97–98; MOWA Band, "Five Points."

101. BAR, "Technical Reports: MBCI," 54, 61, 102, 111.

102. BAR, "Technical Reports: MBCI," 68, 83, 87, 117.

103. Memorandum, Holly Reckord to Deborah Maddox, 11 March 1998, no box, folder "Mowa Choctaw BIA Recognition Folder, 1 of 2," Callahan Papers.

104. BAR, "Technical Reports: MBCI," 58, 71; Wilford "Longhair" Taylor to Sonny Callahan, 20 January 1998, folder "Mowa Choctaw BIA, 1 of 2," Callahan Papers.

105. Phillip Martin to Daniel K. Inouye, 12 July 1991, box 8, Matte Papers.

106. Johnnie Andrews, Jr., "Origins of the Mowa Band of Choctaws: A Critique," commissioned by PBCI, preface, 3; "Poarch Boss: MOWAs Not Going by the Rules," *Mobile Press-Register*, 22 May 1991.

107. Tullis, interview by author.

CHAPTER 5

1. Poteete, interview by author; "So-called 'Southern Cherokees' Claims False," *Cherokee Advocate* 24, no. 3 (2000).

2. King, interview by author. Chief Chad Smith calls a legal definition of Indian a "safe harbor" with little ambiguity—you are either a citizen of a federally recognized tribe or not. Garroutte, *Real Indians*, 31.

3. Cobb, "Devils in Disguise," 465–90; "Indians Claim Outsiders Stoke Cherokee Dispute," newspaper clipping, no date, Vertical Files, Special Collections (SC), NSU; "Report of Meeting of the Inter-Tribal Council of the Five Civilized Tribes," 11 September 1974, box 34, folder 4, Bartlett Collection.

4. "Indian Chief Tells Askew: Tribes Are Cropping up All over Florida," *St. Petersburg Times*, 3 March 1976.

5. "Swimmer Files for Re-Election," *Cherokee County Chronicle*, 31 March 1983; Ira Philips to Ross Swimmer, 8 February 1984, and Ross Swimmer to Lamar Alexander, 8 May 1984, box 9:1, folder 3, Swimmer Papers; Jack Baker, interview by author.

6. Wilma Mankiller, Resume, Vertical Files, SC, NSU; "Cherokee Leader Will Use Position for Economic Development," *Tulsa World*, 17 November 1985; "Chief Mankiller Seeks Full Four-Year Term," *Cherokee Advocate*, March 1987; "Cherokee Leader Faces Determined Election Foes," *Tulsa Tribune*, 22 April 1987; campaign letter, "Cherokee Nation Deputy Chief," Vertical Files, SC, NSU; Richard Allen, interview by author.

7. Senate, Committee on Indian Affairs, *Federal Recognition*, 13 July 1995, 217–41; OFA, "List of Petitioners," 15 February 2007, http://www.bia.gov/ (accessed 6 May 2008); *Northern Cherokee Newsletter*, December 1984, box 20, folder 3, Swimmer Papers; Cherokee Nation, Fraudulent Indian Task Force (FITF), "Wannabe Tribe List," http://taskforce.cherokee.org (accessed 14 November 2008).

8. See generally Taylor, *The States and Their Indian Citizens*, and M. Miller, *Forgotten Tribes*, ch. 6.

9. Allen, et al., "Stealing Sovereignty"; Federal Regional Council of New England, Memo on Federal Recognition, 30 January 1975, box 277, folder "Region I," RG 220, NACP; Sturm, "States of Sovereignty."

10. Ross Swimmer to Lamar Alexander, 8 May 1984, Tomah to Red Clay Brothers, 4 May 1984, Leonard Bradley to Etowah Cherokee Nation, 3 February 1984, and Alvin O. Langdon to Hugh Gibbs, 1 November 1980, box 9:1, folder 3, Swimmer Papers; BAR, "Ethnohistorical Report: Southeastern Cherokee Confederacy (SECC)," 42; "Group Aims to Preserve Indian Heritage," *Sarasota Herald-Tribune*, 15 July 1980; Department of the Interior, "Final Determination That the SECC et al. Do Not Exist as Indian Tribes," 26 September 1985, 50 *Federal Register* 50, no. 187 (26 September 1985), 39047.

11. "Georgia, Oklahoma Indians in Dispute Over Housing Fund," *Rome News-Tribune*, 16 March 1994.

12. Frank Pollard to Wilma Mankiller, 23 March 1995, box 3, folder 3, and Wilma Mankiller to Zell Miller, 4 May 1993, box 16, folder 9, Mankiller Papers; "Tribes Dispute Rising Claims of American Indian Roots," *Wall Street Journal*, 30 October 1996; Janda, *Beloved Women*, 120.

13. Resolution 00-008, Joint Council of the Cherokee Nation and the Eastern Band of Cherokee Indians, 9 April 2008, FITF files; Resolution No. 09-07, Inter-tribal Council of the Five Civilized Tribes, 21 May 2009, transcribed on Indianz.com, http://ns2.indianz.com/boardx/topic.asp?TOPIC_ID=37248 (accessed 7 Oct 2012).

14. Allen, interview by author; "Tennessee Lt. Governor Pushing Indian Tribe Legislation," *Cherokee Phoenix Online*, http://cherokeephoenix.org/ (accessed 9 June 2009); House Bill 1692, Tennessee State Legislature, transcribed on Indians.com, http://ns2.indianz.com/boardx/topic.asp?TOPIC_ID=36663 (accessed 7 October 2012); Alfred Berryhill, Second Chief Muskogee Nation, testimony on HB 1692 and SB 1978, 12 May 2009 and Hank Hayes, "Tennessee

House Panel OKs Native American legislation," *timesnews.net*, 6 May 2009, http://www.timesnews.net/article/php? (accessed 16 June 2009); Joyce Bear, interview by author.

15. Stowe, "Uncolored People," 74; Waters, *Ethnic Options*, 147; Waters, "Optional Ethnicities: For Whites Only?" 96–107; Nagel, *American Indian Ethnic Renewal*, 11, 20–25. Speaking for an earlier period (the late nineteenth century) historian Robert H. Wiebe also found that white ethnic groups such as Germans, Italians, and Poles largely had the choice to identify with their ancestral heritage or not. Wiebe, *Who We Are*, 87.

16. Baker, interview by author; Patti Jo King, interview by author; Allen, interview by author. Christina Taylor Beard-Moose has detailed feelings of disdain, amusement, and anger among Cherokees in North Carolina about the "Cherokee princess" phenomenon. Beard-Moose, *Public Indians*, 126–28.

17. Thornton, *The Cherokees*, 74–75; Waters, *Ethnic Options*, 156–64; Sturm, *Blood Politics*, 207; Omi and Winant, *Racial Formation*, 80–81; Hamill, *Going Indian*; Meyer and Royer, *Selling the Indian*, xii–xviii.

18. "Creek Indian Nation's Rebirth Proclaimed by Descendants, *Tampa Times*, 18 October 1976, available at "Series of Articles from the Tampa Times Newspaper," http://www.southernhistory.us/TampaTimes.htm (accessed 24 February 2010).

19. Baker, interview by author; Cara Cowan Watts, e-mail correspondence with author.

20. King, interview by author; Allen, interview by author; Lambert, *Choctaw Nation*, 41, 190–97; Fixico, "Witness to Change," 2–4; Cowan Watts, e-mail correspondence.

21. Allen, interview by author.

22. Barker, "Indian U.S.A.," 43; Parsley, "Regulation of Counterfeit Indian Arts," 487–514; Hapiuk, "Of Kitsch and Kachinas," 1009–75; See generally McLerran, *A New Deal for Native American Art*.

23. Barker, "Indian U.S.A.," 43–45; Criss Smith, interview by author; LaVelle, Review of Ward Churchill; King, interview by author. While the exact numbers are debated, some individuals did refuse to enroll and accept allotment in Indian Territory. Chang, *The Color of the Land*, 96–97.

24. "Indian Circle Links Tribal Websites," *Seminole Tribune*, 8 May 1998, http://www.seminoletribe.com/tribune/98/may9/indiancircle.shtml (accessed 11 June 2009; page discontinued); King, interview by author; Criss Smith, interview by author; Root, *Cannibal Culture*, 81–83.

25. Criss Smith, interview by author; King, interview by author; Chad Garrison, "Going Native," *Riverfront Times*, http://www.riverfronttimes.com/2006-11-01/news/going-native (accessed 19 May 2011).

26. Wernitznig, *Going Native*, 10; "Cherokees Cry Foul: Fake Cherokees Cashing In On Music Industry," *Free Press*, 13 September 2007, http://www.free-

press-release.com/news/200709/1189741684.html (accessed 9 October 2012), and "Walela, Douglas Blue Feather, Rita Coolidge among Fake Native American Recording Artists," *Free-press-release.com*, 28 January 2008, http://www.free-press-release.com/news/200801 (accessed 16 June 2009); "Rita Coolidge to Appear in Major Native American Conference," New Mexico Film Office, http://www.nmfilm.com/ (accessed 22 July 2009; page discontinued); Walela Web Site, http://www.walela.com/IndianArtistArticle.html (accessed 22 July 2009; site discontinued).

27. Five Tribes Foundation, Report on Area Arts and Crafts Program, 30 June 1973, box 18, folder 150, Keeler Papers; "Truth in Advertising Act," Cherokee Nation, http://taskforce.cherokee.org/ (accessed 14 November 2008); "Mankiller Committed to Solving Rural Cherokee Problems," *Tahlequah Daily Press*, 5 April 1987.

28. "Citizenship Defined," *Tahlequah Daily Press*, 10 September 2008; "Truth in Advertising for Native Art Act," Cherokee Nation, http://taskforce.cherokee.org/ (accessed 14 November 2008); Travis Snell, "Art Act in Effect at Holiday," *Cherokee Phoenix*, no date, http://www.cherokeephoenix.org/ (accessed 9 June 2009).

29. Mooney, interview by author; Cain quoted in Travis Snell, "Art Act in Effect at Holiday," *Cherokee Phoenix*, no date, http://www.cherokeephoenix.org/ (accessed 9 June 2009); Harjo quoted in Betty Smith, "Indian Identity Remains in Question," *Tahlequah Daily Press*, 1 September 2008, http://www.tahlequahdailypress.com/ (accessed 20 February 2009); Lerch, *Waccamaw*, 135–36.

30. Allen, interview by author; Allen, "The Impact of New Age Shamans," 12–15. See generally Winzeler, *Anthropology and Religion*; Wallis, *Shamans/Neo-Shamans*; Wernitznig, *Going Native*.

31. King, interview by author; Root, *Cannibal Culture*, 88–101.

32. King, interview by author; Traditional Elders' Circle resolution of 1980, quoted in Root, *Cannibal Culture*, 95. See also: Fikes, *Carlos Castaneda*, and Castaneda, *The Teachings of Don Juan*.

33. "'Peyote Priest' Could Lose His Freedom," *Arizona Daily Star*, 7 January 2001; Debbie Hummel, "Utah High Court OKs Non-Indian Peyote Use," Associated Press, no date (June 2004), http://www.cognitiveliberty.org/news/utah_peyote_case.html (accessed 29 July 2009); "Bill Would Require Proof to Use Peyote," *Daily Herald Post*, 18 January 2006; Fikes, *Carlos Castaneda*, xxvi–vii; Castaneda, *The Teachings of Don Juan*.

34. Allen, interview by author; Allen, "The Impact of New Age Shamans," 7; Editorial, *Indian Country Today*, 21 August 1995; Richard Peacock, "Tribal Wisdom: A Native American View of Male and Female," interview with Harley Swiftdeer Reagan, *In Context: A Quarterly of Humane Sustainable Culture* (Spring 1987), http://www.context.org/ICLIB/IC16/Reagan.htm (accessed 22

February 2010); Root, *Cannibal Culture*, 88–90; newspaper clipping, *Phoenix New Times*, 13 June 2002, in FITF files.

35. AIM, Ministry for Information, posting, http://www.aimmovement. org/moipr/churchill05.html (accessed 11 June 2009; site discontinued); "Tribe Snubs Prof," *Rocky Mountain News Online*, 18 May 2005, http://www. rockymountainnews.com/drmn/local/article (accessed 11 June 2009; page discontinued); Churchill, "Using Indian Names for Sports Teams," 18–25; "Honest Injun? The Incidence of Fake Indians Is Almost Epidemic," *National Review*, 28 March 2005; "Steve Russell: Fighting the Ferengi Clan," *Indian Country Today*, 5 June 2009; King, interview by author; two interviewees' names withheld here by request when discussing a sensitive matter.

36. Allen, interview by author; Scott Jaschik, "Concern over Michigan Tenure Case," 10 March 2008, http://www.insidehighered.com/news/2008/03/10/ smith (accessed 30 July 2009); Steve Russell, "Addressing Ethnic Frauds," *Indianz.com*, 4 April 2008, http://ns2.indianz.com/News/2008/008005.asp (accessed 9 October 2012); South End Press, http://www.southendpress.org/ authors/258 (accessed 30 July 2009).

37. Cornsilk, quoted in Nagel, "False Faces," 93.

38. Mary Annette Pember, "Ethnic Fraud?," *Diverse: Issues in Higher Education*, 1 November 2007, http://diverseeducation.com/article/9984 (accessed 12 November 2012); Pewewardy, "Will the 'Real' Indians Please Stand Up?," 36–42; various anonymous interviews, 1998–2009, names withheld by request when discussing this sensitive issue; "Admission to Haskell Indian Nations University," http://haskell.edu/ (accessed 7 December 2009); Sunray, interview by author.

39. Dub Maxwell to Parent/Guardian, no date, and "Administration Budget Contract," Lost Cherokee Nation and Wonderview School District, 8 March 2004, in FITF files; Craig Henry, "Indian Grant Money Went to Wrong Students," *Native Journal*, 22 June 2006; Max Brantley, "When Is an Indian Not an Indian? Arkansas Schools Are Finding out the Hard Way," *Arkansas Times*, 22 September 2005, http://www.arktimes.com/arkansas/when-is-an-indian-not-an-indian/Content?oid=865649 (accessed 10 October 2012); Northern Cherokee Nation of Arkansas, Application Letter, no date, Vertical Files, OHS.

40. PowerPoint presentation, FITF files; BAR, "Evaluation of the Kaweah Indian Nation (KIN) Petition," and "Recommendation for Proposed Finding against the Kaweah Indian Nation," 13 June 1984, KIN, OFA; *Southeastern Cherokee Confederacy News*, March 1980; BAR, "Proposed Finding against the Southeastern Cherokee Confederacy (SECC)," September 1985, SECC, OFA; "Kaweah Chief, Tribe Sports Tumultuous History," *JournalStar.com*, 23 June 2007, http://journalstar.com/ (accessed 10 October 2012); Allen, interview by author; "Statement of Jacqueline Johnson," NCAI website, http://www.ncai.org/ (accessed 11 June 2009); Roxana Hegeman, "Unrecognized Indian Tribe

Found Guilty of Defrauding Immigrants," AAANativeArts.com, http://www. aaanativearts.com/ (accessed 10 October 2012); Roxana Hegeman, "Fraud Trial Begins for Disputed Chief," *USA Today*, http://usatoday30.usatoday. com/news/nation/2008-08-05-2588347752_x.htm (accessed 10 October 2012); "American Indian Tribe Called Bogus," Associated Press, azcentral.com, http://www.azcentral.com/offbeat/articles/2008/05/05/20080505sham-tribe0505-ON.html (accessed 11 June 2009).

41. Pewewardy, "Beyond Our Names"; Omi and Winant, *Racial Formation*, 18. See also Weaver, "Indigenous Identity."

42. "The Five Civilized Tribes Intertribal Council Mascot Resolution, Resolution No. 2001-08," available at BRIDGES, University of North Dakota, http://www.und.nodak.edu/org/bridges/itcfct.html (accessed 3 March 2008); "Sucking the Quileute Dry," *New York Times*, 8 February 2010.

43. "Tribe Names Can't Be Trademarks Court Rules in Mohegan," *Indian Country Today*, 28 February 2001; *Cherokee Nation Notice of Opposition, In re Cherokee Nation v. Southern Cherokee Nation*, 7 February 2007, in FITF files.

44. Testimony of Wilma Mankiller, Senate, Committee on Indian Affairs, *Federal Recognition*, 13 July 1995, 211–16.

45. King, interview by author; various confidential correspondences, 1998–2010; Baird, "Are the Five Tribes of Oklahoma 'Real' Indians?"

46. Testimony of Michell Hicks, House, Committee on Natural Resources, *Hearing on HR 898: Recognition of the Lumbee*, 1 April 2004, 33–40.

47. Baker, interview by author; House, Committee on Natural Resources, *Hearing on HR 4228 and S 282*, 17 May 1994; Senate, Committee on Indian Affairs, *Hearing on S 611*, 28 April 1989; Testimony of Phillip Martin, Senate, Select Committee on Indian Affairs, *Federal Acknowledgment*, 5 May 1989, 268–71.

48. Senate, Select Committee on Indian Affairs, *Federal Recognition of the Lumbee*, 12 August 1988, 35.

49. Chad Smith, e-mail correspondence to Cherokee citizens, 22 May 2009, posted on http://www.timesnews.net/ (accessed 16 June 2009).

50. Mooney, interview by author; Cowan Watts, e-mail correspondence with author.

51. Chad Smith, correspondence with author; Poteete, interview by author.

52. Russell, "Fighting the Ferengi Clan," *Indian Country Today*, 5 June 2009; King, interview by author.

53. Chad Smith, editorial, *Indian Country Today*, 9 March 2007; Jeninne Lee-St. John, "The Cherokee Nation's New Battle, *Time.com*, 21 June 2007, http://www.time.com/time/nation/article/0,8599,1635873,00.html (accessed 16 June 2009); "Freedmen Protest Chief's Award," *Cherokee Phoenix*, 9 June 2009.

54. "Non-Recognized 'Cherokee Tribes'," *Cherokee Phoenix*, archives, no date, http://www.cherokeephoenix.org/ (accessed 9 June 2009).

55. Cherokee Nation (Fraudulent Indian) Task Force, http://taskforce. cherokee.org (accessed 14 November 2008); Poteete, interview by author; Allen, interview by author; Baker interview by author; Sunray, interview by author.

56. "Questions Stoke Ward Churchill's Firebrand Past," *Denver Post*, 13 February 2005, http://www.denverpost.com/harsanyi/ci_0002709008 (accessed 10 October 2012); King, interview by author; Sunray, interview by author.

57. Wilford "Longhair" Taylor, to Cherokee Nation, 8 September 2006, in possession of author.

58. Sunray, interview by author; Sturm, *Blood Politics*, 203; Jacobs quoted in "Cowan's 'Indian wars,'" *Tahlequah Daily Press*, 29 August 2008; Conley quoted in "Art Act in Effect at Holiday," *Cherokee Phoenix Online*, http://www. cherokeephoenix.org/2389/Article.aspx (accessed 9 June 2009); Murray quoted in "Who's Appropriating?," letter to the editor, *Tahlequah Daily Press*, 3 September 2008.

59. King, interview by author.

60. See, for example, Senate, Select Committee on Indian Affairs, *Federal Recognition of the Lumbee*, 12 August 1988, *Recognition of the MOWA Band*, 28 March 1990; House, Committee on Natural Resources, *Federal Recognition*, 31 March 2004.

61. "Testimony of Leon Jones, Senate, Committee on Indian Affairs, Hearing on S 611," 24 May 2000, http://www.senate.gov/~scia/2000hrgs/s611/ jones.pdf (accessed 23 September 2008; page discontinued).

62. Gail Thrower, interview by author.

63. "Testimony of Leon Jones, Hearing on S 611," 24 May 2000; Chad Smith, editorial, *Indian Country Today*, 9 March 2007.

64. "GOP Candidate Says Cherokees Aren't Real Indians," *Indianz.com*, 17 September 2004, http://64.38.12.138/News/2004/004263.asp (accessed 10 October 2012).

65. King, interview by author.

66. Testimony of Eddie Tullis, House Subcommittee on Native American Affairs, *Federal Recognition*, 22 July 1994, 127; Tullis, interview by author.

CHAPTER 6

1. Eddie Tullis to Framon Weaver, 20 June 1981, folder 21002, Callahan Papers; Tullis interview by author; Framon Weaver to Whom it May Concern, 4 August 1981, box 4, Matte Papers; Johnston, interview by author; Dial quoted in Senate, Select Committee, *Oversight Hearing on Federal Acknowledgment Process*, 26 May 1988, 34.

2. Castile, "Commodification," 745; Paredes, "Paradoxes of Modernism," 355; Nagel, "False Faces," 93; Jaimes, "American Indian Identification," 123–30; Churchill, "The Crucible," 40–44. See also Olzak, *Ethnic Competition*, 1–28.

3. Lumbee River Legal Services (LRLS), "Petition for Federal Acknowledgment," Volume II, 3–4, and Volume I, 38–40, 53–64, LT, OFA; Dial and Eliades, *The Only Land*, 8–9; American Indian Policy Review Commission (AIPRC), *Task Force Ten Final Report*, 151; Blu, *Lumbee Problem*, 79–81.

4. LRLS, "Petition," Vol. I, 51–52, Vol. II, 4–5; Blu, *Lumbee Problem*, 78–79; Lowery, *Lumbee Indians*, 27, 50, 92–93; AIPRC, *Task Force Ten Final Report*, 149–52; "Notice of Receipt of Petition," 5 March 1979, HF, OFA; Martin cited in Senate, Select Committee, *Recognition of Mowa Band of Choctaw Indians*, 26 June 1991, 244–45.

5. LRLS, "Petition," Vol. I, 65–75; Lowery, *Lumbee Indians*, 89–119.

6. Blu, *Lumbee Problem*, 72; Lowery, *Lumbee Indians*, 121–35, 149–80, 200–208; LRLS, "Petition," Vol. II, 26.

7. House, Committee on Interior, *A Bill to Amend the Act relating to the Lumbee Indians*, 22 January 1974, box 105, folder 902, Steiger Papers; LRLS, "Petition," Vol. II, 26–32.

8. Act No. 79-228, *Alabama Laws, Volume I, 1979*, 350, box 9, Matte Papers; Weaver, interview by author; *Congressional Record—Senate*, May 6, 1987, S 6096; Matte, interview by author; Stoeffle, interview by author; Laura Williams to Chairman Weaver, 22 July 1991, box 8, Matte Papers; "New Ways to Recognize Tribes Splits Indians, *New York Times*, 4 August 1991.

9. BAR, "Proposed Finding against MOWA Band of Choctaw Indians," 16 December 1994, MBCI, OFA; "U.S. Senate Recognizes Mowa Band of Choctaws," *Gadsden Times*, 13 March 1994; MOWA Band, Legal Brief to Appeals Board, folder 21002, Callahan Papers; Taylor, interview by author; Chief Longhair Taylor, "State of the Tribe Address," 1997, and "Mowa Indians Seek Callahan's help," undated clipping, folder "Mowa Choctaws BIA Recognition," Callahan Papers; Tullis, interview by author; Davis, interview by author.

10. Davis, interview by author; Lewis, interview by author; House, Committee on Interior, *A Bill to Amend the Act relating to the Lumbee Indians*, 22 January 1974, HF, OFA; Ruth Locklear, interview by author; Sider, *Living Indian Histories*, xliii–xlix; Hunt, interview by author; LRLS, "Petition"; Sider, *Lumbee Indian Histories*, 157–58.

11. Arlinda Locklear, interview by author; Senate, Select Committee, *Federal Recognition of the Lumbee Tribe*, 12 August 1988, 119–20.

12. Locklear, interview by author; Senate, *Report to Accompany S. 420*, 25 November 2003; House, Committee on Natural Resources, *H.R. 898, to Provide for the Recognition of the Lumbee Tribe*, 1 April 2004; House, Committee on Natural Resources, *H.R. 31, Lumbee Recognition Act*, 18 March 2009; Ruth Locklear interview by author; Hunt, interview by author; "Lumbees Likely

to Wait Again on Federal Recognition," *Fayetteville Observer*, 4 October 2010, http://www.fayobserver.com/ (accessed 9 November 2010).

13. Sunray, interview by author.

14. Senate, Select Committee, *Federal Acknowledgment Administrative Procedures Act of 1989*, 270–71; Phillip Martin to Honorable Daniel K. Inouye, 12 July 1991, box 8, Matte Papers; MOWA Choctaw Recognition Committee, "Tomorrow, I Will Still Be Choctaw: The Mowa Band of Choctaw Fight for Federal Recognition," 2003, Jacqueline A. Matte personal papers, Birmingham, Alabama; BAR, "Proposed Negative Finding against Federal Acknowledgment of the MOWA Band of Choctaw," 16 December 1994, MBCI, OFA.

15. Senate, Select Committee, *Federal Recognition of the Lumbee Indian Tribe*, 12 August 1988, 16, 19, 22, 24.

16. Senate, *Report to Accompany S. 420*, 25 November 2003, 1–3; LRLS, "Petition," Vol. 1, 66; Blu, *Lumbee Problem*, 36; Dial and Eliades, *The Only Land*, 8–9.

17. Swanton, *Indian Tribes*, 81; Swanton, *Indians of the Southeastern*, 110; Lowery, *Lumbee Indians*, 107.

18. LRLS, "Petition," Vol. I, 8–17, and Vol. II, Chart I; Senate, Committee on Indian Affairs, *To Provide for the Acknowledgment of the Lumbee Tribe*, 12 July 2006, http://www.Indian.Senate.gov/ (accessed 20 January 2010).

19. House, Committee on Natural Resources, *H.R. 31, Lumbee Recognition Act*, 18 March 2009, 34–36; Matte, *They Say the Wind*, 161; Taylor, interview by author; Sunray, interview by author; Senate, Select Committee, *Indian Federal Recognition Administrative Procedures Act of 1991*, 22 October 1991, 46.

20. Blu, *Lumbee Problem*, 39; Forbes, *Africans and Native Americans*, 3–4, 65, 89–90; Perdue, *Native Carolinians*, 45; Dial and Eliades, *The Only Land*, 1.

21. LRLS, "Petition," Vol. 1, 14. This quote, with slightly different wording, is found in Blu, *Lumbee Problem*, 39.

22. Lowery, *Lumbee Indians*, 607.

23. Senate, Committee on Indian Affairs, *To Provide for the Acknowledgment of the Lumbee Tribe*, 17 September 2003, 31; Senate, Select Committee, *Federal Recognition of the Lumbee Tribe*, 12 August 1988, 144.

24. Austin, interview by author; BAR, "Status of Acknowledgment Cases," 29 October 1999, http://www.doi.gov/bia/bar/indexq.htm (accessed 6 April 2000; page discontinued).

25. Senate, Select Committee, *Federal Acknowledgment Process Oversight Hearing*, 26 May 1988, 2–4; Senate, Select Committee, *Federal Recognition of the Lumbee Tribe*, 12 August 1988; interview, identity withheld by request; Austin, interview by author.

26. Leon Jones, testimony on *S. 611*, 24 May 2000, in possession of author; Arlinda Locklear, interview by author. See M. Miller, *Forgotten Tribes*, ch. 5, "A Matter of Visibility: The United Houma Nation's Struggle for Tribal Acknowledgement."

27. Berry, *Almost White*, 161; Quinn, interview by author.

28. Quinn, interview by author; Arlinda Locklear, interview by author; Gross, "Of Portuguese Origin"; Miles, "Uncle Tom Was an Indian," 137–60; David Wilkins, speech on Indian-Black relations, in possession of author; Hunt, interview by author; Ruth Locklear, interview by author; Cooper, interview by author; Taylor, interview by author.

29. House, Committee on Natural Resources, *Lumbee Recognition Act*, 18 March 2009, 31–36; Heinegg, *Free African Americans*; interviewees' names withheld by request. There are also several older tests that use blood-typing methods that also question the percentage of Indian ancestry of the groups. One set of studies found that the Lumbee people possessed approximately 42 percent European, 48 percent African, and 10 percent Native American ancestry. The same works also found that the MOWA Band had almost exclusively European and African ancestry. Recent DNA studies also have found that the MOWA Band members may possess little Native American DNA. Pollitzer, "The Physical Anthropology"; Estes, "Where Have All the Indians," 96, 127; "Mapping Mankind Part 2," WKRG.com, http://www.wkrg.com/local/article/mapping_mankind1/6849/Nov-13-2007_11-21-am (accessed 19 May 2011; page discontinued).

30. LRLS, "Petition," Vol. I, 66–69. See generally Bragi, *Invisible Indians*.

31. MOWA Band, recognition materials, folder "MBCI-Response of Mowa Band to Dec. 16, 1994 Proposed Finding," Callahan Papers; Gail Thrower interview by author; photos, Poarch Band of Creek Indians Museum, Poarch Band of Creek Indians Reservation, Poarch, Alabama.

32. Interviewee's name withheld by request.

33. "Press Release: BIA Declines Recognition to Alabama Group," 16 December 1994, folder "Mowa Choctaw BIA Recognition," Callahan Papers; BAR, "List of Petitioners by State, 3 March 1998," http://www.doi.gov/bia/petstate.html (accessed 15 July 1998; page discontinued); Shapard, interview by author; interviewee's name withheld by request.

34. Heading quotes Wilford "Longhair" Taylor in "MOWA Indians Seek Callahan's Help," undated clipping, folder "Mowa Choctaw BIA Recognition," Callahan Papers; "Indians Pressing for National Recognition," *Times Daily (Florence, AL)*, 15 March 1992; LRLS, "Petition," Vol. I, 40; Senate, *Report to Accompany S. 420*, 25 May 2003, 2; McCulloch and Wilkins, "Breaking into the Intergovernmental Matrix"; House, Committee on Natural Resources, *Federal Recognition of Indian Tribes*, 22 July 1994, 78; Senate, Select Committee, *Federal Recognition of the Lumbee Indians*, 12 August 1988, 8–10.

35. Baumgartner et al., *Lobbying*, 20–42.

36. Senate, Select Committee, *Oversight of the Federal Acknowledgment Process*, 21 July 1983, 8; Shapard, interview by author; Deputy Secretary quoted in Senate, Select Committee, *Recognition of Certain Indian Tribes*, 18 April 1978, 19;

Baumgartner et al., *Lobbying*, 20–42; Swimmer quoted in Senate, Select Committee, *Federal Recognition of the Lumbee Tribe*, 12 August 1988, 9; Congressional Budget Office to Ben Nighthorse Campbell, 21 November 2003, and testimony of Aurene Martin quoted in Senate, Committee on Indian Affairs, *Lumbee Recognition*, 17 September 2003; Austin (BIA employee cited), interview by author. In contrast to the Lumbee case, the perceived low cost of acknowledging the small Jena Band of Choctaws (approximately 200 members) was cited in hearing reports as a favorable factor in passing the law. House Subcommittee on Native American Affairs, *Jena Band of Choctaw Indians Confirmation Act*, 22 July 1993.

37. *Ysleta del Sur and Alabama and Coushatta Restoration Act*; Cooper, interview by author; M. Miller, *Forgotten Tribes*, 253–55.

38. Arlinda Locklear, interview by author; Taylor, interview by author; Matte, interview by author; Sunray, interview by author; Wilkins, interview by author; Mississippi Band of Choctaw Indians to Daniel K. Inouye, 12 July 1991, and Memo: Laura Williams to Chairman Weaver, 22 July 1991, box 8, Matte Papers; "Watt Lies behind These Remarks," *Akwesasne Notes*, Late Winter 1983, 24, "Bills, Budgets, and Bureaucratic Policies," *Akwesasne Notes*, Summer 1986, 8; John Lewis, "Reaganomics and American Indians," *Indian Affairs*, December 1982, 7; Senate, Select Committee, *Federal Recognition of the Lumbee Indians*, 12 August 1988, 144; Project Leader, "Trip Report: Western Washington Area," 7–10 March 1979, HF, OFA; "Remarks of Marvin J. Franklin at the NCAI 30th Annual Meeting, Tulsa, Oklahoma, October 30, 1973," box 113, folder 10, Tyler Papers; Wilkins, "Breaking into the Intergovernmental Matrix," 140; Absentee Shawnee Tribe of Oklahoma, Resolution No. AS-76-13, "Objecting to the Federal Recognition of the Lumbee Tribe," 1 October 1975, box 74, folder 4, Steed Collection.

39. Statement of Michell Hicks, House Natural Resources Committee, *Lumbee Recognition*, 18 March 2009, 37–38; "U.S. House Backs Lumbee Recognition," *Fayetteville Observer*, 4 June 2009.

40. Light and Rand, *Indian Gaming*, 65–66, 143; Mason, *Indian Gaming*, 4; Lane, *The Return of the Buffalo*; Arlinda Locklear, interview by author; M. Miller, *Forgotten Tribes*, ch. 2 and ch. 5. For challenges to the identity of the Pequots, see Benedict, *Without Reservation*. In Alabama, prominent land owner Riley Boykin Smith objected to a MOWA bill, fearing the group might use their federal status to claim his family's land. Jo Bonner to Mike Sharp, 2 December 1997, folder "Mowa Choctaw BIA Recognition," Callahan Papers; Jill Peters, interview by author.

41. *Seminole Tribe of Florida v. Butterworth*, 658 F.2d 310 (1981).

42. "Indian Gaming," *NARF Legal Review*, Fall 1985, 1; General Accounting Office, *Indian Issues*; Frey, "Preface," *The Annals of the Academy*, 8–9; *California v. Cabazon Band of Mission Indians*, 480 U.S. 202 (1987); House, Committee on

Interior, *Indian Gaming Regulatory Act, Hearing on HR 964*, 25 June 1987, 76–78; Anders, "Indian Gaming," 98–108; Christiansen, "Gambling," 44–45; House, Committee on Interior, *Indian Gambling Control Act*, 25 June 1985; Senate, Select Committee, *Gaming Activities on Indian Reservations*, 18 June 1987; *Indian Gaming Regulatory Act of 1988*.

43. "The Palace, Creek Bingo House," brochure, and "Poarch Creek Indian Economic Development," folder "Poarch Creek Indians-19," Callahan Papers.

44. "Alabama's Indians Say No to Gambling" *Mobile Press-Register*, mid-1990s era clipping, box 4, Matte Papers; Pearl River Resort web page, http://www.pearlriverresort.com (accessed 1/18/2011); Choctaw Chronology, http://www.choctaw.org/history/chronology/chronology6.html (accessed 18 January 2011; page discontinued); Garry Mitchell, "Creeks' New Casino Hotel Changes Atmore Landscape," October 2008, http://indiancountrynews.net/ (accessed 21 October 2009); Harrah's Cherokee, http://www.harrahscherokee.com/ (accessed 18 January 2011); "Tribal Casinos Report Growth," *(St. George, Utah) Spectrum & Daily News*, 19 June 2008.

45. Cooper, interview by author; "Simmonds Clan," *New York Times*, 14 January 1996; "Indians Picket Casino," *Arizona Daily Star*, 18 September 2000; Karla Martin, "Gaming and Native Education."

46. Taylor quoted in "Alabama Choctaws See Rival Tribes," *Boston Globe*, 2 December 2002; Taylor interview by author; Shapard, interview by author.

47. Kaiser, *So Damn Much Money*, 18–21. See M. Miller, *Forgotten Tribes*, ch. 3 and ch. 6.

48. Kaiser, *So Damn Much Money*, 3–18; "A High-Stakes Gamble," *Washington Post*, national weekly ed., 21–27 March 2005, 9–11; "A Jackpot from Indian Gaming Tribes, *Washington Post*, 22 February 2004.

49. House Committee on Interior, *Federal Acknowledgment of Various Indian Groups* (Jena Band, Mowa Band, et al.), 8 July 1992, 57; "Newest Casino Proposal Throws SW Louisiana into Tizzy," *Beaumont Enterprise*, 16 February 2002; "Texas Tribes Fight to Revive Gambling," December 2008, htpp://indiancountry news.net/ (accessed 21 October 2009); "A High-Stakes Gamble," *Washington Post*, national weekly ed., 21–27 March 2005, 9–11.

50. Newest Casino Proposal Throws SW Louisiana into Tizzy," *Beaumont Enterprise*, 16 February 2002; "Texas Tribes Fight to Revive Gambling," December 2008, htpp://indiancountrynews.net/ (accessed 21 October 2009); "A High-Stakes Gamble," *Washington Post*, national weekly ed., 21–27 March 2005, 9–11; Matte, interview by author; Johnston interview by author; Taylor, interview by author.

51. Hixenbaugh, interview by author; Ruth Locklear, interview by author; Arlinda Locklear, interview by author; House, Committee on Natural Resources, *Lumbee Recognition Act*, 18 March 2009; "Lumbees Visit Key Senators in Recognition Push," *Robesonian*, no date, http://www.lumbeetribe.com/ (accessed

5 November 2010); "Lumbees Likely to Wait Again," *fayobserver.com*, 4 October 2010, http://www.fayobserver.com/ (accessed 9 November 2010).

52. "House Once Again Passes Lumbee Recognition Bill," *Indianz.com*, 4 June 2009, http://64.38.12.138/news/2009/014879.asp (accessed 12 October 2012).

53. Baumgartner et al., *Lobbying*, 9, 62.

54. Eddie Tullis, To Whom it May Concern, 10 September 1990, folder "21002 Mowa Band," Callahan Papers; Jacqueline Matte to H. L. "Sonny" Callahan," folder "21002 Mowa Band, 1991," Callahan Papers; Johnnie Andrews, Jr. to Daniel Inouye, 4 September 1990, box 8, Matte Papers; "New Ways to Recognize Tribes Split Indians, *New York Times*, 4 August 1991; Mississippi Band of Choctaw Indians to Honorable Daniel K. Inouye, 12 July 1991, and Laura Weaver, Memorandum to Chairman Weaver, 22 July 1991, box 8, Matte Papers.

55. Hixenbaugh, interview by author; Arlinda Locklear, interview by author.

56. Arlinda Locklear, interview by author; Ruth Locklear, interview by author; Milton Brown to Jo Bonner, no date, folder "MBCI-Response to Proposed Finding," Callahan Papers; House, Committee on Natural Resources, *Lumbee Recognition Act*, April 2004, 3.

57. See, for example, Pat LaGrange to Sonny Callahan, 16 February 1990, Jack Greer to Sonny Callahan, 21 January 1991, folder "21002 Mowa Band, 1991," Callahan Papers; Gov. Fob James to Chief Wilford Taylor, 24 April 1996, folder "MBCI-Response to Dec. 16, 1994, Proposed Finding," Callahan Papers; Senate, Select Committee, *Federal Recognition of the MOWA Band*, 26 June 1991, letter from Tunica-Biloxi Tribe, 334; House, Committee on Natural Resources, *Lumbee Recognition Act*, 18 March 2009, 65–79.

58. Miller, interview by author.

59. Mason, *Indian Gaming*, 104–19; Matt Connor, "Against All Odds," *Indian Gaming Business*, Fall 2001; "Distributive Justice against Lumbee Recognition," *Indian Country Today*, 9 April 2004; L. A. Williams, "Federal Lumbee Recognition Will Always Pose a Casino Threat," http://christianactionleague.org/ (accessed 27 October 2009); Brooks testimony in *Lumbee Act 2004*, 99–100; Cooper, interview by author.

60. House, Committee on Natural Resources, *Federal Recognition and Acknowledgment Process*, 31 March 2004, 6, 90–91. Benedict's controversial book *Without Reservation* argued that the Mashantucket Pequots tricked the government into recognizing them, that they were not Pequot Indians. Benedict, *Without Reservation*. See also Eisler, *Revenge of the Pequot*.

61. "Ramapoughs Seek Federal Tribal Status," *New York Times*, 6 September 1987; Austin, interview by author; "Another Tribal Nation? And Another Casino?," *New York Times*, 18 February 1996; "Second Tribe Recognized as a Nation: Mohegans May Build State's 2d Casino," *New York Times*, 8 March 1994; "U.S. Denies Tribal Status, Foiling Plans for a Casino," *New York Times*, 18 September 1996;

"North Carolina Group Says Lumbee Recognition Means Casino," 26, February 2003, *Indianz.com*, http://64.38.12.138/News/show.asp?ID=2003/02/26/lumbee (accessed 12 October 2012); Cooper, interview by author; Taylor, interview by author.

62. See Senate, *Report to Accompany S. 420*, 25 November 2003, 3; Senate, Committee on Indian Affairs, *Lumbee Recognition*, 17 September 2003, 24. See also Mowa Files, Callahan Papers.

63. Sunray, interview by author; "North Carolina Commission of Indian Affairs Commission Members, 1999," NCCIA.

64. Martin quoted in House, Committee on Natural Resources, *Federal Recognition and Acknowledgment Process*, 31 March 2004, 64–65; Hicks quoted in House, Committee on Natural Resources, *H.R. 898, To Provide for the Recognition of the Lumbee Tribe*, 1 April 2004, 33.

65. Hicks quoted in House, Committee on Natural Resources, *H.R. 898, To Provide for the Recognition of the Lumbee Tribe*, 1 April 2004, 34; Jenkins, interview by author; "Bill Gives Lumbee Decision to Indian Bureau," 22 March 2003, *Fayetteville Observer*, House, Committee on Natural Resources, *H.R. 31, Lumbee Recognition Act*, 18 March 2009, 31; Taylor, interview by author; Arlinda Locklear, interview by author.

66. Mark Locklear, "17 File as Deadline Ends for Lumbee Elections," *Robesonian*, http://www.robesonian.com/view/full_story/1646791/article-17-file-as-deadline-ends-for-Lumbee-elections (accessed 20 February 2011); Arlinda Locklear, interview by author; Hunt, interview by author; Hixenbaugh, interview by author; Arlinda Locklear, "An Open Letter," 18 December 2010, http://lumbeesovereigntycoalition.wordpress.com/ (accessed 12 October 2012).

67. Shapard, interview by author; Hunt, interview by author; Arlinda Locklear, interview by author; Hixenbaugh, interview by author; AndersonTuell, http://andersontuell.com (accessed 19 January 2011).

68. Shapard, interview by author; Billy Hunt, interview by author; Arlinda Locklear, interview by author; Hixenbaugh, interview by author; Anderson-Tuell web page, http://andersontuell.com (accessed 19 January 2011); Mason, *Indian Gaming*, 122; "Nipmuc Tribal Decision Delayed," *Boston Globe*, 14 December 2000; OFA, "List of Petitioners by State," 15 February 2007, http://www.bia.gov/ (accessed 6 May 2008); "Indian Affairs Decisions on Schaghticokes Probed," *Hartford Courant*, 23 April 2004; "Potential Indian Casino Blocked by Federal Decision," *Las Vegas Sun*, 6 December 2002; "Head of BIA Apologizes to Indian Tribes," *Arizona Daily Star*, 9 September 2000. Names of interviewees withheld by request when discussing this issue. Working for the Office of Federal Acknowledgment has provided staff with fairly well-paid and long-lasting careers. Lower-profile BIA acknowledgment staff members have left the office to work for unrecognized or recently recognized tribes. Others who once worked for unacknowledged tribes, most significantly Jack

Campisi, now head programs for recently acknowledged tribes. Austin, interview by author; "Federal Employees, 2008," Asbury Park Press, http://php. app.com/fed_employees/results.php? (accessed 11 January 2011); Quinn, interview by author.

69. Cooper, interview by author; Hunt, interview by author; Taylor, interview by author; Arlinda Locklear, interview by author; Miller, interview by author; Russell Barsh, e-mail correspondence with author.

Bibliography

ARCHIVAL MATERIALS:
PRIVATE AND PUBLIC COLLECTIONS

Alabama Coushatta Indians, Vertical File, University of Texas Institute of Texan
  Cultures, San Antonio
Dewey F. Bartlett Collection, Carl Albert Center, Monnet Hall, University of
  Oklahoma, Norman
Sonny Callahan Papers, University Archives, University of South Alabama,
  Mobile
Brenda Dardar Personal Files, Raceland, Louisiana
Tom Diamond Personal Papers, Law Offices of Diamond, Rash, Gordon,
  and Jackson, El Paso, Texas
Peter Domenici Papers, Center for Southwest Research, University of New
  Mexico, Albuquerque
Caroline Dorman Collection, Cammie G. Henry Research Center, Watson Mem-
  orial Library, Northwestern State University of Louisiana, Natchitoches
Fraudulent Indian Task Force, Office Files, Cherokee Nation Headquarters,
  Tahlequah, Oklahoma
Records of the Governor's Commission of Indian Affairs, Louisiana State
  Archives, Baton Rouge
Institute of Texan Cultures, San Antonio
Lyndon Baines Johnson Papers, Lyndon Baines Johnson Presidential Library,
  Austin, Texas
  Indian Affairs Files
  White House Central Files

J. Bennett Johnston Papers, Special Collections, Louisiana State University, Baton Rouge

W. W. Keeler Papers, Cherokee Cultural Center, Tahlequah, Oklahoma

Wilma Mankiller Papers, Western History Collections, Monnet Hall, University of Oklahoma, Norman

Jacqueline Matte Papers, Department of Archives, University of South Alabama, Mobile

Mowa Band of Choctaw Indians Cultural Center, Mowa Choctaw Reservation, Mt. Vernon, Alabama

National Archives, Washington, D.C.
 Record Group 75, Records of the Bureau of Indian Affairs
  John C. Collier Files
  Central Classified Files, 1907–1939

National Archives, College Park, Maryland
 Record Group 48, Records of the Office of the Solicitor
  Chronological Correspondence and Memorandum Files, 1930–1938
  General Correspondence and other Records, 1937–1958
 Record Group 220, Records of Special Commissions, Records of the American Indian Policy Review Commission

North Carolina Commission on Indian Affairs, Raleigh

Northeastern State University, Special Collections, Tahlequah, Oklahoma

Office of Federal Acknowledgment (formerly Branch of Acknowledgment and Research), Bureau of Indian Affairs, Department of the Interior, Washington, D.C.
 History Files
 Jena Band of Choctaw Indian Files
 Kaweah Indian Nation Files
 Lower Muskogee Creek Tribe Files
 Lumbee Tribe Files
 Mowa Band of Choctaw Indian Files
 Poarch Band of Creek Indian Files
 Principal Creek Nation Files
 Southeastern Cherokee Confederacy Files
 Tunica Biloxi Files
 United Houma Nation Files

Oklahoma Historical Society, Oklahoma City

Poarch Band of Creek Indians Cultural Center, Poarch Creek Reservation, Atmore, Alabama

John Rhodes Papers, Special Collections, Hayden Library, Arizona State University, Phoenix

State of Louisiana, Office of Indian Affairs, Baton Rouge, Louisiana
 Office Files

Sam Steiger Papers, Department of Archives and Manuscripts, Cline Library, Northern Arizona University, Flagstaff

Ross Swimmer Papers, Cherokee Cultural Center, Tahlequah, Oklahoma

Tom Steed Collection, Carl Albert Center, Monnet Hall, University of Oklahoma, Norman

Texas Indian Commission Records, Texas State Archives, Austin

Texas Indian Commission Vertical File, Center for American History, University of Texas at Austin

S. Lyman Tyler Papers, Special Collections, Marriott Library, University of Utah, Salt Lake City

Morris King Udall Papers, Special Collections, Main Library, University of Arizona, Tucson

Stewart Lee Udall Papers, Special Collections, Main Library, University of Arizona, Tucson

Richard C. White Papers, Sonnichsen Special Collections, University of Texas at El Paso

U.S. GOVERNMENT DOCUMENTS, PUBLICATIONS, AND REPORTS

American Indian Policy Review Commission (AIPRC). *Final Report*, vols. 1 and 2. Washington, D.C.: Government Printing Office, 1977.

————. *Final Report, Appendices and Index*, vol. 2. Washington, D.C.: Government Printing Office, 1977.

————. *Meetings of the American Indian Policy Review Commission*, vol. 4. Washington, D.C.: Government Printing Office, 1976.

————. *Report on Terminated and Nonfederally Recognized Indians: Task Force Ten Final Report to the American Indian Policy Review Commission*. Washington, D.C.: Government Printing Office, 1976.

Department of the Interior. *Opinions of the Solicitor of the Department of the Interior relating to Indian Affairs, 1917–1974*. Washington, D.C.: Government Printing Office, 1974.

General Accounting Office. *Indian Issues: Improvements Needed in Tribal Recognition Process, GAO-02-49*. Washington, D.C.: General Accounting Office, 2001.

Indian Claims Commission. *Final Report*. Washington, D.C.: Government Printing Office, 1978.

U.S. Congress. House. Committee on Interior and Insular Affairs. *H.R. 12216: A Bill to Amend the Act relating to the Lumbee Indians of North Carolina*. 93rd Cong., 2d sess., 22 January 1974.

————. *H.R. 9054, A Bill*. 95th Cong., 1st sess., 12 September 1977.

———. *Indian Gambling Control Act: Hearing on H.R. 1920 and H.R. 2404.* 99th Cong., 1st sess., 25 June 1985.

———. *Indian Gaming Regulatory Act: Hearing on H.R. 964 and H.R. 2507.* 100th Cong., 1st sess., 25 June 1987.

———. *Federal Acknowledgment of Various Indian Groups: Hearing on H.R. 3958, H.R. 1475, H.R. 2349, H.R. 5562, H.R. 3607.* 102d Cong., 2d sess., 8 July 1992.

———. *Indian Federal Acknowledgment Process: Hearing on H.R. 3430.* 102 Cong., 2d sess., 15 September 1992.

U.S. Congress. House. Committee on Interior and Insular Affairs. Subcommittee on Indian Affairs and Public Lands. *Federal Recognition of Indian Tribes: Hearing on H.R. 13773 and Similar Bills.* 95th Cong., 2d sess., 10 August 1978.

U.S. Congress. House. Committee on Natural Resources. Subcommittee on Native American Affairs. *Auburn Restoration and MOWA Band Recognition: Hearing on H.R. 4228 and S. 282.* 103rd Cong., 2d sess., 17 May 1994.

———. *Federal Recognition: Hearing on H.R. 898.* 108th Cong., 2d sess., 31 March 2004.

———. *Federal Recognition of Indian Tribes: Hearing on H.R. 2549, H.R. 4462, H.R. 4709.* 103rd Cong., 2d sess., 22 July 1994.

———. *Lumbee Recognition Act: Hearing on H.R. 31.* 111th Cong., 1st sess. 18 March 2009.

———. *To Provide for the Recognition of the Lumbee Tribe: Hearing on H.R. 898.* 108th Cong., 2d sess., 1 April 2004.

U.S. Congress. Senate. Committee on Indian Affairs. *To Confirm the Federal Relationship with the Jena Band of Choctaw Indians of Louisiana.* 103rd Cong., 1st sess., 30 June 1993.

———. *Federal Recognition Administrative Procedures Act: Hearing on S. 479.* 104th Cong., 1st sess., 13 July 1995.

———. *Federal Recognition Administrative Procedures Act of 1997,* 20 March 1997.

———. *To Provide for the Acknowledgment of the Lumbee Tribe.* 12 July 2006.

U.S. Congress. Senate. Committee on Interior and Insular Affairs. Subcommittee on Indian Affairs. *Establishment of the American Indian Policy Review Commission: Hearings on S.J. Res. 133.* 93rd Cong., 1st sess., 19 July 1973.

U.S. Congress. Senate. Select Committee on Indian Affairs. *A Bill to Establish an Administrative Procedure and Guidelines.* 95th Cong., 1st sess., 15 December 1977.

———. *Federal Acknowledgment Administrative Procedures Act of 1989: Hearing on S. 611.* Part 1. 101st Cong., 1st sess., 28 April 1989.

———. *Federal Acknowledgment Administrative Procedures Act of 1989: Hearing on S. 611.* Part 2. 101st Cong., 1st sess., 5 May 1989.

————. *Federal Acknowledgment Process: Hearing before the Select Committee on Indian Affairs.* 96th Cong., 2d sess., 2 June 1980.

————. *Federal Acknowledgment Process: Oversight Hearing.* 100th Cong., 2d sess., 26 May 1988.

————. *Federal Recognition of Certain Indian Tribes: Hearing on S. 611.* 95th Cong., 1st sess., 27 September 1977.

————. *Federal Recognition of the Lumbee Indian Tribe of North Carolina: Hearing on S. 2672.* 100th Cong., 2d sess., 12 August 1988.

————. *Federal Recognition of the MOWA Band of Choctaw Indians: Hearing on S. 362.* 102 Cong., 1st sess., 26 June 1991.

————. *Gaming Activities on Indian Reservations and Lands: Hearing on S. 555 and S. 1303.* 100th Cong., 1st sess., 18 June 1987.

————. *Indian Federal Recognition Administrative Procedures Act of 1991: Hearing on S. 1315.* 102d Cong., 1st sess., 22 October 1991.

————. *Oversight of the Federal Acknowledgment Process: Hearing before the Select Committee on Indian Affairs.* 98th Cong., 1st sess., 21 July 1983.

————. *Recognition of Certain Indian Tribes: Hearing on S. 2375.* 95th Cong., 2d sess., 18 April 1978.

————. *Recognition of MOWA Band of Choctaw Indians; Aroostook Band of Micmacs Settlement Act; Ponca Restoration Act; and Jena Band of Choctaw Recognition Act: Hearing on S. 381, S. 1413, S. 1747, S. 1918.* 101st Cong., 2d sess., 28 March 1990.

————. *To Provide for the Acknowledgment of the Lumbee Tribe: Hearing on S. 420.* 108th Cong., 1st sess. 17 September 2003.

COURT CASES, PLEADINGS, STATUTES, AND ADMINISTRATIVE AND LEGISLATIVE ENACTMENTS

An Act relating to the Lumbee Indians of North Carolina, 7 June 1956, 70 Stat. 254–255.

An Act to Settle Certain Claims of the Mashantucket Pequot Indians, P.L. 98-134, 18 October 1983, 97 Stat. 851.

California v. Cabazon Band of Mission Indians. 480 U.S. 202 (1987).

Cherokee Nation of Oklahoma v. Babbitt. 117 F.3d 1489 (D.C. Cir. 1997).

Greene v. Babbitt. 64 F.3d 1266 (9th Cir. 1995).

Indian Education Act. 45 C.F.R. Part 100a.

Indian Gaming Regulatory Act of 1988, P.L. 100-497, 102 Stat. 2467.

Indian Reorganization Act of 1934, Act of June 18, 1934, 48 Stat. 984.

Indian Self-Determination and Education Assistance Act of 1975, P.L. 93-638, 88 Stat. 2203.

Mashpee Tribe v. New Seabury Corp. 592 F.2d 575 (1979).

Maynor v. Morton. 510 F.2d 1254 (1974).

Montoya v. United States. 180 U.S. 261 (1901).

Native American Graves Protection and Repatriation Act, P.L. 101-601, 16 November 1990, 104 Stat. 3048.

Passamaquoddy v. Morton. 528 F.2d 370 (1975).

Preference in Employment. 25 C.F.R. Part 1.2.

Procedures for Establishing That an American Indian Group Exists as an Indian Tribe. 25 C.F.R. Part 83.1–13.

Seminole Tribe of Florida v. Butterworth. 658 F.2d 310 (1981).

Snyder Act, 25 U.S.C.A. § 13.

United States v. Candelaria. 271 U.S. 432 (1926).

United States v. John. 437 U.S. 634 (1978).

United States v. Joseph. 94 U.S. 614 (1876).

United States v. Kagama. 118 U.S. 375 (1886).

United States v. Sandoval. 231 U.S. 28 (1913).

United States v. Washington. 520 F.2d 676 (1975).

Ysleta del Sur Pueblo and Alabama and Coushatta Indian Tribes of Texas Restoration Act, Public Law 100-89, 18 August 1987, 101 Stat. 666.

BOOKS, ARTICLES, AND THESES

Albers, Patricia C., and William R. James. "On the Dialectics of Ethnicity: To Be or Not to Be Santee (Sioux)." *Journal of Ethnic Studies* 14 (Spring 1986): 1–21.

Allen, Richard L. "The Impact of New Age Shamans on Cherokee Culture: Identity and Cultural Theft." Paper presented at the Southwest/Texas Popular Culture Association Annual Meeting, Albuquerque, New Mexico, 12 February 2003.

Allen, Richard, Cara Cowan Watts, John Parris, Troy Wayne Poteete, Teri Rhoades, Tonia Williams, and Kathleen Wesho-Bauer. "Stealing Sovereignty: Identity Theft and the Creation of False Tribes." Paper presented at the Sovereignty Symposium XX, 30 May 2007.

American Indian Journal 4, no. 5 (1978). Special issue on tribal recognition.

Anders, Gary C. "Indian Gaming: Financial and Regulatory Issues." *Annals of the Academy of Political and Social Science* 556 (March 1998): 98–108.

Anderson, Terry. "Federal Recognition: The Vicious Myth." *American Indian Journal* 4, no. 5 (1978): 7–19.

Atkinson, Ronald R. "The Evolution of Ethnicity among the Alcholi of Uganda: The Precolonial Phase." *Ethnohistory* 36, no. 1 (1989): 19–43.

Axtell, James. *The Indians' New South: Cultural Change in the Colonial Southeast.* Baton Rouge: Louisiana State University Press, 1997.

Ayers, Edward L. *The Promise of the New South: Life after Reconstruction.* New York: Oxford University Press, 1992.

Baird, W. David. "Are the Five Tribes of Oklahoma 'Real' Indians?" *Western Historical Quarterly* 21, no. 1 (1990): 5–18.

Barker, Joanne. "Indian U.S.A." *Wicazo Sa Review* (Spring 2003): 25–79.

———. *Native Acts: Law, Recognition, and Cultural Authenticity.* Durham, N.C.: Duke University Press, 2011.

Barth, Fredrik, ed. *Ethnic Group Boundaries: The Social Organization of Cultural Difference.* London: Allen and Unwin, 1969.

Bates, Denise Eileen. "Up from Obscurity: Indian Rights Activism and the Development of Tribal-State Relations in the 1970s and 1980s Deep South." PhD diss., University of Arizona, 2007.

Baumgartner, Frank R., Suzanne De Boef, and Amber E. Boydstun. *Lobbying and Political Change: Who Wins, Who Loses, and Why.* Chicago: University of Chicago Press, 2009.

Beals, Ralph L. "The Anthropologist as Expert Witness: Illustrations from the California Indian Land Claims Case." In *Irredeemable America: The Indians' Estate and Land Claims,* edited by Imre Sutton, ch. 6. Albuquerque: University of New Mexico Press, 1985.

Beard-Moose, Christina Taylor. *Public Indians, Private Cherokees: Tourism on Tribal Ground.* Tuscaloosa: University of Alabama Press, 2009.

Benedict, Jeff. *Without Reservation: The Making of America's Most Powerful Indian Tribe and Foxwoods, the World's Largest Casino.* New York: Harper Collins, 2000.

Berkhofer, Robert F. *The White Man's Indian: Images of the American Indian from Columbus to the Present.* New York: Knopf, 1978.

Berry, Brewton. *Almost White.* New York: Collier-Macmillan, 1963.

Berry, M. "The Alabama and Coushatta Indians of Texas." *Texas Geographic Magazine* 7, no. 2 (1948): 20–23.

Biolsi, Thomas. *Organizing the Lakota: The Political Economy of the New Deal on the Pine Ridge and Rosebud Reservations.* Tucson: University of Arizona Press, 1992.

Bird, S. Elizabeth. "Introduction." In *Dressing in Feathers: The Construction of the Indian in American Popular Culture,* edited by Elizabeth S. Bird. Boulder: Westview Press, 1996.

Blu, Karen. *The Lumbee Problem: The Making of an American Indian People.* Lincoln: University of Nebraska Press, 2001.

———. "Region and Recognition: Southern Indians, Anthropologists, and Presumed Biology." In *Anthropologists and Indians in the New South,* edited by Rachel A. Bonney and J. Anthony Paredes, 71–85. Tuscaloosa: University of Alabama Press, 2001.

Bond, Horace Mann. "Two Racial Islands in Alabama." *American Journal of Sociology* 36, no. 4 (1931): 552–67.

Bonney, Rachel A., and J. Anthony Paredes, eds. *Anthropologists and Indians in the New South.* Tuscaloosa: University of Alabama Press, 2001.

Boulware, Tyler. *Deconstructing the Cherokee Nation: Town, Region, and Nation among Eighteenth-Century Cherokees.* Gainesville: University of Florida Press, 2011.

Bowman, Greg, and Janel Curry-Roper. *The Houma People of Louisiana: A Story of Indian Survival.* Golden Meadow, LA: United Houma Nation, 1982.

Brackenridge, Henry Marie. *Views of Louisiana: Together with a Journal of a Voyage up the Mississippi River in 1811.* Chicago: Quadrangle Books, 1962.

Bragi, David Arv. *Invisible Indians: Mixed-Blood Native Americans Who Are Not Enrolled in Federally Recognized Tribes.* Tucson: Grail Media, 2005.

Brown, Anthony D., ed. *New Directions in Federal Indian Policy: A Review of the American Indian Policy Review Commission.* Los Angeles: Regents of the University of California, 1979.

Brown, Sharon Sholars. "The Jena Choctaw: A Case Study in the Documentation of Indian Tribal Identity." *National Genealogical Society Quarterly* 75, no. 3 (1987): 180–93.

Bryant, Alfred Jr., and Teresa D. LaFramboise. "The Racial Identity and Cultural Orientation of Lumbee American Indian High School Students." *Cultural Diversity and Ethnic Minority Psychology* 11, no. 1 (2005): 87.

Burt, Larry. *Tribalism in Crisis: Federal Indian Policy, 1953–1961.* Albuquerque: University of New Mexico Press, 1982.

Campisi, Jack. "The Iroquois and the Euro-American Concept of Tribe." *New York History* 78, no. 4 (1997): 455–72.

———. *The Mashpee Indians: Tribe on Trial.* Syracuse, N.Y.: Syracuse University Press, 1991.

———. "The New England Tribes and Their Quest for Justice." In *The Pequots in Southern New England: The Fall and Rise of an Indian Nation,* edited by Laurence M. Hauptman and James D. Wherry, 179–93. Norman: University of Oklahoma Press, 1990.

———. "Resurgence and Recognition." In *Handbook of North American Indians: Southeast,* edited by Raymond D. Fogelson, 760–68. Washington, D.C.: Smithsonian Institution, 2005.

Campisi, Jack, and William A. Starna. "Why Does It Take So Long? Federal Recognition and the American Indian Tribes of New England." *Northeast Anthropology* 57 (Spring 1999): 1–17.

Carillo, Jo. "Identity as Idiom: Mashpee Reconsidered." In *Readings in American Indian Law: Recalling the Rhythm of Survival,* edited by Jo Carillo, 43–49. Philadelphia: Temple University Press, 1998.

Carmer, Carl. *The Stars Fell on Alabama.* New York: Farrar & Rinehart, 1934.

Carter, Forrest. *The Education of Little Tree.* Albuquerque: University of New Mexico Press, 1986. First published 1976 by Delacorte Press.

Castaneda, Carlos. *The Teachings of Don Juan: A Yaqui Way of Knowledge.* Berkeley: University of California Press, 1968.

Castile, George Pierre. "The Commodification of Indian Identity." *American Anthropologist* 98, no. 4 (1996): 743–49.

Castile, George Pierre, and Gilbert Kushner, eds. *Persistent Peoples: Cultural Enclaves in Perspective.* Tucson: University of Arizona Press, 1981.

Cattelino, Jessica R. *High Stakes: Florida Seminole Gaming and Sovereignty.* Durham, N.C.: Duke University Press, 2008.

Chafe, William H. *Remembering Jim Crow: African Americans Tell about Life in the Segregated South.* New York: New Press, 2001.

Champagne, Duane. *Social Order and Political Change: Constitutional Governments among the Cherokee, the Choctaw, the Chickasaw, and the Creek.* Palo Alto, Calif.: Stanford University Press, 1992.

Chang, David A. *The Color of the Land: Race, Nation, and the Politics of Landownership in Oklahoma, 1832–1929.* Chapel Hill: University of North Carolina Press, 2010.

Christiansen, Eugene M. "Gambling and the American Economy." *Annals of the Academy of Political and Social Science* 556 (March 1998): 45.

Churchill, Ward. "The Crucible of American Indian Identity: Native Tradition versus Colonial Imposition in Postconquest North America." In *Contemporary Native American Cultural Issues,* edited by Duane Champagne, 40–44. Walnut Creek, Calif.: Altamira Press, 1999.

———."The Tragedy and the Travesty: The Subversion of Indigenous Sovereignty in North America." In *Contemporary Native American Political Issues,* ed. Troy Johnson, 17–72. Walnut Creek, Calif.: Altamira Press, 1999.

———. "Using Indian Names for Sports Teams Harms Native Americans." In *Native American Rights: Current Controversies,* edited by Tamara L. Roleff, 18–25. San Diego: Greenhaven Press, 1998.

Clarkin, Thomas. *Federal Indian Policy in the Kennedy and Johnson Administrations, 1961–1969.* Albuquerque: University of New Mexico Press, 2001.

Clifford, James. *The Predicaments of Culture: Twentieth Century Ethnography, Literature, and Art.* Cambridge, Mass.: Harvard University Press, 1988.

Clifton, James A. "Avocation Medicine Men, Inventive 'Traditions' and New Age Religiosity in a Western Great Lakes Algonquian Population." In *Present Is Past: Some Uses of Tradition in Native Societies,* edited by Marie Mauzé, 145–57. Lanham, Md.: University Press of America, 1997.

———. *The Invented Indian: Cultural Fictions and Government Policies.* New Brunswick, N.J.: Transaction Publishers, 1990.

Cobb, Daniel M. "Devils in Disguise: The Carnegie Project, the Cherokee Nation, and the 1960s." *American Indian Quarterly* 31, no. 3 (2007): 465–90.

Cobb, Daniel M., and Loretta Fowler, eds. *Beyond Red Power: American Indian Politics and Activism since 1900.* Santa Fe: School for Advanced Research Press, 2007.

Cohen, Anthony P. *The Symbolic Construction of Community.* New York: Tavistock, 1985.

Cohen, Felix S. *Handbook of Federal Indian Law.* Albuquerque: University of New Mexico Press, 1970.

Conley, Robert J. *The Cherokee Nation: A History.* Albuquerque: University of New Mexico Press, 2005.

Cornell, Stephen. "Discovered Identities and American Indian Supra Tribalism." In *We Are a People: Narrative and Multiplicity in Constructing Ethnic Identity,* edited by Paul Spickard and W. Jeffrey Burroughs, 104–12. Philadelphia: Temple University Press, 2000.

———. *The Return of the Native: American Indian Political Resurgence.* New York: Oxford University Press, 1988.

Cowger, Thomas. *The National Congress of American Indians: The Founding Years.* Lincoln: University of Nebraska Press, 1999.

Cramer, Renee. *Cash, Color, and Colonialism: The Politics of Tribal Acknowledgment.* Norman: University of Oklahoma Press, 2005.

Cromer, Marie West. *Modern Indians in Alabama: Remnants of the Removal.* Birmingham, Ala.: M. W. Cromer, 1984.

Daniel, G. Reginald. "Passers and Pluralists: Subverting the Racial Divide." In *Racially Mixed People in America,* edited by Maria P. P. Root, 91. London: Sage, 1992.

Davis, Marianna W. *South Carolina's Blacks and Native Americans, 1776–1976.* Columbia, S.C.: State Human Affairs Commission, 1976.

Debo, Angie. *And Still the Waters Run: The Betrayal of the Five Civilized Tribes.* Princeton, N.J.: Princeton University Press, 1940.

———. *The Rise and Fall of the Choctaw Republic.* Norman: University of Oklahoma Press, 1934.

———. *The Road to Disappearance: A History of the Creek Indians.* Norman: University of Oklahoma Press, 1941.

Deloria, Philip. *Indians in Unexpected Places.* Lawrence: University Press of Kansas, 2004.

———. *Playing Indian.* New Haven: Yale University Press, 1998.

Deloria, Vine, Jr. *American Indian Policy in the Twentieth Century.* Norman: University of Oklahoma Press, 1985.

———. *Custer Died for Your Sins: An Indian Manifesto.* New York: Avon Books, 1969.

———. *The Nations Within: The Past and Future of American Indian Sovereignty.* New York: Pantheon Books, 1984.

Deloria, Vine, Jr., and Clifford M. Lytle. *American Indians, American Justice.* Austin: University of Texas Press, 1983.

Deloria, Vine, Jr., and David E. Wilkins. *Tribes, Treaties, and Constitutional Tribulations.* Austin: University of Texas Press, 1999.

Denison, Andrew. *Demanding the Cherokee Nation: Indian Autonomy and American Culture, 1830–1900*. Lincoln: University of Nebraska Press, 2004.

Dial, Adolph L., and David K. Eliades. *The Only Land I Know: A History of the Lumbee Indians*. San Francisco: Indian Historian Press, 1975.

Dole, Gertrude E. "Tribes as the Autonomous Unit." In *Essays on the Problem of Tribe*, edited by June Helm, 83–86. Seattle: University of Washington Press, 1968.

Doster, James F. "The Creek Indians and Their Florida Lands, 1740–1823." In *American Indian Ethnohistory: Florida Indians*, 181–286. New York: Garland, 1974.

Downs, Ernest C. "The Struggle of the Louisiana Tunica Indians for Recognition." In *Southeastern Indians since the Removal Era*, edited by Walter Williams, 72–89. Athens: University of Georgia Press, 1979.

———. "A National Conference on Tribal Recognition." *American Indian Journal* 4 (May 1978): 2–6.

Downs, Ernest C., and Jenna Whitehead, eds. "The Houma Indians: Two Decades in a History of Struggle." *American Indian Journal* 2, no. 3 (1976): 2–22.

Drechsel, Emanuel J. "Mobilian Jargon in Southeastern Indian Anthropology." In *Anthropologists and Indians in the New South*, edited by Rachel A. Bonney, and J. Anthony Paredes, 75–83. Tuscaloosa: University of Alabama Press, 2001.

Drechsel, Emanuel J., and Majuakane Drechsel. "An Ethnohistory of 19th Century Louisiana Indians." Special Collections. Louisiana State University. 1997.

Dunbar, William. *Life, Letters, and Papers of William Dunbar*. Jackson: Press of the Mississippi Historical Society, 1930.

Duncan, Andy. *Alabama Curiosities: Quirky Characters, Roadside Oddities and Other Offbeat Stuff*. Guilford, Conn.: Morris Book, 2005.

Duthu, Bruce, and Hilde Ojibway. "Future Light or Feu-Follet?" *Southern Exposure* 13, no. 6 (1985): 24–32.

Eisler, Kim Isaac. *Revenge of the Pequots: How a Small Native American Tribe Created the World's Most Profitable Casino*. New York: Simon and Schuster, 2001.

Ellis, Clyde. "'More Real than the Indians Themselves:' The Early Years of the Indian Lore Movement in the United States." *Western Historical Quarterly*, Autumn 2008, 3–22.

Ellsworth, Lucius F., and Jane E. Dysart. "West Florida's Forgotten People: The Creek Indians from 1830 until 1970." *Florida Quarterly* 59, no. 4 (1981): 430–33.

Estes, Roberta. "Where Have All the Indians Gone? Native American Eastern Seaboard Dispersal, Genealogy and DNA in Relation to Sir Walter Raleigh's Lost Colony of Roanoke." *Journal of Genetic Genealogy* 5, no. 2 (2009): 96–130.

Evans, W. McKee. "The North Carolina Lumbees: From Assimilation to Revitali-
    zation." In *Southeastern Indians since the Removal Era*, edited by Walter L.
    Williams, 49–71. Athens: University of Georgia Press, 1979.
Faiman-Silva, Sandra. *Choctaws at the Crossroads: The Political Economy of Class
    and Culture in the Oklahoma Timber Region*. Lincoln: University of Nebraska
    Press, 1999.
Field, Les W. "Complicities and Collaborations: Anthropologists and the 'Unac-
    knowledged Tribes' of California," *Current Anthropology* 40, no. 2 (1999):
    193–209.
Fields, Barbara Jeanne. "Slavery, Race and Ideology in the United States of
    America." *New Left Review* 181 (May–June 1990): 95–118.
Fikes, Jay. *Carlos Castaneda, Academic Opportunism and the Psychedelic Sixties*. Santa
    Monica: Millennia Press, 1993.
Finger, John R. *Cherokee Americans: The Eastern Band of Cherokees in the Twentieth
    Century*. Lincoln: University of Nebraska Press, 1991.
Fischer, Ann. "History and Current Status of the Houma Indians." In *The Ameri-
    can Indian Today*, edited by Stuart Levine and Nancy O. Lurie, 212–35.
    Baltimore: Penguin Books, 1972.
Fixico, Donald L. *Daily Life of Native Americans in the Twentieth Century*. West-
    port, Conn.: Greenwood Press, 2006.
———. *Termination and Relocation: Federal Indian Policy, 1945–1960*. Albuquer-
    que: University of New Mexico Press, 1986.
———. "Witness to Change: Fifty Years of Indian Activism and Tribal Politics."
    In *Beyond Red Power: American Indian Politics and Activism since 1900*, edited
    by Daniel M. Cobb and Loretta Fowler, 2–15. Santa Fe: School for
    Advanced Research Press, 2007.
Forbes, Jack D. *Africans and Native Americans: The Language of Race and the
    Evolution of Red-Black Peoples*. Urbana: University of Illinois Press, 1993.
Foreman, Grant. *The Five Civilized Tribes*. Norman: University of Oklahoma
    Press, 1934.
Frank, Andrew K. *Creeks and Southerners: Biculturalism on the Early American Fron-
    tier*. Lincoln: University of Nebraska Press, 2005.
Frey, James H. "Preface." In "Gambling: Socioeconomic Impact and Public
    Policy." Special issue, *Annals of the Academy of Political and Social Science*
    556 (March 1998).
Fried, Morton. "The Myth of Tribe." *Natural History* (April 1975): 12–20.
———. *The Notion of Tribe*. Menlo Park, Calif.: Cummings, 1975.
———. "On the Concept of 'Tribe.'" In *Essays on the Problem of Tribe*, edited by
    June Helm, 1–11. Seattle: University of Washington Press, 1968.
Friedman, Jonathan. "The Past in the Future: History and the Politics of Iden-
    tity." *American Anthropologist* 94, no. 4 (1992): 837–59.

Galloway, Patricia, and Clara Sue Kidwell. "Choctaws in the East." In *Handbook of North American Indians: Southeast*, edited by Raymond D. Fogelson, 499–518. Washington, D.C.: Smithsonian Institution, 2005.

Garroutte, Eva Marie. *Real Indians: Identities and the Survival of Native America*. Berkeley: University of California Press, 2003.

Gatschet, Albert S. "The Shetimasha Indians of St. Mary's Parish, Southern Louisiana." *Transactions of the Anthropological Society of Washington* 2 (1882–1883): 148.

Getches, David H., Charles F. Wilkinson, and Robert A. Williams, eds. *Federal Indian Law: Cases and Materials*. 3d ed. St. Paul: West, 1993.

Gilbert, Harlen, Jr. "Memorandum concerning the Characteristics of the Larger Mixed-Blood Racial Islands of the Eastern United States." *Social Forces* 24, no. 4 (1946): 438–47.

Goldberg-Ambrose, Carole. "Of Native Americans and Tribal Members: The Impact of Law on Indian Group Life." *Law and Society Review* 28, no. 5 (1994): 1123–48.

Goldfield, David R. *Black, White, and Southern: Race Relations and Southern Culture, 1940 to the Present*. Baton Rouge: Louisiana State University Press, 1990.

Grabowski, Christine Tracey. "Coiled Intent: Federal Acknowledgment Policy and the Gay Head Wampanoags." PhD diss., City University of New York, 1994.

Green, Daniel Edward. *The Creek People*. Phoenix: Indian Tribal Series, 1973.

Green, Michael D. *The Politics of Indian Removal: Creek Government and Society in Crisis*. Lincoln: University of Nebraska Press, 1982.

Green, Michael K., ed. *Issues in Native American Cultural Identity*. New York: Peter Lang, 1995.

Green, Rayna. "The Tribe Called Wannabee: Playing Indian in America and Europe." *Folklore* 99, no. 1 (1988): 30–55.

Greenbaum, Susan. "In Search of Lost Tribes: Anthropology and the Federal Acknowledgment Process." *Human Organization* 44, no, 4 (1985): 361–67.

———. "What's in a Label? Identity Problems of Southern Indian Tribes." *Journal of Ethnic Studies* 19, no. 2 (1991): 107–24.

Greenberg, Adolph M., and James Morrison. "Group Identities in the Boreal Forest: The Origin of the Northern Ojibwa." *Ethnohistory* 29, no. 2 (1982): 75–102.

Gregory, Hiram F. "Jena Band of Louisiana Choctaw." *American Indian Journal* 3, no. 2 (1977): 2–16.

———. "The Louisiana Tribes: Entering Hard Times." In *Indians of the Southeastern United States in the late 20th Century*, edited by J. Anthony Paredes, 162–82. Tuscaloosa: University of Alabama Press, 1992.

———. "Survival and Maintenance among Louisiana Tribes." In *Handbook of North American Indians: Southeast*, edited by Raymond D. Fogelson, 653–58. Washington, D.C.: Smithsonian Institution, 2005.

Griessman, B. Eugene, ed. "The American Isolates." *American Anthropologist* 74, no. 5 (1972): 1276–98.

Griessman, B. Eugene, and Curtis T. Henson, Jr. "The History and Social Topography of an Ethnic Island in Alabama." *Phylon: The Atlanta University Review of Race and Culture* 36, no. 2 (1975): 105.

Gross, Ariela. "Of Portuguese Origin," *Law and History Review* 25, no. 3 (2009).

Hagan, William T. "Full Blood, Mixed Blood, Generic, and Ersatz: The Problem of Indian Identity." *Arizona and the West* 27 (Winter 1985): 309–26.

Halter, Marilyn. *Shopping for Ethnicity: The Marketing of Ethnicity.* New York: Schocken Books, 2000.

Hamill, James. *Going Indian.* Urbana: University of Illinois Press, 2006.

Hapiuk, William J. "Of Kitsch and Kachinas: A Critical Analysis of the Indian Arts and Crafts Act of 1990." *Stanford Law Review* 53, no. 4 (2001): 1009–75.

Harmon, Alexandra. *Indians in the Making: Ethnic Relations and Indian Identities around Puget Sound.* Berkeley: University of California Press, 1998.

———. "When Is an Indian Not an Indian? The "Friends of the Indian" and the Problem of Indian Identity." *Journal of Ethnic Studies* 18, no. 2 (1990): 95–113.

Hauptman, Laurence M. *Tribes and Tribulations: Misconceptions about American Indians and Their Histories.* Albuquerque: University of New Mexico Press, 1995.

Heinegg, Paul. *Free African Americans of North Carolina, Virginia, and South Carolina.* Baltimore: Clearfield, 1997.

Helm, June, ed. *Essays on the Problem of Tribe: Proceedings of the 1967 Annual Spring Meeting of the American Ethnological Society.* Seattle: University of Washington Press, 1968.

Henry, Frances, ed. *Ethnicity in the Americas.* The Hague: Mouton Publishers, 1976.

Hertzberg, Hazel. *The Search for an American Indian Identity: Modern Pan-Indian Movements.* Syracuse: Syracuse University Press, 1971.

Hobsbawm, Eric, and Terrence Ranger, eds. *The Invention of Tradition.* London: Cambridge University Press, 1983.

Hodge, Frederick Webb. *Handbook of American Indians North of Mexico, Part 2.* Smithsonian Institution Bureau of American Ethnology, Bulletin 30. Washington, D.C.: Government Printing Office, 1907–1910.

Hook, Jonathan B. *The Alabama-Coushatta Indians.* College Station: Texas A&M University Press, 1997.

Hoxie, Frederick E. *A Final Promise: The Campaign to Assimilate the Indians, 1880–1920.* Lincoln: University of Nebraska Press, 1984.

———. "From Prison to Homeland: The Cheyenne River Indian Reservation before World War I." *South Dakota History* 10 (Winter 1979): 1–24.

Hudson, Charles. *The Catawba Nation.* Athens: University of Georgia Press, 1970.

————. *The Southeastern Indians.* Knoxville: University of Tennessee Press, 1976.

Hutchinson, Elizabeth. *The Indian Craze: Primitivism, Modernism, and Transculturation in American Art, 1890–1915.* Durham, N.C.: Duke University Press, 2009.

Innes, Pamela. "Creeks in the West." In *Handbook of North American Indians: Southeast,* edited by Raymond D. Fogelson, 393–403. Washington, D.C.: Smithsonian Institution, 2004.

Jaimes, Marie Annette. "American Indian Identification/Eligibility Policy in Federal Education Service Programs." PhD diss., Arizona State University, 1990.

————, ed. *The State of Native America: Genocide, Colonization and Resistance.* Boston: South End Press, 1992.

Janda, Sarah Eppler. *Beloved Women: The Political Lives of LaDonna Harris and Wilma Mankiller.* DeKalb: Northern Illinois University Press, 2007.

Johnson, Katie N., and Tamara Underiner. "Command Performances: Staging Native Americans at Tillicum Village." In *Selling the Indian: Commercializing and Appropriating American Indian Cultures,* edited Carter Jones Meyer and Diana Royer, 44–61. Tucson: University of Arizona Press, 2001.

Jojola, Ted. "Absurd Reality II: Hollywood Goes to the Indians." In *Hollywood's Indian: The Portrayal of Native Americans in Film,* edited by Peter C. Rollins and John E. O'Connor, 12–21. Lexington: University of Kentucky Press, 1998.

Jolivette, Andrew, ed. *Cultural Representations in Native America.* Lanham, Md.: Altamira Press, 2006.

Josephy, Alvin M., Jr., Joane Nagel, and Troy Johnson, eds. *Red Power: The American Indians' Fight for Freedom.* Lincoln: University of Nebraska Press, 1999.

Kaiser, Robert G. *So Damn Much Money: The Triumph of Lobbying and the Corrosion of American Government.* New York: Knopf, 2009.

Kauanui, J. Kehaulani. *Hawaiian Blood: Colonialism and the Politics of Sovereignty and Indigeneity.* Durham, N.C.: Duke University Press, 2008.

Kelly, Lawrence C. *The Assault on Assimilation: John Collier and the Origins of Indian Policy Reform.* Albuquerque: University of New Mexico Press, 1983.

Kelly, Michael J. "Treaty with the Cherokee, Nov. 28, 1785." In *Treaties with American Indians,* Vol. II, edited by Donald L. Fixico, 285–86. Santa Barbara: ABC-Clio Press, 2008.

Kersey, Harry A., Jr. *An Assumption of Sovereignty: Social and Political Transformation among the Florida Seminoles, 1953–1979.* Lincoln: University of Nebraska Press, 1996.

Kickingbird, Kirke. "The American Indian Policy Review Commission: A Prospect for Future Change in Federal Indian Policy." *American Indian Law Review* 3, no. 2 (1975): 251.

Kidwell, Clara Sue . *The Choctaws in Oklahoma: From Tribe to Nation, 1855–1970.* Norman: University of Oklahoma Press, 2007.

―――. "Choctaws in the West." In *Handbook of North American Indians: Southeast*, edited by Raymond D. Fogelson, 522–30. Washington, D.C.: Smithsonian Institution, 2005.

―――. "Termination of the Choctaw." In *Beyond Red Power: American Indian Politics and Activism since 1900*, edited by Daniel M. Cobb and Loretta Fowler, 126–35. Santa Fe: School for Advanced Research Press, 2007.

King, Duane H. "Cherokees in the West: History since 1776." In *Handbook of North American Indians: Southeast*, edited by Raymond D. Fogelson, 354–71. Washington, D.C.: Smithsonian Institution, 2005.

Klopotek, Brian. "The Long Outwaiting: Federal Recognition Policy in Three Louisiana Indian Communities." PhD diss., University of Minnesota, 2004.

―――. *Recognition Odysseys: Indigeneity, Race, and Federal Tribal Recognition Policy in Three Louisiana Indian Communities*. Durham, N.C.: Duke University Press, 2011.

Kniffen, Fred B., Hiram F. Gregory, and George A. Stokes. *The Historic Indian Tribes of Louisiana: From 1542 to the Present*. Baton Rouge: Louisiana State University Press, 1987.

Krech, Shepard. *The Ecological Indian: Myth and History*. New York: Norton, 1999.

Kroeber, A. L. "Nature of the Land-Holding Group." *Ethnohistory* 2, no. 4 (1955): 302–14.

Kroeber, Karl, and Clifton Kroeber, eds. *Ishi in Three Centuries*. Lincoln: University of Nebraska Press, 2003.

LaGrand, James B. *Indian Metropolis: Native Americans in Chicago, 1944–1975*. Urbana: University of Illinois Press, 2002.

Lambert, Valerie. *Choctaw Nation: A Story of American Indian Resurgence*. Lincoln: University of Nebraska Press, 2007.

Lane, Ambrose. *Return of the Buffalo: The Story behind America's Gaming Explosion*. New York: Bergin and Garvey, 1995.

LaVelle, John. Review of *Indians are U.S.?*, by Ward Churchill. *American Indian Quarterly* 20 (Winter 1996): 109–18.

Lawrence, Bonita. *"Real" Indians and Others: Mixed-Blood Urban Native People and Indigenous Nationhood*. Lincoln: University of Nebraska Press, 2004.

Lerch, Patricia Barker. "Indians of the Carolinas since 1900." In *Handbook of North American Indians: Southeast*, edited by Raymond D. Fogelson, 328–40. Washington, D.C.: Smithsonian Institution, 2005.

―――. "State Recognized Indians of North Carolina." In *Indians of the Southeastern United States in the Late Twentieth Century*, edited by J. Anthony Paredes, 44–71. Tuscaloosa: University of Alabama Press, 1992.

―――. *Waccamaw Legacy: Contemporary Indians' Fight for Survival*. Tuscaloosa: University of Alabama Press, 2004.

Lewis, David, and Ann Jordan. *Creek Indian Medicine Ways: The Enduring Power of Myskoke Religion*. Albuquerque: University of New Mexico Press, 2002.

Liebow, Edward B. "Category or Community? Measuring Urban Indian Social Cohesion with Network Sampling." *Journal of Ethnic Studies* 16, no. 4 (1989): 67–97.

Light, Steven A., and Kathryn R. L. Rand. *Indian Gaming and Tribal Sovereignty: The Casino Compromise.* Lawrence: University Press of Kansas, 2009.

Lofton, Teresa Constance. "Reclaiming an American Indian Identity: The Ethnic Renewal of the Lower Muskogee Creeks." PhD diss., Georgia State University, 2000.

Logan, Michael H., and Stephen D. Ousley. "Hypergamy, Quantum, and Reproductive Success: The Lost Indian Ancestor Reconsidered." In *Anthropologists and Indians in the New South,* edited by Rachel A. Bonney and J. Anthony Paredes, 184–202. Tuscaloosa: University of Alabama Press, 2001.

Lovegrove, Michael W. *A Nation in Transition: Douglas Henry Johnston and the Chickasaw, 1898–1939.* Ada, OK: Chickasaw Press, 2009.

Lowery, Malinda Maynor. *Lumbee Indians in the Jim Crow South: Race, Identity, and the Making of a Nation.* Chapel Hill: University of North Carolina Press, 2010.

Lurie, Nancy Oestreich. "An American Indian Renascence?" In *The American Indian Today,* edited by Stuart Levine and Nancy O. Lurie, 295–327. Baltimore: Penguin Books. 1968.

———. "Problems, Opportunities, and Recommendations." *Ethnohistory* 2 (Fall 1955): 357–75.

———. "Report on the American Indian Chicago Conference." *Current Anthropology* 2, no. 5 (1961): 478–500.

Martin, Joel W. "My Grandmother Was a Cherokee Princess: Representations of Indians in Southern History." In *Dressing in Feathers: The Construction of the Indian in American Popular Culture,* edited by Elizabeth S. Bird, 129–45. Boulder: Westview Press, 1996.

Martin, Karla, and Natalie Adams. "Gaming and Native Education: A Qualitative Exploration of USET Tribes," Archived Information, Office of Indian Education, http://www2.ed.gov/rschstat/research/pubs/oieresearch/conference/martin_200604.pdf (accessed 6 November 2012).

Mason, W, Dale. *Indian Gaming: Tribal Sovereignty and American Politics.* Norman: University of Oklahoma Press, 2000.

Matte, Jacqueline. "Extinction by Reclassification: The MOWA Choctaws of South Alabama and Their Struggle for Federal Recognition." *Alabama Review* 59 (July 2006), 168–80.

———. *They Say the Wind is Red: The Alabama Choctaw, Lost in Their Own Land.* Montgomery: NewSouth Books, 2002.

Matusow, Allen J. *The Unraveling of America: A History of Liberalism in the 1960s.* New York: Harper and Row, 1984.

Mauzé, Marie, ed. *Present Is Past: Some Uses of Tradition in Native Societies.* Lanham, Md.: University Press of America, 1997.

Mazurek, Joseph P., ed. *American Indian Law Deskbook.* Niwot, CO: University Press of Colorado, 1998.

McCall, George J., and J. L. Simmons. *Identities and Interactions: An Examination of Human Associations in Everyday Life.* New York: The Free Press, 1978.

McCulloch, Anne Merline, and David E. Wilkins. "'Constructing' Nations Within States: The Quest for Federal Recognition by the Catawba and Lumbee Tribes." *American Indian Quarterly* 19, no. 3 (1995): 361–90.

McIlwraith, Thomas. "The Problem of Imported Culture: The Construction of Contemporary Sto:lo Identity." *American Indian Culture and Research Journal* 20, no. 4 (1996): 41–70.

McLerran, Jennifer. *A New Deal for Native Art: Indian Arts and Federal Policy, 1933–1943.* Tucson: University of Arizona Press, 2009.

Merrell, James H. *The Indians' New World: The Catawbas and Their Neighbors from European Contact through the Era of Removal.* Chapel Hill: University of North Carolina Press, 1989.

Meyer, Carter Jones, and Diana Royer, eds. *Selling the Indian: Commercializing and Appropriating American Indian Cultures.* Tucson: University of Arizona Press, 2001.

Miles, Tiya. "Uncle Tom Was an Indian." In *Confounding the Color Line: The Indian-Black Experience in North America,* edited by James Brooks, 137–60. Lincoln: University of Nebraska Press, 2002.

Miller, Bruce G. *Invisible Indigenes: The Politics of Nonrecognition.* Lincoln: University of Nebraska Press, 2003.

Miller, Mark Edwin. *Forgotten Tribes: Unrecognized Indians and the Federal Acknowledgment Process.* Lincoln: University of Nebraska Press, 2004.

Moermon, Michael. "Being Lue: Uses and Abuses of Ethnic Identification." In *Essays on the Problem of Tribe,* edited by June Helm, 153–67. Seattle: University of Washington Press, 1968.

Mooney, James. *History, Myths, and Sacred Formulas of the Cherokees.* Fairview, NC: Bright Mountain Books, 1992.

Murphy, Laura Frances. "Among the Cajans of Alabama." *Missionary Voice,* November 1930, 18–21.

———. "The Cajans of Mobile County, Alabama." Master's thesis, Scarritt College, 1935.

Nagel, Joane. *American Indian Ethnic Renewal: Red Power and the Resurgence of Identity and Culture.* New York: Oxford University Press, 1996.

———. "False Faces: Ethnic Identity, Authenticity, and Fraud in Native American Discourse and Politics." In *Identity and Social Change,* edited by Joseph E. Davis, 81–106. New Brunswick, N.J.: Transaction Publishers, 2000.

Nichols, Roger L. "Indians in the Post-Termination Era." *Storia Nordamericana* 5, no. 1 (1988): 83–91.

Novak, Michael. *The Rise of the Unmeltable Ethnics*. New York: MacMillan, 1971.

Oakley, Christopher Arris. *Keeping the Circle: American Indian Identity in Eastern North Carolina, 1885–2004*. Lincoln: University of Nebraska Press, 2005.

Obermeyer, Brice. *Delaware Tribe in a Cherokee Nation*. Lincoln: University of Nebraska Press, 2009.

Officer, James. "The Bureau of Indian Affairs since 1945: An Assessment." *Annals of the Academy of Political and Social Science* 436 (March 1978): 61–72.

Olzak, Susan. *Ethnic Competition: The Dynamics of Ethnic Competition and Conflict*. Palo Alto, Calif.: Stanford University Press, 1992.

Omi, Michael, and Howard Winant. *Racial Formation in the United States: From the 1960s to the 1990s*. New York: Routledge, 1986.

Paredes, J. Anthony. "Back from Disappearance: The Alabama Creek Indian Community." In *Southeastern Indians Since the Removal Era*, edited by Walter L. Williams, 123–41. Athens: University of Georgia Press, 1979.

———. "The Emergence of Contemporary Eastern Creek Indian Identity." In *Social and Cultural Identity: Problems of Persistence and Change*, edited by Thomas F. Fitzgerald, 63–80. Athens: University of Georgia Press, 1974.

———. "Federal Recognition of the Poarch Creek Indians." In *Indians of the Southeastern United States in the Late 20th Century*, edited by J. Anthony Paredes, 120–39. Tuscaloosa: University of Alabama Press, 1992.

———, ed. *Indians of the Southeastern United States in the Late 20th Century*. Tuscaloosa: University of Alabama Press, 1992.

———."Indigenous Renascence: Law, Culture and Society in the 21st Century: In Defense of the BIA and NPS." *St. Thomas Law Review* 10, no. 35 (1997), 35–43.

———. "Kinship and Descent in the Ethnic Reassertion of the Eastern Creek Indians." In *The Versatility of Kinship*, edited by Linda S. Cordell and Stephen J. Beckerman, 166–73. New York: Academic Press, 1980.

———. "Paradoxes of Modernism and Indianness in the Southeast." *American Indian Quarterly* 19, no. 3 (1995): 341–59.

———. "'Practical History' and the Poarch Creeks: A Meeting Ground for Anthropology and Tribal Leaders." In *Anthropological Research: Process and Application*, edited by John J. Poggie Jr., Billie DeWalt, and William W. Dressler, 209–26. Albany: State University of New York Press, 1992.

———. "Some Creeks Stayed: Comments on Amelia Rector Bell's 'Separate People: Speaking Creek Men and Women.'" *American Anthropologist* 93, no. 3 (1991): 697–99.

Paredes, J. Anthony, and Rachel A. Bonney, eds. *Anthropologists and Indians in the New South*. Tuscaloosa: University of Alabama Press, 2001.

Paredes, J. Anthony, and Kaye Lenihan. "Native American Population in the Southeastern States, 1960–70." *Florida Anthropologist* 26, no. 2 (1973): 45–56.

Parenton, Vernon J., and Roland J. Pellegrin. "The 'Sabines': A Study of Racial Hybrids in a Louisiana Coastal Parish." *Social Forces* 29, no. 1 (1950): 148–54.

Parsley, Jon Keith. "Regulation of Counterfeit Indian Arts and Crafts: An Analysis of the Indian Arts and Crafts Act of 1990." *American Indian Law Review* 18, no. 2 (1993): 487–514.

Paschal, Rachael. "The Imprimatur of Recognition: American Indian Tribes and the Federal Acknowledgment Process." *Washington Law Review* 66 (1991): 209–28.

Pascoe, Peggy. "Miscegenation Law, Court Cases, and Ideologies of 'Race' in Twentieth Century America." In *Interracialism: Black-White Intermarriage in American History, Literature, and Law,* edited by Werner Sollers, 202–4. New York: Oxford University Press, 2000.

Perdue, Theda. *Cherokee Women: Gender and Change, 1700–1835.* Lincoln: University of Nebraska Press, 1998.

―――. *Native Carolinians: The Indians of North Carolina.* Raleigh: North Carolina Department of Cultural Resources, 1985.

―――. "A Sprightly Lover Is the Most Prevailing Missionary." In *Light on the Path: The Anthropology and History of the Southeastern Indians,* edited by Thomas J. Pluckhahn and Robbie Etheridge, 165–71. Tuscaloosa: University of Alabama Press, 2006.

Peroff, Nicholas C. *Menominee Drums: Tribal Termination and Restoration, 1954–1974.* Norman: University of Oklahoma Press, 1982.

Peterson, John H. "The Indians in the Old South." In *Red, White, and Black: Symposium on Indians in the Old South,* edited by Charles M. Hudson, 116–33. Athens: University of Georgia Press, 1970.

Pewewardy, Cornel. "'Beyond Our Names: Uncovering Identity' Resource Guide." *Tribal College Journal* 19, no. 3 (2008), http://www.tribalcollege journal.org/archives/6203 (accessed 15 October 2012).

―――. "Will the 'Real' Indians Please Stand Up?" *Multicultural Review* 7, no. 2 (1998): 36–42.

Philp, Kenneth R. *Termination Revisited: American Indians on the Trail to Self-Determination, 1933–1953.* Lincoln: University of Nebraska Press, 1999.

Pierce, Earl Boyd, and Rennard Strickland. *The Cherokee People.* Phoenix: Indian Tribal Series, 1973.

Pollitzer, William S. "The Cajuns of Southern Alabama: Morphology and Serology." *American Journal of Physical Anthropology* 47, no. 1 (1977): 1–6.

―――. "The Physical Anthropology and Genetics of Marginal People in the Southeastern United States." *American Anthropologist* 74, no. 3 (1972): 719–34.

Porter, Frank W., III. "In Search of Recognition: Federal Indian Policy and the Landless Tribes of Western Washington." *American Indian Quarterly* 14, no. 2 (1990): 113–32.

―――. *Nonrecognized American Indian Tribes: An Historical and Legal Perspective.* Chicago: Newberry Library, 1983.

————, ed. *Strategies for Survival: American Indians in the Eastern United States.* Westport, Conn.: Greenwood Press, 1986.

Posey, Darrell A. "Origin, Development and Maintenance of a Louisiana Mixed-Blood Community: The Ethnohistory of the Freejacks of the First Ward Settlement." *Ethnohistory* 26, no. 2 (1979): 177–92.

Price, Edward T. "A Geographic Analysis of White-Negro-Indian Racial Mixtures in the Eastern United States." *Annals of the Association of American Geographers* 43, no. 2 (1953), 138–55.

————. "Mixed-Blood Populations of the Eastern United States as to Origins, Localizations, and Persistence." PhD diss., University of California, Berkeley, 1950.

Pritzer, Barry, ed. *A Native American Encyclopedia: History, Culture, and Peoples.* Oxford: Oxford University Press, 1999.

Prucha, Francis Paul. *The Great Father: The United States Government and the American Indian.* Abridged edition. Lincoln: University of Nebraska Press, 1986.

————. *The Indian in American Society.* Berkeley: University of California Press, 1985.

Quinn, William W., Jr. "Federal Acknowledgment of American Indian Tribes: Authority, Judicial Interposition, and 25 C.F.R. § 83." *American Indian Law Review* 17, no. 1 (1992): 37–69.

————. "Federal Acknowledgment of American Indian Tribes: The Historical Development of a Legal Concept." *American Journal of Legal History* (October 1990): 331–64.

————. "'Public Ethnohistory?' Or, Writing Tribal Histories at the Bureau of Indian Affairs." *Public Historian* 10, no. 2 (1988): 71–76.

————. "Southeastern Indians: The Quest for Federal Acknowledgment and a New Legal Status." *Ethnic Forum: Journal of Ethnic Studies and Ethnic Bibliography* 13, no. 1 (1993): 34–52.

————. "The Southeast Syndrome: Notes on Indian Descendent Recruitment Organizations and Their Perceptions of Native American Culture." *American Indian Quarterly* 14, no. 2 (1990): 147–54.

Raibmon, Paige. *Authentic Indians: Episodes of Encounter from the Late Nineteenth Century Northwest Coast.* Durham, N.C.: Duke University Press, 2005.

Rafert, Stewart. *The Miami Indians of Indiana: A Persistent People, 1654–1994.* Indianapolis: Indiana Historical Society, 1996.

Richman, Robin. "Return of the Red Man." Special issue, *Life*, 1 December 1967.

Robin, C. C. *Voyage to Louisiana, 1803–1805.* New Orleans: Pelican Publishing, 1936.

Roediger, David R. *The Wages of Whiteness.* New York: Verso, 1991.

Rogers, Obra. "Among the Cajuns of Alabama," *Trained Lay Worker* 2, no. 5 (December 1929): 1.

Root, Deborah. *Cannibal Culture: Art, Appropriation and the Commodification of Difference.* Boulder, CO: Westview Press, 1996.

Root, Maria P. P. "Within, Between, and Beyond Race." In *Racially Mixed People in America,* ed. Maria P. P. Root, 1–5. London: Sage Publications, 1992.

Rose, Wendy. "The Great Pretenders: Further Reflections on White Shamanism." In *The State of Native America: Genocide, Colonization, and Resistance,* edited by M. Annette Jaimes, 404–15. Boston: South End Press, 1992.

Rosen, Lawrence. "The Anthropologist as Expert Witness." *American Anthropologist* 79 (1977): 555–73.

Rosenthal, H. D. *Their Day in Court: A History of the Indian Claims Commission.* New York: Garland Publishing, 1990.

Ross, Norman A., ed. *Index to the Decisions of the Indian Claims Commission.* New York: Clearwater Publishing, 1973.

Ross, Thomas E. *American Indians in North Carolina: Geographic Interpretations.* Southern Pines, NC: Karo Hollow Press, 1999.

Roth, George. "Federal Tribal Recognition in the South." In *Anthropologists and Indians in the New South,* edited by Rachel A. Bonney and J. Anthony Paredes, 49–70. Tuscaloosa: University of Alabama Press, 2001.

———. "Overview of Southeastern Indian Tribes Today." In *Indians of the Southeastern United States in the Late 20th Century,* edited by J. Anthony Paredes, 183–201. Tuscaloosa: University of Alabama Press, 1992.

Rountree, Helen. "Indian Virginians on the Move." In *Indians in the Southeastern United States in Late 20th Century,* edited by J. Anthony Paredes, 9–28. Tuscaloosa: University of Alabama Press, 1992.

———. *Pocahontas' People: The Powhatan Indians of Virginia through Four Centuries.* Norman: University of Oklahoma Press, 1990.

Royce, Anya Peterson. *Ethnic Identity: Strategies of Diversity.* Bloomington: Indiana University Press, 1982.

Shanley, Kathryn. "The Indians America Loves to Love and Read." In *Native American Representations: First Encounters, Distorted Images, and Literary Appropriations,* edited by Gretchen M. Bataille, 26–51. Lincoln: University of Nebraska Press, 2001.

Sheridan, Thomas, and Nancy J. Parezo, eds. *Paths of Life: American Indians in the Southwest and Northern Mexico.* Tucson: University of Arizona Press, 1996.

Shuck-Hall, Sheri. *Journey to the West: The Alabama and Coushatta Indians.* Norman: University of Oklahoma Press, 2008.

Sibley, John. "Historical Sketches of the Several Tribes in Louisiana South of the Arkansas River and Between the Mississippi and the River Grand." In *Report to the President: Travels in the Interior Parts of America Communicating Discoveries Made in Exploring the Missouri, Red River and Washita by Captains Lewis and Clark, Doctor Sibley, and Mr. Dunbar.* London: J. G. Barnard, 1807.

Sider, Gerald M. *Living Indian Histories: Lumbee and Tuscarora People in North Carolina.* Chapel Hill: University of North Carolina Press, 2003.

———. *Lumbee Indian Histories: Race, Ethnicity, and Indian Identity in the Southern United States.* Cambridge: Cambridge University Press, 1993.

Slagle, Alogan. "Unfinished Justice: Completing the Restoration and Acknowledgment of California Indian Tribes. " *American Indian Quarterly* 13, no. 4 (1989): 325–45.

Smith, Donald B. "From Sylvester Long to Chief Buffalo Child Long Lance." In *Being and Becoming Indian: Biographical Studies of North American Frontiers,* edited by James A. Clifton, 185–202. Chicago: Dorsey Press, 1989.

Snipp, C. Mathew. *American Indians: The First of This Land.* New York: Russell Sage Foundation, 1989.

Speck, Frank G. "The Houma Indians in 1940." *American Indian Journal* 2, no. 1 (1976): 3–15.

———. "Notes on the Social and Economic Conditions among the Creek Indians of Alabama in 1941," *America Indigena* 7 (July 1947), 194–98.

Spicer, Edward Holland. *A Short History of the Indians of the United States.* New York: Van Nostrand Reinhold, 1969.

Spicer, Edward Holland, and Raymond H. Thompson, eds. *Plural Society in the Southwest.* New York: Interbook, 1972.

Stanton, Max E. "A Remnant Indian Community: The Houma of Southern Louisiana." In *The Not So Solid South,* edited by J. Kenneth Morland, 82–90. Athens, GA: Southern Anthropological Society, 1971.

———. "Southern Louisiana Indian Survivors: The Houma Indians." In *Southeastern Indians Since the Removal Period,* edited by Walter Williams, 90–109. Athens: University of Georgia Press, 1979.

Starna, William A. "'Public Ethnohistory' and Native-American Communities: History or Administrative Genocide?" *Radical History Review* 53 (Spring 1992): 126–39.

———. "The Southeast Syndrome: The Prior Restraint of a Non-Event." *American Indian Quarterly* 15, no. 4 (1991): 493–502.

———. "We'll All Be Together Again: The Federal Acknowledgment of the Wampanoag Tribe of Gay Head." *Northeast Anthropology* 51 (Spring 1996): 3–12.

Steiner, Stan. *The New Indians.* New York: Dell, 1968.

Steinman, Erich. "Settler Colonial Power and the American Indian Sovereignty Movement: Forms of Domination, Strategies of Transformation." *American Journal of Sociology* 117 (January 2012): 1073–1130.

Stockel, Henrietta H. *Shame and Endurance: The Untold Story of the Chiricahua Apache Prisoners of War.* Tucson: University of Arizona Press, 2004.

Stopp, G. Harry, Jr. "On Mixed-Racial Isolates." *American Anthropologist* 76 (1974): 343–44.

Stowe, David W. "Uncolored People: The Rise of Whiteness Studies." *Lingua Franca* (September/October 1996): 68–77.

Sturm, Circe. *Blood Politics: Race, Culture, and Identity in the Cherokee Nation of Oklahoma.* Berkeley: University of California Press, 2002.

———. "States of Sovereignty: Race Shifting, Recognition, and Rights in Cherokee Country." In *Beyond Red Power: American Indian Politics and Activism since 1900,* edited by Daniel M. Cobb and Loretta Fowler, 229–35. Santa Fe: School for Advanced Research Press, 2007.

Sutler-Cohen, Sara C. "(Dis) Locating Spiritual Knowledge: Embodied Ideologies, Social Landscapes, and the Power of the Neoshamic Other." In *Cultural Representations in Native America,* edited by Andrew Jolivette, 43–63. Lanham, Md.: Altamira Press, 2006.

Suttles, Gerald D. *The Social Construction of Communities.* Chicago: University of Chicago Press, 1972.

Sutton, Juanealya McCormick. *The Man behind the Scenes: Neal (Pappy) McCormick & Hank Williams.* DeFuniak Springs, FL: J. M. Sutton, 1987.

Swanton, John Reed. *Aboriginal Culture in the Southeast.* Smithsonian Institution Bureau of American Ethnology, Forty-second Annual Report 1924/25. Washington, D.C.: Government Printing Office, 1928.

———. *Indians of the Southeastern United States.* Smithsonian Institution Bureau of American Ethnology Bulletin no. 137. Washington D.C.: Government Printing Office, 1946.

———. *Indian Tribes of the Lower Mississippi Valley and Adjacent Coast of the Gulf of Mexico.* Smithsonian Institution Bureau of American Ethnology, Bulletin 43. Washington, D.C.: Government Printing Office, 1911.

Taylor, Theodore W. *The States and Their Indian Citizens.* Washington, D.C.: Department of the Interior, 1972.

Thornton, Russell. *The Cherokees: A Population History.* Lincoln: University of Nebraska Press, 1990.

Tolley, Sara-Larus. *Quest for Tribal Acknowledgment: California's Honey Lake Maidus.* Norman: University of Oklahoma Press, 2006.

Tureen, Thomas N. "Federal Recognition and the *Passamaquoddy* Decision." RG 220, NACP.

Usner, Daniel H. *American Indians in the Lower Mississippi Valley: Social and Economic Histories.* Lincoln: University of Nebraska Press, 1998.

Van Rheenen, Mary B. "Can You Tell Me Who My People Are? Ethnic Identity among the Hispanic-Indian People in Sabine Parish, Louisiana." Master's thesis, Louisiana State University, 1987.

Van Slyk, Abigail A. *A Manufactured Wilderness: Summer Camps and the Shaping of American Youth, 1890–1960.* Minneapolis: University of Minnesota Press, 2006.

Walker, Amelia Bell, "Instant Indians: An Analysis of Cultural Identity in the American South." *Southern Anthropologist* 6, no. 2 (1977): 15–27.

Wallis, Robert J. *Shamans/Neo-Shamans: Ecstasy, Alternative Archaeologies, and Contemporary Pagans*. London: Routledge, 2003.

Waters, Mary. *Ethnic Options: Choosing Identities in America*. Berkeley: University of California Press, 1990.

———. "Multiple Ethnicities and Identities in the United States." In *We Are a People*, edited by Paul Spickard and W. Jeffrey Burroughs, 23–31. Philadelphia: Temple University Press, 2000.

———. "Optional Ethnicities: For Whites Only?" In *Rethinking the Color Line: Readings on Race and Ethnicity*, 2d ed., edited by Charles A. Gallagher, 96–107. Boston: McGraw Hill, 2004.

Watt, Marilyn. "Federal Indian Policy and Tribal Development in Louisiana: The Jena Band of Choctaws." PhD diss., Pennsylvania State University, 1986.

"We Are Here Forever: Indians of the South." Special issue, *Southern Exposure* 13, no. 6 (1985).

Weatherhead, L. R. "What Is an 'Indian Tribe'? The Question of Tribal Existence." *American Indian Law Review* 8, no. 1 (1980): 1–47.

Weaver, Hillary N. "Indigenous Identity: What Is It and Who Really Has It?" *American Indian Quarterly* 25 (Spring 2001): 240–55.

Weibel-Orlando, Joan. *Indian Country, L.A.: Maintaining Ethnic Community in Complex Society*. Urbana: University of Illinois Press, 1991.

Wernitznig, Dagmar. *Going Native or Going Naïve? White Shamanism and the Neo-Noble Savage*. Lanham, Md.: University Press of America, 2003.

White, Benton R., and Christine Schultz White. "Phillip Martin." In *The New Warriors: Native American Leaders since 1900*, edited by R. David Edmunds, 195–210. Lincoln: University of Nebraska Press, 2001.

White, Richard. *The Roots of Dependency: Subsistence, Environment, and Social Change among the Choctaws, Pawnees, and Navajos*. Lincoln: University of Nebraska Press, 1983.

Wiebe, Robert H. *Who We Are: A History of Popular Nationalism*. Princeton, N.J.: Princeton University Press, 2002.

Wilkins, David E. *American Indian Politics and the American Political System*. Lanham, Md.: Rowman and Littlefield, 2002.

———. "Breaking into the Intergovernmental Matrix: The Lumbee Tribe's Efforts to Secure Federal Acknowledgment." *Publius: The Journal of Federalism* 23, no. 4 (1993): 123–42.

Wilson, Raymond. "Russell Means." In *The New Warriors: Native American Leaders since 1900*, edited by R. David Edmunds, 144–55. Lincoln: University of Nebraska Press, 2001.

Wilson, Terry P. "Blood Quantum: Native American Mixed Bloods." In *Racially Mixed People in America*, edited by Maria P. P. Root, 111. London: Sage Publications, 1992.

Winston, George T. "The Relationship of the Whites to the Negroes," reprinted in *The South Since Reconstruction*, edited by Thomas D. Clark, 313. Indianapolis: Bobbs-Merrill, 1973.

Winzeler, Robert L. *Anthropology and Religion: What We Know, Think, and Question*. Lanham, Md.: Altamira Press 2008.

Woodward, C. Vann. *The Strange Career of Jim Crow*. New York: Oxford University Press, 1974.

Woodward, Grace Steele. *The Cherokees*. Norman: University of Oklahoma Press, 1963.

Wray, Matt. *Not Quite White: White Trash and the Boundaries of Whiteness*. Durham, N.C.: Duke University Press, 2006.

Wright, J. Leitch. *Creeks and Seminoles: The Destruction and Regeneration of the Muscogulge People*. Lincoln: University of Nebraska Press, 1986.

————. *The Only Land They Knew: American Indians in the Old South*. Lincoln: University of Nebraska Press, 1999.

Young, Mary Elizabeth. *Redskins, Ruffleshirts and Rednecks: Indian Allotments in Alabama and Mississippi, 1830–1860*. Norman: University of Oklahoma Press, 1961.

INTERVIEWS AND PERSONAL CORRESPONDENCE

Due to the sensitive nature of many topics in this study, many interviewees' names have, by request, been withheld from citation.

Allen, Richard, Cherokee Nation citizen and policy analyst. Interview by author, 24 June 2009, Tahlequah, Oklahoma.

Arnould, Pat, United Houma member and deputy director of Governor's Office of Indian Affairs. Interview by author, 11 January 1999, Baton Rouge, Louisiana.

Austin, Steve, Branch of Acknowledgment ethnohistorian. Interviews by author by telephone, 20, 30 October 1998, and 1 April 1999. Interview by author in person, May 1999, Washington, D.C.

Baker, Jack, Cherokee Nation councilman. Interview by author, 22 June 2009, Oklahoma City, Oklahoma.

Bear, Joyce, Muscogee Nation cultural preservation officer. Interview by author, 17 November 2001, Little Rock, Arkansas.

Billiot, Reggie, former chief of the Biloxi-Chitimacha Confederation of Muskogees. Interview by author, 14 January 1999, Houma, Louisiana.

Cooper, Jim, enrolled citizen, Eastern Band of Cherokee Indians, and businessman. Interview by author by telephone, 7 December 2010.

Darcy, Cindy, former Native American affairs advocate, American Friends Service Committee. Interview by author by telephone, 24 May 1999.

Dardar, Brenda, United Houma Nation chairperson. Interview by author, 13 January 1999, Raceland, Louisiana.

Davis, Chad, American Indian affairs liaison for senator Richard Shelby. Interview by author by telephone, 9 October 2008.

DeMarce, Virginia, Branch of Acknowledgment. Interview by author by telephone, 21 February 2002.

Duthu, Bruce, Houma Indian and scholar. Interview by author by telephone, 6 January 2010.

Dysart, Jane, scholar of Eastern Creeks. Interview by author by telephone, 5 March 2010.

Gindrat, Helen, former United Houma Nation chairperson. Interview by author by telephone, 28 January 1999.

Gregory, Hiram (Pete), Anthropology Department, Northwestern State University. Interview by author, 11 January 1999, Natchitoches, Louisiana.

Hixenbaugh, Mike, journalist, *Fayetteville Observer*. Interview by author by telephone, 7 December 2010.

Hunt, Billy, enrolled Lumbee and tribal asset manager. Interview by author by telephone, 10 December 2010.

Jenkins, Venita, journalist, *Fayetteville Observer*. Interview by author by telephone, 17 December 2010.

Johnston, Todd, Mowa Choctaw leader. Interview by author, 13 October 2008, Mt. Vernon, Alabama.

King, Patti Jo, Cherokee Nation citizen and scholar. Interview by author, 23 June 2009, Norman, Oklahoma.

Lambert, Valerie, Choctaw Nation citizen and scholar. Interview by author by telephone, 29 May 2009.

Lewis, Jeff, Native American affairs officer for U.S. senator John Breaux (D-La.). Interview by author by telephone, 8 January 1999.

Locklear, Arlinda, enrolled Lumbee and lawyer. Interview by author by telephone, 8 December 2010.

Locklear, Ruth, enrolled Lumbee and head of tribal enrollment. Interview by author by telephone, 20 December 2010.

Lofton, Teresa, scholar of Lower Muskogee Creek Tribe. Interview by author by telephone, 25 August 2010.

Lyon, Nicholas, non-enrolled Eastern Cherokee descendant, resident of Cherokee, North Carolina. Interview by author, 11 December 2009, Cedar City, Utah.

Matte, Jacqueline, Mowa Choctaw tribal historian. Interview by author by telephone, 7 November 2008, and e-mail correspondence, fall 2008.

McClurken, James, anthropologist for Grand River Band of Ottawa Indians and Nipmuc Nation. Interview by author by telephone, 21 February 2002.

Miller, Don, Native American Rights Fund attorney. Interview by author by telephone, 11 January 2000.

Mooney, Tom, archivist at Cherokee Cultural Center. Interview by author, 25 June 2009, Tahlequah, Oklahoma.

Paredes, J. Anthony, former Poarch Creek anthropologist. Interview by author by telephone, 14 March 2002 and 1 April 2010.

Peters, Jill, Senate Indian Affairs Committee staff, U.S. senator John McCain's office. Interview by author by telephone, 16 February 1999.

Poteete, Troy Wayne, Cherokee Nation Supreme Court justice. Interview by author, 24 June 2009, Webbers Falls, Oklahoma.

Quinn, William, Jr., former ethnohistorian, Branch of Acknowledgment. Interview by author, 5 November 1998, Phoenix, Arizona.

Reckord, Holly, Branch of Acknowledgment. Interview by author by telephone, 1 December 2000.

Richardson, Gregory, executive director, North Carolina Commission of Indian Affairs. Interview by author by telephone, 30 March 2010.

Roth, George, Branch of Acknowledgment and Research. Interview by author, 27 May 1999, Washington, D.C..

Shapard, John "Bud," former chief, Branch of Acknowledgment and Research. Interview by author by telephone, 6 July 2010.

Smith, Chad, principal chief Cherokee Nation. Correspondence with author, 17 November 2001.

Smith, Criss, Navajo/Creek artist. Interview by author, 30 June 2009, Holbrook, Arizona.

Smith, Rose, member of the Lower Muskogee Creek Tribe. Interview by author by telephone, 2 March 2010.

Stoeffle, Richard, Bureau of Applied Anthropology, University of Arizona. Interview by author, 10 April 1998, Tucson, Arizona.

Sunray, Cedric, Mowa Choctaw member and spokesperson. Interview by author by telephone, 14 November 2008. Interview by author in person, 23 June 2009, Norman, Oklahoma.

Taylor, Wilford, chief of the Mowa Band of Choctaw Indians. Interview by author, 14 October 2008, Mt. Vernon, Alabama.

Thrower, Gail, Poarch Band of Creek Indians enrolled member and head of enrollment. Interview by author, 16 October 2008, Poarch Creek Indian Reservation, Alabama.

Thrower, Robert, enrolled member and cultural preservation officer, Poarch Band of Creek Indians. Interview by author, 16 October 2008, Poarch Creek Indian Reservation, Alabama.

Tilden, Mark, Native American Rights Fund attorney. Interview by author by telephone, 21 February 2002.

Trulock, Wilma, former member and tribal officer, Lower Muskogee Creek Tribe. Interview by author by telephone, 4 March 2010.

Tullis, Eddie, former chairman of the Poarch Band of Creek Indians. Interview by author by telephone, 4 March 2010.

Verret, Kirby, former United Houma Nation chairman. Interview by author, 13 January 1999, Houma, Louisiana.

Watts, Cara Cowan, Cherokee Nation councilwoman. E-mail correspondence with author, 4 July 2009.

Weaver, Galasneed, Mowa Choctaw elder and educator. Interview by author, 14 October 2008, Mt. Vernon, Alabama.

Wilkins, David, Lumbee scholar. Interview by author by telephone, 19 November 2009.

Zeidler, James, senior research scientist and associate director for cultural resources, Center for Environmental Management of Military Lands, Colorado State University. Interview by author, 14 April 2011, Phoenix, Arizona.

OTHER PERIODICALS CONSULTED

Afro-American (Baltimore)
Akwesasne Notes
Alabama Indian Advocate
American Indian Journal (Institute for the Development of Indian Law)
American Indian Law Newsletter
Arizona Daily Star
Arkansas Times
Atlanta Constitution
Atlanta Journal and Constitution
Baton Rouge Morning Advocate
Beaumont Enterprise
Boston Globe
Cherokee County Chronicle
Cherokee Phoenix
Daily Press (Mobile, Ala.)
DeFuniak (Florida) Herald
Denver Post
Fayetteville (N.C.) Observer
Florala (Ala.) News
Free Press (Columbus, Ohio)
Gadsden Times
Gallup Independent
Hartford Courant
Houston Chronicle
Indian Affairs: Newsletter of the Association on American Indian Affairs
Indian Country Today

Indian Gaming Business
Indian Voice (Sumner, Wash.)
Las Vegas Sun
Louisiana Life
Macon Telegraph
Missionary Voice (Board of Missions of the Methodist Episcopal Church)
Mobile Press-Register
Muskogee Phoenix
Muscogee Nation News
NARF (Native American Rights Fund) Announcements
NARF Legal Review
National Review
Native Journal (Sherwood Park, Alberta)
Native Nevadan
Neka-Camon (Louisiana Governor's Commission on Indian Affairs)
News and Courier (Charleston, S.C.)
New Yorker
New York Times
Northern Cherokee Newsletter
Ocala Star-Banner
Poarch Creek News
Robesonian (Lumberton, N.C.)
Rome (Georgia) News-Tribune
St. Petersburg Times
San Francisco Chronicle
Sarasota Herald-Tribune
Sarasota Journal
Seminole Tribune
Shreveport Times
Southeastern Cherokee Confederacy News
Southern Exposure
Spectrum & Daily News (St. George, Utah)
State Times (Baton Rouge)
Tahlequah Daily Press
Talking Bayou: United Houma Nation Newsletter
Talking Leaf
Texas Highways
Thomasville Times-Enterprise
Times Daily (Florence, Alabama)
Times-News (Burlington, N.C.)
Times-Picayune
Trained Lay Worker

Tuscaloosa News
Tulsa Tribune
Tulsa World
Village Voice
Wall Street Journal
Washington Post
Wassaja (San Francisco)

Index

CPSIA information can be obtained
at www.ICGtesting.com
Printed in the USA
FSOW02n1028111214
3821FS